CW01021467

The Politics of Opera in Handel's Britain

The Politics of Opera in Handel's Britain examines the involvement of Italian opera in British partisan politics in the first half of the eighteenth century, which saw Sir Robert Walpole's rise to power and George Frideric Handel's greatest period of opera production. McGeary argues that the conventional way of applying Italian opera to contemporary political events and persons by means of allegory and allusion in individual operas is mistaken; nor did partisan politics intrude into the management of the Royal Academy of Music and the Opera of the Nobility. This book shows instead how Senesino, Faustina, Cuzzoni, Farinelli, and events at the Haymarket Theatre were used in political allegories in satirical essays directed against the Walpole ministry. Since most operas were based on ancient historical events, the librettos – like traditional histories – could be sources of examples of vice, virtue, and political precepts and wisdom that could be applied to contemporary politics.

THOMAS MCGEARY has written extensively about the reception of Italian opera in eighteenth-century Britain and his editions and translations of Arnold Schoenberg and Harry Partch received ASCAP-Deems Taylor awards. His research has been supported by fellowships from institutions including the Newberry Library/British Academy, Paul Mellon Centre for British Art, and the American Handel Society, and his articles on art, music, and literature in eighteenth-century Britain have appeared in, among others, *Music and Letters, Journal of the Royal Musical Association, Journal of Eighteenth-Century Studies, Early Music, Burlington Magazine,* and *Philological Quarterly.*

The Politics of Opera in Handel's Britain

THOMAS MCGEARY

CAMBRIDGE UNIVERSITY PRESS

CAMBRIDGE
UNIVERSITY PRESS

University Printing House, Cambridge CB2 8BS, United Kingdom

Cambridge University Press is part of the University of Cambridge.

It furthers the University's mission by disseminating knowledge in the pursuit of
education, learning and research at the highest international levels of excellence.

www.cambridge.org
Information on this title: www.cambridge.org/9781316620229

© Thomas McGeary 2013

First published 2013
First paperback edition 2016

A catalogue record for this publication is available from the British Library

Library of Congress Cataloguing in Publication data
McGeary, Thomas, 1948–
    The politics of opera in Handel's Britain / Thomas McGeary.
        p.   cm.
    Includes bibliographical references and index.
    ISBN 978-1-107-00988-2 (hardback)
    1. Opera–Political aspects–Great Britain–History–18th century.   I. Title.
    ML3918.064M35 2013
    782.10941′09033–dc23
    2012029729

ISBN 978-1-107-00988-2 Hardback
ISBN 978-1-316-62022-9 Paperback

Contents

Figures

Tables

Preface

This book began developing more than fifteen years ago. My initial work on the reception and introduction of Italian opera in Britain dealt with the aesthetic and critical issues raised when justifying and criticizing the new art form. I had remaining unused many squibs and satires on opera found in sources diverse as lead essays in newspapers and high-literary verse satire. Although these sources did not deal with critical or aesthetic issues, they did seem to be important and characteristic British responses to opera and its star singers, the castratos.

The realization that satiric allegories on Italian opera were being used for partisan political purposes led to the present study. The *Deborah*–Excise allegory in the *Craftsman* has often been recognized as a satire linking Handel and Walpole. Other *Craftsman* essays discussed in the following pages have been previously reprinted without comment as if they were bona fide journalism, not satiric allegories.

A general awareness of the high pitch of Tory–Whig party strife in the early decades of the century and of the politicization of the stage throughout the period has predisposed modern scholars to find partisan or topical politics in the management of the opera companies and the opera librettos themselves. My years of immersion in the topical political journalism and pamphleteering of the day, the ninety or so opera librettos, the unquestionable partisan politics of other literature of the period, and the biographical profiles of the opera sponsors led to a reconsideration of the topical political involvement of the world of Italian opera.

The question of the politics of opera can be explored at many levels. From a modern historical vantage point, Italian operas in London might be studied as an expression of the values of its sponsors and audience, as a site expressing class values at a time of the rising middle classes, for their potential as social–political critique of the court or monarchy, as showing how operatic themes reflect transformations in political thought from absolutism to republicanism and democracy, how opera replicates the structures of power and values that organize social life, or as a force in nationalism and forging national identity.

From experience that such inquiries – carried out at high levels of ab-straction and generalization about British politics, society, and culture – are usually unsatisfactory, this study quite deliberately takes a more radical his-torical focus: attempting to discover by recourse to the rich contemporary print culture the political meaning Italian opera – as a genre, institution, or individual operas – would have had for the audiences or libretto readers of Handel's day; how opera was invoked or enlisted for "political work" in the rough-and-tumble of partisan politics of the day; how audiences might have related the opera librettos to current political life.

Not fitting with this brief of partisan, topical politics are numerous poems, plays, political essays, and high-literary satires that engage Italian opera in contesting issues of cultural politics, answering the questions What sort of nation do we want Britain to be? What forms of art contribute to our ideal of Britain? These issues will be explored in a companion study, *Opera and Cultural Politics in Britain, 1700–1742*.

For assistance in providing the time and access to the primary materials necessary for this work (especially in the years before ECCO), I am grateful to the William Andrews Clark Memorial Library, the Newberry Library, and the NEH Summer Fellowship program for residence fellowships, and for travel awards, to the Newberry Library/British Academy, The Handel Institute, and the Paul Mellon Centre for British Art, London.

Throughout the research and writing of this study, I have benefited from the advice, assistance, and encouragement of Lorenzo Bianconi, Donald Burrows, Xavier Cervantes, John Dussinger, Robert Hume, David Hunter, Harry Johnstone, Paulina Kewes, the late N. Frederick Nash, Suzana Ograjenšek, John Roberts, Ruth Smith, Carole Taylor, Stephen Taylor, David Vickers, Carlo Vitali, and Howard Weinbrot.

I am grateful to the staff at the William Andrews Clark Memorial Library, the Newberry Library, the Henry E. Huntington Library, the Houghton Library, and numerous public record offices, but especially at Bury St. Edmunds. The library at the University of Illinois, Urbana–Champaign provided unparalleled access to rare and modern materials; Kathryn Danner and her interlibrary loan staff cheerfully and unfailingly fulfilled my requests for material.

Notes on sources

Fuller information on the operas, singers, musicians, and the opera companies mentioned in this book can be found in the entries in the *Cambridge Handel Encyclopedia* (2009) and the *New Grove Dictionary of Opera* (1992). The sources, plot summaries, and textual histories of Handel's operas are given in thorough detail in Winton Dean and John Merrill Knapp, *Handel's Operas, 1704–1726* (1995), and Winton Dean, *Handel's Operas, 1726–1741* (2006). The operas of the Royal Academy of Music from 1726 to 1728 have been studied by Suzana Ograjenšek, and David Vickers has studied those of Handel's Second Academy period. The political background of the period can be conveniently surveyed in greater depth in the biographies of Walpole, Bolingbroke, George I and II, and Stanhope by J. H. Plumb, William Coxe, Isaac Kramnick, Ragnhild Hatton, Jeremy Black, Andrew Thompson, and Basil Williams. Further background for the period can be found in the surveys by Geoffrey Holmes and Daniel Szechi, *The Age of Oligarchy: Pre-Industrial Britain, 1722–1783* (1993), Geoffrey Holmes, *The Making of a Great Power, Late Stuart and Early Georgian Britain, 1660–1722* (1993), Jeremy Gregory and John Stevenson, *Britain in the Eighteenth Century, 1688–1820* (2000), and Paul Langford, *A Polite and Commercial People: England, 1727–1783* (1989).

Since quotations are taken wherever possible from original sources and to reduce the bulk of the notes, modern reprints of documentary sources are not cited unless they are a full reprint of an important source. Modern reprints of much of the documentary material about Handel and Italian opera are found in O. E. Deutsch, *Handel: A Documentary Biography* (1955), soon to be superseded by the forthcoming *George Frideric Handel: Collected Documents*, the *Händel-Handbuch* (1985), Elizabeth Gibson's study of the Royal Academy of Music (1989), and the online Handel Reference Database ichriss.ccarh.org/HRD. Many of the documents are calendared in Milhous and Hume, *A Register of English Theatrical Documents, 1660–1737* (1991).

Wherever possible, I have made fresh transcriptions from manuscript sources, even when readily accessible in printed sources such as the Historical Manuscripts Commission reports. Consulting the original manuscript sources frequently provides more accurate readings or passages fuller than those in the published transcripts. Manuscript transcriptions reproduce original spelling, abbreviations, and punctuation. Only in rare cases, where meaning requires it, have I provided editorial punctuation in square brackets.

Likewise, I have been able to consult in almost all cases the original issues, usually in folio half-sheet format, of newspapers and periodicals, instead of the later collected reprint editions or the paraphrased and excerpted texts in the *Gentleman's Magazine* or the *London Magazine*. This approach has yielded numerous and important remarks and satires on opera in news columns or advertisements that are omitted in the collected editions and, hence, have hitherto gone unnoticed. Dates and issue numbers are those given in the original issues (those in the *Craftsman*, it must be noted, are occasionally changed in the collected edition). Texts are frequently more complete in the original issues than the collected editions. I indicate quotations from the original texts of periodicals by including the issue number with the date.

In quotations from printed sources, italic and roman are occasionally reversed when an original passage is set in all italics. For dates, the old style calendar years are used, unless noted, except that the New Year is assumed to begin on January 1.

Frontispiece: George Frideric Handel; mezzotint engraving by John Faber the Younger (1749), after painting by Thomas Hudson. Photo: courtesy of the Gerald Coke Foundation, The Foundling Museum, London.

1 | Introduction

Even before Italian opera was first produced in London in 1705, Italian music and singers had been politicized. In the early years of Queen Anne's reign, issues of national identity, religion, gender, and Tory–Whig politics were implicated in the controversy about Italian and English music and the partisanship over the singers Margarita L'Epine and Catherine Tofts. All-sung, Italian-style opera quickly became the most prestigious theatrical entertainment of London's cultural elite. It was a focus of social life, a recurring topic in literature, and, just as quickly, a lightning rod that sparked responses from all quarters reflecting diverse moral, aesthetic, and political concerns.[1] The objections to opera raised in its first decade became a constant refrain in criticism for the remainder of the century and beyond.

Literary critics claimed opera was an irrational, sensuous art form, sung in a foreign language that violated verisimilitude and decorum. Dramatists and friends of British theater saw opera and highly paid singers as threats to native talent and dramatic traditions. Social reformers and moralists, continuing in the vein of Jeremy Collier, condemned opera as an expensive offspring of luxury that led to vice, sensuality, and effeminacy, and whose castrato singers posed a sexual threat to women and gender norms. Nationalists objected to the presence of a foreign art on the London stage, especially at times when Britain was engaged in Continental wars.

These often irrational and no less xenophobic attacks are frequently (and mistakenly) taken to characterize the British response as a whole to Italian opera, and have often distressed lovers of opera and Handel, who take the outcry as evidence the British were incapable of appreciating either opera or his music. As this book will show, much of the satire of Italian opera had ulterior partisan political motives and targets.

This exploration of Italian opera and politics brings together two fields represented by George Frideric Handel and Sir Robert Walpole. It begins with the founding of the Royal Academy of Music in 1719–20, which coincides with Handel's return to writing operas after a five-year hiatus and with the beginning of Walpole's rise to power as prime minister in 1721–22. Handel was emerging as Britain's pre-eminent musical figure, whose creative output in 1720–42 was devoted primarily to composing thirty-nine Italian operas (including arranging pasticcios). Politically, the era was dominated by Walpole, who was the target of twenty years' worth of partisan satire and attack. The year 1742 provides a convenient conclusion; in that year Walpole fell from power, by which time Handel had ceased producing full seasons of opera and had turned to presenting shorter seasons of oratorio (see Epilogue).

This study is not an attempt to systematically explore the possible political content of each of Handel's London operas. It principally shows how, at various moments of political crisis, events at the Haymarket Theatre (also known at the time as the King's Theatre) and its star singers were politicized in partisan polemic.

The politics of individual Handel operas are examined because several of them have been given political interpretations by modern scholars. In Chapter 8, though, partly to redress the slighting of non-Handelian operas in modern scholarship, the political content of Italian operas is considered without giving any special mention of their composer.

The phrase "politics of opera" invites the question: What is the relation of the operas being produced in London to contemporary partisan politics? Given there were upwards of ninety new operas produced from 1720 to 1742, this is a daunting question, no less because the question can be approached in many ways. Indeed, many opera historians have taken it for granted that London's Italian operas were politically and topically engaged. The opera historian Reinhard Strohm has confidently claimed:

> We must remember that Handel was writing operas in London, where the opera was of major political importance and inseparable from very concrete social conditions, and that he himself played a part in the development of those conditions. It is no secret, for example, that contemporary political events played a part in determining the choice of an opera's subject.[2]

"One should not ignore the political implications of [*Rinaldo*] and other Handel librettos," cautions the music historian Curtis Price.[3] The historian Paul Monod maintains that Handel's operas "contain veiled hints about politics [and] impart valuable information about the pervasive influence of politics on the arts during the early 1700s."[4] And the historian William Weber states that "the operatic *querelles* in London during the early part of the century were closely related to party politics."[5] Instead of the high level of abstraction of such claims, this study explores the relation of opera to politics with greater precision, with attention focused on the specifics of the partisan politics of the day.[6]

It would in many ways be attractive to find that in an era when partisan politics saturated social life and literature, the operas of Handel and his fellow composers reflected, articulated, or debated the political events and issues of the day; that opera and dramatic music helped shape the political culture and ideology of the day. In considering the relation of opera to politics, much depends on what question is being addressed, for opera, like any cultural product, can be political in many ways.

To the question whether or how opera contributes to the fundamental political concern of achieving the public good, critics and moralists saw Italian opera as a decisive factor, both as symptom and cause, in their vision of a British society and culture in decline. In high-literary works, such as Alexander Pope's *Dunciad* (1728) and his formal verse satire of the 1730s, to the theatrical farces of Henry Fielding, Italian opera symbolized the false taste in the arts and sciences that was overrunning Britain. To the broad political question "What sort of culture do we want to foster?"[7] some contemporaries replied it was one absent Italian opera, a by-product of luxury with its foreign, effeminizing castrato singers. False taste and the fashion for opera had political implications as well; they were a sign of the perilous state of Britain's arts and sciences and, by implication, a rebuke to the royal family, ministry, and ruling elites. Propagandists in the political opposition of the 1720s and 1730s repeatedly pointed to Italian opera as proof of the corruption and luxury sweeping over London caused by Walpole's ministry.[8]

The content of individual librettos could be political in various ways. Operas have politics as a theme. Librettos on historical subjects represent kings and queens, courtiers, generals, usurpers, tyrants, and Roman consuls and dictators engaged in actions that occur in the political realm: deposing tyrants and usurpers, arranging succession to the throne, discovering the rightful ruler, suppressing rebellion, waging war, dispensing justice, and fending off conquerors. In this sense, as Strohm notes, "Princes and rulers, political and military power, states and nations, were among the most significant themes Italian *opera seria* was expected to address."[9]

Operas produced at seventeenth- and eighteenth-century European absolutist courts for dynastic events are frequently built around allegorical programs populated with symbolic figures, heroes, or mythic characters who represent the virtues, nobility, and heroism of the dynasty or the prince in the audience. These court operas serve to flatter and legitimate the prince and his rule.

Where operas were produced as a communal undertaking, as in the family-owned theaters in seventeenth-century Venice that presented seasonal offerings for the public, the choice of story could speak to a state's mythology, nationalism, and self-image. Early Venetian operas presented the history (or presumed pre-history) of the republic and its mythical origins with the Fall of Troy.[10] London operas on Roman subjects could flatter aristocratic Britons who idealized and assimilated the ideals and arts of ancient Rome in their quest to create an oligarchy of virtue.[11]

Operas can be political in the didactic sense by holding up examples of tyrants and just rulers, and conveying universal lessons about the exercise of political power. Using episodes drawn from history, plots teach the fate of empires and republics, show honor and glory achieved by those who sacrifice for their country, illustrate the wise exercise of power, show the just punishments befitting tyrants, urge devotion to duty and public virtue, show the dangers of rulers led astray by illicit love and unbridled passions, and represent the lustrous examples of rulers exhibiting self-mastery of passions and granting clemency to malefactors. Here, opera would be at one with the professed purpose of history and dramatic poetry: to show the beauty of Virtue and its rewards, the deformity of Vice and its punishments; to encourage the former and frighten from the latter. The lessons are made all the more compelling and attractive by the embellishments of theatrical spectacle. As the librettist Metastasio lamented to his friend Farinelli, he had "wasted his entire life in order to instruct mankind in a pleasing way."[12]

An opera on a historical subject could be made topical or relevant to politics of the day by the technique of parallel and application. A London opera-goer (or libretto reader) could draw from the episode represented on stage a universal lesson or precept of political wisdom; then the opera-goer could apply the precept to the circumstances of the day to illuminate, advise, or judge a specific person or situation. This approach of parallel and application accords with the classical humanist expectation that history or dramatic poetry teaches best by example, not through inculcation by direct moralizing.

At a more philosophical level, operas can be political in the sense that their action, dispensation of poetic justice, or text can state doctrines of political theory or endorse forms of political organization and activity, such as ideas about the duties and obligations of rulers, citizens, and subjects.[13] In the sense of politics as the struggle for control of government and power, London opera – as an institution or genre – was put to symbolic use in satire by opposition propagandists in their media campaign to oust Walpole from his place as prime minister.

However, when opera historians approach the politics of individual Italian operas in London, they usually proceed on the "generic expectation" that operas are allegorical or allusive of contemporary politics and the monarch, statesmen, or the royal family.[14] This approach short-circuits the process of extracting precepts, making parallels, and applying the precepts and instead draws direct identifications between characters or events in the operas and eighteenth-century persons or circumstances.[15] For example, Lucius Cornelius Sulla has been seen as representing the Duke of Marlborough or the Hanoverian Elector Georg Ludwig; Floridant, as George II while Prince of Wales; or Richard the Lionheart, as George I or II.[16]

This book develops two complementary arguments. It argues there is no basis for the generic expectation that the librettos of individual Italian operas on historical subjects are, or were intended and received as, allegorical or allusive of contemporary topical politics; nor is the title-hero to be identified with the reigning monarch or a statesman. When modern allegorical political interpretations are examined, we find that the allegories are incomplete and lack coherence and the relationship claimed to current politics is inconsistent and unconvincing. The operas proposed as allegories are quite unlike what Handel's contemporaries would have known and recognized as allegories. Rather than interpretations that need improving, the premise upon which they are based is faulty.

Yet we need not remain suspended in indecision about assessing the politics of opera librettos. The other undertaking of this book is to examine unmistakable partisan stage works and journalistic essays of the later seventeenth and early eighteenth centuries to identify those features that mark them as having been intended, written, and received as political and allegorical. The relevant context for assessing the politics of opera is not just the contemporary political world, but the whole range of political and polemical works with which political operas might share methods and aims. My goal is to find what Robert Hume calls the "extrinsic evidence with which to validate" political interpretations.[17] In this way, we can attempt to recover the political meanings London operas had for Handel's audiences.

Once we remove the blinders worn as a consequence of the generic expectation, we find that Italian opera – the events at the Haymarket Theatre and those involving its star singers – was engaged in far more varied and significant ways in the daily partisan politics of Hanoverian Britain. A principal way opera is politicized exploits the age-old all-the-world's-a-stage topos. In partisan periodicals and newspapers, propagandists occasionally wrote what appear on the surface to be straightforward journalistic accounts of disputes and squabbles at the opera house – the rivalry between partisans of Faustina and Cuzzoni, Handel's raising of ticket prices for *Deborah*, his dismissal of Senesino, and the supposed capture of Farinelli by the Spanish court in 1737. Upon close examination and with an eye on current politics, these journalists' accounts turn out to be extended parallels between occurrences at the opera house and domestic or foreign political events. They function as part of the sustained opposition propaganda campaign to discredit the policies of Walpole's ministry and force his removal. Opera as a form of dramatic poetry and history could also function as a source for universal precepts and exempla about political experience that could be applied by audience members or libretto readers to the political situation of their day.

An examination of the Royal Academy of Music and the Opera of the Nobility shows that the claims about the influence of politics upon their founding and management are not borne out. Granted, there was partisanship within the Royal Academy about singers and composers, and London recognized the rivalry between Handel's company and that of the Nobility opera; but careful consideration of the full array of evidence reveals the companies operated above the fray of partisan politics. If there was an eighteenth-century generic expectation about Italian opera, I suggest it was that the opera stage was not where one expected to find topical, partisan allusion and allegory.

These complementary arguments are developed in the following chapters. Chapter 2 sets the stage for understanding the relation of opera and politics by examining the generic expectation that operas were allegorical or allusive of contemporary topical politics and that the title-hero is to be identified with contemporary statesmen or members of the royal family. The circumstances of the Continental courts where allegorical operas did celebrate the royal dynasty and monarch are contrasted to the opera system in London to suggest that operas on historical subjects in London cannot generically be expected to have plausible political allegorical applications.

Since political interpretations for Handel operas have been proposed as allegories, this chapter also examines critical writing on allegory and allegorical works of the period to recover what the early eighteenth century thought about allegory and would have recognized as allegory. From a broad range of Restoration and early eighteenth-century plays and satires that were undoubtedly intended and received as political, I develop criteria to suggest whether a work was written or received as political. These criteria point to the type of extrinsic evidence that could validate allegorical or political readings of individual operas.

The political scene beginning with the rise of Robert Walpole as prime minister, which roughly coincides with the founding of the Royal Academy of Music in 1719–20, is surveyed in Chapter 3. Claims that external politics affected the founding and governance of the Royal Academy are examined; in general the Academy's founding, membership, and direction occurred without the intervention of partisan politics. The political interpretations that have been proposed for several of Handel's operas from these years are examined; here and elsewhere, such interpretations are shown as incomplete and inconsistent readings that do not correspond adequately with the political circumstances of the day. No extrinsic evidence supports these readings.

Chapter 4 traces the rise of the political opposition to Walpole in the mid 1720s and examines one way the opera company at the Haymarket Theatre was enlisted in partisan politics. The opposition newspaper the *Craftsman* carried a number of accounts of events at the opera house involving the singers Faustina, Cuzzoni, and Senesino. These pieces of counterfeit journalism are actually allegories of the disputes between Britain and Spain over Gibraltar and the impending conference at Soissons intended to prevent war between the two countries; their partisan purpose was to indict the foreign diplomacy of the Walpole ministry.

The establishment of the opera company run jointly by Handel and Heidegger is described in Chapter 5. As with the Royal Academy of Music, events at the Haymarket Theatre were allegorized by the political opposition in partisan political satires directed against the king and the Walpole ministry.

The Opera of the Nobility, founded in 1733 to rival Handel, has conventionally been taken as an episode where opera became involved with partisan politics. Chapter 6 examines the claims that Prince Frederick, as leader of the political opposition, set himself at the head of this company in opposition to Handel to spite his sister or father. Using a variety of evidence, the chapter shows that much of this oft-told story is a fiction, deriving from John, Lord Hervey's spiteful and unreliable memoirs. If the Opera of the Nobility itself was not a tool of partisan politics, the political opposition took up the occasion of its star singer Farinelli's departure to the Spanish court in 1737 – breaking his contract with the opera directors and remaining "detained" in Madrid – as a means of indicting the Walpole ministry's claimed failure to defend British merchant shipping from Spanish depredations and captures.

A number of allegorical theater and operatic works that celebrated weddings and birthdays of the Hanoverian family were produced in that decade. Similar, in their use of emblematic allegory, to the operas produced at Continental absolutist courts, these musical dramatic works show by contrast how politically unengaged were the realist-mode Italian operas based on historical subjects.

Chapter 7 charts the rise in the mid 1730s of a renewed opposition to the Walpole ministry, often called the Patriot opposition. Topical and politically allusive dramas produced by playwrights in the Patriot circle provide the broader background of politically engaged dramatic works against which the political engagement of Italian operas can be assessed. The full context of these undoubtedly partisan plays – the biography of the author, context, political content, and contemporary response and government reaction – is presented in depth to show how these plays fulfill the criteria presented in Chapter 2 for recognizing partisan political works.

Chapter 8 turns to politics in the librettos of individual operas. Most Italian operas are based on events and persons from (real or fictive) ancient history. If, as some contemporaries wrote, we consider opera librettos as histories and dramatic poetry, we can apply to opera the same technique that contemporaries used for reading history, the *ars historica*, to suggest one way Handel's contemporaries could have related operas to current politics. Operas on historical subjects could be the source of exempla and precepts that the opera-goer could derive and apply to current politics. Plot events, statements by characters, or dispensation of justice in operas also present ideas about political theory and the role and duties of citizens, subjects, and rulers. Although operas present absolute monarchs as legitimate rulers and plots often feature their overthrow, the operas do embody principles of natural law such that they would not be subversive of Britain's monarchy.

Setting opera in its political context must start with an adequate understanding of British political history. Many political interpretations of operas and accounts of politics in the opera companies and of opera's role in British politics are unsatisfactory because they are faulty or simplistic accounts of the politics of Britain, or they do not accord well with the pertinent and contested partisan issues of the day. British political history of the eighteenth century has been a lively and contentious field, and understanding of it has changed substantially.

The traditional view is that eighteenth-century British politics was a conflict between Whig and Tory marked by the ascent of progressive, liberal Whiggism over conservative Toryism. In 1929, however, Lewis Namier proposed a startling revision of this view,[18] showing that the conventional conflict of Whig and Tory ideology could not adequately interpret the events and motivations of politicians in the 1760s. Instead of party ideology, what existed was an administration party and an opposition; politicians were motivated by family and regional connections, self-interest, and the hopes of achieving political power. Subsequently, Robert Walcott transported the "Namier Revolution" to British politics before 1760 and denied that two unified parties existed.[19] Rather, in the period of Queen Anne, the Commons had seven major segments or connections, composed of shifting alliances based on family, professional, or regional connections or dependency on a territorial magnate.

Walcott's revisionary attempt stimulated a burst of new archival and documentary research, leading to a general agreement by historians that (with certain subtle qualifications) the principal element in British politics from 1689 to 1715 was indeed the party strife between Whig and Tory that did reflect well-defined positions on important issues of church, state, and foreign policy.[20] But after the accession of George I in 1714, the Tories were so discredited in the eyes of the king for their role in negotiating what the king and Whigs saw as the shameful Treaty of Utrecht that betrayed Britain and her allies by a separate peace with France, and the Whigs had established such an effective political oligarchy, that Tories were virtually barred from government and, except for those who accommodated themselves with the Whigs, spent the following half-century "in the wilderness."[21] The Tory and Whig labels and distinctions survived but mattered little for the reality of daily politics, although the ruling Whig oligarchy was riven by internal conflict.

With the rise to power of Robert Walpole in 1721–22, as J. H. Plumb argued, the rage of party, the instability of brief and mixed ministries, and the confusion of political life was replaced by a period of political stability.[22] Plumb found three principal causes for the emergence of stability: the development of a Whig oligarchy of great wealthy landowners who wielded social and economic power and by these means dominated politics; the rapid expansion of the executive and bureaucracy with its attendant places, offices, pensions, and honors that built up a large court party that could control Parliament; and the emergence of single-party government such that the Tories ceased to pose any challenge to Whig power.

The election of 1722 was the watershed that consolidated rule by the Whig oligarchy. Unlike Anne, George I was willing to govern with single-party ministries and endorse measures supporting the Whigs; consequently, day-to-day politics became a struggle between various Whig factions (with occasional Tory support) for control of government. For the period covered by this study, the dominant political reality was Walpole's control of government and the attempts by dissident Whigs and Tories to drive him from office.

With time, though, questions arose about the degree of political stability achieved.[23] In 1970 Romney Sedgwick and Eveline Cruickshanks showed the Tory party was effective in many constituencies and maintained considerable solidarity in Parliament; not until 1727 did Tory strength in the Commons sink as low as that of the Whigs in the waning years of Anne's reign.[24] They also showed Jacobite activity was far from extinct. Giving a fuller account of the survival of the Tory party, in 1982 Linda Colley argued the Tories retained an ideological identity, were capable of concerted political action, and nurtured ambitions for political success.[25] Historians, though, have generally considered that Colley has overstated the strength and effectiveness of the Tory party.[26]

The recovery of Jacobitism as a political force was the most sustained challenge to the Plumb stability thesis. Sedgwick and Cruickshanks asserted that "up to 1745 the Tories were a predominantly Jacobite party, engaged in attempts to restore the Stuarts by a rising with foreign assistance."[27] A wide range of poetry, popular culture, imagery, and dissent was uncovered to show Jacobitism was a cultural, social, and religious movement supported by popular or "plebian" activity.[28]

But the significance of Jacobitism as a threat to the Hanoverian succession has likewise been held to be overstated, despite the fears of it aroused by Walpole's ministry.[29] The number of Jacobites in the Tory party was much smaller than claimed by Sedgwick and Cruickshanks.[30] The Jacobite invasion of 1715, the Swedish Plot (1717), the Ormonde invasion (1719), and the '45 demonstrate by their very failure to mobilize the populace the political stability achieved. Arguments exposing the Earl of Burlington, Jonathan Swift, and Alexander Pope as Jacobites or crypto-Jacobites have been strongly challenged.[31] The large amount of scholarship about Jacobitism and Walpole's incessant fanning of fears about Jacobites should not be mistaken for Jacobitism's actual political importance.

Stuart loyalism figures prominently in the revisionist account by J. C. D. Clark, who argues that a long eighteenth-century Britain can properly be called an *ancien régime*: a stable conservative society where culture, politics, and ideology were dominated by the three pillars of aristocracy, crown, and church. It was a period marked by ideological polarity between Stuarts and Hanoverians.[32] Clark's revisionist history provoked heated response.[33] Critics routinely complained that he minimized the forces of modernization or transformation, including commercialization, capitalism, new patterns of consumer consumption, urbanization, secular enlightenment, and science. Social historians argued there was socio-economic change, and indeed some was momentous.[34]

Many historians, though, found aspects of Clark's account salutary and had already come to many of his conclusions: the basis of society was hierarchical, society was generally conservative in its adherence to traditional institutions and values, aristocratic authority remained dominant, and the political nation was successful in maintaining stability and cohesion.[35]

This consensus about early Hanoverian Britain accords well with the social world of opera in London. The direction, subsidy, patronage, and audience of opera were dominated by a small elite of mostly Whig aristocrats, gentry, merchants, financiers, and professionals.[36]

Traditional political history has tended to concentrate on the "high politics" of Parliament, ministry, and foreign diplomacy, giving little consideration to how governance may have been affected by extra-parliamentary public opinion. Nicholas Rogers, Kathleen Wilson, and H. T. Dickinson[37] have shown that a lively, popular British political culture existed that influenced the political process.[38] A broad range of popular opinion – found in print media and circulating in taverns, clubs, coffee houses, playhouses, and crowd activity – could exert pressure at times of political crisis to pose a challenge to the ministry.[39] At such moments of political crisis, opposition propagandists used satire and allegories of events and singers at the Haymarket Theatre to stir dissatisfaction with Walpole's conduct of domestic and foreign affairs.

2 | Opera and political allegory: When is it an allegory? When is it political?

This chapter's point of departure is the fact that attempts at finding the politics of individual Italian operas in London have predominantly been guided by the "generic expectation"[1] (to use Robert Hume's term) that Italian operas are allegorical or allusive of contemporary political events, and their title-heroes are to be identified with the monarch, members of the royal family, or political figures. The practice seems premised on the fact that many Continental Baroque operas were court events, celebrating the ruling prince, family, or dynastic events, and – perhaps reflecting a vestige of the belief that the arts express the spirit of their times – on the assumption that London operas would share this feature. Hence, the allegory or allusion is assumed to be "there" in an opera, waiting to be discovered by the modern scholar.

While political interpretations of Italian operas abound,[2] and several writers do provide rationales for allegorical interpretations,[3] none confront the question succinctly stated by John Wallace: whether the "political meanings are 'in' the work, or if we have put them there."[4] The question can be reframed as a distinction between allegories, parallels, or applications to contemporary events that are invited, directed, or intended by the author and those that Alan Roper calls "reader's applications," which "depend upon the unpredictable responses of readers,"[5] or as Robert Hume frames it, "the difference between textual meaning and susceptibility to application."[6]

This chapter attempts to provide criteria for answering the obvious questions "When is an opera political?" "When is it allegorical?" Or, as Robert Hume asks, "How do we prove that a play was written to make a political point?"[7] Our goal is to provide a broad backdrop of politically engaged stage works against which we can assess the politics of individual Italian operas.

After examining the assumptions that might make the generic expectation plausible, we show that the circumstances of opera production in London differ sufficiently from Continental practices to call into question the extension of Continental practice to operas produced in London. From examining stage works that were unquestionably political and recognized as such in their day, the chapter will develop criteria that can help identify possible "political" operas. Critical writings on allegory by John Hughes and Richard Blackmore teach us how contemporaries understood allegory and what they would have recognized as allegory. Chapters 4 and 5 will present cases of partisan journalism that employ allegories using opera to exemplify the period's customary political use of allegory, application, and personation.[8] By examining the political allegories proposed for three early Handel operas (*Rinaldo* [1711], *Teseo* [1713], and *Silla* [1713]), we see the inherent limitations and difficulties of the generic expectation approach, suggesting that its method and its results are flawed, unconvincing, and unhistorical.[9] Our goal is to escape presentism and attempt to recover political meanings as possibly designed by librettists or as members of Handel's audiences would likely have sought or understood them.

Two immediate qualifications are necessary. First, this inquiry does not propose that political or allegorical interpretations of individual Italian operas are not possible or justified, nor that only a single political interpretation was shared by members of Handel's audience. Rather, while accepting that context and reader response do cause a text's meaning to change and vary for individual readers, the goal is to narrow the range of interpretations to historically plausible and valid interpretations that reveal how Handel and his contemporaries – librettists, opera managers, audiences – would have understood the political role, function, and significance of Italian operas.[10]

Second, the question of the politics of individual operas has arisen primarily with librettos in a realist mode based on episodes drawn from ancient or medieval history. A group of overlooked allegorical operas, serenatas, or masques did celebrate weddings and birthdays of the Hanoverian royal family – and these are uncontestably allegorical and allusive of the royal family and, hence, do carry topical political significance. Of realist-mode operas on historical subjects, *Riccardo primo* is exceptional for having political application to the king, but not in the way usually ascribed to it.

Interpreters of the politics of Italian opera in London have proceeded on the generic expectation that, as stated by Neal Zaslaw, "the contents of staged works were usually taken to stand for current leaders and current events no matter how distant in time, place or overt subject the plots may have been."[11] Reinhard Strohm concurs that "In opera libretti of the Baroque period, and not only in Handel's, all representations of history have some bearing on the present,"[12] and adds furthermore that the title-heroes of operas such as *Alessandro* (1726), *Admeto* (1727), and *Riccardo primo* (1727) are to be read as "allegories of the Hanoverian ruler."[13]

There are many reasons why Italian operas might be expected to be allegorical or allusive of contemporary politics and monarchs in early Hanoverian Britain. From its origin in early seventeenth-century Italy, much

Baroque opera was court-sponsored, and many operas, serenatas, and *feste teatrali* were produced for the absolutist princely courts at Paris, Vienna, Dresden, Florence, Naples, and elsewhere as affairs of state, mounted to celebrate political and dynastic events. T. C. W. Blanning has shown how Baroque operas emanating from absolutist courts functioned as part of a "representational culture" that projected and legitimated princely authority.[14] Serving as an *instrumentum regni* to represent the power, glory, and majesty of a prince and his court, opera – uniting dramatic poetry, music, costume, dance, and theatrical spectacle – filled the stage with allegorical, emblematic, and mythological figures, divinities, and ancient heroes, who represent the classical virtues of the prince, royal couple, or dynasty whom the opera is honoring. Engraved illustrations in printed librettos broadcast the splendor of the elaborate theatrical sets and costumes.

Elaborate examples of such court-sponsored operas are the allegorical musical-theatric works produced for the Habsburg court.[15] The most famous, and likely the most spectacular operatic production of the century, was the allegorical *Il pomo d'oro*, the culmination of the celebration of the royal Austro-Spanish wedding between Emperor Leopold I and the infanta Margarita Teresa. Two years in preparation, this *festa teatrale* containing a prologue, five acts, and sixty-six scenes, was performed at the Hoftheater in Vienna on July 13–14, 1668. With music by Antonio Cesti to a libretto by Francesco Sbarra, it was published in score with engravings of the twenty-three stage sets.[16] *Costanze e fortezza*, an allegorical three-act *festa teatrale* by Pietro Pariati and Johann J. Fux presented before the Habsburg court at Prague on August 28, 1723, celebrated the birthday of the empress as well as the coronation of the emperor and empress as King and Queen of Bohemia. The stage sets by Giuseppe Galli Bibiena were illustrated in seven plates published with the libretto.[17]

Recognized as affairs of state and representations of political power are the *tragédies en musique* produced at Versailles and then at the Académie Royale de Musique in Paris by Jean-Baptiste Lully and Philippe Quinault from 1673 to 1687.[18] The mythological–allegorical prologues, usually self-contained miniature dramas acted out by gods, nymphs, and demons, served as royalist propaganda to flatter Louis XIV, glorify his martial exploits, or celebrate the return to peace. Lully's dedications, as in the cases of *Bellérophon* (1679), *Persée* (1682), and *Amadis* (1685), explicitly link the opera's hero and the Sun King. Especially resonant in these French operas were the heroic deeds of Hercules, Perseus, Theseus, Roland, Amadis, and Renaud, behind whom the courtiers saw (or were invited to see) their monarch. The operas, as Robert Isherwood summarizes, "served the monarchy by presenting attractive explanations of the king's motives for waging war and by representing the king as he wished to appear to his subjects – a peaceful, amorous, benevolent, indestructible hero."[19]

Many of England's own Restoration operas, dramatic operas, and masques were royalist celebrations and allegories of state affairs.[20] *Ariane, ou le mariage de Bacchus* (1674) celebrated the marriage of James, Duke of York to Mary of Modena, conducted by proxy the previous year.[21] In the prologue, the rivers Thames, Tiber, and Seine are represented by three nymphs who pay homage to Albion (Charles II) and Albanius (his brother James). Toward the end, a nymph representing the river Po enters to join her "Divine Marie" to the British hero.[22] The following year, *Psyche* (1675), Thomas Shadwell's reworking of the libretto of the Molière–Lully *Psyché*, was adapted to suggest, according to Curtis Price, that the royal marriage was not the threat and disaster as feared by Shaftesbury and others. In this *tragédie-ballet*, the marriage of Psyche and Cupid parallels that of Mary and James, and Psyche's being sent to Venus' "Rock upon the Sea" parallels Mary's being escorted to Britain.[23]

John Dryden's royalist all-sung masque *Albion and Albanius* (1685) with music by Louis Grabu was the most thoroughly worked-out political allegory on the Restoration stage.[24] Its three acts are peopled with allegorical and mythological figures who, while conversing amidst changes of spectacular scenery and machines, represent the history of the Restoration and the rescue and revival of Augusta (London), and extol the triumph of justice and order by Albion and Albanius (Charles II and his brother James) over anarchy and rebellion. *Albion and Albanius* was originally an act of the prologue to Dryden and Purcell's *King Arthur* (1691), a work planned as part of a royalist campaign to celebrate Charles II's providential deliverance from the 1683 Rye House Plot.[25] Although privately rehearsed before Charles, its public presentation was delayed, perhaps because of the elaborate machines and scenery needed. But Charles died on February 6, 1685, and it was not publicly performed until June 3, now before James II. Dryden was able to adapt the work to its new circumstances with the addition of some twenty to thirty lines, and so to salvage the allegory of the piece and make it "entirely of a Piece" (preface). After a few performances, news of Monmouth's landing reached London on June 13, and further productions were halted.

In the new reign, *Albion and Albanius* was a retrospective allegorical tribute to the late king. At the curtain, a drooping Augusta is surrounded by falling towers and signs of disorder: Democracy and Zeal are in charge. Archon (General Monck) defeats Democracy and Zeal, Albion and Albanius deliver Augusta, and the principal events of Charles' reign are described with the aid of allegorical stage sets and enacted using allegorical characters. The masque ends with Charles' death represented as a divine apotheosis (announced by Phoebus) followed by prophecies by Venus of a glorious reign for Albanius and a view of Windsor Castle.

The original version of the main piece *King Arthur* is lost. King Arthur was an appropriate patriotic subject that offered ample opportunity for allegory – although the political meaning is much disputed. The 1691 reworked version as a dramatic opera dramatizes two rival claimants for the English throne: Arthur leads the Christian Britons against the Saxons, led by King Oswald, who is aided by the evil wizard Osmond. Oswald and Osmond lust after Arthur's beloved Emmeline. With the aid of Merlin and the spirit Philidel, Arthur prevails over the traps set by Osmond and is united with Emmeline. At the close, Arthur and Oswald forge a peace.

It is likely there was originally some parallel between Charles and his recently defeated Whig parliamentary enemies and Arthur and his Saxon enemies.[26] But upon its performance in June 1691 in the wake of the Glorious Revolution, its allegory is ambiguous: it has been given a Jacobite or Williamite reading (Arthur could be James or William), or seen as a "backhanded compliment" (both laudatory and seditious) to William, a king Dryden had no sympathy for.

After the Glorious Revolution, many London dramatic works had strong political elements. The dramatic opera *Brutus of Alba: or, Augusta's Triumph* (1696) celebrates William III through its numerous allusions to his military, personal, and political career. William was abroad fighting the French in 1696, and the opera celebrates his return to Dover by a masque performed by Augusta, Thamesis, Apollo, Neptune, and others. The masque also joins William in mourning the late Queen Mary, "this fair Isle's Imperial Queen."[27] The signing of the Peace of Ryswick is celebrated in Peter Motteux's masque and musical interlude *The Taking of Namur and His Majesty's Safe Return* (1695) and *Europe's Revels for the Peace* (1697).[28] At the Haymarket Theatre, George Granville's patriotic dramatic opera *The British Enchanters* (1706), based on the 1684 *Amadis* of Quinault and Lully, presents Marlborough, like Amadis, as a great warrior returned from foreign wars.[29]

Much of the drama and poetry of the Restoration and early Hanoverian period was also deeply and pervasively political in genesis, content, and reception.[30] In an era before poetry was primarily self-expression, England's writers used literature to do "political work" in the strongest sense of boldly addressing and trying to shape public opinion about the crucial political events, ideas, and personalities of the day – in effect writing pieces of partisan propaganda. Many writers held official, ministerial, and diplomatic posts (among them Dryden, Halifax, Addison, Steele, and Prior). Dryden, writes Phillip Harth, epitomized "the public poet ... the public orator who writes occasional poems in which he speaks to his contemporaries on current issues and seeks to influence them."[31] Literary texts of the Restoration, Stephen Zwicker observes, "were central to the celebration of civic persons and institutions, to polemic and party formation, to the shaping of public opinion, indeed to the creation of political consciousness itself."[32]

About the spoken theater, in a passage often cited to justify political interpretations of Italian opera, John Loftis states:

> More perhaps than any other literary form, drama felt the impress of national politics. Theatres are sensitive at any time to political currents because they depend on public favour; and the theatres of the Augustan age ... were emphatically no exception ...
>
> Party leaders recognized the value of the theatres as organs of propaganda, in touch with the small group that was dominant politically; and at their bidding playwrights and actors became the spokesmen of faction.[33]

These Continental precedents and the politicized nature of English opera, drama, and poetry might indeed justify the generic expectation that Italian opera in London was politically allegorical or allusive.

But despite the apparent relevance of this background and context, it is unwarranted to generalize and extrapolate to Italian opera in London. Overlooked has been Lorenzo Bianconi's important point: "Clearly, not only the artistic and/or institutional constitution of opera varies widely from one country to another; different, too, are the various expressions of power, social structure, cultural conditions, literary, theatrical and musical traditions."[34] The organization, patronage, and governance of the London opera companies and the very nature of the librettos themselves suggest no reason to accept the generic expectation that Italian operas, with the exception of the Hanoverian celebratory pieces (see Appendix 5), are politically allegorical or allusive of the royal family or current political events.

Bianconi distinguishes several systems for producing opera, which range from complete subsidy and artistic control by a court (private patronage and invited audience) to capitalist/commercial models dependent on the market place and satisfying the playing public, along with hybrid forms. Court-sponsored opera was found in Vienna, Paris, and other German or Italian princely courts; public theaters were found in Hamburg; and impresario systems where management is devolved to a promoter who receives civic, noble, or aristocratic backing was typical of Venice and Florence.

Court-sponsored operas were products of poets, musicians, artists, and scenery designers often retained by the court. Performed privately a few times for invited privileged guests, the operas were not revived or put into repertory (exceptionally, those for Versailles were also repeated in Paris and entered repertory). As ceremonial affairs for special diplomatic or court occasions and tied to state protocol, the librettos address or allegorize the ruler to demonstrate and express the power and majesty of the prince, his reign, and dynasty. The Viennese operas, notes Bianconi, "though invariably newly composed, are stylistically quite invariable, true to their very function as one-off symbols and focal points of court celebration and rejoicing (as such, indeed, destined to a permanent place on the shelves of the Imperial library)."[35]

London's Italian opera system did not follow Continental patterns in a number of ways.[36] The operas produced at Vienna, Dresden, and other princely courts were usually allegorical and political in ways quite unlike those operas in London that are claimed to be political allegories. In the works for the Habsburg court, such as *Il pomo d'oro* (1668), *Il fuoco eterno custodito dalle Vestli* (1674), *La conquista del vello d'oro* (1678), and *Il Palladio in Roma* (1685), a mythological–allegorical program suitable for the occasion was purposely devised by the court poet through which the contemporary rulers, royal couples, or dynastic houses are allegorized through figures on stage; in the process, they gain the virtues and heroic status of the figures on stage. Characteristically, the singing characters in most of these celebratory operas were allegorical, emblematic, and mythico-historical figures: their presence is an obvious cue that the audience has entered the realm of allegory. For the benefit of audience members, prefaces, keys, and arguments spelled out the thoroughgoing allegorical program and the relations between the mythico-allegorical characters and the royal houses, persons, or nations represented.

A 1676 dramatic chamber composition[37] for the engagement of Archduchess Maria Antonia with King Carlos II of Spain has a typical allegorical program representing a double union presided over by Hymen, goddess of marriage:

> Hercules = 15-year-old Spanish king
> Omphale = Maria Antonia, daughter of Leopold I
> Hesperia = Spain
> Istria = Danube River
> Hymen

More abstract is the program for the three-act *Il fuoco eterno custodito dalle Vestali* (1674),[38] presented for the birth of the first child (a daughter) of Leopold I:

the eternal fire of Vesta = the House of Esterhazy
Publius Scipione = Emperor Leopold
the grounded ship = unfulfilled expectation of an heir
extinguishing the fire in the Temple of Vesta = death of
Empress Margarita Teresa

The libretto was illustrated with twelve stage sets.

The English court operas and the Restoration examples mentioned above are quite obviously symbolic–allegoric occasional works, intended to be applied to the monarch, dynasty, or royal family present at the opera. Robert Hume surveyed the political–allegorical interpretations offered for more than forty Restoration operas and readily admits clear allegory (usually in the royalist-celebratory mode) in *Ariane* (1674), *Psyche* (1675), *Albion and Albanius* (1685), *The Grove* (1700), and *The British Enchanters* (1706). But he concludes from his survey that otherwise there is no generic expectation that operas are either political or allegorical.[39]

By contrast, the Handel operas claimed to be politically allegorical or allusive are in a dominantly realist or mimetic mode. The problem arises from the attempt – in lieu of accompanying cues in title pages, dedications, prefaces, prologues, keys, or arguments spelling out the allegorical program – to apply such realist, historical plots to then current political persons and situations of Great Britain. Significantly, the generic expectation is fulfilled on precisely those occasions when London theater managers and impresarios did intend to celebrate weddings and birthdays of the royal family. These Hanoverian celebratory pieces do use allegory in the manner of Continental court operas.

The organization of the London opera companies, their financing, audience, repertory system, and the frequent revivals and adaptations made to operas all argue against seeing them as functioning similarly to court-sponsored operas. By the time of the introduction of Italian opera, the British court and monarch lacked the political authority and means to produce operas for themselves and guests as affairs of state and to celebrate the monarch's reign.

Robert Bucholz has charted the decline of court culture in late-Stuart Britain.[40] For a brief period early in the reign of Charles II, the exuberant "Merry Monarch" spent lavishly on the arts and exercised his expected role as a patron and impetus for artistic innovation. But his financial resources and limited attention span precluded any systematic promulgation of a royalist propaganda program, such as existed at the Continental courts. William III was decidedly uninterested in the arts, and, not insignificantly, the burning-down of Whitehall Palace in January 1698 meant the loss of a court theater large enough for plays or operas.

By the time of Queen Anne's reign, the court's position in England's cultural life had diminished. Absent a cultural program at court, artists and connoisseurs were on their own to find patronage and guidance in cultural fashions. Cultural leadership and patronage thus devolved to the great aristocrats, clubs and academies, impresarios and concert managers, and public (especially in literature and music).[41] Symptomatically, when two operas were produced at court for the queen's birthday on February 6 (*Arsinoe* in 1705 and *Camilla* in 1707), both were in production at the theaters.

The introduction of Italian-style opera in 1705 was due to the competition between the theater managers John Vanbrugh and Christopher Rich. Subsequently, various impresarios, a chartered royal company, or groups of aristocrats produced Italian opera as commercial enterprises largely dependent on subscriptions and subsidies, fickle and fashionable taste, and the variable supply of star singers. The impresarios and opera companies were largely free of royal control, although they were subject to some directives from the Lord Chamberlain, royal input about singers, or the threat of censorship.[42] The Royal Academy of Music at the Haymarket Theatre was guaranteed a £1,000 royal subsidy beginning in 1720, but was still greatly dependent for its viability on subscriptions and public ticket sales; the monarch never covered the debts of the companies.[43]

As Bianconi and Walker observe, in systems of court or aristocratic subvention, where opera is first and foremost an instrument of political authority and serves as an *instrumentum regni*, the addressee of the production is the promoter.[44] Not insignificantly, when the Royal Academy of Music produced its inaugural opera *Numitore* (1720), the libretto was dedicated to the directors of the Academy (Figure 2.1), who are listed in full on the dedication page.

What little we know about how librettos were chosen and adapted suggests it is unlikely there was much if any consideration of making them apply to contemporary British politics. Rather than purpose-written librettos that might be directly relevant to contemporary events (such as the Continental court operas, *The Beggar's Opera* [1728], or the Patriot dramas of the 1730s), most London operas on historical subjects were based on pre-existing librettos,[45] and many hands were involved in choosing and adapting them.[46] The Royal Academy's agent in Italy, Owen Swiney, took it upon himself to vet, obtain, or recommend librettos for

NUMITORE.

D R A M A.

Da Rapprefentarfi

Nell' R E G I O T E A T R O d' *H A Y - M A R K E T.*

P E R

L' *Accademia Reale di Mufica*

Di P A O L O A N T O N I O R O L L I, Segretario *Italiano* della Medefima.

Poftquam cæpit agros extendere victor, & urbem Latior amplecti Murus——— Acceffit numerifque modifque licentia major.

La Mufica è del Signor G I O V A N N I P O R T A, Virtuofo di S. E. il Signor Duca di *Wharton.*

Le Scene fono del Signor R O B E R T O C L E R I C I, Ingegnero della Reale Accademia.

L O N D O N:

Printed for T H O. W O O D in *Little Britain.*

M. D C C. X X.

Figure 2.1 Title page of *Numitore*, produced at the Haymarket Theatre, London, 1720. Photo: courtesy of the Newberry Library, Chicago.

London.[47] Directors occasionally chose or suggested librettos.[48] Several operas were begun or composed and then put aside for a later season, and several librettos were chosen to ensure prominent roles for stars in the companies at that time. Many directors of the opera companies had brought back librettos or even full scores from their Grand Tours to Italy.[49] Nicola Haym, one of the Royal Academy's London secretaries, had a collection of over 260 titles that served as source material for London operas.[50] Composers had some input in choosing librettos. Handel apparently had a collection of librettos gathered from operas he had seen produced in Germany and Italy.

Giuseppe Riva in London wrote to Lodovico Muratori, a colleague in Italy, to explain that a libretto being sent could not be used that season "since our composers have chosen their librettos for the coming season and are already at work on them."[51] Librettos undergoing adaptation for London in 1726 had goals other than political application. Riva added that the librettos "have to be reformed, or I should rather say deformed, in order to bring them into the shape which the English public favors." Riva had easily fathomed the English taste:

> people like very few recitatives, thirty airs and one duet at least distributed over the three acts. The subject must be simple, tender, heroic – Roman, Greek or possibly Persian, but never Gothic or Lombard. For this year, and for the next two, there must be two equal parts in the operas for Cuzzoni and Faustina. Senesino takes the principal male character and his part must be heroic.[52]

With the exception of *Riccardo primo* (1727) and the Hanoverian celebratory works, there are no signs that the choice of, or adaptations made to, a source libretto were done to allude or apply to the specifics of British politics or the royal family.[53] The case of *Teofane* is instructive. Produced at Dresden at a new court theater seating 2,000 in 1719 with music by Antonio Lotti for the marriage of Frederick Augustus to the Habsburg Archduchess Maria Josepha, it was probably seen by Handel. The subject of the marriage of the Saxon Emperor Otto II to Theophanu, daughter of the Byzantine emperor, was a fitting subject to celebrate a dynastic wedding. Each of the three acts was followed by an allegorical scene. When the libretto was set by Handel and produced in London as *Ottone* (1723), the adaptations – and especially the removal of the allegories that concluded each act – were made precisely to eliminate the political or dynastic topicality.[54] The contrast is manifest in the libretto title pages (Figures 2.2 and Figures 2.3). The addressee and occasion of *Teofane* dominate the page, whereas the title-page layout of *Ottone* is uniform with other London printed opera librettos where the dedicatee's name is relegated to an interior dedication page.

Had London librettists, opera directors, or managers intended to make their operas politically topical by allegory, allusion, parallel, or application, it is plausible to assume the librettos would have been purpose-written, have recognizable allegorical and topical content, and contain dedicatory epistles, prologues, textual cues, epilogues, or keys to direct the audience to the intended interpretation or application. The Royal Academy, the Handel–Heidegger partnership, and the Opera of the Nobility were managed, patronized, and subsidized primarily by Whig aristocrats, courtiers, and office holders dependent upon the court and ministry. The most obvious

TEOFANE
DRAMMA PER MUSICA
rappresentato
Nel Regio Elettoral Teatro di Dresda
IN OCCASIONE
Delle felicisfime NOZZE
De' Serenisfimi Principi
FEDERIGO AUGU-STO,
Principe Reale di Pollonia, & Eletto-
rale di Saffonia,

e
MARIA GIOSEFFA,
Arciduchefla d' Auftria.

DRESDA,
Per Gio: Corrado Stössel, Stampatore di Corte.
M DCC XIX.

Figure 2.2 Title page of *Teofane*, produced at Dresden, 1717. Photo: courtesy of the Sibley Music Library, Eastman School of Music, University of Rochester.

political content for such operas would be validation or celebration of the Hanoverian family. However, when the generic expectation leads to interpretations that are subversive or critical of the Hanoverians, the method must be suspected of being flawed and unhistorical.

Politics

The possibility that political interpretations not intended by the author or manifested in the work could be spun from the most innocuous text was recognized by eighteenth-century writers themselves. The author of one

OTTONE,

Re di GERMANIA.

DRAMA.

Da Rapprefentarfi

Nel REGIO TEATRO
d' *HAY-MARKET,*

PER

La Reale Accademia di Mufica.

LONDON:

Printed by THO. WOOD in *Little Britain.*

M. DCC. XXIII.

Figure 2.3 Title page of *Ottone*, produced at the Haymarket Theatre, London, 1723. Photo: courtesy of Newberry Library, Chicago.

play in 1702 complained of the "Malice of those Persons, who have endeavoured to pervert the Genuine Meaning of some Sentences, and give them a wrong Turn of Design, which was never in the view of the Author."[55] Lewis Theobald may be recalling Joseph Addison's *Cato* (1713) when he wrote in 1717 about audiences politicizing plays:

Party and private Sentiments have so great a Prevalance, that the chief View with them [the audience] is to wrest an innocent Author to their own Construction, and form to themselves an Idea of Faction from Passages, whence the Poet little suspected it should arise … [They] sit stupidly listening for accidental Expressions struck out of the Story, which speak the Sense of their own Principles and Perswasion. Such an

Application of Passages is grown so Epidemical, that a War of *Whig* and *Tory* is carried on by way of *Clap* and *Hiss* upon the meaning of a single Sentence, that, unless Prophetically, could never have any Relation to Modern Occurrences.[56]

Jonathan Swift lamented that "Nothing is more frequent than for Commentators to force Interpretation, which the Author never meant."[57] So as expected, after *Gulliver's Travels* appeared, John Gay wrote to Swift predicting the tale will "meet with people of greater perspicuity, who are in search for particular applications in every leaf."[58]

We need not be paralyzed trying to ascertain whether an Italian opera was political or topical and whether modern political interpretations are plausible and historical. There is a wide range of seventeenth- and eighteenth-century plays and allegorical narratives in partisan periodicals that were recognized in their time as topical and political, from which we can derive criteria for assessing whether an opera was intended as, has the features of, or was received as political.

The Restoration was a super-heated political milieu where politics was a no-holds-barred blood sport. The theater was part of the political arena of the day, and playwrights, plays, masques, and dramatic operas had partisan agendas and applications that contemporaries were quick to note.[59]

A series of crises – Titus Oates' allegations of a plot to destroy the Anglican establishment and return Britain to Catholic rule (the Popish Plot),[60] the Rye House Plot (a Protestant scheme to assassinate the king), a series of parliamentary bills to exclude James, Charles' Catholic brother, from the throne (the subsequent Exclusion Crisis, 1678–81),[61] and Monmouth's Rebellion – all found their way into literature and drama. Politically dangerous intentions, sympathies, loyalties, or insurrection were suspected everywhere, especially on the stage. Both heroic tragedy and comedy risked offending one party or the other: Whigs sniffed out evidence of Catholic sympathies, and Tories rooted out treason against the monarchy. Even basic themes and tropes themselves could be politically charged.[62]

Providing a vehicle for topical comment under the cover of distant events, Shakespeare was rewritten to court current political topicality.[63] From October 1678 to June 1682, nine Shakespeare plays were altered for production, and two of them were suppressed by the Lord Chamberlain (Nahum Tate's *The History of King Richard the Second* [1680] and John Crowne's *Henry the Sixth, The First Part* [1681]). Later, Colley Cibber's 1699 adaptation of *Richard III* was cut by order of the Lord Chamberlain to remove the first act, for fear its characterization of Henry VI would remind the audience of James II.[64] Michael Dobson shows how the adaptations of some plays "participate in and enact the ideological turmoil of this extraordinary passage of constitutional history": *Titus Andronicus* (1678) became "a satire on Oates and the Whigs"; *Troilus and Cressida* (1679), a "guarded royalist polemic"; *King Lear* (1681), "a bastard's rebellion is crushed and the legitimate monarch triumphantly restored"; and *Cymbeline* (1682), a "vindication of a virtuous British princess … celebrating the … political success of her royal father."[65] Cautionary lessons about the consequences of banishment and rebellion would be especially applicable to England during the reign of Charles II.

A number of plays that became enmeshed – intentionally or not by the author – in partisan politics provide the relevant context for assessing how Handel's contemporaries might have approached politics in the theater. Produced in the aftermath of the Exclusion Crisis and Monmouth Rebellion was the Tory Thomas Otway's play *Venice Preserv'd, or A Plot Discovered* (February 9, 1682). Based on a historical event of 1618, the play dramatizes the plotting of conspirators against the Venetian Senate. Ultimately, one of them betrays the plot, and the conspirators are put to death. There is abundant evidence the play was perceived as highly partisan.[66] In his epilogue, Otway predicted that the Whigs will "damn this Play." It indeed won immediate Tory favor and the court attended special performances.

Otway's prologue made certain the audience recognized the play's relation to its times:[67]

> In these distracted times, when each man dreads
> The bloody stratagems of busy heads;
> When we have feared three years we know not what,
> Till witnesses begin to die o'th' rot,
> What made our poet meddle with a plot?

Modern critics have inconsistently and variously interpreted *Venice Preserv'd* as a political allegory, in which the Venetian conspirators represent the Whig exclusionists, conspirators, revolutionaries, or the Popish Plot; and the Venetian Senate variously represents the English court, Parliament, or Whig leaders.[68]

Phillip Harth shows that for an English audience the Venetian conspiracy would resemble only the Popish Plot. Attempts by modern interpreters to see Tory political partisanship in the allegory or the parallel of the Venetian conspiracy to contemporary England, Harth demonstrates, are mistaken and contradict the experience of most readers and audiences. The partisanship of the play lay not with topical parallel, he argues, but with the two comic "Nicky-Nacky scenes," in which Otway invented the character of Antonio to viciously characterize the Whig Earl of Shaftesbury according to all the prevailing Tory stereotypes of him. Significantly, when the topicality of the play passed, these scenes were later dropped.[69] What was attractive to Tories in power at the time was application of the universal precept: men should be loyal to the state to avoid the consequences of rebellions and insurrection.

John Dryden and Nathaniel Lee's *The Duke of Guise* (November 28, 1682), originally titled *The Parallel*, is based on the episode of the civil unrest produced in late sixteenth-century France by the Catholic League.[70] The elements of the historical situation – a Catholic childless king (Henri III/Charles II) with a collateral Protestant heir (Duke of Guise/Duke of Monmouth); the States General (Parliament), with support of the people, wishing to exclude the heir from the throne; the duke's adherents plotting a Holy League (Whig Association); the king summoning the States General away from Paris to Blois (Oxford Parliament); and imminent civil war – all had many parallels with contemporary English politics.

If any in the audience were too dull to notice the topical parallels, Dryden helpfully began his prologue "Our Play's a Parallel" and proceeded to spell out the parallels. In presenting their historical parallels, Dryden and Lee faced an embarrassing circumstance they could not evade: Henri III was guilty of treachery and murder in arranging the Duke of Guise's death. When news of the play got abroad in July 1682, the Lord Chamberlain temporarily banned the play at the request of the Duke of Monmouth, who was shown in the play ultimately assassinated by orders of Henry III/Charles II. Dryden showed the Lord Chamberlain the play's source and convinced him the parallel between Monmouth and the Duke of Guise derived from the historical source.

Even before the play was published, Whig pamphleteers revived the malicious and treasonous parallels and charged that Dryden and Lee were advocating assassination of Monmouth.[71] Dryden was forced to follow up with *The Vindication* (1683), asserting (rather lamely and unconvincingly) that the parallel between the French League and Whigs was a parallel not of men, but of the times. A contemporary newsletter reported the impact of Dryden's play:

July 29, 1682. A play having been made [by] Mr. Dryden tearmed ye Duke of Guise [it being] supposed to Levell att the villifying the Duke of Monmouth & many other protestants & great Interest made for the Acting thereof but bringing to the knowledge of his Matie the same was forbidd for though his Maties pleasure is to be dissatisfyed and angry with the Duke of Monmouth, yet hee is not willing that others should abuse him out of a naturall affection for him.[72]

Even though not carried through consistently, the play's parallels do have an application to contemporary England that serves Tory propaganda: showing the dangers of civil war posed by the Whigs and defending Charles' strong actions as reasonable and proper in response to the Exclusion Crisis.

Dryden's *The Spanish Fryar* (1680) started out innocently enough as what he called a "Protestant Play."[73] When first performed, the play's anti-Catholic sentiments fitted the times, especially in the comic character of the fat pimp, Father Dominic. In the play's serious plot, the reigning Queen of Aragon had inherited the throne from a usurper; she agrees to the murder of the rightful imprisoned king to secure her claim to the throne. When revived in 1686, after the accession of the Catholic James II, the play was quickly forbidden by the Lord Chamberlain.

When anti-Catholicism was once more in season, Queen Mary carelessly ordered, to her later embarrassment, a performance of the play on May 28, 1689. The audience and queen quickly saw the parallel of the usurper Queen of Aragon to Mary, who now shared with William the throne abandoned by her father. The Earl of Nottingham described that night at the theater:

Some unhappy expressions [referring to the queen as a "usurper"] … put her in some disorder, and forced her to hold up her fan, and often look behind her and call for her palatine, and hood, and any thing she could next think of, while those who were in the pit before her turned their heads over their shoulders, and all in general directed their looks towards her, whenever their fancy led them to make application of what was said. [74]

The episode, wrote Nottingham, "furnished the town with discourse for near a month."

Most celebrated as a party play of the period is the Whig Joseph Addison's *Cato* (April 14, 1713) premiered during the Tory ministry of Oxford and Bolingbroke. Larded with noble paeans to Stoic virtue, it presents as an *exemplum virtutis* the suicide of the republican martyr for liberty, Cato of Utica. The great-grandson of Cato the Censor, he follows the path of heroic virtue and would rather die by his own hand than live under the tyranny of Julius Caesar.

Addison drafted the play sometime after 1691 while at Oxford, and it was read by Dryden. He continued to work on it while on his Grand Tour, and showed it to Jonathan Swift, Colley Cibber, and Richard Steele when he returned in 1704. It was then an incomplete torso of four acts. According to his biographer Thomas Tickell, his friends "prevailed with him to put the last finishing to it, at a time when they thought the doctrine of Liberty very seasonable."[75] Sometime before its premiere, Addison showed the play to the staunch Whig Lady Mary Wortley Montagu, upon whose advice he added "some stronger Lines on Liberty" throughout the play.[76]

On its opening night, Steele and the Whig Kit-Cats packed the house with a partisan audience who showered the play with applause. The play had twenty performances through May and closed only because cast member Mrs. Oldfield was reaching the end of her pregnancy. Tonson purchased the copyright for the unheard of sum of £107 10s and the printed play ran to eight editions in the year. Partisans of both parties claimed *Cato* as their own, as a near contemporary wrote in a prologue for a revival in 1717:

> Contending Parties all his Words apply'd,
> And strove to lift the Patriot on their Side;
> Nay, by how natural an Application,
> He chim'd with every Faction in the Nation.[77]

A play extolling liberty above tyranny could have universal application as an injunction to be vigilant for liberty against encroachments by the rule of one man.[78] But liberty had long been the Whig cry, so amid the Whig–Tory strife of the last years of Queen Anne's reign, a play by a Whig declaiming for liberty was unavoidably topical and seen (and cheered) as a Whig play. Colley Cibber saw that *Cato* seemed "plainly written upon what are called *Whig* Principles."[79] By contrast, the Tory ministry could easily be seen as sympathetic to tyranny, for it had concluded a speedy peace with the absolutist Louis XIV, a peace seen as betraying the Protestant Succession and favorable to the interest of the Pretender.

While there was little disagreement that *Cato* was a Whig piece, confusion arose when it came to making specific personal identifications. Shortly after the premiere, the Countess of Bristol reported to her husband, "the Tory's say Cato is meant for my L:d T[reasurer]"[80] (or Robert Harley, Earl of Oxford). "The Key or Explanation to the History, and Play of Cato"[81] (?1713) claims Caesar as a partisan of "the Tyrannical Party" (p. 8), whereas Cato represents "the Duke of *Marlborough*, famous not only for his great Success in War, but also for his Admirable Sedateness and Presence of Mind in time of Battle" (p. iii). Fleshing out the roster, he continues: "As for *Lucius* and *Sempronius*, the first is made a *Coward*, and the other a *Turn Coat*" – clearly intended as Oxford and Bolingbroke – "two great *Ministers* of *State*, now in Favour." The added epithets, "whose Fame for Loyalty to their *Queen*, Love to their *Country*, and Zeal for the *Church of England*, will never Decay," are certainly Whiggish irony.

The "Key" hammers home the personation of Cato for Marlborough:

> Great *Marlborough* is the Hero whom the *Play*,
> Did Lively represent the other Day,
> Before the Audience of the *British* Stage,
> For He's the Hero of the present Age:
> Whilst *Cato*'s Virtues are esteem'd Divine,
> In Famous *Marlborough* they'll ever shine;
> Nay, Future Ages to their Seed shall Tell,
> That *Marlborough*'s Fame, did *Cato*'s Fame Excell.[82]

To deflate the Whig claim that Cato represents Marlborough, the author of *Mr. Addison Turn'd Tory: or, the Scene Inverted: Wherein It Is Made Appear That the Whigs Have Misunderstood that Celebrated Author in His Applauded Tragedy, Call'd Cato* (1713) demonstrates that Marlborough rather resembles the tyrant Caesar, and that Cato resembles the Tory minister the Earl of Oxford. To counter Whig appropriation of the play, Oxford, sitting in a box next to the author and his friends, likewise applauded the Whig lines to show the lines carried no offense or application to Tories. Since rumor had it that by the strokes against a tyrant the play must mean either Oxford or Bolingbroke,[83] the Tories during a performance took a collection in the boxes and Bolingbroke summoned Booth, a known Tory who played Cato, to his box and gave him a purse of fifty guineas "For his honest Opposition to a perpetual Dictator,"[84] now conflating Booth with Cato and thus identifying Caesar with Marlborough, who had asked the queen to make him Captain General for life.

But the staunch Whig John Dennis, ever alert to the moral lessons conveyed by art, saw that tying Cato to Marlborough had the effect contrary to supporting liberty: "Shewing a Man of consummate Virtue unfortunate only for supporting Liberty, must of Necessity in a free Nation be of pernicious Consequence, and must justly raise the highest Indignation in all true Lovers of Liberty."[85]

From these plays, *Tamerlane* (to be discussed below), narrative fiction in partisan newspapers (Chapters 4 and 5), and a group of plays from the 1730s (Chapter 7), we can identify circumstances and textual features that mark these works as intended and received as political:

There is usually biographic or documentary evidence of the author's goals or motives in writing the work.

The politics of the work has a relation to the author's own political biography and his political allegiance and circumstances.

There is often paratextual material such dedications, prefaces, or keys containing hints at the political application.

There are textual cues or aspects of plot and character that direct or invite comparisons to the real-world person or situation implicated.

The issues raised in the work resonate with the prominent political issues of the day.

There is ample evidence that contemporaries remarked on the politics and political applications.[86]

There is evidence of official response, such as censorship, prohibition, or replies in official journals.

There is a clear answer to the question *Cui bono?* The play promotes or advocates the interest of a political party or faction.

None of the Italian operas on historical subjects that have been claimed to be politically topical – with the exception of *Riccardo primo* (1727), which carries a dedicatory poem to George II – have any such corresponding features or circumstances.[87]

What made Addison's *Cato* so susceptible to reader application and to conflicting political interpretation by its contemporaries is instructive. While Addison probably began the play without thought to topical application, at the time he was completing it under Lady Mary's guidance, he larded it with Whiggish sentiments – unmistakably making it a party piece. It is the lack of textual cues or distinctive features given to Cato beyond his thumping for liberty that allows him to be opportunistically identified with Marlborough or Oxford.

The case of Addison's contemporaries finding contradictory personations in *Cato* is similar to the cases where, in the absence of cues in the text, modern interpreters discover contradictory personations for the same operatic character in *Silla* (1713) or *Floridante* (1721). These interpretations must be seen as reader applications, not part of the textual meaning of the operas. But there is this significant difference: in the case of *Cato*, we have contemporary comment that compels our attention to what these reader interpretations reveal about the political climate of the day and how contemporaries appropriated *Cato* to do political work.

To see how the generic expectation about opera has worked out in practice, we can examine the political–allegorical interpretations that have been offered by modern scholars for three Handel operas – all written during the height of Tory–Whig strife during the reign of Queen Anne. Brian Trowell proposed a political allegory for Handel's first London opera *Rinaldo*, which premiered on February 24, 1711. Trowell suggests that given the context of the times – the threat of armed invasion by Jacobites, the War of the Spanish Succession, the perceived subversive threat of Italian opera, and the imminence of Handel's employer, the Elector of Hanover, as the next king of England – "the choice of subject for the new opera was likely also to have been significant … It was no doubt easy, in 1711, to reinterpret its symbolism [the story of Rinaldo and Armida] and substitute the northern Protestant alliance for the Crusaders, and for the alluring but insidious pagans, their Catholic opponents."[88]

The context for February 1711 is the concluding years of the War of the Spanish Succession. Britain, the Dutch United Provinces, and Austria were allied against France over the question of the succession to the Spanish throne. The Grand Alliance of 1701, led by the Duke of Marlborough and Prince Eugene of Austria, sought to prevent Philip of Anjou, the French dauphin, from assuming the throne of Spain and thus uniting France and Spain under the Bourbons. From the Whig vantage point, a successful war would realize William III's goal to contain Louis XIV's ambitions toward universal monarchy in Europe and secure the Protestant succession in Britain.

That *Rinaldo* had an original Italian libretto by Giacomo Rossi, derived from a scenario by the Whig Aaron Hill and adapted from an episode in Tasso, rather than an adaptation of an earlier source libretto, does initially suggest that it could have been written to carry allegorical significance. Of the cast – Godfrey, general of the European forces; Eustacio, his brother; Rinaldo; Argantes, King of Jerusalem; the Magician; the Herald; Arminda, the enchantress Queen of the Amazons; Almirena, daughter to Godfrey and betrothed to Rinaldo; and assorted spirits, furies, and soldiers – Trowell merely divides it into Crusaders and pagans, paralleling the Protestant alliance and its Catholic opponents:

Protestant alliance	Catholic opponents
Godfrey	Argantes
Eustacio	Armida
Rinaldo	Mermaids
Almirena	Spirits
	Furies

Nothing in the preface or dedication to Anne connects the production with politics or the war, or makes any hint to relate the Crusaders to the Protestant alliance; nothing in the libretto itself cues the audience to look for contemporary analogs or allegory; and the narrative of *Rinaldo* has no credible analogs to the progress of the war.

Beyond the convenient good–evil polarity aligning the Crusaders/ Protestant alliance against pagans/France and Spain from the original source in Tasso, Trowell's proposed allegory has too many inconsistencies, loose ends, and gaps to suggest the libretto was intended as, or taken as, a contemporary political allegory. The supposed allegory is too imprecisely drawn. There was, strictly speaking, no northern Protestant alliance at the time; the Grand Alliance also included Catholic Austria and Portugal; and for a while, the Duchy of Parma was an ally. The Crusaders/Protestant alliance identification has to disregard the fact the original Crusaders were Roman Catholics, who in 1711 were both enemies and allies of the Protestants.

It is not clear how one would align Godfrey, Rinaldo, and Eustacio with the Alliance powers (Britain, the United Provinces, and Austria); Argantes, possessor of Jerusalem, would have to be Louis XIV; but this leaves his Armida unaccounted for. Any contemporary allegory of the War of the Spanish Succession would certainly focus on a Marlborough figure, and Godfrey (described as "Capitano Generale" in the *Personaggi*) is the best candidate; but Rinaldo is, in fact, the hero of the opera. While the Crusaders sought to capture Jerusalem, the Grand Alliance had the capture of no single city as its goal in its two-fronted war in the Low Countries and Spain, and was in fact responding to French aggression and fears of France as a universal monarchy. Nor can Rinaldo's dalliance and enchantment by Armida, his deliverance by Godfrey, and capture of Jerusalem be reconciled with the events of the war. Hill was a pedestrian but competent writer, and we could expect that had he wanted an allegory, he was certainly capable of devising a plot that paralleled the war and made a political point.

Of equal importance, there is no contemporary comment recognizing the allegory or political application. Given the heated political pamphleteering occurring during the Tory ministry – at the height of the *Examiner* and *Medley* exchanges between Swift and Arthur Mainwaring,[89] for example – it is unlikely a work celebrating the war aims of the previous Whig ministry would not have drawn comment from ministry polemicists. Moreover, it is curious that an opera validating the Whig cause of the war against absolutism would be the subject of such satire by the staunch Whig Joseph Addison in the *Spectator* papers of March 1711.

To the extent that *Rinaldo* would celebrate the Grand Alliance, it would be Whiggish; but if so, we are left to puzzle why, after September 1710 (the Fall of the Whigs), a Tory ministry with the Duke of Shrewsbury (a Whig turned Tory collaborator) as Lord Chamberlain would allow performances of the opera, for a celebration of the war would embarrass the Tories and Anne, the dedicatee of the opera.

Handel's *Teseo* (January 10, 1713) has been found to take a parti-san political position. As Paul Monod states, "Handel's operas ... con-tain veiled hints about politics [and] impart valuable information about the pervasive influence of politics on the arts."[90] The libretto, adapted by Nicola Haym from Quinault's *Thésée* (1695), relates – with the usual minor characters, subplots, tangled love triangles, and vengeful spurned lovers – how Theseus, a foreign prince, and Agilea, a princess under Egeus' protection, are united, overcoming the malicious interference by Egeus and the enchantress Medea. The ultimate moral is the triumph of virtuous love.

Monod uses the "tagging" approach we saw used for *Rinaldo*, whereby contemporary counterparts are found for characters in the opera; but his account disregards many characters and the main thread of the narrative. From the full cast –

Egeus, King of Athens	Arcanus, confident of Egeus
Agilea, princess under his care	Medea, enchantress
Clitia, Agilea's confident	Minerva and priests
Theseus, foreign prince	Chorus of Atheneans

– Monod aligns Theseus with William III and Egeus with James II. The opera, he states, asserts the Hanoverian right to the British throne:

By the end of 1712, the main political issue in England was the succession to the throne ... The plot of *Teseo* leaves no doubt as to who had the best claim. The chorus of Athenians, "the will of the people," applauds the eponymous hero of the opera [Theseus/William III] as their true monarch. As a successful war leader who rises to the throne through popular approval, Teseo resembles William of Orange, and the flawed, misguided King Egeo is reminiscent of James II.[91]

In January 1713 the raging political issue of the moment was the pending peace with France and its betrayal (in Whig eyes) of Hanover and the Allies. At the moment of the opera, the succession issue was settled by law, not by popular acclamation: the Crown would pass to Electress Sophie of Hanover and her heirs. The crisis of the day was whether the Tory ministers Oxford and Bolingbroke would be able to engineer the conversion of the Pretender (son of James II) to the Anglican faith so he could resume his place in the succession. In the event, he chose not to.

As with *Rinaldo*, there are no circumstances in Haym's or the manager Swiney's biographies or cues in the dedication, preface, the libretto itself, or reception to hint the opera was intended or perceived as politically alle-gorical or allusive. Nothing in the libretto suggests contemporary analogs to Theseus and Egeus. The proposed analogs are so inexact, inconsistent, or lacking connection with the contemporary British political situation that the entire allegorical program is unpersuasive.

Since the allegorical interpretation seems to be set about 1688 with Egeus/ James as King of Athens/England, we would expect the political analogs to be the invitation to William by the "Immortal Seven," his invasion, James' flight to France, or the Convention Parliament that offered the Crown to William and Mary. But in the opera, Theseus/William is fighting in Athens/ England to preserve the throne of Egeus/James. Monod does not account for the fact that at the final scene Theseus is revealed as Egeus' son incognito. In any case, it was William's wife Mary who had the more direct right to the throne by blood as James II's daughter. But importantly, the right of Egeus/James to the throne is never questioned. Theseus is acclaimed by the people as Egeus' successor – not to supplant him – because Egeus' son is believed absent from the kingdom. Other critical plot elements have no contemporary analogs: such as the fact that Egeus and Theseus both are suitors for Agilea, the role of the enchantress Medea as a rival to Agilea for Theseus, and Medea's transformation of the palace into a desert and her torment of Agilea and Theseus. Nor is it clear why a Tory ministry would sanction an opera so clearly Williamite and Whiggish.

One of Handel's most puzzling operas is *Silla*, whose dedication is signed by Rossi, June 2, 1713, three months after the Peace of Utrecht was signed. While scores and a single copy of the libretto survive, there is no evidence that the opera was ever performed or, if so, when and where.[92] On the basis of the stage sets described, it would have required performance at the Haymarket Theatre (at the time, called the Queen's Theatre).[93] With a fulsome dedication to the French Ambassador Extraordinary Louis-Marie D'Aumont Rochebaron, the opera, if produced, would probably have been part of the lavish entertainments D'Aumont mounted in London to project the status and power of France.[94]

The story of the general Lucius Cornelius Sulla, who returns to Rome to become a wanton and dissolute tyrant, is argued by Duncan Chisholm to be part of a Tory or the French ambassador's attack on the Whig hero the Duke of Marlborough.[95] As Chisholm rightly demonstrates, at the time Marlborough was indeed subject to vicious comparisons with evil Roman figures, such as Sejanus, Catiline, and Caesar. The Marlborough–Sulla identification, though, is more likely to be a case of reader application rather than one put there by the author or recognized by the audience. Most significantly, as Chisholm shows, D'Aumont wrote home to his ministry at length describing events of his embassy, but makes no mention of the opera. The opera is not mentioned in the Colman opera register,[96] nor is there any comment in the London newspapers, manuscript newsletters, or private correspondence. Unlike Nicholas Rowe's play *Tamerlane* (1701), which hints at its own intended parallels, the retelling of the return of Sulla shows no signs of being adapted to give Sulla the traits for which Marlborough was reviled by the Tories: his prolongation of the war, his tyranny over the queen, his avarice and wealth accumulated from use of public funds, and his ambition to be Captain General for life.[97] Aside from the parallel of a victorious commander, Sulla's domestic conquest and murder of a domestic rival, his mass slaughter of Romans, and his designs on other men's wives have no counterparts in Marlborough's career at that time.

By the time of the opera's presumed production in June 1713, it is not clear who would have benefited from a censure of the self-exiled Marlborough. The Captain General was then already in disgrace: the Queen had stripped him of his command on December 31, 1711. Tories had indicted Marlborough and the Whig politician Robert Walpole for their alleged war profiteering in January 1712; on December 1, 1712, Marlborough began his self-imposed exile on the Continent; in March 1713, the ministry had concluded what Whigs said was a "shameless" peace with France that betrayed the Grand Alliance and the interests of Hanover and Great Britain; and an angry Anne would suspend work on Blenheim in June. In retrospect, the Marlborough–Sulla interpretation would have revived claims that the Tories had betrayed the interests of the Grand Alliance and the elector.

Another interpretation proposed by Ellen Harris presents *Silla* as an allegory of the arrival (at some unforeseen date) of Elector Georg Ludwig of Hanover to London as King George I. But the correspondences are tenuous. In this reading, Georg's future arrival in London supposedly parallels Sulla's return and conquest of Rome; his parliamentary-sanctioned accession to the throne, Sulla's becoming dictator. Georg's earlier repudiation and imprisonment of his wife and his taking mistresses in Hanover parallel Sulla's dissolute behavior upon his return.[98] But at the presumed time of the opera's production – June 2, 1713 – Georg Ludwig had been the heir to the British throne for five days, the dowager Electress Sophia having died on May 28, so the opera was not likely devised to defame him.

A Marlborough or Georg Ludwig supposedly paralleled by Sulla does not serve the character-destroying work that Chisholm and Harris suppose. The plots of many operas are driven by tyrants and malefactors, and an eighteenth-century audience or reader would have followed the plot to its conclusion and its dispensation of poetic justice before passing moral judgment. Whatever political work the opera might do in blackening the character of Marlborough or Georg Ludwig is undercut by the *lieto fine*.

A crucial element of the plot must be considered. In Act III, scene x, Sulla and his wife, Metella, declare their love as Sulla embarks on a ship bound on a secret mission to Sicily. After the ship departs, Metella describes a storm at sea with a comet, lightning, and thunder; Sulla's ship is wrecked and Metella rescues him. At the *scena ultima*, they enter a square in Rome just at the moment that Mars has revealed himself in a cloud. Sulla falls to his knees, renounces his titles, begs forgiveness from Mars for his crimes, and says he will seek better days with his wife. In the *coro*, the cast assure us that those caught in storms can hope for relief from heaven.

Thus, instead of a portrayal of a tyrant and his misdeeds, *Silla* is a providential tale of divine intervention coupled with a *deus ex machina* that restores freedom and liberty to Rome; Sulla is represented as an exemplar of a ruler who yields to divine omens and authority, repents, and turns to a virtuous life of retirement. Given the full arc of the opera's plot, it becomes harder to reconcile Sulla as an allegory for Marlborough or Georg Ludwig. Since Marlborough had already voluntarily done six months earlier what the opera's denouement represents Sulla honorably doing, the opera might just as well be endorsing Marlborough's actions. And if the opera is a damning portrait of Marlborough, why Handel, a representative to London of the elector (and so identified in the libretto), would collaborate in a work indicting the military genius guaranteeing the Protestant succession of his employer in Hanover needs to be explained.

The generic expectation leads, as we see in the cases of *Rinaldo*, *Teseo*, and *Silla*, to allegorical interpretations that are incomplete, inconsistent, and fail to relate adequately to the circumstances of contemporary politics. Interpreters treat as allegories stage works that exhibit no signs of being intended, devised, written, adapted, or perceived as topically allegorical or allusive. Moreover, the opera characters lack distinctive traits that would identify them with contemporary counterparts.

Allegory

If we are interested in rescuing interpretation and understanding of Italian operas as an historical undertaking, teaching us how operas were received and understood by Handel's contemporaries, we must accept that not all works should be subject to allegorical reading. As C. S. Lewis cautions,

No story can be devised by the wit of man which cannot be interpreted allegorically by the wit of some other man ... Therefore the mere fact that you *can* allegorize the work before you is of itself no proof that is an allegory. Of course you can allegorize it. You can allegorize anything, whether in art or real life. I think we should take a hint from the lawyers. A man is not tried at the assizes until there has been shown to be a *prima-facie* case against him. We ought not to proceed to allegorize any work until we have plainly set out the reasons for regarding it as an allegory at all.[99]

This caution returns us to our previous distinction between works that are by intent, form, and content recognizable as allegories and what Rosamond Tuve calls "imposing of allegory upon an already extant artistic fiction."[100]

Again, we need not be paralyzed in trying to evaluate in an historical sense whether an opera was intended or received as an allegory. Numerous critical essays and literary texts give us a good idea of what the period meant and understood by allegory.[101] Allegory was primarily a dual-level narrative or an extended metaphor. All the major literal characters and actions in the text – whether epic poem or prose narrative – have a fairly consistent, stable, and parallel relationship with their analogs in the figurative level. Allegory is usually found in extended narratives such as epics and romances or prose works of a visionary, fanciful, dream-like nature. Such works often violate probability or nature, and this very non-realistic fable or plot implies a hidden, parallel fable of human passions, temptations, vices, and virtues.[102]

The most extensive account of allegory is provided by the poet and librettist John Hughes. For him, an allegory is "a Fable or Story, in which, under imaginary Persons or Things, is shadow'd some real Action or instructive Moral."[103] Characteristic of an allegory is what Sir Richard Blackmore calls its "double Sense": "there is both a *Literal* Sense obvious to every Reader, and that gives him satisfaction enough if he sees no farther; and besides another *Mystical* or *Typical* Sense, not hard to be discover'd by those Readers that penetrate the matter deeper."[104] Hughes applies to allegory an image from Aesop: "as Grapes on a Vine are cover'd by the Leaves which grow about them, so under the pleasant Narrations and Fictions of the Poets, there are couch'd many useful Morals and Doctrines."[105]

Many of Hughes' examples are epics, a genre that was expected to be allegorical and to teach moral lessons.[106] Most definitions of epic followed Le Bossu, stressing its moral function: "Epic is a discourse invented by art to form the manners by such instructions as are disguised under the allegories of one important action."[107] Examples cited by Hughes as allegories include Milton's *Paradise Lost*, Aesop's *Fables*, Spenser's *Fairy Queen*, Virgil's *Aeneid*, the stories of Circe and Calypso (from Homer's *Odyssey*), Alcina (from Ariosto's *Orlando furioso*), and Armida (from Tasso's *Gerusalemme liberata*). The fabulous character of the literal level of these stories cued the reader that these were allegories, that there was "another Meaning under these wild Types and Shadows."[108] The London Italian operas that could invite allegorical moral interpretation would be those with prominent elements of mythology or romance: *Rinaldo* (1711), *Calypso and Telemachus* (1712), *La conquista del vello d'oro* (1738), *Alcina* (1735), *Orlando* (1733), and others based on mythology.

Hughes sets out four criteria for a good allegory, the last two being of most relevance: an allegory must be "lively, and surprising"; characterized by "Elegance, or a beautiful Propriety"; "every where consistent with itself" with the persons sustained "in their proper Characters"; and "clear and intelligible: the Fable being designed only to clothe and adorn the Moral, but not to hide it."[109]

Numerous essays in the *Tatler* and *Spectator* confirm this sense of allegory as an extended dual-level narrative that conveys moral instruction. The brief stories related in the essay are usually cast as dreams or visions.[110] In almost all cases, the actual allegorical narrative is preceded by a short introduction or framing device that invariably consists of Mr. Bickerstaff or Mr. Spectator relating the events inducing him to fall asleep to dream the vision. In these short narratives, the human actors represent passions, virtues, vices, and various affections of the mind.[111]

Quintilian is a classical touchstone for the view that allegory's virtue lay in its immediate and vivid conveyance of meaning: "When, however, an allegory is too obscure, we call it a riddle: such riddles are, in my opinion, to be regarded as blemishes, in view of the fact that lucidity is a virtue."[112] An allegory that is obscure violated Hughes' criteria that it be "clear and intelligible." "A Moral which is not clear," he continued, "lies at the Mercy of every fanciful Interpreter."[113] Dryden prided himself that the allegory of *Albion and Albanius* was "so very obvious, that it will no sooner be read than understood."[114] An opera such as *Silla*, whose allegory is so opaque that it is amenable to multiple and contradictory readings, would violate the period's expectations about allegory.

Named characters in epic or drama, even when figures supposedly drawn from history, were not expected to be accurate representations of the historical figure but universal characters or abstractions of virtues, vices, passions, or human faculties. A commentator on Addison's *Cato* stated:

> Dramatic *Action* ought to be General and Allegoric, not Particular; because Particular Actions can't have a General Influence … Thus it is with *Cato*; for it not only shews what *Cato* did, but what any other Hero with his *Manners*, and Qualifications, in the same Circumstances, Notions, and Passions, wou'd have done.[115]

John Dennis grants that poets need to take names from history "to give the Action an Air of Truth." But even these named persons "remain at the bottom Universal and Allegorical."[116] For Dennis,

As the Action of a Dramatick Fable is universal and allegorical, the Characters are so likewise … When a Dramatic Poet sets before us his Characters, he does not pretend to entertain us with particular Persons … but proposes to lay before us general and allegorical Fantoms, and to make them talk and act as Persons compounded of such and such Qualities, would talk and act upon like Occasions, in order to give proper Instructions.[117]

The idea that poetic dramatists were creating universal types, rather than attempting historical portrayals, suggests that when viewing operas, Handel's contemporaries were seeing character types, from which they were to draw moral lessons, not to match them with real persons of the day. In his libretto for *Giulio Cesare* (1724), Nicola Haym admitted he violated historical truth when he had Sextus (son of Pompey) kill Ptolemy, murderer of his father, even though Ptolemy had been vanquished by Caesar. Haym thought it necessary to contrive this circumstance to show what a son should do "in Revenge for his Father's Murder" (argument).

Were a contemporary inclined to allegorize *Rinaldo*, it would most probably have been along moral – not topically political – lines, consistent with the principles set out by Hughes, Blackmore, and Dennis. An interpretation would probably have followed Tasso's own cue, provided in "The Allegory of the Poem," which sets out the allegorical sense concealed under the veil of the actions. Jerusalem is the symbol of man's pursuit of earthly happiness; Godfrey and Rinaldo represent the opposed faculties of the soul, "the rational and irascible faculties." The Christian Crusade is Everyman's struggle to reconcile his soul's two elements in the pursuit of earthly felicity. For Tasso,

The army, composed of its various leaders and the other Christian soldiers, signifies mature man, who is compounded of body and soul – the soul considered not as simple, but as divided into many and various faculties. Jerusalem – a strong city, situated in rough and mountainous country, toward which are directed all the endeavors of the army of the faithful, as toward an ultimate end – signifies civic felicity, to the degree befitting Christian man … Godfrey, who is captain of all this assembled force, stands for the intellect … Rinaldo, Tancred, and the other princes stand for the other faculties of the soul … The two sorcerers … are two diabolic temptations that exercise their envy on two faculties of our souls from which all sinfulness proceeds … Armida is the temptation that sets snares for the appetitive faculty … Rinaldo, who in the action is in the second rank of honor, should in the allegory also be placed in the corresponding rank … The irascible is that which is least distanced from the nobility of the mind … This faculty, impetuous, violent and untamed [is] principally signified by Rinaldo.[118]

Most likely, then, Handel's audience would have allegorized *Rinaldo* as asserting the importance of keeping steadfast to a noble goal and avoiding impetuous behavior and sensuous temptation. The moral was in part actually pointed in the text: Godfrey admonished Rinaldo, "Yet in the Road to Glory fall not back, / But pass by Love when thy fair Fame invites Thee."[119] Rinaldo failed to heed these commands, and so was "Stain'd with the Guilt of soft and untim'd Love."[120]

In the higher literary genres, allegory tended to be universal and moralistic. There are, however, genres where thoroughgoing, dual-level allegories were intended and expected to be put to political use: partisan narrative prose. Examples include Mrs. Delariviere Manley's *Secret History of Queen Zarah* (1705), an attack on the Duchess of Marlborough; John Arbuthnot's five *John Bull* pamphlets, allegorical narratives that are part of the political propaganda on the War of the Spanish Succession (1712);[121] *The History of Prince Titi* (1736), an allegory of the royal family featuring Prince Frederick; and *The Statesman's Progress: or, a Pilgrimage to Greatness* (1741), a full allegory of the political career of Walpole as "Badman."

Political periodicals such as the *True Briton*, *Mist's* and *Fog's Weekly Journal*, the *Craftsman*, the *Grub-street Journal*, and *Common Sense* used purpose-written, thoroughgoing narrative allegories in political essays with parallels to persons and events of the day. Given the venue, framing devices, verbal cues, and subject matter, it is clear the reader was invited to look for counterparts in the outside political world. From periodicals of the Walpole era, such strict political allegories include the stories of Don Fernando (Walpole) and the Bishop of Tortoso in the *True Briton* (1723);[122] "The Vision of Camilick," "The History of the Norfolk Steward," and "The Allegory of the Tree of Corruption" in the *Craftsman*;[123] and "The Vision of the Golden Rump" in *Common Sense*.[124] In Chapters 4 and 5, we encounter in partisan periodicals purpose-written, dual-level narrative allegories that draw out analogs between singers and events at the opera house at the Haymarket and the world of domestic or foreign political affairs.

John Hughes also recognizes allegory in painting, where the double sense of the literal and mystical meaning is consistently carried out in the design, and the emphasis again is on abstraction and moral lessons. Britons would have been familiar with allegorical paintings by Rubens and more recently by Verrio, Laguerre, Pellegrini, the Ricci brothers, Thornhill, and others that decorated the ceilings, walls, and staircases of the many splendid mansions and country seats then being built in London and the country.[125] In such visual allegories, there is an overarching, unifying iconographic program and a clear, one-to-one correspondence between each person portrayed and a mythological or allegorical character. Iconographical handbooks guided both painter and viewer in establishing and decoding the allegorical conventions.

Hughes cites one of Rubens' paintings in the *Life of Marie de' Medici* cycle then in the gallery at the Palais du Luxembourg, Paris (now at the Louvre), "The Majority of Louis XIII" or "The Ship of State," which celebrates Louis XIII coming of age.[126] Hughes spells out the correspondences: "the Government of *France* [is represented] by a Galley. The King stands at the Helm; *Mary* of *Medicis*, the Queen Mother and Regent, puts the Rudder in his Hand; Justice, Fortitude, Religion, and Publick Faith are seated at the Oars; and other Vertues have their proper Employments in managing the Sails and Tackle."[127] Well-known allegories of state in England at the time included Rubens' ceiling of the Banqueting House at Whitehall (1634–35)[128] and Sir James Thornhill's walls and ceilings of the painted halls at the Royal Hospital for Seamen at Greenwich (*c.*1708–27)[129]

Neo-classical criticism of the later seventeenth and eighteenth centuries was sensitive to the genre of literary and dramatic works. Much contemporary criticism and literary theory considered how well suited were the subject, genre, style, content, and diction of a work to its chosen purpose or occasion. It is consistent with eighteenth-century critical thought to argue that – as a generic expectation – London opera audiences did not routinely look to realist-mode opera librettos on historical or mythological stories as vehicles for political comment, allegory, parallel, or topical allusion.

Parallel and application, personation

If Handel's contemporaries were not likely to look for political allegory in realist-mode operas on historical subjects, they were indeed familiar with stage works that were intended to be applied to contemporary politics in several other, less strict ways. Plays might relate to contemporary politics by means of parallel plots, character types, satirical remarks, personal references, generalized warnings, themes, and tropes.[130] Two methods especially pertinent to operas that might have political application were parallel history (parallel and application) and personation.[131]

As we saw, *Venice Preserv'd*, *The Duke of Guise*, *The Spanish Fryar*, and *Cato* were written as, or seen as, retellings of historical events with applications to contemporary events. John Wallace describes the writer's method of parallel history: after choosing his moral, "He assembled selectively from history a plot, or episodes and characters, and presented them with a seeming impartiality so that their inferences could not be missed in careful scrutiny." The reader's task was to reverse the process and extract precepts of morality or political wisdom from the situation represented in the historical or dramatic narrative; then if he wished, he was free to apply the precept to his own time to instruct or judge a particular person or situation.[132]

Lessons or precepts that could be derived from historical episodes might be the dangers of rebellion, the consequences to the state of a ruler's illicit love, the danger of letting power fall into the hands of evil councilors or favorites, the self-destructiveness of over-ambition, the virtues of clemency, reminders of the cause of downfall of empires, that fate opposes immoderate conquest, not to trust fortune at times of prosperity, that even a too-virtuous prince can commit violence out of jealousy, that a prince should not leave his seat of government when the senate is too powerful, and the necessity of sovereignty based on strength – all lessons that could apply at the time of a play's or opera's original production (if intended) and at later moments in time as well.

Confusion arises when modern readers transform the persons and situations in parallel histories into specific, topical allusions and allegories instead of deriving universal precepts. As Wallace cautions, "To allegorize the historizing poems is to defeat the purpose for which they were written."[133] This technique of parallel and application accords with the classic, prevailing expectation that drama was inherently "general" and taught universal lessons. The point of poetic drama was to generalize to the higher degree of precept and moral lesson (further discussed in Chapter 8).

How one of Handel's contemporaries might have drawn a parallel and application from a historical text to his own times is shown by a 1737 letter by the celebrated physician Dr. Edward Barry. After reading Charles Rollin's *Ancient History*,[134] Barry wrote to John Boyle, fifth Earl of Orrery, son of Charles Boyle, fourth Earl and a Jacobite member of Earl Cowper's Lords opposition in 1720–22.[135] After the Atterbury Plot broke in the summer of 1722, the fourth earl was sent to join the accused chief plotter, Francis Atterbury, Bishop of Rochester, in the Tower on September 27 on the basis of information provided by Christopher Layer. Layer was executed as a traitor on May 17, 1723, and his head mounted on the Temple Bar.[136] Another conspirator, George Kelly, was sentenced and imprisoned but managed to escape. In the event, Walpole did not have enough evidence to risk a trial of Orrery, who was released on bail on March 12, 1723. As Walpole discovered, the evidence provided by Layer and the intercepted mails between the plotters and the Pretender's agents in France was so slight that, if presented in the Commons, it may well have been considered false information. As a last-ditch effort, Walpole resorted to the extra-legal expedient of trying

Atterbury in the Lords, which did not have to follow rules of procedure and evidence. Tried in May, Atterbury was convicted and sent into exile.

After reading Rollin's *History*, which he commends for dwelling on any "Circumstance which might improve the mind of his Reader," Dr. Barry remarked to Orrery about an episode in the history of Artaxerxes that occurred after his war against Cyprus:

> I was particularly pleased with the following passage, and having lately read the trial of the Bp of Rochester and George Kelly[137] it probably made a greater Impression on me ... One of the King's favourites [Orontes], envious of the merits of one of his best Officers [Tiribasus], accused him privately, and endeavoured to make his Fidelity suspected; on a fair and impartial Examination he was cleard, and all the King's [Artaxerxes'] indignation fell on the perfidious Informer [Orontes].[138]

By appointing a panel of three great lords of Persia to examine the charges of Orontes, Artaxerxes, writes Barry, "gave a fine example of the just rigor which ought to be exercised against false Informers."

Barry was probably struck by parallels between the situation of Tiribasus and Atterbury as victims of false testimony. In his continuation, Barry spells out the universal lesson to kings about the benefits of not using false testimony:

> The wise Prince knew that one of the true Signs of a prudent Government was to have his Subjects stand more in fear of the Laws than of Informers, and thought that to have acted otherwise would have been a direct Violation of the most common Rules of natural Equity and humanity. It would have been opening a Door to Envy, Hatred, Calumny, and Revenge: it would have been exposing the honest simplicity of his subjects to the cruel Malice of detestable Informers ... it would have been divesting the Throne of the most noble privilege belonging to it, namely, of being a Sanctuary for Innocence and Justice against Violence and Calumny.[139]

By his mention of the Atterbury trial, Barry is directing application of this precept drawn from ancient history to King George and his ministers about the benefits to the kingdom of avoiding "the cruel Malice of detestable Informers" and the possible crisis of public faith in the laws and government of Britain. Barry is advocating to Orrery that a "just rigor" and "indignation" should have fallen on Robert Walpole for the use of Layer's false testimony against Atterbury: "A single example of this kind against informers convicted of falsehood, would for ever shut the door against calumny." Such an application, we can imagine Barry thinking, would have been very sympathetic to Lord Orrery, whose father was so accused by Walpole.

When eighteenth-century political writers did intend to comment on a contemporary political or royal figure, they rely on a much looser form of parallel called personation, which draws general similarities of character between one or two major figures in a play or narrative and contemporary counterparts.[140] Concentrating on selected similarities, personation transfers the moral qualities of the literary or historical character to vilify or praise the contemporary person by association. In John Gay's *Beggar's Opera*, for example, the character of Macheath was immediately recognized as applicable to Walpole. Even though there were no strict biographical parallels between their lives, the traits of robber, plunderer, womanizer, and betrayer of friends were seen to characterize Walpole.

A piece of advice for writing libels against the government described the process:

> You are to make yourself thoroughly acquainted with the Doctrine of Parallels, from *Sejanus* to *Menzikoff*, and learn all the Secrets of Falshood [sic] and Misrepresentation; you are to aggravate Circumstances in one Place, omit in another, and reconcile the whole with a certain modern Art, call'd *Lying*, to make the Pictures answer in every Feature, or, in School-Language, make the Simile run upon all Four.[141]

Writers for opposition periodicals of the 1720s and 1730s ransacked ancient, modern, and English history for stories of wicked ministers and politicians, which they retold – or printed verbatim from sources – in the columns of the *True Briton*, the *Craftsman*, and *Common Sense*. Favorite subjects were the careers of Sejanus, Catiline, Wolsey, and Menzikoff, which were retold with the clear intent of hinting to readers the dangers of powerful royal favorites. By well-placed disclaimers, epithets, and other cues the reader is "invited" or "directed" to apply the evil and corrupt minister to Robert Walpole. The purpose is two-fold: to remind King George of the danger of giving too much power to a royal favorite, and to caution Walpole about the consequences to those who abuse power and royal favor.

Personation could work ironically, as in the case of the *Craftsman's* personation of Walpole by John Kipling, the treasurer at the Haymarket Theatre. In a form of mock panegyric, Kipling is praised for those traits of honesty that Walpole lacks (discussed in Chapter 4). If the unflattering application is made to a person in power, the historical distance provides the author some protection against charges of libel or slander. Protection was provided by the old adage, "Application makes the ass," which turned the indictment upon the person's defenders.

A paradigmatic example of how personation was built into a play such that its political implications were unmistakable is Nicholas Rowe's *Tamerlane*, produced in late 1701 and one of the most popular political plays of the eighteenth century. *Tamerlane* celebrated the Whig hero William III and Whig constitutional principles and, by contrast, vilified William's Continental enemy Louis XIV. As a Whig party piece, it was sporadically performed in the years after its premiere but was not performed during the high-water years of the Tory ministry in 1711–14. Thereafter, the play was performed on November 4, William's birthday, in almost every season of the century.[142]

Bajazet is an evil figure of unrestrained cruelty. Tamerlane typifies a great conqueror and good ruler. Both have potential applications at many moments and places in history. In 1701, Tamerlane was intended to stand for William as an ideal king, conqueror, and champion of religious toleration, and Tamerlane's victory over Bajazet becomes a dramatization of providential conquest of good over evil, English Protestant liberty over French absolutism.[143]

Rowe's dedication and Samuel Garth's prologue clinch the personation between Tamerlane and William. Rowe, somewhat disingenuously, tries to discredit those who believe that "in the Person of *Tamerlane* I have alluded to the greatest Character of the present Age." But he concedes:

There are many Features, 'tis true, in that Great Man's Life, not unlike His Majesty: His Courage, his Piety, his Moderation, his Justice, and his Fatherly Love of his People, but above all, his Hate of Tyranny and Oppression, and his zealous Care for the Common Good of Mankind, carry a large Resemblance of Him. (b1r)

The suggestion that Louis XIV is William's foe follows from Rowe's remark that "there wants nothing to his Majesty but such a deciding Victory, as that by which *Tamerlane* gave Peace to the World." Here the panegyric on William becomes a Whig summons to Britain at the eve of the outbreak of the War of the Spanish Succession.

Samuel Garth's unused (but later widely reprinted) prologue for the original production is more direct:

> Today a Mighty Hero comes, to warme
> Your curdling Blood & bids you Brittains arme;
> To Valour much He owes, to Virtue more;
> He Fights to Save & Conquers to Restore;
> …
> Such Brittains is the Prince that you Possess
> In Councell Greater & in Camps no less
> Brave but not Cruell, Wise without Deceit
> Born for an Age curs'd with a Bajazet.[144]

The technique of personation allowed a historical figure to be adapted to ever newer circumstances as writers carefully crafted new applications to new monarchs. In 1723, when the *History of … Tamerlaine the Great* was translated and dedicated to the young Frederick, future Prince of Wales, then living in Hanover, the original personations devised by Rowe were no longer appropriate, so the translator easily shifted the personation to glance favorably on the monarch of the time: "[Tamerlaine] is resembled by that great and living pattern … your Royal Grandfather, King George [I]."[145]

But a dozen years later, a letter to the opposition newspaper the *Craftsman* could use Tamerlane to let loose an innuendo against George II.[146] By carefully planting the terms "Prime Minister" and "*Tyranny* unpunish'd," the writer recalls two common opposition themes: the danger of monarchs relying on favorite ministers and the charge that Walpole's regime was eroding British liberties. Turning the description of Tamerlane into an anti-type of George II (by ironic inversion), the writer observes, "He always governed the State Himself, without having Recourse to a Prime Minister [Walpole]; … and none under his Government ever exercised *Violence* and *Tyranny* unpunish'd." The claim "He esteem'd *Learning* and *learned Men*, and it was his constant Endeavour to render *Arts* flourishing throughout his Empire" was surely intended to reflect ironically on the monarch who had elevated Colley Cibber as Poet Laureate.

Given the widespread politicization of Rowe's *Tamerlane*, the subject would be a good candidate for an opera libretto turned to political use. But Handel's opera *Tamerlano* from 1724, adapted from an earlier libretto, lacks any cues in the text, preface, or dedication drawing attention to a contemporary political application. Complicated by numerous love subplots, the opera focuses on the haughty Bajazet's refusal to submit to Tamerlane's authority, even at the cost of his own freedom, the death of his daughter, and his own suicide.

Parallel history and personation can be "directed" or "invited" by textual cues, demonstrable parallels, or adaptation of a source. Or they may be "reader's applications" that the text merely permits and which depend upon the responses of readers.[147] In which case, it is the reader himself who has drawn a universal precept, lesson, or moral from the particular text and applied it to his own times. Hence, when "Philo-Briton" prefaces a long extract in the *True Briton* from a historian with "As no Application can possibly be made to our present Happy Times," it is an open invitation to a reader to find the application, as well as a disingenuous defense against libel.[148] It is such reader applications that make Shakespeare's plays seem to have universal, perennial political application. Further examples of the use of parallel, application, and personation in partisan political writings and applied to opera will be seen in Chapter 4.

There are no signs that any Italian operas on historical subjects, with the exception of *Riccardo primo* (1727), were chosen or adapted to have parallels or personations with contemporary Hanoverian politics or persons. Even if no operas had intended or directed parallel and application to the times, opera-goers could have extracted from the historical episodes presented onstage moral precepts, examples, or lessons of political wisdom to apply to the circumstances of their own day. This approach will be discussed further in Chapter 8.

When is it political? When is it allegory?

Drawing on the plays surveyed above, the theory of allegory by Hughes, Blackmore, and Dennis, the insights of Wallace, Hume, and Roper, the political allegories examined in Chapters 4 and 5, and the Patriot dramas examined in Chapter 7, I propose criteria that can be used to identify works that, on historical grounds, were likely intended, written, and received as topically political using techniques such as allegory, personation, or parallel and application. Italian operas that are claimed to be topically political should, I suggest, exhibit these features.

By proposing this cluster of criteria, I try to avoid the reductive fallacies that the meaning of a text can be identified with a single element, whether the author's intention, its textual meaning or verbal content, its context, or reader reception. Rather, the understanding of a work's historical political meaning occurs at a nexus of authorial intent and biography, the work's genre and formal features, textual meaning, the political effect of the work, relation to the political issues of the day, and contemporary reception.[149] My goal is to propose some bounds for political readings that are historically plausible and valid, and that reveal the political significance Italian operas could have had for Handel's contemporaries. Some works will defy simple judgment, but these following criteria should help focus discussion.

> First, allegory is foremost a formal device. Paradigmatic allegories have features such as framing devices, extended romance plots, and allegorical, mythic, or symbolic figures. These features cue the reader that the work is what Angus Fletcher calls a "ritualized form" that is "intended to elicit from the reader some sort of exegetical response."[150] While Continental court operas, English Restoration operas such as *Albion and Albanius*, and the Hanoverian celebratory pieces have numerous cues that the works are allegories, none of the Italian operas

on historical subjects proposed as political allegories have any formal devices hinting at an allegorical meaning.

Genre and venue alert readers to politics and allegory. Readers of the *True Briton*, *Fog's* and *Mist's Weekly Journals*, the *Craftsman*, *Common Sense*, and political pamphlets would have expected the narratives to be political and to harbor allegories satirizing the ministry. The known political bias of the newspaper would have guided the application of the allegories, histories, and personations. The opera house, the evidence suggests, was not a venue where an audience would normally have expected to look for partisan politics, whereas the playhouses were.

There are signs of intention. Political works can be shown to emanate from authors whose political circumstances and other known works are consistent with the political positions espoused in the work. In discerning political meaning, it is legitimate and indeed necessary to appeal to authorial intent to validate textual meaning and motive to affect public opinion.[151] Interpreters of the politics of Italian operas generally avoid enquiring why the Royal Academy directors, Rolli, Haym, Handel, or Heidegger chose or adapted an opera, devised the allegory, or benefited from engaging in politics – especially when their allegorical interpretations render the opera's content subversive or critical of the monarch.

Textual cues are present. When a political writer retells a historical episode to make a political point or writes a purpose-made story, he plants unmistakable textual cues, such as an ironic disclaimer or character epithets, to invite or direct the application to contemporary political circumstances. Cues are also contained in dedications, prologues, or advertising text in newspapers. Plays or operas cannot make their political points if the audience or reader are not cued in. No such paratextual features (except the dedicatory poem to *Riccardo primo*) have been found to indicate operas on historical subjects had a topical significance.

Where a political allegory, application, or personation is found in a work, the political point chimes with other contemporary partisan polemic, which helps shape the identification and application of an individual work. We should expect the partisan political import in operas to be similar to that found in other contemporary political writing. Modern interpretations of operas, however, tend to have strained and tenuous engagement with the prevailing partisan issues of the day.

There is usually evidence that contemporaries noticed and commented on the political content. One form of contemporary response was the publication of keys to explain the allegory to the uninitiated.[152] Quite often, the ministry of the day was aware of the partisan attack and responded by attacking the satirists in the government press, suppressing or censoring the work, or, in extreme cases, jailing the printer or calling the author to the bar. No corroborating evidence of contemporary response to operas claimed to be political has been offered by modern interpreters.[153]

The crucial test for determining a political work is that there is an answer to the question *Cui bono?* Political texts do "political work"; some political faction benefits. Political works are not constructed merely as copybook exercises. The sting of each satire, the accepted truth of the innuendo, or the application of the historical personation blackens a political opponent or benefits some faction of the day. Political interpreters of Italian operas have failed to show how Rolli, Haym, Handel, Heidegger, the Royal Academy of Music, or the Opera of the Nobility benefited from the politicized operas.

These criteria can serve to guide evaluation of whether the politically topical allegory, personation, or parallel is "in" the textual meaning of the opera and is historically plausible, or whether it is the result of reader application, "put there" by modern interpreters.

One might try to salvage the political readings of *Rinaldo*, *Teseo*, *Silla*, and other Handel operas discussed in following chapters by recasting them as personations or parallel histories instead of stricter allegories. But even so, these operas lack the other features that would mark them as political works. The portrayal of the dictator Sulla in Handel's *Silla* would be a good candidate for a personation; but the libretto is devoid of any cues to guide the application to any contemporary person. As in the case of *Cato*, that Sulla can suggest the Duke of Marlborough or the Elector Georg Ludwig would confirm the idea that no specific personation was intended or present in the text.

A challenge to this approach of delimiting plausible, historically justified political interpretations is offered by the claim that texts are open to multiple readings.[154] It is, of course, a fact of literary life that readers with different orientations, reading experiences, backgrounds, or interests will respond differently to a text and that texts acquire new meanings over time.

But the application of this principle whereby multiple and even contradictory meanings are offered of a work, as if all are equally valid and not subject to evaluation, is untenable and abandons the historical enterprise,[155] reflecting instead a modern critical climate that privileges ambiguity, pervasive irony, subversive readings, reader response, and textual instability. The approach flies in the face of the spirit of early eighteenth-century neoclassical art and criticism that stressed clarity and explicitness of meaning, representation of general nature, universality over personal expression, verisimilitude and decorum, and adherence to rules and genres.[156] Instruction and moral didacticism, imitation of nature, and moving the passions are rendered futile or ineffective if the precepts, exemplars, and moral center of the work are equivocal or ambiguous. Of course, we cannot control for the variety of readings by individual past audience members, but our goal in the first instance must be the common, broad, context-specific meaning the opera likely had for the general audience targeted by the librettist, producer, and composer.[157]

Lessons from contemporary interpretations of opera

Instructive in recovering how London audiences of Handel's era would have been inclined to respond to operas are several overlooked contemporary comments on specific operas and a related genre, the masque.[158] In accord with the prevailing notions of the purposes of art, the interpretations consider the operas in terms of their moral function: whether they encourage virtue and discourage vice. When, in 1726 and 1737, political writers relate *Camilla* (1706) to current, topical politics, these are readers' applications certainly not intended or built in to Bononcini's original opera, which was premiered in Naples in 1696.

William Law's denunciation of the masque *Apollo and Daphne; or, the Burgomaster Trick'd* (January 14, 1726) in *The Absolute Unlawfulness of the Stage-Entertainment Fully Demonstrated* (1726) follows from a severely religious and moralistic standpoint.[159] In this extended attack on playhouses as grossly sinful in their own nature, Law fulminated for nine pages against "the present celebrated Entertainment of the *Stage*, which is so much to the Taste of this Christian Country, that it has been acted almost every Night this whole Season, I mean *Apollo* and *Daphne*."[160] The very opening scene, "a *magnificent Palace discover'd: Venus attended with Graces and Pleasures*,"[161] according to Law, "supposes the Audience to be fit for the Entertainment of *Lust* and *Wantonness* … an Entertainment fitter for *publick Stews*, than for People who make any Pretences to the Holiness and Purity of the Spirit of Christ."[162] While Law does not allegorize the figures of Apollo and Daphne, his interest is clearly the moral impact of the masque on the viewer.

An interpretation of Joseph Addison's *Rosamond* (1707) was offered in 1731 by "The Traveller" in the *British Journal* because "the present prevailing Taste of most, who frequent our Theatres, seems to be confined to Operas."[163] The Traveller believes operas have the same effect on the human mind and the same moral end as dramatic poetry, which is "the Encouragement of Virtue," which it achieves by means of its fable.

Writing as if he had not seen *Rosamond* performed and is relying only on the printed text, the Traveller is certain that "if set to good Music and well performed," it would answer the purpose of the encouragement of virtue, and he points out the intended moral:

Some of the ill Consequences which attend an unlawful Love [i.e., between Henry II and Rosamond] are shewed in the Fate of *Rosamond*; nor does the Poet depart from Probability in his Representation of the Resentment of a jealous Wife [Queen Eleanor]; one of the Effects of whose Jealousy was the Death of her Rival [Rosamond].[164]

The Traveller's remarks suggest that a moral reading of *Rosamond* that draws out the ill consequences of Henry's unlawful love of Rosamond and Queen Eleanor's acting on her jealousy is more satisfactory historically than the more common political readings.[165] The moral lesson – avoiding unlawful love such as Henry's – could, of course, be applied at any time to any public figure.

The period's most detailed reading of an Italian opera libretto is of Handel's *Alcina* (1735). Writing to the *Universal Spectator* several months after its premiere, "Henry Stonecastle" was put to reflecting about *Alcina* after overhearing a young gentleman who thought he was being "very witty upon Opera's, in general, and on that of *Alcina* in particular," by claiming he could find "no Allegory in the whole Piece ... and nothing of a Moral."[166]

Stonecastle holds that "the Theatre is allow'd to call upon the Sister Arts, Poetry, Painting and Musick" and to use all means for conveying a "Moral in the most agreeable Manner, and to allure us into Virtue by flattering our Senses." Morals are conveyed when the vicious are exposed and punished, the virtuous applauded and rewarded, and the wiles of villainy not crowned with success. Stonecastle offers a rare commendation of the librettos of Italian opera in regard to their poetic sources:

the Italian Poets, from whom the Opera's are taken, have more strictly adher'd to the first Design of Poetry, viz. the rendering Virtue amiable and Vice odious, than have our modern Writers; their Allegories are delightful and contain excellent Morals.[167]

Stonecastle's allegorization of *Alcina* works well, of course, because the episode from Ariosto's *Orlando furioso* is a fable of magical enchantment: Rogero is carried by a Hypo-griffin to the island of Alcina and is warned of the enchantments of her palace; he resolves instead to go to the palace of Logistilla. Rogero, though, is captured by monstrous forms and taken to Alcina's palace, where "he is drown'd in Luxury, grows effeminate, [and] forgets his betroth'd Wife and Friends." Meanwhile Bradamante, to whom he is engaged, surrenders a virtuous ring to the good enchantress Melisso, who takes the ring to Rogero on the island of Alcina. The ring breaks Alcina's enchantment, and she appears to Rogero as "the most deform'd and forbidden of her Sex." Her enchantment over him is broken, and Rogero and Melissa escape. In his description of the allegory, it is clear Stonecastle is telling the story from Ariosto's poem, not the opera libretto.

In *Alcina* Stonecastle finds a "beautiful and instructive" narrative allegory, wherein Rogero is Everyman and the actions and characters in the plot allegorize Vice or Virtue and symbolize moral behavior in life's course of choices between good and evil. Stonecastle allegorizes every element of the plot. Thus, for example, the Hypo-griffin that carries Rogero to Alcina's island figures "the Violence of youthful Passions, which hurries us into the Air, that is, beyond the Bounds of Reason." Alcina's beauty and inconstancy "proves the short Duration of all sublunary Enjoyments, which are lost as soon as attain'd." Rogero's being attacked by the monstrous forms figures "the Vices which continually make War upon us, and his making a Stand against them for some Time, shews the first Struggling of a virtuous Mind." Bradamante's ring "figures to us Reason, which when we listen to it will strip vicious Pleasures of their Paint and gaudy Trappings, shew them in their innate Deformity, and necessarily cause our Abhorrence and Flight, as it did that of Rogero; by which we are taught that we ought rather to fly from, than enter the List with sensual Pleasures."[168]

Stonecastle's moralizing essay is the longest contemporary response to a specific Italian opera. His allegorization is a thoroughgoing, dual-level, narrative allegory, to which the opera adapts unusually well. He does not draw identifications with contemporary political figures but holds up characters and actions as exempla of vice or virtue.

The most popular opera of the period, Giovanni Bononcini's *Camilla*,[169] was the subject of two political applications. When revived in December 1726 at Lincoln's Inn Fields, one "Nicholas Observation" sent his observations to *Mist's Weekly Journal* (no. 87, December 17, 1726), a periodical of High Tory–Jacobite sympathies. Nicholas Observation admits he admires "the Moral of this Opera mightily," by which he probably means the poetic justice meted to King Latinus and Camilla. His discussion focuses on Latinus, the villainous king who holds the dominions of Camilla, the rightful ruler.

The character (or performer) of King Latinus in *Camilla* had always been held up to ridicule. In a fictional letter to the *Spectator* in 1711, Richard Steele has the supposed singer of the role regret that his character "never failed to make all that beheld him merry at his Appearance."[170] A month before the 1726 revival, one "Hampshire Yahoo" wrote to the *London Journal* about his seeing *Camilla*, noting the objection "that neither the Person nor Habit [costume] of *King Latinus* were proper to raise that Reverence and Admiration which generally waits upon Princes." His appearance was "the absolute Burlesque of Majesty" and he was "always deposed by the Audience upon Sight."[171]

Nicholas Observation alternately describes the character Latinus and the Mr. Pearson who sang the role,[172] making a mischievous personation between Latinus and George I in order to cast aspersions on the king's dignity, mildly accuse the Hanoverians of being usurpers, and express hope for the return of James III (that is, that the poetic justice in the opera – restoration of Camilla – might apply to the Pretender):

Latinus [George I] … is represented by a meagre Jaw'd Candle Snuffer that can't so much as act the Part of a King for half an Hour; they have put on him a large Plume of Feathers, and a long Train, which seem to make him very uneasy, and the Moment he enters the People hiss at him as if he was a real Usurper, when, God knows, I dare swear, the poor Wretch had rather be at home [Hanover] by his Fire-Side, than be the true Possessor of those Territories [Great Britain], he is now only suppos'd to command; but the Fellow finds himself well paid for his Pains, and so very impudently comes and keeps *Camilla* out of her Right, till by a Stratagem she gets the better of him and his Son, and regains her Father's Throne.[173]

Nicholas Observation draws his lesson: "Though I am not for changing of Kings without an absolute Necessity; yet, methinks, 'twere better to let the Man (who never was cut out for a Monarch)[174] go home to his Wife and Children, if he has any, and set another Prince in his Room."

Another political reading of *Camilla* using the devices of parallel and application appeared eleven years later in the opposition journal *Common Sense* (no. 46, December 17, 1737). "Camillus" writes musing that in terms of ease or happiness, that of "Regality is least desirable." He recalls the two kings Latinus and Turnus in the opera and notices that another character, Metius, afforded him "great Speculation, and which seems to be a Satyr on

Prime Ministers in general, and yet at the same Time points out to them Conduct not as honest, but as Political as they can wish." According to Camillus, Metius as a type gives insight into "the miserable Situation of a first Minister."

Reading in an opposition journal, one would have scant doubt as to whom we are invited to compare Metius. Camillus casually drops pointed verbal cues to direct the application: Metius is "the Prime Minister," a "cunning Minister," he had served two successive kings, and he is in love and is resolved to have a mistress (Walpole had kept Molly Skerrett since autumn 1724). His case gives insight "into the miserable Situation of a first Minister. The State of *Tantalus* is full as eligible. He is in perpetual Expectation, and perpetual Fear of Death." (Camillus is probably recalling here the assassination threats against Walpole during the Excise Crisis in 1733; see Chapter 5.) "As he lives, so he must die, like a Dog flung out on the next Dunghill; a Rotten Carcass, the true Emblem of his Rotten Mind."

Camillus draws a lesson on the state of prime ministers:

There is so general a Corruption spread over the whole Earth, that a good Man will not be a great Man [an epithet for Walpole], and a great Man cannot be a good One. – The Man of Honour shuns the World and seeks Retirement: … whilst the bold, intruding Knave, makes his Way as near as possible to the Throne, and gives up Conscience to Ambition, Integrity to Avarice, and Sincerity to false Pride.[175]

In both cases, we can find the anti-Hanoverian and anti-Walpole sentiments are not "in" the opera, but are reader applications and are consistent with the politics of the writer or periodical; and the political viewpoint conveyed actually does some propaganda work on behalf of a partisan faction of the day.

This chapter clears the way for understanding the relation of politics and individual Italian operas, as opposed to opera as an institution, in early Hanoverian Britain. I suggest there can be no generic expectation that London Italian operas on historical subjects were allegorical or allusive of topical politics, statesmen, or the royal family. The assumption itself is unwarranted: there are too many differences between the circumstances of operas produced at Continental courts and in Restoration England and those of the Italian operas produced in eighteenth-century London to accept that the London operas functioned as did other Baroque allegorical operas.

When the interpretations offered on the basis of the expectation – such as for *Rinaldo, Teseo, Silla,* and others to be discussed in following chapters – are examined, they fail as convincing, consistent, comprehensive historical readings and are, instead, a reader's application based not in the textual meaning of the libretto but on the general susceptibility of any text to application. The relations claimed to contemporary politics are unsatisfactory; the method is so poorly theorized that multiple or contradictory interpretations are offered for a libretto (such as *Silla* and *Floridante*); and there are no satisfactory answers to the questions of how the politics of the opera served the interests of the opera's producer or advanced the interest of a partisan faction. If there was a generic expectation about individual Italian operas, it was, I suggest, that the opera stage was not the place to seek application to contemporary partisan politics.

One group of operas does follow the model of Continental court operas. On occasions to mark Hanoverian weddings and birthdays, the opera managers and producers were quite capable of using the apparatus of symbolic and emblematic allegory to celebrate members of the royal family, much along the lines of other Baroque operas. These Hanoverian celebratory pieces (see Appendix 5) show by contrast how little engaged with topicality or the royal family were the other Italian operas on historical subjects.

The criteria proposed to help determine in an historical sense when works were political and topical and whether allegory, personation, or application were at work can be used to guide future political interpretation of individual operas. Without the blinkers of the generic expectation approach, the following chapters explore the more subtle and varied ways Italian opera – both as an institution and individual librettos – were or might have been politicized in Hanoverian Britain.

3 | Politics in the Royal Academy of Music

The accession of Elector Georg Ludwig as King George I of Great Britain on August 1, 1714, transformed English politics and ensured the triumph of the Whigs. After a decade of heated Tory–Whig strife, Britain settled into a period of stability under the Whig oligarchy.

Even as elector, George knew the Whigs were his true friends and despised Oxford and Bolingbroke for deserting the Allies in the midst of a war that was pushing France to defeat and for concluding a secret, separate peace with France.[1] Jonathan Swift described the fierce and thorough purge of Tories from government offices after the Accession:

Upon Queen Anne's death the Whig faction was restored to power, which they exercised with the utmost rage and revenge; impeached and banished the chief leaders of the church party, and stripped all their adherents of what employments they had.[2]

With great prescience, Bolingbroke lamented, "The grief of my soul is this, I see plainly that the Tory party is gone."[3] In fact, the Tory party was effectively proscribed from office for nearly fifty years.[4] There was in turn generous bestowing of honors on Whigs. Marlborough was restored to his post as Captain General; among younger Whigs, Robert Walpole became Paymaster of the Forces; William Pulteney, Secretary at War; James (later Viscount) Stanhope and Charles (later Viscount) Townshend, Secretaries of State.

In the general election of 1715, Whig propaganda claimed a Tory victory would mean the Pretender's restoration through French arms, British subjugation to France and the Pope, and an end to the Church of England. Much Tory electoral propaganda recklessly insulted the king and vilified the Whigs. Francis Atterbury's *English Advice, to the Freeholders of England* (1714), asserting that all "the Dangers and Miseries, to which we are exposed, are entirely owing to the Whigs" (p. 29), was so inflammatory, the king issued a proclamation for discovery of the author.

George exhorted voters "to have a particular Regard to such as showed a Firmness to the Protestant Succession when it was most in Danger."[5] Thus denounced by the king and tainted with Jacobitism, the Tories suffered their biggest loss since the Revolution. J. H. Plumb describes the outcome: "With a majority in the Commons, and most of the court offices in their pockets, the Whig leaders went about making the world safe for the Whigs."[6]

After their electoral defeat, other events hastened the ruin of the Tories. In Parliament, the triumphant Whigs destroyed the Tory leadership by impeaching Oxford, Bolingbroke, and others for treason by betraying Britain by the Peace of Utrecht and their intrigues with the Pretender. Oxford was sent to the Tower; Bolingbroke's flight to France in late March 1715 and brief service to the Pretender only confirmed to Whigs his guilt and the impression that Tories were in fact crypto-Jacobites.

The Jacobite threat was brought home by the inept and ill-fated rebellion (the "Fifteen") when the Earl of Mar raised the Pretender's standard in Scotland on September 6, 1715, followed by defeat at Preston and James' flight back to Paris the following February.[7] The Jacobite rebellion was fatal to the Tories in another way, for Whigs invoked it to justify the Septennial Act of 1716, which prolonged parliaments to seven years and prevented the confusion caused by another general election. By the 1722 election, the Tory cause would be even more hopeless as a steady stream of Tories defected to the Whig party. For the next half century, politics in Britain is less one of Tory–Whig strife, as in the reign of Queen Anne, than of a series of quarrels and maneuvers between various Whig factions scheming to gain mastery of government.

The Whig Schism and royal feud

Opera might have been expected to thrive in London with the accession of George I, who, of all the arts, seemed most inclined toward music. In the early years of his reign, royal attendance at about half the operas performed each season brought generous payments to performers and management.[8] After the peak 1711–12 season in which seven operas (including revivals) were given sixty-two performances, productions declined until the 1716–17 season when six operas were given thirty-two performances. For the following two seasons, Heidegger produced no operas at all.[9]

The lapse in opera productions from June 1717 until April 1720 has been related to the schism in the Whig party and the feud between the king and the Prince of Wales that disrupted social activities of the nobility, the primary supporters of opera. The suggestion is that the nobility's divided loyalty inhibited their attending the opera, bringing about its demise. Conversely, the revival of opera in April 1720 is said to be related to the mending of the schism in politics and the royal family, symbolized by the king and prince attending the premiere of Handel's *Radamisto* (1720).[10] Attractive as this narrative might be for putting opera at the center of politics, the timing of some events does not agree and others may just be coincidence.

George I and the Prince of Wales had been on poor terms since they came over from Hanover. The king lived a life apart from his subjects, surrounded by his German ministers and mistresses. The prince and princess took up the social slack and kept a fashionable court. In 1717 the simmering ill will at court broke out into a public feud, which coincided with a political split among the ministerial Whigs.[11] From the beginning of the new reign, Whig leaders had been at odds. In 1716 the ministry was divided over the king's efforts to use British power to protect his Hanoverian interests, maintain the balance of power in the Baltic, and achieve rapprochement with France. Sympathetic to the king's European interests were his ministers Charles, Earl of Sunderland and James, Earl Stanhope.

Before going abroad from July 1716 to January 1717, the king slighted the prince by making him regent but without many of the usual powers; the prince was further humiliated when the king forced him to remove as chamberlain his favorite adviser, the Duke of Argyll. While the king was abroad, the prince and princess held court, dined in public, and entertained lavishly at Hampton Court, exceeding anything known at the king's court. Entertaining without distinction of party, they nonetheless showed open favor toward the Tories and opposition Whigs, who flocked to their court. As ministers, Walpole and Townshend attended the prince.

Abroad in Hanover with Stanhope, Sunderland, and his German ministers, the king received reports of his son's entertaining, ambitions to gain public popularity, encouraging the political opposition, and – abetted by Walpole and Townshend – plotting to oppose the ministry in the coming Parliament. Irritated over Townshend's disagreement with his Northern policies, delay in getting an Anglo-French alliance signed, and alleged encouragement of the prince, the king removed Townshend as Secretary of State on December 12, 1716, replacing him by Stanhope the following day. For the sake of Whig unity, Townshend swallowed his pride and accepted rustication as Lord Lieutenant of Ireland.

The following spring, the prince absented himself from Parliament and the Cabinet. Walpole and Townshend worked against the court in Parliament and encouraged their supporters likewise. Townshend's vote against the annual Mutiny Bill, essential for the king to keep a standing army, was the last straw, and George dismissed him on April 9. The following day, Walpole led a massive resignation of Whigs, creating a considerable parliamentary opposition of Whigs and Tories. The resignations of Walpole and Townshend set off a minor pamphlet war between their vindicators and those who vilified them as "defectors" and "betrayers" whose resignations proved their motive was self-interest and whose actions only revived Jacobite hopes.[12] The Whig Schism – between Stanhope and Sunderland in the ministry and Walpole and Townshend – would last six years.

The schism was felt in London's social life. In the summer of 1717, prevented by domestic crises from going abroad, the king broke his usual habits. Determined to increase his own popularity, eclipse his son and his supporters, and support the ministry by courting wavering politicians, he felt compelled to hold a season of drawing rooms, balls, concerts, plays, open dinners, and social events at Hampton Court and London. It was this summer of royal public display that saw the water party accompanied by Handel's *Water Music* on July 17, 1717.[13]

Relations between the king and prince broke off completely in December when the king forced the prince to accept the Duke of Newcastle as godfather to his son. After the christening, the prince accosted the duke and uttered what Newcastle thought was a challenge to a duel. Incensed at this behavior, the king expelled the prince and princess from St. James's Palace on December 2, 1717, and took control of the royal children. The exiled prince set up a rival court at Leicester House. The king made it known that those who attended the prince's court were not welcome at St. James's and were expected to resign any appointments they held from the prince. For two years, the rival courts mirrored the split between the ministry and opposition Whigs as the prince's court became the social center of the Whigs and Tories opposed to his father's ministry. In December 1719 Walpole and Townsend scored a signal victory on behalf of the prince by defeating the ministry's Peerage Bill, designed to limit the number of peers the next monarch could create.[14]

Early in April 1720, rumors flew of a reunion of the Whigs and a reconciliation of the royal family. Behind the scenes, on April 10 Walpole received through James Craggs the Younger an offer of reconciliation if the prince were to send a contrite letter to the king, who would invite him to court. A draft letter was circulated the following week, and the prince duly appeared before the king on St. George's day (Saturday, April 23). The following day, Whigs of the old Cabinet appeared at court and the king and prince attended chapel together. On Wednesday April 27, both attended the premiere of Handel's *Radamisto*. Despite the reconciliation, relations between the king and prince remained strained and chilled for all to see.

The political reunification of the Whigs was symbolized by a dinner held on April 25 at Sunderland's home. Walpole and Townshend were taken back into the ministry in June, with Walpole reappointed as Paymaster of the Forces, and Townshend as Lord President of the Council. With Townshend, Walpole, and Pulteney no longer in opposition, the Whig schism now moved behind the scenes as Walpole and Sunderland struggled to secure majorities in Parliament and control of the government.

Founding of the Royal Academy of Music

The resolution of the royal feud and the revival of opera is most likely just coincidence. The more probable causes for the resumption of opera were the economics of opera production and the pent-up aristocratic demand for opera. The groundwork for the resumption of opera was well underway before the royal feud and political schism were healed.

The early phase of the divided court and social life probably did not affect opera-going, for attendance had already been declining since the 1714–15 season (see Table 3.1); the manager John James Heidegger had given his last production of the 1716–17 season on June 29, well before the royal rupture in December 1717.

Faced with the silent opera house, Britain's cultural elite realized they would have to take matters into their own hands if they wanted opera. Opera was expensive to produce, and in London – by contrast to Continental courts and aristocratic academies – impresarios had to rely on patrons willing to commit to subscriptions, a fickle box office, and an uneven supply of singers and new operas. Since its introduction to London in 1705, Italian opera had been produced by a series of managers or impresarios. The usual pattern of financing was to offer for each new opera a subscription to an initial, limited number of performances (usually six), supplemented by individual ticket sales; if successful enough, the run could be extended to additional individual performances. The impresario was thus dependent upon attracting and pleasing an elite, limited London audience – and expenses always outran receipts. Even the ten consecutive performances of *Rinaldo* in the 1714–15 season, which is often held up as proof of that opera's popularity, ran at a deficit.[15] Table 3.1 shows the steadily mounting losses incurred by Heidegger. After a disastrous 1716–17 season, Heidegger wisely chose to abandon losing money on an unprofitable entertainment.

About the circumstances of opera in London at the end of the 1716–17 season, Judith Milhous and Robert Hume observe:

Table 3.1 Finances of Heidegger's opera company, 1713–14 to 1716–17

Season	Performances	No. of Operas	Income	Expenses	Loss
1713–14	31	4	£4,255	£4,604	£349
1714–15	42	6	£5,700(?)	£6,700	£1,000(?)
1715–16	29	5	na	na	na
1716–17	32	6	£2,197+(?)	£4,533+(?)	£2,336(?)

Figures marked with "?" are estimates.
Sources: Adapted from Judith Milhous and Robert D. Hume, "Heidegger and the Management of the Haymarket Opera, 1713–17," *Early Music* 17 (1999), 81; and Winton Dean and Merrill Knapp, *Handel's Operas, 1704–1726*, rev. edn. (Oxford: Clarendon Press, 1995), 156.

The company needed a substantial dollop of capital and a royal subsidy. It needed to mount lavish productions of new operas by major composers – as for example Handel and Bononcini. It needed major singers from the continent and some variety from season to season. Prices must be raised even higher (from 8s to half a guinea in the event) and annual subscriptions obtained from a substantial number of the gentry in order to fund these improvements. Heidegger and his predecessors had been fatally dependent on walk-in trade and one-off subscriptions to particular new productions.[16]

Careful attention to chronology shows that even at the nadir of the royal rupture, there were plans afoot to found a new opera company, which went on apace without the prospect of a reconciliation. In January 1719 (almost a year and a half before the reconciliation) several gentlemen petitioned the king to establish opera in London in the form of a joint-stock company. Their goal was to provide London with regular seasons of international-caliber opera befitting such a "great and opulent City" as London. They hoped a reserve of capital from shareholder subscriptions (and in the event supplemented by an annual royal bounty) would put opera on a firm financial basis. Capital was amassed by the new system of the joint-stock company, which spread the risk among shareholders, who expected a financial return.[17]

Handel had been about to depart to Europe on personal business in February 1719, but he abruptly cancelled the trip so he could, as he wrote to his brother, remain and attend to "important affairs, and on which, I dare say, my fortune depends."[18] Presumably he wanted to be in London to ensure his participation in the new opera company.

A "Proposall for carrying on Operas by a company and a Joynt Stock" was drafted in April. It set out governance, the means of raising the £10,000 capital from subscribers, plans for assigning boxes and hiring musicians, and an optimistic estimate of the 25 percent dividends to be paid to the shareholders. The projectors gained the involvement of several Londoners with practical experience in opera production, including Vanbrugh, Handel, and Heidegger. Handel was engaged not as principal composer, but as "Master of the Orchester with a Sallary" (the salary is not known). He came to share composing duties with Giovanni Bononcini and Attilio Ariosti.

The king ordered the Royal Academy of Music incorporated on May 9, and five days later the Duke of Newcastle issued Handel with a warrant to travel to Europe to assemble a company of singers.[19] The royal charter was granted on July 27. By its terms, the king settled an annual bounty or subsidy of £1,000 on the Academy for the duration of its twenty-one-year charter.[20] The king also made payments when members of the royal family attended performances. The Academy hoped to raise £10,000 in subscriptions of £200 shares, and by the end of the summer, sixty-three peers, aristocrats, and gentry had subscribed for £200 shares. Ultimately, there were seventy-three shareholders, who pledged upwards of £15,000.[21] The shareholders, who would elect directors, had to put up only £40 of each £200 share. They were liable for further calls on their shares, but it was not expected that more than 25 percent of the subscription would be called. The governor of the Academy, the Lord Chamberlain, was the king's permanent representative on the board with a veto over the board's decisions. The Crown presumably had the right to forbid or censor any opera production as it could other theater productions; but the only evidence of royal influence on the Academy was when George I made known his wishes about the hiring of Cuzzoni and Faustina and apparently settling a dispute among other singers. In the first short season, the Academy offered only twenty-two performances of three operas. In subsequent full seasons, the Academy staged from thirty-nine to about sixty-three performances, in most seasons between fifty-one and about sixty-three performances.[22]

Although it planned to open in March 1720, the company began its season on April 2 with Giovanni Porta's *Numitore*. Preparations for this production were certainly underway well before news circulated of the court and Whig reconciliation in early April. That Handel's *Radamisto*, the second opera of the season, was the one attended by the king and prince for their public display of reconciliation may just be fortuitous.[23] Nothing in the libretto alludes to the event: Handel's dedication to the king commends his protection of music and his "most Refined Taste in the Art," and the title page announces the opera as performed "for the Royal Academy of *Musick*" (see Figure 3.1).

Il RADAMISTO.

O P E R A.

Da Rapprefentarfi

Nell' REGIO TEATRO
d'*H A Y-M A R K E T.*

PER L'

Academia Reale di Mufica.

Stampata in *L O N D R A* per T. Wo o d
in *Little Britain,* il M DCC x x.

Figure 3.1 Title page of *Radamisto*, produced at the Haymarket Theatre, London, 1720. Photo: courtesy of the Newberry Library, Chicago.

The direct involvement of Lord Burlington and other Whig connoisseurs and patrons suggests the Royal Academy was part of the broader campaign to improve and cultivate the arts in Britain on the basis of Italian models. The Proposal sets out the undertakers' belief in the national importance of the Academy:

Opera's … are an Encouragement and Support to an Art that has been cherished by all Polite Nations. They carry along with them some Marks of Publick Magnificence and are the great Entertainment which Strangers share in. Therefore it seems very strange that this great and opulent City hath not been able to support Publick Spectacles of this Sort for any considerable time.[24]

Implicit in the Proposal is the belief that an opera company would demonstrate Britain's parity with Europe as a seat of taste and politeness to accompany its growing commercial and military power. Charles Burney would later state, as the proud owner of the original signed and sealed patent roll of the Academy, that the document was "a memorial of our prosperity, good-humour, patronage of polite art, and happiness."[25] Over the years, the company attracted some of Europe's most prominent singers and composers. The castrato Francesco Bernardi, called Senesino, arrived in September 1720; the composer Giovanni Bononcini arrived the following month. The soprano Francesca Cuzzoni arrived in December 1722, and the soprano Faustina Bordoni followed in the spring of 1726. Early attempts to recruit the rising star Carlo Broschi, called Farinelli, though, were unsuccessful.[26]

Despite the annual royal subsidy and £15,000 pledged capital, the company still had to cater to public taste by raising season subscriptions and attracting the walk-in opera-goer. What was intended as capital invested in a profit-making stock company soon became subsidies by the shareholders. In time, despite the payment of one 7 percent dividend in February 1723, twenty-one calls on shareholders ultimately consumed each pledged £200 share.

Like Britain's mixed constitution, the Royal Academy of Music was a unique hybrid. Since the royalist excesses of the court of Charles II, English monarchs, dependent on annual grants by Parliament, had kept relatively modest court establishments by comparison with other Continental rulers, reaching a low point in the final years of Anne's reign.[27] After the Glorious Revolution, a court-supported opera, whose role was to serve as outward expression of the majesty of the court and glorify the ruler (as had been the case with many operas of the reigns of Charles II and James II), would have been, even if financially possible, inappropriate and uncongenial to English sensibilities.[28]

As a profit-oriented opera house open to the paying public, the Royal Academy resembled the commercial opera houses in Hamburg and Venice. Yet because of the royal patent, bounty, and veto and governance by aristocrats who were often court office holders (see Appendix 1), there is an element of an opera produced by and for the court and aristocrats, but one without the political or dynastic functions of typical Continental court operas. Unlike them, the Royal Academy productions, amounting to a whole season, were not limited to celebrating specific state events nor limited to the court and invited guests. In Lorenzo Bianconi's sense, the operas were addressed to the Academy and its sponsors, not the monarch.[29]

The printed libretto of the first opera *Numitore* (1720) is instructive. The title page (Figure 2.1) clearly announces the Academy is the sponsor and recipient of the opera, and it is dedicated to "Alli Nobilissimi Signori Li Sig.i Directtori della Reale Accademia di Musica," who are named in full on the dedication page. The title-page epigram, "But when a conquering race began to extend its domain, and a greater wall embraced its cities … then both rhythms and melodies were allowed greater freedom,"[30] alludes to the founding of Rome, the subject of the opera (the restoration to the throne of Numitor, grandfather of Romulus and Remus) – suggesting the Academy is primarily a reflection of the growing eminence of Britain, not its royal family.

The rise of Walpole

After the unification of the ministerial Whigs, two events, the South Sea Bubble crisis and the Atterbury Plot, ensured the rise to ministerial prominence of Robert Walpole and his ultimate dominance of British politics for two decades.[31]

By 1719 the nation had amassed some £31 million in debt. In January 1720, the Commons accepted a proposal from the South Sea Company to take over the national debt and convert it into dividend-paying South Sea stock in return for fixed interest paid by the government. Since the amount of stock given for a unit of public debt was not fixed, the Company had an ulterior motive for manipulating a rising stock value.[32] To ease passage of the proposal, the Company bribed courtiers, ministers, and politicians with gifts of stock, which they could sell at a profit. Stanhope and Sunderland personally guided the bill through the Lords, and on April 7 it received royal assent. The country went wild speculating in South Sea stock. From its level of 128 on January 1, 1720, stock peaked at 1,050 on June 24, in great part due to stock manipulation by the Company.[33]

The late realization that the Company had no profits to pay dividends brought a bitter dose of reality, and the bubble burst in September 1720, with the Company's stock dropping to 180. Thousands suffered losses, yet some individuals made huge, honest profits. The bursting of the bubble ruined credit and fortunes, and plunged the country into a financial crisis and even fears of a Jacobite coup. Arthur Onslow, later Walpole's Speaker of the House, thought the rage against the government so great, "the King being at that time abroad, that could the Pretender then have landed at the Tower, he might have rode to St. James's with very few hands held up against him."[34]

In parliamentary trials for corruption in February and March 1721, Charles Stanhope, Secretary of the Treasury, and Sunderland narrowly escaped conviction. Walpole had spoken in defense of both, which earned him the charge that he was shielding the court and the company directors from incriminating testimony about their role in the bribery. For his role in preventing full retribution and confiscation of wealth as demanded by the Commons and the public, Walpole would thereafter be known as the "screen" or "screenmaster" to recall his role in the scandal. But Walpole knew that public abuse was irrelevant: what was important was his standing with the king and ability to manage his affairs in Parliament.

The Sunderland–Stanhope ministry slowly dissolved: James Stanhope died of a stroke on February 5, after a strenuous speech in Parliament; Secretary James Craggs the Younger died on February 16; Postmaster James Craggs senior committed suicide on March 16. Although narrowly acquitted, Sunderland felt obligated to resign his Treasury post on April 3, 1721. Walpole assumed his post and now became First Lord of the Treasury, Chancellor of the Exchequer, and Paymaster General; but he was still locked in a struggle with Sunderland for complete power. He now consolidated his position; his brother-in-law Townshend had filled Stanhope's place as Secretary of State. He filled government posts with other family members and shored up his position in the Commons by appointments to other junior posts. While the Commons enacted revenge on the malefactors, Walpole saw through a rescue scheme that received royal assent on July 29, and Parliament was dismissed on August 10.

The South Sea scandal ruined or eliminated Walpole's political rivals, and his management of the aftermath demonstrated his mastery of the Commons. Through his financial knowledge, directing retribution and revenge onto the directors, and limiting the scope of the investigations, Walpole saved the court and ministry from outright scandal and restored faith in the nation's financial system. Despite public indignation at the exposure of public corruption, the March 1722 parliamentary election returned a safe, solid Whig majority for the ministry and dealt a serious blow to Tories.

Public anger over the South Sea scandal and the corruption it revealed revived Jacobite hopes and brought their greatest chance for success since the death of Queen Anne. In spring 1721, leading Tories (if not Jacobites) including the Earl of Strafford, Lord North and Grey, and Francis Atterbury, the Bishop of Rochester, began corresponding with the Pretender in Italy and his agents in Paris, urging them to exploit the volatile situation in Britain. In early 1722, appeals for money were sent to

European courts, and general plans were underway for a spring invasion and insurrection.[35]

Unknown to Atterbury and the conspirators, Walpole's officers were intercepting their mail and discovered the plotting. In April, the Duke of Ormonde's invasion from Spain was thwarted, and the Jacobite threat faded away. Troops were encamped in Hyde Park on May 7, and Townshend announced the plot to the Lord Mayor the following day. Arrests began the following week and culminated on August 24 in the arrest of Atterbury and his commitment to the Tower for high treason. Lord North and Grey and the Earl of Orrery were arrested in September on the evidence of Christopher Layer and followed Atterbury to the Tower.

Walpole knew the plot was by now utterly harmless, but exploited it for his political advantage. Sunderland, who owed his narrow escape in the Lords to Atterbury and other Tories, probably would not have prosecuted the plotters as severely as Walpole. But with his sudden death on April 19, Walpole seized the opportunity to discredit his former rival, inflict a mortal blow on the Tories, and cement himself in the king's favor by prosecuting the plotters. The arrest of the bishop and his humiliating treatment in the Tower aroused public expressions of sympathy for the bishop. Walpole's political future now rested on proving the conspiracy.

The new Parliament sat early on October 9, and habeas corpus was promptly suspended, leaving the conspirators at the mercy of the ministry. Despite exhaustive investigation, Walpole had no legally valid evidence against Atterbury and two other conspirators, Plunkett and Kelly, and had to settle for a Commons bill of pains and penalties against them. In the May 1723 parliamentary inquiry, Layer was found guilty and subsequently executed. Atterbury was tried and convicted, and on May 27 the king assented to his exile. Lords North and Grey and Orrery were released on bond, and Atterbury departed for exile in France on June 18, 1723. Walpole's relentless persecution of Atterbury and the hapless plotters was so successful, he afterwards opportunistically raised the specter of Jacobitism and tarred the political opposition as Tory and Jacobitical to strengthen support for the Hanoverian succession.[36]

Despite containing the South Sea crisis and the successful prosecution of the Atterbury plotters, the Stanhope–Sunderland and then the Walpole–Townshend ministries were plagued by dissent in the Whig ranks and assaults from the press.[37] Outrage at the corruption revealed by the scandal and calls for vengeance upon the malefactors were topics of early essays by Thomas Gordon and John Trenchard in the *London Journal* and *British Journal* running from 1720 to 1723.[38] Disgusted at the Whig ministry, Earl

Cowper, the highly respected former Whig Lord Chancellor, in January 1721 began organizing in the Lords a new opposition of dissident Whigs, Hanoverian Tories, and Jacobites.[39] The Duke of Wharton launched the *True Briton* (1723–24) to denounce Walpole's prosecution of Atterbury as a violation of the constitution and British liberties.[40] In its skill in ransacking history for evil ministers and use of narrative allegories to apply to Walpole, the *True Briton* anticipates the techniques and themes of later opposition periodicals like the *Craftsman* and *Common Sense*.

Nevertheless, Walpole strengthened his hold on power and created the Robinocracy that would endure twenty-one years. By his policies and management of the Commons, he reduced the national debt, increased financial confidence in the government, kept Britain out of expensive Continental wars, and established a strong executive. J. H. Plumb records his achievement:

Aided both by events, and by the tidal sweep of history, a politician of genius, Robert Walpole, was able to create what had eluded kings and ministers since the days of Elizabeth I – a government and a policy acceptable to the Court, to the Commons, and to the majority of the political establishment in the nation at large. Indeed, he made the world so safe for Whigs that they stayed in power for a hundred years.[41]

Internal politics of the Royal Academy

Given the politicization of London's theaters and the divisive partisan politics of the day, the inevitable factions in the management of the Royal Academy might be expected to align with the partisanship of the political world at large. This possibility is no doubt sanctioned by Charles Burney, who – after noting that oppositions are inherent to popular governments – stated that "political animosities were blended with Musical faction" in the Academy.[42]

It seems to be an article of faith among many opera historians that the factions in the Royal Academy did mirror national party politics. Yet no writer has ever named the partisan allegiance of any director. On the basis of the observations that the public was accustomed to party strife being expressed in the theaters and that parties were divided between Drury Lane and Lincoln's Inn Fields, Hans Dieter Clausen states that "since opera was presented in only one theater, party-strife was acted out within the directorate" of the Royal Academy.[43] He identifies, but names no members of, an "anti-George" faction in the directorate.[44] O. E. Deutsch, following

Sir John Hawkins, states that Bononcini's patrons were Whigs, while the Tories favored Handel.[45] Jane Clark asserts that "the directors of the opera always had a strong Jacobite element."[46] For Ellen Harris, "In its early years, the Academy had two internal, political factions: the opposition party – Jacobite, Catholic, and Italian, represented by composer Giovanni Bononcini and librettist Paolo Rolli – and the court party, represented by Handel and the librettist Nicola Haym."[47] On the basis of allusions in librettos, she suggests the anti-Hanoverian librettos stem from the Rolli–Bononcini faction, whereas the pro-Hanoverian librettos came from Handel and Haym.[48]

As might be expected in an enterprise with an elected directorate trying to staunch a constant drain on its capital, hire Europe's finest musical talent, and balance the demands of the partisans of rival composers and singers, there was dissention within the Academy, which was often gleefully reported by contemporaries. They often compared the factions to political parties, but none, though, align any directors with a party. Giuseppe Riva, Modenese diplomatic secretary, partisan of Bononcini and Cuzzoni, and strong antagonist of Handel, reported on operatic affairs to friends on the Continent and frequently noted the divisions and squabbles in the Academy. In March 1721, he wrote to Agostino Steffani:

The malignant spirit of parties, which is so natural to the English mind, has been introduced into the Academy of Music, with the result that at present things are going sideways, and there is everything but harmony.[49]

Less than two months later, he reported again to Steffani:

The Royal Academy of Music has succeeded in becoming a kind of South Sea Company. Everything went marvellously well at the beginning, but as it progressed the devil entered and sowed discord among the singers, subscribers and directors. The parties have started making insulting remarks to each other, and everyone has been carried away by mad passion.[50]

Early in January 1723, Friedrich Ernst von Fabrice wrote to Graf Flemming:

There are two factions, the one for Hendell, the other for Bononcini, the one for Cenesino [Senesino] and the other for Cossuna [Cuzzoni]. They are as animated against each other as the Whigs and Tories, and sometimes even divide the directors.[51]

A year later, he reported that the squabbles within the Academy often provided the public with "the most diverting scenes."[52] A little earlier that year, the *Weekly Journal*, like its successors, *Mist's* and *Fog's Weekly Journals*, not favorably disposed toward opera, enjoyed reporting,

We hear there have been strange Commotions in the State of Musick in the Opera House in the Hay-Market, and that a civil Broil arose among the Subscribers at the Practice [rehearsal] of the new Opera of *Vespasian* [premiere, January 14, 1724], which turn'd all the Harmony into Discord; and if these Dissentions do not cease, it is thought *Opera* Stock will fall.[53]

And at the beginning of the final season, Handel's friend Mary Delany could observe, "I doubt operas will not survive longer than his winter, they are now at their last gasp ... The directors are always squabbling, and they have so many divisions among themselves that I wonder they have not broke up before."[54]

The most famous dramatization of the conflict in the Royal Academy is John Byrom's epigram, first printed in June 1725:

> Some say, that Seignior *Bononchini*,
> Compar'd to *Handel's* a meer Ninny;
> Others aver, to him, that *Handel*
> Is scarcely fit to hold a Candle.
> Strange! that such high Disputes shou'd be
> 'Twixt *Tweedledum* and *Tweedledee*.[55]

While factions were certainly rife in the Royal Academy, no evidence suggests any alignment along Whig–Tory lines, nor for that matter a strong Tory or Jacobite presence.

Profiles of the shareholders and directors for the early years of the Royal Academy (see Appendix 1) show that, where political allegiances are known or can be inferred, the eighty or so original shareholders are primarily Whig courtiers and government officeholders, all of whom were serving at the pleasure of the king.[56]

That most shareholders are Whigs reflects the Whig oligarchy's domination of the British political and commercial world after 1714. By point of reference, the 1722 House of Commons (of 558 seats) was 70 percent Whig, giving the government a strong majority of 220, or 40 percent.[57] The Lords was somewhat less Whiggish, at about 60 percent Whig.[58] Since the initial organization of the Royal Academy occurred during the Whig Schism, the shareholders also include a number of schismatic Whigs allied with Walpole, Townshend, and the Prince of Wales. There are a few Tories; but by this date, most of those who remained were increasingly shedding their Tory colors and joining the Whigs, and were reconciling themselves to the government and the Hanoverian succession. As Linda Colley has argued, they saw themselves as a "loyal opposition."[59]

On the basis of the political alignments of the shareholders and directors, it becomes difficult to support the idea of a significant or effective Jacobite, "anti-George," or opposition faction in the Royal Academy. The Royal Academy directors, who managed its seasons, were chosen by the shareholders. When it came to electing them, the predominantly Whig shareholders seem not to have held politics against anyone and voted in two Tories, including the Tory member of Earl Cowper's parliamentary opposition Robert Benson, Lord Bingley (see Appendix 1).

The Bononcini affair

Politics has been seen in the dismissal of the composer Giovanni Bononcini from the Academy in late September or early October 1722; the Academy's secretary Paolo Rolli was dismissed soon afterward. The accepted account, first proposed by Lowell Lindgren,[60] notes that the dismissals occurred in the wake of the Jacobite scare following Walpole's round-up in early August 1722 of suspects in the Atterbury Plot. A consequence of the witch-hunt was a "Jacobite paranoia, the effect of which was disfavour for any Roman Catholic in London."[61] Bononcini's association with "the most conspicuous Jacobites," Francis Atterbury and the Duchess of Buckingham, and his Catholicism caused the Academy directors to suspect him as a Jacobite and dismiss him.

Clausen similarly explains that the discovery of the plot on behalf of the Pretender weakened the "anti-George faction" in the Academy's directorship and led to the dismissals of Bononcini and Rolli.[62] Clausen's idea of a weakened "anti-George" faction that backed Bononcini and Rolli assumes that the few Tories in the Academy were anti-Hanoverian and it was their influence that kept Bononcini employed until they were discredited.[63] The likely Tory candidates would be Dr. John Arbuthnot and Lord Bingley; but these two have not been suspected of being Jacobites. In any case, curiously for one who may have been "anti-George," Bingley later became a privy councilor and treasurer of the household to George II.

Upon careful examination of the events and Bononcini's supporters, the Jacobite explanation for Bononcini's dismissal loses credibility: it relies on coincidence, association, tendentious interpretation of documents, and a selective use of evidence to make it seem that contemporaries would have considered that Bononcini was patronized by Jacobite sympathizers and was himself suspect. Significantly, the diligent archival searches of scholars of Jacobitism have never unearthed any mention of Bononcini or Rolli in secret or intercepted Jacobite correspondence. There are more plausible and better-documented explanations for Bononcini's dismissal.

One of Bononcini's supposed Jacobite associates was Francis Atterbury, Dean of Westminster and Bishop of Rochester. For the state funeral of the Duke of Marlborough at Westminster Abbey on August 9, 1722, Bononcini composed the anthem; the dean presided over the service just two weeks before his arrest on August 24. Lindgren suggests that Atterbury appointed and commissioned Bononcini to compose the anthem, implying contemporaries would associate Bononcini with the Jacobite Atterbury.

But there is little reason to believe contemporaries would have made such an association. Reporting on plans for the funeral, the *Post Boy* stated that "The Dean of Westminster hath appointed Dr. Crofts [*sic*] to compose an Anthem."[64] Lindgren correctly observes the paper published a retraction in its next issue: "We were misinform'd in our last, as to Dr. Croft's composing an Anthem at the Funeral of the late Duke of Marlborough."[65] But this correction, which does not mention the true composer of the anthem nor who commissioned it, cannot be construed, as does Lindgren, as a public notice of "Atterbury's apparent role in commissioning the anthem."[66]

There is, however, ample evidence that Atterbury did not in fact commission the anthem, nor, more importantly, that contemporaries might have thought he did. Atterbury was unlikely to have taken much interest in the ceremony honoring the great Whig hero. As he wearily complained to Alexander Pope, he would be going in a few days reluctantly up to the Abbey, "till I have said, Dust to Dust, and shut up the last Scene of Pompous Vanity" on a man, his biographer wrote, "he had never honoured in life."[67] The service for the duke was a state funeral directed by his widow, Sarah, the dowager duchess.[68] Even direct evidence cited by Lindgren points to the fact that the commission came instead from the Marlborough family and the king.

On August 3, Giuseppe Riva wrote from London to Modena about the duke's funeral: "Giovan Bononcino ... has been chosen by the King and the two duchesses, the mother [Sarah, the dowager duchess] and daughter [Henrietta] to compose the music for this great occasion."[69] About a year after the funeral, the Earl of Godolphin wrote to Sarah, his mother-in-law, apparently advising the executors about paying Bononcini for the anthem:

Since the Dutchess of Buckingham's present to Bononcini was a hundred pound [*sic*], I am, I confess, of my Lord De-la-Warr's mind, that the Duke of Marlborough's

Executors should not give him less; tho' had there not been that Precedent for it, and had the gratuity been given at the time the Musick was made, Perhaps half the sum would have been very thankfully accepted.[70]

Godolphin apparently believed that Bononcini should have been grateful for £50 for composing the anthem: but with the passage of time, and the precedent of the Duchess of Buckingham's payment, probably for the music to her late husband's plays (see below), the executors were honor-bound to pay Bononcini's demand for £100. Sir John Hawkins, relying on one of the daughters of the duchess, states the commission came from the family.[71]

Indeed, contemporaries would more likely associate Bononcini with the Marlborough family than with Atterbury. As was well known, Bononcini's connections with the great Whig family continued after the funeral. Between 1724 and 1732, he was the resident composer and music director for Henrietta, the younger Duchess of Marlborough and dedicated his *XII Sonatas for the Chamber* (1732) to the dowager duchess.

Bononcini's other patron and Jacobite acquaintance who is supposed to have brought suspicion on him was Catherine Sedley, Duchess of Buckingham, illegitimate daughter of James II. The first public link between Bononcini and the duchess cited by Lindgren is her subscription to his *Cantate e duetti* (1721; published in early 1722). Tory subscribers included Lord Bathurst, Lord Bingley, the Earl of Peterborough, the Duchess of Shrewsbury, and Alexander Pope. The *Cantate* amassed a large and prestigious list of 243 or more subscribers,[72] including members of the royal family and numerous peers and aristocrats. But these few Tories are insufficient to suggest Bononcini was perceived as a Tory or Jacobite favorite.

Bononcini was, in fact, greatly favored publicly by the Whigs. W. A. Speck examined the subscription list to the *Cantate e duetti* and found it "received a disproportionate number of Whig subscribers presumably because he stayed in England as the guest of the Duke of Marlborough, the Earl of Sunderland and other Whig peers."[73] As Table 3.2 shows, the directors were lavish in their support of Bononcini, subscribing among them to fifty copies (21 percent) of his *Cantate*. Some of these Whig oligarchs subscribed to thirty (Lord Carleton), twenty-five (Duke and Duchess of Queensberry, each), or fifty-five (Countess of Sunderland) copies, whereas Pope and the Duchess of Buckingham put down for only one copy apiece. One of Bononcini's longest-standing supporters was the great Whig family the Marlboroughs; among his hosts at Twickenham (and subscribers to the *Cantate*) were the court Whigs Lady Mary Wortley Montagu (also a protector of the Catholic singer Anastasia Robinson) and her husband;[74]

Table 3.2 Bononcini subscriptions by directors of the Royal Academy of Music, serving 1720–21

Director	Political allegiance[1]	Copies subscribed
Thomas Holles, Duke of Newcastle (Governor)	Whig courtier	1 copy
Lord Bingley (Deputy Governor)	Tory; member of Lord Cowper's Lord's opposition	1 copy
Duke of Portland	Whig courtier	—
Duke of Queensberry	(Whig) courtier	25 copies; his wife, 25 copies
Earl of Burlington	Whig courtier	—
Earl of Stair	Whig courtier	1 copy; his wife, 1 copy
Earl of Wadeck[2]	—	—
Lord Chetwynd	Whig MP and office holder	—
Lord Stanhope (later Earl of Chesterfield)	Whig MP and office holder (court of Prince of Wales)	1 copy
James Bruce (Treasurer)	(Whig) office holder	1 copy
Colonel (James) Blathwayt	(Whig) office holder	5 copies
Thomas Coke of Norfolk (later Earl of Leicester)	Whig MP (1722–28)	1 copy
Conyers D'Arcy	Whig MP	—
Brig.-Gen. (James) Dormer	(Whig) office holder	1 copy
Brian Fairfax	(Whig) office holder	—
Colonel (James) O'Hara	(Whig) office holder	1 copy
George Harrison	Whig MP	—
Brig.-General (Robert) Hunter	(Whig) office holder	1 copy
William Pulteney	Schismatic Whig MP	10 copies
Sir John Vanbrugh	Whig	—
Major-General (George) Wade	Whig MP and office holder	—
Francis Whitworth	Whig MP	1 copy
		50 copies (out of 238 total)

[1] Given the fact of the Tory proscription after 1714, court and government officeholders and military officers are presumed Whig (indicated by brackets) in lieu of other identification.

[2] O. E. Deutsch, *Handel: A Documentary Biography* (New York: W. W. Norton, 1955), 123, and others following him, silently and without explanation converts Malcolm's "Earl of Wadeck" to "Earl of Waldegrave." He is more likely Count Frederik Anton Ulrich van Waldeck-Pyrmont (1676–1728).

Source: Dedicatees of Alexander Malcolm, *A Treatise of Musick, Speculative, Practical, and Historical* (1721). Biographical information adapted from Appendix 1.

and another Whig patron was the Earl of Bristol, who sponsored a private rehearsal at his home of *Crispo* on June 5, 1721.[75]

The subscription list to Bononcini's *Cantate*, headed by the Prince and Princess of Wales and their daughter Princess Anne, suggests patronage of the publication was not a place to look for supposed signs of Jacobite sympathy. The publication verges instead on being a Hanoverian celebration, for it was obsequiously dedicated "alla sacra maestà di Giorgio rè della Gran Britagna," who paid £50 for the dedication.[76] The significance of the duchess' name on the subscription list evaporates in light of the overwhelming Whig support for Bononcini and the fact that her subscription was entered on her behalf (possibly without her authorization or knowledge) by Alexander Pope.[77]

The second link between Bononcini and the duchess is his composing of choruses for a projected performance at Drury Lane in 1722–23 of her late husband's play *Julius Caesar*.[78] From Shakespeare's *Julius Caesar*, the duke had crafted two plays;[79] after each of its first four acts, each play was to have sung choruses in the Greek manner with instrumental accompaniment. The texts of two choruses (in addition to two by the duke) had been written at the duke's request by Pope around 1714–16 and published in his *Works* (1717). Bononcini composed the choruses for *Julius Caesar*, while John Galliard composed those for *Marcus Brutus*.

The musical requirements were beyond the usual forces of Drury Lane and required special arrangements. The choral parts were to be taken by members of the Chapel Royal. For the remaining parts, in September 1722 Pope asked the Earl of Egmont (then Lord Percival) on behalf of the duchess to intercede with General Robert Hunter, one of the directors of the Royal Academy, that "in case any voice, or part of the Instrumental Musick shou'd be wanted, they wou'd permit them to perform in it for a few nights, supposing those nights not to interfere with the Operas."[80] Several days later, Pope learned from Egmont that the request for use of the chief singers was denied, but that he might have "Bosci, & any of the instrumental musick on Such nights as did not interfere with the Operas."[81] The plays and choruses were announced in the newspapers through December, and the choruses and instrumental music were in rehearsal at Buckingham House in January 1723, with Mrs. Robinson, Mrs. Barbier, and Mrs. Clark as singers, instrumentalists of the Royal Academy, and men from the Chapel Royal.[82]

In the event, neither play with its music was produced. On January 12, 1723, the *London Journal* explained the failure of a public performance of the first play: "His Majesty would not allow that the Gentlemen of the Royal Chappel, who are to be the Performers, should appear upon the Theatre."[83]

Lindgren casts doubt on the veracity of the reason for the refusal; but the reason given for the king's objection to his Chapel Royal singers performing on stage is so plausible there are no good grounds to reject it or believe it is a ruse.[84]

The Jacobite scenario for Bononcini's dismissal can also be discounted for the compelling reason that two of Bononcini's acquaintances document an utterly plausible and characteristic reason: a contractual or monetary disagreement between Bononcini and the directors. In the key piece of evidence about Bononcini's dismissal, the Countess of Bristol wrote from Richmond to her husband on October 5, 1722: "Bononcini is dismiss'd the Theatre for Operas which I beleiv you and some of your family will regret; the reason they give for it, is, his most extravagant Demands."[85] That is, he probably asked too high a salary or favorable conditions for a benefit for the coming season.[86]

The countess had preceded this sentence with a piece of news about Walpole's taking-up of Christopher Layer for questioning: "they say Mr: L — r Squeeks finely [.] there are Several people more nam'd that they say are to be taken up, but that is too tender a point to touch upon, unless it were done." Lindgren proposes that because the countess had just previously mentioned the Jacobite plot, she "clearly implied" that the directors' reason of extravagant demands was fictitious or a cover-up for the real reason. But rather, the phrase "but that is too tender a point to touch upon, unless it were done" suggests instead she was not going to mention names on the basis of hearsay until the suspects were apprehended.

About the same time (October 1722), the Catholic soprano Anastasia Robinson reported to Giuseppe Riva the same impasse and attributed it to disputes about Bononcini's demands about a benefit (and possibly salary):

I have great hopes Signor Bononcini's demands may be agreed too, tho in another form then that which he propos'd, the di[ffi]culty is to get the benefit day certain, for they would have it to depend on their favour and generosity (a wretched dependance indeed).[87]

Robinson's following remarks, Lindgren states, specify "Bononcini's Roman faith as the reason why the Academy would not give him a contract":[88]

I took the liberty to say what they designed doing, must be by contract, for tho Bonocini [*sic*] was a papist, yet he had been long enough in this heretick unbelieving country, to loose all his faith.[89]

But Lindgren surely mistakenly interprets the phrase "tho Bononcini was a Papist" (which is gratuitous, for certainly the directors had long known this). Robinson is not attributing an anti-Catholic motive to the directors. Rather, in an exaggerated way she is saying he had been in Protestant England long enough to have lost his faith in the director's honesty about the benefit and must take the precaution of getting a contract.

Given the precarious finances of the Academy, such cautions were prudent. The Academy's musicians did have reason to distrust its directors. About a year previously (August 26, 1721), Riva had written to Steffani in Hanover:

The affairs of the Academy of Music are in disarray. They have not yet finished paying their debts for the season [ending in July 1721]. Oh what wits these English have! Oh, and then they complain that they have been swindled by foreigners! They deserve it, because they do not keep their promises, and anyone who knows their nature sees that they must be taken on the wing.[90]

There is corroboration about Bononcini's "extravagant Demands" and quarrelsome nature. In his letter to the duchess quoted above, Godolphin apparently believed that Bononcini should have gratefully accepted £50 for composing the anthem: but with the passage of time and the Duchess of Buckingham's payment, the executors were obligated to pay Bononcini's demand for £100. A decade later, when Bononcini was employed by the Duchess of Marlborough, John, Lord Hervey wrote about receiving a letter from her "filled with complaints of Bononcini." Hervey seemed to think Bononcini was on the verge of losing his appointment with the duchess: "I really think 'tis an odd whim of him who recieves [*sic*] five hund.d pounds a year for playing on the violóncello four hours in a week, to risque the losing it by running after a desperate debt w.ch to be sure can be but inconsiderable."[91] Bononcini and the duchess ended up quarrelling, and he left her service sometime in 1732.[92]

All told, the accounts by the Countess of Bristol and Anastasia Robinson agree so fundamentally there is no reason to doubt that it was "his most extravagant Demands" and lack of deference to superiors that led to a contractual impasse and Bononcini's parting from the Royal Academy. The explanation invoking "Jacobite paranoia" and disfavor for Roman Catholics is also unsatisfactory because it overstates the persecution of Roman Catholics due to the legal proscriptions, which were laxly enforced.[93] The other foreign Catholic composers, singers, and musicians at the Royal Academy were not affected by the Atterbury scare and anti-Catholic bias. Their Catholicism did not prevent many of them receiving gifts from royal family members and aristocrats for publication dedications, benefit tickets, and lessons. Bononcini's place was in fact filled by a Catholic monk, Attilio

Table 3.3 Composers of operas produced by the Royal Academy of Music

Season	Bononcini	Handel	Ariosti	Other
1719–20	0	1	0	2
1720–21	2 ⅓*	⅓	0	1 ⅓
1721–22	2	1	0	0
1722–23	1	2	1	0
1723–24	2	1	2	0
1724–25	0	3	2	0
1725–26	0	2	1	0
1726–27	1	1	1	0
1727–28	0	3	1	0

* Fraction indicates one act of *Muzio Scevola*.

Ariosti; and Rolli's place, by the Italian (and presumed Catholic) Nicola Haym. Somehow, though, Bononcini's supposed Jacobitism was not such a stigma, because the Academy later mounted four of his operas (Table 3.3).

Political allegory in the operas of the Royal Academy

On the basis of the generic expectation that operas allegorize or allude to contemporary politics and that opera heroes refer to the current monarch, royal family, or statesmen, opera historians have sought to find the topical politics in the librettos of operas produced by the Royal Academy. The interpretations all happen to be of Handel operas: *Muzio Scevola* (1721), *Scipione* (1726), *Floridante* (1721), *Ottone* (1723), *Admeto* (1727), and *Riccardo primo* (1727). Three representative interpretations are examined below.

Handel's *Muzio Scevola* (April 15, 1721) presents the heroism and courage of Mucius Scaevola, Horatio, and the Roman Amazon warriors in defense of Rome and her liberty. The fate of liberty in Republican Rome was a subject that resonated deeply with British Whigs. The central action of the story was the attempt of Mucius Scaevola to enter the invading Etruscan camp, disguised in Tuscan robes, to assassinate Porsena, who was besieging Rome and attempting to restore the Roman throne to its last king, the tyrant Tarquin. Mucius stabbed the secretary by mistake. Seized by the guards and brought before Porsena, he thrust his right hand into an altar fire to demonstrate his fortitude and told Porsena that 300 other, equally determined Romans had entered his camp, each avowed to assassinate him. Astonished at the courage of Mucius and what he and his countrymen would suffer on their country's behalf, Porsena made peace with Rome.

Reinhard Strohm sets the opera in a political context by citing the libretto's dedication to George I as a "kind of peace-offering to the king that ... can be read into the dramatic action of the piece."[94] But it is not clear what the Royal Academy and Rolli would have been atoning for, and the fulsome dedication to the king is not especially significant, since the Royal Academy directors or librettists dedicated twenty-eight of their thirty-three operas to the royal family, nobility, and directors (see Appendix 2).

Strohm finds some analogs between the opera and contemporary events:

> the conservative aristocracy are identifiable with the defenders of Roman republican liberty, while George I is identified with the Etruscan king Porsenna who represents a threat to that liberty but who nobly abandons his plans of conquest and betroths his daughter to the Roman hero Orazio ... Rome's own native oppressor, Tarquinius, is not included in this political compromise. The most formidable enemy of the London aristocracy at this time was the Whig leader, Sir Robert Walpole, who was prime minister after 1722 ... and the object of attack in *Muzio Scevola*.

This allegorical interpretation is too inconsistent and leaves too much unaccounted for. If George I is the Etruscan King Porsena, an invading threat to British liberty, he is certainly an unflattering parallel to the British monarch, and it is not clear what invading country he represents and to what country's throne he would be attempting to restore Walpole (Tarquin) as king. Most crucially, a complete allegorical reading of *Muzio Scevola* must surely provide an analog for the principal figure and main action of the opera: Mucius Scaevola's attempted assassination of the besieging King Porsena (George I); at which point, though, we would have the implausibility of the Royal Academy producing on the London stage an opera symbolically advocating regicide.

Other parallels with contemporary history are also faulty. Strohm implausibly sets the aristocracy against George I and calls the king's minister Robert Walpole "the most formidable enemy of the London aristocracy at this time," which disregards the great number of aristocrats who held household or government posts and honors at the pleasure of the king and his minister.

At the time of the premiere (April 15, 1721), Walpole was still locked in a power struggle with Sunderland. At the time, contemporaries would not have seen him as an oppressor or enemy of the aristocracy; rather, he was reviled as the factious politician who divided the Whig party or abused as "the screen" for his parliamentary defense of Sunderland and Stanhope and shielding the court and ministry from the enquiry arising from the South Sea Bubble. In the latter role, he might likely have been seen as a friend to the court.[95]

The politics of *Muzio Scevola* are likely much more at the level of patriotic ideology and are announced in the libretto's title-page epigraph drawn from Cato's speech in Addison's play:

> Do thou, great Liberty, inspire our Souls,
> And make our Lives in thy Possession happy,
> Or our Deaths glorious in thy just Defence.
>
> *Cato*, III.v, ll. 79–81

These lines suggest the opera's subject was chosen to show Mucius Scaevola as a worthy Roman, noble for his self-sacrifice for the good of the Republic.

Rolli's dedication to the king invokes the favorite Whig theme of the Progress of Liberty and enlists George not as an invading threat but in the great cause of establishing Roman liberty in Britain:

[The subject] is the birth of Roman liberty: having been driven out of its great but unfortunate homeland … which finally found great safety and glorious shelter in the happy realms of Your Majesty. Happiest of realms! So different from all others; your realms truly enjoy Roman liberty.[96]

Rolli further asserts, let Roman history be read and there will be found many more a Brutus, Mucius Scaevola, or Scipio. Rome and Britain are similar in the glory of their arms, laws, and literature; all that happens in Britain can be found in Roman history. Rolli lists all George's virtues that make him worthy the obedience of a people who resemble ancient Rome.

If contemporaries saw political significance in *Muzio Scevola*, it was more likely as an *exemplum virtutis*: an object lesson of public spirit, civic virtue, and patriotic sacrifice. Perhaps Britons in the audience flattered themselves they were capable of such sacrifice.

The Royal Academy opera that has drawn the most attention for topical, political relevance is *Floridante* (December 9, 1721). That several contradictory interpretations have been proposed for the opera highlights the problems arising from the generic expectation in the absence of cues in the libretto to direct the personation and application to current events or persons. The idea that the opera had topical relevance seems to be inferred from a letter by the Tory Dr. William Stratford, Canon of Christ Church, Oxford, written from London to the Tory Edward Harley, second Earl of Oxford, in the country. Apparently referring to the production on December 16, Stratford wrote to Harley on December 19, 1721:

Some things have happen'd at a new opera which have given great offence. It is called Floridante. There happens to be a right Heir in it that is imprison'd. At last the Right Heir is deliver'd and the chains put upon the oppressor. At this last circumstance, there happen'd to be very great and un[-]seasonable Clapping, in the Presence of Great ones. You will hear more when You come to town.[97]

Stratford's account, mentioning the delivery of a rightful heir, has been the basis for frequent statements suggesting, as Ellen Harris writes, that *Floridante* "is the only libretto that Handel set to music known to have been interpreted politically at the time of its first performance."[98]

But Stratford's letter, as we will see, is misleading and has sent scholars on the wrong track about the role of the right heir and enchainment of the oppressor. Additional cues from the dedication and the title-page epigraph have been taken to swell Stratford's implication into the presence of subversive or embarrassing politics in the opera.

Elizabeth Gibson originally suggested that

Handel's dedication of this opera to the Prince of Wales was tactless: the composer could not have been unaware that the plot paralleled the troubles between the Prince and George I. The subject dealt with the trials of a Prince of Thrace, whom a jealous father tries to deprive of his rights to the throne.[99]

Donald Burrows seconded the allegorical interpretation and suggested the dedication to the Prince of Wales was perhaps intended to balance the dedication to the king in *Radamisto*, "but it may accidentally have helped to stir the embers of political controversy."[100] The dedication to the Prince of Wales, however, was (as in the case of *Muzio Scevola*) probably of little such significance. Gibson adds that the title-page epigraph drawn from Quintilian –

Illud adjiciendum videtur, duci Argumenta non e confessis tantum, sed etiam a Fictione.

I think I should also add that arguments are drawn not merely from admitted fact, but from fictitious suppositions.[101]

– was "perhaps intended to limit the immediate comparison."[102] Rather than trying to limit comparison to an offensive dedication, the epigraph is just a Latin version of the common statements frequently made by librettists when adapting episodes from classical history. They acknowledge a kernel of historical truth and admit that subplots, usually involving young lovers, are invented. Typical is the statement from the libretto of *Alessandro Severo* (1738): "This true history, accompany'd by some probable incidents, forms the present drama." The anonymous librettist of *Lucio Papirio dittatore* (1732) wrote, "To the Truth of this History is subjoined the Probability of the Episodes upon the Subjects of Love." And Samuel Humphreys probably wrote the disclaimer to the libretto of *Catone in Utica* (1732): "To this

Historical Truth is added the Probability of those Incidents of Love that are represented in this Performance."

The interpretation that the plot dealing with the trials of a prince of Thrace, whom a jealous father tries to deprive of his rights to the throne, parallels the trouble between George I and his son is based on these analogs:

Floridant (Prince of Thrace, rightful heir) = George Augustus, Prince of Wales
Orontes (jealous father, oppressor) = King George I
Persia = Britain

But these parallels have no obvious relation and many points of contradiction to the recent feud between George I and his son. Most crucially, and contrary to the assumption of most interpretations, the libretto reveals that *Orontes is not Floridant's father* and that *the rightful heir is instead Elmira*. In *Floridante*, a Persian general (Orontes) overthrew and murdered his own king and became a tyrant. Orontes has raised the king's daughter Elmira (hence, the rightful heir) as his own daughter. Orontes is jealous of Floridant because of their rival love for Elmira. Early in the opera, Floridant, a prince of Thrace and in service to Orontes, has returned from a conquest over Tyre and expects to marry his betrothed Elmira. In the meantime, Orontes had decided to marry Elmira himself and banishes and then imprisons Floridant (disguised as a Moor, he had tried to assassinate Orontes). Finally, the people under Timantes, a captured Tyrean prince, overthrow and imprison Orontes, free Floridant, and recognize Elmira as queen (who takes Floridant as her consort).

It is difficult to see how this plot allegorizes contemporary events in Great Britain. George (Orontes) would better be portrayed as jealous of the popularity of his son, but who is already married. Nor at any time had the king exiled and imprisoned the prince, nor had the prince attempted parricide. Most seriously, following Stratford's letter leads to the interpretation that the opera represents King George as a tyrant and oppressor and that the audience is applauding the oppressor's justified imprisonment. There is little reason why Rolli and the predominantly Whig directors of the Royal Academy would broach an event that had so embarrassed the court and the Whig party and characterize their king as a tyrant. Overall, the political point the libretto would be making or who would benefit by raising the scandal is not clear.

Another tack in allegorizing the opera is taken by Ellen Harris, who supposes that those in the audience clapping were Jacobites: for them, the rightful heir Floridant is the Pretender and Orontes the oppressor is King George.[103] This reading, though, suggested by the fact that Stratford and Harley were Tories, is no more plausible: most obviously because the Pretender was in Italy, did not return victorious to Britain, and was not imprisoned by George, who was not a general who murdered his own king to gain the throne.

The restoration of the rightful heir is such a common conclusion of opera librettos (see Appendices 2 and 4) that there is no reason *Floridante* or any other opera should be taken as referring specifically to the restoration of the British Crown to a rightful British heir. It is difficult to understand why the audience applauding the liberation of one falsely imprisoned and the enchainment of a tyrant was a politically seditious action. Moreover, given the overwhelming Whig dominance of the Royal Academy and its audience, it strains credulity to presume those in the audience believed their monarch did not rightfully occupy the throne (and would parallel Orontes). It may be that the affront was the disruption of theatrical decorum by applause during royal attendance (or some incident not related in Stratford's letter).

Yet another set of personations and parallels for *Floridante* is found by Konrad Sasse and endorsed by Reinhard Strohm. For Sasse, "certain political currents here also played a role."[104] Of concern was Britain's policy toward France:

The new ministry under Walpole was again under Whig leadership, the same party that prior to the Bolingbroke administration had been led by the Duke of Marlborough, who then being victim of defamatory accusations had been dismissed by Queen Anne, despite his great success as field marshal in the War of the Spanish Succession …

This new Walpole Whig ministry, however, pursued a politics different than the old one under Marlborough, for the latter [i.e., Marlborough] had been an arch-opponent of France and the former [i.e., Walpole] now represented a politics of negotiation …

With the parallel of the disgraced Prince Floridant to the dismissed Duke of Marlborough and the military glory they both won, the perilous moment in the opera finds its counterpart for the king: His reign could not permanently hold in check a politics of negotiation with France, such as followed the dismissal of the duke, that would not, as in 1708, once again promote a Stuart rebellion. Indeed, it would actually come to that in 1744.[105]

We can go straight to the central problem: there is no obvious reason to parallel Floridant with the Capitan General Marlborough except for the minimal coincidence that both were victorious generals dismissed by their monarch, but for different reasons. Beyond that, the personation and parallels are weak or inconsistent.

In the opera, Orontes (Anne/George) exiled Floridant (Marlborough) because of jealousy over Elmira, the rightful heir, and then imprisoned him after Floridant's attempt to assassinate him. The parallel would also require Marlborough to be prince of another country, fighting on behalf of Britain.

Anne dismissed Marlborough in December 1711 because his service as Captain General was no longer needed due to the Harley–St. John ministry's ending the war effort against France. Even before his dismissal Marlborough had been charged by the Tories with war profiteering and prolonging the war for his own benefit. He went into voluntary exile in December 1712. At the time of the opera, Marlborough was past his glory. His health had broken in 1716 with the death of his favorite daughter and the effects of several debilitating strokes; Sarah was acting for him in politics, and his military duties were administered on his behalf. By 1718 he and Sarah were isolated from the court, and his loss of an appeal in 1721 to the House of Lords about debts over the building of Blenheim Palace[106] marked the end of his public life and the end of his reputation and influence. He would die in June 1722, six months after the opera's premiere.[107] It is not at all obvious that Marlborough would at the time have been seen as such an important public advocate of anti-French policy that he warranted such an allegorization.[108]

Strohm follows Sasse and considers the opera an "anti-Hanoverian work," concurring that Floridant is to be identified with the Duke of Marlborough. But Strohm adds further difficulties by introducing the Orontes–George parallel and a Floridant–Timantes reconciliation:

The dramatic action of the piece involves the reconciliation of the 'Generale' (Floridante) with his former French [Tyrean] enemy (Timante) to unite against the 'Tirano' (Oronte) … easily identified with Great Britain. The tyrant and usurper is eventually dethroned. In the circumstances in which Britain found herself in 1721 the piece could be seen as a challenge to George I, the Hanoverian intruder, who himself pursued a pro-French policy, but only when he had reason to fear too close a link between his own nobles and France. If Walpole was the object of attack in *Muzio Scevola*, in *Floridante* it is the king himself.[109]

Pat Rogers calls this "an astonishingly garbled passage."[110]

In this interpretation, it not clear why King George, who had parliamentary sanction for his British crown and had not gained it by killing and deposing his king, would parallel a tyrant, usurper, and intruder. There are no cues to indicate that Timantes or Tyre should be equated with France (except that Marlborough's enemy was French); nor would there be any British parallel to Timantes, the Tyrean prince captured by Floridant and who roused the people of Persia to rescue Floridant and restore Elmira to the throne. And of course in Britain, there was no rightful heiress to be restored to the throne.

Strohm's attempt to make the opera repudiate George's pro-French policy seems at odds with the libretto itself: a policy of reconciliation with one's former enemy is validated in the opera by virtue of Floridant's reconciliation with his former enemy Timantes and the latter's raising the Persian people against the tyrant Orontes. This reading is also inherently implausible since it ignores implications of the identification of Timantes as a French general and Orontes as George: it presumes that a captured ex-French general is rousing forces in London to depose George to free the imprisoned Floridant (Marlborough).

Nor is it clear who would benefit by questioning George's pro-French policy. Almost a decade after the Peace of Utrecht (1713), the significance of relations with France had changed. By 1720 a pro-French policy was now in the interest of the king. Stanhope had negotiated an Anglo-French alliance in 1716, which secured recognition of the Hanoverian succession, gained French aid to protect George's Hanover electorate, and removed James III from France (removing the threat of French aid to the Pretender). Stanhope also negotiated the Triple Alliance between Britain, France, and the United Provinces in 1717, and in 1718 the Quadruple Alliance, in which Britain joined the French, Austrians, and Dutch against Spain; a new Triple Alliance between France, Britain, and Spain was concluded in 1721.[111] It does seem unlikely that Rolli, Handel, or the Whig- and ministry-dominated directorate of the Royal Academy would publicly rebuke the king's foreign policy – let alone in such an obscure and indirect manner as in an Italian opera libretto.

Of the Royal Academy operas said to refer to the reigning monarch, a case can be made for Handel's *Riccardo primo* (November 11, 1727), although not in the allegorical way usually proposed whereby the title hero represents the British monarch. Strohm argues that the subject of *Riccardo primo* was chosen to celebrate George II, who had acceded to the throne on June 11, 1727:

> *Riccardo Primo* formed part of the celebrations of the coronation of George II and was therefore related to an actual political event, but it also expressed – and far more clearly than Handel's earlier operas – a current political ideology. The new king is celebrated in the person of his famous predecessor Richard Lionheart and the old absolutist – or new imperialistic – conception of the British Empire is given an historical justification ... Handel's only opera plot taken from English history must therefore be seen in connection with other "commemorative-ceremonial-patriotic works" of the year 1727.[112]

Few Britons of the day would have considered their constitutional monarchy, commonly thought to have its origins in the ancient constitution of the Saxons, absolutist, an epithet they usually flung at France.

Handel completed the autograph of *Riccardo primo* on May 16, 1727, so presumably the opera was planned for the end of the 1726–27 season, following the run of Bononcini's *Astianatte* (1727), whose last performance was on June 6. George I had set out for Hanover on June 3 in good health but died suddenly at Onsabrück. The news of the king's death, reaching London on the afternoon of June 14, closed the theaters for the season; Prince of Wales George Augustus was proclaimed king on June 15 and crowned on October 11. Strohm, taking the change of monarchs into account, suggests the opera was first intended for the Prince of Wales.[113]

The claim that *Riccardo* was a commemorative–ceremonial–patriotic work for the coronation of George II is unfounded. On August 12, 1727, the coronation was proclaimed for October 4, but was adjourned to October 11. The orders for the coronation specified the participants of the procession, the coronation ceremony itself, and the evening's banquet (including the ceremony of the King's Champion). The day concluded with the usual "Bonfires, Illuminations, Ringing of Bells, and publick Demonstrations of general Joy and Satisfaction." Handel's contribution to the coronation proper was the four coronation anthems. No sources mention any additional public events, such as performances at theaters, which were closed that day.[114] *Riccardo* had a public rehearsal on November 8 at the Haymarket Theatre;[115] its first public performance followed a full month after the coronation. The timing does not suggest a connection with the coronation; and in fact George apparently only saw the opera once, on December 5, on the eighth of eleven performances. Better operas as candidates for celebrating the new reign would be *Admeto* or *Teuzzone*, which were playing at the Haymarket Theatre in October and November.

The opera's episode from Richard's crusade does little to celebrate him. In the opera, the tyrant Isacus refuses to allow Richard's fleet to land at Limissus, on Cyprus, where Richard's bride Constantia is to arrive. Isacus deceives Richard by sending his daughter Pulcheria in the place of Constantia. In retaliation, Richard enlists the aid of Orontes and attacks and besieges Isacus in his castle; Pulcheria obtains Richard's pardon for her father, and Richard's nuptials with Constantia are celebrated. Were it not that George II was already married, the subject might be better suited for a wedding occasion.

Nor was Richard the Lionheart universally seen as a British Worthy. A Norman who spoke no English and acquired the British crown by dynastic accident, he spent only eight months in England. Despite his present image, eighteenth-century British historians found little to commend in Richard's character.[116] "After commending his Valour, which was something like a brutish Fierceness," wrote Rapin de Thoyras in his canonic Whig *History of England*, "in vain do we seek in him some other Virtue to afford matter for his Panegyrick ... We find in him abundance of Vices, and some of the most enormous." He concludes that "all those that have writ his Life agree, that Pride, Avarice and Lust were his three reigning Vices."[117]

John, Baron Somers in 1702 is unrelenting in his appraisal of him as

the worst of all the *Richards* ... the Unsteadiness of his Judgment made his Government very uneasie and distasteful to almost all sorts of Men ... He was an ill Son ... an ill Brother ... an ill Man ... a worse King ... most unworthy the Affections of his Subjects ... He rak'd more Money by unparallel'd Taxes upon the Nation, than any King before him: His Voyage to the *Holy Land* par'd it to the Bones, by many unjust ways; but his unlucky Return quite Ruin'd it.[118]

For an opposition writer in 1733, Richard was such an odious figure, he and his Bishop of Ely served as a parallel with George II and Walpole.[119] A year later, Richard comes off no better in the hands of the ministerial writer John, Lord Hervey; defending the ministry in 1734, Hervey described "that *Royal Don Quixote*, and warlike Enthusiast, *Richard* the First ... who exhausted the Treasure of his Kingdom, to raise his Fame upon Earth; and spilt the Blood of his Subjects, to purchase Glory in Heaven."[120] Winton Dean slyly notes, "A native Englishman might have permitted himself a cynical smile at an entertainment in which an Italian and an ex-German compared another ex-German to a Norman who spoke no English as a paragon of British virtue and honour."[121]

J. Merrill Knapp is closer to the mark when he suggests that the choice of the libretto "probably had nothing to do with British history and the monarch but with the equal musical opportunity it accorded the three stars: Faustina as Pulcheria; Cuzzoni as Constanza; and Senesino as Riccardo Primo. The two collaborators [Handel and Rolli] were primarily men of the theatre first and not politicians."[122]

The history of the opera suggests how it did play a role in boosting British patriotism – yet without allegorizing George "in the person" of Richard. The source libretto, *Isacio Tiranno*, produced in Venice in 1710, likely was chosen because, as Knapp suggested, it offered two major roles for Faustina and Cuzzoni. In it, the title-character Isacus was a ruthless tyrant; Richard himself has only one aria – so the choice of subject had little to do with Richard. In the first version of the London libretto, as completed by an unidentified librettist in May 1727, the role of Richard was expanded, no doubt to give the *primo uomo* Senesino an adequate role (the role of the tyrant was reserved for the bass Giuseppe Maria Boschi).[123] Nothing in this May 1727 version gives Richard any exceptional or noteworthy status that might refer to George I or the Prince of Wales.

In late summer or fall, after the accession of George II, the Royal Academy directors probably decided that *Riccardo* could be turned into a patriotic piece to honor the new king. Rolli drastically overhauled the May 1727 libretto and further expanded the role of Richard, for which Handel provided additional music. It took some creative work for Rolli to transform the historical Richard from an odious, impious despoiler of his country into an honorable and virtuous king. Rolli's Richard is a celebration of an English soldier-king, who, in the November 1727 version of the libretto, is repeatedly praised for his generosity, magnanimity, and clemency.[124] History offered few other English examples of the soldier-king (the common choices were Edward III, the Black Prince, and William III).[125]

In the revised version, *Riccardo* becomes a patriotic piece, celebrating British military valor and a warrior-king. In the first scene of Act III, as he prepares to attack Isacus, Richard's big *scena* of accompanied recitative exhorting his troops becomes a paean to British glory, virtue, and magnanimity:

> O you, who with me, on the Banks of *Thames*,
> Where Virtue, Liberty and Courage reigns,
> Were born to Acts of Justice, and of Honour,
> Follow your King …
> It is the constant Practice of the *Britons*
> To make the haughty bend,
> And grant to all beside full Peace or Pardon.

> O voi che meco del Tamigi in riva
> Patria di Libertà Virtù Valore,
> Nati siete all' Imprese
> Di Giustizia e d'Onore,
> Seguite il vostro Re: …
> Usate prove de' *Britanni* sono
> Debellare I superbi,
> E concedere altrui pace o perdono.
>
> III.i, pp. 56–7

To the libretto, Rolli added a fulsome dedicatory poem addressed to George II, which cites Richard as George's warrior predecessor and stresses the attributes Rolli had recently provided him in the libretto:

> Great KING, ready to arms in one glance, whose
>   paramount dominion
>   Stretches over all the seas and so many realms,
>   The Royal [opera] Stage offers you your warlike
>   Predecessor, Richard the Lionheart,
> In deeds of valor, quick as an arrow,
>   Ardent, fierce, but nobly fierce,
>   Great, loving, amiable, true,
>   Swift to victory, but not slow to pardon.
> But if you yearn for a more lively image of the
>   strong Hero,
>   Turn your generous mind, O great KING,
>   To your own thoughts; think about yourself:
> Then, having equaled him [Richard] in proofs of
>   Honor and Valor,
>   Say that in your hand you hold the destiny
>   Not only of the orient [like Richard] but, like Jove,
>   of the world.[126]

> Gran RE ch' ai [hai] sommo e pronto in armi
>   a un guardo
>   Su tutt' i mari e in tanti Regni impero,
>   T' offre la Regia Scena il tuo guerriero
>   Predecessor, Cuor di Leon, Riccardo,
> Rapido all' Opre di Valor, qual dardo,
>   Ardito, Fier, ma nobilmente Fiero,
>   Grande, Amoroso, Affabile, Sincero,
>   Al vincer, ratto: al perdonar, non tardo.
> Ma se più al vivo Eroe sì forte espresso
>   Brami, o gran RE; tua generosa Mente
>   Volgi alle proprie Idee; pensa a te stesso:
> Poi d' Onor e Valor, pari alle prove;
>   Di' che in tua man, non sol dell' Oriente,
>   Ma i Destini del Mondo ai [hai], come Giove.

Rolli's text does not identify George with Richard; his strategy asks George to see the Richard on stage (not necessarily the historical one) as a warrior-king with virtues worth emulating. But for a more lively image of a king who will conquer not just the Near East but the world, George may look to himself. The trope that Rolli is using in the dedication and opera is not allegory but the *speculum regni*, the Mirror for Princes. Rolli is holding up for George the operatic Richard as an *exemplum* of the virtues he should see in himself;

and obliquely Rolli is using the *laudando praecipere*, exhorting him to practice those virtues by praising him for already possessing them.[127]

The interpretations of these three operas have been examined at length to suggest that the generic expectation approach is inherently misguided and unproductive. That the search for the politics yields such multiple and conflicting interpretations, and yields interpretations critical of the monarch or his politics, suggests the expectation fails to provide a reliable and historically valid interpretive methodology.

None of these Royal Academy operas (except *Riccardo*) have any cues in their librettos that suggest application to current politics or rulers was intended. Unlike most other readily recognizable topical political works, no contemporary responses about the allusions or allegories have been found. The comment that is supposed to be a contemporary's recognizing the topicality of *Floridante* turns out, upon examination, to be a chimera. To take up the distinctions of John Wallace and Allan Roper, we can confidently say that the allegories are not "there," were not "put there" by the librettists. What we have are modern post hoc reader applications that impose allegories on otherwise non-allegorical works and that do not lead us to better understanding of how politics may have worked in these operas.

Were the Royal Academy librettists wanting to personate or allegorize the reigning Hanoverian monarchs, we could expect they would have done so using purpose-written mythological–emblematic allegories along the lines of Continental Baroque court operas, whose allegorical program would have been stated by prefaces, dedications, keys, or advertisements. The musical works produced for the marriages of George II's children show the London stage was quite capable of unabashed royal celebration along the lines of Continental court opera (see Appendix 5).

Another political aspect of Royal Academy operas has been proposed on the basis of their subject matter. Ellen Harris observed that the majority of Royal Academy operas are set in oriental locations, areas where much of Britain's overseas trade at the time was conducted by the East India Company, the Levant Company, and others. Such settings, Harris argues, were a "deliberate, tactical choice" by the directors "to keep the image of the East in front of those who might assist them politically" and further their mercantile investments "by voting the appropriations necessary to defend British trade and dominion."[128]

In one sense, the large number of oriental settings is unremarkable and needs no special explanation. For Harris, the Orient is so vast and elastic a concept – it encompasses Spain, North Africa, the Near and Middle East, and South Asia – that it includes all the lands of recorded ancient history except Europe and the Italian and Greek peninsulas: so it is no wonder we find most operas on historical subjects are set in what Harris calls the Orient.[129]

It is unlikely, though, that operas on oriental subjects were deliberately chosen or had any effect in promoting the financial interests of the Academy directors. Most crucially, of the fifty-nine known directors of the Royal Academy, only two are shown to have been directors of the East India Company; we are invited to assume on the basis of no documentation that other directors had significant financial interests in companies trading in the Orient.[130] We do not know, in fact, how personally involved the directors were in choosing librettos for the Royal Academy, their motivation, or how they might have made their intention known.

The actual settings of most operas are of little significance. Often the only revealing indication of location is in the argument of the printed libretto itself. Most stage sets, which are generic throne rooms, royal apartments, prisons, courtyards, and gardens, rarely reflect any local color and were often shared between operas. Librettists thought nothing of changing the location of an opera[131] while leaving intact what is surely the most important and dominant feature of an opera, the characters and their dramatic and moral conflicts. Of some opera, set in the Orient, the principal participants are often not the native inhabitants, but Roman or Greek conquerors, as in *Giulio Cesare* (1724), *Scipione* (1742), or *Alessandro* (1741).

No suggestions are offered about how awareness by opera-goers of the oriental settings a millennium or more ago would translate into parliamentary or ministerial support for Britain's Eastern trade. The Orient of the operas had little to commend or attract the sympathy of the Academy's audience: the societies were feudal empires, ruled by absolute monarchs with authoritarian power over their families and subjects. For many Roman historians and their British readers, the East was the origin of the luxury and effeminacy that corrupted the Roman Republic and Empire.

Presumably, though, protection of trade was such a national imperative, it did not need an assist by reminders from watching operas. Other more pragmatic matters – availability of source librettos, suitability of roles for current singers, moral and ethical didacticism, interest in heroic subject matter – were probably far more important considerations in the choice of opera librettos than promoting the investment and mercantile interests of its directors and shareholders.[132]

The Royal Academy of Music arose from the desire of Britain's elite to establish on a secure footing an Italian opera company that would reflect Britain's stature as a European power, if not rival those on the Continent. The initial petitioning, incorporation, solicitation of shareholders, and election of directors were carried out unaffected by the Whig Schism and royal quarrel.

Rather than an opera company that enacted or reproduced the partisanship of contemporary politics, the Academy's shareholders and directors – pursuing their aim of producing world-class opera but caught in internal disputes about how to do so – seem to have operated independently of partisan politics. At the first election for directors, at least two Tories (John Arbuthnot and Robert Benson, Lord Bingley) were elected by predominantly Whig shareholders.

Consistent with this image of a politically tolerant opera directorate, is the unlikelihood that Bononcini was dismissed because of his suspected Jacobite associations or sympathies. A directorate dissociated from partisan politics is also consistent with the Academy's operas lacking the topical political allusions and allegories claimed for them. However, if the Academy's directorate and the operas themselves were not involved in partisan politics, other events at the Haymarket Theatre and the rivalries between partisans of their singers could be turned to political advantage, as will be seen in following chapters.

4 | The opera house, allegory, and the political opposition

After the furor of the Atterbury trial, the following two sessions of Parliament were relatively tranquil. In April 1724 Walpole engineered the rustication of Secretary of State William Carteret, Sunderland's protégé, to Ireland as Lord Lieutenant, effectively removing the last legacy of the Sunderland–Stanhope faction and his only remaining serious rival. As one observer wrote at the close of the 1723–24 session, "There is nothing disposed of here but by the interest of one great man who has made himself so useful to the nation that we cannot be without him."[1] By 1725, Walpole had full control of Parliament and the ministry. He was now securely in the king's favor, shown most notably by his becoming a Knight of the Bath on May 27, 1725, and progressing to the Garter a year later, the first commoner to be so honored since 1660.

Meanwhile, an organized opposition to Walpole's ministry emerged in the parliamentary session of 1724–25.[2] Two major figures were his former Whig colleague William Pulteney and Henry St. John, Viscount Bolingbroke, Walpole's implacable Tory foe from the days of Queen Anne. A friend and adherent of Walpole while the two were in opposition, Pulteney grew disappointed at the slow pace of his political advancement and openly broke with Walpole in the Commons on April 8, 1725, over the Civil List debt; following up in debate the next day, he accused Walpole of waste, corruption, and financial mismanagement.[3] Walpole replied to the charges, but had a trump card to play: he had Pulteney dismissed from his place at court. By the end of the session, Pulteney was the leader of a small group of dissident Whigs.

To avoid trial for treason after the Whigs gained control of Parliament in 1714, Bolingbroke fled to France, temporarily entering the Pretender's service, thus forever tainting himself with Jacobitism – a fact opposition writers never hesitated to raise to discredit him. While in self-exile, Bolingbroke schemed behind the scenes to persuade the government to allow him to return to England.[4] Influenced by bribes to his mistress, King George finally granted Bolingbroke a pardon on May 25, 1723, allowing him to return and regain his estates; Walpole (against his better judgment) complied with the king's wishes, but opposed Bolingbroke's resuming his seat in the Lords, thus preventing him from participating in politics. Realizing Walpole's removal

was necessary if he were to enter the Lords, Bolingbroke – ignoring the grati-
tude many thought he ought to have felt – concentrated his energies toward
uniting those disaffected with Walpole and turning him out of office.

In the summer of 1726, Bolingbroke's Dawley estate became a seedbed for
political activity directed against Walpole's ministry. His principal allies were
the Whigs Daniel and William Pulteney; the Tory leader in the Commons, Sir
William Wyndham; the leader of the Jacobite interest, William Shippen; and
the Country Whig, Samuel Sandys. At Dawley Bolingbroke also entertained
the Scriblerians Pope, Bathurst, Swift, Arbuthnot, and Gay, who contributed
to the literary campaign against Walpole. Also sympathetic to the opposition
campaign against Walpole were lesser country gentry, high-church clergy,
small merchants and craftsmen, and the City of London.[5]

In Parliament this coalition used a broad array of tactics in an endless
campaign to obstruct Walpole and his legislation. The opposition relent-
lessly attacked standing armies, Britain's alliance with France, the subor-
dination of British interests to those of Hanover, pay for Hessian troops,
Walpole's foreign policy of peace at any price, the growing power of his
ministry, and, above all, the effects of his corrupt political methods. Despite
its wealth of political and literary talent, the opposition was too fragmented
to achieve its goal; an opposition united only to remove Walpole from office
was no agenda for political success.

The opposition was momentarily heartened with the accession of George
II on June 11, 1727, and the possibility of a new ministry. At first George
indicated his intention to place Speaker of the Commons Sir Spencer
Compton at the head of the Treasury. But Queen Caroline's influence and
Walpole's parliamentary skill at increasing the Civil List and the queen's
jointure made the king realize his own interests were best served by retaining Walpole at the Treasury, with Townshend and Newcastle as Secretaries
of State.[6] Caroline would prove to be Walpole's strongest ally at court. The
later resignation of Townshend in 1730 gave Walpole control over both
financial and foreign policy, and he emerged as a prime minister of unprecedented longevity and power. Bolingbroke's hopes of finding favor with
the new king remained futile.

The opposition and its polemics

Drawing heavily on Old Whig and Country ideas, Bolingbroke's political
journalism and pamphleteering provided the philosophical underpinning
for a principled opposition.[7] Opposition rhetoric conveniently divided the

political landscape to its own advantage. It claimed the high ground of standing for virtue, liberty, and patriotism, adhering to strict Whig principles, and protecting the British Constitution. To the ministry was ceded corruption and self-interest.

Mounting a multimedia campaign, the opposition loosed against Walpole a toxic flood of pamphlets, satiric verse, ballads, newspapers, broadsides, and cartoons. It seized any opportunity to satirize, libel, and embarrass him and so hopefully to weaken his authority. The implication was always the same: Walpole's removal would reverse the nation's decline by restoring political virtue, the balanced constitution, and liberty. There was no imaginable political, social, aesthetic, or moral vice the opposition could not claim due to Walpole: he was leading Britain into domestic tyranny; he was corrupting taste in the arts; he was ruining trade and failing to protect British merchants from Spanish pirates.

Walpole was personally demonized as a corrupt and evil minister who attempted arbitrary government: he diverted public money for his own use or the bribery of MPs, promoted faction to divide the opposition, spread rumors of Jacobite threats to justify a standing army, maintained rule by corruption and servile placemen, and fostered luxury throughout the country to divert attention from his misdeeds. He was compared with all the evil ministers of Roman or English history. The themes of trickery and cheating are brought together in personations of Walpole as a gamester or card player. All these characters suggest his manipulation of public and political life by fraud and deception.[8]

Opposition engravings, woodcut prints, and illustrated broadsides developed their own easily recognizable visual codes and allusions. Walpole – with his star and garter – is shown riding in triumph on a chest of money, screening persons from parliamentary inquiry, controlling MPs like a puppeteer, and ignoring Spanish depredations on British merchants.[9] From these anti-ministerial prints and engravings emerged the distinctive British political cartoon.

In this media campaign, Walpole was known by a string of nicknames, personifications, and catchwords: the Great Man, the Great One, Brazen Face, Sir Robert Brass, Bob Fox the Juggler, Sir Blue String, Sir Blazing Star, the Knight of the Blazing Star, the Norfolk Steward, the Norfolk Dumpling, the Norfolk Projector, Bob-Lyn, the Blunderer, and the Screen-master. To the politically attuned, the presence of even one of these names in the most harmless print, ballad, or poem set off long trains of associations and innuendo damning Walpole and the ministry. One of these epithets casually placed in an otherwise harmless story about a corrupt statesman or the downfall of a royal favorite from the past turned it into an allegory on the prime minister.

The principal voice of the opposition was the periodical the *Craftsman* (later retitled the *Country Journal*), which molded political opinion against the Walpole administration for over fifteen years. Launched on December 5, 1726, its purported author was "Caleb D'Anvers, of Gray's Inn, Esquire." At its peak in early 1731, the *Craftsman* probably reached a circulation of at least 10,000, and was read in Europe and America as well.[10] Other periodicals poised against the ministry had distinctive viewpoints and motives: Nathaniel Mist's *Weekly Journal, or British Gazette* (1716–25), later *Mist's Weekly Journal* (1725–28) and then *Fog's Weekly Journal* (1728–37), were Tory if not crypto-Jacobite. Ostensibly established in defense of Alexander Pope, the *Grub-street Journal* (1730–37) offered a mock defense of a Grub-street society that satirized Walpole's writers, who were often those hapless scribblers pilloried in Pope's *Dunciad* (1728). Later, *Common Sense* (1737–43) and the *Champion* (1739–43) were voices of the Patriot opposition. Through their literary satire, these papers subjected the Walpole administration to what J. H. Plumb called "an endless stream of vilification and criticism which made not only England but Europe roar with delight."[11]

Throughout opposition polemic, Italian opera is singled out as symptom and agent of the corruption of morals and taste spawned by Walpole's ministry. Opera appears in opposition periodicals in various ways, but always to discredit and undermine the legitimacy of the ministry. The *Craftsman* used the Royal Academy of Music, its singers, and its personnel as the basis for allegories on Britain's domestic and foreign affairs (explored in this chapter). With its strongly moralistic social critique, *Mist's Weekly Journal* directly denounced opera (along with masquerades, pantomimes, rope-dancing, and ballad operas) as an example of the degeneracy of taste that was driving true drama from the stage.[12] *Fog's Weekly Journal* most often indicted opera as an example of the luxury and effeminacy overrunning Britain.[13] The *Grub-street Journal* attacked opera and its devotees as the debasement of taste occurring under Walpole. In the wake of the singer Farinelli's three stellar seasons and then unannounced departure to Spain, *Common Sense* invoked opera-lovers and Farinelli to embarrass the ministry for failing to prevent Spanish captures of merchant shipping and to goad Britain into war with Spain (see Chapter 6).

To respond to opposition attacks, Walpole's ministry subsidized several newspapers, most importantly the *Free Briton*, *Daily Courant*, *Hyp-Doctor*, and *London Journal*, many sent free through the Post Office. These were consolidated into the *Daily Gazetteer* on June 30, 1735. Between February 1731 and February 1741, the treasury paid out £50,077 18s to authors and printers of periodicals.[14] Despite Jonathan Swift's epithet, "Bob, the Poet's Foe," the stream of poems and odes in praise of Walpole that filled the pamphlet shops shows he rewarded poets willing to tune their lyres to his praises.[15] Walpole's writers attacked the motives and principles of the opposition, accusing them of faction and dissent and, hence, encouraging the Jacobites. Walpole also used the power of the Treasury to harass the opposition press: blocking circulation through the mail, seizing libelous issues, raiding printing shops to seize documents, and jailing printers.[16]

The opposition campaign to drive Walpole from office and his ministry's defense of him and campaign of abuse against the opposition dominated British politics and much of its literature, both high and low, until his fall from power in 1742. This opposition campaign provides the backdrop for the partisan use of Italian opera explored in this and later chapters. If Italian operas in London were intended (by selection, revision, or adaptation) to be involved in topical politics, we would expect the domestic and foreign issues raised in the attack and defense of Walpole and his ministry to be reflected in the librettos of individual operas and work to benefit one side or the other.

The techniques of irony, innuendo, allegory, personation, and parallel and application employed by the opposition had been well honed in earlier periodicals. A complete inventory of such techniques was compiled in *The Art of Railing at Great Men: Being a Discourse upon Political Railers Ancient and Modern* (1723).[17] These include the "fabulous or *allegorical* Mode," the "*Ironical* or *Mock Panegyrick*,"[18] "that of *drawing Parallels*," and the "Lying Mode." The basic technique is irony, and even the dullest readers of the *Craftsman* would have seen the satire applied to opera in "Philomath's" statement:

I have always look'd upon it as a laudable Inclination in my Countrymen, and therefore have been a constant Advocate for the Importation of *Italian Operas* and *Singers, Dancing-Posture-Ballance Masters, Tumblers, Rope-Dancers* and *Harlequins*; all which I could prove to have been of so much Advantage to our *most excellent Ministry*, and consequently so necessary to the Well-being, nay even the Preservation of the Kingdom, that the annual Expence of them is a mere Trifle, in Comparison with the great Benefits We reap from them.[19]

Two techniques were commonly used to involve opera in political satire. In the "fabulous or *allegorical* Mode," the "Ambiguity or *double Entendre* of a Fable raises the Curiosity of every Reader, to discover the secret Sting which it contains." Such a mode is "an eternal Recourse for Slander," for it allows the writer "to say the same dreadful ill Things of Beasts, which are daily utter'd in Coffee-House and Clubs against our national Governours."[20]

Although usually not fables in the common sense of using animals, opposition allegories, commonly found in periodical essays, use the framing devices of dreams and visions to present Walpole presiding over the political corruption of Great Britain. He was the Norfolk Steward who rises to power only to betray his master's trust.[21] On the "Island Fortunata," he is a devouring monster ravaging Great Britain.[22] A vision of an autopsy on a gigantic carcass allegorizes the corruption of the body politic of Great Britain.[23] Walpole perched in the Tree of Corruption throwing to those below golden apples that corrupt all who eat of them allegorizes his corruption of politics by money.[24] Bolingbroke's "The First Vision of Camilick" envisions the Magna Carta hovering over armies of faction and reconciling them.[25] The notorious "Festival of the Golden Rump" is a ceremony of courtiers worshiping the posterior of a satyr-like statue of George II.[26] A variant of the Persian letter technique has travelers writing about a foreign country that is Great Britain in disguise.[27] These allegories applied to topical politics exemplify the usual eighteenth-century approach to allegory as described by John Hughes and Richard Blackmore (in Chapter 2), which is a thoroughgoing narrative with consistent correspondences between the literal and allegorical levels.

The historical mode, or that of "*drawing Parallels,*" is a veiled technique to impugn contemporary ministers:

There is scarce a Character of Antiquity that is remarkable for Pride, Avarice, Corruption, Ambition, or Domination, (all Words of great Use to *Political Railers*) which has not been drawn forth in the blackest Colours, and by the Addition of Modern Incidents adapted to some of our Contemporaries.[28]

Drawing parallels or making past evil statesmen personate a contemporary minister implies both have committed the same crimes against the public.[29]

An early issue of the *Craftsman* rhetorically asked, "How easy is it to turn over *Tully*, *Tacitus*, or *Livy*, and when you have found a good strong Sentence or two upon *Corruption*, to insert it in any Paper? The Author need never be at the trouble to make the Application. Every Child in the Street knows well enough upon whom to fix it."[30]

Using the technique of personation, Walpole was compared to a gallery of Roman and British evil ministers and favorites: Sejanus (under Tiberius), Robert, Earl of Oxford (Richard II), Mortimer (Edward II), Gaveston (Edward II), Cardinal Wolsey (Henry VIII), Buckingham (Charles I), Earl of Strafford (Charles I), Vasconcellos (Queen Regent of Portugal), Duke of

Ripperda (King of Spain), Knez Menzikoff (the Czar), and others. These abused their position and led the ruler and nation to ruin.[31] One tract, *A Short History of Prime Ministers in Great Britain* (1733), a résumé of British kings and the evil consequences and sorry ends of their prime ministers, was an opposition handbook for parallel and application.[32] Drawing portraits of past statesmen to be applied by the knowing reader to Walpole was a defense from charges of libel and put the ministry in a bind, for to object to the personation was to admit its truth. The ministry, in its turn, compared Walpole to Britain's great ministers, including William Cecil, Lord Burghley.[33]

A paradigmatic example of personation used ironically is a *Craftsman* essay from February 1727 that leads the reader to believe it is first praising the integrity of John Kipling, the treasurer of the Royal Academy of Music.[34] Caleb D'Anvers desires to recommend to posterity worthy men of virtue; when such an ornament of the age is found in lower life, all the better, for then a writer cannot be charged with flattery or mercenary motives.

D'Anvers praises his unnamed subject's virtue and integrity: he manages a public revenue without adding a shilling to his own fortune; people pay their taxes voluntarily because they are satisfied with his public service; he is uncorrupt himself and will not suffer his officers to plunder by his authority; the public's treasure is expended with frugality and prudence; and he permits no embezzlement and promptly provides accurate accounts when asked. In short, he is "a *Treasurer* with *clean* and *empty* Hands!"

A reader of the *Craftsman*, no doubt by now reading the essay as an ironic panegyric of Robert Walpole, would certainly have been surprised to be told he "must, by this Time, perceive that I can mean no body, in my Description of the fore-going character, but that very worthy and excellent man Mr. Kiplin, *Treasurer to that Honourable Corporation, the Royal Academy of* Musick." Kipling is contrasted to Robert (Robin) Sidney, Earl of Leicester, Robert (Robin) Harley, Earl of Oxford, and the Earl of Clarendon. Unlike them, Kipling is neither fat nor full, has never made a penny of his master, and lacks immense riches. Happy it is for the Royal Academy to have "so worthy and uncorrupt a Man in the management of the *Treasure* of it! with what Contempt do I look down on the *Greatest* men, when I compare them with Mr. Kiplin, and find them inferior to him in virtue and integrity?"[35]

Now, there is no reason why the *Craftsman* would go to such lengths to praise as a "model of Virtue and Integrity" someone so removed from the public eye as the treasurer of the Haymarket Theatre, unless to use the panegyric as a pretext for innuendo that Walpole lacks the very traits

Kipling possesses. Although never naming him, carefully placed epithets and phrases – "Publick Revenue," "Taxes," "Minister," "Great Man," "Fat and Full," "immense riches," "secret Service," as well as the pointedly repeated word *treasurer* and name *Robin* – leave no doubt who is the object of the directed application. Using Pope's principle that "Praise undeserv'd is scandal in disguise,"[36] the panegyric on Kipling becomes a libel-proof way to accuse Walpole of the vices of dishonesty, corruption, and theft of public funds.

Ironically comparing Walpole to persons in the theater world is a step toward a favorite opposition device, the *totus mundus historiam* topos: satirizing the government by allegorizing it in terms of the stage. The *Craftsman*, noting Shakespeare's phrase "All the world's a stage, and the men and women in it merely players,"[37] observed

There are Vocations and other Circumstances in Life much more theatrical than Those mention'd by Him [Shakespeare], and the Top of all is the *ministerial Play*, which is somewhat like the *what d'ye call it*, or a *tragi-comical Farce*, and as expensive to the Spectator as an *Oratoria*.[38]

Showing Britain's world of politics and the ministry as a farce, comedy, fair-booth puppet show, or squabble at the opera house affronts Walpole's dignity and undercuts his pretence to legitimacy. Walpole's skill at manipulation and retaining control of government, much of it hidden from view through corruption of elections and placemen, led to his being depicted as a puppeteer, stage manager, magician, wizard, juggler, Harlequin, or Punch. Paul Langford finds the theatrical topos in satiric prints was so powerful because "it reinforced a popular belief that the existing regime was by its very nature in a sense false, deceiving and theatrical."[39] It is this long-standing and instinctive satiric use of state–theater parallels that animates the allegorical satires on the Royal Academy of Music presented below.

One fully worked out satire analogizing opera and the world of politics is a mock playbill announcing the opening session of Parliament on Tuesday, January 14, 1735, as if it were a comedy. The Earl of Egmont describes the circumstances of the playbill's distribution at a masquerade attended by the king on Thursday, January 16:

At the Ball or Masquerade in the Haymarket … there was an incident that has made good deal of noise.

After the King had been there some time (for whose pleasure these masquerades were first set up & have been hitherto continued during the winter) there came in a Harlequin and Punchanello follow'd by divers others in different dresses with bundles of printed play bills in their hands, one of which Harlequin gave the King, and then all throwing down their papers disappeard.[40]

Egmont transcribed the handbill:

BY PERMISSION
This is to give Notice to all Gentlemen and Ladies. & others
That
At the OPERA House in the HAYMARKET
This present Evening will be presented the comicall and diverting Humours of
PUNCH.

And on Thursday next by the Norfolk Company of artificiall *Commedians at ROBINS great Theatricall Booth PALACE YARD* will be presented a comical and diverting *PLAY* of Seven *ACTS* calld COURT and COUNTRY in which will be revived yᵉ: entertaining Scene of

The Blundering Brothers
with the Cheats of
RABBI ROBBIN

Prime Minister to King *SOLOMON*. the whole concluding with a grand *MASQUE* call'd the *DOWNFALL of SEJANUS*, or the
STATESMAN OVERTHROWN
with Axes, Halters Gibbets & other Decorations proper for the Play.
to begin exactly at Twelve o'Clock.

N.B. These are a new sett of Puppets as big as the Life yᵉ chief part of which have been brought up from all parts of yᵉ Country at very great Expence
VIVANT REX *ET* REGINA

In the playbill, the business of the seven-year Parliament is reduced to the dignity of a theatrical-booth puppet farce presented by a band of Norfolk comedians, with Sir Robert and his brother Horatio as the Blundering Brothers and King George as Solomon.[41] The allusions to the puppets echo charges that Walpole bought and manipulated MPs; the masque of Sejanus (a common evil-minister parallel to Walpole) represents a wished-for demise of Walpole's career and his condemnation and execution by Parliament. Egmont concludes with the wry comment, "Those who know the times, know the Satyr of this." The ideas in the farcical playbill were developed at length in *C— and Country. A Play of Seven Acts* (1735).[42]

Reading these political allegories, parallels, and personations at some two hundred years' remove, we need not be caught in the dilemmas raised in Chapter 2, whether they were put there in the text by the author or are a modern reader's invention. Knowledge of the likely authorial intent, venue of publication, cues in the text, political context, similarity to other contemporary propaganda, and evidence of contemporary response leave no doubt about the intended and perceived political allegory and application.

Contemporaries were in no doubt about the politics of the innuendo and application of the propaganda, and ministry and opposition argued their use and mis-use.[43] Frustrated at the difficulty of responding to innuendo, the ministry complained the opposition has offered up *"Visions, Dreams, Emblems, Pictures,* and *Hieroglyphicks,* instead of plain *Declarations* of *ministerial Guilt,* or unsophisticated *Recitals of Grievances* lying upon the People."[44] When the government arrested opposition printers, seized papers, or replied in kind to its attacks, the opposition disingenuously protested: "How invidious is it in any Man to wrest an Author's meaning, and draw Parallels where none were design'd."[45] And in mock objection to the ministry's finding parallels and applications in historical essays where none supposedly were intended, the *Craftsman* objected that "the whole *English History* might be prov'd a Libel upon the *present Government* by the same Rule of Interpretation."[46]

These techniques of irony, parallel, innuendo, personation, and directed application are put to use famously in John Gay's *Beggar's Opera* (1728), which was immediately recognized to reflect on the ministry, Walpole, and the court – all to the benefit of the opposition. By 1728 the charges against Walpole were so familiar, it was easy to recognize their partisan sting: Walpole betrayed his friends, his wealth arose from bribes and corruption, and he was robbing the public. Gay's technique in the *Beggar's Opera* is described by John Loftis:

Not an allegorical play nor even one with characters consistently identifiable with living figures, it scores its hits by way of a succession of political parallels, each established briefly and then obscured as different character relationships emerge. Thus Macheath the robber of the public gives way as a symbol of Walpole to Peachum the screen, the receiver of stolen goods, who with his brother-in-law plies a profitable trade in legitimate peculation. All this is reinforced by deft allusion to vices that had long been charged to Walpole – graft, bribery, treachery, and adultery.[47]

Macheath exposes that all ranks of society alike are robbers and thieves, and Gay carefully plants cues to direct this universal truth to Walpole and his ministry.[48] Gay's names for one of the thieves in Peachum's crew make use of common epithets for Walpole: "Robin of Bagshot, alias Gorgon, alias Bluff Bob, alias Carbuncle, alias Bob Booty" (I.iii), as do references to Macheath as "a great man" (I.xi). Macheath's claim that "Money well timed, and properly applied, will do anything" (II.xii) suggests his political methods. The married Walpole's keeping a mistress Maria (Molly) Skerrett finds parallels in Peachum's remark that Robin "spends his life among women" (I.iv) and in Macheath's two women (Polly Peachum and Lucy Lockit) who claim him in prison (III.viii).

Commenting on the ballad opera, the *Craftsman* showed how such innuendo worked:

there are such Things as *Innuendo's*, (a never-failing Method of explaining *Libels*) … Nay the very *Title* of this Piece and the *principal Character*, which is that of an *Highwayman*, sufficiently discover the mischievous Design of it; since by this Character every Body will understand *One*, who makes it his Business arbitrarily to *levy* and *collect* Money on the People for his *own Use*, and of which he always dreads to give *any Account* – Is not this *squinting* with a Vengeance and wounding *Persons in Authority* through the Sides of a *common Malefactor*?[49]

Such was the perceived abuse of Walpole, that Gay's sequel, *Polly* (1729), was suppressed.

The political climate and techniques of partisan journalism of the 1720s and 1730s provide the context and models for the opposition use of Italian opera and events at the Haymarket Theatre in its political propaganda.

The Royal Academy of Music and European politics

As part of its unrelenting attack on Walpole and his ministry, the *Craftsman* seized on incidents at the Haymarket Theatre and turned them into thinly veiled allegories on the world of domestic and foreign politics. Often presented as letters from readers or even as news accounts, these satiric allegories have all the appearance of straight journalism; but readers of opposition periodicals were accustomed to pierce the veil and see their analogs to real-life political affairs. The satire and allegories testify to the *Craftsman's* ability to turn virtually any event, no matter how slight or removed from politics, into an opportunity to harass and embarrass the ministry.

By comparison with other direct attacks on Walpole, these opera-house allegories are restrained, but they did serve the opposition's purposes. They kept foremost in the public's mind the ministry's supposed misdeeds and mishandling of domestic and foreign policy and at the same time kept the ministerial writers busy on the defensive. Given the Academy's royal charter, the king's annual bounty, regular royal attendance, and court and ministerial membership in the Academy's directorate, any ridicule directed at opera also glanced at the court and ministry.

Gibraltar and European politics

Events in the final two seasons of the Academy (1726–28) ran strikingly parallel to affairs on the Continent. Europe was split into two alliances on the brink of war, whereas the Academy's audience was split between partisans of the "Rival Queens" Francesca Cuzzoni and Faustina Bordoni for the place of prima donna. The *Craftsman* exploited the coincidences for partisan purposes in a series of allegorical essays.

The major powers of Europe were involved in a whirl of hostilities, alliances, and treaties – all with the goal of maintaining a balance of power that would preserve peace and security. Britain was worried by growing Spanish naval power and commercial aspirations in the Americas.[50] Spain resented Britain's treaty-guaranteed trading rights in the West Indies that undermined its own commerce with its colonies.

The flashpoint of contention was Britain's possession of Gibraltar, captured from Spain in the War of the Spanish Succession. By the Treaty of Utrecht (1713), Spain ceded Gibraltar and Minorca to Britain and granted Britain the *asiento*, the concession to supply slaves to the Spanish colonies. Spain still hoped to recover Gibraltar and periodically threatened British commercial privileges in the West Indies; yet despite a decade of treaty making, Britain and Spain slowly drifted toward hostilities over possession of Gibraltar.

In June 1717, England, France, and the United Provinces signed the Triple Alliance, which guaranteed the terms of the Treaty of Utrecht and expelled the Pretender from Avignon. After Spain conquered Sardinia in August, the Alliance was reconstituted with the emperor as the Quadruple Alliance, which regulated Spanish territorial claims, granted Tuscany, Parma, and Placentia to the eldest son of the Spanish Queen, Elisabeth Farnese, and scheduled a congress to settle other matters.

Some in the ministry believed Gibraltar had little commercial or military significance and that its continued possession would just antagonize Spain.[51] While on a trip to Madrid in August 1718, Secretary of State James Stanhope had secretly agreed to restore Gibraltar as an inducement for Spain's joining the Quadruple Alliance and to assure better Anglo-Spanish relations. Whether the return was in exchange for money or an equivalent was disputed. War briefly broke out between Britain and France against Spain in 1718–20; so when Spain did join the Quadruple Alliance on May 20, 1720, the British considered the intervening war invalidated the secret offer of Gibraltar. In following years, recovery of Gibraltar became a matter of principle for Philip, the Spanish king.

When news of the ministry's offer to restore Gibraltar became public, there was clamor in the press and pre-emptive efforts by Parliament to prevent the return. Pamphlets demonstrated how Gibraltar secured British naval power in the Mediterranean, provided security to British trade, and prevented French attempts at naval power. As part of the British dominions, it could only be yielded by Parliament.[52] In the midst of the domestic crisis following the collapse of the South Sea Bubble in September, pursuing the restitution of Gibraltar would have been political suicide for the ministry. Indeed, the first of Thomas Gordon's *Cato's Letters* on November 5, 1720, asked, "Can it be imagined, that men of honour would forfeit their reputation, patriots sacrifice a bulwark of their country, or wise men venture their heads, by such a traitorous, shameful and dangerous step?"[53]

Stanhope's sudden death on February 5, 1721, removed the principal advocate of restitution from the ministry, and his successors had little interest in bringing the matter before Parliament. George I sent Philip a private letter in June 1721 promising "to make use of the first favourable opportunity to regulate this article with the Consent of my Parliament."[54] Philip mistakenly assumed this was a definite promise and used the letter to insist on Gibraltar's return.

A crisis arose on a new front early in 1725. In March, the French broke off the pending marriage of the young Louis XV to the Infanta and returned her to Spain. Affronted, Spain withdrew from the Quadruple Alliance and entered into the first Treaty of Vienna with Austria on April 30 and May 1. Among its terms, Emperor Charles VI pledged to influence England to abandon Gibraltar and Minorca (location of Port Mahon) and promised the succession of the duchies of Parma and Tuscany to Don Carlos. In June, Philip again threatened English commercial privileges unless Gibraltar was restored; the ministry in turn ordered the Gibraltar defenses strengthened.

Panicked by the Austrian–Spanish alliance, on September 3 Britain, France, and Prussia created the Alliance of Hanover. Joining later were the United Provinces, Portugal, Sweden, and Denmark, the latter two induced by annual subsidies; subsidies to the landgrave of Hesse secured troops for British service. The treaty's signatories pledged to resist attacks on Gibraltar and Minorca; Europe was now ranged between two alliances, and war seemed imminent.

In response to the Vienna alliance, Britain dispatched fleets to the Baltic, the coast of Spain, and the West Indies. In September 1726, Admiral Hosier blockaded Porto Bello, the Spanish fort in Panama, intending to frustrate the Vienna allies by preventing return of the treasure-laden Spanish galleons. The six-month expedition was an infamous failure,[55] but the blockade provoked Spain into besieging Gibraltar in December 1726, and Britain sent troops and ships as reinforcements. On January 1, 1727, the Spanish ambassador broke off relations with Britain, and Spain began bombarding Gibraltar on February 22. That the Anglo-Spanish conflict remained localized to Gibraltar was chiefly due to the pacific tendencies of Walpole and Cardinal Fleury, the French chief minister, who worked to reconcile Spain and Britain.

With Parliament set to open on January 17, 1727, the ministry and opposition contested the strength of the ministry's commitment to retain Gibraltar. Writing for the ministry, Bishop Benjamin Hoadly readily admitted the importance of Gibraltar as "a great *Defence* and *Advantage* to our extended *Navigation*." While silent on the king's promise of restoration, Hoadly reiterated that Gibraltar and Port Mahon were secured to Britain by alliances and treaties, including ones by the Spanish king himself.[56] Despite Hoadly's admissions, Bolingbroke raised the specter of a Gibraltar in danger by repeating the popular belief that British right "is come, by dint of N—n [Negotiation], from being indisputable, to be called in question."[57] The uncertain peace and Spanish depredations on British merchants in the West Indies led to calls for war against Spain.[58]

In the spring of 1727, with Gibraltar under siege, the *Craftsman* and the ministerial *British Journal* sparred over Italian opera, specifically the effect of luxury and its offspring opera, on Britain's moral character and public spirit. The exchange was forecast in the *Craftsman* for February 17: "We have receiv'd several ingenious Letters from our Correspondents; particularly one concerning *Luxury* and *Musick*, which shall be speedily publish'd."[59]

In what may have been a pre-emptive strike, a little over two weeks later the *British Journal* carried a letter providing a sophisticated defense of Italian opera.[60] The *Journal's* correspondent notes that Italian opera is now "the universal Entertainment of the polite Part of the World" and of "Men of the finest Parts and best Understandings"; "Every one is delighted with it but the Criticks, who still keep up their antient Enmity against it." Offering a many-pronged defense of opera, the writer points out it is unjust to say that the sole pleasure of good music consists in the sense of sound; the delight is the "Operation of the Mind" upon the sound. There is no reason to degrade music as an irrational pleasure, because it is capable of expressing with equal force and delicacy "all the nobler Passions and Affections of the Mind" and offering "proper Employment to the Understanding," as do painting or poetry.

The *Craftsman's* promised letter from its correspondent, actually Bolingbroke,[61] duly appeared on March 13. Printed while Gibraltar was under bombardment by the Spanish, the letter's comments on the effects of opera upon the nation's manners now had considerable political bite. Caleb D'Anvers, as editor, apologizes to the beau monde of both sexes for printing a letter that so directly impugns "their most darling Entertainments." Brimming with irony, his statement that he wishes Britain may prove "the singular Instance of a Nation, upon whose Morals Luxury, Corruption and unmanly Diversions shall have no Influence" suggests their effects are already present. But he offers that if any of the gentlemen of the Royal Academy will prove "that no bad Consequences ought to be justly apprehended from such *Entertainments* in a *warlike* and *Trading* Nation," he will print such a justification if they submit one.

In his letter, Bolingbroke admits that at such a moment it may seem trifling to "Discourse on *Operas* and the gayer pleasures of the Town," but he fears "they will bear too great a part in the success of a War, to make the consideration of them foreign to it." Ransacking history, he points to past nations ruined by luxury and pleasure and rehearses the commonplaces that luxury enervates and effeminates men, rendering them incapable of achieving virtue or fulfilling their civic duties.[62] The effects of luxury are the same, no matter the nation.

Bolingbroke hints that Walpole is one of those wily statesmen (a "darling Son of *Machiavel* and *Tacitus*") who leads his people into slavery by the "Baits of Pleasure." The greatest danger of operas and masquerades is not their considerable expense, but the "Tendency which they have to deprave our manners": "the soft *Italian* musick relaxes and unnerves the Soul, and sinks it into weakness; so that while we receive their Musick, we at the same time are adopting their manners." Returning to the foreign political crisis at hand, he closes, "What effect *Italian* Musick might have on our polite Warriors at *Gibraltar*, I can't take upon me to say; but I wish their Luxury at home, may not influence their Courage abroad." The supposed danger to British troops abroad from opera at home was the occasion for Bolingbroke to restate the dangers of luxury in order to emphasize once again the consequences to the nation of Walpole's continuing corruption of politics.

The ministry did not allow the *Craftsman*'s denunciations of luxury and opera to go unanswered, for the following month, a correspondent to the *British Journal* offered a common ministerial rebuttal by impugning the motives of those offering "General Satires and Reflections on whole Societies of Men, made without any manner of Distinction." Such "grievous Complaints and Murmurings against the Age" arise from the "Ill-nature … Spleen and Disgust" of Malcontents and those disappointed in not achieving what they thought their merit deserved.[63] A glance at the flourishing arts, sciences, learning, and commerce of Britain will show the supposed ill effects from luxury are not occurring.

Faustina, Cuzzoni, and the Preliminaries of Paris

While the Alliances of Hanover and Vienna were veering toward war, London's Royal Academy broke out into its own internal conflict: the headline-making feud that broke out in 1726 between partisans of Faustina and Cuzzoni. In the summer of 1727, the *Craftsman* used the rivalry as the basis for three allegorical letters on British foreign affairs and Gibraltar; the final one is as complex an allegory as the later and better-known allegory on Handel's *Deborah* and Walpole's Excise scheme (see Chapter 5).

Faustina and Cuzzoni had shared the stage without reported incident in Venice in the seasons 1718, 1719, and 1721, where pairs of prime donne were common.[64] In London there is no record of any personal animosity between them except in the satires or comic pieces in the print media, which likely exaggerate the partisanship of London audiences to crown one of them as prima donna into animus between the singers.

Francesca Cuzzoni's much-anticipated debut with the Royal Academy of Music was on January 12, 1723, in Handel's *Ottone*. The pastime of ranking singers was already set with Cuzzoni's arrival, when a newspaper wrote, "She far excells Seigniora *Duristante*, already with us, and all those she leaves in *Italy* behind her."[65] The Faustina–Cuzzoni rivalry was prepared as early as March 30, 1723, when a brief news item reporting a successful benefit for Cuzzoni mentioned the possibility of Faustina's coming to London and claimed her voice "exceeds that we have already here."[66] A press report in September 1725 plants a hint about her role: "Signiora *Faustina*, a famous Italian Lady, is coming over this Winter to rival Signiora Cuzzoni."[67]

Faustina made her debut on May 5, 1726, in Handel's *Alessandro*, an opera featuring two principal female roles. Already by May 14, the two singers had been dubbed "the Rival Queens" by the anti-ministerial and opera-antagonist *Mist's Weekly Journal* as it delightedly apprised the public of the rivalry between them:

By our last Letters from St. James's Coffee-House we have received Advice, that Things have taken a more happy Turn than could have been expected in so short a Time; for the rival Queens *Faustina* and *Cuzzoni*, whose Jealousy of each other's Power might have divided us into Party and Confusion, have been prevail'd upon to speak to each other, and, some Advices say, even to sup together, without Suspicion of Poison of either Side.[68]

A laconic afterthought scores a satiric hit against the undue importance placed on opera: "I know that some People will dispute the Truth of this Piece of News, because South-Sea [stock] has not rise[n] upon it."

The animosity between partisans of the singers warmed again the following season, for the spoken prologue at a revival of *Camilla* at Lincoln's Inn Fields Theatre on November 19, 1726, remarked how between the "Rival Queens, such mutual Hate / Threats hourly Ruin to yon tuneful State" at the Haymarket Theatre.[69] The following month, *Mist's* reported another reconciliation, beginning with the phrase customarily used when reporting diplomatic news ("Our last Advices") and continuing in terms of ministers, treaties, and negotiations:

> Our last Advices from the Haymarket take Notice of a second Reconcilement betwixt the Rival Queens, Cuzzoni and Faustina; an unhappy Breach being made betwixt them since their first Reconcilement, occasioned by one of them making Mouths at the other while she was singing. This Treaty has been three Months in negotiating, and could never have been brought about had it not been for the great Skill and Address of some of the ablest Ministers of the Royal Academy. What makes this Piece of News the more acceptable is, its falling out at such a Juncture; for if the Emperor, or King of Spain should have the Rashness to enter into a War with us, we don't fear now but that we shall have better Singing than they.[70]

The final sentence may be a squib against the ministry: in case of war, the Faustina–Cuzzoni reconciliation will guarantee Britain musical superiority; but the innuendo is that Austria or Spain will have military superiority because British ministers have been attending to music instead of statecraft.

Audience members showed their loyalty to their favorite singer by hisses and catcalls directed at her rival. On one occasion, an apology for a disturbance was sent on behalf of Cuzzoni by Mary, Countess of Pembroke, to the Princess of Wales, whose daughter, Princess Amelia, was in the audience.[71] The feud's notorious climax occurred at the June 6 performance of Bononcini's *Astianatte* on what would be the final evening of the 1726–27 season, with Princess Caroline in attendance. The *London Journal's* account on June 10 ironically commented on the audience's behavior:

> On Tuesday Night last, a great Disturbance happen'd at the Opera, occasion'd by the Partizans of the two celebrated Rival Ladies, *Cuzzoni* and *Faustina*. The Contention at first, was only carried on by Hissing, on one Side, and Clapping, on the other; but proceeded [*sic*] at length, to the delightful Exercise of Catcalls, and other Indecencies, which demonstrated the inimitable Zeal and Politeness of that Illustrious Assembly. *N.B.* The Princess Carolina[72] was present; but no Regards were of Force to restrain the glorious Ardour of the fierce Opponents.[73]

The disturbance was the freshest gossip about town. As John, Lord Hervey informed a correspondent on June 13, 1727,

> As to Opera Feuds they are hotter than ever: I suppose you have heard already y.ᵗ both Cuzzoni & Faustina were so hiss'd & catt-call'd last tuesday y.ᵗ yᵉ Opera was not finish'd y.ᵗ Night, nor have yᵉ Directors dared to venture yᵉ representation of another since.[74]

But it was not the fear of audience disturbances at the opera that prematurely ended the season. Although operas were not given on the usual opera nights of June 10 and 13, it was the arrival on the afternoon of June 14 of news of the death in Onsabrück of George I that shuttered the theaters.

The outbreaks at the opera house amused the town, and reports of them found their way into innumerable poems, pamphlets, and plays.[75] In June the author of "A Full and True Account of a Most Horride and Bloody Battle between Madam Faustina and Madam Cuzzoni"[76] is dismayed that the skirmishes seen so often among lady rivals in trade "should reach the *Hay-Market*, and inspire Two Singing Ladies to pull each others Coiffs, to the no small Disquiet of the Directors, who (God help 'em) have enough to do to keep Peace and Quietness between 'em." The following month, *The Contre Temps; or, Rival Queans* developed the feud into a short theatrical farce.[77] In the Temple of Discord, crowded with peers and beaux armed with catcalls and whistles, Heidegger tries to get the singers to settle their feud, which has eclipsed all other civil or foreign disputes. With a glance at Continental politics that satirizes those who have taken the feud too seriously to the neglect of attending to foreign affairs, Heidegger exclaims,

> Nor *Gibraltar* we seek, nor *Port-Mahon*;
> Possessing you, makes all the world our own:
> Who wails expiring *Sp—n*, or dead *Cza—na* [Czarina]?
> Leave us kind heav'n! – *C—z—ni* and *F—s—na*.
> *Contre Temps*, p. 6

To opera-goers, Cuzzoni and Faustina are worth all of Gibraltar and Port Mahon. Heidegger's proposals of peace and equal celebrity are rebuffed; verbal sparring turns to boxing and then to blows with crowns and scepters until Faustina flees.

The Royal Academy directors had decided between the pre-eminence of the two singers in early June 1727 and planned not to rehire Cuzzoni.[78] According to the Countess of Pembroke, the king sent a message to the directors that "if they dismist Cuzzoni they shoud not have ye Honour of his presence or what He was pleasd to allow them [his £1,000 annual bounty]."[79] In the end, royal wishes prevailed, and Cuzzoni was rehired for what would be the Academy's last season.

Abundant testimony confirms that partisanship developed around the feud, both within the Royal Academy and London society at large, but no source mentions factions that reflect political alignment. One example is instructive. Sir John Hawkins prints an "Epigram on the Miracles wrought by Cuzzoni" from the Harleian manuscripts that mentions three subscribers of the Academy who supported Cuzzoni:

> Boast not how Orpheus charm'd the rocks,
> And set a dancing stones and stocks,
>   And tygers' rage appeas'd;
> All this Cuzzoni has surpass'd,
> Sir Wilfred seems to have a taste,
>   And Smith and Gage are pleas'd.[80]

Hawkins identifies the Cuzzoni partisans as Sir Wilfred Lawson, Simon Smith, Esq., and Sir William Gage. Two were MPs. Sir William Gage voted regularly with the ministry, supporting Newcastle's interests, whereas Sir Wilfred Lawson began voting with Pulteney and the opposition in January 1724.[81] Simon Smith remains unidentified.

Sir Robert Walpole was a partisan of Faustina, as was Lady Delawarr, whereas, as we have seen, the king favored Cuzzoni, who was also favored by Lady Walpole, the Countess of Pembroke, and the Duke of Rutland.[82] The fashionable young lady about town in the poem "The Discontented Virgin" (March 1727) reveals that the Prince and Princess of Wales (who lived at Leicester House) concurred with the king, while the courtiers the Earl and Countess of Burlington favored Faustina:

> At *Leicester Fields* I give my Vote
>   For the fine-piped *Cuzzoni*;
> At *Burlington*'s I change my Note,
>   *Faustina* for my Money.[83]

The feud probably had no political alignment because it antedated the political opposition that arose in the summer of 1726.[84]

The rivalry continued through the final season of the Academy, for on February 23, 1728, the French traveler César de Saussure reported that "The Court and town, men and women, are divided into two parties, one admiring Faustina and the other the Cozzoni, and both parties load their respective favourite with presents, compliments, and flatteries."[85]

While the siege of Gibraltar was underway, King George persuaded the French to move forces toward the Rhine to protect Hanover from Prussian and Austrian attack, and the ministry drew up plans for war. Determined to avoid war, Cardinal Fleury threatened the emperor unless he agreed to preliminary articles that would arrange a prompt peace. Inclined now toward peace, the emperor abandoned his obligations to Spain and in May 1727 joined England, France, and the United Provinces in signing the Preliminary Articles for a General Pacification, ratified shortly afterward by Spain. A triumph for Fleury's diplomacy, the Preliminaries of Paris provided that Spain would raise the siege of Gibraltar, England would recall her fleets, hostilities would cease, and the emperor and France would mediate between England and Spain. Rights of territorial possession accorded by previous treaties were affirmed; all other issues were deferred to a European congress to be convened at Soissons on June 14, 1728.

Dissatisfied with the Preliminaries, Spain refused to fulfill its obligations. Pressing its own interpretation of them, it demanded that right of possession of Gibraltar and Minorca be discussed at the congress; Britain in turn refused to withdraw its fleet from Spanish waters. Walpole now had to deal with pro-war factions at home, demands that Gibraltar not be discussed at the congress, and criticism of his reliance on Fleury's diplomacy.[86]

While Britons awaited the official text of the Preliminaries, various supposed translations of them appeared in the press.[87] In three consecutive issues in May and June 1727, the *Craftsman* used anxiety that Britain would cede important points,[88] such as possession of Gibraltar, to badger and harass the ministry and imply possible betrayal of Britain's interests.[89] Pointedly it asked whether Britain was guaranteed "the Right of Possession" of Gibraltar by the Preliminaries or whether "it is to be *debated* at the *Congress*."

In the third of these issues for June 10, appearing the same day as the ministerial *London Journal*'s account of the disturbance between supporters of Cuzzoni and Faustina at the opera, a letter from "Phil-Harmonicus" used the Faustina–Cuzzoni dispute to press opposition concerns about foreign policy and the fate of Gibraltar. The satiric allegory relating opera to European politics is hinted from the outset: "Since our *publick* Quarrels are *in so fair a way* of being adjusted, I am sorry to see our *private* [operatic] *ones* increase."[90] Since his letter appears directly following the foreign affairs section, which had commented on the siege and status of Gibraltar in the Preliminaries, the phrase serves as an ironic comment on the success of British diplomacy.

The ostensible occasion of Phil-Harmonicus' letter was his attendance at the opera when the Faustina–Cuzzoni feud broke out in Bononcini's *Astianatte* and his amazement during one of the finest songs he had ever heard at what he took to be a new instrument – harsh, out of tune, and out of time – accompanying Cuzzoni. The sounds, he is told, are but catcalls issued by Faustina's supporters "as a sound to Battle between the *Rival Queens* and their mighty Parties." Phil-Harmonicus is let into the secret of the quarrel: the dispute is about the right of pre-eminence between the singers. Since "a *Rupture* seems so near, in which both the *Rivals* may suffer," he proposes "a *Congress* for adjusting their Rights," for which he offers eight "*Preliminary* Articles."

The timing of his letter leaves no doubt that his real topic is the competing claims of Britain and Spain for Gibraltar. His proposals parallel those of the Preliminaries of Paris, which set the groundwork for the projected Congress of Soissons, and his series of numbered articles mimics those of the Preliminaries, which had just been widely printed in newspapers.[91] Phil-Harmonicus' proposal has these analogs:

Royal Academy = Europe/Countries meeting at the
Congress of Soissons
First part in the opera = Gibraltar
Faustina = Spain
Cuzzoni/Cuzzoni's voice = Britain/Britain's right to Gibraltar
Senesino = Cardinal Fleury
Singer = a European country

As with other *Craftsman* allegories, the parallels occasionally shift slightly. Phil-Harmonicus' preliminary proposals are

1. That *Senesino* be desired to assist as *Mediator*, and to use his well-known Abilities to lay [*sic*: allay?] the Passions of these fair Antagonists.

2. That as in all other *Congresses* the *longest Heads* are thought the most proper for *Plenipotentiaries*, the *longest Ears* [those with Midas' (or ass's) ears] shall carry it here, being the best qualified for so important a Charge [judging between singers].

3. That it shall be debated in the *Congress*, whether *Cuzzoni* has a *Voice* or not; and if she has, whether the Property of it is in *herself*, or in the *Academy* [to be settled by the Congress of Soissons].

The opera–Gibraltar correspondence is most pertinent in the fourth article:

4. That it be decided in the *Congress*, whether the *first Part* in the *Opera*, which has been for some Years in possession of *Cuzzoni*, and of which no *Singer* cou'd ever justly disposses her (tho' she has been warmly attacked *this Winter*) shall *remain* with her, or be *given up* to the *Faustina*, either for or without an *Equivalent*.

The fifth article alludes to opposition suspicions about the status of Gibraltar:

5. That all *Rights* and *Possessions* in the *Academy* shall remain on the Foot of the former *Treaties* and *Conventions* between the contracting Parties; unless *either* of them hath departed from her Right, by any *secret Engagements* [George's letter or Stanhope's promise], which shall be decided at the *Congress* proposed.[92]

6. That from the first meeting of the *Congress* there shall be a *Cessation* of *Cat-calls* [warfare].

The next and final two articles are the usual ones dealing with treaty ratification. Phil-Harmonicus closes believing that "every Man, who has the *Musick and Good* of his *Country* at heart, will agree with me, that it is a pity such Dissentions shou'd arise in a Christian Country, and that any *Discord* shou'd prevail in the House of *Harmony*."

So far, the allegory is rather innocuous; but once established, Phil-Harmonicus put it to stronger use the following month when he again wrote the *Craftsman* from the Haymarket Theatre:

You seem to have the *Royal Academy of Musick* so much at Heart, that I cannot forbear troubling you, a second time, with some farther account of the melancholly declining State, in which that Society [Royal Academy] is at present involved.[93]

He reports that, although the Preliminaries for a pacification are signed and a congress agreed upon, "the dispute between the two celebrated *Rival Singers*, concerning the *first part* in the *Opera*" is far from being accommodated. At this point, in the guise of discussing the opera, Phil-Harmonicus reiterated the opposition accusation about the ministry's conduct of the negotiations:

yet most People are very uneasy for the Event, because one of the *most material Articles* is worded in such a *dark* and *mysterious* manner as gives too much Ground to suspect that it was done on purpose, in order to conceal a *Difficulty*, which it will be hard to get over.[94]

The difficulty is the fifth article, which is so worded that it might allow Faustina (Spain) to raise the king's letter promising return of Gibraltar. Then continuing the allegory, Phil-Harmonicus states the opposition fear that at the Congress Philip will attempt to use George's secret letter to extort Gibraltar from Britain:

The *Right of Possession* [of Gibraltar] is certainly in *Cuzzoni* [Britain], which she hath enjoy'd without molestation, for some years, and is confirm'd to her by diverse *Treaties* between her and the *Academy* [European alliances]. *Faustina* [Spain], on the other hand, insists that *Cuzzoni* hath consented and promised to yield up that *Right* to her, by a *secret Stipulation*, under her *own hand* [George's letter], which she is ready to produce. *Cuzzoni* seems to prevaricate a little in this Affair; for as she cannot well deny her own *hand writing*, she would persuade the World that it is only a *sort of a Promise* ... to make *Faustina* easy for the present.[95]

Phil-Harmonicus believes this stipulation and the inclinations of the foreign singers (allies), some of the directors (ministers), and the mediator Senesino (Cardinal Fleury) toward Faustina (Spain) jeopardize Cuzzoni's (Britain's) chances of success at his congress.

Under the pretext of discussing the Academy and opera directors, Phil-Harmonicus then implies the whole range of opposition charges against the ministry: that some of the ministers and Fleury secretly wish to return Gibraltar; the Walpole administration is unnecessarily raising taxes for the Civil List and army; the public Treasury is nearly empty despite the raising of vast sums; and Britain's European allies threaten to abandon England unless subsidies for troops are paid.

In closing, Phil-Harmonicus turns to John Kipling, the treasurer of the Royal Academy, and it is clear again that Walpole is meant. All these events are the more surprising, he ironically writes,

> when we consider the frugal Management and unblemished Integrity of Mr. *Kiplin*, the Treasurer, whom every Man acquits of any bad Design … So universal is the Resentment grown against this *Gentleman* (whether he deserves it or not, I shall not determine) that it is thought, nothing will pacify the true Friends of the *Opera* and redeem their Affairs, till They see him removed and the management put into other Hands.[96]

The Beggar's Opera and the Academy's final season

The high point of the 1727–28 theater season was the January 29, 1728, premiere and unprecedented sixty-three unbroken performance run of John Gay's *Beggar's Opera*. It was immediately obvious to all what sort of political mischief the ballad opera was up to, and opinion in favor of and against it align with the opposition and ministry. With only some understatement did John, Lord Hervey record that the *Beggar's Opera* "was thought to reflect a little upon the Court."[97] Colley Cibber, also loyal to the Whig government, a patentee of the Drury Lane Theatre and future Poet Laureate, refused to produce the ballad opera for political reasons, and it was taken up by John Rich at Lincoln's Inn Fields.[98] The *Craftsman* quickly noted, "The Waggs say it has made *Rich* very *Gay*, and probably will make *Gay* very *Rich*."[99]

The ministerial press in general reviled the ballad opera for the immorality of setting up highwaymen and thieves as heroes and undermining opera and serious British drama. Certainly responding to ballad opera was a letter to the ministerial *London Journal* in March regretting the neglect of the Italian opera despite "that excessive Fondness for *Italian* Operas, which has of late Years over-run the Nation."[100] The surprising neglect of Italian opera, now playing to near-empty houses despite three splendid new operas, the correspondent attributes to the fickle taste of Englishmen, who were so converted to the Italian taste that they accepted nothing but the best talent from Italy and have made it "as compleat as an Entertainment of that sort, in respect of the Musick and Voices, (which are the essential Parts of an Opera,) was capable of being." But the best voices, composers, musicians, and stage decorations had only raised disputes and divided the audience into factions quarreling about two perfect, but different voices. He deplores that performance nights for Italian opera conflict with those of the ballad opera, whereby its full houses demonstrate that the British had only a "violent Affection" for opera, rather than "a true Taste of good Musick." One advantage does come from the smaller audiences for the opera: it diminishes the number of false friends of the opera who indulge in catcalling the singers, and so true lovers of music can enjoy opera without interruption.

The following week in the same journal, "Philopropos" complains that its pleasant and memorable tunes and adaptation to the vulgar taste make the moral contagion of the *Beggar's Opera* – showing the unpunished triumph of villainous highwaymen and their lives "agreeable, and full of Mirth and Jollity" – all the more widespread. The ballad opera fails to do what Addison expects: to laugh men out of Vice and Folly.[101] The same day in the *Weekly Journal*,[102] Dorimant speaks out against the town's prevailing applause for the *Beggar's Opera* and Miss Polly Peachum: their popularity proves the foolishness of the audiences, the stupidity of the kingdom, and "the Degeneracy of Taste" that has prevailed for some years. The fashion for Gay's opera has shown all the pains and expense of the Royal Academy of Music have been "to no Manner of Purpose at all."

With its swipes at the ministry as a gang of thieves and parody and satire of Italian opera, the *Beggar's Opera* was welcomed by the opposition. The *Craftsman* in February 1728 was delighted at its success: "The *British Opera*, commonly called the *Beggars Opera*, continues to be acted, at the Theatre in Lincoln's-Inn Fields with general Applause, to the great Mortification of the Performers and Admirers of the *Outlandish Opera* in the Haymarket."[103] That May, Jonathan Swift, no friend of either Walpole or opera, approved Gay's opera because it "exposeth with great Justice, that unnatural Taste for *Italian* Musick among us, which is wholly unsuitable to our Northern *Climat*, and the *genius* of the People, whereby we are over-run with *Italian-Effeminacy*, and *Italian* Nonsense."[104]

Opposition propaganda exploited the opera's popularity and inflamed Gay's general reflections on politics and society into highly partisan attacks. Three weeks after it opened, in a letter to the *Craftsman*, "Phil. Harmonicus" rejects the excuse that the ballad opera is general satire and asserts it is "the most venemous *allegorical Libel* against the *G—t* [Government] that hath appeared for many Years past." Consequently, pretending he is a friend to the ministry, he proposes that restraints be put on performances of the ballad opera, which he justifies because it conveys "not only *Scandal* and *Scurrility*, but even *Sedition* and *Treason*."[105]

To prove the need for restraints, he points out the application of the *Beggar's Opera*. Dismissing the idea that Lockit is designed for Walpole ("the *Keeper* or *prime Minister* of *Newgate*"), he asserts that it is Macheath (with "a tolerable *Bronze* upon his Face") who is designed "to asperse *somebody in Authority* ... at the Head of a Gang of *Robbers* ... [and] often call'd a *Great Man.*" The opera abounds in "*satirical* strokes upon *Ministers, Courtiers* and *Great Men,*" says Phil. Harmonicus, and he carefully makes explicit many of the innuendos of the plot: "that *Courtiers have less Honesty than Highwaymen,*" "that *some Persons* have been well paid for *saving,* or *screening* their *former Acquaintance,*" "that *great Statesmen frequently betray their Friends,*" and "*that* every Courtier *is corrupted* either *with* Vice or a Bribe, *or* with Both." His letter was soon reprinted with a key to cue any contemporary who needed help to interpret the opera as a libel upon the ministry and court.[106] Using the persona of a friend to the ministry to justify restraint on the ballad opera gives him the occasion to reiterate its abuse of Walpole.

Another writer to the *Craftsman* – noting the stinging indictment of Walpole through the character of Macheath – surmised Gay had been secretly put to work by Walpole himself that he might be esteemed "a less *infamous Character*" as a "*Plunderer of his Country.*"[107] Writing to the *Craftsman* a year later, "Hilarius" chides the paper for being the instigator of the idea that the satire of "the Character of *Macheath*" applied "to *some Persons in Authority.*"[108] His mock rebuttal of the supposed attacks against Walpole only serves to identify and sharpen them. Shortly thereafter, Caleb D'Anvers kept the identification alive by claiming he had almost decided to stop mentioning the word "*Mackheath*" (among names of other statesmen, including Catiline and Sejanus) because "a *certain Person*" (Walpole) had taken "a particular Fancy, from time to time, to declare that *He* was allegorically meant under all these Titles."[109]

Several fictions about *The Beggar's Opera* must be dismissed. Despite its notoriety and obvious embarrassment to Walpole and the ministry, Gay's ballad opera did not contribute to the fall of Walpole,[110] who remained in power until 1742. Another fiction that Gay's opera crippled or caused the demise of Italian opera in London has its source in Pope's footnote on Gay in the *Dunciad Variorum* (April 1729):

Furthermore, it [the *Beggar's Opera*] drove out of *England* the *Italian Opera,* which had carry'd all before it for ten years: That Idol of the Nobility and the people, which the great Critick Mr. *Dennis* by the labours and outcries of a whole life could not overthrow, was demolish'd in one winter by a single stroke of this gentleman's pen.[111]

Pope's statement about Gay's ballad opera to the contrary, Italian opera retained its foothold in Britain. Two new Italian operas were produced in the following months, so that including revivals, there were upwards of thirty-three opera performances that season after the *Beggar's Opera* closed.[112] While the Royal Academy did fold after the 1727–28 season, opera productions were resumed by Handel and Heidegger in December 1729, and thereafter Italian opera prevailed throughout the rest of the century and beyond, even at two periods being offered by competing companies. In later editions of the *Dunciad*, Pope emended the phrase to "drove out of *England* for that season" in order to reflect correctly just the hiatus between the Royal Academy and the Handel–Heidegger partnership. Nevertheless, at the time, Italian opera's survival was doubtful, and the success of the *Beggar's Opera* was a convenient excuse for its lapse.

Another fiction is its supposed aim to drive out Italian opera. A great deal of the fun of *The Beggar's Opera* is its good-humored and self-conscious send-up of the conventions and plot devices of Italian opera.[113] As the ballad opera opens, Gay's Beggar apologizes that he has not "made my opera throughout unnatural, like those in vogue." He touches on all its topics of parody or burlesque: "I have introduced the similes that are in all your celebrated operas: the swallow, the moth, the bee, the ship, the flower, etc. Besides, I have a prison scene, which the ladies always reckon charmingly pathetic."[114] Alluding to the recent Faustina–Cuzzoni scandal, the Beggar says he has "observed such a nice impartiality to our two ladies that it is impossible for either of them to take offense." In the final scene when Macheath is about to be hanged, the Beggar agrees with the Player that "an opera must end happily" and gives the highwayman a reprieve: "In this kind of drama 'tis no matter how absurdly things are brought about" (III.xvi).

However, even granting that Gay's ballad opera parodies and burlesques conventions of Italian opera, it is not an attack on Handel or opera.[115] It has none of the indictments of opera's great expense, effects on native drama, vicious ridicule of castratos, and denunciations of its effeminacy found in other genuine attacks on opera. Yet, the parody and burlesque do political work by ridiculing a favorite entertainment of Walpole, the court, and aristocracy, and in so doing indicts the taste of the political leaders of the nation.

The demise of the Royal Academy cannot be laid to the supposed triumph of *The Beggar's Opera*. Ruinous expense and insufficient income, the loss of novelty occurring with any new entertainment, and mismanagement all played greater roles in the dissolution of the Academy. During the 1726–27 season, the directors made three calls on shareholder capital, bringing the calls on the initial investment to 89 percent.[116] The perilous state of the Academy's finances was revealed in its final 1727–28 season, which opened earlier than usual in September, perhaps as a means to eke out extra income. Nevertheless, cash was short, and by the season's end (on June 1, 1728), there were four more calls, exhausting the shareholders' investments and the Academy's cash reserves.[117] Correspondence of opera enthusiasts in the winter and spring of 1728 mentions the divisions and quarrels among the directors, dissatisfaction with singers and their demands for payment, the popularity of *The Beggar's Opera*, and dwindling attendance at the opera – all raising fears opera would not survive the summer. Most ominously, as early as November 1727, it was reported that Senesino and Faustina threatened not to return for another season.[118]

Four general meetings of shareholders were held in May and June 1728 to settle finances and "to receive any further Proposals that shall be offered for Carrying on the Operas."[119] The *Daily Courant* announced the agenda for the last meeting on June 5: "recovering the Debts due to the Academy, and discharging what is due to Performers, Tradesmen, and others; and also to determine how the Scenes, Cloaths, &c. are to be disposed of, if the Operas cannot be continued."[120] The season had already closed on June 1. As feared, the principal singers slipped away back to Italy: Senesino and Faustina, in July; Cuzzoni, a month later.[121]

But all hope for opera was not abandoned. The Royal Academy's charter was still valid for another twelve years, and as early as May, thirty-five peers and gentry pledged a capital infusion of £200 "to the corporation of the Royal Academy of Musick towards carrying on of Operas which are to begin in October 1728."[122] Heidegger left for France and Italy in June to recruit singers for another season.[123]

The Congress of Soissons and the Treaty of Seville

The final season of the Royal Academy coincided with the run-up to the Congress of Soissons, planned to convene on June 14, 1728. With pressure from Fleury, Spain and Britain were finally brought to peace with the Convention of the Pardo, signed on March 6, 1728. Spain promised to raise the siege of Gibraltar, and Britain agreed to recall her fleets from Spanish waters and discuss at the Congress alleged British contraband trade in the Indies. The ministry proclaimed the Convention a vindication of Walpole's conviction that negotiation was better than war.

The Congress of Soissons ultimately failed to settle any of the outstanding issues disrupting the peace. Spain demanded the return of Gibraltar on the basis of George's promise of 1721, whereas the British claimed that George had only promised to present the question to Parliament, and that the 1718–20 war voided the obligation. Sensitive to public opinion, Secretary Townshend warned one of the British emissaries in June:

You cannot but be sensible of the violent and almost superstitious zeal … among all parties in this kingdom, against any scheme for the restitution of Gibraltar … The bare mention of a proposal, which carry'd the most distant appearance of laying England under an obligation of ever parting with that place, would be sufficient to put the whole nation in a flame.[124]

A provisional treaty was circulated in August among the delegates, but failed primarily because Spain baulked at any agreement that precluded raising its claim to Gibraltar. The Congress came to a standstill by the end of 1728. The British government continued to be attacked at home for failing to prevent Spanish depredations on British shipping, and cries for war with Spain continued.[125]

Over the summer of 1728, with both the outcome of the Congress of Soissons and the future of the Royal Academy of Music uncertain, the *Craftsman* continued its allegories about the Royal Academy and European diplomacy as a means to harass and discredit the ministry. On July 6, the periodical carried a brief item on the departure for Paris and Italy of Senesino and Faustina that was a gibe at the lack of diplomatic progress at the Congress: "Some say they [Senesino and Faustina] design a short Stay at *Soissons* for the Entertainment of several Persons of Quality, and to shew an Example of *Harmony*."[126]

The now-familiar parallel between the Royal Academy and Congress of Soissons was developed at length in a letter to the *Craftsman* for August 31. After summarizing the previous preliminary proposals for a congress that would settle the disputes between Cuzzoni and Faustina at the Haymarket, the writer continues:

But alas! it is too well known how this Assembly broke up; that they wrangled, for some time … without so much as once mentioning the *material Points* in Debate. This did, of Consequence, very deeply affect every Man, who had any real Concern for the *Musical* Government of *Great Britain*, which now seems to be in the utmost Danger, and hath raised a general Indignation against *Those*, who have reduced it to this Extremity. I need not mention *these Men*. They are sufficiently denoted by the daily Exclamations of the *Subscribers* against them; but it can not be amiss, for the

Instruction of *other States* and *Societies*, to recapitulate their Proceedings, for some Years past, on this Affair; from whence the monstrous Absurdity and Madness of their Conduct will appear, and I hope be a Warning to all true Lovers of *Musick* and *Harmony*.[127]

The principal parallels of the unfolding are

Royal Academy/Haymarket = Congress of Soissons/Europe
first part of the opera = right to Gibraltar
Faustina = Spain
Cuzzoni = Britain or King George
harmony = peace
musical government = political government
managers = secretaries of state
connoisseurs, friends, or subscribers of opera = Britons, MPs,
Parliament, taxpayers

The letter-writer recalls the origins of the Cuzzoni and Faustina rivalry: "Madam *Faustina* [Spain] was pleased, upon her coming over hither, to set up a Claim to the *first Part in the Opera*, against her Competitor *Seigniora Cuzzoni*, (who had long possess'd it) by virtue of a *former, secret Promise* [George I's letter] … of the said *Cuzzoni* to surrender it [Gibraltar] to Her," but "great Numbers of the *best Friends* of the *Opera* expressed the utmost Abhorrence of such a Design and would not, upon any Terms, be induced to consent that she should give up so material a Right."

To Faustina's "*powerful Alliances* amongst the chief Nobility and Gentry of the Kingdom" [representing the Treaty of Vienna], "*Cuzzoni* began to think herself in imminent Danger and applyed herself, with the utmost Diligence, to the forming of counter *Alliances*" [Treaty of Hanover]. The letter-writer gets off an unmistakable accusation at the ministry: "*Cuzzoni* … having intrusted the Management of her Affairs in the Hands of *unskilful Persons* [ministers] (who seemed to know no other Methods of *Negotiation*, than *Threats*, *Blusters* and *Bribes* [subsidies]) they were not able, by all their Endeavours, to turn the *Balance* on her Side."

In further passages, the British expedition against Spain in the West Indies, the diplomatic rupture between England and Spain, Spanish reprisals against British merchant shipping, the siege of Gibraltar, the proposal of the Congress of Soissons to settle disputes, Cardinal Fleury's actions as mediator, the break-off of the Congress, and France's rapprochement with Spain – all evidence of the ministry's mismanagement of foreign affairs – are alluded to in terms of the opera house.

The ministry's failure to obtain an explicit Spanish renunciation of Gibraltar is again criticized:

> It is pretended … that *Cuzzoni* is now left absolutely in Possession of her *Right*, which remain'd somewhat doubtful during the *Struggle last Winter*; [and] whereas *Faustina*, by deserting her Ground, seems to give up her Pretensions … but I would willingly ask *these Gentlemen* … whether the *Connoiseurs of Musick* would not be glad to have a *safe, honourable* and *lasting Accommodation* concluded with *Faustina*.[128]

Senesino's and Faustina's departure in July is used to belittle Fleury's influence with the Spanish court: "The *same Gentlemen* endeavour to alleviate our Sorrows and remove our Discontents, under these *melancholy* and most *unharmonious* Circumstances, by assuring us that *Senesino* will *come over to us* again, and that He is *gone off* at present only with a Design to reconcile *Faustina* to our Interest and Proposals."

In closing, the letter turns to a more literal account of the decline of opera affairs. Opera-goers cannot rely on the cessation of hostilities between Faustina and Cuzzoni and "do not seem inclinable to come into *another Subscription* [treaty], to support the Expence of so many Performers, till They are convinced of a *perfect Agreement*." Finally, the letter-writer gets off a parting shot at the ministry and an endorsement of the satire of *The Beggar's Opera*:

> But let these Affairs end how They will, the Management of them hath, without doubt, been exceedingly *ridiculous*, if not *worse*, and Mr. *Gay* had too much Reason, in his *Beggar's Opera*, to expose it [the ministry] to the Contempt of the whole Town.[129]

The failure at Soissons was ridiculed in other opposition satires for being devoted only to the ministers' pleasures and entertainment. *The Norfolk Congress: or, a Full and True Account of their Hunting, Feasting and Merry-making* (November 1728) compares the assembly at Soissons to one of Walpole's extended hunting parties at Houghton, his Norfolk estate.[130] With Parliament due to sit on January 21, 1729, ministerial and opposition writers continued their polemics about the government's handling of foreign affairs and Gibraltar.[131]

A war between Britain and Spain seemed likely but was averted when the Spanish queen joined Britain and France and signed the Treaty of Seville on October 29, 1729. Britain's commercial privileges in the West Indies were restored; Spain released the *Prince Frederick* and offered recompense for other seizures; and Don Carlos' rights to succeed to the duchies of Parma and Tuscany were secured by stationing Spanish troops in the provinces. The Treaty of Seville kept an uneasy peace between Britain and Spain for a decade, but at home it did not prevent a paper war breaking out as the ministry and opposition disputed the treaty's success in securing Gibraltar.[132]

That December *Fog's Weekly Journal* got off a squib against both opera and the ministry's handling of the peace, finding a reason for the failure of its diplomacy:

They write from St. James's, that the Politicks of that Quarter are not employ'd in Speculations about the *Peace*, but about the *Opera*, for the Fate of which the wise Men of Goatham are under great Concern; in fine, they apprehend no less than its Downfall, because there appears no very good *Harmony* at its first setting out.[133]

Despite the group of aristocrats who pledged money for the opera, uncertainty about the Royal Academy and the outcome of the Treaty of Seville continued through the summer and fall of 1728. Some, such as "Mrs. Pen. Prattle," the fictional writer of *The Parrot*, had already given up opera as lost by October:

How fickle is the Humour of this World! since Michaelmas Lamps have been lighted, I have not heard one Sigh at the Fall of *Opera's*. The two *Signiora's* that some time ago were considerable enough to run us into Parties, and to create Debates about their respective Excellencies, are now gone off unlamented, hardly spoken of; for my own part, I retained the Gentility of my *Goust* [goût] to the very last, and with great Concern bid adieu to my dear *Cuzzoni*.[134]

Mrs. Prattle supposes that the singers have left in her charge all the opera properties from the Haymarket Theatre to be auctioned, "that the good People of *England* might have more than Songs for their Money."[135]

Heidegger returned to London in November without a cast of singers; and it was this outcome, not the success of *The Beggar's Opera*, that caused, as a newspaper reported, that the "Italian Opera's are now entirely laid aside in this Kingdom for the present."[136] At the news, Anne, Countess of Albemarle concluded several days later, "so no operas this winter."[137]

From its inception, the Royal Academy was doomed by unrealistic expectations and inherent financial weakness. Despite a royal charter and bounty, underwriting capital of almost £20,000, involvement of the experienced manager Heidegger, splendid productions with Europe's greatest singers and composers, and generally good attendance, in Milhous and Hume's assessment, a company that paid huge sums to singers, consistently ran a deficit, devoured all its capitalization, and was run by an amateur committee was ultimately doomed to collapse.[138] Nonetheless, for nine seasons, the Academy achieved its goal of giving London opera productions rivaling any on the Continent – and even to declare a dividend for one of the seasons.

Given its public visibility and association with the court and ministry, events at the Royal Academy and its personnel – from opera stars Faustina,

Cuzzoni, and Senesino down to the lowly treasurer John Kipling – were irresistible subjects for the opposition to use in its ongoing practice of exploiting any social or public event to abuse the Walpole ministry.

In the last two seasons of the Academy, using the all-the-world's-a-stage topos, the *Craftsman* took up the rivalry of Faustina and Cuzzoni that was amusing London society and – noticing the coincidence with the unfolding British–Spanish conflict over Gibraltar and the run-up to the Congress of Soissons – strung out a series of counterfeit letters from readers containing allegories about the contest of Faustina and Cuzzoni for pre-eminence at the Haymarket Theatre as a means to discredit the ministry's conduct of foreign diplomacy.

5 | Handel's Second Academy

After Heidegger's disappointing return from the Continent in November 1728 without a cast of singers,[1] the directors of the Royal Academy of Music called a final General Court of shareholders for January 18, 1729, to consider some proposals "for carrying on Operas; as also for disposing of the Effects belonging to the said Academy."[2] But since their charter still ran until 1741, the Academy decided to give up active management of opera and, as the Earl of Egmont recorded, "to permit Hydeger and Hendle to carry on operas without disturbance for 5 years and to lend them for that time our scenes, machines, clothes, instruments, furniture, etc."[3]

There were no operas for the 1728–29 season, but Heidegger continued with his proven money-maker, mounting another series of masquerades from December 18, 1728, to May 13, 1729. Handel made another try to recruit singers and set out for Italy on February 4, 1729.[4] Unable to engage any of the Royal Academy's previous singers or the rising star Carlo Broschi, called Farinelli, he did manage to assemble a cast and returned on June 29.[5] *Fog's Weekly Journal* used the news to strike at the fashion for opera: it followed accounts of a "Distemper" ravaging the West Country by giving more significant news: "But these Advices affect not us, for we have receiv'd from Italy the joyful News, that *Mynheer Hendel* has made up a Company of *Singers*; so that we shall have *Italian Operas* next Winter."[6]

Still obscure are the practical arrangements of the Handel–Heidegger partnership, often called Handel's Second Academy, which lasted until the 1733–34 season.[7] Heidegger, who held the lease on the King's Theatre, presumably handled the managerial end, while Handel ran the musical department. Probably because he was handling all the musical duties of the company, in these seasons Handel relied more than usual on revivals and pasticci. In creating these pasticci from the music of the latest Italian composers, including Hasse, Vinci, and Orlandini, Handel was introducing London audiences to the latest in the increasingly popular *galant* Neapolitan style – a style noticeably different from his own.

The royal family took a direct interest in the Handel–Heidegger venture. After the January 1729 meeting, Paolo Rolli wrote to Senesino (now in Italy) that Handel's "new plans find favor at Court" and that the royal wishes about singers were made known. The king would contribute a prom-ised sum if both Cuzzoni and Faustina returned, his usual bounty if only Cuzzoni (his favorite) alone, and none at all if only Faustina was hired.[8] In the event, neither of the Rival Queens returned, and the king subscribed his usual £1,000 bounty. Just when the season was underway, a dispute arose between two singers, which, as John, Lord Hervey reported, had to be set-tled by "royal interpositions."[9]

The first season's subscription, according to the fourth Earl of Shaftesbury, was conducted "under the Patronage of The Princess Royal,"[10] although what role Anne, Handel's pupil, actually took is unknown. By the middle of February 1729, Handel's friend Mary Delany reported that the subscription for the upcoming season "goes on very well, to the great satisfaction of all musical folks."[11]

In late September, London was expecting the arrival from France of the singers hired by Handel.[12] As seems to have been customary, the singers per-formed privately before the royal family. On October 23, Princess Amelia wrote to her governess Lady Portland, "We have heard now all the Singers and are mightily satisfied it is the compleatest troop one could have expected."[13] However, Rolli, not a great fan of Handel, shared his decidedly different opinion with Giuseppe Riva in Vienna: "Do you really want me to give you musical news? If everyone were as well satisfied with the company as is the Royal Family, we should have to admit that there never had been such an Opera since Adam and Eve sang Milton's hymns in the Garden of Eden."[14]

Opera resumed after a year-and-a-half interval on December 2 with Handel's *Lotario*. His first new operas of the 1729–30 season were not suc-cesses, and he soon turned to revivals and pasticci. The castrato Bernacchi's failure to please London audiences forced Handel to approach Senesino. Through Francis Colman, Senesino's services were obtained in August 1730 for 1,400 guineas.[15] He returned to London in October to replace Bernacchi and appeared with great success in two revivals in the 1730–31 season.

The years 1732–33 saw renewed interest by theater managers and audi-ences in dramatic music sung in English.[16] From March 1732 through May 1733, under the direction of Henry Carey, Thomas Arne, Sr and Jr, and John Frederick Lampe, eight English operas in the Italian style were pro-duced, at times by two competing companies at the Little Theatre in the Haymarket and Lincoln's Inn Fields Theatre. Also part of the initiative was William De Fesch's oratorio *Judith* (February 16, 1733). In the spirit of these undertakings, Aaron Hill, earlier a promoter of Italian opera during Queen Anne's reign, wrote to Handel in December 1732 imploring him to turn to composing dramatic music in English to "deliver us from our *Italian* bondage; and demonstrate, that *English* is soft enough for Opera."[17]

Just before these English companies started up was an event that would prove a milestone in Handel's career. On February 23, 1732, the first of three private performances of his *Esther* (composed for James Brydges, the future Duke of Chandos, and probably first performed at Cannons in 1718 and 1720)[18] was presented at the Crown and Anchor Tavern by Bernard Gates, using for most of the singers members of the Chapel Royal and the Westminster choir. The first oratorio publicly given in Britain apparently was presented with stage action, "after the Manner of the Ancients," with the choruses placed between the stage and the orchestra.[19]

According to Charles Burney, Princess Anne asked Handel to produce *Esther* himself, "exhibited in action at the Opera-house in the Hay-market."[20] But before he could do so, another pirated version was produced at the York Buildings on April 20. To undercut the competition and boost his own production, Handel revised and expanded his original, which premiered on May 2; there was no stage action and the music was "disposed after the Manner of the Coronation Service."[21]

Two performances in May 1732 of *Acis and Galatea* (originally produced by Handel for James Brydges in 1718) as part of Thomas Arne's English productions in May 1732 likewise prompted Handel to mount an expanded production of his own work on June 10. Fleshed out with arias from his Italian cantata *Aci, Galatea e Polifemo* and the *Brockes Passion*, this *Acis and Galatea* was a bilingual production with only two of the characters and the chorus singing in English. It was given with scenery and decorations, but no stage action. In September, as part of a series of benefit concerts, Maurice Greene produced a short English oratorio *The Song of Deborah and Barak*, which was no doubt a spur for Handel to tackle the same subject for a new oratorio *Deborah* first performed on March 17, 1733.[22]

Handel's first public productions of dramatic music in English were largely a response to English works mounted by other concert promoters appealing to audience interest in English dramatic music. His primary interest for almost another decade remained Italian opera. Rather than a sudden volte-face with *Deborah*, Handel only gradually turned to oratorio and disengaged from Italian opera (see Epilogue).

Political satire and the Second Academy

During the Handel–Heidegger partnership, Bolingbroke and the *Craftsman* continued their well-honed technique of finding parallels between the operatic and political worlds that could be turned into satiric allegories against Walpole. As the dominant figure in London's music life, and perhaps because he shared Walpole's corpulence and favor with the royal family, Handel was a natural surrogate for Walpole. These satires have often been taken uncritically as evidence of the public's animus against Handel or as sources of biographical evidence. The thrust of these satires, as their publication in an opposition periodical should indicate, was part of the ongoing campaign to discredit Robert Walpole by means of theater–ministry parallels. It is Walpole who is demeaned by the suggestion that the world of politics is little different from the opera world at the Haymarket, although in the case of the *Deborah*–Excise satire, the public anger at Handel's raising ticket prices seems accurately invoked.

Strada and the Belloni letter

A minor squabble involving Handel's singer Anna Strada del Pò, her husband Aurilio del Pò, and the composer Giovanni Bononcini was turned by Bolingbroke into an elaborate attempt to discredit Walpole's practice of tarring the opposition with the brush of Jacobitism.[23] Bolingbroke announces that the lead essay in the *Craftsman* for August 12, 1732, is a commentary on "*the Pedantry of Politicks*," which, "of all Sorts of *Pedantry*" in learning or taste, is the worst for "the pernicious Effects" it often produces.[24] The Political Pedant concerns himself with treaties and negotiations, subjects not to be trifled with like mere systems of philosophy.

As an example of the "Pitch of Absurdity" to which political pedantry can lead even sober persons, Bolingbroke prints a letter supposedly from a Countryman and admirer of Bononcini. The Countryman writes of going up to London recently to hear "some Musick" of Bononcini at the opera house. Disappointed in the performance, he went to pass the evening in conversation with some fellow music-lovers. The conversation turned to various stories about "the *two late famous Antagonists*" Faustina and Cuzzoni and then to Bononcini's concert about which there was a diversity of opinions why it was not continued. One music lover put the blame for the failure squarely on Strada's husband and read aloud Aurilio del Pò's notice from the *Daily Post* for June 9, 1732:

Whereas Signor Bononcini intends after the Serenata composed by Mr. Handel has been performed, to have one of his own at the Opera-house, and has desired Signora Strada to sing in that Entertainment:

Aurelio del Po, Husband of the said Signora Strada, thinks it incumbent on him to acquaint the Nobility and Gentry, that he shall ever think himself happy in every Opportunity wherein he can have the Honour to contribute to their Satisfaction;

but with respect to this particular Request of Signor Bononcini, he hopes he shall be permitted to decline complying with it, for Reasons best known to the said Aurelio del Po and his Wife; and therefore the said Aurelio del Po flatters himself that the Nobility and Gentry will esteem this a sufficient Cause for his Non-compliance with Signor Bononcini's Desire; and likewise judge it to be a proper Answer to whatever the Enemies of the said Aurelio del Po may object against him or his Wife upon this Occasion.[25]

The story the Countryman relates has a basis in fact. Handel presented *Acis and Galatea* at the Haymarket Theatre on June 10, 13, 17, and 20, 1732; and Bononcini planned to produce a "Pastoral Entertainment" at the same theater later, which was widely announced in the newspapers for June 24.[26] The day before the run of *Acis and Galatea* began, newspapers did print del Pò's notice that was read aloud to the company. It is not known why del Pò did not wish his wife to sing in Bononcini's serenata; perhaps he did not want to disoblige Handel, in whose company she was a regular performer, by singing for a competing concert. After Handel's run of *Acis and Galatea*, Bononcini did present a single performance of his pastoral entertainment, given by royal command and attended by members of the royal family.[27]

Unraveling how the remainder of the Countryman's letter about Bononcini's serenata involved opposition politics requires reviewing the scandal involving the Charitable Corporation that struck London and the House of Commons earlier that year. This scandal was one of several that were held up as examples of the fraud and corruption of Walpole's ministry. Chartered on December 22, 1707, the Charitable Corporation provided relief for the industrious, deserving poor by providing them small sums at legal interest upon pledges.[28] In October 1731, the cashier George Robinson, the warehouse keeper John Thomson, and one of the managers of the Corporation fled to France. It was discovered that these three and three directors (including Archibald Grant and Sir Robert Sutton) had embezzled upwards of £453,000 of shareholder money.

In February 1732, the Commons was petitioned to investigate the frauds and provide relief to the sufferers. Robinson and Thomson were declared felons and their estates forfeited; for their roles in the frauds, Robinson, Sutton, and Grant were expelled from the Commons.[29] On May 16, while the Commons committee was in the midst of its investigations, the committee chairman received several letters from the Parisian banker Robert Arbuthnot. One letter was from John Angelo Belloni, the Rome banker for the Stuarts, dated May 4, 1732 (NS), to the committee investigating the frauds. The letters were laid before the House, and a committee appointed to translate Belloni's letter from the French.[30]

Arbuthnot reported that Belloni had secured Thomson's arrest in Rome, obtained all his effects and full disclosure of his actions, and sent to him all Thomson's papers with orders to his friends to deliver up his effects.[31] However, these papers were only on deposit with Arbuthnot until Thomson's conditions, spelled out in the memorandum, were met. Thomson wanted his debts paid; in return, his books and papers would lead to the recovery of tens of thousands of pounds.

It was Belloni's letter addressed to the parliamentary committee that became the center of interest (given here in the official translation):

> Gentlemen,
>
> It is with much Pleasure, that *I* embrace an Opportunity, which hath presented itself, to shew *my* Esteem and *my* Affection for the *English Nation*, in contributing to the Advantage of many Persons of the said Kingdom; and consequently to the Satisfaction of the Parliament, and of the Nation itself.
>
> As the Frauds, which have been committed in the Management of the Charitable Corporation, have made much Noise every where, *we have here* been touched in a lively Manner with the Evils which they have occasioned; and *we are sensible* of the Interest that the Nation hath in their Remedy, which could not be effected, but by seizing of the Person, the Papers, the Books and Effects of the *Sieur Thomson*, to which the Parliament had not as yet been able to attain.

Then Belloni describes how Thomson was arrested and repeats the conditions that must be met before Thomson's papers are handed over to the committee.

> Having thus *acquitted myself of my Commission*, nothing remains for me, but to intreat you to be persuaded of my *Respect for the Nation*, and the *Ambition which I shall always have to contribute to its Advantage.*
> I have the Honour to be, Gentlemen,
> Your most Humble, and most Obedient Servant,
> *John Angelo Belloni.*[32]

From the persons involved (Arbuthnot was said to be an avowed Jacobite and Belloni to be the Pretender's banker in Rome), the arrest of Thomson only to protect him rather than return him to England, and Thomson's papers being turned over only on certain evasive conditions, Parliament saw the whole affair as a contrivance of the Pretender to show his zeal in having justice done for the English people. On May 23, the Commons declared Belloni's letter to be

> an insolent and audacious Libel, attempting by false and insidious insinuations, to impose upon the Parliament, and *British* Nation … to amuse the unhappy Sufferers of the Charitable Corporation with vain and deceitful Hopes of Relief; that the said

Paper is in itself absurd and contradictory, conceived, at the Beginning, in Terms, and in the Stile, of Power and Authority … but concluding in the Person and Character of a private Banker of *Rome* … and that this whole Transaction appears to be a scandalous Artifice, calculated purely to delude the Unhappy, and to disguise and conceal the wicked Practices of the professed Enemies to his Majesty's Person, Crown, and Dignity.[33]

On June 1, the ministerial *Free Briton* gave up all news and advertising to devote its full four-page issue to use the Belloni letter to discredit Jacobitism. The ministry's propaganda campaign was spread in newspapers and by broadsides throughout the kingdom.[34]

William Arnall, the ministerial author and editor of the *Free Briton*, grants that the mismanagement of the Charitable Corporation was a villainy worse than the South Sea Bubble because the sufferers were the common people who trusted all their savings to the Corporation. The person protecting this "*Spoiler of his Majesty's Subjects*" is none other than the Pretender – an enemy of the government and British liberty. Arnall claims that Thomson had plundered the Corporation for the benefit of the Jacobites and that his patrons in Paris were also notorious Jacobites.

By philological analysis, Arnall demonstrates Belloni's letter was written by the Pretender:

the Letter is divided into *two Parts*, the *first* of which runs in the Particle *on*,[35] and is in the Style of great Authority; for which Reason *on* hath been rendered [in the Parliamentary translation] in the *first Person plural*, or the *Style Royal*. The second Part uses the Particle, *Je*, or *I*, the *first Person singular*, and is writ in the Style and Character of a *private Banker* at *Rome*.[36]

A mere banker, Arnall claims, would not presume to address Parliament and Great Britain, to arrest Thomson in Rome, provide him protection, and arrange to restore his papers to Parliament. The Belloni letter, Arnall continues, was designed to establish "a *Canal of Correspondence* between the Pretender and the *British House of Commons*."

The Belloni letter featured in ministerial and opposition polemics. In three consecutive issues that June, the *Grub-street Journal* used the letter as part of its ongoing campaign of quibbling and fault finding with ministerial writers.[37] The first issue disputes on grammatical grounds Arnall's attempt to render *on* in "the *first Person Plural*, or the *style Royal*" and to show its use is "altogether inconsistent with *the style of great authority*." The other two issues deny that Thomson was a notorious Jacobite or that the Pretender had designs to share in the plunder of the Charitable Corporation.

With Arnall's *Free Briton* paper in the background, we can follow the remainder of the Countryman's letter and find the point of Bolingbroke's satire about political pedantry. After del Pò's notice from the *Daily Post* was read, a fat, elderly gentleman in the company astounded the others with his heated assertions that the *Daily Post* notice is no *"very innocent Advertisement"* from "a poor *Italian*, who lets out his Wife to sing for Hire." Mimicking Arnall's philological analysis, he asks,

Pray observe the Words, and the Manner in which this Paragraph is drawn up. – "*He thinks it incumbent upon Him to acquaint the* Nobility *and* Gentry" (Don't you mark the Pompousness of the Style?) "*that He shall ever think Himself happy in every Opportunity, wherein He can have the* Honour *to contribute to their Satisfaction*;" (pray observe how artfully He introduces it!) "*but hopes He shall be permitted to decline complying with this Request of* Bononcini, *for Reasons Best Known to the said* Aurelio del Pò *and his Wife*;" What Dignity! What Authority discovers itself in every Line?[38]

The fat, elderly gentleman is incredulous the other gentleman insists the letter is "*No* Libel … *no Attempt against the Government!*" An old lady hastily interrupts and guesses the identity of the writer:

as if every Body did not know who was meant by *Aurelio del Po*; but He should have cloak'd it better, if He design'd it should pass. Every Body knows whose Name begins with a *P.* and every Body knows that it is pronounc'd in the Beginning like those two Letters *P.O.* [i.e., Pulteney]. What! I suppose We shall hear, by and by, that Mr. *P.* is no Enemy to his Country; though all the World knows that He is for suspending the *Habeas Corpus Act*; for *Pensionary Parliaments*; for arbitrary Power in the *Crown*; for *Corruption* and *Taxes*; for a *general Excise, a standing Army*, and all the *bad Things* one can possible think of.

Here the Countryman breaks in, thinking the old lady mistaken, since the description seems "the very Reverse of *that Gentleman's* Character." Bolingbroke, of course, expects alert readers of the *Craftsman* would recognize the irony: these characterizations are not of William Pulteney, but are a litany of stock opposition charges against Walpole. Asked by the Countryman how she knew this about Pulteney, the old lady answered,

have We not the Blessings of a *Whig Ministry*; and are not the *Whig Principles* directly opposite to *such Measures*? … nothing can be plainer; for if He [Pulteney] opposes a *Whig Ministry*, must not He of Course be for every Thing, that is contrary to *Whig Principles*?

Here Bolingbroke mocks a ministry that attacks the opposition while at the same time claims to be upholding true Whig principles.

At this point the fat, elderly gentlemen rouses himself and says he can prove "nobody could pen this Advertisement but the *Pretender* Himself" – at which point half the company burst out in loud laughter. Undeterred, the Countryman continues,

but it is evident to me that this *Aurelio* – Why, did you never hear of *Marcus Aurelius*, the famous Statue on a Horseback; and what, I pray, is a Man on Horseback; but a *Chevalier?* Now, We all know who the *Chevalier* is [the Pretender].

At this, a sober fellow who had sat quietly in a corner cried out,

Ay, 'tis plain, … 'tis very plain that *Aurelio* stands for the *Pretender*, *Po* for the *Pope*, and *Del* for the *Devil*. Heaven shield us from such Advertisements!

A young lady demurs, but the fat, elderly gentleman continues that every word shows that no one could write with such elegance but the Pretender:

Who could assume so much *Dignity* and *Majesty* but *one*, who calls Himself a *Monarch* … And would an *Italian*, would a *singing Woman's Husband* presume to make Use of such a Stile, or have the Insolence to *offer Terms*, in this Manner, to the *Nobility* and *Gentry* of *Great Britain?* No, no, it must be the *Pretender*, who hath endeavoured to impose upon the Nation, under this Disguise, and to open a Correspondence with the *Royal Academy of Musick*.

The Countryman closes his letter leaving it up to Mr. D'Anvers how to expose and put a stop to such "a strange Way of forcing Constructions."

In the years leading to 1732, there were signs of Jacobite threat to Britain. By 1730, the Anglo-French Alliance was breaking down, and in spring 1731, the international scene was tense as British, French, and Spanish fleets were arming. In April, Secretary of State Newcastle believed, "It is certain the Jacobites begin to conceive hopes of France, and thereupon the greatest attention imaginable should be given to that."[39] At the end of June 1731, the press was reporting movements of French troops toward the Channel. Reports that the Pretender and other Jacobites had been invited to Paris fueled fears of a French-led Jacobite invasion. Britain experienced a brief war panic: Sir Charles Wager was ordered to assemble a squadron, and troops were deployed along the coast.[40] In the spring of 1732, diplomatic reports that the Pretender was preparing for a journey led to speculation he would board a ship at Barcelona and lead a Spanish fleet against Britain. In response to the Spanish and French naval preparations, British naval strength was increased that summer.

The Commons' and *Free Briton*'s construing the Belloni letter as a Jacobite intrigue served Walpole by raising fears of a Jacobite threat to the Hanoverian succession. Having once benefited from exploiting the

Atterbury Plot, Walpole continued to alarm the nation with charges of plots and invasions, while ministerial papers constantly tried to discredit the opposition by charging that it served Jacobite interests and enemies of the Protestant succession. As Speaker Onslow later remarked, Walpole pursued with great delight "his plan of having everybody to be deemed a Jacobite who was not a professed and known Whig."[41]

In August 1732, then, the fat, elderly gentleman's outlandish demonstration that Aurilio del Pò is the Pretender satirizes the tactics used in the *Free Briton* to prove Belloni's letter originated with the Pretender; it defends the opposition by disarming by ridicule the ministry's attempt to discredit the opposition by tainting it with Jacobitism. As well, it encourages the practice of reading *Craftsman* allegories as directed at Walpole and the ministry.[42]

Deborah and the Excise

In March 1733, events in the Commons and Haymarket Theatre coincided to yoke Walpole and Handel together as projectors who, each in his way, schemed to fleece their publics. On March 14, Walpole unveiled to the Commons details of his Excise plan to achieve a more thorough and efficient revenue service by collecting duties on tobacco and wine when they were withdrawn from bonded customs warehouses for retail, rather than subjecting them to duties upon import. The proposal would require an additional 150 excise officers who could search the homes and shops of merchants for contraband; a system of judges would be set up to adjudicate disputes between merchants and excisemen.[43] Walpole argued the plan would remove incentives for smuggling, eliminate fraud, recoup money otherwise lost to the Treasury, and benefit the common trader and consumer through lower prices.

News of the as-yet-unspecified Excise was already circulating well before Parliament sat on January 16, 1733. In the previous October, the opposition unloosed its full arsenal of pamphlets, newspaper articles, ballads, and prints to vilify Walpole and the Excise, flooding the country with a torrent of propaganda that deliberately misrepresented almost all aspects of the undisclosed plan and used the occasion to arouse patriotic resentment against oppression.[44]

To opposition propagandists, the Excise meant loss of liberties, increased power of the ministry and Crown, a danger to trade, an increased tax burden on the poorer parts of society, tyranny by excisemen, and a new system of courts. Propagandists raised the specter of a country overrun by an army of excise officers and of merchants hauled before commissions appointed by the Treasury. Through corruption and patronage Walpole would personally benefit from the increased revenue.

A vivid expression of the fears aroused by the Excise is conveyed in a print illustrating a ballad *Britannia Excisa*. Drawing a chariot bearing Walpole is "that monster the Excise! that plan of arbitrary power!" Some of its mouths gulp down all possible excisable articles, while another mouth spews back a stream of coins into Walpole's outstretched hand.[45] One member of the ministry, writing to an ambassador abroad, reacted to the campaign of disinformation: "There is not a Cobler but is made to believe that he is to pay an Excise before he eats his bread & Cheese and drinks his pot of Beer."[46]

While the Excise was before the Commons, mobs assembled in the Court of Requests, the lobby, and stairs of Westminster. City, trading, and merchant groups presented petitions and threatened unconstitutional actions to influence their MPs. Across the country, mobs demonstrated, meetings of merchants and importers resolved to oppose the plan, ministerial journals and pamphlets were burned, and instructions and deputations were sent to MPs.[47] Walpole dismissed the multitude of petitioners as "sturdy beggars,"[48] an epithet that became an opposition watchword demonstrating Walpole's contempt for London's merchants.

Walpole carried the first resolution on March 14, 1733, by 265 votes to 204. But support gradually waned: on its first reading, the bill carried, 232 to 176, but support fell on further procedural divisions. On April 10, the ministry prevailed by only seventeen votes against the City of London's petition opposing the Excise. The second reading of the bill was scheduled for the next day; but in the face of fierce public outcry and dwindling parliamentary support, and convinced his majority would vanish, Walpole abandoned the Excise by postponing the second reading until a day that Parliament would not sit.[49]

At news of Walpole's abandoning the Excise, the country rejoiced. Bonfires and illuminations burned, bells rang, and Walpole blazed in effigy. The populace broke out into such rejoicing "as went beyond all Limits of Decency, and even to Licentiousness."[50] For months after, pamphlets still maligned Walpole and the proposal and numerous anti-Excise plays and ballad operas reached the stage.[51]

Three days after the Excise was presented to the Commons, Handel outraged his own public at the March 17, 1733, premiere of *Deborah* by not honoring their season tickets and charging doubled ticket prices. Contemporary accounts of the affair differ slightly but agree on the town's displeasure with Handel. According to the memoir by Handel's friend the fourth Earl of Shaftesbury,

In the Spring of 1733, Mr Handell finding that the Oratorio of Esther, had been well received, the Oratorio of Deborah, which he [had not] reckoned into the number of the 50 Opera's Subscribed for, and – as he had taken great Pains, and as this was a new kind of Musick attended with some Extraordinary Expence, and moreover for his own Benefit, he took double Prices, vizt a Guinea for Pit & Box's. This Indiscreet Step disgusted the Town, and he had a very thin House.[52]

At the end of March, Anne, Viscountess Irwin, reported on the premiere of *Deborah* to her father:

last week we had an Oratorio: Compos'd by Hendel out of ye Story of Barak & Deborah ye latter of wch name it bears[.] Hendel thought encourag'd by the Princess Royal it had merit enough to deserve a Guinea & ye first time it was perform'd att ye price, exclusive of subscribers tickets, there was but a 120 people in the House: the subscribers being refus'd unless they woud pay a Guinea they insisting upon ye right of their silver tickets forc'd into the House & carry'd their point[;] this gave occasion to the eight lines I send you in wch they have done Hendel the Honour to joyn him in a dialogue with Sr Robert Walpole. I was att this entertainment on teusday [*sic*] [;] 'tis excessive noisy a vast number of instruments & Voices who all perform att a time, and is in musick what I fancy a French ordinary in Conversation.[53]

The eight lines enclosed (not preserved) are probably similar to those quoted below. From Lady Irwin's account it is clear that Handel was not counting *Deborah* among the operas the subscribers expected admission to on Saturday, the usual night of the opera.

The Prussian envoy to Great Britain, Count Degenfeld, wrote back to King Frederick William I on April 17 and remarked on Handel's unpopularity and the subsequent boycott:

As the Musical Composer Hendel would needs set the operas [the oratorio *Deborah*] at a higher price, and receive a whole Guinea for coming in, instead of ½ an one, so this displeased the frequenters of operas in such manner, that nobody would go to them unless they were put upon the old foot again, and this he was forced to comply with.[54]

In Degenfeld's account we see confusion about the genre of *Deborah* and oratorios. A report in the *Daily Journal* also refers to "the Opera called *Deborah*."[55]

Several circumstances may explain why Handel denied admission to subscribers and raised ticket prices. The advertisements for *Deborah* read in part: "N.B. *This is the last Dramatick Performance that will be exhibited at the King's Theatre till after Easter*. The House to be fitted up and illuminated in a new and particular manner."[56] A little-noted report in the *Daily Advertiser* amplifies Handel's reason for the price rise:

On Saturday Night last [March 17] the Royal Family were present at the King's Theatre in the Haymarket, to see Mr. Handell's new Oratorio; an Entertainment, perhaps, the most magnificent that has ever been exhibited on an English Theatre … The Disposition of the Performers was in a Taste beyond what has been attempted. There was a very great Number of Instruments by the best Hands, and such as would properly accompany three Organs. The Pit and Orchestre were cover'd as at an Assembly, and the whole House illuminated in a new and most beautiful manner.[57]

Several points are worth noting from these printed notices. Handel had gone to some expense to light the house and engage a large number of performers (recall Lady Irwin's comment about excessive noise). The disposition of the performers coupled with the pit and orchestra being covered (i.e., covered with planking to be level with the stage) suggest Handel reduced the capacity of the main floor. The expense for decorations and reduced capacity suggest the need for increased revenue. In the event, like Walpole, Handel relented in the face of public pressure. When productions of *Deborah* resumed after Holy Week, the advertisements stated: "The Silver Tickets of the Subscribers to the Opera will be admitted," and the gallery tickets were priced at five shillings.[58]

What was seen as Handel's greed in raising ticket prices prompted two satires comparing *Deborah* to Walpole's equally ill-fated Excise. In mid March, an epigram (such as the one Lady Irwin sent) reporting a dialogue between Walpole and Handel was circulating in London.[59]

The following *Epigram*, which has run about in Manuscript for two or three Days past, does not want *Epigrammatick wit*. It needs no Explanation to People who know what is done in the World.

> *A Dialogue between two Projectors.*
> Quoth W— [Walpole] to H—l [Handel] *shall we two agree,*
> *And Join in a Scheme of Excise*? *H.* Caro si.
>   Of what Use is your Sheep if your Shepherd can't sheer him?
> At the *Hay-Market* I, you at *We—er* [Westminster]
>   *W. Hear Him.*
> Call'd to Order the Seconds appear'd in their Place,
> One fam'd for his Morals [Sir William Yonge], and one
>   for his Face [Heidegger];[60]
> In half they succeeded, in half they were crost;
> The *Tobacco* was sav'd, but poor *Deborah* lost.

The increased prices for *Deborah* were indeed lost. The phrase "the Tobacco was sav'd" makes sense if, at the time of the epigram's writing in mid March, the Excise seemed likely to pass.

The Handel/Walpole–*Deborah*/Excise conceit is expanded in an elaborate allegory by Bolingbroke that appeared the following month in the *Craftsman*.[61] Although Handel, *Deborah*, and the Haymarket Theatre are the literal basis of the allegory, in the guise of describing Handel's imperious behavior, the allegory raises before the reader all the stock opposition charges against Walpole and the Excise. Bolingbroke's allegory reveals considerable knowledge about the opera company and its recent management; but distortions, embellishments, or additions are blended into the narrative that are not appropriate to Handel and *Deborah* and that actually only apply to Walpole and the Excise.

The context and target of the allegory were clear to contemporaries. When the *Bee* reprinted Bolingbroke's allegory, it hinted at the real target, Walpole, introducing it as

an Account of an Attempt which has been lately made by the famous Mr. *H—l*, upon the Liberties and Properties of all who love Operas: It may not be amiss to inform our Country Readers, that tho' there is some *Foundation* for a Letter of this kind from what happen'd lately at the Oratorio of *Deborah*, (upon which Accident he may see an Epigram in our *Bee, No. VIII* [recte: VII].) yet that Mr. *D'Anvers* is generally thought to have something more in his View.[62]

The principal parallels used in the allegory follow (although occasionally not used consistently) and should make the meaning clear.[63]

Handel = Walpole

oratorios/*Deborah* = the Excise scheme

the opera/Haymarket = government/Treasury/customs

orchestra/musicians = Members of Parliament

Handel's partner Heidegger = Walpole's brother Horatio

annual subscribers = merchants

Handel's doorkeepers at the opera = customs officers

audience/town = the nation/Parliament

music = government measures

Montagnana = King George

Strada = Queen Caroline

judges of music = Excise judges

auditors at the opera = MPs who first voted for the Excise

Even if the allegory did not appear in the *Craftsman*, the changes rung on stock opposition themes in Bolingbroke's introduction and the directed target of the application are unmistakable.

SIR,

… As I know your Zeal for Liberty, I thought I could not address better than to you the following exact Account of the noble Stand, lately made by the polite Part of the World, in Defence of their Liberties and Properties, against the open Attacks and bold Attempts of Mr. *H—l* upon both. I shall singly relate the Fact, and leave you, who are better able than I am, to make what Inferences, or Applications may be proper.[64]

Bolingbroke begins by alluding to Walpole's principal role in the ministry, his mastery of government by controlling Parliament by placemen, and his great wealth amassed while at the head of the Treasury. Also alluded to are common opposition charges: that George II was manipulated by the queen and Walpole and that Walpole promoted servile placemen and officials in preference to more talented ones – all of which are said to have parallels in Handel's management of the opera at the Haymarket.

The Rise and Progress of Mr. *H—l's* Power and Fortune are too well known for me now to relate. Let it suffice to say that he was grown so insolent upon the sudden and undeserved Increase of both, that he thought nothing ought to oppose his imperious and extravagant Will. He had, for some Time, governed the *Opera's* [ministry], and modell'd the *Orchestre* [Parliament], without the least Controul. No *Voices*, no *Instruments* [government appointees] were admitted, but such as flatter'd his Ears, though they shock'd those of the Audience. *Wretched Scrapers* [placemen] were put above the *best Hands* in the *Orchestre*. No *Musick* [government measures] but *his own* was to be allowed,[65] though every Body was weary of it; and he had the Impudence to assert, *that there was no Composer in* England *but Himself.* Even *Kings* and *Queens* [singers] were to be content with whatever low Characters he was pleased to assign them, as is evident in the Case of Signior *Montagnana*[66] [King George II]; who, though a *King*, is always obliged to act (except an angry,[67] rumbling Song, or two) the most insignificant Part of the whole Drama [government]. This Excess and Abuse of Power soon disgusted the Town; his Government grew odious; and his *Opera's* [Treasury] grew empty. However this Degree of Unpopularity and general Hatred, instead of humbling him, only made him more furious and desperate. He resolved to make one last Effort to establish his Power and Fortune by Force, since he found it now impossible to hope for it from the good Will of Mankind. In order to [do] This, He form'd a *Plan*, without consulting any of his *Friends*, (if he has any) and declared that at a proper Season he would communicate it to the Publick; assuring us, at the same Time, that it would be very much for the Advantage of the Publick in general, and of *Opera's* [the Treasury] in particular. Some People suspect that he had settled it previously with Signora *Strada del Po*[68] [Queen Caroline], who is much in his Favour; but all, that I can advance with certainty, is, that he had concerted it with a *Brother of his own* [Heidegger], in whom he places a most undeserved Confidence.

A lengthy section (not quoted here) satirizes Horatio Walpole and his services as minister abroad. The allegory then continues:

Notwithstanding all these and many more Objections, Mr. *H—l*, by and with the Advice of *this Brother*, at last produces his *Project* [*Deborah*/Excise]; resolves to cram it down the Throats of the Town; prostitutes *great* and *awful Names*, as the Patrons of it; and even does not scruple to insinuate that they are to be Sharers of the Profit. His *Scheme* set forth in Substance, that the late Decay of *Opera's* [revenue] was owing to their *Cheapness*, and to the great *Frauds* committed by the *Doorkeepers* [customs officers]; that the *annual Subscribers* [merchants] were a Parcel of *Rogues*, and made an ill Use of their Tickets, by often *running* two into the Gallery[69] [underreporting the weight of cargoes]; that to obviate these Abuses he had contrived a Thing, that was better than an *Opera* [customs], call'd an *Oratorio* [the Excise]; to which none should be admitted, but by *printed Permits*, or Tickets of one Guinea each, which should be distributed out of *Warehouses of his own*, and by *Officers of his own naming*; which *Officers* could not so reasonably be supposed to cheat in the Collection of *Guineas*, as the *Door-keepers* [customs officers] in the Collection of *half Guineas*;[70] and lastly, that as the very being of *Opera's* [government] depended upon *Him singly*, it was just that the Profit arising from hence should be for his *own Benefit*. He added, indeed, one Condition, to varnish the whole a little; which was, that if any Person should think himself aggriev'd, and that the *Oratorio* was not worth the Price of the *Permit*, he should be at Liberty to appeal to *three Judges of Musick* [excise officers who would adjudicate disputes], who should be oblig'd, within the Space of seven Years at farthest,[71] finally to determine the same; provided always that the said *Judges* should be of his Nomination, and known to like no other Musick but his.[72]

This last point on appealing Excise decisions raised a prominent opposition theme: the loss of British liberties. William Pulteney claimed that under the Excise, merchants would have been "tried in a *summary* and *arbitrary* Manner by Judges whom the Crown shall please, from time to time, to appoint."[73] That is, appeals would be to judges named by Walpole. The opposition objected that a merchant charged with violating the Excise had to prove his own innocence and had no right of trial by jury.[74]

The allegory continues:

The Absurdity, Extravagancy, and Oppression of *this Scheme* disgusted the whole Town. Many of the most constant Attenders of the *Opera's* resolv'd absolutely to renounce them, rather than go to them under such Extortion and Vexation.[75] They exclaim'd against the *insolent and rapacious Projector of this Plan*. The King's old and sworn Servants, of the two Theatres of *Drury-Lane* and *Covent-Garden* [the two houses of Parliament], reap'd the Benefit of this general Discontent, and were resorted to in Crowds [crowds that gathered outside Parliament], by way of

Opposition to the *Oratorio*. Even the fairest Breasts were fir'd with Indignation against this *new Imposition*. Assemblies, Cards, Tea, Coffee, and all other Female Batteries [deputations, pamphlets, and petitions] were vigorously employ'd to defeat the *Project*, and destroy the *Projector*. These joint Endeavours of all Ranks and Sexes succeeded so well, that the *Projector* had the Mortification to see but a very thin Audience at his *Oratorio*: and of about two hundred and sixty odd, that it consisted of, it is notorious that not ten paid for their *Permits*, but, on the contrary, had them given them, and Money into the Bargain for coming to keep him in Countenance [Walpole's bribes to MPs].[76]

The thin audience of about "two hundred and sixty odd" are the thin majority that voted for the Excise on its first reading in the Commons. These, it is imputed, were merely Walpole's placemen, beholden to him because of their appointments or seats they had won through Treasury influence.

The concluding section purports to describe Handel, but here the guise is much thinner and Bolingbroke is defaming Walpole:

This Accident [loss of the Excise/boycott of *Deborah*], they say, has thrown Him into a deep *Melancholy*, interrupted sometimes by *raving Fits*; in which he fancies he sees ten thousand *Opera* devils coming to tear Him to Pieces; then he breaks out into frantick, incoherent Speeches; muttering *sturdy Beggars, Assassination*, &c. In these delirious Moments, he discovers a particular Aversion for the *City*. He calls them all a Parcel of *Rogues*, and asserts that the *honestest Trader among them deserves to be hang'd* – It is much question'd whether he will recover; at least, if he does, it is not doubted but he will seek for a Retreat in his *own Country* [Norfolk/Germany] from the general Resentment of the Town.

Handel's imagined return to Germany parallels Walpole's customary trips to Houghton in Norfolk for the summer.[77]

Commentators frequently miss the fact that Walpole is the real subject of Bolingbroke's allegory. On the basis of the allegory, wrote one, "Handel was apparently subject to fits of raving about the treatment *Deborah* received," and another that Handel was exhibiting "mental imbalance and irrational behavior … in the wake of *Deborah*'s failed premiere."[78] Contemporaries did attest Walpole's disappointment at abandonment of the Excise, but nothing approaching raving fits or delusions as imputed with malice by Bolingbroke. John, Lord Hervey witnessed how after the vote on the Excise, Walpole

was never more struck with any defeat or less able to disguise his being so than this night. He stood some time after the House was up, leaning against the table with his hat pulled over his eyes … whilst his enemies with the gaiety of so many bridegrooms seemed as just entering on the enjoyment of what they had been so long pursuing.[79]

William Pitt recalled Walpole gave up the Excise "with sorrow, with tears in his eyes, when he saw, and not till he saw it impossible to carry it through the House."[80]

The government MP Sir Thomas Robinson described Walpole's exit through the Court of Requests, where the

lower sort of people, flushed with victory and drink … insulted and made several attempts on the projector [Walpole], and many blows past on both sides. It begun by a person seizing him by a great loose coat he had over his shoulder, which giving way saved him; otherways in all probability he might have been pulled down, and if so he must certainly have been trod to death.[81]

An opposition tract has his foes delighted in imagining a Walpole afraid of assassination: "Nothing renders the *Projector* more ridiculous than his continual Apprehensions of *Plots* and *Assassination*; which seem to haunt Him by Night and by Day, like a bad Conscience, and disturb all his golden Dreams of Power."[82] After citing some of Walpole's previous fears about assassinations, the tract continues: "He now concluded that his Time was come. The Case of Julius Cæsar ran strangely in his Head, and possess'd Him with a full Opinion that the *Nones of April* would prove as fatal to *Him*, as the *Ides of March* were to the other." The comparison of Walpole to Julius Caesar was a common opposition innuendo hinting that Walpole was a tyrant and threat to liberty.[83]

Walpole's fears of assassination were not unfounded; veiled calls for it had spread in the opposition press, set off possibly inadvertently several months earlier in *Fog's Weekly Journal* (no. 223, February 10, 1733), whose writer relates how the Revolution of Portugal in 1640 transferred to the House of Braganza the crown of that kingdom, ruled by a vice-queen under the dominance of Miguel Vasconcellos, an archetypal evil minister and enemy to his country, whose power over the queen, devising new methods of taxation, and diverting revenue to his own use, make Vasconcellos personate Walpole. The Portuguese revolution was effected by citizens storming the palace and discovering the minister cowering in a clothes press beneath a heap of paper. Speechless from fear, he was shot in the head – "by that Means they prevented Tyranny from ever rising again." The writer's application to Britain is "that a few Gentlemen of Courage, and publick Spirit, may be able to rescue their Country from Slavery." A ministry tract denounced the issue as "a *Panegyrick upon* Assassinations," inciting a "Party of Ruffians to butcher the Principal Minister," which would transfer the crown to the Pretender.[84] The *Journal* later claimed the ministry had "drawn an harmless inoffensive Letter into Sedition and Defamation."[85]

Fog's letter about Vasconcellos[86] closed with a possibly fictitious anecdote, which the writer says prompted the account of Vasconcellos.

There happen'd an Accident when I was last at the Opera of *Julius Cæsar*, which will serve to explain this Part of *Vasconcellos*'s Character, and from which indeed I took the Hint of writing this Paper. A Piece of the Machinery tumbled down from the Roof of the Theatre upon the Stage just as *Senesino* had chanted forth these Words;
  Cesare non seppe mai, che sia timore.[87]
  Cæsar does not know what Fear is.
The poor Hero was so frightened, that he trembled, lost his Voice, and fell a-crying. – Every Tyrant or Tyrannical Minister is just such a *Cæsar* as *Senesino*.

The opposition's parallel of Walpole with Julius Caesar, joined with Senesino's playing Julius Caesar in the opera, suggests that Walpole, like Vasconcellos, is really timid, easily frightened, and an easy quarry for assassination.

Bolingbroke closes his allegory by appending a slightly different version of the epigram that had been circulating since mid March and signs the letter "P—lo R—li," for Paolo Rolli.[88] The fictional signature was likely Bolingbroke's ruse to have Rolli, someone knowledgeable about operatic matters and an antagonist to Handel, serve as a plausible writer for an attack on Handel.[89]

The political point of Bolingbroke's burlesque on Handel's *Deborah* was apparent to the Walpole apologist John "Orator" Henley, who responded to Bolingbroke's "breaking in on Mr. *Hendel's Oratorio*" three days later in his *Hyp-Doctor*,[90] a periodical undertaken to defend Walpole and abuse, ridicule, and mock the opposition. Henley takes the *Craftsman's* presumed Jacobitism as the key to the *Deborah*–Excise allegory.

Using the Royal Academy as synonymous with the Haymarket Theatre, Henley slightly recasts the allegory by lining up musicians/MPs who are for oratorio/the Royal Academy/ministry/Handel/Walpole against those in favor of opera/Italian music/Jacobitism. The Protestant Handel/Walpole deserves to lead the Royal Academy/ministry because "he gives Time and Note, [and] we are more secure of a Good Harmony." Tory or Jacobite MPs are "*English* blind Fiddlers *out of Play* [office], and disaffected Patriots *out of Tune*" who play the "Unnatural Discord" of "*Romish Sonatas*."

Henley charges it is no proof of the musical quality/Patriotism of a performer/MP for having been turned out from the concert/orchestra/Parliament for clashing with the head of the Royal Academy/ministry/Handel/Walpole. Bolingbroke, a dismissed lord, is a "*broken Fiddler … who would Spoil* the Music [nation's domestic harmony], because he has *no part* in the *Oratorio*/Ministry." With "Orator" Henley, we have for once a ministerial writer taking up the opera house–ministry metaphor favored by opposition writers and turning it against them to charge the opposition with sowing political discontent and advancing the cause of Jacobitism and the Pretender.

The Chesterfield affair

One consequence of the Excise was that George II, presumably at Walpole's instigation, dismissed from regimental posts or household offices peers who had spoken out against it, including the Dukes of Bolton and Montrose and Lords Stair, Cobham, Chesterfield, Clinton, Westmoreland, and Marchmont.[91]

The Earl of Chesterfield's dismissal was quickly put to political use by the opposition. A minor journalistic skirmish began when on April 21, 1733, the *Craftsman* reported in its news column:

On *Friday* [April 13], in last Week, the Day, which gave the finishing Stroke to the *Excise Project* in Parliament, his Grace the Duke of *Grafton* was sent to the Earl of *Chesterfield*, to signify his Majesty's Pleasure to him that he should resign his Staff, as Lord Steward of the Household. The next Morning (as we are inform'd) his Lordship sent it, accompany'd with a very dutiful and respectful Letter to his Majesty.[92]

The *Craftsman* rehearsed Chesterfield's honors and service to the king and nation, and closed with a snipe at the king's petty retribution against a loyal servant: "The World seems greatly astonish'd at so unexpected an Event, and Those, who are most zealous for the present Royal Family, grieve to see so *able* and *faithful a Servant* dismiss'd, in so critical a Conjuncture."

The next issue of the ministerial *Free Briton* (no. 179, April 26, 1733) rebuked the *Craftsman* for using Chesterfield's name and character to censure the king. The writer accused the *Craftsman* of insolence for upbraiding the king's behavior to Chesterfield and of "Invasion of his *personal Liberty*" and "*Royal Dignity*" in a way ill-becoming any private person. It was impudent to claim the world is astonished and grieved that the king would exercise his "undoubted Right to dismiss his Servants at *his own* Pleasure."

In self-vindication, the *Craftsman* (no. 359, May 19, 1733) followed with an elaborate mock legalistic defense against the *Free Briton's* arraignment of "high Crimes and Misdemeanors" and turned it against the ministry: for every good subject has a right to be astonished and grieve over the loss of an able minister such as Chesterfield. The world should really grieve, the writer claims ironically, "that a *great Minister* [Walpole] should be baulk'd in his Design of passing the most beneficial Law in the World" and that "*so unable and so* unfaithful a *Servant*" and "*so worthless a Wretch*" is "*continued in Power.*" The *Free Briton* strung out the controversy in three subsequent issues in May and June,[93] quibbling about a letter Chesterfield sent to the *Free Briton* and charging that the astonishment felt by the *Craftsman* was really that the Excise failed to be the occasion to usher in a new ministry.

While this exchange was running in the press, Handel and Heidegger's 1732–33 opera season was winding down. In his dealings with his musicians, Handel had apparently fallen out with Senesino. On June 2, the *Craftsman* (no. 361) began its news columns with the following item:

> We are credibly inform'd that one Day last Week Mr. *H—d—l*, Director-General of the Opera-House, sent a Message to Signior *Senesino*, the famous *Italian* Singer, acquainting Him that He had no farther Occasion for his Service; and that *Senesino* reply'd the next Day by a Letter, containing a full Resignation of all his Parts in the *Opera*, which He had perform'd for many Years with great Applause. – We hope the polite Mr. *Walsingham* [pseudonym of William Arnall] will give us Leave to observe, upon this Occasion, *that the World seems greatly* Astonish'd *at so unexpected an Event; and that all true Lovers of Musick* Grieve *to see so* fine a Singer *dismiss'd, in so critical a Conjuncture.*

While we should be cautious about accepting this notice as a document of Handel's dismissal of Senesino and his reply,[94] Senesino did announce from the stage his dismissal by Handel after his final performance in *Griselda* on June 9. The *Daily Advertiser* carried a full report:

> After the Performance was over, Signor Senoseni [*sic*] took his Leave of the Audience in a short Speech, acquainting them, as he said with Regret, "That he had now perform'd his last Part on that Stage, and was henceforward discharg'd from any Engagement: He thank'd the Nobility for the Great Honours they had done him in an Applause of so many Years, and assured them, that whenever a Nation to whom he was so greatly obliged, should have any further Commands for him, he would endeavour to obey them."[95]

The *Craftsman* obviously made its report and editorial comment about Handel's dismissal of Senesino such a close paraphrase of its earlier report of the king's dismissal of Chesterfield to antagonize the *Free Briton* and remind the public of the king's retribution against a politician who had spoken out against the unpopular Excise. Added innuendo keeps alive the opera–ministry parallel and implication that the king and Walpole's management of government has sunk to the level of squabbles in the opera house.

Politics of *Sosarme*

One opera from the Second Academy may have been influenced by political concerns. Maintaining good foreign relations may have slightly affected the naming of countries and characters of Handel's *Sosarme, re di Media* (February 15, 1732). At the time he began composing, the opera was set in Coimbra, Portugal, and its title was *Fernando, re di Castiglia.* Winton Dean has noted that after composing the first two acts of the opera, Handel went back, changed the setting to Sardis, and altered all but one of the characters' names before completing the score.[96] The principal plot elements (using the original names) – the rebellion of the rightful heir Alfonso against his father (Dionisio), the minister Altomaro's attempt to place his grandson Sancio on the throne, and the king needing to be rescued by his Castilian neighbor Fernando – would have cast the Portuguese, one of Britain's oldest allies, in an unflattering light. At some point then, Dean suggests, the offensive parallels were drawn to the attention of Handel or his librettist, and Handel altered the location and characters.

With *Sosarme*, we again find that applying the generic expectation that politics is to be found by allegorizing the characters and events in an opera leads to unsatisfactory results. Konrad Sasse offered a reading of *Sosarme* that relates the libretto directly to domestic politics (using the revised character names): "There was great discord at court between the king and the Prince of Wales. Thus the opera is also based on such a conflict between the King Haliate [George II] and his son Argone [Frederick, Prince of Wales]."[97] Sasse's key for *Sosarme* has these analogs: Argone (Prince Frederick), eldest son of Haliate, King of Lydia (King George), by Queen Erenice (Queen Caroline), is jealous that Haliate, under the urging of the evil councilor Altomaro (Walpole) has decided to make as his successor Melo, his natural son by Anagilda and grandson of Altomaro. Argone has raised a civil rebellion against his father and with his followers captured and occupied the palace and capital city, which Haliate is besieging and forcing into starvation. Ultimately, Sosarme, neighboring king of Media, achieves a reconciliation.

Reinhard Strohm, amplifying Sasse's interpretation, argues that the change to Sardis notwithstanding, the opera "still shows a son rebelling against his father, which was interpreted as a reference to George II and the Prince of Wales."[98] Strohm offers no instances of any contemporary actually making such an interpretation. But rebellious sons are so common in opera plots that there is no reason to believe that the father–son conflict is a specific allusion to George II and Frederick.

But the year 1732 is still too early to speak of a royal feud. At the time, relations between George II and Frederick had not openly deteriorated; Frederick still lived with the royal family and, as newspapers regularly reported, attended public events with them (such as chapel, operas, and hunts) and invited them to his concerts and other entertainments. Frederick's well-known defiance of his father, expulsion from St. James's, and establishment of a separate household did not occur until 1737 (see further in Chapter 6).

The differences between the civil war engaged in by the operatic characters in *Sosarme* and the circumstances of Frederick and his father in 1732 are so great as to call the whole allegorical interpretation into doubt. Frederick did not raise a rebellion against his father's palace; George did not have a second wife; and while Altomaro could make an analog to Walpole, and Melo might be seen as a parallel to Frederick's brother, the Duke of Cumberland, the genealogy of Melo makes this implausible. And it is not clear which foreign country would reconcile the king and prince, which rescue in itself would be an insulting suggestion to George.

Finally, it is not clear what Handel or his librettist hoped to achieve by the allegory. Moreover, publically drawing attention to royal family matters and the need for outside rescue for Great Britain would be so offensive that it is implausible that Handel and Heidegger would have any motive to mount an opera that would indict their royal master. While Dean's rationale for the changes in the libretto in the midst of composing *Sosarme* is plausible, any topical allegorization of the affairs of the British royal family is not.

As in the years of the Royal Academy of Music, the *Craftsman* seized on events at the Haymarket and satirically put them to use in its continuing propaganda campaign to harass and ridicule the Walpole ministry. Bolingbroke invented a group of music lovers discussing a letter from Aurelio del Pò relating to Bononcini's pastoral serenata to ridicule the ministry's use of the Belloni letter to tar the opposition as Jacobitical; the allegory on *Deborah* supposedly written by Paolo Rolli rehearses the opposition's charges of Walpole's Excise as a threat to British liberties; and Handel's dismissal of Senesino was used to remind readers of the king's dismissal of an opposition peer, Lord Chesterfield, for speaking out against the Excise.

In the wake of the Excise, the election of 1734 was highly contested and expensive. Walpole won a fifty-seat majority, but the Commons would never again be as compliant as before the Excise. Bolingbroke was unable to reconcile the differences between opposition Whigs and Tories and Jacobites, and the parliamentary opposition could not replicate the momentary success on the Excise issue. Under continuous attack by Walpole's pamphleteers and realizing he was a liability to the opposition, Bolingbroke went into another self-imposed exile in France in May 1735, bitter that despite his efforts on behalf of the opposition there was no hope of being restored to his seat in the Lords. As he wrote to Sir William Wyndham from Paris, "My part is over, and he who remains on the stage after his part is over, deserves to be hissed off."[99]

6 | Rival opera companies and Farinelli in Madrid

The 1732–33 season closed on June 9, 1733, with Senesino's announcement from the stage of his dismissal from the opera by Handel. The following month, Handel took his singers and musicians to Oxford to produce a series of concerts and oratorios as part of the end-of-term Act of Convocation. In the meanwhile, a group of aristocrats disaffected with Handel's management of the opera, and still harboring resentment over the raised ticket prices for *Deborah*, took advantage of Senesino's dismissal and began planning a company to be directed by him that would rescue opera from Handel's domination. Except for the loyal Strada del Pò, Handel's other singers decamped to the new company.

The first mention of the rival opera company, conventionally known as the Opera of the Nobility, is a newspaper notice on June 13:

The Subscribers to the Opera in which Signor Senesino and Signora Cuzzoni are to perform, are desired to meet at Mr. Hickford's Great Room in Panton-street, on Friday next [June 15] by Eleven o'Clock, in order to settle proper Methods for carrying on the Subscription.[1]

The directors set their sights high and sent for Cuzzoni, the rising star Farinelli, and the composer Nicola Porpora.

A general court of the subscribers was called for the following Friday, and the directors announced "the first Call of Ten Guineas on each Subscriber, to be collected by Mr. Joseph Haynes."[2] Presumably, the total subscription was the customary twenty guineas for about fifty performances.

Despite Handel's being occupied preparing for his concerts in Oxford, Handel and Heidegger began their subscription for the following season, as reported on June 22:

We hear that Subscriptions are actually in great forwardness for having two different Opera's next Winter, one at the King's Theatre in the Haymarket, under the Direction of Messrs. Handel and Heydegger, and the other to be at one of the Playhouses …

Signor Carastini, Signor Schaltzs, and Signiora Durastanti, are engag'd by Mr. Handel to come over from Italy to perform … as is likewise Signora Antonina from Portugal.[3]

Less than two weeks later, the dowager Duchess of Leeds almost gleefully reported to her stepson, the young Duke of Leeds,

I am at Present in top spirits wth ye certainity [*sic*] of having a very good opera here next winter, in opposition to Handell ... [The] subscription for this is full, & Handel has not got 20 subscribers yet, so most people think he will drop his opera.[4]

Further news favorable for the rival company appeared several days later:

Letters from Turin that came last Wednesday, mention Signora Cuzzoni being on her Departure for England. And it is not doubted but that she is already on the Road, so that in all likelihood Opera's next Winter will be perform'd here to the greatest Advantage.[5]

Cuzzoni, however, would not arrive until April the following year. By late July, the Nobility opera had recruited a "Mr Mattis," an Oxford violinist, for their orchestra.[6]

Handel's new singers Carestini and Durastanti arrived in early October, and Londoners received a preview of the season:

There are to be two Italian Operas this Winter, one at the Hay-market, under the Direction of Mr. Handel; and another at Mr. Rich's Theatre in Lincolns-Inn-Fields, under the Direction of Signor Senoseni; and we hear that both will open about the middle of Next Month, great Preparations of fine Cloaths and Scenes having been made in order thereto.[7]

No doubt because the rival company had to fit up the old Lincoln's Inn Fields Theatre, Handel stole the march and began his season on October 30 with the royal family (including Prince Frederick) in attendance for the pasticcio *Semiramide*, with music mostly by Vinci to a libretto by Metastasio.[8] Only after Handel halted productions for the holidays, did the Nobility opera begin its season on December 29 with *Arianna in Nasso* by its principal composer Porpora, thus avoiding head-to-head competition with Handel for its opening night. The rival company may have been offering enticements for its new patrons: it priced its gallery seats starting at 4s (instead of Handel's 5s) and gave librettos gratis to the subscribers instead of for the usual price of a shilling.[9]

For the 1733–34 season, London opera-goers enjoyed the spectacle of two opera companies engaged in the mutual assured destruction of competing for their limited patronage. Writing on December 13, Handel's future librettist Charles Jennens was quite realistic:

How two Opera Houses will subsist after Christmas, I can't tell; but at present we are at some difficulty for the support of One; & Mr. Handel has been forc'd to drop his Opera three nights for want of company.[10]

For its second season, the Opera of the Nobility was able through its contacts in Italy to recruit the "blazing star" Farinelli, who arrived in October 1734 for three seasons with the company.[11] For two seasons, London's opera stage hosted Europe's two most celebrated castratos, Farinelli and Senesino. Farinelli's debut brought rapturous accolades, and his first benefit concert on March 15, 1735, was quite possibly the most celebrated and stellar single musical event of the century.

The formation of the Opera of the Nobility in rivalry to Handel is the episode most often cited as the intrusion of partisan politics into the world of opera. In the often-told, though varied, account, Frederick, Prince of Wales developed a hostility toward Handel to spite his father or eldest sister, Anne, the Princess Royal. At the head of the political opposition, he established the Opera of the Nobility, supported by opposition politicians, as a means of antagonizing his father and Walpole. The royal family and society chose sides and exclusively patronized one company or the other. Versions of this account and Frederick's motivation have been repeated and embellished and passed into conventional wisdom,[12] although several more recent biographers have retreated from it. A full reconsideration shows that the conventional account of the political motivation of this episode is largely a fiction. But first, a brief account of the pivotal character, Prince Frederick, is necessary.[13]

Frederick Louis, the future Prince of Wales, had remained in Hanover to represent the electoral interest after George I's accession in 1714. When his father became George II, he probably considered, as in his own case, the mischief an heir apparent could cause colluding with opposition politicians and saw no need to call Frederick to Britain. The ministers, though, believing the heir should reside in Britain, prevailed and Frederick arrived at St. James's on December 4, 1728, and was invested as Prince of Wales the following month.

Frederick's reputation has suffered from his youthful amatory adventures, his supposed hostility to Handel, the charge that he was the naïve tool of opposition politicians, his feud with his parents, and the hostile and spiteful accounts of him in John, Lord Hervey's memoirs, which take every opportunity to blacken his character and behavior. A posthumous doggerel dubbed him "Poor Fred," and even one of Frederick's biographers did him no honor by repeating the tag as the title of a book.

Unlike his father and grandfather, Frederick was a personable and social figure and made efforts to mix and ingratiate himself with his future subjects. Meeting him in Hanover, Lady Mary Wortley Montagu described him at age nine as having "something so very engaging and easy in his behaviour, that he needs not the advantage of his rank to appear charming … I was surpriz'd at the quicknesse and politenesse that appear'd in every thing he said, joyn'd to a person perfectly agreable."[14] The month after his arrival in Britain, Anne, Viscountess Irwin wrote, "there's a frankness and affability in his way very different from his rank, and very engaging."[15] The Earl of Egmont noted, "The Prince has a particular art of engaging persons to esteem him."[16]

Frederick cultivated his popular appeal and image as a dutiful, concerned future monarch through public appearances and acts of charity, which were widely reported in the press.[17] He cultivated the merchant and trading interests of Bath, Bristol, and London and spoke in support of trade and commerce, which endeared him to a large part of the public and aligned him with the political opposition, which pushed for an aggressive assertion of treaty-guaranteed trading rights in the West Indies.

One area where his reputation has recently undergone deserved rehabilitation is his arts patronage, and he is now seen as a sincere and knowledgeable connoisseur of the arts. His interest in the arts helped establish the prestige of his own court, forged bonds with fellow aristocrats, set the tone of his future reign, and encouraged the nation's artists.[18] An avid collector and patron of sculpture and painting, he took an early interest in documenting the royal collections at Hampton Court.[19] Probably under the influence of William Kent and Alexander Pope, he took up landscape gardening and actively supervised planting his own gardens.[20] In 1749, Frederick expressed interest in an academy for British painters, which was a subject for a planned commemorative painting.[21]

An avid theater-goer, his attendance at a play would result in a bounty to the theater.[22] As a patron of letters, Frederick was third only behind George III (his son) and the Earl of Chesterfield in receiving dedications of books in the eighteenth century.[23]

Frederick was a generous patron of music, opera, and oratorio.[24] At his residences, he hosted rehearsals of operas and oratorios.[25] An amateur cellist and composer, he kept a musical establishment and held frequent series of musical entertainments that were widely reported in the newspapers. Charles Burney would later repeat anecdotes about Handel at rehearsals and entertainments at the prince's home.[26] The prince was one of Farinelli's most lavish patrons, and the two played duets, Farinelli singing to Frederick's cello playing.[27]

As was the pattern with Hanoverian monarchs, Frederick had strained relations with his father, and Hervey's memoirs report the king and queen's disdain for their son – although Hervey's memoirs must be suspect of his own animus against Frederick. A mounting series of crises marked Frederick's worsening relationship with his parents. While Frederick was still in Hanover, the king thwarted his desired marriage with his cousin, the Princess of Prussia. In Britain, Frederick chaffed under his parents' tight and confining control, was kept short of money, and not allowed to have his own residence. His father and Walpole no doubt were attempting to forestall a situation similar to when George II as Prince of Wales had established a court to rival his father's.

Associating Walpole with his parents' treatment of him, from his earliest days in Britain, Frederick befriended members of the opposition, whose antipathy to Walpole he came to share. As early as February 1729, it was observed that "whoever was so [in favor] with the Prince must of consequence be out with the King."[28] By 1733, Frederick's household had become a gathering place of leaders of the opposition. Although he did not take a direct role in politics, Frederick extended patronage to writers and politicians and spent money backing opposition candidates in elections; he had his own electoral interest in the Duchy of Cornwall.

The king tried to reconcile Frederick and Walpole in June 1733 by offering him a choice of three princesses to marry, choice of his own servants, and a settlement of £80,000. The prince politely declined the offer, excusing himself from reconciling with Walpole.[29] Princess Anne, his younger sister, was married in March 1734 and received a jointure of £80,000 from Parliament. Frederick considered the marriage of his sister before him and the amount of her jointure an insult.[30]

In late June 1734, Frederick offended his father when, it was believed on the advice of the opposition, he burst into his father's presence with three demands: permission to serve in a campaign in the Rhine, to receive an allowance equal to what the king had enjoyed while Prince of Wales, and to be married. Indignant at the prince's demands, the king hinted he would consider the second request, but was silent about the others. Walpole urged moderation, the queen softened the king's anger, and a complete rupture was prevented.[31] Clearly, it was not in the king's interest in effect to grant £100,000 to help support the opposition to him and the ministry.

King George finally arranged a marriage for Frederick with Princess Augusta of Saxe-Gotha and sent Lord Delawarr, treasurer of his household, in March 1736 to escort the princess from Germany to Britain. The royal wedding on May 4 was celebrated with productions by both Handel and the Nobility opera. The marriage increased Frederick's popularity, and the opposition turned the debate on the motion for a congratulatory address to the king into a partisan affair. In their speeches, William Pitt and George

Lyttelton lavished warm panegyric on the prince; but their cool praise of the king and censure of Walpole served only to widen the breach between the king and his son.[32] Frederick now felt his income was insufficient for his enlarged household and continued to resent not being able to name his own servants, although in a sign of his contrariness, he refused his father's offer that he could name some of them, insisting on naming them all.[33]

Frederick and the Opera of the Nobility reconsidered

The image of a Handel-spiting Frederick as the founder of the Opera of the Nobility with a political motivation seems to have begun with R. A. Streatfeild in 1909, who portrays Frederick as Handel's "redoubtable antagonist" who, because of his known hostility to the king and Sir Robert Walpole,

threw himself into the arms of the Opposition … To suit his own purposes he pretended to despise Handel's music, and he carried his perversity so far as to combine with several of the influential subscribers in founding a rival enterprise at Lincoln's Inn Fields with Porpora as leading composer.[34]

A biography of Frederick that appeared soon afterwards dramatizes the division of society:

No sooner had his sister's protégé [Handel] established his opera at the Haymarket Theatre than he [Frederick] forthwith started an opposition opera at the Theatre in Lincolns Inn Fields … All the adherents of the Prince … ceased their patronage of Handel's theatre, and transferred it to the Prince's undertaking in Lincolns Inn Fields.[35]

In 1923 Newman Flower puts the beginning of Frederick's animus against Handel around the time of the premiere of *Deborah*:

On 17 March [1733] *Deborah* was given for the first time … The King, Queen and the Royal Family were present, with the exception of Frederick, Prince of Wales, who had begun to show his open hostility to Handel for no other reason than because his father was loud in his praise.[36]

Flower cites no evidence for royal attendance. However, newspapers report Frederick – in company with his parents – attended four of the six performances of *Deborah*, including its premiere.[37]

 Flower describes how the feud "flamed up more furiously than ever, owing to the Prince having thrown himself into the battle against Walpole … The King had refused to pay his debts, and had openly excommunicated him from the Court." Flower's embellishment draws together several unrelated events. The refusal to pay Frederick's debts occurred in 1728 when the king refused to settle Frederick's accounts from Hanover;[38] the expulsion from court actually occurred in the summer of 1737. Flower then refers to the June 15 meeting "held at the behest of the Prince" and describes how "the Duke of Marlborough gladly arrayed himself beside the Prince as his principal supporter in the coming attack."[39] No documentation survives for the Duke of Marlborough's involvement with the Nobility opera.

The origin for Streatfeild's and Flower's accounts of Frederick and the Nobility opera quite certainly lies in John, Lord Hervey's memoirs, first published in 1848, which both cite elsewhere in their books. In Hervey's version, the target of Frederick's spite was not the king or Handel, but his sister Anne and her continued support of her music teacher Handel.

Another judicious Subject for his Enmity, was her suporting Hendel ... against several of the Nobility who had a Pique to Hendel, & had set up another Person [Senesino] to ruin him. Or to speak more properly and exactly the Prince in the beginning of his Enmity to his sister set himself at the Head of the other Opera, to irritate her.[40]

Hervey describes the king and queen's stubborn loyalty to Handel during the first 1733–34 season:

The King & Queen were as much in earnest upon this Subject as their Son & Daughter ... They were both Hendelists & sat freezing constantly at his empty Haymarket-Opera; whilst the Prince with all the chief of the Nobility went as constantly to that of Lincoln's-in-Fields. The Affair grew as serious, as that of the <u>Greens</u> and the <u>Blues</u> under Justinian at Constantinople; an anti-Hendelist was look'd upon as an anti-Courtier; and voting against the Court in Parliament was hardly a less remissable, or more venial sin than speaking against Hendel or going to the Lincoln-in-Fields-Opera.[41]

What Flower and Hervey describe rather resembles the events in the turbulent summer of 1737; then, offended by Frederick's spiriting the Princess of Wales away from Hampton Court to St. James's to give birth, the king banished Frederick and his household from St. James's and forbade from his presence those who attended Frederick's court (see below).

That the various accounts of Frederick as founder of the Opera of the Nobility targeting the king or his sister, the division of the court and society, and the alignment of the Nobility opera with opposition partisan politics are largely a fiction is shown by a wide range of contemporary evidence: Lord Hervey's bias against Frederick, the circumstances of the founding of the Nobility opera, eighteenth-century accounts of the two companies, political profiles of the directors, and patterns of attendance and payment by Frederick and the king.[42]

As suggested above, Streatfeild and Flower based their accounts on the memoirs of Lord Hervey. In everything dealing with Frederick, however, Hervey's judgments must be suspected of reflecting his own personal bitterness and vengeance against the prince.[43] Hervey and Frederick became acquainted during Hervey's visit to Hanover in 1716. Frederick was called to Britain in December 1728, and Hervey became vice-chamberlain of the household two years later. In the routine and intimacy of court life, they became close friends.[44] For one or more reasons that are not clear, Frederick and Lord Hervey had a bitter falling out in the spring of 1732, resulting in mutual antipathy.[45] Hervey's account of his rupture with Frederick must have been so inflammatory that the May 1730 to late-summer 1732 portion of his memoirs was destroyed by a descendant,[46] yet surviving portions are vitriolic enough.[47]

As vice-chamberlain, Hervey became an intimate and favorite of Queen Caroline and surpassed Frederick in her affection. By the time the memoirs resume in mid 1732, Hervey was taking her side in the family disputes, and Hervey had no reluctance to record the king and queen's most hostile and insulting remarks about their son. By then, Frederick had befriended many of the peers in the political opposition to Walpole, while Hervey was taking part in government pamphleteering. Hervey's memoirs must be taken as a highly partisan account of court life, which take every opportunity to maliciously defame Frederick. It serves his personal purposes, then, to describe Frederick as conspiring against Handel, a musician favored by Frederick's parents and sister.

Several points about the founding and organization of the rival opera emerge: there is no evidence of Frederick's involvement in the formation of the rival opera; political alignment or motivation is never mentioned in sources; the two companies are often just mentioned as rivals for London's limited opera audience; much of the opera world is dissatisfied with Handel and wants to support Senesino; the focus is on the conflict between Handel and Senesino; and the rival company was often referred to as Senesino's opera or directed by him.

The principal organizers of the rival company were John West, seventh Baron Delawarr (later first earl), and William, second Earl Cowper.[48] The day after the June 1733 meeting, Delawarr wrote to the Duke of Richmond describing plans for the new company and soliciting a subscription:

There is A Spirit got up against the Dominion of Mr Handel, A Subscription carry'd on, and Directors chosen, who have contracted with Senisino, and have sent for Cuzzoni, and Farrinelli, it is hoped he will come as soon as the Carneval of Venice is over, if not sooner. The General Court gave power to contract with any Singer Except Strada, So that it is Thought Handel must fling up, which the Poor Count [Heidegger] will not be sorry for, There being no one but what declares as much for him [Heidegger], as against the Other [Handel], so that we have A Chance of Seeing Operas once more on A good foot. Porpora is also sent for. We doubt not but we shall have your Graces Name in our Subscription List. The Direct^{rs}. chosen are as follows. D. of Bedford, L^{ds}. Bathurst, Burlington, Cowper, Limmerick, Stair, Lovel, Cadogan, DeLawarr, & D. of Rutland. Sr John Buckworth. Henry Furnese Esq. S^r Mi^d. Newton; There seems great Unanimity, and Resolution to carry on the Undertaking comme il faut.[49]

Early accounts are silent about political partisanship. In September, the Duke of Newcastle, then a secretary of state, one of Walpole's staunchest allies, and one who might be aware of political opposition, merely mentions how Handel "might gett the better of his enemies, for he will have the advantage in performers."[50] Later that month, a German correspondent wrote to the agent Giovanni Zamboni in London, "Don't forget to tell me whether the *contre-opéra* has begun and how Handel has fared up to now."[51] Paolo Rolli wrote in December 1733 only of "the Opera of the Nobility" (*l'Opera de' Signori*).[52] When James Brydges, Duke of Chandos, who earlier had been Handel's patron at Cannons, wrote to Lord Delawarr giving him his proxy for an upcoming General Court, he refers only to "the sub[s]cribers to the Academy of Musick."[53] On January 1, 1734, the Prussian minister in London reported back to Berlin about the first production of the Opera of the Nobility, *Arianna in Nasso*:

Last Saturday was the opening of the new *Opera*, which the *nobility* has undertaken since they were not satisfied with the *conduct* of the *director* of the old Opera, *Handel*, and to humiliate him, planned a new one, to which over two hundred people *subscribed*, and each one contributed 20 *guineas*. The premier singer, named *Senesino*, is pictured on the *ticket* of the subscribers with the inscription: *Nec pluribus impar*.[54]

The ticket represented a scene "with Senesino, drest like a Heroe, in a Singing Posture."[55]

In several contemporary accounts, it is Handel and Senesino who head the rival companies. The author of *Do You Know What You Are About? or, A Protestant Alarm to Great Britain* (1733) satirizes the opera rivalry as a division between Handel and Senesino, who "are playing at Dog and Bear, exactly like the Two Kings of *Poland*,[56] contending for the Empire of

Doremifa." The writer attributes Senesino's "implacable hatred to *Handel*, for making him sing in the English Oratorios, whereby he incurr'd the Pope's Displeasure."[57] The *Daily Advertiser* in October refers to the companies under the direction of Handel and Senesino.[58] In his opera register, Francis Colman identifies the two opera theaters as "Handells House" and "Senesino's House."[59] The Abbé Prévost reports for his French readers: "You know already that Senesino quarreled irreconcilably with Mr. Handel, and formed a schism in the troupe, and that he rented a separate theatre for himself and his partisans."[60] And again later he puts the partisanship between "Mr. Handel, enjoying the continued patronage of the King and the Royal Family ... and all the gentlemen of the Court who idolize Signor *Senesino* [and who are] prodigal of their guineas in order to raise him above his rival."[61] While abroad in Turin, the Earl of Essex received a report in January 1734 about the opera world, where "between the Competition of the Two Houses neither of them is full enough to pay much more than the Charges; but I think Senesino has the better of it."[62]

In the same month, when the *Grub-street Journal* proposed a mock set of articles of peace to end the dispute between the managers and actors at the Drury Lane Theatre, it proposed Handel, Heidegger, and Senesino as guarantors of the agreement.[63] At the end of the first season, Essex's business agent calculated the financial ruin: "They say hendell has lost £3000 and Senesino £1500 by the Season."[64] A comic allegory of Handel and the rival opera in *Harmony in an Uproar* (1734) makes no mention of political partisanship, and in fact writes that Frederick "only laugh'd at them in his Sleeve."[65]

Contemporaries, then, saw the leader of the rival opera company as Senesino,[66] and there is no awareness of partisan politics in the rivalry or suggestion that Frederick founded or directed the company. Handel's associates and eighteenth-century biographers also make no mention of Frederick's direct instigation, targeting Handel or the king, or political motivation. They put the cause as Handel's difficulties with Senesino and his singers and the debacle of the ticket prices for *Deborah*.

Handel's friend the Earl of Shaftesbury put the origin at the misunderstanding between Handel and Senesino and Handel's raised ticket prices for *Deborah*, and referred to the company "where Senesino was to have the principal part."[67] John Mainwaring, Handel's first biographer, reported that

occasioned by the disagreement between Handel and his Singers, many of the Nobility raised a new subscription in order to carry on another Opera at Lincoln's-inn-fields, in which they could have Singers and Composers of their own chusing.[68]

John Hawkins noted the nobility raised a subscription for an opera at Lincoln's Inn Fields so they could run an opera without being subject to the control of composers or singers.[69] Following Mainwaring and Hawkins, Charles Burney states it was the nobility's siding with Senesino and Cuzzoni in their differences with Handel and their offense at the raised prices for *Deborah* that prompted their support for a rival opera company.[70]

Walpole's biographer William Coxe, publishing his *Anecdotes of George Frederick Handel* in 1799, put the impetus for the "birth to a rival Opera" as the opposition to Handel that was excited by the affair of the first performance of *Deborah*.[71] Since Coxe had published just the previous year his three-volume *Memoirs of the Life and Administration of Sir Robert Walpole*, we might have expected him, sympathetic to both Walpole and Handel, to have noted any political involvement of the Opera of the Nobility.

An important point in Delawarr's letter to Richmond is the silence about Frederick's involvement – which presumably might be a draw for attracting subscribers. Of the potential directors named, nine had been directors of the Royal Academy of Music, confirming that a primary motivation was promotion of opera. It is even possible the company being founded was a rump of the old Royal Academy of Music, mounting an interim company in anticipation of the expiration of the Handel–Heidegger five-year lease on the Haymarket Theatre.[72]

Political profiles of the Nobility opera's directors (see Appendix 3) reveal that instead of a group of opposition peers and politicians, the directors are roughly equally divided between court office holders and those in the opposition. The one independent director is Burlington, who had been a courtier but resigned his places in May 1733 and thereafter avoided the world of politics and did not join the opposition.[73] It is not known whether Richmond responded to Delawarr's solicitation with a subscription; but at the time, he was a courtier.[74] Once again, it seems the world of opera was unaffected by partisan politics.

But most significantly to confound the traditional account that the opera was partisan and targeted against the royal family or king, the two principal managers of the Nobility opera, Lord Delawarr and Earl Cowper, were courtiers and favorites of the king. In addition to their places at court (see Appendix 3), each executed important missions for the king while heading the rival opera. Delawarr accompanied the king to and from Hanover for his summer visit in 1735, and in March–April 1736 was sent as ambassador to Saxe-Gotha to conclude Frederick's marriage with Princess Augusta and escort her to Britain.[75] The king sent Cowper, one of his gentlemen of the bedchamber, on a royal yacht to Holland in September 1733 to escort Prince William of Orange to Britain for his marriage to Princess Anne.[76] Hawkins reported that he participated in concerts for the royal family in Queen Caroline's library in Green Park.[77] In October 1734, Cowper was Farinelli's first host in England and presented him at court.[78]

Moreover, were there political motivation behind the Opera of the Nobility's planning, we would expect to find Bolingbroke, Pulteney, Carteret, Cobham, and other opposition politicians included as organizers or potential subscribers – especially in June 1733, several months after the Excise Crisis, when partisan politics were still at high pitch and the king had just dismissed several peers. Nor is any mention of the company's formation found in the opposition political journals the *Craftsman*, the *Grub-street Journal*, or *Fog's Weekly Journal*.

Rather than seeing his courtiers Delawarr and Cowper as betraying him, the king rather felt they were embarrassing themselves. The king, reported Hervey, took no part in the opera rivalries other than to subscribe his £1,000 to Handel when his company occupied the Haymarket Theatre, but he added:

that he did not think, setting one self at the Head of a Faction of Fidlers a very honorable Occupation for People of Quality; or the Ruin of one poor Fellow so generous or so good-Natured a Scheme as to do much honour to the undertakers whether they succeeded or not; but the better they succeeded in it the more he thought they would have reason to be ashamed of it.[79]

Despite his mean opinion of it, the king avidly attended operas produced by the Nobility opera.

Another of the Hervey–Streatfeild–Flower claims is belied by the pattern of royal attendance at operas. Hervey implied there was exclusive attendance of the royal family and nobility at one or another of the companies.[80] The documented attendance of the royal family for the first season casts doubt on Hervey's account. Their majesties availed themselves of the additional opportunities for opera offered by the Nobility opera and attended its first performance. The Prussian minister continued his account: "This new *Opera* was first called the *Opera* of the rebels. But since the whole Court attended the first *Overture*, it has thereby become *legitimate* and *loyal*."[81] This is certainly an unlikely comment were the Nobility opera received as an affront to the king. That first season, Frederick attended at least twelve of Handel's productions (Table 6.1).

But Hervey's memoirs even disregard his own first-hand experience; he wrote once of returning with the king from a performance of the Nobility

Table 6.1 Attendance by Prince Frederick and the king and queen at the rival opera companies

| | Prince Frederick | | King and/or queen | |
| | Handel | Opera of the Nobility | Handel | Opera of the Nobility |
Season				
1733–34	12	6[1]	22	1[1]
1734–35	none recorded	6	8	5
1735–36	none recorded[1]	8	3[1]	4
1736–37[2]	8	4	4	3

[1] Short season.

[2] King away in Hanover part of the season.

Sources: Attendance is documented in *The London Stage, Part 3: 1729–1747*, ed. Arthur H. Scouton (Carbondale: Southern Illinois University Press, 1961). Dates have occasionally been supplemented by notices in London daily newspapers.

opera's *Adriano in Siria* on November 25, 1735, attended as well by the princesses.[82] The king took considerable interest in this opera. Since he thought it "to be rather too long, M. Veracini has shorten'd it, and his Majesty has declar'd his Intention of being present at it," reported a newspaper.[83] Contemporary newspapers give ample evidence that members of the royal family attended performances of both companies (see Table 6.1). The notices can only be taken to give minimum figures, since many attendances were not reported in the press.[84]

Frederick's support of both companies was well known at the time, for Princess Caroline wrote to her sister Anne, now Princess of Orange and living in Holland, on December 17, ?1734: "The operas are going very badly … My brother [Frederick] patronizes both, but he does not see it do the managers any great good."[85] Like the royal family, members of the Granville and Wentworth families and the Earl of Egmont also attended performances of both companies, as revealed in their letters and diaries.[86] Even Thomas Coke (later Earl of Leicester), one of the directors of the Nobility opera, patronized both opera companies, with consequences that he reports to Lord Burlington: "I am sorry to hear Operas do so badly, you know as a virtuoso I encourage both, & have subscribed to Hendell, for w[ch] I have been severely reprimanded by my brethren."[87]

The royal family's attendance at the Opera of the Nobility is confirmed by other evidence. Queen Caroline's library contained librettos of ten Nobility operas.[88] Four librettos of Nobility operas survive in bindings bearing the arms of George II.[89] And when she became Princess of Orange, Handel's pupil Anne acquired the music of the Nobility operas *Polifemo* (1735) and *Adriano in Siria* (1735).[90]

The pattern of royal payments and bounties also belies the conventional account of exclusive partisanship. Table 6.2 summarizes the disbursements of Frederick and his father to the rival opera companies beginning 1733–34. Frederick's household account books show he was giving bounties of £250 to Handel for at least the two seasons prior to the founding of the Nobility opera, and for two seasons of the rivalry gave an equal bounty to both companies.

The anomalous three seasons of 1734–37 when the king gave his bounty to the Nobility opera are not signs of his withdrawing his patronage from Handel; rather he seems to be following precedent that the king gave a yearly bounty to the opera company in the King's Theatre in the Haymarket. It is also curious that, if the Opera of the Nobility were an affront to him or an agent of the opposition, the king would grant them his £1,000 annual payment, for after the failure of the Excise, he had no qualms about stripping of their offices peers who opposed the Excise or other government measures.

Finally, were the Opera of the Nobility an agent of Frederick and the opposition, we might expect the operas to have oppositional political content, along the line of the Patriot dramas examined in Chapter 7. Appendix 4 provides summaries of the Opera of the Nobility's librettos, none of whose subjects show sign of being chosen or adapted for contemporary partisan application. Opposition newspapers give no special notice to Nobility operas nor make any topical application of their librettos. The one exception, *Festa d'Imeneo*, for Frederick's wedding is patriotic panegyric suitable to the occasion (see below).

Admittedly, there are no reported payments to Handel and attendance at his operas by Frederick in the two seasons 1734–35 and 1735–36. These gaps have been taken as signs of a break with Handel. Any number of reasons might explain why no payments or attendance are recorded. Frederick, always living beyond his means, was crippled by debt in the years 1735–36 and forced to economize.[91] For the 1735–36 season, a possible explanation for the lack of a season bounty is that Handel's season ran only from March 3 to June 9, 1736, for sixteen performances, in comparison to the Nobility opera's full season of fifty-five performances running from October 28, 1735, to June 22, 1736. The attendance reports in the newspapers are demonstrably on the low side,[92] and so nothing precludes an occasional attendance for which payment may not be reflected in the accounts. Even conceding that Frederick did not significantly patronize Handel for two seasons, this

Table 6.2 Payments from Prince Frederick and the king to the rival opera companies

Season	Handel	Opera of the Nobility
	Payments from Frederick	
1731–32	£250[1] (KT)	—
1732–33	£250[1] (KT)	—
1733–34	£250 (KT)	£250 (LIF)
1734–35	none recorded	£250 (KT)
1735–36	none recorded	£250 (KT)
1736–37	£250 (CG)	£250 (KT)
	Payments from the king[2]	
1731–32	£1,000 (KT)	—
1732–33	£1,000 (KT)	—
1733–34	£1,000 (KT)	—
1734–35	—	£1,000 (KT)
1735–36	—	£1,000 (KT)
1736–37	—	£1,000 (KT)

[1] Payments recorded in British Library, Add. MS 24,403, ff. 14v (June 30, 1732) and 63r (July 5, 1733).
[2] Payments recorded in O. E. Deutsch, *Handel: A Documentary Biography* (New York: W. W. Norton, 1955), 295, 317, 370, 394, 412, 439.
Key:
KT = King's Theatre, Haymarket
LIF = Lincoln's Inn Fields Theatre
CG = Covent Garden Theatre
Sources: Except where noted, Frederick's payments from Carole Taylor, "Handel and Frederick, Prince of Wales," *Musical Times* 125 (1984), 89–92.

absence does nothing to undermine the major argument that Frederick was not involved with the founding of the Nobility opera or that there was no partisan motivation in the operatic rivalry.

There may not even have been as much (or any) ill feeling between the composer and prince as is often supposed. Even late in the 1735–36 season, there were gestures by Handel toward Frederick. Frederick married Augusta, Princess of Saxe-Gotha, at the Chapel Royal in St. James's Palace on April 27, 1736. For the wedding of his "antagonist," Handel composed his second wedding anthem, "Sing unto God." Even though the wedding anthem was probably part of Handel's duties as composer to the Chapel Royal,[93] as opera impresario, he provided celebration of the wedding in the form of "eight Operas, for the Entertainment of her royal Highness the future Princess of Wales."[94] These were performances of *Ariodante* (May 5, 1736) and the new *Atalanta* (May 12, 1736). The special care Handel took with the production is reflected in the elaborate stage set (see the description printed in Appendix 5).

For the first night of *Atalanta*, Frederick commanded Addison's *Cato* at Drury Lane, where the royal box was "adorned in a compleat, rich, and elegant manner."[95] The choice of Addison's *Cato*, with its exhortations to liberty, may have been as much a patriotic gesture as an attempt to slight Handel. But his absence at *Atalanta*'s premiere does not preclude attendance at other of Handel's operas later in the season.[96] Handel began his next opera season early on November 6, 1736,[97] at the command of the Prince and Princess of Wales with *Alcina*. For the occasion, a newspaper reported, a special box for the couple was decorated with

white Sattin, beautifully Ornamented with Festons [*sic*] of Flowers in their proper Colours, and in Front was a flaming Heart, between two Hymeneal Torches, whose different Flames terminated in one Point, and were surmounted with a Label, on which were wrote, in Letters of Gold, these Words, Mutuus Ardor.[98]

Later that month, *Atalanta* was repeated by command of the prince and princess on November 20 and 27, 1736 (the first for his birthday), both times with the fireworks.

The conventional account of the Opera of the Nobility, the fact of the "oppositional allegiance of the Nobility company," Hervey's veracity, and the "general political cast to the rivalry" have recently been reasserted by Suzanne Aspden. The "accretion of fact" (such as presented above), she asserts, does not convincingly deal with Hervey's account, which she accepts without reservation, and only bypasses "much contemporary reportage that promoted or reinforced the opera companies' supposed politicization."[99] Upon close examination, the literary reports adduced and the competing Ariadne operas (see below) merely reflect what is not in doubt: that the two companies were – and were seen as – rivals. The literary accounts cited do not express the opposition program against the ministry and are political only in the most general sense of commenting on persons or events in the public arena.[100]

It would be remiss not to acknowledge Frederick's special interest in the Opera of the Nobility and its singers. When he visited Farinelli in August 1770, Charles Burney reported that Farinelli told him "of the part which the late Prince of Wales took with that [opera company] managed by the nobility."[101] For the 1736–37 season, Frederick personally promoted the Nobility opera, for one of the directors, Sir John Buckworth, informed the Earl of

Essex, that "the Subscription [is] in the Prince's Hands, who labours hard for our Interest."[102] Nonetheless, Frederick attended both companies and gave each an equal bounty that season (see Tables 6.1 and 6.2).

The Nobility opera and its singers performed especially for the prince. *Arianna in Nasso*, its first opera of the opening season, was rehearsed at Frederick's house in Pall Mall on Christmas Eve, 1733.[103] In the following November another Nobility opera, a revival of Handel's *Ottone* (1723), was performed there before Frederick, in which both Farinelli and Senesino performed.[104] The Nobility opera presented a special production of the serenata *Festa d'Imeneo* to honor Frederick's wedding on May 4, 1736, with elaborate sets by William Kent (see below).

Frederick bestowed generous gifts on Farinelli: for his celebrated benefit concert on March 15, 1735, Frederick presented him with 200 guineas.[105] The following month it was reported that since Farinelli "hath constantly attended at all his royal highness' concerts of vocal and instrumental music, since he came from Italy," Frederick gave him "a fine wrought gold snuff-box, richly set with diamonds and rubies, in which was enclos'd a pair of brilliant diamond knee-buckles, as also a purse of 100 guineas."[106] Frederick's household accounts reveal he paid £46 for the snuffbox and £47 for the knee-buckles.[107]

Frederick also took an interest in the Nobility opera's principal composer Nicola Porpora. He soon acquired manuscript scores of four of Porpora's operas produced in the first two seasons: *Arianna in Nasso* and *Enea nel Lazio* (1733–34 season) and *Polifemo* and *Ifigenia in Aulide* (1734–35 season).[108] Porpora dedicated his *Twelve Italian Cantatas* (1735) and *Sinfonie da camera a tre istromenti* (1736) to Frederick.

Frederick's patronage of both Handel and the Nobility opera can be seen as part of his genuine interest in promoting music, painting, literature, and theater. Publicly supporting the arts would enhance his standing with the aristocracy, present him as an arts patron, and build support for his future role as king. His patronage of both companies may also reflect his adoption of the ideal of a king who rises above faction and unifies his country: in this case, by appearing as the Maecenas who patronized all the worthy musicians in his realm.

The parliamentary sessions of 1734–36 were relatively quiet and tranquil, and domestic issues gave little opportunity to the opposition. It was not until 1737 that partisan politics and Frederick's relations with his father reached crises. The severity of these events of 1737 has often been unwittingly transported back to 1733 as the context for the founding of the Opera of the Nobility. The Parliament that sat on February 1 was unusually restless and unruly. The opposition found several issues it could use to challenge Walpole and the court: Frederick's allowance and the Princess of Wales' jointure, the Licensing Act (see Chapter 7), and growing public indignation over increasing Spanish depredations upon British merchant shipping in the West Indies. The opposition scored a success when Walpole's measures to punish Edinburgh for the Porteous Riots of the previous year were opposed in both houses by members of the government.

Bolingbroke had apparently hinted to Frederick as early as 1735 that he might gain independence from his father and apply to Parliament for the full portion of the civil settlement that his father had refused him. The idea lay dormant until February 1737, when it was taken up by the opposition and turned into a political issue. It was considered especially appropriate that the prince's settlement be increased now that he was married. On February 22, both houses moved an address to the king to settle £100,000 on the prince and a jointure on the princess. The government saw the motion as disrespectful to the king, fomenting a division in the royal family, and in effect putting one-eighth of the Civil List into the hands of those opposed to the king and his ministers.[109] The measure failed in both houses. In the Commons, the opposition again revealed its disarray: forty-five Tories absented themselves, refusing to vote for a measure they considered an interference with the royal prerogative. The princess, though, received her jointure.[110] Nonetheless, Frederick continued to wait upon his parents at court.[111]

Frederick's actions later that summer brought the tensions with his parents to the breaking point on July 31. When the princess began labor while at Hampton Court, Frederick rushed her to St. James's, where she delivered a daughter.[112] Although the prince justified his action by pointing out that midwives, nurses, and doctors were wanting at Hampton Court, the king saw the action as dangerous to the princess and child, and a spiteful, disrespectful act to prevent a potential heir being born at court. Despite a series of submissive and penitential letters from Frederick, the king would not pardon what he took as defiant contempt of his authority. Finally, on September 10, citing his "undutiful Behaviour," the king banished the prince, his family, and all persons attached to him from his palace. Seeing Frederick as a tool of the opposition, he commanded him to sever all ties with those in the opposition. In addition, the following day, the king announced those with appointments at both courts would have to renounce one of them.[113]

Banished from court, Frederick established his household at Norfolk House, in St. James's Square, which became a social and political center of the opposition, thus dividing London politically and socially as in the days when his father was Prince of Wales. The defection of peers from the government that began in the aftermath of the Excise grew as young, ambitious politicians saw that their path to power lay allied with the future king. The death of Queen Caroline on November 20 deprived Walpole of his greatest support of political influence with the king, and it was believed he could not govern the king as well as she had done.

Operas produced by the rival companies

In lieu of the Hanoverian court directly mounting either public or private theater works to mark royal occasions, as in the years of the Restoration or on the Continent, it fell to theater and opera managers to mount public works celebrating royal events.[114] These stage works present their Hanoverianism not by allegorizing members of the royal family by the figures in episodes from history, but in straightforward panegyric sung by the allegorical–emblematic figures in the serenata, cantata, or masque and addressed to the audience or royal family members.

The royal event receiving the widest public celebration in the early Hanoverian period was the wedding of Princess Anne to Prince William IV of Orange. The engagement was announced on May 8, 1733; William arrived in Britain on November 7 for a ceremony initially scheduled for November 12. Because of William's delicate and precarious health, the ceremony was postponed several times before being held on March 14, 1734. London's theater managers went all-out, attempting to exploit patriotic sentiment by mounting a variety of musico-dramatic works celebrating the event (see Appendix 5).[115]

That season the rival opera companies each produced an opera on the Ariadne subject. The Opera of the Nobility opened its season with *Arianna in Nasso* (December 29, 1733), set by Porpora to a libretto adapted by Paolo Rolli. Handel, already well into his own season, followed four weeks later with *Arianna in Creta* (January 26, 1734) to a libretto by Pariati. Whether the similar subjects were a coincidence or the result of rivalry is uncertain.[116] Handel's opera deals with the earlier part of the myth: Theseus' arrival in Crete from Athens, his fight with the Minotaur in the labyrinth, and his marriage to Ariadne, daughter of King Minos. The Nobility's opera presents a fuller version of the myth: Theseus emerges from the labyrinth, Theseus and Ariadne flee to Naxos, and Theseus betrays Ariadne, who is rescued by Bacchus.

The generic expectation leads Suzanne Aspden to see the two Ariadne operas as related to the royal wedding of the following March. The parallels between the myth and the royal marriage, she claims, are "several and obvious."

Britain, like Crete, was an island that in recent days had become a major maritime power. William of Orange (the Third, of course, but also the new William, for those heartily disaffected with the recent rule), like Theseus, was both the rescuer of a nation threatened by a hidden monster (Catholicism, the Excise, Walpole's government in general) and the enlivener of nation and constitution. Anne and Britannia, like Ariadne, were concerned for their lovers, waiting interminably, even fearing abandonment.[117]

There are, though, no hints at all from prefaces, dedications, text, or contemporary sources that in any way connect the operas to the royal couple or wedding.

The relation of the Theseus–Ariadne myth to the arrival of either William is strained and relies on a simplified version of the myth and an unsystematic matching of analogs between the myth and British history of 1688 or 1734 that are too discrepant to bear comparison. The analogy brings under a single term too-disparate elements: the "hidden monster" represents the Minotaur, a religion, a parliamentary proposal, and a ministry. It is not clear in what sense Catholicism under James II, the Excise, or Walpole's ministry are "hidden." William III arrived with his wife Mary, so presumably Ariadne, as England personified as Britannia is now his "lover." William IV played no role in the defeat of the Excise, which was withdrawn after the wedding date. Ultimately it is Bacchus and Ariadne who are united in the myth, so the William IV analog has to shift from Theseus to Bacchus – and with it comes a tactless imputation of the future marital infidelity of William. But the foul-breathed, hunchback dwarf William is not a likely parallel to the valiant hero Theseus, let alone Bacchus, who rescued Ariadne.[118]

The proposed allegory does not account adequately for the central significance of Theseus' mission to Crete/England. In fact, it is not Crete/Britain that is "threatened by a hidden monster," for the Minotaur is securely sequestered in the center of the labyrinth on Crete. It is Athens/Holland that is freed from the barbaric tribute of the sacrifice to the Minotaur of the youth demanded by King Minos/George II from a defeated Crete in return for peace. Herein is the key to the moral of Handel's opera. During the first scene in the throne room, "The Stone, on which is engraven the Agreement of *Athens* falls down and break to Pieces. Four *Cupids* fly thro' the Air." This action embodies the allegorical moral: the steadfast love of Theseus and Ariadne will triumph over the enmity between Crete and Athens.

Further discrepancies between the myth and the arrival of William and the wedding arise when we look at the specific operas. In Handel's *Arianna in Creta*, Theseus/William arrives in Crete/Britain as part of a group of male and female youth who are sent from Athens/Holland to be sacrificed in games or fed to the Minotaur as tribute by King Minos/George II. By defeating the Minotaur, Theseus frees Athens from further tribute and wins the love of Ariadne/Anne. In the meantime, Ariadne is jealous that Theseus loves Carilda. In the Nobility's *Arianna in Nasso*, Theseus is married to Anthiope, Queen of the Amazons, who – seeking revenge for his unfaithfulness – pursues Theseus and Ariadne to Naxos (not back to his homeland Athens).

In these allegorizations, the operas "play out problems of the wedding of Anne and William." Handel's opera could be seen to be "disloyal to the royal family" and Rolli's "casts doubt on it"; but how the plots of the operas express their disloyalty or doubts about the wedding is not clear. Some sense of the motivation or intention of Handel and the directors of the Nobility opera and likely audience response must be considered. It is not plausible that operas celebrating a royal wedding would have subversive allegorical meanings about the royal family, from whom Handel and audience members had pensions and places.

But the major reason we need not accept Handel's *Arianna in Creta* as referring to the royal wedding is that Handel produced for that occasion the serenata *Il Parnasso in festa* at the King's Theatre on March 13, 1734 (see Appendix 5). Two days before the premiere, a newspaper announced:

for the Solemnity of the approaching Nuptials, there is to be perform'd ... a Serenata, call'd *Parnasso in Festa*: The Fable is Apollo and the Muses celebrating the Marriage of Thetis and Pelus ... People having been waiting with Impatience for this Piece, the celebrated Mr Handel having exerted his utmost Skill in it.[119]

Its premiere on the eve of the wedding was attended by the king and queen, royal family, and the Prince of Orange. Its subject, the marriage of Thetis and Pelus, is certainly appropriate for a wedding. In the first act, Apollo with the Muses, Orpheus, Mars, nymphs, and shepherds join to praise the god of wedded love and faith and to sing the hymeneals of Thetis and Peleus. In the second act, Calliope sings of Orpheus and the power of his music, Apollo recalls his Daphne, and Orpheus sings of Eurydice. Apollo and Orpheus then put aside thoughts of their own loves and sing of Thetis and Peleus.

Mars sings of what blessings await them, and a Grand Chorus sings their triumphs and proclaims their glory and love:

> But on the Race of *Peleus, Jove*
> Propitious will for ever prove.
> 'Tis *Jove's* Decree
> That They shall ever happy be.

> Alla stirpe di *Peleo*
> Un supremo fato arride
> Giove il vuole
> In eterno fiorirà.
>
> pp. 46–7

The serenata was repeated thereafter, attended several times by the royal couple.

For Frederick's marriage with Princess Augusta on May 4, 1736, each of the rival opera companies presented a work to celebrate the occasion, both in the true allegorical mode. The Nobility opera led off with the serenata *Festa d'Imeneo per le reali nozze di Frederico Prencipe Reale di Vallia* (*The Feast of Hymen for the Royal Wedding of Frederick, Prince of Wales*) on May 4, 1736, with music by Porpora to a libretto by Paolo Rolli (see Appendix 5). The elaborate sets were designed by William Kent, who had been appointed as Frederick's architect in 1732.[120]

In the Baroque allegorical mode, Hymen, Neptune, Mercury, Venus, Pallas, Bellona, and a chorus of sea gods address the two royal houses and alternate in declaring (among much else) that Wisdom's daughter brought Augusta to Britain; that Britain will enjoy propitious days, liberty, and power under Frederick and Augusta; and that love, virtue, and beauty are united in the royal pair. Moreover, every nation shares Britain's joy in the marriage, Fame sounds Britannia's glories, the three kingdoms ardently wish a bright succession of Frederick's virtues, and, finally, Rome is now revived in Great Britain. Flattering Frederick's interest in the arts, Apollo sings:

> royal Frederick so sweetly wakes
> The golden strings of my inchanting lyre,
> And sheds protection round my warbling Sons.

> Perchè l'Arte immortal della mia Lira
> Frederico Real possiede e ammira.
>
> pp. 12–13

Invoking two of England's heroes whom Frederick succeeds, Hymen envisions a temple by the Thames enshrining Alfred, "conqueror of the *Danes*" and founder of fleets, and Edward, "Wales's black Prince," who brought the French king and son to London in triumph. The nationalistic allusions to Alfred and Edward and prophecies of Britain's future under Frederick are fitting tribute to a Hanoverian prince.

Later that month, Handel mounted the pastoral *Atalanta. An Opera … On Occasion of an Illustrious Marriage* (May 12, 1736) (see Appendix 5). The subject had been widely used on the Continent as eminently suited for royal weddings. Set in Arcadia, shepherds and shepherdesses pursue interests in love and hunting. The usual amatory misunderstandings and confusions between two couples (some persons are royalty in disguise) are resolved. At the point in the source libretto where the two couples recognize each other and sing of their love, *Atalanta* introduces an apotheosis of a series of choruses and instrumental symphonies in which "Mercury descends on a Cloud, attended by the Loves and Graces" to bless the union of the royal couple in the audience. The chorus members (hitherto Arcadian shepherds) step forward and declare:

> From the Hero never springs
> > A Race of base unworthy Kings.
> From Sires like this illustrious Pair's divine,
> > Great Souls are form'd to bless the Royal Line.

> Dalla stirpe degli Eroi
> > Alma vil nascer non può.
> Dai piu illustri Genitori
> > Di quei sposi gloriosi
> > L'alma grande si formo.
> > > pp. 32–3

At the climax, "The Scene opens and discovers Illuminations and Bonfires, accompanied by loud Instrumental Musick."

These three works and *Proteo* (April 17, 1741) are within the tradition of continental Baroque allegorical theatrical works populated with deities and mythic or symbolic figures who address the royal couple in the audience. They demonstrate that London's theater managers were capable of using the conventions of Baroque symbolic allegory to refer transparently to the royal family on notable occasions – unlike the references to the royal wedding in the Ariadne operas, which have to be decoded, only to reveal subversive intent.

Farinelli and war with Spain

Farinelli gave his final performances for the Opera of the Nobility in June 1737; the following month, he left to spend a second summer in Paris. The directors had already contracted with him, and his return for the following season was expected. His second Parisian visit was not as profitable as he would have wished,[121] and he accepted an invitation to the Spanish court, where he arrived on August 7.[122] His arrival in Madrid was widely noted in the diplomatic community.[123]

How Farinelli charmed the Spanish court has become a staple of musical mythology that turned him into a latter-day Orpheus.[124] King Philip V of Spain was suffering from depression and melancholy. As the story goes, to amuse the king and rouse him from his depression, Queen Elisabeth arranged for Farinelli to sing outside the king's chamber. So charmed was he by Farinelli's singing, that Philip's melancholy was cured, and Farinelli became a royal favorite on whom the king and members of the royal family heaped appointments and gifts that surpassed those he received in Britain.

The Spanish court prevailed on Farinelli to break his contract with the Opera of the Nobility and remain in Madrid, where he was to spend his next twenty-three years, rising to a position of great power at court. Farinelli's defection from the Nobility opera caused ripples in the diplomatic world as the opera directors in vain enlisted the ministry to enforce their contract.[125]

The growing realization of London's opera-going public that Farinelli would not return for another season coincided with the growing tensions between Britain and Spain known as the Depredations Crisis, which culminated in the War of Jenkins' Ear in October 1739. The causes of the crisis and ensuing war lay in the commercial rivalry between Britain and Spain in the West Indies, Spain's attempt to monopolize trade with its possessions despite the privileges granted to Britain by the Treaty of Utrecht (1713), and the openly known fact that British merchants were carrying out an enormous illegal trade and smuggling with Spanish America.[126] The crisis flared up in 1737 as Spain tried to control British smuggling by licensing *guarda costas* (essentially privateers, often no more than pirates) that boarded and searched British trading ships, seized contraband goods, and often captured seamen or forced them to work their passage back home. The British, quite fairly, claimed that zealous Spaniards often committed atrocities against their ships and seamen, seizing legally traded goods and imprisoning British sailors, and demanded reparations from Spain for unlawful seizures, whereas the Spanish king in turn claimed the South Sea Company was not paying his full share of trading profits.

To merchants and the City of London, the government seemed powerless or unwilling to control Spanish captures of ships, crewmen, and cargoes. In October and November 1737, newspapers printed merchant petitions and letters from ships' captains telling of piratical seizures of ships and cruel treatment of their crews.[127] The reports fired indignation over British honor insulted, sailors imprisoned, property plundered, and treaties and rights of navigation violated. The *Craftsman* especially took up the merchants' cause: demanding satisfaction for their losses, accusing the ministry of failing to protect shipping and freedom of navigation, and promising its efforts to make trade secure from "pyratical Depredations and cruel treatment of our Seamen."[128] Even the ministerial *Daily Gazetteer* had to admit "The Clamours against the *Spaniards* are very loud, and the Sufferers impatient for Relief."[129]

The parallel of the Spanish court's recruitment of Farinelli and Spain's capturing British merchant ships and depriving the South Sea Company of its rights guaranteed by treaty was quickly noted by the opposition and put to political use to call attention to Walpole's handling of the Depredations Crisis as a means of agitating for war with Spain. As early as September 10, 1737, when London was first learning Farinelli would be spending the coming opera season in Madrid, *Common Sense* printed a letter from "C. J." that scores hits at the ministry's conduct of relations with Spain. With his shifting ironic and literal tone, C. J. strikes a wide range of targets. From the account above, the literally accurate parts of the letter are recognizable.

Viewed from the anti-opera orientation of *Common Sense*, Spain is doing Britain a favor by detaining Farinelli:

please to acquaint your Readers, that his Catholick Majesty, to make some Amends for his taking our Ships in the *West-Indies* ... has been graciously pleas'd to free us from a very unnecessary National Expence, by obliging the famous *Farrinello* to spend the succeeding Winter at *Madrid*. The illustrious *Eunuch*, indeed, pleaded the Ingagements he was under to the Royal Academy of Musick in *England*, and how Inconsolable the fine *British* Ladies wou'd be for the Loss of their darling Warbler ...

When *Don T—s G—o* [Thomas Geraldino, Spanish emissary to Britain] notified this extraordinary Event at Court, several pretty Gentlemen and Ladies, whom the Depredations in *America* never in the least affected, were Thunder-struck at the fatal Report, and were no sooner recovered from their Surprize, but several indecent Expressions were thrown out against his *Spanish* Majesty, for this unheard of Outrage; nay, 'twas resolv'd, humbly to address his Majesty, that he would be pleas'd to send positive Orders to Mr. *Keene* [British minister to Spain], to demand immediate Satisfaction for this flagrant Instance of arbitrary Power. Cries a Lady of exquisite Taste, What are the taking a few Ships, and the cutting off the Ears of the Masters of our Merchantmen [i.e., Captain Jenkins' ear], to the Loss of our dear, dear *Farrinello*?[130]

C. J.'s letter exploits a supposed gap between the interests of the merchants and traders and those of the ministry and cultural elite. By ridiculing those apolitical persons of the beau monde (but really meaning the ministry) who only expressed selfish concern and outrage for the loss of Farinelli (when their real patriotic concern should be for captured British shipping), C. J. calls attention to the Walpole ministry's supposed indifference to the plight of the merchants and ineffectual efforts to protect their shipping.[131]

Misplaced or exaggerated grief of opera-lovers for the loss of Farinelli quickly became an object of satire. A correspondent to the Duke of Leeds, who had met Farinelli in Italy and was one of his greatest friends and patrons in England, wrote to him on September 6, 1737 – when there still seemed hope Farinelli might return – that Farinelli's return was worth yielding Gibraltar, over which Spain and England had quarreled since of the Treaty of Utrecht (1713):

All the news I can learn here is … that we shall certainly have Fari: again who is now detained at the Court of Spain; for the great wits say there is a Treaty on foot by which we are to give the King of Spain an Equivalent which they say will be Gib: [Gibraltar].[132]

In November 1737, the *Craftsman* indicted political Epicureans who sided with the party that gave "most Encouragement to their Pleasures." They shun serious discourse and would rather talk of "the Character of the new *Singing-man*, that is come over, or who appear'd the best dress'd at the *last Birth-day*." The caricature of these "beaux Esprits" is a lively inversion of the *Craftsman*'s values: "They make a Jest of the *Spanish Depredations*, as a Thing of little or no Moment; but will never forgive his *Catholick Majesty* for making Prize of *Farinelli*." The writer doubts the political Epicurean has enough spirit even to "rise up as one Man against any *Minister* [Walpole], who should attempt to deprive Them of their favourite *Operas, Ridottos*, and *Masquerades*." The essay's conclusion states the merchants' case against Spanish depredations, reports on a recent petition to the king, and approves a rising spirit on behalf of the merchants.[133]

Exploiting for political purposes Farinelli's residence in Madrid is the after-piece the *Coffee-House* by the opposition poet and pamphleteer James Miller.[134] The farce, probably planned for performance in late 1737, was postponed when the theaters were closed following the death of Queen Caroline on November 21.[135] When Bawble, "a solemn Beau," is informed of the melancholy news of Farinelli's departure to Spain, he exclaims, "We are all ruin'd! Poor *Faronello*, dear celestial Faronello's lost! … Alas! we can do nothing but bewail our Misfortune." He breaks into a lament, marked "largo," expressing misplaced or exaggerated sorrow over Farinelli's departure and detention at Madrid:

> What dire Misfortune hath befel
> Each quav'ring Beau and tuneful Belle!
> Lost *Faronello*'s killing Note,
> For *Spain* has caught him by the Throat.

The final stanza brings Bawble among the fashionable elite so outraged at the loss of Farinelli they would trade all British merchant ships and sailors for his return:

> O cruel *Spain*! will nought suffice?
> Will nought redeem this lovely Prize?
> Take all our Ships, take all our Men,
> So we enjoy but him again.[136]

Bawble's willingness to exchange Farinelli for all of Britain's shipping indicts yet again the indifference of opera-goers (and by implication the ministry) to merchant losses.

The *Coffee-House* was one of the first plays to be reviewed by the Lord Chamberlain's office under the 1737 Licensing Act (see Chapter 7). The licenser (or perhaps someone in the theater) apparently thought the original final lines of Bawble's lament

> Ruin'd, Lords and Commons all
> From St. *James*'s to *Guild-Hall!*

so associated the court and ministry with those overly aggrieved at Farinelli's loss, and hence indifferent to British shipping, that for performance "St. *James*'s" was changed to the less political "Grosvenor's Square."[137]

In that December, *Common Sense* carried a letter from "Nonsense, a Terrestial Goddess," whose satiric allegory continues the *Craftsman*'s ploy of drawing parallels between the worlds of opera and politics[138] and again shows *Common Sense*'s sympathy with British merchants and commercial interests. Nonsense, a sister of Pope's Dulness and Fielding's Goddess of Nonsense, angrily protests her exclusion from the pages of *Common Sense*.[139] Claiming her power is so universally acknowledged that she has the Poet Laureate Colley Cibber and all "the Ladies, Poetasters, and the M— [Minister]" on her side, she boasts of her many followers at the Haymarket opera house, where Common Sense dares not appear. At this point in the allegory, the Haymarket Theatre stands for the ministry. Angelo Cori, one of the composers for the company that succeeded the Opera of the Nobility at the Haymarket Theatre (see Epilogue), stands for Walpole's brother Horatio. Nonsense boasts that the Haymarket Theatre is the *Sanctum Sanctorum* of *Nonsense*, and owes its present Glory to the happy Administration of those two Demi-Gods, my Vice-Gerents, *Angelo Cori* and *John James Heidegger*. – The Merits of *John James* are known and confess'd at all the Courts of Europe; and they have rais'd such Envy in the *Spanish* Ministers (who are making continual Depredations on the *English*) that those Rapacious *Dons* have seiz'd the Charming *Farinelli* as counterband Goods. *John James* bears the Loss [of Farinelli] with an Equanimity and Calmness that renders him, if possible, more than ever the Delight of Mankind.[140]

In her allegory, Heidegger's bearing of the loss of Farinelli with "Equanimity and Calmness" parallels the usual opposition charge that Walpole was passive and timid in the face of insults to British honor and ineffectual in obtaining redress for depredations.

Writing in support of the ministry in the *Nonsense of Common-Sense* the following January, Lady Mary Wortley Montagu ridicules the opposition's clamor for war with Spain – and its satire of opera-lovers who lament Farinelli's detention – in a mock letter from one Signior Balducci who is promoting his invention of mechanical statues. He has invented one that can imitate "exactly the Voice of any *Singer* that ever did, or even can appear upon the Stage" and perform at sight "the most difficult Piece of Musick the learned Mr. *H—l* can compose." The statues so excel real singers, they will no longer feud or overstep their roles. He promises he could even make a surrogate of Farinelli and "remove one of the Reasons we have for ... being involved in a War with *Spain*."[141] Lady Mary mocks those who clamor for war by reducing the *causus belli* with Spain as of little more significance than regaining an opera singer.

By early 1738 popular sentiment for war grew as no resolution to the Depredations Crisis seemed at hand. Parliament sat on January 24, and an unruly Commons began examining the ministry's handling of Spanish depredations. In March the Commons received petitions from shipowners and merchants complaining of their losses to *guarda costas* and asking the house to put an end to all "Insults and Depredations" on British shipping.[142]

Public indignation was inflamed in mid March when London learned that thirty-one sailors captured off Cuba had been forced to work their passage home and were now "groaning in the Fetters and Dungeons" in Cádiz.[143] To dramatize Spanish insults and cruelties, the Commons ordered Captain Robert Jenkins to appear on March 28 so he could tell how a Spanish privateer seized his brig in 1731, cut off his ear (among other cruelties), and told him to take it to King George.[144] Jenkins' ear became the symbol of Spanish cruelty and gave its name to the ensuing war.[145] Despite the popular clamor, Walpole was eager to avoid war, he said, "as long as there is any prospect of obtaining redress in a peaceable manner,"[146] by which he meant negotiating with Spain.

During the 1738 summer parliamentary recess, *Common Sense* carried fictional news items from Madrid, whose editorial comment kept before readers the opposition's case against the government's handling of the Depredations Crisis.[147] On June 3, certain news from Spain is said to be of greater consequence to friends of "a great Man" (Walpole) than a preceding item about diplomacy: the Spanish King now prefers the voice of a gift nightingale to "the Musick of Farinelli's Pipe." As a result, "our Politicians at the last Levee have form'd Hopes that Farinelli may be restored to this Nation again." The following ironic editorial comment – mocking those so eager to recover Farinelli that they disregard what should be their real concern – restates the opposition's patriotic concerns.

Let the Spaniards take our Ships, let them drive us out of our Colonies, nay let them cut off our Ears, if they return us Farinelli – Ask all the affected Ladies about Court, ask our new promoted Heroes that behave so valiantly at a [military] Review, what is the Ruin of a thousand Merchants, what the Interest of a dirty Nation, in Comparison of a Song?[148]

After delays caused by the slow pace of Spanish diplomacy, a settlement between Spain, Britain, and the South Sea Company was incorporated into the Convention of the Pardo, signed in Madrid on January 14, 1739 (NS), which was a preliminary to negotiations to begin in Madrid within eight months.[149] The Convention's terms confirmed the opposition's worst fears about Walpole's pacific policy toward Spain, and the country was flooded by opposition pamphlets denouncing the Convention as a national humiliation,[150] while the ministry reiterated that the Convention was merely a preliminary for a treaty that would settle outstanding issues.[151]

Negotiations ultimately deadlocked over demands by the South Sea Company and the Spanish king. With the collapse of the Convention, Walpole relented and against his better judgment declared war against Spain on October 19, 1739. With ringing of bells, bonfires, fireworks, and cheering of crowds, the country celebrated and looked forward to humbling Spain as in the days of Elizabeth and Cromwell. The Prince of Wales drank a toast to the war's success.[152]

There is no question but that London's opera world recognized the rivalry between Handel and the Opera of the Nobility. Some opera-goers patronized only one company,[153] while many others exploited the opportunity and attended both. But Hervey, Streatfeild, Flower, Chrysander, Deutsch, and others misrepresent the exclusivity of the patronage of the royal family and other opera-goers and the antagonism of Frederick toward Handel.

Likewise mistaken is the notion that Frederick was a founder of the Nobility opera with a partisan political motivation. The most convincing explanation for the company's founding is that a group of aristocrats and gentry from across the political spectrum – dissatisfied with Handel's management of the opera – established a company with the recently dismissed Senesino at its head to produce opera to their liking. Like his father, Frederick gave bounties to and attended performances of both companies, and in following years patronized Handel's oratorio seasons.[154] Frederick, then, was not exclusive in his patronage, and the gap in his recorded attendance and payments to Handel was temporary.[155]

If it was not the rivalry between the two opera companies that had partisan overtones, the same was not true of "Spain's detention" of the Nobility opera's star singer Farinelli. Such was Farinelli's impact on London's cultural consciousness, far beyond the limited circle of those who ever heard him sing, that even in his absence after summer 1737, his detention was exploited in popular media by the opposition in their agitation for war with Spain. Taking his entering the service of the Spanish court as a parallel to Spanish captures of British shipping and mocking London's opera-goers for their misplaced lamentations over the loss of Farinelli was a way to indict Walpole's ministry for its indifference to the loss of British trade, ships, sailors, and national honor at the hands of the Spanish.

7 | Politics, theater, and opera in the 1730s

The Excise Crisis revealed how a mobilized public opinion could affect parliamentary legislation. Even though Walpole withdrew the Excise, the opposition would not let the issue drop, and the Excise lingered as a topic for pamphleteering and an issue in the June 1734 general election; but the opposition was unable to capitalize on public anger to drive Walpole from office. With Bolingbroke discredited and now in a second exile in France, a dispirited and divided opposition lost momentum, and a political calm settled as the opposition reached its nadir in 1735.

In the wake of the Excise arose a revived opposition to Walpole's ministry. One casualty of the crisis was Sir Richard Temple (later Viscount Cobham), military hero from the Marlborough campaigns, who was dismissed in June 1733 from his army commands in retaliation for his speaking out against the Excise. Using his wealth and influence, Cobham threw himself into organizing an opposition to Walpole; in elections in 1734 and 1735 he succeeded in placing his nephews and relations, variously known as "Cobham's Cubs" or the "Boy Patriots," in Parliament where they became leading members of what is known as the Patriot opposition.[1] Cobham's estate at Stowe became a meeting place for opposition politicians and hosted visits from Alexander Pope and Frederick, Prince of Wales. The ideals of the Patriot opposition were even embodied in the statuary and monuments in his garden.[2]

Rallying under the Patriot's banner, the revived opposition took Frederick as its figurehead and looked to him as a future Patriot King who would rise above political parties, restore virtue and the British constitution, and redeem the nation from the corruption of Walpole's regime. The image of a messianic leader was articulated in Bolingbroke's *The Idea of a Patriot King*, written in England 1738–39 and circulated in manuscript in Patriot circles.[3] Motivated by virtue and opposed to corruption, these dissident Whigs could claim to be true patriots, offering a vision for Britain's greatness after Walpole and George II passed from the scene. Allied with the future king, the new opposition could escape the taint of Jacobitism.

Discouraged by the lack of patronage from the court, turned out by Walpole, or opposed to his policies, a new generation of writers cast their lots with the circle now forming about Frederick and wrote plays, satires, verse, and pamphlets reflecting the Patriot program. George Lyttelton, who became secretary to Frederick in August 1737, seems to have been a catalyst for much of the literary activity. By the end of the decade, the group included James Thomson, David Mallet, Richard Glover, Mark Akenside, James Hammond, Paul Whitehead, James Miller, Lyttelton, and Pope. Although direct personal links to Lyttelton or Frederick cannot always be documented, some writers had long-standing grievances with Walpole or the government; others were drawn to the Patriot cause by personal associations with the circle of Cobham, Lyttelton, and Pope.[4]

The rhetoric and ideology of Patriot literature continues Bolingbroke's indictment of a Britain overcome by luxury, corruption, false taste, and faction – all traced to Walpole's management of politics. Woven throughout many high-literary works are references to topical politics, Britain's forlorn state, her loss of liberty and virtue, and decline of the arts and sciences. Walpole is portrayed as failing to protect British shipping and sailors from Spanish depredations in the West Indies. The innuendo, as in most opposition propaganda, is clear: Walpole's removal will rectify these ills and rescue Britain. The political force of Patriot literature was recognized and answered by the ministry. With the ministerial journals consolidated in the *Daily Gazetteer* in June 1735 and financed by the Treasury, Walpole's propagandists systematically refuted the writings and attacked the persons of opposition writers, whom they called "False Patriots" and promoters of faction.[5]

On the positive, hortatory side – a facet generally lacking in earlier Scriblerian satire and most of the opposition periodical press – Patriot literature now prominently celebrated British national pride, virtue, and liberty. Paeans to Frederick and praise of opposition statesmen abounded even in bitter satire. As a rebuke to contemporary statesmen and prevailing taste, Patriot literature held up a canonic group of past British Worthies for emulation and proof of Britain's native genius.

Part of the Patriot literary campaign are a series of plays on historical subjects produced in 1738–40. With these dramatic pieces we are not caught in the dilemma of trying to decide whether the politics is "really there" or is "in the eye of the interpreter." These works demonstrate the principle that politics usually works by means of directed personation and parallel and application. The political effectiveness of the plays arises when characters on stage make speeches about evil ministers, statesmen, or tyrants of the past that could function as surrogates for contemporary partisan propaganda applicable to a contemporary political figure (usually Walpole). Serving opposition partisanship are speeches in defense of liberty or denouncing tyranny and corruption. The question *Cui bono?* has a clear answer: the plays disparage Walpole and his ministry, charge him with fostering tyranny and corruption, and consolidate sentiment among the political public to oppose his measures. The personal histories and associations of the authors put them in the Patriot camp and confirm the political intentions of the plays.

Contemporaries recognized the plays as partisan. There are comments on them in personal correspondence or the political press, and the ministry reacted to protect Walpole by banning or attacking them and their authors in the government journals – attesting to their perceived (or feared) political effectiveness.[6] The historical setting provides the excuse that the statements are being made of a fictional or historical character of the past. The ministerial writers are again in a bind. If they claim the statements libel the prime minister, they call attention to the statements and concede their application and validity. Nonetheless, ministerial writers attempted to disarm and subvert the effectiveness of the Patriot plays. Set against these topical stage works and the various techniques they use, we can see by contrast how distant from topical politics are Italian operas on historical subjects.

The Licensing Act and the politicization of drama

By the mid 1730s, there was general disgust at the increasing immorality and licentiousness of plays, objection to the violence, drunkenness, and prostitution in the theater neighborhoods, and dissatisfaction with the inability of the courts and city government to regulate the stage. Since *The Beggar's Opera* of 1728, the increasing politicization of the stage was directed primarily at Walpole. Even revivals of Shakespeare plays such as *Richard II* could be seen to reflect on contemporary politics.[7] As one observer noted, "the spectators were ready to apply all that was uttered in the theatre to the transactions of the day and to the ministry."[8]

After allowing Walpole to suffer the abuse of *The Beggar's Opera*, the ministry was more attentive to the stage, and in following years banned or suppressed partisan plays, including John Gay's *Polly* (1729), William Hatchett's *The Fall of Mortimer* (1731), and Walter Aston's *The Restauration of King Charles II* (1732). In *Polly*, Gay's sequel to his *Beggar's Opera*, courtiers are transported felons and a Walpole parallel – "an *infamous, over-grown Robber* so much to the Life"[9] – is their chief. John, Lord Hervey reported Walpole had the Lord Chamberlain suppress *Polly* rather than allow himself to be shown on the stage in the person of a highwayman.[10] *The Fall of Mortimer* sets up obvious parallels between Walpole and the evil minister Roger Mortimer, who is the source of all forms of corruption in the land. The young King Edward III is advised of Mortimer's treachery by a "Patriot Band" and Mortimer is hanged.[11] *Fog's Weekly Journal* made certain the public saw the application by printing excerpts from the play.[12] *The Restauration of King Charles II*, with its Jacobitical plot of a country uniting against a repressive government and restoring an overseas Stuart king to his rightful throne, would obviously be objectionable to the Hanoverians.

Most responsible for the ultimate regulation of the stage was the playwright Henry Fielding. His early plays are political in the sense that their burlesque and satire touch on politicians, the royal family, and electoral and ministerial corruption. But since their targets are usually politicians of both ministry and opposition, rarely are they specifically partisan.[13] As Robert Hume points out, since the genres were parody and burlesque, the charges were probably not taken too seriously.[14]

Fielding's first political work, *The Welsh Opera* (April 22, 1731),[15] is a ballad opera that burlesques the life and loves of the royal family and the prime minister transposed to a Welsh cottage. Touched on are Frederick's rumored impotence and amours with his mother's ladies-in-waiting, Walpole and his mistress Maria Skerrett, and Queen Caroline's influence over the king. However, the passing topical jibes at a household mismanaged by its servants do not amount to enough to give the farce a sustained partisan thrust. Fielding's own politics at the time are not known for certain and have been the subject of long debate; but as an impecunious playwright, he seems to have held out hopes of ministerial patronage.[16] Unsuccessful, Fielding then threw in his lot with the opposition. His contacts were Lord Chesterfield and George Lyttelton, the latter a childhood friend from Eton and a member of Frederick's circle.[17]

The first parliamentary attempt at regulating the stage – though for moral, not political reasons – was thwarted. On March 5, 1735, the opposition London Alderman Sir John Barnard asked the Commons for a bill to limit the "number and scandalous abuses of the Play-Houses" to prevent "corrupting the Youth, encouraging Vice and Debauchery, and being prejudicial to Trade and Industry." Barnard's bill reaffirmed the Lord Chamberlain's right to forbid plays, prohibited the establishment of any new theaters, and would bar anything "profane, obscene, or offensive to piety or good manners."[18] The bill met little opposition, for the idea that theaters should be regulated seemed reasonable enough; there was even objection the bill did not go far enough in regulating plays or theaters.[19]

Although the bill was not aimed at operas, the opposition MP James Erskine was led to count opera among the prevailing theatrical ills. He declared in debate supporting the bill:

> It is astonishing ... to all Europe, that Italian eunuchs and signoras should have set salaries equal to those of the Lords of the Treasury and Judges of England, besides the vast gains which these animals make by presents, by benefit nights, and by performing in private Houses; so that they carry away with them sums sufficient to purchase estates in their own country, where their wisdom for it is as much esteemed, as our vanity and foolish extravagance laughed at and despised.[20]

In a facetious objection to Barnard's bill, the *Craftsman* for June 28, 1735, used the tried and tested all-the-world's-a-stage topos to take a swipe at both opera and Horatio Walpole, Robert Walpole's brother and foreign ambassador.[21] Drawing a parallel between ambassadors and strollers (a legal term for actors), the writer thinks the bill would be too hard on Horatio, "*one of the greatest political Strollers*, that any Age, or Nation hath ever produced." Since Italian strollers (singers) are so encouraged in Britain, the writer asks the bill to admit a clause in favor of native strollers, so Horatio would not be treated as a mere vagabond.

Despite its popularity, Barnard's bill failed. At the last minute, Walpole attempted to amend the bill to allow the Lord Chamberlain to censor plays. The idea of putting such power over plays into the hands of a single member of Walpole's ministry was obviously anathema to Barnard and others. The House voted to delay consideration of the bill beyond the working period of the session, and the bill died the same death as Walpole's Excise. Even in its failure, the consequences of Barnard's bill were far reaching. A proposal for regulating the theaters had received general assent. The bill's failure encouraged – if not provoked – playwrights and managers to exploit their freedom, and following seasons saw even more politically seditious satire directed at the prime minister.

In the following year, Fielding started The Great Mogul's Company, opening on March 5, 1736, with the hugely successful *Pasquin: A Dramatic Satire on the Times*, rivaling *The Beggar's Opera* with thirty-five performances. *Pasquin* is highly topical and political, but not yet partisan and anti-ministerial. Representing a playhouse rehearsal, there are two plays within the play: a comedy ("The Election") and a tragedy ("The Life and Death of Common Sense"). True to the poet Trapwit's claim in the prologue, the comedy will "maul 'em" all: "both Whig and Tory; / Or *Court* and *Country* Party." In "The Election," a burlesque of a country election, candidates of both court (Lord Place and Colonel Promise) and country (Sir Harry Fox-Chace and Squire Tankard) bribe electors with cash and gifts. Fustian's tragedy shows Queen Ignorance and her attendants invading the realm of Queen Common Sense and murdering her. Its satire, like that of Alexander Pope's *Dunciad* (1728), lashes serious subjects including opera, pantomime, lawyers, physicians, and divines. The Earl of Egmont recorded, "It is a good satire on the times and has a good deal of wit," but noted no partisan implications.[22]

While the play may not be a party piece, it does exemplify what Brean Hammond identifies as Fielding's cultural politics: not narrowly partisan politics but a "cultural or aesthetic commitment" whose targets are similar to those of the cultural project of the Scriblerians – dunces, pedants, unintelligent theatrical entertainment, theater managers, political corruption, Lewis Theobald, and Colley Cibber.[23] Fielding's cultural politics subsumes the frequent satiric strokes against opera, castratos, and Farinelli that pervade his plays and their prologues and epilogues. Such a broad cultural politics, obliquely indicting the nation's culture and its rulers, nonetheless indirectly serves the opposition agenda.

The following season, though, Fielding's company transgressed from cultural politics to what the ministry called "the bringing of Politics on the Stage."[24] Some of that season's plays were not printed, perhaps because Fielding wanted to suppress evidence of how libelous they were, but two that survive in printed form, *The Historical Register for the Year 1736* and *Eurydice Hiss'd: or a Word to the Wise* (both published May 12, 1737), are subversive enough. Parodying the published annual report of the year's political events from which it takes its name, *The Historical Register* (March 21, 1737) is a medley of satirical rehearsal scenes touching on the fashions and politics of the day, the theater, Patriot politicians, and taxation by the ministry. Some scenes are innocuous, but several are acidic attacks on Walpole.[25]

In one scene, the author Medley has invited Lord Dapper and Sourwit to a rehearsal of a farce. When asked by Sourwit how the political is connected with the theatrical, Medley explains, using the all-the-world's-a-stage topos: "When my politics come to a farce, they very naturally lead to the playhouse, where, let me tell you, there are some politicians too, where there is lying, flattering, dissembling, promising, deceiving, and undermining, as well as in any court in Christendom."[26] He explains how his farce resembles politics:

there [is] a strict resemblance between the states political and theatrical. There is a ministry in the latter as well as the former, and I believe as weak a ministry as many poor kingdom could ever boast of. Parts are given in the latter to actors with much the same regard to capacity as places in the former have sometimes been, in former ages, I mean.

As the ministerial papers had objected, Fielding had brought politics onto the stage, ridiculed Walpole, and shown "all Government is but a Farce."

Eurydice Hiss'd, introduced as an afterpiece on April 13, 1737, again is cast as a rehearsal play exploiting stage–politics parallels. The author Spatter introduces a levee held by the poet Pillage, "a very Great Man," who has written a farce about to be played.[27] As Spatter explains to the critic Sourwit, he had to make his "Great Man not only a poet but a master of a playhouse and so, sir, his levee is composed of actors soliciting for parts, printers for copies, boxkeepers, scene-men, fiddlers and candle-snuffers." The device allows Fielding to compare Pillage's recruiting actors to perform his farce to Walpole's running the government by bribery and corruption. Honestus, who refuses a bribe to applaud Pillage's new play and objects to raised ticket prices (recalling the *Deborah*/Excise affair), is a mouthpiece for Patriot virtues. The Earl of Egmont recognized the levee scene was "a satire on Sir Robert Walpole." The night he saw it, he reported that the Prince of Wales loudly applauded all the "strong passages" in favor of liberty.[28]

Fielding's pointedly partisan plays finally spurred the government into action and to charge Fielding as a creature of the opposition.[29] The ministry's sensitivity to Fielding's attacks is revealed by "An Adventurer in Politics," who wrote to the *Daily Gazetteer* in May 1737, charging his abuses of liberty justified the necessity of restraining the stage. Ridiculing electoral corruption – as ill judged as Gay's "turning *Highwaymen*, *Pickpockets*, and *Whores*, into *Heroes* and *Heroines*" – made a "Minister appear ridiculous to a People," turned patriotism into jest, and impudently compared the ministers of the time "to *Farce-Actors*."[30] Fielding, writing as "Pasquin," defended himself in the opposition journal *Common Sense*, to which the Adventurer replied in turn.[31]

In May 1737, Parliament began consideration of the Licensing Act, which would transform the British theater. Interestingly, at that stage there is no record that Walpole was involved with the bill, which began in the Commons as amendments to the Vagrancy Act of 1714.[32] With objections to licentiousness of the plays and theaters increasing, the bill sped quickly to passage; even the opposition accepted the implicit charges against the theaters. During debate, Walpole announced his intention to allow the prior licensing of all plays by the Lord Chamberlain. As justification, he presented the most licentious passages from *The Golden Rump*, a farce attacking the king and Walpole.[33]

The bill passed on June 1, 1737, and limited all acting to the two patent theaters at Covent Garden and Drury Lane or the licensed King's Theatre at the Haymarket (thus shuttering Fielding's playhouse); it required all plays and entertainments to be submitted to the Lord Chamberlain's office for approval before acting.[34] The passage of the Act prevented Fielding continuing his final season as projected.

The bill received little opposition in the Commons, where it appears that only Pulteney spoke against it, asserting that restraining the "Writers for the Stage, was a certain preamble to the taking away the Liberty of the Press in general."[35] When it was taken up in the Lords on June 2, the opposition's Lord Chesterfield delivered a celebrated speech against the bill's censorship of the theaters. Joining his contemporaries in deploring the state of the stage, Chesterfield agreed that recent productions certainly deserved censure or prosecution, but opposed the new law "as an unnecessary, and as a dangerous One," for present law is sufficient for punishing the offender. Chesterfield's most telling point (taken up repeatedly thereafter against the government) was that "a Restraint on the Liberty of the Press ... will be a long Stride towards the Destruction of Liberty itself." Chesterfield's speech did little to hinder the bill, which passed the Lords on June 6 and received royal assent on 21 June.[36]

While the bill was working its way toward passage, it became a flashpoint in the print warfare between the government and opposition. The opposition press, reiterating points from Chesterfield's speech, claimed the bill portended general restrictions on liberty and freedom of the press.[37] The ministerial *Daily Gazetteer* devoted an unprecedented fifteen issues to the bill, stating it posed no threat to liberty and casting its opponents as "*Patrons* of *all Licentiousness*" and "Scurrilities of the Stage" intent on bringing politics and "the *Personal* Abuse of *Majesty*" itself" onto the stage; only enemies of the government would prevent the Lord Chamberlain prohibiting "*Seditious* and Immoral Plays."[38]

While the ministry and opposition clashed over the bill, it did not escape the notice of opposition writers that the Licensing Act would also apply to the operas and oratorios produced at the Haymarket and Covent Garden Theaters, and they used the ongoing political debate to set off squibs at opera and embarrass the ministry. Even before the bill passed the Commons, "A. B.," a correspondent to the oppositional *Fog's Weekly Journal*, doubted the stage would be reformed until "we see a reformed Taste in the Town" and expected "the Theatres will continue as immoral as ever."[39] But sharing *Fog's* general concern about the degeneracy of the stage and hostility toward opera, A. B. hopes the Lord Chamberlain might use his powers against the operas on account of "the exorbitant Sums carry'd out of the Kingdom by the *Italians*" and their contributing to "the enervating of our Youth." A. B. thinks there might be a great party to defend opera on the grounds of "the Innocence of this Diversion," but introduction of some sense would be necessary to render opera "an agreeable Amusement for your *Time Killers*." Yet since the Italian poets would rather throw up their pens than write sense, he doubts this will come to pass.

In a parting shot at the irrationality of opera, A. B. provides unintended support for the argument that topical or political allusions and allegory are not to be expected in opera librettos. Were it not for their expense and tendency for effeminacy, A. B. has no wish for the fall of operas. But since, unlike English plays, they lack sense, they are harmless to those in public office. His proof –

For as they [operas] will never deviate into Wit, so there is no Danger of their being Satyrical upon any [person], and a M—r [Minister] may blunder or plunder, or both, without any Apprehension of being exposed on the *Italian* Stage in *London*.

– is a master stroke of innuendo accusing Walpole of being an error-prone statesman and robber of the public purse.

Resigned that the bill would probably become law, a writer for the *Craftsman* on June 4 saw that some good to the nation might arise. "If therefore it should be thought necessary to lay any farther Restraint upon the *most useful Sort of dramatical Entertainments*," he declared he hoped "our *Italian Opera's* will fall the first Sacrifice, as they not only carry great Sums of Money out of the Kingdom, but soften and enervate the Minds of the People."[40] Later that month, agreeing with the stated design of the bill, "to put a Stop to the *Luxury*, *Extravagance* and *Corruption* of the Age," the *Craftsman* was optimistic that this meant that "We shall hear of no more *Italian Operas*."[41]

Because the Licensing Act applied to all stage entertainments, librettos of operas and oratorios were required to be approved by the Lord Chamberlain (or his deputy, the licenser) before performance. About a year later, this fact was used in another opposition gibe at the ministry over the Act. As an advocate of "Punch, Master of the Artistical Company of Comedians in the Haymarket," "A. D." wrote to *Common Sense* for May 13, 1738, presenting Punch's complaint that, although Handel performs on Wednesdays and Fridays in Lent, Punch has been restrained from doing so.[42] Everyone knows Handel's entertainments are "calculated for the Quality only, and that People of moderate Fortunes cannot pretend to them, although as Free *Britons*, they have as good a Right to be entertained with what they do not understand as their Betters." A. D. does not know whether Handel has a license from the church or licenser of the stage, but believes Punch has just as good a right to perform.

The supposed prevention of Punch's acting is held up as an example of the ministry's feared abuse of the Licensing Act to censor the stage, invade property, prevent Punch earning a livelihood, and deny Britons "those Amusements and Recreations which have been always thought inoffensive, and which none but superstitious Beasts ever found Fault with." After printing Punch's petition to be allowed to perform, A. D. reassures that since the sanction for oratorios is their being founded on scriptural history, Punch's performances will be on similar subjects, such as the "Life and Death of *Haman*, Prime Minister to King *Ahasuerus*" – a sly way of bracketing Walpole with a Biblical king's favorite and evil minister. The observation that "between the Acts *Punch* will perform several serious Dances to the Organ" surely holds up Handel to slight ridicule by comparing his organ performances during oratorios to dances by a wooden puppet.

The politics of Patriot drama

In their campaign against the Walpole ministry, opposition writers used epic and tragedy as vehicles for Patriot polemic. Historical subjects were chosen for their application to the contemporary political scene – not intended for thoroughgoing allegory but for the looser technique of personation and application. Spoken by characters in the play, set-speeches are carefully crafted as if directly addressed to or about Walpole or members of the royal family. These opposition works serve as examples of how partisan works are readily recognizable and meet the benchmarks set out in Chapter 2. They suggest what we would expect to find in Italian opera librettos on historical subjects were they intended, structured, written, and received as politically topical – and especially the issues that might be raised in the Nobility operas, were the company, as claimed, organized by Frederick and the opposition.

A model from the Patriot circle for putting historical subjects to partisan use is Richard Glover's blank-verse epic *Leonidas* (April 16, 1737). Merchant and opposition MP Glover was one of the most popular men in the City for his advocacy of the merchant's cause against the government's failure to protect British shipping in the West Indies against Spanish depredations. The nine-book epic tells how the Spartan King Leonidas (491–480 BC) and his small band heroically perished while resisting Xerxes' much larger Persian force at the pass of Thermopylae.[43] Throughout the text are hortatory set-speeches indicting luxury and corrupt ministers, reiterating Patriot values, and rallying calls to war (intending Spain).

The first hint that *Leonidas* was a party work is the dedication to Lord Cobham. When George Lyttelton commended the poem in *Common Sense*,[44] his precis of the poem's "great and instructive Moral" hit all the hot buttons of opposition polemic – praise of "Virtue, Publick Spirit, and the Love of Liberty" and the erosion of British liberties – and leaves no doubt how to apply the poem at that time. Although the Persian invasion and decisive battle had no analogs with Britain, in *Leonidas*, the oppression occurs in Persia under the tyrant Xerxes, but the intended parallel and application is the supposed enslavement of Britain under the Walpole ministry.[45] By commending Glover for avoiding "the Imputation of writing *for a Party*" by going to Greece for an event that had no parallel to contemporary times, Lyttelton plants the innuendo that there *is* a contemporary application.

Lyttelton's praise of *Leonidas* in *Common Sense* had the ulterior purpose of increasing its readership and directing the point of its application. But his puff was deflated by a long three-part letter to the *Weekly Miscellany*.[46] Ironically praising *Leonidas*, the author dismisses the achievements of Homer, Virgil, and Milton and satirically elevates Glover's correctness and flat, prosaic diction into great beauties.

Unintimidated by the threat of censorship imposed by the Licensing Act, a group of writers in the Lyttelton–Frederick circle took the Patriot propaganda campaign to the theater in a series of historical application plays. Frederick, an avid theater-goer, used his influence to get them produced, and Pope helped revise at least one of them.[47] Thomas Davies later described the strategy. The poets David Mallet and James Thomson were appointed secretaries to Frederick and employed to vindicate his cause by attacking Walpole's administration.[48] Although not deeply versed in political argument, the plays were, wrote Davies, "supposed capable of interesting the public in favour of their master's cause by the art of working up a fable in a tragedy, and in the drawing [of] characters, and giving them such language, as an audience could not fail properly to apply."[49]

The first Patriot play to test the Licensing Act was an adaptation of Aeschylus' *Agamemnon* (April 6, 1738) by James Thomson, by now the celebrated author of *The Seasons*. We can document how Thomson, a writer of impeccable Whig credentials, drifted into the Patriot circle, which helps confirm his works as vehicles for opposition polemic. Dedications of his early poems show his Whig sympathies. When Sir Isaac Newton died in

March 1727, Thomson quickly published a *Poem to the Memory of Sir Isaac Newton* (May 8, 1727), dedicating it to Sir Robert Walpole and praising him as Britain's "most illustrious *Patriot*" who is "balancing the Power of *Europe*, watching over our common Welfare."

Two years later, Thomson anonymously published *Britannia* (1729), which shows him caught up in the fervor of contemporary politics. *Britannia* was part of the general public clamor against Walpole's humiliating course of peace and diplomacy toward Spain in the face of its continuing depredations on British shipping. In an allegorical tableau, Britannia sits in despair on a stormy, wind-beaten shore. The Muse records her lament and address to the nation. The cause of her despair is "the insulting *Spaniard*" who fearlessly seizes British shipping while Britain meekly endures a "false peace," in contrast to the days of Elizabeth when the English easily defeated the Armada (lines 23–89). The opening indictment of the ministry is balanced by a Whig paean to the benefits of peace to trade and commerce. But nothing better justifies abandoning peace, Thomson urges, than threats to trade and commerce. Britannia cautions Britain that luxury and corruption destroy liberty and urges virtue and public spirit. After panegyric to the royal throne and Prince Frederick, Britannia disappears in the gale.

Both poem and poet were received as political. Samuel Johnson saw it as "a kind of poetical invective against the ministry, [by which] piece he declared himself an adherent to the opposition."[50] Ministry and opposition newspapers selectively quoted from the poem to turn it to their own purposes.[51] A ministerial writer quoted the forty-seven lines extolling the government's peace measures, whereas *Fog's Weekly Journal* printed the opening eighty-one lines describing the causes of Britannia's despair, breaking off at the point of the invading Spanish Armada. The ministry later rebuked Thomson for ingratitude and libeling the ministry after having received £50 from Walpole for the poem on Newton.[52]

At the time, Thomson had not abandoned his ministerial Whig allegiance (or at least hopes for patronage), judging by a subsequent dedication of his first play *Sophonisba* (March 1730) to Queen Caroline and by the numerous courtiers and government members who subscribed to *The Seasons* (June 1730), where *Autumn*, completing the cycle, is dedicated to the new speaker of the Commons, Arthur Onslow. In November 1733, Thomson accepted the post of secretary of briefs from Lord Chancellor Charles Talbot, who at the time was a Walpole supporter. But in the following year, Talbot became disaffected over the government's refusal to appoint Thomas Rundle to the See of Gloucester. Talbot's son William declared against Walpole, voting the following year against the ministry. By 1733, Thomson's friend and patron George Bubb Dodington was in open opposition. Most likely, then, Thomson slowly drifted with his friends and patrons into opposition.

Upon his return from accompanying Talbot's son to Italy, Thomson began publishing the installments of *Liberty* (1735–36), a five-part Whig panegyric to the Progress of Liberty from her rise and fall in Greece and Rome, her flight northward, and her "excellent Establishment in Great Britain" (dedication).[53] In an opposition gesture, the first book (as well as the completed poem) was dedicated to Frederick, in whom "the Cause and Concerns of Liberty have so zealous a Patron" and who unites "the noblest Dispositions of the Prince, and of the Patriot" (dedication). At the end of Part 1, a paean to the royal family in the voice of Goddess Liberty includes a lengthy and prominent tribute to Frederick, who "burns sincere" for liberty and will encourage the arts (Part 1, lines 359–78). The oppositional stance of *Liberty* arises less from overt denunciations of Walpole or his ministry, than in rehearsals of Bolingbrokeian political ideas, patriotic exhortations, and praise of Frederick as champion of constitutional liberties.[54]

In the final part, Liberty, now settled in Britain, declares, "On Virtue *can alone* my Kingdom *stand,* / *On* Public Virtue, every Virtue join'd" (Part 5, lines 93–4). This variation on the Progress of Liberty topos – the new theme of Liberty in danger – carries an implicit and tactless affront to the king's ministry. It is understood, of course, that the danger to liberty stems from Walpole's corrupt management of politics.[55] A prospect of Britain's future passes before the poet in a vision: kings who value only merit and virtue, a new race of noble and generous youth, arts and sciences that flourish, rising public works, and arts that pursue social ends and temper the passions.

While Thomson was abroad, the Countess of Hertford had apparently given Frederick a volume containing his *Seasons* and *Britannia*. Frederick's approbation gave Thomson hope "of seeing the fine arts flourish under a Prince of his so noble equal humane and generous dispositions; who knows how to unite the soveraignty of the prince with the liberty of the people, and to found his happiness and Glory on the publick Good."[56] Thomson's later additions to *The Seasons* further politicize the poem; he mentions Patriot statesmen and dedicated the 1744 edition of the final poem to Frederick.[57]

When Chancellor Talbot died in February 1737, Thomson lost his secretarial sinecure. Now secretary to Frederick, Lyttelton sent for Thomson and learning of his poverty, obtained for him in August a £100 pension. Public evidence of Thomson's allegiance to the opposition appeared on September 13, 1737, with the publication of an ode to Frederick on the birth of his daughter, the Princess Augusta.[58] Thomson tactlessly slights the reigning monarchs as he sings "the promis'd Glories" of the coming reign of Frederick; and the reflection that this will occur "When *France* Insults, and *Spain* shall Rob no more" (line 30) is a sharp indictment of Walpole's foreign policy. The slight poem of only five stanzas reflected so poorly on the king and his government that the *Daily Gazetteer* devoted an entire lead essay to personal invective against the "impudent" poet and to exposing the insults, libels, and affronts of the poem.[59]

1737–38 season

It was as a poet aligned with the opposition and a pensioner of Prince Frederick that Thomson adapted *Agamemnon* to advance the Patriot cause. Pope commended it to the theater managers and attended the disappointing first night, when the play was met with hissing and catcalls in the last two acts. The next morning, Pope met with others at the playhouse and pruned and reorganized the play, which went on to a respectable run of nine performances.

There are broad and unflattering parallels in the play with the royal family. Alert members of the audience would find Agamemnon's return to Argos with a concubine after ten years in Troy recalls King George's recent return from an extended trip to Hanover where he dallied with his German mistress Madam Wallmoden (she was later called for, and arrived in London on June 12, 1738). Queen Clytemnestra, with her reliance on Egisthus as counselor and conspiracy with him to corrupt Argos in Agamemnon's absence, could parallel the late Queen Caroline and Robert Walpole, who were widely believed to have ruled over George.[60] These might be innocuous enough coincidences (not enough for a thorough-going allegory), but the partisanship in the speeches is surely intentional and dangerous, echoing similar themes in other Patriot opposition works.

On one level, the play offers the age-old caution to a ruler about placing too much power and trust in advisors and ministers. While the parallels to the king and queen are not consistently carried out (Caroline, for example, never plotted to murder her husband as did Clytemnestra), Thomson certainly intended denunciations of Egisthus to be construed as attacks on Walpole. When Agamemnon charges Egisthus with usurping power, corrupting the people, and failing to protect the arts (II.v), the accusations echo stock opposition attacks on Walpole's government. When Agamemnon asks how his country became so dissolute during his absence, Arcas' explanation could apply as well to Walpole's corruption of politics:

> These Cities [in Mycenae] now with Slaves and Villains
>   swarm.
> At first *Egisthus* [Walpole] …
> By hidden Ways proceeded, [under]mining Virtue:
> He Pride, he Pomp, he Luxury diffus'd;
> He taught them Wants, beyond their private Means:
> And straight, in Bounty's pleasing Chains involv'd,
> They grew his Slaves.
>
> III.ii

Thomas Davies[61] recalled that one speech of Agamemnon's denouncing his wicked minister who betrayed him struck directly at Walpole and was greatly applauded:

> But the most fruitful Source
> Of every Evil – O that I, in Thunder,
> Could sound it o'er the listning Earth to Kings! –
> Is Delegating Power to wicked Hands.
>
> III.ii

The hortatory moralizing comes from the bard Melisander and the loyal servant Arcas. Asserting the right of a virtuous mind to speak the truth, Melisander denounces traitors and even suggests that the King deserves blame for giving too much power to an evil minister (III.i). Later when Agamemnon asks Arcas whether remain any "Faithful Few! to save the sinking State?" his reply –

> A Band of generous Youth, whom native Virtue,
> Unbroken yet by Avarice and Meanness,
> Fits for our purpose
>
> III.ii

– obviously points to the young Patriot opposition. The opposition's idea of justice for Walpole emerges when after Agamemnon's death, Cassandra prophesies Egisthus' death as a "trembling Coward" (V.ix).

The Lord Chamberlain did not find the play dangerous enough to ban.[62] Queen Caroline's death in the previous November, John Loftis suggests, "removed its sting, and may have had something to do with the fact that it was licensed."[63] While he did not ban the play, the Lord Chamberlain (or perhaps the theater manager) was at least attentive enough to censor six lines of the spoken prologue, written by David Mallet, that alluded to the Licensing Act and impugned Parliament. The players, the speaker said in the struck lines, know "Our last best Licence" must flow from the influence-free audience in the theater: "One Place, – unbiass'd yet by Party-Rage, – / Where only Honour votes."[64]

1738–39 season

The high water of the Patriot drama campaign was the 1738–39 season. With the involvement of Frederick, Lyttelton, and Pope, tragedies based on the historical subjects Mustapha, Gustavus Vasa, and Edward and Eleonora were prepared for the stage by Mallet, Henry Brooke, and Thomson. Speeches in the plays contain Patriot polemic and thinly veiled attacks on the king, Walpole, and the ministry. That the lines struck home is shown by contemporary notices and the ministry's response in the *Daily Gazetteer*.

An avid theater-goer, Frederick promoted the Patriot plays, and at his direction Charles Fleetwood, manager at Drury Lane, mounted David Mallet's *Mustapha* on February 13, 1739.[65] Mallet read the script to Pope, who attended the first-night performance, and dedicated the published play to Frederick, remarking on "that generous protection the politer arts now meet with from the Prince of Wales." For Mallet, to wish every blessing to the prince was "to wish the future happiness of Great Britain."

The first night was an opposition occasion. Davies reported there were assembled "all the chiefs in opposition to the court; and many speeches were applied by the audience to the supposed grievances of the times, and to persons and characters."[66] One writer observed even "the dullest Auditors of the Galleries" "chuckled and clapt" because the play "stung the great Folks!" and everyone wondered how "it got through the Licenser's Hands."[67]

Lady Hertford wrote about the play from London the following week to Henrietta Louisa, Countess of Pomfret, then traveling abroad, "I hear other People say there are many Party-strokes in it."[68] After she received the play, Lady Pomfret noted the obvious party applications and remarked, "I think the malice of it is more visible than the wit."[69]

Mustapha is set at the Turkish court of Emperor Solyman the Magnificent. The wicked vizier Rustan (Walpole) and the Empress Roxolana (Queen Caroline) conspire to mislead Solyman (King George) into believing his virtuous, popular son Mustapha (Frederick) is disloyal (III.iii). Mustapha is falsely charged, and Solyman has him executed – again the example points up the dangers of a wicked principal minister. A caution about evil ministers could be applied by audiences at any time, but the application to Walpole is directed by the context.[70] A speech by Achmet, friend of Mustapha, denouncing the wicked vizier and the arts by which he rose to greatness, could be applied to Walpole, and the vizier's plotting with

Solyman and Roxolana against the popular royal heir could parallel the estrangement of Frederick and his parents and Frederick's increasing popularity. Although Frederick would not share Mustapha's fate, the speeches extolling Mustapha's virtue and patriotism were no doubt intended to flatter Frederick and the Patriots.

As in most Italian opera librettos, central to the plot is a moral choice confronting a character. In this case, Mustapha could kill his father and gain his empire by committing untold horrors, or die guiltless under false suspicion but having led an honorable life. Mustapha holds up for emulation the example of a virtuous prince who chooses the latter course (III.vii).

After *Mustapha* with its clearly directed parallels and applications, the Lord Chamberlain grew more attentive, and the two other Patriot plays planned for the season were banned. On March 16, three days before its scheduled premiere and after five weeks of rehearsal and with no explanation from the Lord Chamberlain's office, Henry Brooke's *Gustavus Vasa, the Deliverer of His Country* (1739) became the first play to fall victim to the Licensing Act. The suppression drew forth one of Samuel Johnson's earliest satires, *A Compleat Vindication of the Licensers of the Stage* (May 25, 1739).[71] Published by subscription on May 5, 1739, the play gained thereby a wider audience and greater reward for the author. The subscription list, containing no supporters of the Walpole ministry, suggests subscribing to the play was a sign of solidarity with the opposition.[72]

Lady Hertford continued to keep Lady Pomfret informed about Patriot plays, writing in March, "By an odd caprice of Fortune Gustavus Vasa is not to be acted at last thô there does not appear to me, half so much in it to incurr the displeasure of the Licenser, as there is in Mustapha."[73] Benjamin Victor thought both *Mustapha* and *Agamemnon* contained far more politically objectionable passages, which he called "party clap-traps, *designedly introduced*," than *Gustavus Vasa*, whose sentiments naturally arose from the business of the scene. He admitted that "the tyrant, *Christern* [*sic*], King of Denmark, has, indeed, a most accomplished Wicked Minister, and there, perhaps, the cap fits, but surely those who make the *application*, make the *libel!*"[74]

The play's prologue encourages the application to Britain at the time.[75] While "this Night" no doubt refers to the play's opening scene at the copper mines in Dalecarlia, Sweden, it could also be taken by an attentive audience to glance at present-day Britain:

> *Britons!* this Night presents a State distress'd,
> Tho' brave, yet vanquish'd; and tho' great, oppress'd;
> Vice, rav'ning Vulture, on her Vitals prey'd,
> Her Peers, her Prelates, fell Corruption sway'd.

Using an incident in Swedish history, *Gustavus Vasa* shows the inevitable triumph of liberty over tyranny. Sweden is suffering under the tyrannical rule of Cristiern, King of Denmark, who has usurped the Swedish crown. He is about to attack Dalecarlia, the last resort of expiring liberty in Sweden. Gustavus, cousin to the lately defeated Swedish king, appears as a stranger laboring in the copper mines. He soon reveals himself (almost like a messiah) to his fellows to rouse and lead a smaller band of virtuous Dalecarlians to defeat the attacking usurper Cristiern and restore liberty. *Gustavus Vasa* is more overtly political than other such dramatic works in the sense that it does raise political ideas. Beyond posing the unproblematic choice between tyranny and freedom, the play takes stands on issues of political theory: the source of a ruler's legitimacy (not through conquest and usurpation, as with Cristiern), the source of the law's legitimacy (from the people), and the duty of a prince (not to ignore the people's needs and enslave them).

The ministerial *Daily Gazetteer* recognized that efforts were made to have the play "thought a *design'd Satire* upon *some Personages*."[76] The obvious parallel is between Walpole and Trollio, Cristiern's scheming minister who suborns and manipulates men by appealing to their base passions. After his defeat, Cristiern murders Trollio (a veiled hint to the king to dispense with Walpole?). Trollio's own description of his methods could be taken as an opposition portrait of Walpole's corruption of politics:

> Vice and Frailty are the Statesman's Quarry,
> The Objects of our Search, and of our Science;
> Mark'd by our Smiles, and cherish'd by our Bounty.
> 'Tis hence, you lord it o'er your servile Senates;
> How low the Slaves will stoop to gorge their Lusts
> When aptly baited: Ev'n the Tongues of Patriots,
> (Those Sons of Clamour) oft relax the Nerve
> Within the Warmth of Favour.
>
> IV.i

In his preface to the subscribers, Brooke says he took his subject from one of "those *Gothic* and *glorious* Nations" from whom Britain has inherited her "*Sparks* of Liberty and Patriotism." His single and great moral was "*Patriotism*, or *the Love of Country*," embodied in the character of Gustavus. The play's epilogue enjoins the reader to liken Gustavus to William III, and so honors "The Deliverer of our Country," who freed England "From blood-stain'd Tyrant, and perfidious Priest."

There are so many foreign usurpers of thrones in plays and opera librettos of the time, that it strains plausibility to give the play Jacobite implications, as does J. C. D. Clark, who suggests the "sensational" play was an

easily decoded Jacobite allegory, whereby Gustavus (with the better hereditary claim) would stand for the Pretender returning to depose the usurper
(George II) and his wicked minister (Walpole).[77] Such a reading, offering a
vision for the future, would, however, affront opposition Whigs (many of
whom subscribed to the printed play) and deny Frederick, the opposition's
figurehead, his rightful succession to the throne. If Clark's was such an easily decoded reading, it is highly unlikely that a theater manager, operating
at the pleasure of the king and in the wake of the Licensing Act, would
risk producing such a play, or that the licenser would pass it. As Howard
Weinbrot points out, although the play "is in opposition to Walpole, it also
is loyal to the German Hanoverians."[78]

That the political focus of the play was on Trollio/Walpole is confirmed
by *The Fate of Favourites: or, a Looking-Glass for S***** [Statesmen].
Addressed to the Subscribers of Gustavus Vasa, the Deliverer of His
Country* (1739).[79] The pamphleteer includes Walpole among those evil
royal favorites whose only interest is enlarging their own power, and
whose rule ruins a state and destroys the people. As in other opposition polemic, Walpole is paralleled to Sejanus, a favorite of the wicked
Emperor Tiberius. A parallel to Britain after the Licensing Act is drawn
when the pamphleteer recalls that Tiberius (unlike Julius Caesar or
Augustus) suppressed free speech.

The Lord Chamberlain's suddenly forbidding *Gustavus Vasa*, as expected,
drew attention to the play. Brooke exploited the prohibition in his subscription advertisement for the printed play, confident "the Sentiments
are just, and no way unbecoming a free Subject of Britain to publish, or
highest Powers – to approve."[80] To encourage subscriptions, "A. Z." wrote
to *Common Sense* (no. 114, April 7, 1739). To allay suspicion that the play
deserved encouragement only for being prohibited, A. Z. submitted the
play's prologue for examination and urged readers to read Brooke's translation of Torquato Tasso, *Jerusalem, An Epic Poem* (1738).

The ministry reacted to the subscription campaign for *Gustavus Vasa* the
following month with a pamphlet by one "Country Correspondent," who
complained the poetry of this "darling Patriot" made him worthy of being
"Poet Laureat to the Goths" or "Secretary to the Vandals."[81] Ridiculing the
promotion of the play and its wild diction and figures of speech, he feigns
he couldn't tell whether they raised wonder or laughter. In all, it was perhaps better that it had not been acted, though the preface was worthy of
being set to recitative by Lord Flame in *Hurlothrumbo* (1729).

Two days before its planned first performance, Thomson's next play,
Edward and Eleonora, was banned on March 27. Davies thought it "was

excluded the stage, because the licenser saw, as he imagined, a formidable attack upon the minister."[82] Considering that the Lord Chamberlain had the play for over a month, such a precipitous action was, as James Sambrook suggests, "admonitory and vindictive."[83] The prohibition was again turned to advantage, and the play was prominently advertised and published by subscription. Advertisements disingenuously denied the play had any political application and feigned ignorance at why it was banned. Thomson "had no other Intention but to paint Virtue and Vice in their Proper Colours," and "how Moral Reflections and Sentiments of Liberty should offend, in a free Nation, he will not enquire."[84]

The sentimental play is based on an apocryphal story of the last crusade at the siege of Jaffa in 1272. When Prince Edward (later King Edward I) is stabbed by a poisoned dagger, his wife Eleonora sucks out the poison and saves his life. She in turn falls mortally ill, but is cured by the Sultan of Jaffa, a virtuous, tolerant pagan. The Lord Chamberlain must have found a number of "clap-trap" set-speeches by Edward and his advisor and friend the Earl of Gloster objectionable; gratuitous to the plot, the speeches are opposition propaganda in their application to the king and Walpole.[85] Denouncing his father Henry III's ministers back in England, Edward (as Prince Frederick) could be describing Walpole's ministry as he comments while reading dispatches from home:[86]

> Is there a Curse on human Kind so fell,
> So pestilent, at once, to Prince and People,
> As the base servile Vermin of a Court,
> Corrupt, corrupting Ministers and Favourites?
> IV.viii

Gloster, a mouthpiece for opposition views, urges Edward to give up the crusade and return to England, an "unhappy Country":

> Exhausted, sunk; drain'd by ten thousand Arts
> Of ministerial Rapine, endless Taxes,
> …
> Who knows what evil Counsellors, again,
> Are gather'd round the Throne.
> I.i

Gloster summons Edward "on the firm Base / Of well-proportion'd Liberty," to build *England's* rising Grandeur." His pleas to Edward later touch on volatile topics such as political corruption, the Spanish depredations on British shipping, and a call to war:

> O save our Country, Edward! save a Nation,
>
> …
>
> Robb'd of our antient Spirit, sunk in Baseness,
> At home corrupted, and despis'd abroad.
> Behold our Wealth consum'd, those Treasures squander'd,
> That might protect and nourish wholesome Peace,
> Or urge a glorious War; on Wretches squander'd,
> A venal Crew that plunder and disgrace us.
>
> II.ii

Gloster's exhortations to the royal heir Edward could be seen as applying to Frederick, Bolingbroke's idea of the Patriot King who would embody virtue, eliminate corruption, rise above faction, and redeem Britain. The plot's emphasis that reason must control the passions and that a ruler must subordinate private interest to the public good are lessons to Frederick how to rule as a wise king.

Lady Pomfret regarded the subject of Edward and Eleonora as an exemplum of conjugal love.[87] Since Thomson dedicated the printed play to the Princess of Wales, the expressions of love between the couple could be a tribute to his patrons the royal couple.

An unnoted aspect of this season of Patriot dramas are three pamphlets presenting the historical backgrounds to *Mustapha*, *Gustavus Vasa*, and *Edward and Eleonora*.[88] Treating the plays quite objectively and without any obvious application to contemporary Britain, the overblown puffs of the plays and their authors must have been intended nonetheless as part of a deliberate effort to promote the plays.

Ministerial attacks on Patriot drama

Spurred by the public attacks on Walpole, puffs in the opposition press, and successful subscription campaigns, the ministry tried to undermine the Patriot plays and limit their political damage in its own offensive of essays in the *Daily Gazetteer* in April–June 1739. Combining *ad hominem* attacks on the "*protesting Poets*" Thomson and Brooke with serious criticism of the poetic deficiencies of their plays, the ministerial writer "Algernon Sidney" sought to undercut their credibility and, presumably, limit their wider circulation and partisan effect.

In two essays in April, Sidney chides Thomson and Brooke for complaining about the banning of their plays.[89] The Lord Chamberlain had allowed *Agamemnon* despite the "mean Intention too apparent in several Parts of it." In their subscription solicitations, the "*grumbling Bards*," like opposition leaders, are pursuing their own private interest in parading "the paltry thread-bare Pretence" that their plays were only rejected for their party content and expressions of "*flaming Ardour* for Liberty." Out of concern for the dignity of the Muses, Sidney is concerned that dramas inspired by political interest are offered "as the *genuine Growth of Parnassus*." Sidney charges the "wide-mouth'd *Grumblers*" were using the excuse of being banned to deceive the public into thinking the plays are works of dramatic genius. He even turned Thomson's prostitution of the "*Tragick Muse*" to the government's advantage, claiming it was a "melancholy Instance of the Advantages arising from our full Enjoyment of Liberty."

After *Gustavus Vasa* and *Edward and Eleonora* were published, Sidney rose again to attack each play,[90] exposing Brooke's attempt to benefit from appearing in "the *unpoetical* Light of a modern *Patriot Advocate*" and elicit sympathy for his play's being banned for political reasons. Any supposed harm to Brooke had been undone by the successful subscription campaign. Since Thomson's earlier plays were "too void of Fancy, and too destitute of Imagination" to succeed on the stage, Sidney surmises his motives for the present play "can scarcely be supposed *poetical* ones." The Licensing Act, Sidney points out, allows the Lord Chamberlain to reject pieces he judged "unfit for Representation on the Stage," leaving the implication that he was sparing the public from poor plays. Sidney drives home the point by marching through the defects of each tragedy – from choice of subject, historical accuracy, plot construction, and violation of verisimilitude to unnatural diction.

These efforts to discredit the Patriot dramas suggest their personations and applications stung enough that the government had to defend Walpole. The Lord Chamberlain passed *Agamemnon* and *Mustapha* perhaps out of inattention or a calculation that the plays would pass unnoticed and prohibition would only call attention to them; but *Gustavus Vasa* and *Edward and Eleonora* were too obviously party clap-trap to allow on the stage.

Arminius in play and opera

The Germanic hero Arminius, who defeated three Roman legions at the Teutoberg Forest in AD 9, was the subject of an opera by Handel and a Patriot drama in the 1730s. The history of Arminius, set in lower Germany in the general area of modern Hanover and Brunswick, would have special meaning for the Hanoverian dynasty and broader appeal to Britons at large for representing the defense of Northern liberty against Roman tyranny. A comparison of their stage treatments shows how one was designed to have partisan political application and the other steered clear of any topicality.

In the 1739–40 season, *Arminius* by Thomson's friend William Paterson was banned on January 4, 1740, before it reached the stage.[91] Whatever the licenser thought, *Arminius* is unashamedly Hanoverian, as revealed immediately in the published dedication to Prince Frederick's younger brother the Duke of Cumberland. The dedication draws on the tradition that the Hanoverian family is allied by blood to the ancient Germanic Cherusci, the tribe of Arminius. Paterson hopes the duke will prove "equally useful and ornamental to *Great Britain*." A decade later, Frederick planned to install Arminius in a Mount Parnassus in his gardens at Kew, his own version of Cobham's Temple of British Worthies.[92]

The prologue celebrates the Whig topos of the Progress of Liberty from enslaved, corrupt Rome to the rugged, free North – a common theme of Patriot ideology:

> Liberty forsook degenerate *Rome*,
> Strait to the Regions of the rugged *North*,
> She took her Flight in Search of manly Worth;
> In Search of guiltless uncorrupted Plains,
> Where generous Nature scorn'd to stoop to Chains;
> Where Luxury ne'er mix'd the baneful Bowl,
> Nor sordid Interest had enslav'd the Soul.

Driving the play, set on the Roman frontier, is the conflict between the two Cherusci leaders and their stances toward Rome. Segestes, jealous of the younger Arminius for supplanting him in leadership, wants peace and goodwill with Rome; by an alliance with Rome he will gain power.

Arminius, the popular champion of freedom against Roman corruption and slavery, asserts (like Cato of Utica) that peace with a tyrant is dishonorable; death is better than slavery. For him, Rome, "who treads on Necks of Kings," is the "proud Oppressor" spreading its terrors over "a ruin'd World" (p. 18).

Arminius and the Roman general Varus are rivals for the hand of Artesia, Segestes' daughter; Sigismund (son of Segestes) and Arminius' sister are lovers. Facing the subsidiary characters is the choice between peace, submission, and slavery under Rome or the freedom, virtue, and valour worthy of the free nations of the North. After Arminius' treacherous capture by Segestes and then his release, Arminius' forces defeat the Romans at the Teutoberg Forest, slaughtering three of Varus' legions. In defeat, Varus falls on his sword, and Arminius, out of love for Artesia, extends clemency to her father Segestes and directs burial honors for Varus.

Much of the play harmlessly enough celebrates virtue, freedom, triumph of honorable love, patriotic self-sacrifice, and the myth of the Gothic

North. But the now-alert licenser found objectionable material, most of it in speeches with intended application to Walpole. Already in the prologue, several lines –

> Our Scene displays – How nobler, kinder far,
> Than a false treacherous Peace is open War.

– could be construed to indict Walpole's timid policy toward Spanish depredations and urge war against Spain.

Segestes obviously personates Walpole, and speeches by or about him could be applied to Walpole's inept management of the war. Segestes says of Arminius:

> [He] loads me with Reproaches for the Peace
> I have concluded – says I have betray'd
> The Freedom of my Country, yielded up
> The Glory of the *Germans*, and become
> A tame submissive Slave.
>> I.i

Segestes justifies his pacific alliance with Rome, by following

> The undisputed Maxims of all Kings,
> Who shift Alliance and make Peace or War,
> As suits their Interest most; nor ever deem
> Their Glory sully'd by such prudent Measures.
> …
> And better far to see a People flourish
> Beneath indulgent Peace, than from false Views
> Of wild Ambition and unhallow'd Fame,
> To plunge them headlong into Seas of Blood.
>> II.iii

Segestes' rationale could be a fair description of Walpole's justification for avoiding conflict with Spain.

The play could not have been banned as anti-Hanoverian, Jacobitical, or treasonous. Most likely, the Lord Chamberlain realized that the theme of liberty and resistance to tyranny and the applications to Walpole would be recognizable as opposition party clap-trap. J. C. D. Clark has argued Paterson's *Arminius* belongs to the Tory Jacobitical Anglo-Latin tradition.[93] But as Howard Weinbrot rightly points out, *Arminius* is anti-Roman in spirit and asserts the superiority of Britain's northern German heritage to slavish Rome.[94]

Three years before Paterson's *Arminius* was banned, Handel produced an opera *Arminio* on the same subject on January 12, 1737.[95] A comparison with

Paterson's play shows how an Italian opera on a subject with political reson-
ance manages to steer wide of potential application to contemporary politics.

Some plot elements are common to Paterson's play and *Arminio* due
to their common source in Tacitus:[96] the enmity between Arminius and
Segestes; Segestes' alliance with Rome; the love triangle between Arminius,
Varus, and Segestes' daughter (now Arminius' wife); Sigismond's conflict
between duty to his father and love for Arminius' sister and German liberty;
Arminius' release from captivity by Sigismond (out of his love for Arminius'
sister); the Germans' defeat of Varus; and Arminius' pardon of Segestes.

In the libretto's treatment of the story, Arminius is a minor and passive
figure. He spends most of the opera as a prisoner of Varus awaiting execution, and the plot is motivated by the efforts of Arminius' wife and sister
to win his release from prison through manipulation of Sigismond. Like
Cato of Utica, Arminius would rather die than live under the rule of Rome.
Absent are Segestes' set-speeches in favor of peace with Rome or the denunciations of Roman corruption and attempts at enslavement that could be
applied to Walpole and his ministry. Once Arminius is freed and Varus'
troops defeated, the *lieto fine* celebrates Arminius' freedom and union
with his wife, Arminius' reconciliation with Segestes, and the marriage of
Arminius' sister and Sigismond. The moral of the opera sung by the *coro* is
quite anodyne:

> A capir tante dolcezze
>   Troppo angusto è 'l nostro cor.
> Cangia in gioia le tristezze
>   Generoso un bel Valor.
>
> To contain such sweetness
>   Too narrow is our heart.
> A fine, generous valor
>   Changes sadness into joy.
>
> *Arminio*, III.ix, p. 43
> [trans. provided]

In Paterson's play, the final moral spoken by Arminius is politically potent:
a celebration of opposition ideals of virtue and public spirit as opposed to
the private corruption fostered by Walpole:

> 'Tis Virtue only that gives true Renown,
> Gives blameless Glory, Peace, and lasting Joy.
> …
> Who saves the Publick, saves his private Bliss.
>
> *Arminius*, p. 62

The unsatisfactory nature of the generic expectation is again revealed by the attempts to find the politics of *Arminio* by seeking analogs between the opera's characters and the royal family and court. Reinhard Strohm states that the fate of the couple Arminius and Tusnelda "must be understood as referring directly to the Prince of Wales and his wife."[97] Nothing in the libretto or plot, however, hints at such an identification of the couples. Aside from an opening *scena* and love duet in the *scena ultimata*, Arminius and Tusnelda play a small role in the opera. Little is similar in the couples' fates. Arminius is in jail for most of the opera awaiting execution by the Roman general Varus to whom Arminius has given Tusnelda for protection; he is freed by the efforts of Tusnelda and his sister Ramisa and then leads the German tribe's defeat of Varus.

Robert Ketterer proposes instead that the royal family's feud is the context and, therefore, the royal references must be to the tribal leader Segestes and his son Sigismond. For Ketterer "stress should be put on the message of reconciliation between estranged members of the governing family." But this rather misrepresents the importance of the Segestes–Sigismond reconciliation in the opera (and the application to George and Frederick). The Segestes–Sigismond reconciliation is not the goal of the action, nor are any beneficial consequences of the reconciliation to the German tribe extolled. The reconciliation is a last-minute implication (it is not explicitly stated to occur) of Arminius' granting clemency to Segestes, embracing him as a friend, and uniting the lovers Sigismond and Ramisa, thus removing the cause of Sigismond's conflict with his father – but nothing is said or exchanged between Segestes and Sigismond. The importance of family reconciliation cannot be seen as promoted by the *lieto fine* into a moral or precept to be taken away from viewing the opera. The *coro* celebrates how "A fine, generous valor / Changes sadness into joy."

The following month Handel produced another opera *Giustino* (February 16, 1737) that has been given a political interpretation. Konrad Sasse's reading again reveals his Marxian orientation. For Sasse, "This work deals above all with the social rise of a man from simple peasant to a hero crowned with glory. In that respect, the work is typical of the possibility of such a rise for Everyman from the people."[98] Strohm elaborates, "Guistino could be taken to represent the interests of the middle class – a simple man reaching the pinnacle of social success by his own abilities."[99]

In the opera, Vitalian, tyrant of Asia Minor, has besieged Emperor Anastasius at Constantinople. We first encounter Justin as a peasant farmer who leaves his plow to aid his emperor. After many deeds of valor and battle against Vitalian's troops, surviving false accusations of being a traitor, and the revelation of his royal birth (he is Vitalian's brother), Justin overthrows the usurping tyrant and obtains Leocasta as his bride. In these adventures, goddess Fortuna intervenes to guarantee his success.

But the Sasse–Strohm interpretation is historically anachronistic. Justin is not a member of a middle class (bourgeois) but is still a vassal in a feudal agricultural system and engaged in warfare in service of his emperor. He does not rise by virtue of middle-class values as an Everyman engaged in class struggle. Rather, he succeeds by virtue of his courage and warlike deeds of valor, assisted by divine intervention, whose application to Britain would have been far-fetched. The plot does not exemplify the myth of a middle-class rise by merit; it shows success is at least partly due to a noble birth, following a path set by Fate, and the assistance of Fortune and the Gods – hence still compatible with an *ancien régime* society.[100]

The Sasse–Strohm reading offers no hint of authorial intention or what political work the opera might do. The London opera companies, subscribers, and audience were predominantly an elite drawn from the aristocratic, gentry, and urban professional orders.[101] It is unlikely that Handel had any interest in representing the progress or success of a middle-class hero (say, as in Lillo's *London Merchant* or Hogarth's apprentice in *Industry and Idleness*) or thought he might gain increased attendance from members of a middle class seeing themselves represented in the opera.

Alfred

The only Patriot dramatic piece to achieve any afterlife on the stage is the masque *Alfred* by David Mallet and James Thomson, now recalled chiefly as the source of the patriotic favorite "Rule, Britannia." Rehearsed first at Drury Lane on July 28, 1740, with music by its resident composer Thomas Arne, the masque was first performed before the Prince and Princess of Wales in the garden of their Thames-side estate Cliveden on August 1.[102] Sung in English, *Alfred* represents one of Britain's native alternatives to Italian opera, such as advocated by some in the Patriot circle.[103]

The Saxon King Alfred, a canonical figure in opposition mythology, embodied the central Old Whig and opposition doctrine that English liberties and constitutional government began in Saxon times (not as government writers had it, after 1688).[104] Sometime about 1735, Alfred was installed by Lord Cobham in his Temple of British Worthies at Stowe, where an inscription celebrates Alfred as

> The mildest, justest, most beneficent of Kings;
> who drove out the Danes, secured the seas, protected learning;
> establish'd juries, crush'd corruption, guarded liberty;
> and was the founder of the English Constitution.

The inscription could work in two ways. Alfred is a contrast to King George who supposedly lacks these qualities; conversely, he serves as a model for Prince Frederick. Frederick himself entered into the identification when in 1735 he erected in his garden at Carlton House a statue of Alfred, which bore an epigraph citing Alfred as the founder of the liberties and common-wealth of England. The *Craftsman* pointedly endorsed Frederick's choice, writing that it foretold that "He will think Himself under an obligation, whenever He comes to the Throne, to preserve the *Liberties of our antient Constitution.*"[105]

The masque is set on the Isle of Athelney, Somerset, where Alfred, defeated by the Danes, is hiding in disguise, surrounded by enemies and sheltered by shepherds. Alfred is heartened by the presence of his loving queen, family, and a Hermit, who has seen Britain's glorious future, "when guardian laws / Are by the patriot, in the glowing senate, / Won from corruption," when invincible liberty prevails over tyranny, and Britain's empire rules the seas (I.v) – a situation by implication still not achieved in Britain.

Alfred states an agenda for Frederick as king (and a rebuke to George II) when he asks the Hermit whether the duty of a king is not

> To be the common father of my people,
> Patron of honor, virtue and religion;
>
> …
>
> If not to raise our drooping *English* name,
> To clothe it yet with terror; make this land
> Renown'd for peaceful arts to bless mankind,
> And generous war to humble proud oppressors:
> If not to build on an eternal base,
> On liberty and laws, the public weal.
>
> I.v

The climax of the masque is the Hermit's vision (II.iii), in which the Genius of England brings forth the spirits of three future British heroes: Edward III, Elizabeth I, and William III – each a British Worthy of opposition propaganda and myth. Finally, a future king arises,

> Good without show, above ambition great;
> Wise, equal, merciful, the friend of man!
>
> II.iii

Alfred's comrade, the Earl of Devon, then returns with news of the defeat of the Danes. Alfred's identity is revealed, a Bard sings "Rule, Britannia," and the Hermit prophecies the future glories of Britain's worldwide commercial empire. The masque's last four lines –

> *Britons*, proceed, the subject Deep command
> Awe with your navies every hostile land.
> In vain their threats, their armies all in vain:
> They rule the balanc'd world, who rule the main.
>   II.v

– in their aggressive vision of the extension of British naval power are surely meant as a contrast to Walpole's poor management of the current war with Spain.

The masque works in many ways as Patriot propaganda. Both Alfred and Frederick are kings-in-waiting. The celebration of Alfred's virtues allows oblique flattery of Frederick as the Patriot's figurehead. The Hermit's vision sets the agenda for Frederick's reign, and Alfred serves as an exemplar for Frederick's reign. The masque's celebration of British Worthies offers stark contrast to George and the nation corrupted by the ministry of Walpole.[106]

Alfred was immediately recognized as a partisan piece. Writing to the *London Magazine* in August 1740, "Philomathes" declared nothing gave him greater pleasure than to hear that Frederick was entertaining himself with a masque that showed "our great King *Alfred* ... rising from the *utmost Distress*, to redeem and establish the *Liberties* of his Country." Frederick's pleasure in such a masque may be a pledge

that he will endeavour to build the publick Weal *on Liberty and Laws*; and that he will disdain to think of establishing his Throne upon the *Tongues* or *Swords* of those, who count for Gain ... by sacrificing the *Constitution* and *Liberties* of their Country.[107]

Lady Hertford recognized in the masque "several Party hints, and one invidious Reflexion – which did not need the Pains that has been taken (to Print it in a different Character) to make it absolutely unpardonable."[108] The blue-stocking Elizabeth Montagu described the masque's reception: "Mr Grenville commends it and says it will be published. I own I cannot give much credit to it, for I rather imagine he commends as a patriot than a judge."[109]

Mallet and Thomson enlarged the masque to three acts for intended theatrical performance in 1741, for which the patriotic and political sentiments were expanded. Surprisingly, this version was licensed, but it apparently languished due to Charles Fleetwood's inept management. It was not until the 1744–45 season that *Alfred* was first publicly produced in Dublin and London in yet another version.[110]

In the 1730s, the London stage was politicized to such a degree that the government was moved to license the stage to exercise greater pre-production scrutiny of plays and prevent insult to Walpole and his ministry. The drama of the 1730s – its political intent recognized by friend and foe of the ministry alike – offers a broad context for examining how topical partisan politics was introduced into a dramatic genre comparable to Italian opera.

Like most Italian operas, the Patriot dramas of the 1730s were based on historical subjects. But unlike Italian operas, their subjects were chosen and original texts were written to personate current persons or to be applied to current topical politics; set-speeches were composed that were proxies for opposition propaganda against Walpole's ministry. *Leonidas*, *Liberty*, the Patriot dramas, and their context and reception exhibit the hallmarks proposed in Chapter 2 to identify those works likely intended as, and that contemporary Britons might have recognized as, political. The dramas were produced by poets with known political allegiance and motivation for writing partisan plays; the plays contain cues directing their application; audience members and the ministry recognized their partisan nature; and the partisanship was revealed in the subscription campaigns, government censorship, and campaigns in ministerial newspapers to discredit the plays.

These Patriot dramas demonstrate how we might expect politics to be introduced were opera directors, managers, and librettists trying to give operas topical political application. Moreover, they show how we might expect the Nobility operas to be politicized, were the Opera of the Nobility a politically motivated company, as is often claimed for it. Overall, the political theater of the 1730s shows by contrast the general lack of topical political engagement in Italian operas.

8 | The opera stage as political history

Italian opera's most notorious English antagonist John Dennis found it impossible to conceive that opera could "inspire publick Spirit, and publick Virtue, and elevated notions of Liberty" or play a constructive role in the civic life of Britain.[1] A writer for *Fog's Weekly Journal* (no friend of opera either) echoed Dennis in 1735 when he asked "whether a Man ever returned wiser from an Opera than he was before he went to it" and whether Farinelli's singing ever inspired any opera-goer "with more vertuous or honourable Sentiments in respect to their Country?"[2] If we approach Italian operas as contemporaries approached poetic drama and history with their traditional goals of encouraging Virtue and discouraging Vice, we can suggest how Italian operas, especially those based on episodes from history, might very well have satisfied the unfulfilled expectations of Dennis and the writer for *Fog's* journal.

Many of Dennis' contemporaries did hold that opera could achieve the traditional goals of dramatic poetry. The author of *The Touch-Stone* (1728) emphatically asserts: "A compleat Opera is a regular musical Dramma, and approaches very near to the Excellency of Poetry, (because Virtue may be there inculcated by a proper Fable)."[3] Henry Stonecastle, who had offered the interpretation of *Alcina* examined in Chapter 2, was certain that when an opera

> gives us, in some pleasing Allegory, a Lesson of Morality, I can't but think it preferable to either the Comick Vein or the Tragick Stile ... The Language is ... a just Mean between the Rant of Tragedy and the low wit of Comedy; beside[s], the Italian Poets, from whom the Opera's are taken, have more strictly adher'd to the first Design of Poetry, viz. the rendering Virtue amiable and Vice odious, than have our modern Writers; their Allegories are delightful and contain excellent morals.[4]

English readers were told in 1734 that opera "under proper Regulation ... would be a School both to delight, and to excite in us a Love for Virtue."[5]

Taking these contemporary justifications of opera seriously can be the springboard for exploring how Italian operas (concentrating on those representing historical episodes) could claim the utility of history and dramatic poetry to play a comparable role in the political and civic life of Britons.

Although poetry, history, and philosophy are sister arts, their partisans engaged in the inevitable *paragone* of ranking them. Classical rhetoricians and Renaissance humanists saw history's potential to serve a higher purpose than to be a mere chronicle of events; as part of the *literae humaniores*, history could convey principles of morality and prudence in well-told stories about great men. This role of history was enshrined in what became Cicero's ubiquitous tag: *historia magistra vitae* (history, the great teacher of life).[6] This classical approach to both the writing and reading of history was embodied in the *ars historica*.[7]

History has the advantage over philosophy in that instead of instructing by philosophy's dry moralizing precepts, universal truths about human actions, morality, and the passions were conveyed in stories about great men and made more vivid and admirable by the ornaments of rhetoric and style;[8] hence, in the famous formulation, "history is philosophy teaching by example."[9] As Seneca put it, "The way is long by precepts but short and effective by examples."[10] "The force of Example," explained Cornelius Nepos, "is intelligible to the meanest Capacities."[11]

History was most effective in forming the mind to virtue, as Dryden claims, when "'tis conveyed in verse, that it may delight, while it instructs."[12] For, as Richard Steele chimes, "Virtue sinks deepest into the Heart of Man, when it comes recommended by the powerful Charms of Poetry."[13] History presented on the opera stage could surpass even the charms of poetic drama. A writer in 1730 thought theatrical representations with music the most perfect entertainment that "Humane Wit can invent":

Their Ornaments are Music, Painting, and Poetry; we are by them snatch'd back into former Ages, grow in a Manner cotemporary [with the past] and acquainted with *Cæsar* and *Alexander*, and are made Eye-Witnesses of the Actions of *Cato* and *Lucretia*. Men [on stage] are more legible and expressive Characters than any that fall from the Pen of the most artful Writers.[14]

The following year, a contributor to the *British Journal* maintained that

An Opera, with all the Circumstances necessary to make a Tragedy compleat in the Fable, Sentiments, and Diction, set to Music by a masterly Hand, and performed with Justice to the poetical and musical Compositions, would have an Advantage over Tragedy … Music therefore may be properly sayed, if the Song has any moral Sentiments in it, to be one of the Channels of Morality to the Mind.[15]

The music and the spectacle of drama and opera rendered heroes more admirable and held the audience attentive to the noble actions on stage. If for Giovanni Botero, "l'Historia è il piu vago theatro, che si poss imaginare" ("history is the most pleasing theater imaginable"),[16] then the opera stage is history shown to best advantage.

History was the great font of examples of human experience. Simply put, the historian's task was to incite men to Virtue and frighten them from Vice; to show what to shun and avoid, or to admire and emulate. In history, writes Livy, "you have a record of the infinite variety of human experience plainly set out for all to see; and in that record you can find for yourself and your country both examples and warnings; fine things to take as models, base things, rotten through and through, to avoid."[17] For Tacitus the historian aimed "to ensure that merit is recorded, and to confront evil deeds and words with the fear of posterity's denunciation."[18] Livy, Plutarch, and Petrarch were esteemed for their canonic portraits of virtuous Greeks and Romans.[19] Contrarily, the English *Myrroure for Magistrates* (1559) showed how vice has been punished in great men.[20] Tacitus, especially in his portrait of Tiberius, exposed the means by which tyrants retained power at all costs.

For the classical humanist, the historian's task was by his own pithy observations to point out the political and moral lessons and precepts to be drawn from the examples presented. With skill, even the most graphic depictions of tyranny, lust, or evil could be turned to a positive lesson, illustrating the perils befalling those who succumb to unrestrained lust or ambition.[21] For Jean Bodin, one reads history "to acquire reliable maxims for what we should seek and avoid."[22] So valued were the historian's own *sententiae*, maxims, precepts, and aphorisms, they were collected, arranged, and annotated as the basis for discourses on politics.[23] Tacitus' *Annals* and *Histories* were especially scoured for *sententiae* and precepts for guidance on governing the state.[24] The most famous collections drawing on Tacitus include Justus Lipsius' *Politicorum libri sex* (1589)[25] and Scipio Ammirato's *Discorsi sopra Cornelio Tacito* (1594).[26] Likewise, proverbs, fables, aphorisms, and sayings of great men were collected to provide guidance in the world of politics.[27]

The *ars historica* encouraged active reading.[28] Readers annotated their own copies or wrote into commonplace books the historian's *sententiae*, maxims, precepts, and aphorisms (or devised their own) that could then be applied to politics of their own time.[29] Like histories, operas present virtuous or vicious actions from which an opera-goer could draw precepts and maxims, such as these from Lipsius:[30]

"clemency makes a prince worthy of love, safe, and distinguished" (2.12)

"no power obtained by ill lasts for long" (2.4)

"for those who begin a new reign, the reputation of Clemency is useful" (2.5)

"no one has remained in government for long whose reign was hated" (2.12)

Lessons of history were digested into advice books for princes, a genre begun by Seneca's *De Clementia*, written for the young Nero. Flourishing in the Renaissance, these Mirror for Princes books drew on the great *exempla* and precepts from history to offer advice and models for how to rule as a just prince.[31] The mirror metaphor suggested the prince could see himself in the virtuous deeds presented in the advice book (often dedicated to the prince) – much the same as Rolli encouraged George II to see himself in the dedicatory poem to *Riccardo primo*. Of the thousand or so advice books published 1400–1700, the best known are Machiavelli's *Il principe* (*The Prince*, 1513/32) and Erasmus' *Institutio Principis Christiani* (*The Education of a Christian Prince*, 1516).[32]

History as a mere chronicle of events could be faulted because in its fidelity to the past, it shows, as Francis Bacon observed, "the successes and issues of action not so agreeable to the merits of virtue and vice"[33] – that is, it violates poetic justice when the vicious triumph over the virtuous. In addition to embellishing the images of Virtue, poetry has the advantage over history because, according to Aristotle, rather than merely chronicling the vicissitudes of human life, it deals with higher, universal truths.[34] Sir Philip Sidney's *Defense of Poesy* (1595) scorns history for ties too close to "the particular truth of things." Instead, the "feigned image of poetry" has "the more force in teaching" because it "couples the general notion with the particular example."[35] The poet, writes Dryden, "is not ty'd to truth, or fetter'd by the Laws of History" and so can take the liberty to arrange the plot to provide the proper poetic justice, showing Virtue prevailing and Vice vanquished.[36] Even if what poets tell is false to history, their fables and examples inspire the reader to admire and imitate the heroes they celebrate in their verses. It was on this principle that John Dennis faulted Addison's *Cato*. Showing a just man driven to suicide must "raise the highest Indignation in all true Lovers of Liberty."[37]

Because poetic justice ideally encourages aspirations to nobility and virtue, operas are usually not tragedies that show great men and women brought low due to the indifference of fate. Major protagonists rarely meet doom due to a tragic flaw or resolute adherence to a noble goal.[38] This demand for the joyous ending (*lieto fine*) in operas was the basis for one of the jibes at it in *The Beggar's Opera*: the Player's admonition that to have Macheath hung "is manifestly wrong, for an opera must end happily" (III.xvi).

The lessons of history, drama, or opera were for nothing if not applied to one's own times. Machiavelli urged his prince to read history to see how great men "conducted themselves during war and to discover the reasons for their victories or their defeats, so that he can avoid the latter and imitate the former."[39] Dryden set out the rationale for the modern application of ancient history:

[History] helps us to judge of what will happen, by shewing us the like revolutions of former times. For Mankind being the same in all ages, agitated by the same passions, and mov'd to action by the same interests, nothing can come to pass, but some President [*sic*] of the like nature has already been produc'd, so that having the causes before our eyes, we cannot easily be deceiv'd in the effects, if we have Judgment enough but to draw the parallel.[40]

The contemporary political application of history, poetry, drama, or opera lies in the potential of examples, *sententiae*, and precepts to guide one's own political conduct and to understand and judge the actions and persons of one's own day. This use of history was still alive for Handel's contemporaries. Frederick, the future Prince of Wales was instructed in 1723 that "[History] supplys [the prince] the place of experience, and acquaints him in one short view with what otherwise wou'd cost many years of observation; furnishing his mind with such rules of conduct as may render his people happy, and himself immortal."[41] In 1732 British students at school or university were told that from reading Suetonius they would learn "the dismal Effects of arbitrary Power lodged in the Hands of a single Person" and be "more sensible of the Value of Liberty, and the Happiness they enjoy under the just and legal Government of their native Country."[42]

Virtue and the citizen

The political and moral program of both the *ars historica* and opera librettos is governed by the classical ideals embodied in the writings of Cicero, especially *De Officiis* (*On Duties*), the West's most influential guide to civic behavior.[43] The shorthand for the qualities necessary for the citizen or subject was the term *virtus* (*virtù*), which itself embraced all the other virtues.[44] The British often translated the term as "public spirit." For Cicero, *prudentia*, *justitia*, *fortitudo*, and *temperantia* were the Cardinal Virtues. The health of the state derives from the virtue of its individual citizens and subjects. Most necessary for civic concord was *justitia*, which Cicero analyzes into *beneficentia* (generosity) and *clementia* (mercy).[45] For Sallust, it was "through toil and the practice of justice" that the Republic grew to greatness.[46]

Absolute monarchies and tyrannies could rely on the power of the state to enforce obedience to authority and compel military service. A republic, though, relied on citizens to cultivate virtue and put duty to the public interest above private self-interest. Achieving virtue was both one's personal and civic duty. In "The Dream of Scipio," Scipio Africanus (Publius Cornelius Scipio) appears in a dream before his grandson and exhorts that "for everyone who has saved and served his country and helped it to grow, a sure place is set aside in heaven where he may enjoy a life of eternal bliss."[47] Family and friends are dear, "but one native land embraces all our loves; and who that is true would hesitate to give his life for her, if by his death he could render her a service?"[48] The ideals of devotion to virtue and duty to country appear most prominently in operas set in Republican Rome.

As Caius Fabricius asserts, "Virtue's the only View of noble Acts" ("L'Onesta oprar, di chi ben opra è 'l fine"; *Cajo Fabbricio* (1733), III.xii, pp. 44–5). Sextia, his daughter, proclaims,

> Virtue alone preserves the Power to charm
> A noble *Roman* Breast, and gently warm.

> Di virtù sola
> >   Non d' ostri, e d'ori
> >   Vani Tesori,
> >   Un cor *Romano*
> >   Piacer si fà.
> >   I.v, pp. 12–13

Commitment to virtue, duty, or honor is often expressed as Stoic acceptance of suffering, prison, exile, or death rather accepting an alternative that will commit one to "the scandal and infamy of servitude and debasment" of a dishonorable life without liberty.[49] Achievement of virtue, as the consul Marius Aquilius states, requires suffering:

> To go thro' Toil, my Friends, with Hearts unwearied,
> To suffer Ills with firm unshaken Souls,
> Has ever been the boast of Roman Virtue.

> L'Oprar da forti o Amici
> E da forti soffrir vanto fu sempre
> Dalla virtù Romana; ...
> >   *Aquilio Consolo* (1724), II.iv, pp. 40–1

The most famous example is Cato of Utica's preferring suicide over life under Julius Caesar:

> And if I longer cannot live in Freedom,
> At least when this dire Ruin whelms me down,
> The gazing World shall in that Period see
> The *Roman* Liberties expire with me.

> e se non lice
> Viver libero ancor, si vegga almeno
> Nella fatal ruina
> Spirar con me la libertà latina.
>> *Catone* (1732), III.xi, pp. 56–7

Like Cato of Utica, the Germanic tribal leader Arminius would prefer death instead of a disgraceful liberty under Roman rule.[50]

Even citizens and subjects in Near Eastern monarchies strive for glory, honor, and realizing one's own virtue. For Agenor in *Astarto* (1720),

> The Performance
> Of his duty is the greatest Pleasure of a Subject.

> Umil vasallo
> A 'tutto il suo piacer nel suo servaggio.
>> I.v., pp. 18–19

At the *lieto fine* of *Faramondo* (1737), Pharamond proclaims:

> Virtue, which fortifies the heart,
> Will triumph over love and hate;
> Nay, it has pow'r to conquer fate,
> And make e'en sorrows joys impart.

> Virtù, che rende sì forte un core,
> D' odio, e d' amore – sà trionfar.
> Ancor del Fato vince il potere,
> Fa che al piacere – guidi il penar.
>> III.xv, pp. 68–9

When Arsaces, although innocent but valuing honor more than life, accepts his execution, Megabise observes:

> Neither the grim Looks of Death, Reason, nor
> Friendship can induce a great Soul
> to anything that's mean.

> Nè l'aspetto di morte
> Nè ragion nè amistrade
> Possono indurre un cor grande a viltade.
>> *Arsace* (1721), III.i, pp. 66–7

The term *virtus* is derived from *vir* (man) and essentially means those attributes necessary for a man in his civic role. Hence, virtues are generally construed as masculine in the form of endurance, strength, bravery, and avoidance of softness (effeminacy).[51] The opposition between manly military fitness and effeminacy is drawn by Pyrrhus, King of Epire. Assisting the people of Taurentum in waging war again Rome, he addresses them:

> People of *Tarentum,*
>   Why this effeminate Pomp in a manly Nation?
>   Train up your Youth in military Arts;
>
> Popolo *Tarentin,* qual' è cotesta
>   Femminea pompa iln viril gente?
>   In disciplina
> Militar s' agguerisca
> La gioventu.
>   *Cajo Fabbricio* (1733), I.i, pp. 4–5

But librettos also present examples of females who aspire to attain civic virtue, honor, and glory by sacrifice for the state.[52] In *Muzio Scevola* (1721), Clelia bids farewell to her beloved Mucius Scaevola:

> Let our Country and Liberty be
> preferred to our Love, and let
> not tender Affection retard your
> Valour.
>
> E Patria e Libertà
> Si preferisca al nostr' amor, nè sia
> Tenero affetto remora al valore
>   II.iv, pp. 50–1

Later, Clelia leads a corps of Amazon warriors in defending a portion of the Roman walls against the attacking Etruscans. Then, taken as hostages, they escape the Etruscan camp, flinging themselves into the Tiber, while Clelia proclaims:

> Let an extream Courage be immediately
> engaged towards our Escape, or else let
> an honourable Death crown our Exploits.
>
>   in breve
> O a nostro scampo, estremo ardir s' adopre;
> O un' onorato fin coroni l'Opre.
>   III.vii, pp. 88–9

Porus, King of India, asks his sister Erissena, to show that the same blood, full of virtuous ardor, flows "in a varied sex" ("in vario sesso"; *Poro* (1731), III.i, pp. 50–1). Claudia, in love with Attius Tullus, prince of the Volsci, on command of the Senate and people, must abandon her love because he is an enemy of Rome. Agreeing to do so, she states,

> I feel myself already more a Roman than a Lover.

> Sento che in quest' istante
> Preval Claudia Romana, a Claudia amante.
> *Cajo Marzio Coriolano* (1723), I.vii, pp. 12–13

For females, realization of virtue or honor is usually accomplished by abhorring tyrants and preserving their chastity by refusing to submit to them in marriage. Lidia rebukes the tyrant Amulius, who demands her in marriage:

> You'll see my undaunted Soul, in Extasies of Joy,
> Abhor you whilst I live, and scorn you when I dye.

> Che più lieta vedrai quest' Alma forte
> Odiarti'n vita, e averti a sdegno in morte.
> *Numitore* (1720), II.i, pp. 24–5

Later, in a long scene of recitative, further refusing Amulius, she prefers union in death with her beloved and willingly drinks a cup of poison (II.iv). Zenobia, imprisoned with her husband Radamistus by Tiridates, pleads:

> I am resolute: I'll rather die
> Than fall into the Tyrant's Hands:
> Rouse up, Dear *Radamistus*,
> Your noble Spirit, and kill me here.

> Risoluta; la morte io voglio pria
> Che in man gir del Tiranno;
> Sveglia sù *Radamisto*
> Lo spirto generoso, e qui m'uccidi.
> *Radamisto* (1720), II.i, pp. 26–7

In *Vespasiano* (1724), Arricida, wife of Titus, is the object of the illicit love of Domitian, who is attempting to usurp Titus' crown. She rejects his passionate advances and offer of the crown (I.viii–ix). Commanded to be kept among the Vestal Virgins, she resolves to suffer anything in defense of her honor, proclaiming

> From my bosom, faithful and strong,
>   Tear out, tyrant, even my heart;
> Death will be sweet for me,
>   If in this way Honor will live.

> Dal mio sen costante e forte
> Svelli pur tiranno il Cor;

Sarà dolce a me la Morte
Se così vivrà l'Onor.
I.ix, p. 16
[trans. provided]

Other examples of female virtue and heroism include *Cajo Fabbricio* (1733), where Caius Fabricius gives his daughter Sextia, now an enslaved captive, a dagger, expecting she will kill herself if her captor attempts his unlawful love upon her. Calfurnia, daughter of a Roman consul, refuses to flee from her sacrifice that will ensure her father's conquest of Rome's enemy (*Calfurnia* [1724]). In *Aquilio Consolo* (1724), Lincestes, sister of the tyrant Arrenion, helps Aquilius escape prison and ultimately return with soldiers to overthrow the tyrant. In *Adriano in Siria* (1735), Emirena, the captive daughter of her vanquished father Osroa, offers to sacrifice herself as Adrian's wife to save her father.[53] Both Pulcheria and Constantia are betrayed by Isacus in *Riccardo primo* (1727). Constantia (betrothed to Richard) prefers death to marriage with Isacus, whereas Pulcheria (his daughter) goes as hostage to Richard to force her father to yield Constantia to Richard. In *Lucio Vero* (1727), Queen Berenice would rather die with her husband than marry Lucius Verus. In *Arminio* (1737), Tusnelda prefers death to marriage to the Roman general Varus.

Most librettos embellish their episodes from ancient history. To flesh out the brief historical source into a full evening's entertainment, the librettists, as they often admitted in the arguments prefixed to librettos, devised subsidiary roles and subplots involving invented wives or loves of the main characters, triangles of lovers, lost lovers in disguise, and sons or daughters betrothed against their wishes. Lovers who remain true to each other prevail over obstacles placed in their way by monarchs or fathers and are united in a *lieto fine* as a reward for their fidelity or chastity. Plots never countenance coerced love-matches or marriages based on the illicit use of power or authority by a ruler or father against the wishes of one of the lovers. As Crispus tells Fausta: "Unlawful Love is always a Crime" ("è colpevole sempre / Quell' Amor che non lice"; *Cripso* [1722], I.v, pp. 12–13). Achieving appropriate love matches that ultimately coincide with duty is one of the principal goals of opera plots, with the implication that true, reciprocal love is a worthwhile good for the state.

Librettos dramatize the conflicting demands of civic duty and personal desire.[54] Operas reward rulers and subjects who shun the pleasant and gratifying path of love and private passion in favor of the more demanding but nobler course of virtue, duty, and sacrifice. The opposition between duty and private passion is shown as strong and uncompromising. Tancred reminds that

> A noble Passion excites the Soul to
> generous Actions.Virtue, Enemy to
> Love, is severe and untractable.
>
> Per Alma Generosa
> Nobile Affetto ad Opre belle è sprone.
> Virtù d' Amor nemica
> È selvaggia è feroce.
> > *Erminia* (1723), III.vi, pp. 70–1

Operas acknowledge that the power of love can overwhelm striving for virtue. As Grimoaldo rightly observes, a lover is often deaf to the claims of virtue and civic duty:

> The Voice of Virtue
> Finds no Admittance through a Lover's Ear,
> Of if it does, passes, unheeded, through it,
> And reaches not the Heart.
>
> Le voci di Virtù
> Non cura amante Cor, o pur non sente.
> > *Rodelinda* (1725), II.iv, pp. 38–9

Operas caution the dangers arising from heroes led astray by pursuit of love, disregarding their duty and wandering from the path of virtue. In *Rinaldo* (1711), Godfrey admonishes Rinaldo,

> Yet in the Road to Glory fall not back,
> But pass by Love when thy fair Fame invites Thee.
>
> Sul Sentier della Gloria
> Tu non devi arrestar' il Piè nel Corso.

The sentiment is seconded by Almirena:

> The Force of Love has Valour oft suppress'd,
> And Glory freezes in an amorous Breast.
>
> Che la Face d'Amore
> Spesso gela nel Sen marziale Ardore.
> > I.i, pp. 4–5

Rinaldo fails to heed these commands, and so is "Stain'd with the Guilt of soft and untim'd Love" ("Contaminata da' tuoi molli Amori"; III.iv, pp. 50–1).

Librettos demonstrate that the competing claims of love and duty are to be settled in favor of duty. In *Calfurnia* (1724), Lucio cautions Trebonio that

Rome will disown th' unworthy Man,
Who to his Country's Good and Glory
Prefers an idle Passion.

   Roma non soffre
Un Cittadin protervo
Che più che della Patria è d'amor servo.
I.xiii, pp. 25–7

In *Muzio Scevola*, whose central action is one of the principal touchstones for Republican heroism, Mucius Scaevola makes clear that the demands of honor and virtue on a citizen trump the interests of one's personal life. Before setting out on his attempt to assassinate Porsena, he asks Horatio to carry a message to Clelia, his beloved.

Tell her that nothing but the Zeal for
my Country cou'd possibly prevail
over my Love.

Dille che sol l'affetto
Della Patria prevale all' amor mio:
Dàlle per me dolce amorosa addio.
II.iii, pp. 46–7

Those who do follow virtue are rewarded in the *lieto fine* with love, glory, and happiness. In *Arminio* (1737), Sigismond is torn between duty to his father (who has betrayed the Germans and now sides with the Romans) and love for Ramisa, the sister of Germany's hero Arminius. He throws his lot on the side of German liberty and ultimately gains Ramisa.

For some, the demand of duty over love is simple. In *Calfurnia* (1724), G. Marius tells Trebonius,

You are a Roman …
Let Love no longer burn within your Breast,
When for your Country's Good, your Sword's requir'd;
But at the Trumpet's Call let Love be banish'd,
Chase the deluding Charm, and take to Arms.

Che sei Figlio di Roma
…
Sia l' tuo core amoroso,
Finchè chieda la Patria altro pensiero;
Ma al fragor delle Trombe
Lasci pronto l'Amor, e sia guerriero.
I.ii, pp. 8–9

Mucius Scevola reminds himself that he must put his civic duty above love for Clelia:[55]

> Remember in the first Place, my Heart, that
> you are *Roman*; comply with the Laws of
> Honour: perform first the Duty of a Citizen
> to your Country, and then return to Sighs,
> and languish again. Death will be your
> Happiness. Ah Honour! Ah my Country!
> Ah Peace! Ah Liberty!

> Mio Cor pria ti ricorda
> D' esser Romano; adempj
> Alle legi d' Onor: pria con la Patria
> Usa il dover di Cittadino, e poi
> Torna a sospiri tuoi,
> Torna a languir: Morte il tuo Ben sarà.
> Ah Onore! Ah Patria! Ah Pace! Ah Libertà!
>> III.iv, pp. 82–3

The choice is more difficult for Queen Thomyris. In *Farnace* (1723), she conceals her love for her general Pharnaces, whom she must sentence to death for supposed treason, and admonishes herself:

> Wake out of Lethargy, and chase away
> All those persuading Arguments of Love,
> Which lead astray, and cheat a Woman's Heart:
> Those born to Sceptres, must secure the State,
> And make the publick Good their chiefest Care.
> …
> Nature, Ambition, and the Laws of State,
> To these I thus comply.

> Svegliati dal letargo, e calpestando
> L'empia ragion d'amante
> Doma i sensi mal cauti, alma regnante.
> …
> Natura, Impero, ambition di Regno
> Siete paghi.
>> II.xv, 58–61

Ultimately, his innocence is revealed and Thomyris marries Pharnaces.

Cicero placed duty to state above duty to family. Those who follow their duty to country are rewarded at the *lieto fine* (usually by having the conflict between nation and family reconciled in a single action). The adaptation of an exemplary episode from Republican history (325 BC) in *Lucio Papirio dittatore* (1732) amplifies the conflict. As told in Livy (8.30–35), Lucius Papirius Cursor, dictator in the war against the Samnites, has instructed Quintus Fabius, master of the horse and son of Marcus Fabius, not to attack the enemy until he has returned to Rome and consulted the Auspices. Taking advantage of a propitious opportunity, Quintus Fabius attacks and defeats the enemy. Lucius Papirius sentences Quintus Fabius to death for disobedience. Apostolo Zeno's libretto multiplies the conflicts between duty to the state and family by introducing Papiria as daughter of Lucio Papirio and wife of Quintus Fabius. Delivering the punishment, Lucio Papirio announces:

> Where the Judge sits the Father hears no more.

> Ove il Giudice siede
> Il Padre non ascolta
> > I.xiii, pp. 18–19

Other family members follow Lucio Papirius' renunciation of familial ties. Papiria resolves,

> For where my Country claims it at my Hand,
> I can forget all Ties of Blood and Fondess:

> Dove la Patria il chiede,
> Sangue, ed affetti obblio:
> > I.xv, pp. 22–3

Papiria must decide between loyalty to her accused husband or nation; she determines, "I am a *Roman*, and a Wife no more" ("Son *Romana* ancor Io, Sposa non sono"; II.v, pp. 30–1). Later she tells her husband, "The Wife is lost now in the duteous Daughter" ("Sposa non più, ma figlia"; II.v, pp. 30–1).

Quintus Fabius' father, renouncing his son for his disobedience, says he "Put off the Parent, and assum'd the *Roman*" ("D' esser Padre lasciò, *Romano* apparve"; II.v, pp. 28–9). In both Livy and the opera, the Roman people plead mercy for Quintus Fabius. By yielding to the popular will, Lucius Papirius still fulfills his duty, but now with no violation of his honor.

In a parallel Roman episode, the librettist for *Tito Manlio* (1717) has departed from Livy to achieve a similar end. As told by Livy (8.7–8), Titus Manlius, son of the consul Titus Manlius Torquatus (*c.*340 BC), is sent as head of a cavalry squadron to reconnoiter the rebelling Tusculan cavalry led by Geminus Maecius. Forgetting the consular command that he should not engage the rebels, Titus succumbs to taunts by Geminus and defeats him in one-to-one combat. Titus Manius decrees that Manlius be executed for disobedience (despite his resulting victory), as an example not to undermine consular authority. So far, the father is an exemplar of a stern

Roman who puts duty to the Republic above family ties,[56] and Manlius' fate is a caution against yielding to anger and disobeying consular orders.

Contriving a *lieto fine*, the libretto has Manlius instead only take Geminus' sword during combat. Nonetheless, Titus Manlius insists on the prosecution, asserting

> The Mem'ry of Father's quite extinct
> Since I'm a Consul made.
>
> Di Padre in me la rimembranza è spenta
> Giache consoloe il sono;
> I.vii, pp. 12–13

Showing his own sense of duty, Manlius refuses an opportunity to escape, proudly proclaiming,

> By my Example, you may see
> What Punishment is due to those that don't observe
> The Sov'raign Senates most Supream Commands:
> Of me alone learn how you ought t' obey.
>
> In me si veda
> Qual castigo è donuto a chi non cura
> Dell' eccleso senato il gran commando:
> Da me solo apprendete ad esser cauti.
> III.viii, pp. 50–1

At last, Titus Manlius yields to the *popolar tumulto*, "To save a Hero from an unjust Death" ("Di salvar un Eroe da ingiusta morte"; III.viii, pp. 54–5). As in *Lucio Papirio*, the *lieto fine* transforms Titus Manlius from the stern Roman who puts duty to his country above family, to an exemplar of the dutiful ruler who yields to the will of the people.

While sacrifice for the state was the highest virtue, it was never the case that heroes were asked to sacrifice for a tyrant. The greatest exercise of virtue was in the cause of liberty. Both the opera and printed libretto to *Muzio Scevola* (1721) exhort the defense of liberty. Liberty, the great cry of the Whigs, is extolled in one of the few title-page epigraphs found on the librettos, taken from a speech of Cato in Addison's tragedy:

> Do thou, great Liberty, inspire our Souls
> And make our Lives in thy Possession happy,
> Or our Deaths glorious in thy just Defence.
> *Cato* (1713), III.v, lines 79–81

The myth of Britain as the goal of the Progress of Liberty is set forth in the libretto's dedication to George I by Paolo Rolli:

The subject … is the birth of Roman liberty: having been driven out of its great but unfortunate homeland, that liberty attempted to find refuge in almost all remaining parts of the world: but halted and oppressed by the few, or defeated and exiled by only one, would forever have wandered amid woods and huts had it not finally found great safety and glorious shelter in the happy realms of Your Majesty. Happiest realms! So different from all others; they truly enjoy Roman liberty, while the people possess it, tribunes watch over it, patricians defend it, [and] the sovereign protects it.[57]

Rolli goes on to compare Britain and Rome in their heroes, civic life, and literature, and to extol George as an incarnation of Alexander Severus.

Defense of liberty verged on an absolute duty. When the sacred Lupercalian games are interrupted by armed assault by the tyrant Amulius, Romulus urges his countrymen,

> In just defence of native Liberty
> None ought to spare the shedding all their Blood.
>
> Per conservar la Libertà natia
> Tutto il sanque versar non si risparmj.
> *Numitore* (1720), I.vi, pp. 22–3

The treacherous Maximus uses the call to liberty as he leads troops against his enemy Aetius, exhorting:

> He that loves his Country,
> Let him unsheath his Sword, and follow me.
> Behold the Path that leads to Liberty,
> Which we'll obtain for *Rome* and all the Empire.
>
> Chi vuol salva la Patria
> Stringa il ferro, e mi siegua; ecco il sentiero.
> Onde aurà libertà *Roma*, e l'Imperio.
> *Ezio* (1732), III.xiii, pp. 58–9)

Monarchy and sovereignty

Librettos enter the realm of political philosophy when they deal with the origin of the state, sovereignty, and resistance. Librettos in London would need to deal carefully with portrayals of monarchy, especially in a limited, parliamentary monarchy such as Britain's and with the monarch in attendance in the royal box. They would have to avoid the appearance of glorifying absolute monarchy and arbitrary rule and yet preserve the possibility of deposing monarchs without threatening monarchy itself; they would need to respect the monarch's authority while also presenting the monarch's responsibilities to his or her people.

Most Italian operas in London were adaptations of pre-existing Italian librettos. Thus – with the exception of such librettos as those written for Venice and Hamburg – most operas were originally performed for courts or at theaters in cities ruled by what the British would have considered absolute or even arbitrary rulers, and so we can assume that the political ideas and images of rulers in these source-librettos were originally supportive of, and by no means subversive of, absolute monarchs. There is, then, a potential conflict that needs resolving: How did the representation of absolute monarchs in operas function in Britain – a nation that had practiced regicide, experimented with a republican commonwealth, forced a king to abandon his throne; a nation that had fought a Continental war to limit the aspirations of an absolute universal monarch; a nation that placed parliamentary limits on its monarch and prided itself on having the greatest degree of liberty of any country in Europe.

Despite England's experience with the Commonwealth and Glorious Revolution, early eighteenth-century Britain was fully committed to a monarchical system. As even the canonic statement of Whig principles, *Cato's Letters*, states, "England at present is not capable of any other form of government than what it enjoys, [for] liberty may be better preserved by a well poised monarchy, than by any popular government that I know now in the world."[58]

The most common form of sovereignty found in seventeenth- and eighteenth-century Europe and opera librettos was rule by a limited absolute monarch; Great Britain with its mixed, limited (constitutional) monarchy was a notable exception, with the monarch sharing power with a legislature. The principles underlying sovereignty can be understood against the prevailing theory of Natural Law as the basis for civil society, legitimate rule, and the right of resistance.[59]

The system of modern (as opposed to medieval or scholastic) Natural Law begins with Hugo Grotius' *De Jure Belli ac Pacis* (1625), followed by, among others, the writings of John Selden, Samuel Pufendorf, Richard Cumberland, Thomas Hobbes, and John Locke.[60] Natural Law theorists used human reason as the basis to discover the universal principles that all men would recognize and obey. Two principles are cardinal: that man first existed in a "state of nature," and that man's fundamental motive is self-preservation and protection of his property.

In the state of nature, men make compacts with their fellows, give up certain rights, and delegate power and authority (sovereignty) to a third party, usually a strong ruler, in return for protection, thus creating civil society.[61] Monarchs rule by virtue of this tacit compact. By protecting the people, the ruler in turn retains the people's allegiance, obedience, and support.[62] The laws of nature grant rights and dictate what man is required or forbidden to do.[63] Hence, in the opera *Siroe* (1728) the title character can state simply that "the Laws of Nature" ("Per legge di Natura") bid him to defend his father and king (II.ii, pp. 36–7).

Expressions of this reciprocal compact between ruler and people appear at crucial points in opera plots. Monarchs recognize their contractual responsibility to their subjects, summarized in the ubiquitous tag of Cicero: "Salus populi suprema lex esto" ("Let the safety of the people be the supreme law").[64] As Numitor states to his younger brother, who usurped his throne:

> The People give the Sovereign
> A general Pow'r, that so in their Defence
> It may be used against their Enemies;
> Whereby he keeps in calm Tranquility
> Both his own Throne and others Liberty.
>
> La commun potestate
> Dà il Popolo a Sovran, perchè in difesa
> L'usi a ragion contro a' nemici sui:
> Onde conservi 'n placida quiete,
> Il soglio a se, la libertate altrui.
> > *Numitore* (1720), I.iii, pp. 10–11

Upon his restoration to the throne at the Temple of Mars, Numitor declares to his people in an aria:

> I carry with me to the Throne
> Thoughts of your Happiness,
> Which are the only Thoughts of Kings.
>
> Of Criminals and Flatterers,
> I'll ever be a Judge severe,
> But an indulgent Father to the Just.
>
> Su quel Trono meco viene
> Il pensier del vostro Bene,
> Chè de' Regi il sol pensier.
>
> Contro all'Empio e al Menzognero,
> Sarò Giudice severo,
> Sarò Padre al Giusto e al Ver.
> > *Numitore* (1720), III.iii, pp. 60–1

Arthenice, Queen of Armenia, upon ascending the throne, announces to her subjects:

> More fond you'll find me to defend the Laws,
> Than to impose them with a Sovereign Power.

> Me attenta avreta a custodir le leggi,
> Più che a imporle sovrana.
> > *Ormisda* (1730), I.i, pp. 8–9

About to be crowned, Artaxerxes announces,

> I solemn swear,
> Safety and Ease to all beneath my Reign.

> Perche sicuro
> Ne sia ciascum; solennemente il giuro.
> > *Arbace* (1734), III.vi, pp. 42–3

Although a usurper, Zidiana proclaims to her people:

> Your Welfare, my loyal People, shall be
> The chief Rule and Foundation of my Law;
> On your Safety my best Cares shall attend.

> Norma delle mie Leggi
> Sarà il publico bene: a vostri sonni
> Veglieran le mie cure,
> > *Teuzzone* (1727), I.vii, pp. 24–5

When Aeneas accepts the kingship of the Etruscans, he swears:

> To the Tyrrhen nation
> I promise an equitable reign, and common benefit.

> Alle genti Tirrene
> Prometto il giusto Regno e il comun bene.
> > *Enea nel Lazio* (1734), I.i, pp. 4–5

In response, the people swear their allegiance in return for his protection:

> Ascend that throne, Æneas,
> > Thou art our king:
> The crown and scepter take,
> > We will swear to thee allegiance.
> …
> Protect thy kingdom,
> We'll live, we'll die with thee.

Sopra quel Trono ascendi
  Enea sei nostro Re.
Lo scettro e il serto prendi
  Fede giuriamo a te.

…

Il Regno tuo difendi,
Vivrem, mortem con te.
I.i, pp. 4–5

A king's obligation to those who granted him the throne is the major motive behind Gualtiero's seeming public rejection of his beloved shepherdess Griselda. Gualtiero affirms that

Kings are made by the Subjects; their Affections are our Strength, and likewise our Laws.

Fanno i Popoli il Re, son lor voleri
Nostro Poter, ma nostra Lege ancora.
Griselda (1721), I.ii, pp. 4–5

Subsequently told that his people disapprove of his choice of Griselda as consort, Gualtiero assents:

My People, this is the Day, in which your King is to receive Laws from you: 'Twas an Offence to you to see a Woman sit with me on the Throne, who was born to feed the Flocks: she pleas'd me as such; you disdain her, now I behold her with your Eyes, and cast her off.

Popoli, questo è il giorno, in cui le legi
Da voi prende il Re vostro: a voi fa sdegno
Veder meco su 'l Trono
Donna che nacque a pascolar la Greggia:
Tal Griselda mi piacque,
Tal la sdegnate, al fine,
Miro lei co' vostr' occhj, e la ripudio.
I.ii, pp. 6–7

Instances of the compact are found in librettos when the people often must ratify someone (usually a hero) as the monarch, even if the monarchy is hereditary. However, never is there an outright contested election for the throne; rather, an heir or valorous hero is acclaimed by the people. In the British monarchy, likewise, hereditary succession was not an absolute right; the Revolution Principles and Act of Settlement had affirmed Parliament's right to alter or set conditions to the succession, specifically that the successor be Protestant.

In *Teseo* (1713), as a reward for his valor in battle, the Athenians proclaim "Then let him be our King" ("Egli sia dunque il nostro Rè"; II.iv, pp. 20–1). In *Floridante* (1721), Elmira, whose rightful throne is being held by Orontes, is summoned to the throne by her people, as she is told,

> The city up in arms,
> cries aloud thy name:
> come, O queen, to comfort a
> faithful people that call upon thee.
>
> La città sollevata
> Alto grida il tuo nome:
> Vieni o regina a consolare un fido
> Popolo che t'acclama.
>
> III.viii, pp. 56–7

Teuzzone claims the right of his crown

> by virtue of my Father's
> Written Will, and the choice of the People.
>
> Col pubblico voler quello del Padre.
>
> *Teuzzone* (1727), I.iv, pp. 14–15

These episodes and verses could well be taken to illustrate precepts from Lipsius: "He who is to rule all, must be chosen from all" (2.4) or "the king is created from those who are capable and suitable because of conspicuous virtue, or because of actions originating in virtue" (2.7).

As we saw in *Tito Manlio* and *Lucio Papirio*, rulers occasionally yield to the vox populi's demand for justice or mercy for a civic hero. Probably due to theatrical economy, the crowd is usually only an offstage presence. The rescue of Darius and Statira from an unjust death sentence from the tyrant Sidermes is accomplished by the Persian princes Agesilaus and Artabanus, as announced by Artabanus to Sidermes:

> the general Voice of the all the People
> Demands Darius' and Statira's Freedom.
>
> Ogn' un libero vuol Statira, e Dario,
> E alla tua strage anela.
>
> *Dario* (1725), III.ii, pp. 52–3

In *Ormisda* (1730), it was the offstage camp of soldiers and generals who successfully demanded (in the name of lawfulness and justice) that the rightful heir Cosroes be king.

Natural Law recognizes that sovereignty may take the form of monarchy, aristocracy, or democracy.[65] For theorists such as Jean Bodin, Thomas Hobbes, and Robert Filmer, sovereignty must be absolute – unlimited, irrevocable, irresistible, and undivided.[66] An absolute monarchy creates stability through an authority that can act decisively at moments of crisis.[67] For Britons, the monarchy of Louis XIV exemplified absolutism, although the British often unfairly characterized his rule as arbitrary.[68] Sovereigns are not to be actively resisted by subjects, nor can they be deposed by subjects or the church.

In opera librettos, monarchs shown in Near Eastern courts are absolute. They are allowed great discretion in meting punishment without application to a judiciary, ruling without a legislature or advisory council, declaring and waging war, and commanding marriages or other actions of their family or members of their court. With the few exceptions of Roman emperors and consuls, rulers are not accountable to representative assemblies. All exercise a greater range of rightful power and authority than could the British monarchs.

The most extreme form of absolutism, and one outside the founding conditions of man in a natural state, was a hereditary divine right monarchy, such as described in Sir Robert Filmer's *Patriarcha* (published 1680), whereby the monarch's power derives directly from divine authority, not consent. In Filmer's patriarchal form, the king rules as does a father over his family; there is no state of nature, original compact, or consent; and the monarch's power is unlimited, irresistible, irrevocable, and undivided.[69] In Britain, this doctrine was vigorously refuted by James Tyrrell, the martyr Algernon Sidney, and John Locke.[70]

Librettos generally eschew such an extreme form of divine right. This doctrine is renounced in at least one opera. *Muzio Scevola* (1721) puts into the mouth of Tarquin, the last of the Roman kings, whom the Etruscan King Porsena is attempting to restore to the throne, an articulation of the doctrine supporting arbitrary monarchs. Tarquin instructs Porsena:

> in the mean time maintain the Right of
> Kings, and remember that we are Deities on
> Earth, and that all others are born to Serve
> and Adore us upon the Throne.

> tu intanto
> La ragione dei Re sostieni, e pensa
> Che noi siam Numi 'n Terra, e gli altri sono
> Nati a servirne et adorar su'l Trono.
>   I.i, pp. 12–13

This *jure divino* doctrine is repudiated by virtue of its spokesman and his fate.

But most absolute monarchies were limited. Common law, custom, civil law, or procedures established upon the grant of sovereignty placed limits on the authority, selection, and succession of the sovereign.[71] The monarchy could also be mixed, with authority shared with a legislature, as in Great Britain. As Thomas Gordon stated on behalf of Britons: "They have been always fond of Monarchy modeled and limited by Laws."[72]

Librettos show a king's actions restrained by custom or civil law. As Xerxes is told by Arsamenes,

> It is not lawful, sir,
> That you, a king, shou'd to the throne advance,
> One who is not a sov'reign princess born.
>
> Signor a un Re non lice
> Ergere al Trono chi non è Regina.
> *Serse* (1738), I.i, pp. 8–9

Occasionally, the monarch's will must be legitimated by formal alteration of laws, as in *Artaserse* (1724), where the royal family has recognized a law that requires the death of any unlawfully born son of the king. In the *scena ultima*, in order to effect a happy ending, Artaxerxes formally repeals this "inhumane law" ("La dura Legge") in order to marry his favorite Agamira and to spare his son by her, Darius (known as Cleomenes).

The ancient Near Eastern and Roman courts were pagan in religion; there are occasional sacrifices as entreaties for upcoming military success, but, in general, the world of the operas functions without divine intervention. The few exceptions include *Ifigenia in Aulide* (1735), *Giustino* (1737), and *La conquista del vello d'oro* (1738). This general absence of divine intervention accords well with the progressive trend in seventeenth- and eighteenth-century political philosophy that dispenses with divine right, secularizes politics, and relies on Natural Law and contractual theories of government.

Librettos insist on strict, recognized succession to the throne. Attempts to alter succession and place a person on the throne other than the rightful heir (such as a second son or son of a mistress or second wife) are always thwarted.[73] One hero, Darius, shows his virtue by offering to relinquish his throne should Sidermes prove his rightful lineage and claim to the throne, "for the Subjects Good" ("per il ben de' Vassalli"; *Dario* (1725), I.i, pp. 4–5). The plan of King Ormisda's second queen to put her own son Arsaces on the throne in place of Cosroes is prevented by the offstage camp of soldiers who demand that the rightful heir Cosroes be king (*Ormisda* [1730], III.v). Monarchs who obtain kingdoms by conquest or usurpation are always deposed, and the throne is returned to the rightful ruler (although the early phases of a plot may show the court and people submitting passively to the usurping or conquering monarch). Too numerous to mention are instances of the many usurpers who end up being deposed.

Unlike France, for example, which followed the Salic Law that forbade female succession, Britain and the librettos of many operas recognized succession by the eldest child, who could be a daughter (though males have precedence).[74] In operas, this principle of succession is so well established that there are numerous queens, including Arsinoe (Queen of Cyprus) in *Arsinoe* (1705); Arsinoe (daughter of the King of Caria) in *Antioco* (1711); Camilla in *Camilla* (1706); Thomyris (Queen of Scythia) in *Thomyris* (1707), *L'Odio e l'amore* (1721), and *Farnace* (1723); Elisa in *Astarto* (1720); Elmira in *Floridante* (1721); Cleopatra in *Giulio Cesare* (1724); Adelaide in *Lotario* (1729); Parthenope in *Partenope* (1730); Cleofida in *Poro* (1731); Arthenice in *Ormisda* (1730); Berenice in *Lucio Vero* (1727); and Arianne in *Giustino* (1737).

Female succession is so accepted that in *Semiramide riconosciuta* (1733), when Semiramis, who has been ruling Assyria in man's apparel under the name King Minus, has her identity revealed, she willingly offers to lay down her crown. Yet the people exclaim:

> Live happy, henceforth be our Queen,
> Who 'till now our King has been.
>
> Viva lieta e sia Reina
> Chi fin'or fù nostro Rè.
> III.xiii, pp. 68–9

No issue was as contentious in political philosophy as the right of subjects to resist their sovereign.[75] Having delegated power and authority, do subjects have the right to resist the sovereign's exercise of power or to take back sovereignty and adopt a new form of government? Given their experience of the Commonwealth and Glorious Revolution, and the possible – though distant and unlikely – Jacobite invasion, this was a political issue of great importance to Britons.

Inasmuch as operas do show the successful and legitimate overthrow of sovereigns, they are staking out a position about the right of resistance that would generally be acceptable in Britain, certainly among the Whigs. Advocating resistance to monarchs might be a sensitive issue when a king who chartered and subsidized the opera company is sitting in his royal box. However, the people's right to resistance had been a bedrock principle of the British Constitution and English Whig political thought of the post-Revolution era.[76] John, Lord Hervey, in a ministerial pamphlet from 1734, states the Whig position on resistance: "When the People are injur'd, when they are oppress'd, when their Rights are infring'd, their Liberties invaded, and the Constitution hurt and wounded, let them resist; it is their Interest, and it is their Duty to resist; it is their Nature."[77] To the extent that librettos for London embody the right of resistance, they would be acceptable to Whigs, possibly problematic for Tories, but probably offensive to High Churchmen or Jacobites.

It was commonly agreed that the people could not rightly resist those who legitimately held and used the sovereign power.[78] In the absolute or divinely sanctioned forms of sovereignty, after the compact between sovereign and subjects has been made or the monarch divinely sanctioned, subjects lose any right to resist the sovereign or revoke his power.[79] Subjects must suffer the sovereign's actions even so far that the subject's only recourse was to flee, passively endure unjust injury as part of a subject's lot, or expect that the sovereign would receive divine punishment.[80] Grotius granted that "all men have the right of resisting in order to ward off injury," but the state "in the interest of public peace and order, can limit that common right of resistance ... If, in fact, the right of resistance should remain without restraint, there will no longer be a state, but only a non-social horde."[81]

The problem remained of how to maintain the sovereignty of the state without exposing subjects to arbitrary princes or tyranny and denying their natural rights. Theorists granted the legitimacy of resistance when a ruler violates the people's rights of safety and protection; he breaks the contract and loses his legitimacy and becomes a public enemy or tyrant.[82] As asserted by Pufendorf, "A people can defend itself against the extreme and unjust violence of its prince,"[83] but this right was never to be confused with individual rebellion against authority. The principle of allowing a high degree of resistance to authority was characteristic of the Protestant humanist tradition and later Catholic Counter Reformation.[84]

Drawing the line between a ruler who is merely unpopular or unkind and a tyrant is thus crucial.[85] The distinction was carefully marked by Bodin:

Now the greatest difference betwixt a king and a tyrant is, for that a king conformeth himselfe unto the lawes of nature, which the tyrant at his pleasure treadeth under foot: the one of them respecteth religion, justice, and faith; whereas the other regardeth neither God, faith, nor law: the one of them referreth all his actions to the good of the Commonweale, and safetie of his subjects; whereas the other respecteth nothing more than his owne particular profit, revenge, or pleasure.[86]

With the ruler's legitimacy voided, subjects may exercise their right of self-defense, and the ruler may be deposed. The people thus commit *tyrannicide*, not *regicide*. One removes a king, but not kingship. Another legitimate object of resistance are rulers who obtain thrones by conquest or usurpation; such are justly deposed and the throne is returned to the rightful ruler. Since such usurpers invariably rule tyrannically, they ultimately warrant resistance.

The London opera librettos are fastidious in seeing that acts of resistance occur only against tyrants or usurpers who exercise power oppressively and cruelly. Care is always taken to blacken the character of tyrants and to expose their unjust hold on power in order to justify resistance. Julius Caesar is vilified by Emilia, Pompey's widow, who plots his death:

> Thou knows't him not, he is an impious Wretch,
> And every Crime appears to him a Virtue,
> If it contributes to promote his Power.

> Tu no 'l conosci è un' empio; ogni delitto
> Purche giova a regnar virtù gli sembra.
> > *Catone* (1732), I.xi, pp. 22–3

In *Rodelinda* (1725), Garibaldo describes the reign of the usurper Grimoaldo:

> As he by Tyranny procur'd the Crown,
>   By Blood he must secure his Reign;
> Pity but weakly props a tott'ring Throne
>   Which nought, but Rigour, can maintain.

> Tirannia gli diede il Regno
> Gliel conservi crudeltà;
> Del Regnar base e sostegno
> E il rigor non la pietà.
> > II.iv, pp. 40–1

Those about to overthrow a tyrant justify resistance. In *Radamisto* (1720), for example, Tiridates, king of neighboring Armenia, has overcome Thrace and rules tyrannically. Fraartes and Tigranes, princes of Armenia and Pontus, plot to overthrow him. As a motive, Tigranes states:

> Weary with suffering so cruel a King;
> And with seeing so many Royal Persons in Danger,
> I'm thinking of a no less strange
> Than just and glorious Enterprize.

> Stanco di più soffrir Re sì crudele
> E tant' alme Reali in tal periglio,

> Alzo il pensiero ad una strana impresa,
> Ma gloriosa, e guista.
>
> III.i, pp. 52–3

Tigranes makes clear his motive is not to kill Tiridates or take away his rightful throne, but to remove the means of his tyranny. Fraates replies,

> So glorious an end
> Would even turn Crime into a Virtue.
>
> Un fin sì glorioso
> Può far che sia virtude anche un delitto.
>
> III.i, pp. 54–5

And when Polyxena announces the arrival of Tigranes and Fraates, she tells Tiridates,

> Your Soldiers weary of your Misdemeanours,
> Are up in Arms;
> And *Tigranes* and *Phraates* have join'd them.
>
> Stanchi de tuoi misfatti
> An preso l'armi i tuoi guerrieri; e seco
> Son Tigrane e Fraate.
>
> III.x, pp. 66–7

In *Riccardo primo* (1727), when Richard joins Orontes in a just war attacking Isacus to avenge his deception and betrayal of them both, they emphatically declare him "Perfidious Traitor, Tyrant *Isacus*," "Unjust and ruthless King," "that impious treach'rous Man" ("Perfido Isacio, Traditor, Tiranno!"; "Iniquo Re, spietato"; "O mostrero a quell' Empio"; III.i, pp. 54–5; II.iv, pp. 34–5; II.vi, pp. 42–3).

Resistance to tyrants is usually assumed by a vigilant general, courtier, or foreign prince. Not insignificantly, having resistance led by a general or foreign power avoids condoning mass rebellion by the populace and preserves the general principle of non-resistance by subjects. For Bodin, "so is it a most faire and magnificall thing for a prince to take up armes to relieve a whole nation and people, unjustly oppressed by the crueltie of a tyrant."[87] Grotius concurred that "those who possess rights equal to those kings, have the right of demanding punishments" not only for injuries which affect them but for any that "excessively violate the law of nature or of nations in regard to any persons whatsoever."[88]

In *Dario*, as mentioned, the rescue of Darius and Statira from the tyrant Sidermes was accomplished by the Persian princes Agesilaus and Artabanus. In *Floridante*, the overthrow of Orontes is accomplished by Timante and

Coralbo, a prince of Tyre and a general of Persia. And in *Radamisto*, the overthrow of Tiridates by Fraartes and Tigranes is accomplished by the king's brother and the Prince of Pontus. In *Ormisda* (1730), it was the off-stage camp of soldiers and generals who successfully demanded (on the side of lawfulness and justice) that the rightful heir Cosroes be king.

The librettos for London, then, steer a careful course in representing monarchy, and their presentation of it generally conforms to British expectations. Many operas are set in motion with a tyrant or usurper occupying the throne. Plots are devoted to engineering their overthrow and replacement with a legitimate monarch (by rightful succession or popular choice). Operas offer monarchy as an unquestioned, acceptable form of government. Outright consideration of other forms of government is avoided, and there are no instances of a change of government from monarchy to democracy or aristocracy. Significantly, by endorsing the right of resistance to tyrants who forfeit their right to govern, the librettos endorse Britain's expectations of a limited, constitutional sovereign. Although nothing in contemporary politics or political discourse makes the concept of monarchy problematic and requiring such a defense, librettos reinforce the ideal of monarchy by showing the achievements of beneficent, virtuous monarchs.

Opera as the Mirror for Princes

Operas could fulfill the role of the *ars historica* in the manner of the Mirror for Princes advice books by presenting onstage actions that the prince or ruler could admire and imitate – or distain and avoid – in his or her role as ruler.[89] The virtuous actions were made all the more attractive by the added spectacle, dance, poetry, and music of opera. Henry Felton's remarks in *A Dissertation on Reading the Classics* (1713) could apply equally well to a monarch attending an opera: "[You] will meet with great and wonderful Examples of … Virtue in the *Greeks* and *Romans*, with many Instances of Greatness of Mind, of unshaken Fidelity, Contempt of humane Grandeur, a most passionate Love of their Countrey."[90]

There are two broad traditions of the Mirror for Princes. In the Ciceronian mold, as represented by Erasmus and Francesco Patrizi, humanists urged the prince to cultivate virtue and above all justice as the sure way to gain the love of his people, glory, and fame.[91] A countervailing Tacitean, Machiavellian, anti-Ciceronian strain is represented by Machiavelli, Lipsius, Guicciardini, and Botero.[92] Here, the prince may find it useful to feign virtue and justice;

but necessity, utility, profitable deceit, and prudence must prevail over virtue, justice, and moral obligations as the means for the prince to ensure the maintenance of his rule and preservation of the state. This *ragion di stato* tradition taught the prince the *arcana imperii* (the mysteries of state), those evil deeds, lies, and treachery necessary to rule effectively and maintain one's rule.

In the descriptions of the actions of tyrants, we occasionally get glimpses of the Machiavellian *ragion di stato*. Emilia, Pompey's widow denounces Julius Caesar:

> Thou knows't him not, he is an impious Wretch,
> And every Crime appears to him a Virtue,
> If it contributes to promote his Power.

> Tu no 'l conosci è un' empio; ogni delitto
> Purche giova a regnar virtù gli sembra.
> > *Catone* (1732), I.xi, pp. 22–3

Garibaldo describes how the usurper Grimoaldo retains his throne:

> As he by Tyranny procur'd the Crown,
> > By Blood he must secure his Reign;
> Pity but weakly props a tott'ring Throne
> > Which nought, but Rigour, can maintain.

> Tirannia gli diede il Regno
> Gliel conservi crudeltà;
> Del Regnar base e sostegno
> E il rigor non la pietà.
> > *Rodelinda* (1725), II.iv, pp. 40–1

Machiavellian advice is offered by Sivenio, confederate of the usurper Zidiana,

> Dissimulation is the surest Art
> To govern well.

> La prim' arte in chi regna, il finger sia.
> > *Teuzzone* (1727), I.i, pp. 10–11

And later he asserts,

> Deceit is no Crime when it serves a Cause.

> Error, che giova, è necessario errore.
> > I.iii, pp. 12–13

Stilicon, a conspirator against the emperor Flavius Honorius, declares:

All
Is permitted, when to reign's the question.

Il tutto
Lice all' Uom per regnar.

Onorio (1736), III.iii, pp. 40–1

Whereas a fellow conspirator concurs that

> A fortunate success
> From blackest deeds takes off the stain of infamy.
>
> Fortunato successo
> Toglie l'Infamia ad ogni iniquo Eccesso.

I.ii, pp. 4–5

But such sentiments are repudiated by the plot resolutions. By showing exemplary princes prevailing over tyranny and dispensing justice and clemency, librettos endorse the Ciceronian mode of the Mirror for Princes.

Necessary for a prince striving for virtue is self-mastery of the private passions of love, hatred, or revenge. Such self-conquest ultimately redounds to the ruler's own glory, confirming his virtue and suitability to rule. As Cicero declared, in praising Julius Caesar, "To conquer the will, to curb the anger, and to moderate the triumph … him who acts thus I do not compare to the greatest of men, but I judge him most like to God."[93] Admetus, King of Thessaly, is advised by Hercules at the news of the death of his wife Alcestis:

> If thou'rt a King, act with unconquer'd Pow'r,
> And rule the sorrowing Passions of thy Soul.
>
> Se Re tu sei, da invitto
> Domina del tuo cor l' alto dolore.

Admeto (1727), I.vii, pp. 16–17

Librettos show monarchs caught in conflicts between love and the pursuit of duty and virtue. The stark conflict between love and duty is recognized by Cyrus, King of Persia:

> Love and Monarchy are so severe,
>   That they never suffer
>   More than one to reign at once.
>
> Più d' uno sol che imperi
>   Non soffrono severi
>   Amore e Regno:

L'Odio e l'amore (1721), III.v, pp. 80–1

For the ruler, the passion of love must be suppressed in favor of duty, as Queen Zidiana is counseled:

> Learn to govern your Passions, and be a Queen.

> Regna sovra i tuoi sensi, e sei Regina.
> > *Teuzzone* (1727), I.ix, pp. 28–9

The primacy of duty is clear to the conspirator Agenor. Trying to foil the love of Elisa for Astartus (against whom he is spreading false reports), Agenor is certain:

> He'll please [you] no longer when once he's found
> > a Traytor;
> Reason of State in Princes, always prevails over the
> Tyranny of Love.

> Cesserà di piacer; s' è traditore.
> Preval sempre in chi regna
> Ragion di Stato a tirannia d' amore.
> > *Astarto* (1720), I.ii, pp. 16–17

Several of the most famous examples of self-mastery from antiquity are represented in operas for London. Most celebrated is the Continence of Scipio (from Livy, 26.50), presented in *Scipione* (1726). Publius Cornelius Scipio, a victorious proconsul in Spain, had fallen in love with a beautiful slave-captive; when he discovers she is betrothed, he announces:

> Now the fall'n Enemy has felt his Doom,
> I'll try new Triumphs, I'll myself o'ercome,
> And prove the bravest Conqu'ror at home.

> Dopo il Nemico oppresso
> Voglio esser di me stesso
> Più forte Vincitor.
> > III.viii, pp. 60–1

He demonstrates his virtue and self-mastery when he gives up the slave-captive to her fiancé and hands over as her dowry the ransom offered for her release. Similarly, in *Ormisda* (1730), Cosroes yields Arthenice to her beloved Arsaces, who obtains his rightful kingdom (III.xv).

Alexander the Great displays his noble, compassionate soul throughout *Poro* (1731). Victorious over Porus, Alexander offers to return his kingdom on his admission that he has been conquered and offers him one of Darius' swords (I.ii). He frees Porus' captured sister (I.iii), returns gifts offered by Cleofida (I.ix), prevents Porus from stabbing Cleofida (II.ii), and restores to Porus his freedom, queen, and kingdom (III.xiii) – all examples of mastering his desire for wealth, love, or revenge.[94] In *Adriano in Siria* (1735), the

Emperor Hadrian, "at length gaining a Victory over himself," overcomes his passion for his slave Emirena, "restores to his Enemy his Kingdom; to his Rival his Spouse, and pardoning Idalma, restores his Heart to Sabina [his espoused], and recovers his own Glory" ("che vincitor al fin di se stesso, rende il Regno al nemico, la consorte al rivale, il perdono ad Idalma, il cuore a Sabina, e la sua Gloria a se stesso"; argument). Likewise, Flavio, King of the Lombards, though married and inflamed with love of Theodata, finally yields her to her beloved (*Flavio* [1723], III.vii).

The greatest duty of a ruler – and the one that brought glory and the love of one's subjects – was dispensing justice, and the most glorious form of justice was practicing *clementia* (mercy).[95] For Seneca, "Of all the virtues, in truth, none befit a human being more, since none in more humane."[96] Cicero and Seneca maintained that *clementia* was crucial for a ruler in securing and maintaining his rule, and granting it was one of the noblest prerogatives of a sovereign. Julius Caesar proclaims, "'Tis the Prerogative of Heroic Virtue to pardon Offences" ("Virtù de' grandi è il perdonar l' offese"; *Giulio Cesare* [1724], I.ii, pp. 6–7). Eucherio, confidant of the Emperor Flavius Honorius, advises,

> Magnanimity is never parted from human
> Perfection.
>
> Suol magnanimo spirto
> Accompagnar le perfezzioni umane.
> *Onorio* (1736), I.vi, pp. 12–13

Even Machiavelli could provisionally advise that every prince "must want to have a reputation for compassion."[97]

Classical *clementia* should not be confused with pity or compassion (*misericordia*) – what Augustine calls "a kind of fellow-feeling in our own hearts for the sufferings of others that in fact impels us to come to their aid as far as our ability allows."[98] *Clementia*, for the Stoic Seneca, is a form of self-mastery; it means "restraining the mind from vengeance when it has the power to take it, or the leniency of a superior towards an inferior in fixing punishment."[99] The Roman Stoics actually held pity was a weakness, if not a sickness (*aegritudo*); the ruler or judge should not be moved by the passions into disregarding the rational demands of justice, law, or needs of state.[100] In *Sosarme* (1732), Haliates, King of Lydia, for example, rejects pity as a tool of state: "Pity may guild [*sic*], but not preserve a Throne" ("Pietà fa bello e non sicuro il Trono"; I.vii, pp. 14–15).

The preponderance of operas arrange their plots so that in the *scena ultima* the monarch or rightful ruler dispenses justice, usually in the form of clemency: pardoning malefactors, even those who have attempted assassination or rebellion against them, and uniting pairs of true lovers – thus producing the obligatory *lieto fine*. We can imagine the spectacle of opera contributing luster to this action: the clement ruler at the center of the stage, surrounded by the entire cast, with his deed praised by the final *coro* of soloists and orchestral accompaniment.

It was Ptolemy's lack of mercy toward Pompey – sending his severed head to Caesar – that aroused Caesar's rage against him as a "Barbaro traditor," as he denounced him in an aria:

> The Prince, whose Soul is void
> Of Pity and Compassion
> Deserves not to hold the Reins of Empire
>
> Non è di Re quell core,
> Che donasi al rigore,
> Che in sen no hà pieta
> *Giulio Cesare* (1724), I.iii, pp. 8–9

When revising *Riccardo primo* (1727), to make Richard more of a noble warrior-king, librettist Paolo Rolli emphasized Richard's magnanimity, generosity, self-mastery, and clemency.

Clemency can be extended for reasons of state.[101] It can teach malefactors to reform and confess. In *Poro* (1731), Alexander grants clemency (*perdono*) to the traitor Timagenes, admonishing him,

> from hence,
> Let the severe Remembrance of thy Crime
> Teach thee to act with an unblemish'd Faith.
>
> conservando in mente
> Del fallo tuo la rimembranza amara
> Ad esser fido un altra volta impara.
> III.vi, pp. 56–7

Darius states, "A Crime confess'd deserves some Clemency" ("Il confessato error merta Clemenza"; *Dario* [1725], III.v, pp. 62–3).

Glory comes to the prince who exercises clemency. Queen Thomyris asks her people what punishment Cyrus deserves; they reply he deserves death. She counters it is sufficient punishment that he is overcome. Cyrus and his beloved Telesia, Princess of Scythia, reply:

> *Cyr.* Oh greatness of Soul beyond all Example! *Tel.* Let
> the supream Gods, behold on Earth one like themselves.

Cir. Oh senza esempio Anima grande! *Tel.* In Terra
Veggion chi li somiglia i sommi Dei.
L'Odio e l'amore (1721), III.vii, pp. 84–5

Artaxerxes' clemency toward Artabane and his son (the latter had quelled a
rebellion against him) is praised by his Persian subjects:

> Impartial Prince! Persia adores
>> Mercy seated on the throne,
>> When with pardon it rewards
>> An Hero's loyalty.
>
> Justice is truly lovely,
>> That has Mercy for its Mate.
>
> Giusto Re la Persia adora
>> La Clemenza assisa in Trono
>> Quando premia col perdono
>> D'un Eroe la fedelta.
>
> Da Giustizia è bella allora
>> Ch'è compagna alla Pietà.

Artaserse (1734), III.vi, pp. 50–1

Cletus, leader of a failed rebellion against Alexander the Great, implores
clemency on the grounds of "Our Truth and Valour" ("Nostra fede e valor"),
which Alexander grants, justifying what he does in an aria:

> To pardon Men that are subdu'd,
> To raise the Humble, check the Proud,
> Proofs of truest Grandeur are.
>
> Prove sono di Grandezza
> Perdonar l' Alme soggette,
> Le superbe debellar.

Alessandro (1726), III.vi, pp. 60–1

The most celebrated Roman act of clemency (best known now through
Mozart's 1791 setting of an adaptation of Metastasio's 1734 libretto for the
Prague coronation of Leopold II) is that of the Emperor Titus Vespasian.
Having discovered that he was the intended victim of an assassination plot
by one of his dearest friends Sextus, he remands Sextus to the Senate for
trial. Although the Senate declares Sextus guilty, and his spurned lover
Vitellia admits she instigated the plot, Titus pardons all and embraces his
friend. Sextus proclaims:

> Of all thy noble acts, O gen'rous prince,
> Thy pard'ning crimes, does much the brighest shine.

> O Generoso Augusto,
> Di tue sublimi Imprese
> E la più grande il perdonar le Offese.
>   *La clemenza di Tito* (1737), III.viii, pp. 60–1

Many of the lines above recited or sung by Caesar, Titus, or Alexander could be extracted by a reader of the libretto or remembered by an opera-goer as *sententiae*, precepts, or maxims about the virtue and glory of self-mastery and clemency. The exemplary actions themselves, enhanced by the spectacle of the opera, could be taken to heart by the king, privy councilors, judges, ministers, and other Britons and emulated as they dispensed justice in their daily lives.

A key element of the British legal system was the monarch's prerogative of mercy,[102] which was one of the most venerable signs of the monarch as God's representative on earth. British monarchs swore in the coronation oath to "cause Law and Justice in Mercy to be Executed" in all their judgments.[103] After judicial sessions concluded, judges' reports were sent to the secretaries of state, who approved on the king's behalf the recommendations for mercy. Favorable cases obtained the Great Seal on the authority of a secretary of state or the Privy Council.

William Blackstone summarized the benefits of the royal pardon, of which "the king hath the whole and sole power thereof":

These repeated acts of goodness, coming immediately from his own hand, endear the sovereign to his subjects, and contribute more than any thing to root in their hearts that filial affection, and personal loyalty, which are the sure establishment of a prince.[104]

For Blackstone, "one of the great advantages of monarchy in general, above any other form of government [is] that there is a magistrate, who has it in his power to extend mercy, wherever he thinks it is deserved."[105]

By the 1720s, the granting of royal pardons in capital cases was fully routine. Newspaper columns, while reporting on current capital convictions, also contained reports of those granted reprieves, pardons, or transportations.[106] In eighteenth-century Britain, over 100 people with capital convictions were spared each year.[107] The *exempla* of clemency in the opera librettos not only validate Britain's system of pardons, but align the routine, daily actions of judges, secretaries, and ministers with the great and noble figures shown in the ancient world – in a way providing a link in Britons' self-identification with ancient Rome.[108]

How a Briton actually did draw precepts about clemency and apply them to a current monarch is provided by the writer of *A Free-Holder Extraordinary* (March 6, 1716) in the wake of the "Fifteen" Jacobite rising in Scotland.[109] The rising began when John, Earl of Mar with 600 men raised the Stuart standard at Braemar on September 6, 1715.[110] Troops led by seven Jacobite lords headed south and were defeated by a smaller English force at Preston on November 13, and some 1,600 troops and the lords were taken prisoner; the same day a rebel force was routed at Sheriffmuir. The seven lords and some 130 leading rebel troops were paraded to London for trial. In the following months London witnessed trials and executions of the Jacobite rebels and plotters. Three plotters from Oxford were hanged on November 30. On January 9, 1716, the rebel lords were impeached in the Commons; all were sentenced to death on February 9, but only two were beheaded on February 24. Four more rebels were executed in May and July. Trials for the rebels in Lancashire took place there in January and February, resulting in thirty-four executions.

The *Free-Holder* writer reprinted and commented on episodes reported in William Wotton's *The History of Rome, from the Death of Antonious Pius, to the Death of Severus Alexander* (1701). Each holds up as exemplary a Roman emperor's clemency of rebellious subjects and draws a precept of political wisdom. The first episode presents "that real *Clemency* and Greatness of Soul" of Marcus Aurelius Antonius (reign: AD 161–180). Avidius Cassius, a friend and one of the emperor's best generals, led a civil war against the Empire in which he was killed. Marcus Aurelius wrote to his wife and the Senate, pardoning Cassius' family and accomplices and urging the Senate to impose light punishments on others, stating (as Wotton has him say), "Nothing recommends a *Roman* Emperor so much to his People as *Clemency*." Wotton opines that Marcus believed those pardoned would be his best subjects. The second example is the treatment by Alexander Severus (reign: AD 222–235) toward his rebellious subject Ovinius Camillus, who tried to form a party against the empire. Alexander summoned Camillus, declared him a partner in the empire, and took him on a campaign against the Persians. The *Free-Holder* writer concludes that the example shows "the most generous, if not the most effectual Way of overcoming a Pretender." Alexander believed, he continues, it is not worth securing power "at the Price of any Person's Blood."

Appearing in the wake of the executions of the rebels, the *Free-Holder* writer certainly wants these lessons about the virtues of clemency to be applied to George I; and, hence, held up as a rebuke to him for his own failure to follow the example of the emperors and so to gain the loyalty of the rebels.[111] The application of these Roman emperors to George I relies not on allusion, allegorical identification, or personation but on judging George I in the light of examples and precepts drawn from historical precedents.

In fairness to John Dennis and the writer for *Fog's*, both were surely attending merely to the sensuous, aesthetic aspects of a musical entertainment sung all in Italian – ignoring the verbal content of the libretto. This chapter suggests how an opera might well "inspire publick Virtue" in an opera-goer, who might well "return wiser from an Opera" "with more vertuous or honourable Sentiments."

The contemporary politics of operas on historical subjects, then, is not so much *in* the opera librettos by means of built-in allegory, parallel history, allusion, or personation, as it was in their potential to fulfill the imperatives of the *ars historica*: presenting exemplary episodes from history that show the consequences of tyranny and vice, glory achieved by those who sacrifice for their country, the rewards of devotion to virtue and civic duty, and demonstrations of self-mastery by renouncing illicit love and dispensing justice. These actions, the opera-goers could admire, imitate, and turn into habit in their own lives. From verses in the librettos, readers or audience members could draw *sententiae*, maxims, and precepts that could be applied to understanding and judging the political world of their own times – in the manner we have seen conducted by Edward Barry, the commentators on *Camilla*, and the writer for the *Free-Holder Extraordinary*. From this perspective, operas offer political guidance in the most attractive form, heightened by the delights of poetry, spectacle, and music.

After the Glorious Revolution, as Philip Ayres describes, Britons imagined themselves as virtuous Romans and – in the arts, architecture, and gardening – proclaimed their allegiance to, and gave form or expression to, Roman ideals of liberty and civic virtue – self-fashioning themselves as an "oligarchy of virtue."[112] Seeing and identifying with the exemplary Romans on the opera stage could contribute to Britons' self-fashioning themselves on the models of ancient Romans.

Epilogue

A conjunction of events operatic and political brings this book to a close in 1742. For their 1735–36 and 1736–37 seasons, Handel and the Opera of the Nobility struggled to survive in a city that could barely support one opera company. Senesino and Cuzzoni returned to Italy at the end of the 1735–36 season. Farinelli's unexpected failure to return to London, breaking his contract with the Nobility opera for the coming 1737–38 season, seems to have taken the wind out of that enterprise.

During the last weeks of the 1736–37 season, Handel suffered a 'rheumatic palsie' that prevented his composing or performing at the harpsichord. At this point, Handel – now in poor health, obese, and probably suffering from gout and lead poisoning – apparently chose to abandon producing full seasons of Italian opera under his own direction.[1] Before leaving for Aix-la-Chapelle to spend the summer recovering his health, Handel agreed for £1,000 to write two new operas for Lords Cowper and Delawarr of the Opera of the Nobility for the 1737–38 season.[2] Among the seven operas of that season, Handel provided *Faramondo* (1738), *Serse* (1738), and the pasticcio of his own music *Alessandro Severo* (1738). His agreement also allowed him his own benefit night. Under the title "An Oratorio," his concert program included mostly selections from his English anthems and oratorios, as well as an appearance by Handel himself performing an organ concerto.

Heidegger, manager of the Haymarket Theatre, decided to produce the 1738–39 opera season himself. After failing to raise the needed 200 subscriptions or hire a star singer, even though offering 1,000 guineas, he announced cancellation of the season and refund of subscriptions.[3] Handel took advantage of the empty Haymarket Theatre to produce a short season of English dramatic works and an Italian opera, *Giove in Argo* (1739). Recently returned from his Grand Tour in Italy, where he became an opera enthusiast and promoter, Charles Sackville, Earl of Middlesex, produced the serenata *Angelica e Medoro* (to showcase his mistress) in March–April 1739 at Covent Garden and went on to produce two seasons of Italian opera in 1739–40 and 1741–42.[4] The king and Prince of Wales were able to accommodate both their love of opera and mutual antagonism by deciding the prince would attend opera on Tuesdays and the king on Saturdays so they would not meet.[5]

Handel's 1740–41 season included among English oratorios, odes, or serenatas, his last two Italian operas *Imeneo* (1740) and *Deidamia* (1741). The following season Handel was in Dublin, where *Messiah* (1742) was premiered.

Handel and Middlesex competed head-to-head for the 1739–40 and 1742–43 seasons. Since these two seasons of Handel's were devoted to dramatic works in English, the Handel–Middlesex rivalry was one of the aesthetics of English versus Italian dramatic music. Only now did Handel give up on Italian opera. In 1743–44, he alienated much of the quality of the Town by refusing to compose for Middlesex's company, even though in July 1743 he had agreed to write for them a pair of operas for 1,000 guineas; the town's displeasure with him only increased when he offered his own subscription season, which included the new works *Semele* (1744) and *Joseph and his Brethren* (1744).[6]

Politically, Britain's landscape changed with Walpole's fall from power in February 1742.[7] The collapse of the Convention of the Pardo in June 1739 left Walpole no choice but to declare war against Spain on October 19. Reluctantly drawn into a war the nation had clamored for, his ministry largely mismanaged it. The terms of the Convention, the war's late start, and disastrous army–navy campaigns in the West Indies eroded Walpole's support. The parliamentary elections in the summer of 1741, which would determine Walpole's future as prime minister, were fiercely contested and for him a setback. The dowager Duchess of Marlborough, William Pulteney, and the Prince of Wales spent great sums on the election; the prince himself was said to have spent £12,000.[8]

The newly elected parliament sat on December 1 with a sense of suspense and uncertainty. The make-up of the Commons and Walpole's poor control of it showed his power was on the wane; one estimate has his majority reduced to about eighteen votes. He suffered a surprising series of parliamentary defeats over contested elections in December 1741 and January 1742. Moreover, in Cabinet Walpole was at odds with Newcastle and Hardwicke, who had supported a more aggressive policy toward Spain.[9]

Through the king, on January 5, Walpole made a last, desperate effort to retain his position by trying to detach Frederick from the opposition. If the prince would go to court and beg His Majesty's pardon, the king would increase the prince's allowance by £50,000, pay off his debts, and provide for his servants as vacancies occurred.[10] Frederick's refusal of such an offer as long as Walpole continued in power stiffened the resolve of the opposition.

Realizing he could no longer carry on the king's business, Walpole accepted the necessity of retirement and on February 2, 1742, announced his resignation to the House. Accepting a pension of £4,000 and resigning all his places, on February 18 he advanced to the Lords as the Earl of Orford. After his fall, the *Craftsman* rejoiced with his countrymen for "their happy Deliverance from a most oppressive Bondage of, at least, twenty Years Duration."[11]

After Walpole's fall, Frederick was reconciled with his father, who increased his allowance by £50,000. Many politicians sullied their reputations for their supposed political integrity while in opposition as they shamelessly scrambled for places and peerages. John, Lord Hervey noted the "Hopes and Expectations" of the people turned to "Derision and Odium" as the masks of the Patriots were thrown off, and the conduct of the Patriots fulfilled every prophecy of the *Daily Gazetteer*.[12] The king's disdain for his son and his closest allies for their role in forcing Walpole's removal did not abate, and he continued to inflict spiteful indignities on the prince.

Historians have been more generous in their judgment of Walpole's career than have literary historians, who seem to have accepted as just assessments of him the satire and self-serving propaganda of the Scriblerians and the Patriot opposition. Walpole, historians point out, was effectively using the traditional means of building a loyal and responsive ministry and Parliament. His policies restored confidence after the South Sea Company scandal, kept Britain out of expensive land wars, and assured the stability of the Hanoverian succession; he reduced the land tax, and Britain's trade and commerce increased worldwide. Despite the satirists, by all measures the arts and sciences flourished during a period of peace and increasing prosperity. J. H. Plumb assesses his achievement:

A politician of genius, Robert Walpole, was able to create what had eluded kings and ministers since the days of Elizabeth I – a government and a policy acceptable to the Court, to the Commons, and to the majority of the political establishment in the nation at large. Indeed, he made the world so safe for Whigs that they stayed in power for a hundred years.[13]

With the Great Man, the arch-corruptor of British liberty and the Constitution – against whom the greatest wits of the age directed their lashes and venom for over two decades – gone from the political stage, British political satire lost its energy and spirit, declining into personal caricature and abuse;[14] and with Walpole's exit, passed an era of the vigorous use of Italian opera in the partisan politics of Hanoverian Britain.

Appendix 1: Political affiliation and principal offices of shareholders of the Royal Academy of Music, *c*.1717–22

Original fifty-eight shareholders, July 27, 1719[1]

Henry, Duke of Kent
  Govt. Whig (1717)   PC (1717); KG (1713); Regent of the Realm (1714); Gentleman of the Bedchamber (1714–16); Lord Steward (1716–19); Keeper of Privy Seal (1719–20); Lord Justice of the Realm (1719, 1720, 1723, etc.)

Thomas Holles, Duke of Newcastle (Governor) (five shares)
  Govt. Whig (1717)   PC (1717); Lord Lieut. of Middlesex, Westminster, and Nottinghamshire (1714); Lord Chamberlain (1717–24); KG (1718)

Charles, Duke of Grafton
  Schismatic Whig   PC (1715); Lord High Steward, Coronation of George I (1714); dismissed as Gentleman of the Bedchamber and Lord Justice [I] (1717); Viceroy of Ireland (1720–24); KG (1721); Lord Chamberlain (1724)

Henry, Duke of Portland (three shares)
  Whig   Gentleman of the Bedchamber (1717); Gov. and Vice-Adm., Jamaica (1721)

James, Duke of Montrose
  Whig   Keeper of the Great Seal [S] (1716)

Charles, Duke of Manchester (Deputy Governor)
  Govt. Whig (1717)   Gentleman of the Bedchamber (1714); Carver, Coronation of George I (1714); cr. duke in 1719

James, Duke of Chandos (five shares)
  "Lukewarm" Tory   PC (1721)
  Govt. supporter (1717)

Charles, Earl of Sunderland
Govt. Whig   PC (1714); Sec. of State (1717); First Lord
                             of the Treasury (1718); Groom of the Stole
                             (1719); d. April 19, 1722

Henry, Earl of Rochester
Tory   —

James, Earl of Berkeley
Whig   PC (1717); Gentleman of the Bedchamber
                             (1714); Lord of the Admiralty (1717)

Richard, Earl of Burlington (five shares)
Whig member of Prince   PC (1714); Lord Treasurer [I] (1715); Lord
of Wales' party   Lieut. of Yorkshire and Co. Cork (1715)

George, Earl of Lichfield
Tory; member of Cowper's   —
Lords opposition

Henry, Earl of Lincoln
Govt. Whig (1717)   PC (1715); Gentleman of the Bedchamber
                             (1714); Joint Paymaster-General (1715)

Thomas, Earl of Strafford
Tory; member of Cowper's   —
Lords opposition;

George, Earl of Halifax
Govt. Whig (1717)   PC (1717); Auditor of the Exchequer (1714);
                             Joint Housekeeper of Hampton Court and
                             Ranger of Bushy Park (1716); Lord Justice
                             of the Realm (1720)

Henry, Earl of Thomond [I]
Whig   —

Talbot, Earl of Sussex
Govt. Whig   Gentleman of the Bedchamber (1722)

William, Earl of Cadogan
Govt. Whig   PC (1717); Master of the Robes (1714);
                             cr. earl in 1718

David Colyear, Earl of Portmore
                             PC (1712; resworn, 1721)

Henry (Coote), Earl of Mountrath
  Govt. Whig   PC [I](1718); MP (1715–20)

Henry, Viscount Lonsdale
  Whig   Gentleman of the Bedchamber (1717)

Richard Child, Viscount Castlemaine (two shares)
  Tory under Anne; turned   MP (1708–22); cr. viscount [I] (1718);
  Govt. Whig   cr. Earl Tylney [I] (1731)

James Hamilton, Viscount Limerick [I]
                              cr. viscount 1719

John, Lord Gower
  Tory; member of Cowper's   —
  Lords opposition

Allen, Lord Bathurst
  Tory; member of Cowper's   —
  Lords opposition

Robert Benson, Lord Bingley (Deputy Governor)
  Tory; member of   PC (1714), cr. baronet (1713); Treasurer of
  Cowper's Lords   Household (1730)
  opposition

George, Lord Lansdowne
  Tory   —

Henry, Lord Carleton
  Whig   —

Charles Paulet (styled Marquis of Winchester; later Duke of Bolton)
  MP (1705–10, 1715–17)   PC (1725); Vice-Admiral of S. Wales (1715);
  Govt. Whig (1717)   Lord Lieut. Carm., Glam. (1715), Hants.,
                              Dorset (1722); Gentleman of the Bedchamber
                              [Prince of Wales] (1714–17); Col. Royal
                              Horse Guards (1717); cr. Lord Powlett (1717);
                              KG (1722)

Walter, Lord Chetwynd (Viscount Chetwynd [I] (1717))
  MP (1712–22)   Ranger, St. James's Park (1714); High
  Sunderland Whig   Steward, Stafford (1717)

James Craggs
MP (1713–21)   PC (1718); Cofferer to the Prince of Wales
Sunderland Whig   (1714–17); Sec. at War (1717–18); Sec. of State
                      (1718–21); d. February 16, 1721

Richard Hampden
Whig MP (1701–28)   PC (1718); Treasurer of the Navy (1718–20);
                      Teller of the Exchequer (1716–18); chair-
                      man, Committee of Privileges and Elections
                      (1715–22)

Sir Hungerford Hoskyns, Baronet
MP (1717–22)   —
Admin. Whig

Sir Matthew Decker, Baronet
Whig MP (1719–22)   —

Sir John Guise, Baronet
MP (1705–10, 1722–27)   —
Independent Whig

Sir Wilfred Lawson, Baronet
MP (1718–37)   Groom of the Bedchamber (1720–23)
Admin. Whig

Sir John Jennings
MP (1705–11, 1715–34) Lord of the Admiralty (1714–17, 1718–27);
Admin. Whig   Keeper, Greenwich Park (1720)

Sir George Coke
                                    —

Sir Humphry Howarth
                                    —

Thomas Coke
Tory MP (1710–15)   PC (1708); Vice Chamberlain of the
                      Household (1706)

William Evans   —

Roger Jones
Tory MP (1713–15);   —
inconsistent Whig MP
(1715–22)

James Bruce (Treasurer)
  Tory MP (1708–10)   Joint Comptroller of Army Accounts (1711)

William Pulteney
  Whig MP (1705–42)   PC (1716); Sec. at War (1714); Lord
  Schismatic Whig (1717)   Lieut. E. Riding, Yorks. (1721)

Thomas Coke [of Norfolk]
  Whig MP (1722–28)   KB (1725); cr. Baron Lovel (1728); cr. Earl of
                             Leicester (1744)

Thomas Harrison

                                         —

Benjamin Mildmay
  (?Whig)   Chief Comm. of Salt Duties (1714)

Thomas [recte: George] Harrison

                                         —

George Wade
  MP (1715–48)   Brig.-Gen. (1708); Maj.-Gen. (1714); Col.
  Admin. Whig   Third Dragoon Guards (1717)

Francis Whitworth
  Whig MP (1723–42)   Sec. of Barbados (1719)

William Chetwynd
  Whig MP (1715–27)   Lord of the Admiralty (1717)

Thomas Smith
  Whig MP (1709–13,   —
  1715–22, 1727–28)

Martin Bladen
  Whig MP (1715–46)   PC [I] (1715); Comptroller of the Mint
                             (1714); Sec. to Lords Justice [I] (1715–17);
                             Lord of Trade (1717); Comm. to Court of
                             France (1719–20)

Thomas Gage
  Whig MP (1717, 1721–54)   Cr. viscount [I] (1720)

Francis Negus
  MP (1717–32)   Comm. of the Office of Master of the
  Admin. Whig   Horse (1715–27); Avenor and Clerk Martial
                             (1717)

William Yonge
  MP (1715–55)   Comm. for Stating Army Debts (1717–22);
  Sunderland Whig (1717)   Comm. of Irish Revenue (1723–24); Lord of
                                 the Treasury (1724); Lord of the Admiralty
                                 (1728); KB (1725; succ. as baronet (1731)

Brian Fairfax
  (?Whig)   Comm. of Customs (1723)

Dr. John Arbuthnot
  Tory   —

On undated roster[2]

Kaspar von Bothmer
                                 Hanoverian minister in London

William, Lord North and Grey
  Tory; arrested as   —
  Atterbury plotter, 1722

Christoph Kreienberg
                                 Hanoverian resident in London

Samuel Edwin
  Tory MP (1717)   —

John Blith (? = John Bligh, later Earl of Darnley)
  Irish Whig   —

Additional shareholders proposed by motion, November 30, 1719[3]

Thomas, Duke of Wharton
  Member of Cowper's   —
  Lords opposition (1720–21);
  then government supporter;
  then opposition (1723); later
  flees country and joins
  Pretender

John, Lord Percival
  Whig MP (1727–34)   PC [I] (1714); cr. baron [I] in 1715; court
                                 of Prince of Wales (1717–20); cr. viscount
                                 [I] (1723); cr. Earl of Egmont [I] (1733)

Sir Robert Child
   Tory MP (1710–15)   Kt. (1714); lost Col. of Militia in 1714

Sir John Eyles, Baronet
   Whig MP (1713–34)   —

Mr. Burnett   —

Charles Whitworth, Baron [I]
   Whig MP (1722–25)   Minister, Imperial Diet (1714–16); Envoy, Berlin (1716–17); Envoy, The Hague (1717–21); Minister, Berlin (1719–22); Ambassador, Congress of Cambrai (1722–25)

Major Boyle Smyth (Smith)   —

Sir Thomas Samuel   —

Additional shareholders proposed by motion, December 2, 1719[4]

Sir William Gordon, Baronet
   Whig MP (1708–13, 1714–27)   Comm. for Stating Army Debts (1715–20)

John Proby
   Tory MP (1722–27,   —
   1734–47)

Shareholders known from other sources

Sir Godfrey Kneller, Baronet[5]
                         Gentleman of the Bedchamber (1722)

Robert Walpole[6]
   Whig MP (1701–12, 1713–42)   PC (1714); Paymaster of the Forces
   Schismatic Whig (1717)   (1714–15, 1720–21); First Lord of the Treasury and Chancellor of the Exchequer (1715–17, 1721–42)

Edward, Lord Harley (later Earl of Oxford)[7]
   Tory   —

Political offices are those most antecedent and contemporary to *c.*1717–22 in order to reflect relevant political orientation. Identification of commoners is less certain than for peers and knights.

1 *Source:* Original patent roll (NA C66/3531, no. 3); printed in Judith Milhous and Robert D. Hume, "The Charter for the Royal Academy of Music," *Music and Letters* 67 (1986), 50–1.

2 *Source:* Additional names found on NA LC 7/3 ff. 52–3; printed in Elizabeth Gibson, *The Royal Academy of Music, 1719–1728: The Institution and Its Directors* (New York: Garland Publishing, 1989), 319–20. Gibson suggests a date of May 1719; however, since this list has five more names than on the patent charter, it is likely to date after July 1719 (unless these persons ultimately decided not to become shareholders).

3 *Source:* Judith Milhous and Robert D. Hume, "New Light on Handel and the Royal Academy of Music in 1720," *Theatre Journal* 35 (1983), 152, and Milhous and Hume, "The Charter for the Royal Academy," 57.

4 *Source:* Gibson, *The Royal Academy of Music*, 24.

5 Godfrey Kneller's obligations to the Royal Academy are cited in posthumous Chancery suit cases, which have evidence of calls due to John Kipling, then deputy treasurer of the Royal Academy; see J. Douglas Stewart, *Sir Godfrey Kneller* (Oxford: Clarendon Press, 1983), 85, n. 38.

6 Robert Walpole's account books show he paid all the calls made on shareholders; see Thomas McGeary, "The Opera Accounts of Sir Robert Walpole," *Restoration and Eighteenth-Century Theatre Research* 7, n.s. (1996), 1–9.

7 Gibson, *The Royal Academy of Music*, 22, n. 2.

Sources: Useful in identifying party affiliations for this period are Clyve Jones, "The Impeachment of the Earl of Oxford and the Whig Schism of 1717: Four New Lists," *Bulletin of the Institute of Historical Research* 55 (1982), 66–87 (source for those peers indicated "Government Whigs" for a vote in November 1717); and Geoffrey Holmes, *British Politics in the Age of Anne*, rev. edn. (London: Hambledon Press, 1987), 425–39. Members of Cowper's Lords opposition are known by their frequent appearance as signers of the printed Lords protests. Also: *The History of Parliament. The House of Commons, 1690–1715*, 5 vols. (London: History of Parliament Trust, 2002); *The History of Parliament. The House of Commons, 1715–1754*, 2 vols. (London: History of Parliament Trust, 1970); J. C. Sainty and R. O. Bucholz, *Office-Holders in Modern Britain. 11: Officials of the Royal Household 1660–1837*, 2 parts (London: University of London, Institute of Historical Research, 1997–98); N. B. Leslie, *The Succession of Colonels of the British Army from 1660 to the Present Day* (London: Society for Army Historical Research, 1974); *The Complete Peerage of England, Scotland and Ireland*, ed. George E. Cokayne, rev. edn., 13 vols. (London: St. Catherine Press, 1910–59); also consulted, edition of 1887–98 (London: G. Bell & Sons, 1887).

Appendix 2: Operas premiered at the Royal Academy of Music

1719–20 Season

Numitore (April 2, 1720)
Giovanni Porta (servant of the Duke of Wharton); Paolo Rolli
Dedicatee: Directors of the Royal Academy of Music (including Thomas Coke of Norfolk)

> Numitor, King of Alba and grandfather to Romulus and Remus (mythical founders of Rome), is restored to his throne (lost to usurpation by Amulius) by means of armed assault led by his grandsons Romulus and Remus; Mars announces Romulus and Remus will found Rome.

Radamisto (April 27, 1720)
George Frideric Handel; Nicolà Haym/Domenico Lalli
Dedicatee: George I (signed by Handel)

> Radamistus, Prince of Thrace, recovers his wife Zenobia (whom he mistakenly believes he killed) and kingdom from the tyrant Tiridates, King of Armenia, who had conquered Thrace to satisfy his illicit love for Zenobia.

Narciso (May 30, 1720)
Domenico Scarlatti with additions by Thomas Roseingrave; Rolli/Capece
Dedicatee: Caroline, Princess of Wales

> Ovidian fable of Narcissus and Echo; with story of Procri consenting to marry the hero Cephalus, who kills the boar that is wasting Athens.

1720–21 Season

Astarto (November 19, 1720)
Giovanni Bononcini; Rolli/Apostolo Zeno and Pietro Pariati, after Quinault's *Astrate* and *Amalasunta*
Dedicatee: Richard Boyle, third Earl of Burlington

Astartus (as Cleartes), rightful king of Tyre, whose father was deposed, is discovered and restored by the Phoenicians to his throne, now occupied by Elisa, daughter of the murderer of his father. Inflamed by Elisa's love, Astartus pardons her, and they are united as king and queen.

Arsace (February 1, 1721)
Giuseppe Orlandini, with additions by Philippo Amadei; Rolli/Antonio Salvi, from T. Corneille's *Le comte d'Essex* (1678) on Queen Elizabeth I and the death of the Earl of Essex
Dedicatee: John, second Duke of Montagu

Arsaces (= Earl of Essex), favorite general of Queen Statira (= Queen Elizabeth I), out of remorse for thwarted love, accepts death rather than stain his honor by asking pardon for a crime he is innocent of; his death causes the despair and madness of Statira.

Muzio Scevola (April 15, 1721)
Philippo Amadei, Bononcini, and Handel; Rolli/Nicolò Minato and Silvio Stampiglia
Dedicatee: George I

The heroism and courage in defense of Rome and her liberty by Gaius Mucius Scaevola (late 6th century BC), Horatio, and the Roman Amazon warriors induce the Etruscan King Porsenna to abandon his attempt to restore Tarquin, the last Roman king, to the throne.

L'Odio e l'amore (May 20, 1721)
Bononcini; Rolli/Matteo Noris
Dedicatee: Thomas Pellam-Holles, first Duke of Newcastle

Thomyris, Queen of the Messageti (a Scythian people), is torn between hatred and love of her enemy, the Persian King Cyrus, who killed her son in battle. Forsaking her love for him, she pardons the conquered Cyrus and lets him enjoy the love and throne of Telesia, Princess of Scythia.

1721–22 Season

Floridante (December 9, 1721)
Handel; Rolli/Francesco Silvani
Dedicatee: George, Prince of Wales

The Persian general Orontes overthrew and murdered his own king and became a tyrant. Orontes has raised the king's daughter Elmira as his own daughter.

Floridant, a Prince of Thrace and in service to Orontes, has returned from a conquest over Tyre and expects to marry his betrothed Elmira. Orontes is jealous of Floridant because of their rival love for Elmira. Orontes decides to marry Elmira himself and banishes and then imprisons Floridant (who disguised as a Moor had tried to assassinate Orontes). Finally, the people under Timantes, a captured Tyrean prince, overthrow and imprison Orontes, free Floridant, and recognize Elmira as queen (who takes Floridant as her consort).

Crispo (January 10, 1722)
Bononcini; Rolli/Gaetano Lemer
Dedicatee: Henry Boyle, first Baron Carleton

Crispus (*c.*AD 305–326), son of Constantine I (the Great), finally receives justice, happiness, and his beloved after being falsely accused of the lascivious love of his step-mother Fausta, whose love he refused; Crispus begs of Constantine a pardon for Fausta.

Griselda (February 22, 1722)
Bononcini; Rolli/Zeno, from Boccaccio's *Decameron*
Dedicatee: John Manners, third Duke of Rutland

Gualtiero, King of Sicily, abandons his beloved shepherdess Griselda to follow his duty to his people, who wish him to marry a neighboring princess. Gualtiero pardons the leaders of an insurrection and is reunited with Griselda, who is extolled as an example of humility, virtue, love, and constancy.

1722–23 Season

Ottone, re di Germania (January 12, 1723)
Handel; Haym/Stefano Pallavicino
Dedicatee: George Montagu, second Earl of Halifax

Gismonda, widow of the Langobard king in Rome, wants to place her son Adelbert on the throne instead of Otto. Adelbert, who has been courting Matilda, presents himself as Otto to Theophane, niece of the Byzantine emperor, who has arrived to marry Otto. Otto's troops defeat those of Adelbert and Emireno, leader of the Saracens. Adelbert and Emireno escape, taking Theophane hostage. Theophane and Emireno discover they are brother and sister, and Emireno delivers Adelbert to her as prisoner. Otto pardons Adelbert; Otto and Theophane and Adelbert and Matilda are united; and Gismonda and Emireno repent.

Cajo Marzio Coriolano (February 19, 1723)
Attilio Ariosti; Haym/Pariati
Dedicatee: Henrietta Godolphin, first Duchess of Newcastle

Gauis Marcius Coriolanus (Roman general, 5th century BC) has been captured by Sicinus, his rival in love for Volumnia. Coriolanus, innocent of Sicinus' accusations, is ultimately rescued by Attius Tulius and the Volscians. Veturia, Coriolanus' mother, prevents him from ruining Rome; he pardons Sicinus and is united with Volumnia.

Erminia, favola boschereccia (March 30, 1723)
Bononcini; Rolli/?Petrosellini, from Tasso's *Gerusalemme liberata*
Dedicatees: "Alle Gentilissime Dame della Gran Britannia, Amatrici della Musica"

In a pastoral fable set during the Crusades, three couples (including Erminia, Princess of Antioch, who is searching for Tancred) are confounded until love ultimately triumphs and the three pairs are united.

Flavio, re de' Longobardi (May 14, 1723)
Handel; Haym/?Noris or ?Stampiglia
Dedicatees: Directors of the Royal Academy of Music

Flavius is king of Lombardy. At his court are two pairs of lovers (children of his counselors): Vitige and Theodata (in secret) and Emilia and Guido (formally engaged). Flavius, though married, falls in love with Theodata, whose father Hugo is appointed governor of Britain (which enrages Lotarius). Lotarius, father of Emilia, affronts Hugo, Guido's father. Emilia and Guido's love affair revealed, Lotarius insists on breaking off the wedding. To avenge the family honor, Guido kills Lotarius in a duel. Flavius courts Theodata in Vitige's presence. Circumstances cause the lovers doubts and jealousies. Flavius abandons hopes of marrying Theodata, blesses her union with Vitige, and the love of Emilia and Guido overcomes the death of her father.

1723–24 Season

Farnace (November 27, 1723)
Bononcini; ?Lalli/Lorenzo Morari
Dedicatee: Charles Mordaunt, third Earl of Peterborough

Pharnaces, ignorant that he is an Assyrian prince, is serving as a general for Queen Thomyris of Scythia against Assyria; both are concealing their love for each other. Pharnaces is falsely accused as a traitor to Thomyris and killer of her son; his innocence revealed, Queen Thomyris pardons the false accusers and marries him.

Vespasiano (January 14, 1724)
Ariosti; Haym/Giulio Cesare Corradi
Dedicatee: William Montagu, second Duke of Manchester

Titus Flavius Vespasianus (emperor, AD 69–79) is proclaimed emperor by the troops. Despite having been once pardoned by him, Domitian, Vespasian's son, continues plotting to usurp the crown and to ruin his father. Domitian attempts to assassinate Vespasian, who ultimately again pardons him and gives him command of Asia.

Giulio Cesare in Egitto (February 20, 1724)
Handel; Haym/G. F. Bussani
Dedicatee: Caroline, Princess of Wales

Caesar has pursued Pompey and his wife Cornelia and son Sestus after the battle of Pharslia to Egypt where Cleopatra and her brother Ptolemy are contesting the throne. Ptolemy raises Caesar's contempt for his murder of Pompey (in hopes of gaining Caesar's favor). Caesar falls in love with Cleopatra who seeks his support against Ptolemy. Caesar escapes Ptolemy's attempt on his life and defeats his army with the aid of Sestus, who kills Ptolemy. Caesar places Cleopatra on the throne; they declare their love; she pledges allegiance to Rome; and all welcome the return of peace.

Calfurnia (April 18, 1724)
Bononcini; Haym, after Grazio Braccioli
Dedicatee: Charles Douglas, third Duke of Queensberry and second Duke of Dover

Calfurnia, obeying a false prophecy reported by a jealous lover and leader of a conspiracy, is willing to be sacrificed so her father, the consul Marius (preferring the glory of his country to his own paternal affection), can conquer the Cimbrians. The deceit is revealed, Calfurnia is married, and Marius pardons the conspirators and departs for victory.

Aquilio consolo (May 21, 1724)
Ariosti; ?Haym/Silvani
Dedicatee: none

Aquilius, disguised as a gardener (Erennius) but a Roman consul earlier defeated by Arrenion, the tyrant-usurper of Sicily, is imprisoned by Arrenion because of Aquilius' feigned love for Arrenion's sister Lincestes. She helps him escape and returns with soldiers to overthrow the tyrant and return Sicily to Rome.

1724–25 Season

Tamerlano (October 31, 1724)
Handel; Haym/Agostino Piovene and a 1719 version (*Il Bajazet*)
Dedicatee: John Manners, third Duke of Rutland

> Tamerlane, Emperor of the Tartars, has imprisoned Bajazet, Emperor of the Turks, and Asteria, his daughter. The proud Bajazet desires death rather than captivity. Asteria, loved by Tamerlane (though he is engaged to Irene), herself loves Andronico. After many murder plots, betrayals, crossed love plots, and Bajazet's suicide, Tamerlane announces Bajazet's death has appeased his passion for vengeance; he marries Irene and unites Andronico and Asteria.

Artaserse (December 1, 1724)
Ariosti; Haym, after Zeno and Pariati
Dedicatee: Charles Lennox, seventh Duke of Richmond and first Duke of Lennox

> Artaxerxes, King of Persia, has two lawful male heirs and one son from Agamira, a favorite; all three sons love Aspasia, a Grecian princess, who loves Hidaspes. Spurned by Artaxerxes, Agamira foments assassination plots against him. Artaxerxes learns of the numerous plots but cannot identify the traitors, and launches his own counterplots. He is about to condemn his two sons, Agamira, and Aspasia when the truth is revealed; he joins the pairs of lovers, pardons all offences, and marries Agamira.

Rodelinda, regina de' Longobardi (February 13, 1725)
Handel; Haym/Salvi, from P. Corneille
Dedicatee: William Capell, third Earl of Essex

> Rodelinda, Queen of the Lombards, has been left behind (with their son) by her husband Bertarido, who fled when his country was overrun by the forces of Grimoaldo. The exiled Bertarido has spread rumors of his own death, and Rodelinda, under duress, agrees to marry Grimoaldo. Bertarido returns in disguise and prevents the death of Grimoaldo by a rival; whereupon Grimoaldo, reformed by this act of magnanimity, restores Bertarido's wife and throne.

Dario (April 10, 1725)
Ariosti; ?Haym/?
Dedicatee: none

> Darius, a Persian prince and king, has his rightful hope of the throne thwarted by the arrival of the Scythian Sidermes, who (with the assistance of Artabanus) deceives the council into thinking he is the rightful king. When Statira, Darius' espoused, refuses his love, the tyrannical Sidermes condemns both to death.

Sidermes' own betrayal of Artabanus and treachery cause his downfall; Darius is proclaimed king and banishes Sidermes and Artabanus.

Elpidia, overo li rivali generosi (May 11, 1725)
Leonardo Vinci and Orlandini (arr. by Handel); ?Haym/Zeno
Dedicatee: none

Elpidia, Princess of Apuglia, has fled to Rome and the protection of Belisarius (*c.*AD 505–565). Elpidia will marry the most courageous of her suitors. Olindus and Arminius, Greek princes and rivals for her love, rescue her from Vitiges, King of the Goths; Olindus relinquishes Elpidia to Arminius for saving his life. Through virtue and generosity, the two rivals attain love and happiness.

1725–26 Season

Elisa (January 15, 1726)
Porpora and others (arr. by ?Ariosti); ?Haym
Dedicatee: none

During the Second Punic War (*c.*201 BC), Eliza, daughter of the Carthaginian general Hannibal (247–182 BC) and promised to Prince Sitalces of Numidia, is captured outside Carthage by the Romans led by Publius Cornelius Scipio Africanus Major (236–*c.*184 BC), while Nubians capture Scipio's betrothed. Sitalces, disobediently breaking a truce between Rome and Carthage (due to his passionate love for Eliza), attempts to rescue Eliza and is also captured. Ultimately, Hannibal and Scipio pardon Sitalces, peace is made, and the pairs of lovers are united.

Scipione (March 12, 1726)
Handel; Rolli/?Salvi
Dedicatee (only in Rolli's separately published Italian-only libretto): Charles Lennox, second Duke of Richmond

The episode of the Continence of Scipio. Publius Cornelius Scipio Africanus Major (236–*c.*184 BC), Roman proconsul in Spain (209 BC), demonstrates his personal virtue when he relinquishes a beloved captive slave Berenice to her fiancé Luceo, forgives Luceo's attempt to reclaim her, and refuses her father's proffered ransom for her, which he gives to the couple.

Alessandro (May 5, 1726)
Handel; Rolli/Ortensio Mauro
Dedicatee (only in Rolli's separate Italian-only libretto): Caroline, Princess of Wales

Alexander the Great (356–323 BC) has carried his campaign to India and has breached the walls of Oxidraca. Roxana (a slave) and Lisaura (a Scythian princess) both love Alexander, but Roxana fears Alexander's possible love for Lisaura. Alexander frees Roxana and aided by Taxilis, the Indian King, defeats a rebellion led by his Macedonian captains. Alexander pardons the rebels and pledges his love to Roxana and friendship to Lisaura.

1726–27 Season

Lucio Vero, imperator di Roma (January 7, 1727)
Ariosti; ?Haym/Zeno
Dedicatee: none

Lucius Aurelius Verus (emperor, AD 161–169), chosen by Marcus Aurelius as his successor contingent upon marrying his daughter Lucilla, captured and fell in love with Berenice, Queen of the Armenians and married to Vologesus, King of the Parthians. Lucilla arrives from Rome in a futile attempt to consummate her marriage with Lucius Verus. A rebellion by Flavius foils Lucius' attempted murder of Vologesus and marriage to Berenice; he begs mercy, reunites Vologesus and Berenice, and marries Lucilla.

Admeto, re di Tessaglia (January 31, 1727)
Handel; Rolli or Haym/Mauro, from Antonio Aurelio
Dedicatee: none

Greek myth of Admetus, King of Pherae in Thessaly, married to Alcestis; she sacrifices her life to save that of Admetus, and is rescued from Hades by Hercules and returned to Admetus. A secondary plots deals with the love of Princess Antigona's brother Trasimede for Trajan.

Astianatte (May 6, 1727)
Bononcini; Haym/Salvi, from Racine's *Andromaque*
Dedicatee: Henrietta Churchill, second Countess of Godolphin and junior Duchess of Marlborough (assumed title of duchess in 1722)

Astyanax (son of Hector and Andromache) and widowed Andromache are captive at the court of Pyrrhus, who loves Andromache (thus slighting his betrothed Hermione) and vows to restore Astyanax to his throne. Orestes' demanded sacrifice of Astyanax, his attempted murder of Pyrrhus, and Hermione's kidnapping of Astyanax are thwarted; Pyrrhus frees Orestes, Hermione and Orestes are united, and there is peace between the shades of Hector and Achilles.

1727–28 Season

Teuzzone (October 21, 1727)
Ariosti; ?Haym/Zeno
Dedicatee: Frederick William I, King of Prussia

Teuzzone, rightful emperor of China, is displaced from the throne by Zidiana (the second wife of his deceased father, Troncone), who secretly loves Teuzzone. Teuzzone refuses Zidiana's offer of the throne and marriage, and is condemned. Just as Teuzzone and his fiancée are to be executed, a signed warrant from Troncone declares Teuzzone the heir, and he pardons Zidiana.

Riccardo primo, re d'Inghilterra (November 11, 1727)
Handel; Rolli/Francesco Briani
Dedicatee: George II

During the Third Crusade, Richard and his espoused Costanza (who have never yet met) are separately shipwrecked on Cyprus. The tyrant Isacus captures and falls in love with Costanza, who conceals her identity. Richard, disguised as his own ambassador, goes to Isacus to recover her. Isacus sends instead his daughter Pulcheria to Richard. Aware of the deception, Richard and Orontes, Pulcheria's lover, attack Isacus' castle. Richard pardons Isacus, gains Costanza, and Orontes wins Pulcheria and the throne of Cyprus.

Siroe, re di Persia (February 17, 1728)
Handel; Haym, after Metastasio
Dedicatees: Directors and subscribers of the Royal Academy of Music

Cosroes, King of Persia, is jealous of his elder son Siroes' popularity and wishes to make Medarses (his second son) king instead. Siroes and Emira (infiltrating the court disguised as a man to avenge the death of her father by Cosroes) are lovers. Victim of false accusations by Medarses and Laodice (Cosroes' favorite), Siroes remains silent and would rather die than live dishonored. Ultimately the intrigues against Siroes are overcome. The plotters confess their guilt; Siroes pardons them; and Cosroes unites Siroes and Emira and gives the crown to them.

Tolomeo, re d'Egitto (April 30, 1728)
Handel; Haym/Carlo Capece
Dedicatee: William van Keppel, second Earl of Albemarle

Ptolemy, exiled by his mother Cleopatra III to Cyprus, is living as a shepherd (Osmino), and is sought by his wife Seleuce (shepherdess Delia), but is also pursued in love by Elisa, sister of the king of Cyprus. Alessandro, Ptolemy's brother, has been sent by Cleopatra to murder him. Elisa's attempt to blackmail Seleuce to renounce Ptolemy fails and she threatens both with death. Alessandro tells Ptolemy Cleopatra has died and left the throne to him. Ptolemy and Seleuce are united, and Ptolemy pardons all.

Sources: Elizabeth Gibson, *The Royal Academy of Music, 1719–1728: The Institution and Its Directors* (New York: Garland Publishing, 1989); *The Cambridge Handel Encyclopedia*, ed. Annette Landgraf and David Vickers (Cambridge University Press, 2009); works list (by Anthony Hicks) in Winton Dean, *The New Grove Handel* (New York: W. W. Norton, 1983); Colin Timms, "Handelian and Other Librettos in Birmingham Central Library," *Music and Letters* 65 (1984), 141–67; and George E. Dorris, *Paolo Rolli and the Italian Circle in London, 1715–1744* (The Hague: Mouton, 1967), 269–77.

Appendix 3: Directors of the Opera of the Nobility with political allegiances in June 1733

Directors with Ministerial Allegiance

John Manners, third Duke of Rutland

Whig MP (1719–21); succeeded to title (1721); Lord Lieut. of Leicestershire (1721); Lord of the Bedchamber (1721–27); KG (1722); PC (1727); Chancellor of the Duchy of Lancaster (1727–36). Went into opposition 1736.

Director of Royal Academy of Music (1727–28); subscriber (1728–29).

William, second Earl Cowper

Whig courtier; Gentleman of the Bedchamber (1733–48).

Charles, second Baron of Cadogan

Whig MP (1716–26); Col. of His Majesty's Own (4th) Regiment of Foot (1719); succ. to title (1726); Col. 6th Dragoons (1724); Col. of Inniskilling (6th) Regiment of Dragoons (1734); promoted to Brigadier General (1735); Major General (1739).

Director of Royal Academy of Music (1727–28); subscriber (1728–29).

John West, seventh Baron Delawarr (later first Earl)

Courtier; KB (1725); Gentleman of the Bedchamber (1725–27; vacated on death of George I); Lieut. Col. 1st Reg. of Foot Guards (1730); PC (1731); Treasurer of the Household (1731); ambassador to Saxe-Gotha to conclude marriage of Prince of Wales with Princess Augusta (1736); Col. 1st troop Life Guards (1737); Governor and Captain-General of New Jersey and New York (1737); Captain of the Yeomen of His Majesty's Guard (1737).

Thomas Coke, Baron Lovel (later Viscount and Earl of Leicester)

Whig MP (1722–28); KB (1725); created Baron Lovel (1728); Postmaster General (1733–58); Capt. of the Band of Gentleman Pensioners (1733).

Director of Royal Academy of Music (1720, 1720–21); RAM subscriber (1728–29).

(?)Charles Lennox, second Duke of Richmond and Lennox

Whig MP (1722–23); succ. to title (1723); Royal Horse Guards (1722); KB (1725); KG (1726); aide-de-camp to the king (1726–35); Gentleman of the Bedchamber to George I (1726) and George II (1727); Lord High Constable for Coronation of George II (1727); PC (1735) "as a strong supporter of Walpole's government" (*CP*); Master of the Horse (1735–50).

O. E. Deutsch, *Handel: A Documentary Biography* (New York: W. W. Norton, 1955), 304, on no authority, states he became a director, even though the letter from Delawarr only asks for a subscription.

Deputy Governor of Royal Academy of Music (1726–27, 1727–28); subscriber (1728–29).

Directors with presumed anti-ministerial allegiance

John Russell, fourth Duke of Bedford

Succeeded to title (1732); "entered politics as anti-Walpole Whig" (*CP*).

John Dalrymple, second Earl of Stair

PC (1714); Gentleman of the Bedchamber and Col. of Inniskilling Dragoons (1714); Vice-Admiral of Scotland (1729); dismissed from all offices after Excise Crisis (1733).

Director of Royal Academy of Music (1720–21); subscriber to Handel's 1732–33 season.

James Hamilton, first Viscount Limerick

Whig MP (1724–41); "an opposition Whig" (*HP*, vol. II, 101).
Director of Royal Academy of Music (1726–27, 1727–28); Royal Academy of Music subscriber 1728–29.

Allen, first Baron Bathurst (later earl) (1684–1775)

Tory MP (1705 to 1712); created baron (1712); "an active opponent of the Walpole Administration" (*CP*). Prince of Wales visits him in October 1738.

Sir John Buckworth, second Baronet

MP (1734–41); voted against government in both recorded divisions (*HP*, vol. I, 504).

Director of Royal Academy of Music (1726–27).

Sir Michael Newton

> MP (1722–43). "Though one of the wealthy commoners invested with the order of the Bath when Walpole revived that order in 1725, he voted against the Government in every recorded division till his death" (*HP*, vol. II, 295); step-uncle to Baron Lovel (Thomas Coke).

> Director of Royal Academy of Music (1727–28).

Henry Furnese, esq.

> MP (1720) who went into opposition; lost his seat in 1734; re-entering Parliament in 1738, he voted with Pulteney and the Opposition (*HP*, vol. II, 55–6).

> Royal Academy of Music subscriber (1728–29).

Independent director

Richard Boyle, third Earl of Burlington (1694–1753)

> Architect and patron of the arts; Vice-Admiral of County York (1715); Lord Lieutenant of East and West Riding (1715); Walpole adherent after the Whig party split of (1717); PC (1729); KG (1730); Capt. of the Gentlemen Pensioners (1731–33); breech with the king causes him to resign all offices in May 1733, and thereafter abstains from active politics.

> Director of Royal Academy of Music (1719, 1720, 1720–21, 1726–27, 1727–28); subscriber to Handel's 1732–33 season.

Abbreviations (see sources)
CP = *The Complete Peerage of England, Scotland and Ireland*
HP = *The History of Parliament. The House of Commons, 1715–1754*

Sources: The Complete Peerage of England, Scotland and Ireland, ed. George E. Cokayne, rev. edn., 13 vols. (London: St. Catherine Press, 1910–59); also consulted, where cited, edition of 1887–98 (London: G. Bell & Sons); *The History of Parliament. The House of Commons, 1715–1754*, ed. Romney Sedgwick, 2 vols. (New York: Oxford University Press, 1970); Carole Taylor, "Italian Operagoing in London, 1700–1745" (Ph.D. dissertation, Syracuse University, 1991); J. C. Sainty and R. O. Bucholz, *Office-Holders in Modern Britain* 11: *Officials of the Royal Household 1660–1837*. 2 parts (University of London, Institute of Historical Research, 1997–98).

Tenure of directors of the Royal Academy of Music: Elizabeth Gibson, "The Royal Academy of Music (1719–28) and its Directors," in *Handel Tercentenary Collection*, ed. Stanley Sadie and Anthony Hicks (Ann Arbor, MI: UMI Research Press, 1987), 136–64, at 152.

Subscribers to Royal Academy of Music, 1728–29: West Sussex Record Office. Goodwood MS 143 and 144.

Handel's 1732–33 season: Judith Milhous and Robert D. Hume, "Handel's Opera Finances in 1732–3," *Musical Times* 125 (1984), 86–9.

Appendix 4: Operas (and other works) premiered by the Opera of the Nobility

1733–34 Season

Arianna in Nasso (December 29, 1733)
Nicolò Porpora; Paolo Rolli
Dedication: the Condesa de Montijo, wife of the Spanish ambassador

> Ariadne has helped Theseus escape from the labyrinth, and they flee to Naxos, although Theseus is married to Antiope. Theseus finally accedes to the prophecy of Bacchus and departs with Antiope. Ariadne's rage at betrayal is assuaged when Bacchus arrives to claim her love.

Fernando (February 5, 1734)
Carlo Arrigoni; Rolli/Girolamo Gigli
Dedication: Diana Spencer Russell, Duchess of Bedford

> Ferdinand, King of Castile, has defeated the father of Garcia, now King of Navarre; Fernando has arrived at Navarre to marry Anaguilda, Garcia's sister, but is betrayed and imprisoned by Garcia. Fernando is delivered and pardons Garcia.

David e Bersabea (oratorio) (March 12, 1734)
Porpora; Rolli
Dedication: Mary How Herbert

> David, having fallen in love with Bathsheba, sends her husband Uriah off to certain death at the front ranks of the army. Nathan declares David has despised God's word. David realizes his sins and is penitent. The chorus begs for compassion and mercy; Nathan announces God's pardon of David.

Belmira (March 23, 1734)
(lost)

Enea nel Lazio (May 11, 1734)
Porpora; Rolli
Dedication: Catherine Sheffield, Duchess of Buckingham

Aeneas, arriving in Latium, is elected King of the Tyrrhens; he and Lavinia, Princess of Laurentum, are lovers, though she is promised to King Turnus by her mother. Aeneas defeats Turnus and Camilla (Princess of the Volcians); he spares them and marries Lavinia and receives her kingdom as dowry.

1734–35 Season

Artaserse (October 29, 1734)
Johann A. Hasse and Ricardo Broschi; adapted from Pietro Metastasio

Artaxerxes, the son of Xerxes, King of Persia, is murdered by Artabanes, desirous of the throne. Suspicion first falls on Artaxerxes' brother Darius, but Artabanus places the blame on his own son Arbaces, friend of Artaxerxes and lover of his sister Mandane. Having fled, Arbaces then proves his innocence by killing the leader of a rebellion; Artabanes confesses his guilt, is mercifully exiled by Artaxerxes, and Arbaces and Mandane are united.

Polifemo (February 1, 1735)
Porpora; Rolli

Story of Polyphemus' love for Galatea combined with the episode of Ulysses blinding Polyphmeus. Acis is revived and all ends happily.

Issipile (April 8, 1735)
Pietro Sandoni; Angelo Cori/Metastasio
Dedication: Duchess of Portland

Hypsipyle, daughter of Thoas, King of Lemnos, is engaged to Jason, Prince of Thessalia. The Lemnite women slaughter their husbands (because they have neglected them by dallying abroad with their conquered concubines), but Hypsipyle has hidden her father. Plots of the exiled Learchus (rejected suitor of Hypsipyle) to disrupt the marriage are thwarted. At the climactic moment, Thoas pardons Learchus and unites Jason and Hypsipyle.

Ifigenia in Aulide (May 3, 1735)
Porpora; Rolli

Iphigenia has been lured by her father Agamemnon back to Aulis (on the pretext of a marriage to Achilles) to be sacrificed to atone for her father's killing one of Diana's deer. At the moment of sacrifice, Achilles bursts in with a sword, and Diana appears in a cloud and appoints Iphigenia a priestess in Tauris.

1735–36 Season

Adriano in Siria (November 25, 1735)
Francesco Veracini; Cori/Metastasio
Dedication: Countess of Sunderland

> Emperor Hadrian (AD 117–138), conqueror of Parthia, although engaged to Sabina, is enamored of Emirena, captive daughter of Osroa, the Parthian king. After plots by Osroa (attributed to Farnaspes, who is promised to Emirena) and intrigues by Idalma, who secretly loves Hadrian, Hadrian masters his passions, forgives Idalma, returns the throne to Osroa, unites Emirena and Farnaspes, and marries Sabina.

Mitridate (January 24, 1736)
Porpora (pasticcio?); Colley Cibber, after Nathaniel Lee's *Mithridates*
Dedication: Baroness Loss (wife of the Saxon ambassador to London)

> Mithridates, King of Pontus, renounces his betrothed Ismene and claims Semandra, beloved of his son Xiphares. Xiphares, returned from victory, believes Semandra unfaithful and renounces her. Mithridates' other son Pharnaces conspires with his foe Pompey. In battle, Xiphares defeats Pompey and Mithridates is wounded. Instead of dying alone in shame, he repents; given justice, he asks forgiveness and dies with the sympathy of his general and Xiphares.

Orfeo (March 2, 1736)
Pasticcio after Porpora, Hasse *et al.*; Rolli

> Story of Orpheus and Eurydice with added amatory subplot between Aristæus, a demi-god, and Autonoe, Princess of Thebes.

Onorio (April 13, 1736)
F. Campi; Domenico Lalli, after Sebastiano Biancardi and Giovanni Boldini's adaptation of T. Corneille's *Stilicon*

> Flavius Honorius, emperor of the west (AD 395–423), is a victim of conspiracies led by Stilicon, father of his wife Termantia. Suspected in the plot are Termantia and her brother Eucherio (who loves Honorius' sister Placida). Captured in a battle, the rebel Stilicon is revealed and is exiled by Honorius, who pardons all others, and Eucherio wins Placida.

Festa d'Imeneo (serenata) (May 4, 1736)
Porpora; Rolli
Dedication: Augusta, Princess of Wales

Serenata in celebration of the wedding of the Prince and Princess of Wales with parts for Hymen, Apollo, Neptune, Mercury, Venus, Pallas, Bellona, and chorus of sea gods. Frederick spreads protection to the arts; Great Britain will enjoy prosperity under Frederick and Augusta, in whom love, virtue, and beauty are united. Includes allusions to Alfred and Edward, the Black Prince.

1736–37 Season

Siroe, re di Persia (November 23, 1736)
Hasse; Metastasio

Cosroes, King of Persia, is jealous of his elder son Siroes' popularity and wishes to make Medarses (his second son) king instead. Siroes and Emira (infiltrating the court disguised as a man to avenge the death of her father by Cosroes) are lovers. Victim of false accusations by Medarses and Laodice (Cosroes' favorite), Siroes remains silent and would rather die than live dishonored. Ultimately the intrigues against Siroes are overcome. The plotters confess their guilt; Siroes pardons them; and Cosroes unites Siroes and Emira and gives the crown to them.

Merope (January 8, 1737)
?; Cori/Zeno
Dedication: Duchess of Buckingham

To secure the throne of Mysia for himself, the usurper Polyphontes has unjustly condemned Merope, Queen of Mysia, to death for the murder of her husband, and plots the death of her son Ephitides (known as Cleon), whom Merope believed dead. At the moment of Merope's execution, Ephitides appears, Polyphontes is revealed as the true instigator of the king's death, and the crown is restored to Ephitides.

Demetrio (February 12, 1737)
Johann Baptiste Pescetti; Cori/Metastasio
Dedication: Duchess of Newcastle

Demetrius, son of the deposed king of Syria, has grown up disguised as a Alcestes, a shepherd. Cleonice, daughter of the deceased usurper of the Syrian throne, is torn between duty to wed from among the Syrian nobility and her love for Alcestes. Alcestes' true identity is revealed; Cleonice can reconcile love and duty, and Demetrius gains his rightful throne.

La clemenza di Tito (April 12, 1737)
Pasticcio; Cori/Metastasio

Titus Flavius Vespasianus (emperor, AD 79–81) occupies the throne taken from Vitellio by his father (Vespasianus). Vitellia, daughter of the now-deceased Vitellio, secretly loves Titus and wants to regain the throne but is enraged that Titus has overlooked her as his consort. Vitellia prods her admirer and Titus' friend Sextus into an attempted assassination of Titus. Vitellia confesses her guilt, and Titus forgives everyone.

Sabrina (April 26, 1737)
Pasticcio; Rolli, after Milton's *Comus*

In a forest, Sabrina, a dryad, rescues two couples (on their way to a country seat for one couple's wedding) from the mischief caused by the enchantments of the demigod Comaspe.

Demofoonte (May 24, 1737)
Duni; Cori/Metastasio
Dedication: Duchess of Manchester

Demophontes must sacrifice a virgin each year until a usurper is identified. His son Timantes, refusing Demophontes' command to marry Creusa, is condemned to death with his secret wife, Dircea. Creusa obtains freedom for the pair. It is revealed first that Dircea is Demophontes' daughter, and then that Timante is not Demophontes' son and the unwitting usurper; the marriage of Timante and Dircea is recognized.

Sources: George E. Dorris, *Paolo Rolli and the Italian Circle in London, 1715–1744* (The Hague: Mouton, 1967), 270–7; and Carole M. Taylor, "Italian Operagoing in London, 1700–1745" (Ph.D. dissertation, Syracuse University, 1991).

Appendix 5: Hanoverian celebratory pieces

Marriage of Princess Anne to William, Prince of Orange (March 14, 1734)

The Happy Nuptials
November 12, 1733, Goodman's Fields
Words and music by Henry Carey

> Advertised as "a new Pastoral Epithalamium"[1]

> Revised as *Britannica, or the Royal Lovers*

The Festival, or the Impromptu Revels Masque
November 24, 1733, Little Theatre in the Haymarket
Music by Henry Carey

> Advertised as "An Impromptu Revels Masque, made on the Occasion of the approaching Royal Nuptials"[2]

Britannia; or, The Royal Lovers
February 11, 1734, Goodman's Fields
Words and music by Henry Carey

> Advertised as "Britannia: or, The Royal Lovers. The Landing of Prince Germanicus [William] at the Tower. His Reception. His passing through the City. His first Interview with Britannia. The whole concluding with The Solemnization of the Nuptials in the Temple of Hymen.
>   The House will be adorned with the Portraits of the Royal Family, and his Highness the Prince of Orange; and a new Ceiling-piece of Apollo and the Muses; painted by Mr. Hayman."[3]

Il Parnasso in festa
March 13, 1734, King's Theatre (Handel's company)
Music by Handel; text translated by John Oldmixon

> Advertised as "Parnasso in Festa: or, Apollo and the Muses celebrating the Nuptials of Thetis and Peleus. A Serenata."[4]

The *Daily Advertiser* reported: "We hear, amongst other publick Diversions that are prepar'd for the Solemnity of the approaching Nuptials, there is to be perform'd, at the Opera-house in the Hay-Market, on Wednesday next, a Serenata, call'd *Parnasso in Festa:* The Fable is Apollo and the Muses celebrating the Marriage of Thetis and Pelus. There is one standing Scene, which is Mount Parnassus, on which sit Apollo and the Muses, assisted with other proper Characters emblematically dress'd, the whole Appearance being extreamly magnificent; nor is the Musick less entertaining, being contriv'd with so great a Variety, that all sorts of Musick are properly introduc'd in single Songs, Duettoes, &c., intermix'd with Chorus's something in the Stile of Oratorios. People having been waiting with Impatience for this Piece, the celebrated Mr Handel having exerted his utmost Skill in it."[5]

The following day, the same newspaper reported: "Last Night Mr. Handell's new Serenata, in Honour of the Princess Royal's Nuptials … was received with the greatest Applause; the Piece containing the most exquisite Harmony ever furnish'd from the Stage, and the Disposition of the Performers being contriv'd in a very grand and magnificent Manner."[6]

The Nuptial Masque
March 16, 1734, Covent Garden
Music by John Galliard; words by Edward Phillips

> Published as *The Nuptial Masque; or, the Triumphs of Cupid and Hyman. As It Is Performed at the Theatre Royal in Covent-Garden* (1734).

Love and Glory or Britannia
March 21, 1734, Drury Lane
Music by Thomas Arne; words by Thomas Phillips

> Advertised as "Love and Glory. A Serenata. Compos'd on the present joyous Occasion of the Royal Nuptials."[7]

Aurora's Nuptials
? not performed
Music by John Frederick Lampe

> Published in 1734 as *Aurora's Nuptials. A Dramatick Performance: Occasion'd by the Nuptials of his Serene Highness William, Prince of Orange, with Her Royal Highness Anne, Princess-Royal of Great Britain. As it is represented at the Theatre-Royal in Drury-Lane.*

Britannia and Batavia
? not performed
Words by George Lillo

Published as *Britannia and Batavia: A Masque. Written on the Marriage of the Princess Royal With his Highness the Prince of Orange. By the late Mr. Lillo* (1740).

Marriage of Frederick, Prince of Wales to Augusta of Saxe-Gotha (May 4, 1736)

Festa d'Imeneo
May 4, 1736, King's Theatre (Opera of the Nobility)
Music by Nicolò Porpora; text by Paolo Rolli

> Advertised as "A Theatrical Feast, entitled, The Feast of Hymen. In Honour of the Royal Nuptials of their Royal Highnesses the Prince and Princes of Wales."[8]

> Published as *Festa d'Imeneo per le reali nozze di Frederico Prencipe Reale di Vallia* (1736).

Atalanta
May 12, 1736, Covent Garden (Handel's company)
Music by Handel; libretto adapted from Valeriani, *La caccia in Etolia* (Ferrara, 1715)

> Advertised as "In Honour of the Royal Nuptials of their Royal Highnesses the Prince and Princes of Wales."[9]

The newspapers reported: "Last Night was perform'd at the Theatre Royal in Covent Garden, for the first Time, the Opera of *Atalanta*, composed by Mr. *Handel* on the joyous Occasion of the Nuptials of their Royal Highnesses the Prince and Princess of Wales. In which was a new Set of Scenes painted in Honour to this Happy Union, which took up the full length of the Stage: The Fore-part of the Scene represented an Avenue to the Temple of *Hymen*, adorn'd with Figures of several Heathen Deities. Next was a Triumphal Arch on the Top of which were the Arms of their Royal Highnesses, over which was placed a Princely Coronet. Under the Arch was the Figure of *Fame*, on a Cloud, sounding the Praises of this Happy Pair. The Names *Fredericus* and *Augusta* appear'd above in transparent Characters.

Thro' the Arch was seen a Pediment supported by four Columns, on which stood two Cupids embracing, and supporting the Feathers, in a Princely Coronet, the Royal Ensign of the Prince of Wales. At the farther end was a View of *Hymen*'s Temple, and the Wings were adorn'd with the Loves and Graces bearing Hymenæal Torches, and putting Fire to Incense in Urns, to be offer'd up upon this Joyful Union.

The Opera concluded with a Grand Chorus, during which several beautiful Illuminations were display'd."[10]

Thomas Gray described the illuminations in the last act: "There is a row of blue fires burning in order along the ascent to the temple; a fountain of fire spouts up out of the ground to the ceiling, and two more cross each other obliquely from the sides of the stage; on the top is a wheel that whirls always about, and throws out a shower of gold-colour, silver, and blue fiery rain."[11]

Love and Glory, a Serenata
10 February 1743, Aungier Street Theatre, Dublin
Music by Thomas Arne

Published as *Love and Glory, a Serenata. Compos'd in Honour of the Nuptials of His Royal Highness Frederick Prince of Wales, with the Princess Augusta of Saxe Gotha* (Dublin, 1743).

Marriage of Princess Mary to Frederick II, Landgrave of Hesse-Cassel (May 8, 1740)

Busiri
May 10, 1740, Little Theatre in the Hay-Market
Music by Johann Baptiste Pescetti; words by Paolo Rolli

Advertised as "Busiri, overo Il Trionfo D'Amore."

Published as *Busiri overo in van si fugge amore. Melodrama boschereccio* (1740).

The wedding connection is explicit in lines from the "Epithalamium" of the *scena ultima*: "Of Hesse and Britain happy Hymen join'd / Two famous branches, to supply hereafter, / Like their great Ancestors, a race of heroes." (p. 45)

Birthday of Frederick Prince of Wales

Proteo
April 17, 1741, Hickford's Rooms

Published as *Proteo. Cantata dramatica, per il giorno natalizio di S.A.R. Frederico prencipe reale di Vallia. E prencipe electtorale d'Hanover* (1741).

Frederick's birthday was on January 20.

Advertised as "Proteus, A Musical Dramatic Poem."[12]

Possibly anticipating a royal wedding

Imeneo[13]
Music by Handel; composed in 1738.
November 22, 1740, Lincoln's Inn Fields Theatre

---

1 *Daily Post*, no. 4420 (November 14, 133); *London Evening Post*, no. 939 (November 27, 1733).

2 *Daily Journal*, no. 4017 (November 20, 1733).

3 *Daily Advertiser*, no. 972 (March 12, 1734).

4 *Daily Journal*, no. 4102 (March 11, 1734).

5 *Daily Advertiser*, no. 971 (March 11, 1734); the same notice appeared in the *Daily Journal*, no. 4102 (March 11, 1734).

6 *Daily Advertiser*, no. 974 (March 14, 1734).

7 *Daily Journal*, no. 4110 (March 20, 1734).

8 *London Daily Post, and General Advertiser*, no. 470 (May 4, 1736).

9 *London Daily Post, and General Advertiser*, no. 480 (May 15, 1736).

10 *Daily Advertiser*, no. 1652 (May 13, 1736); *London Daily Post and General Advertiser*, no. 478 (May 13, 1736); *London Evening Post*, no. 1324 (May 11–13, 1736); *Old Whig: or, the Consistent Protestant*, no. 63 (May 20, 1736).

11 Letter of June 11, [1736] to Horace Walpole; in *The Yale Edition of Horace Walpole's Correspondence*, vol. XIII: *Horace Walpole's Correspondence with Thomas Gray, Richard West, and Thomas Ashton*, ed. W. S. Lewis (New Haven, CT: Yale University Press, 1948), 102.

12 *London Daily Post, and General Advertiser*, no. 2022 (April 16, 1741).

13 Possible occasions for its composition are discussed in John Roberts, "The Story of Handel's *Imeneo*," *Händel-Jahrbuch* 47 (2001), 337–84. The opera was first drafted in 1738, and subsequently considerably revised.

Notes

1 Introduction

1 The most thorough bibliography of early criticism of opera is Lowell Lindgren, "Critiques of Opera in London, 1705–1719," *Il melodramma italiano in Italia e in Germania nell' età barocca*. Contributi musicologici del Centro Ricerche dell' A.M.I.S.-Como 9 (1995), 145–65. The most useful extended discussions of the critical response include Sigmund A. E. Betz, "The Operatic Criticism of the *Tatler* and *Spectator*," *Musical Quarterly* 31 (1945), 318–30; Kállmán G. Ruttkay, "The Critical Reception of Italian Opera in England in the Early Eighteenth Century," *Studies in English and American Philology* 1 (1971), 93–169; and Henrik Knif, *Gentlemen and Spectators: Studies in Journals, Opera and the Social Scene in late Stuart London* (Helsinki: Finnish Historical Society, 1995).

   The more recent interest in the role of gender/sexuality in reception of opera is explored in Todd S. Gilman, "The Italian (Castrato) in London," in *The Work of Opera: Genre, Nationhood, and Sexual Difference*, ed. Richard Dellamora and Daniel Fischlin (New York: Columbia University Press, 1997), 49–70; Xavier Cervantes, "'Tuneful Monsters': The Castrati and the London Operatic Public, 1667–1737," *Restoration and 18th Century Theatre Research*, 2nd ser., 13 (1998), 1–24; Thomas McGeary "'Warbling Eunuchs': Opera, Gender, and Sexuality on the London Stage," *Restoration and 18th Century Theatre Research*, 2nd ser., 7 (1992), 1–22; McGeary, "Gendering Opera: Italian Opera as the Feminine Other in England, 1700–42," *Journal of Musicological Research* 14 (1994), 17–34; and McGeary, "Verse Epistles on Italian Opera Singers, 1724–1736," *Royal Musical Association Research Chronicle* 33 (2000), 29–88.

2 Reinhard Strohm, "Handel and his Italian Opera Texts," in *Essays on Handel and Italian Opera* (Cambridge University Press, 1985), 34–79, at 35, 48.

3 Curtis A. Price, "Political Allegory in Late-Seventeenth-Century English Opera," in *Music and Theatre: Essays in Honour of Winton Dean*, ed. Nigel Fortune (Cambridge University Press, 1987), 1–29, at 28.

4 Paul Monod, "The Politics of Handel's Early London Operas, 1711–1718," *Journal of Interdisciplinary History* 36 (2006), 445–72, at 447. Monod treats politics as "the production and consumption of Handel's works, meaning the sponsorship, financing, publishing, staging, performance, and reception of words as well as music" and "questions of power, authority, or legitimacy" (447, 448).

5 William Weber, "Beyond Zeitgeist: Recent Work in Music History," *Journal of Modern History* 66 (1994), 326. Elsewhere Weber writes that "Librettists and composers played upon people's partisan sensibilities with a highly entertaining ambiguity. Musical activities, of course, had long had close links with politics"; Weber, "Musical Culture and the Capital City: The Epoch of the *beau monde* in London, 1700–1870," in *Concert Life in Eighteenth-Century Britain*, ed. Susan Wollenberg and Simon McVeigh (Aldershot: Ashgate, 2004), 71–89, at 81–2.

   Udo Bermbach discusses the politics of Handel's operas in marxian and psychologically influenced readings at the abstract level of direct or indirect thematization of political, moral, and personal interests (leading to an ironic-satiric reading of *Serse*); "Die Verwirrung der Mächtigen: Herrschertugenden und Politik in Georg Friedrich Händels Londoner Opern," in *Wo Macht ganz auf Verbrechen ruht: Politik und Gesellschaft in der Oper* (Hamburg: Europäische Verlagsanstalt, 1997), 38–63, and notes on 292–3.

   John Bokina, *Opera and Politics: From Monteverdi to Henze* (New Haven, CT: Yale University Press, 1997), discusses opera as the history of ideas: how opera reflects and transforms themes and ideas characteristic of contemporary political thought (such as monarchy, republicanism, class relations, status, gender) and the political implications of the representation of passions and emotions for life in the state and society.

6 Construals of politics as "the structures of power and social value that organize human life," "the structures of belief and interest, the ideologies which permeate every level of human existence," "a matter of values and ideals, conceptions of the good life, the good state, and so forth," or as "values" (see these uses in *The Politics of Interpretation,* ed. W. J. T. Mitchell (University of Chicago Press, 1983), 1, 2, 4, and 312), are too abstract to be of use for this study, as would a study of "Dryden's cultivation of obliquity, ambiguity, and paradox in political allusion" or of his "political awareness in imaginative works"; see Howard Erskine-Hill, *Poetry of Opposition and Revolution: Dryden to Wordsworth* (Oxford: Clarendon Press, 1996), 3, 4.

7 As posed by E. D. Hirsch, "The Politics of Theories of Interpretation," *Critical Inquiry* 9 (1982), 244.

8 I have explored these aspects briefly in "Opera, Satire, and Politics in the Walpole Era," in *The Past as Prologue: Essays to Celebrate the Twenty-Fifth Anniversary of ASECS*, ed. Carla H. Hays with Syndy M. Conger (New York: AMS Press, 1995), 347–72. I study this critique of opera as representing false taste, generally carried out in literature, satire, and periodical essays, in a forthcoming study, *Opera and Cultural Politics in Britain, 1700–1742.*

9 Reinhard Strohm, *Dramma per Musica: Italian Opera Seria of the Eighteenth Century* (New Haven, CT: Yale University Press, 1997), 270.

10 Ellen Rosand, *Opera in Seventeenth-Century Venice: The Creation of a Genre* (Berkeley: University of California Press, 1991); Beth Glixon and Jonathan Glixon, *Inventing the Business of Opera: The Impresario and His World in*

Seventeenth-Century Venice (New York: Oxford University Press, 2006); and Dennis Romano, "Why Opera? The Politics of an Emerging Genre," *Journal of Interdisciplinary History* 36 (2006), 401–9. Claudio Monteverdi's *L'incoronazione di Poppea* (1643), for example, portrayed the triumph of Vice over Virtue that could happen in Rome but not in a republic such as Venice; Ellen Rosand, "Seneca and the Interpretation of *L'Incoronazione di Poppea*," *Journal of the American Musicological Society* 38 (1985), 34–71.

11 Philip Ayers, *Classical Culture and the Idea of Rome in Eighteenth-Century England* (Cambridge University Press, 1997).

12 "Perdé tutta la sua vita per istruir dilettando il genere umano." Letter from Metastasio, January 28, 1750, in Vienna, to Farinelli; in *Lettere disperse e inedite Pietro Metastasio*, ed. Giosuè Carducci (Bologna: Nicola Zanichelli, 1883), no. 177, p. 325.

13 For ideology in Hasse's operas, Reinhard Strohm, "Rulers and States in Hasse's *Drammi per Musica*," in *Dramma per Musica: Italian Opera Seria of the Eighteenth Century* (New Haven, CT: Yale University Press, 1997), 270–93. See his note 1 for studies of the political ideologies in Metastasio's libretti.

14 The term "generic expectation" is from Robert D. Hume, "The Politics of Opera in Late Seventeenth-Century London," *Cambridge Opera Journal* 10 (1998), 15–43.

15 This has often been called the "pick-lock" approach, since the interpreter's goal is to find a "key" that will match characters or events in the opera's libretto to contemporary persons or historical situations. Often the method results in "tagging" several main characters in the opera with the name of the contemporary Briton, leaving aside the question of intention, application to other characters or events of the plot, how the interpretation relates to prevailing politics, and who benefits politically.

16 Hume, "The Politics of Opera," 42: "The oft-cited hypothesis that opera protagonists must be identified with the reigning monarch is not borne out by scrutiny of the texts. The results of such legislated application are mostly fatuous." Consequences of this premise are developed at length in Udo Bermbach, "'Dein Wunsch zu regieren muß oberstes Gesetz sein' – Betrachtungen zu Händels Herrschergestalten," *Göttinger Händel-Beiträge* 12 (2008), 33–50.

17 Hume, "The Politics of Opera," 43: "The inclination to construct elaborate parallels and personification readings should be resisted where there is no extrinsic evidence with which to validate them. However ingenious or textually plausible they may seem, they are not a sound form of historical scholarship."

18 Lewis Namier, *The Structure of Politics at the Accession of George III*, 2nd edn. (London: Macmillan, 1957); and Namier, *England in the Age of the American Revolution*, 2nd edn. (London: Macmillan, 1961), 179–215.

19 Robert Walcott, *English Politics in the Early Eighteenth Century* (Oxford: Clarendon Press, 1956).

20 Principal studies are Geoffrey Holmes, *British Politics in the Age of Anne*, rev. edn. (London: Hambledon Press, 1987); J. H. Plumb, *The Growth of Political Stability in England, 1675–1725* (London: Macmillan, 1967); W. A. Speck, *Stability and Strife: England, 1714–1760* (Cambridge, MA: Harvard University Press, 1977); Speck, *Tory & Whig: The Struggle in the Constituencies, 1701–15* (London: Macmillan, 1970); and Henry Horwitz, "Parties, Connections, and Parliamentary Politics, 1689–1714: Review and Revision," *Journal of British Studies* 6 (1966–67), 45–69.

21 The phrase is from Keith G. Feiling, *The Second Tory Party, 1714–1832* (London: Macmillan, 1938), 13.

22 By political stability, Plumb means "the acceptance by society of its political institutions, and of those classes of men or officials who control them"; Plumb, *The Growth of Political Stability in England*, xvi.

Plumb's "stability thesis" became the orthodox interpretation of British political history for the first half of the eighteenth century; see Frank O'Gorman, "The Recent Historiography of the Hanoverian Regime," *Historical Journal* 29 (1986), 1005–20; William Speck, "Whigs and Tories Dim Their Glories: English Political Parties under the First Two Georges," in *The Whig Ascendancy: Colloquies on Hanoverian England*, ed. John Cannon (London: Edward Arnold, 1981), 51–70; and Stephen Taylor, "British Politics in the Age of Holmes," *Parliamentary History* 8 (1989), 132–41. *Britain in the First Age of Party, 1680–1750: Essays Presented to Geoffrey Holmes*, ed. Clyve Jones (London: Hambledon Press, 1987) is devoted to the question of stability in British Politics.

23 See the symposium on Plumb's book, "Sir John Plumb's 'Growth of Political Stability': Does it Stand?" in *Albion* 25 (1993), 237–77; and Geoffrey Holmes, "The Achievement of Stability: The Social Context of Politics from the 1680s to the Age of Walpole," in *The Whig Ascendancy: Colloquies on Hanoverian England*, ed. John Cannon (London: Edward Arnold, 1981), 1–22, and following colloquy. Despite popular and informal resistance to Whig rule, E. P. Thompson argues such popular resistance need not undermine the Plumb stability thesis; Thompson, "Patrician Society, Plebeian Culture," *Journal of Social History* 7 (1974), 382–405.

24 "The Tories," *The History of Parliament. The House of Commons, 1715–1754*, ed. Romney Sedgwick, 2 vols. (New York: Oxford University Press, 1970), vol. I, 62–78. On p. viii Sedgwick acknowledges the account of the Tories is based on the research of Eveline Cruickshanks.

25 Linda Colley, *In Defiance of Oligarchy: The Tory Party, 1714–60* (Cambridge University Press, 1982). Brian W. Hill had earlier stressed the independence of the Tories as a political force, quite distinct from the dissident Whigs who opposed Walpole in the years 1724–42; Hill, *The Growth of Parliamentary Parties, 1688–1742* (Hamden, CT: Archon Books, 1976).

26 Peter D. G. Thomas, "Party Politics in Eighteenth-Century Britain: Some Myths and a Touch of Reality," *British Journal for Eighteenth-Century Studies* 10

(1987), 201–10; Nicholas Rogers, "Party Politics During the Whig Ascendancy," *Canadian Journal of History* 18 (1983), 253–60; Speck, "Whigs and Tories Dim Their Glories"; and Geoffrey Holmes, "Eighteenth-Century Toryism," *Historical Journal* 26 (1983), 755–60.

27 *History of Parliament. The House of Commons*, vol. I, ix.

28 Major studies include *Ideology and Conspiracy: Aspects of Jacobitism, 1689–1759*, ed. Eveline Cruickshanks (Edinburgh: John Donald, 1982); Bruce Lenman, *The Jacobite Risings in Britain, 1689–1746* (London: Eyre Methuen, 1980); Paul K. Monod, *Jacobitism and the English People, 1688–1788* (Cambridge University Press, 1989); Murray G. H. Pittock, *Poetry and Jacobite Politics in Eighteenth-Century Britain and Ireland* (Cambridge University Press, 1994); Pittock, *Jacobitism* (New York: St. Martin's Press, 1998); David Szechi, *Jacobitism and Tory Politics, 1710–14* (Edinburgh: John Donald, 1984); and Frank McLynn, *The Jacobites* (London: Routledge & Kegan Paul, 1985).

On Jacobite themes in literature, *Jacobitism and Eighteenth-Century English Literature*, ed. Ronald Paulson. Special issue of *ELH* 64(4) (Winter 1997); Howard Erskine-Hill, *The Augustan Idea in English Literature* (London: E. Arnold, 1983); and Erskine-Hill, *Poetry of Opposition and Revolution*.

29 Nicholas Rogers, *Whigs and Cities, Popular Politics in the Age of Walpole and Pitt* (Oxford: Clarendon Press, 1989), identifies sites of popular resistance and challenges to the Whig regime. He argues that popular revels and expressions of Jacobite sympathies or symbolism should not be taken as commitment to the Stuarts; Rogers, "Riot and Popular Jacobitism in early Hanoverian England," in *Ideology and Conspiracy: Aspects of Jacobitism, 1689–1759*, ed. Eveline Cruickshanks (Edinburgh: John Donald, 1982), 70–88.

Cautions about accepting the persistence of Jacobitism include David Hayton, review of Monod, *Jacobitism and the English People*, *Scriblerian* 23 (1991), 279–81; Andrew Hanham, "'So Few Facts': Jacobites, Tories and the Pretender," *Parliamentary History* 19 (2000), 233–57; O'Gorman, "The Recent Historiography of the Hanoverian Regime"; Lawrence Lipking, "The Jacobite Plot," in *Jacobitism and Eighteenth-Century English Literature*, ed. Ronald Paulson. Special issue of *ELH* 64(4) (Winter 1997), 843–55; Rogers, "Party Politics During the Whig Ascendancy"; Tim Harris, *Politics Under the Later Stuarts: Party Conflict in a Divided Society, 1660–1715* (Harlow: Pearson Education, 1993), 208–33; Betty Kemp, review of *The History of Parliament. The House of Commons, 1715–1754*, *English Historical Review* 88 (1973), 388–92; and B. W. Hill, "Men and Parliament in the Eighteenth Century," *History* 57 (1972), 234–40.

30 Hanham, "So Few Facts," 254.

31 On Burlington as a Jacobite, Jane Clark, "The Mysterious Mr Buck: Patronage and Politics, 1688–1745," *Apollo* 129 (May 1989), 317–22, and notes on 371; Clark, "Palladianism and the Divine Right of Kings: Jacobite Iconography," *Apollo* 135 (April 1992), 224–9; Clark, "For Kings and Senates Fit," *Georgian Group Journal* (1989), 55–63; Clark, "Lord Burlington Is Here," in *Lord Burlington: Architecture,*

Art and Life, ed. Toby Barnard and Jane Clark (London: Hambledon Press, 1995), 251–310; and Clark, "'His Zeal Is Too Furious': Lord Burlington's Agents," in *Lord Burlington – The Man and His Politics: Questions of Loyalty*, ed. Edward Corp (Lewiston, NY: Edwin Mellen Press, 1998), 181–97.

For the case against Burlington as a Jacobite, Clyve Jones, review of *Lord Burlington – The Man and His Politics*, *Parliamentary History* 18 (1999), 217–19; and Edward Gregg, review of *Lord Burlington – The Man and His Politics*, *British Journal for Eighteenth-Century Studies* 24 (2001), 95–7.

On Jonathan Swift as a Jacobite, Ian Higgins, *Swift's Politics: A Study in Disaffection* (Cambridge University Press, 1994); and Pittock, *Poetry and Jacobite Politics*.

For the case against Swift as a Jacobite, F. P. Lock, *Swift's Tory Politics* (London: Duckworth, 1983); and Lock, "Swift and English Politics, 1701–14," in *The Character of Swift's Satire: A Revised Focus*, ed. Claude Rawson (Newark: University of Delaware Press, 1983), 127–50. J. A. Downie argues Swift was a life-long Whig; Downie, "Swift and Jacobitism," *ELH* 64 (1997), 887–901; Downie, "Swift's Politics," in *Proceedings of the First Münster Symposium on Jonathan Swift*, ed. Hermann J. Real and Heinz J. Vienken (Munich: Wilhelm Fink, 1985), 47–58; Downie, *Jonathan Swift: Political Writer* (London: Routledge & Kegan Paul, 1984); and David Oakleaf, *A Political Biography of Jonathan Swift* (London: Pickering & Chatto, 2008).

On Pope as a Jacobite (in addition to works in note 28), Howard Erskine-Hill, *The Social Milieu of Alexander Pope: Lives, Example, and the Poetic Response* (New Haven, CT: Yale University Press, 1975); Erskine-Hill, "Alexander Pope: The Political Poet in His Time," *Eighteenth-Century Studies* 15 (1981–82), 123–48; Erskine-Hill, *Poetry of Opposition and Revolution*, 57–108; John Morillo, "Seditious Anger: Achilles, James Stuart, and Jacobite Politics in Pope's *Iliad* Translation," *Eighteenth-Century Life* 19 (May 1995), 38–58; Douglas Brooks-Davies, *Pope's "Dunciad" and the Queen of Night: A Study in Emotional Jacobitism* (Manchester University Press, 1985); and John M. Arden, *Pope's Once and Future Kings* (Knoxville: University of Tennessee, 1978).

For the case against Pope as a Jacobite, Chester Chapin, "Pope and the Jacobites," *Eighteenth Century Life* 10, n.s. (1986), 59–73; and J. A. Downie, "1688: Pope and the Rhetoric of Jacobitism," in *Pope: New Contexts*, ed. David Fairer (New York: Harvester Wheatsheaf, 1990), 9–24.

32 J. C. D. Clark, *English Society, 1688–1832: Ideology, Social Structure and Political Practice during the Ancien Regime* (Cambridge University Press, 1985); second edition in 2000 with the title *English Society, 1660–1832: Religion, Ideology, and Politics during the Ancien Regime*.

33 Major critiques of Clark include John Cannon, book review, *British Journal for Eighteenth-Century Studies* 10 (1987), 74–7; H. T. Dickinson, *The Politics of the People in Eighteenth-Century Britain* (New York: St. Martin's Press, 1995), 3–9; Joanna Innes, "Jonathan Clark, Social History, and England's Ancien Regime," *Past and Present* 115 (May 1987), 165–200; G. S. Rousseau, "Revisionist Polemics:

J. C. D. Clark and the Collapse of Modernity in the Age of Johnson," *Age of Johnson* 2 (1988), 421–50 (cites additional reviews); O'Gorman, "The Recent Historiography of the Hanoverian Regime"; Jeremy Black, "England's 'Ancien Regime'?" *History Today* 38 (March 1988), 43–51; and Roy Porter, "English Society in the Eighteenth Century Revisited," in *British Politics and Society from Walpole to Pitt, 1742–1789*, ed. Jeremy Black (New York: St. Martin's Press, 1990), 29–52.

34 *The Cambridge Urban History of Britain*, vol. II: *1540–1840*, ed. Peter Clark (Cambridge University Press, 2000), 453–640; M. J. Daunton, *Progress and Poverty: An Economic and Social History of Britain, 1700–1850* (Oxford University Press, 1995); Paul Langford, *A Polite and Commercial People: England, 1727–1783* (Oxford: Clarendon Press, 1989); John Brewer, *The Sinews of Power: War, Money, and the English State* (London: Century Hutchinson, 1988); Wilfred Prest, *Albion Ascendant: English History, 1660–1815* (Oxford University Press, 1998); and Frank O'Gorman, *The Long Eighteenth Century: British Political and Social History, 1688–1832* (London: Hodder Arnold, 1997).

35 See John Cannon, *Aristocratic Century: The Peerage of Eighteenth-Century England* (Cambridge University Press, 1985); H. T. Dickinson, *Liberty and Property: Political Ideology in Eighteenth-Century Britain* (New York: Holmes and Meier, 1977); J. A. W. Gunn, *Beyond Liberty and Property: The Process of Self-Recognition in Eighteenth-Century Political Thought* (Kingston: McGill-Queen's University Press, 1983), 120–93; and Paul Langford, *Public Life and the Propertied Englishman, 1689–1798* (Oxford: Clarendon Press, 1991).

 Roy Porter shows that social change could be adapted to coexist with and support a stable political order and that the ancien regime adopted new means for maintaining its hegemony and governing a changing society; Porter, "English Society in the Eighteenth Century Revisited."

36 See David Hunter's analysis of Handel's audiences, "Patronizing Handel, Inventing Audiences: The Intersection of Class, Money, Music and History," *Early Music* 30 (2000), 33–49.

37 Rogers, *Whigs and Cities*; Kathleen Wilson, *The Sense of the People: Politics, Culture and Imperialism in England, 1715–1785* (Cambridge University Press, 1995); Langford, *A Polite and Commercial People*; Dickinson, *The Politics of the People in Eighteenth-Century Britain*; and Dickinson, "Popular Politics in the Age of Walpole," in *Britain in the Age of Walpole*, ed. Jeremy Black (London: Macmillan, 1984), 45–68.

38 Dickinson, *The Politics of the People in Eighteenth-Century Britain*, 7.

39 G. C. Gibbs, "Parliament and Foreign Policy in the Age of Stanhope and Walpole," *English Historical Review* 77 (1962), 18–39.

2   Opera and political allegory

1 Robert D. Hume, "The Politics of Opera in Late Seventeenth-Century London," *Cambridge Opera Journal* 10 (1998), 15–43; Hume denies the generic expectation (see esp. 1, 28, 35, 43).

2 Reinhard Strohm, "Handel and his Italian Opera Texts," in *Essays on Handel and Italian Opera* (Cambridge University Press, 1985), 34–79; Konrad Sasse, "Die Texte der Londoner Opern Händels in ihren gesellschaftlichen Beziehungen," *Wissenschaftliche Zeitschrift der Martin-Luther-Universität Halle-Wittenberg. Gesellschafts- und Sprachwissenschaftliche Reihe* 4(5) (1955), 627–46; Curtis A. Price, "Political Allegory in Late-Seventeenth-Century English Opera," in *Music and Theatre: Essays in Honour of Winton Dean*, ed. Nigel Fortune (Cambridge University Press, 1987), 1–29, at 28; Price, "English Traditions in Handel's *Rinaldo*," in *Handel Tercentenary Collection*, ed. Stanley Sadie and Anthony Hicks (Ann Arbor, MI: UMI Research Press, 1987), 120–37; Brian Trowell, "Notes on Rinaldo," in program book for Metropolian Opera, New York, production, in *Stagebill* 11(5) (January 1984); Paul Monod, "The Politics of Handel's Early London Operas, 1711–1718," *Journal of Interdisciplinary History* 36 (2006), 445–72; Duncan Chisholm, "Handel's 'Lucio Cornelio Silla,'" *Early Music* 14 (1986), 64–70; Ellen T. Harris, "With Eyes on the East and Ears in the West: Handel's Orientalist Operas," *Journal of Interdisciplinary History* 36 (2006), 419–43; Harris, *Handel as Orpheus: Voice and Desire in the Chamber Cantatas* (Cambridge, MA: Harvard University Press, 2001), 185–6; Fiona McLauchlan, "Lotti's 'Teofane' (1719) and Handel's 'Ottone' (1723): A Textual and Musical Study," *Music and Letters* 78 (1997), 349–90; and Suzanne Aspden, "Ariadne's Clew: Politics, Allegory, and Opera in London (1734)," *Musical Quarterly* 85 (2001), 735–70.

3 Harris, *Handel as Orpheus*, and Aspden, "Ariadne's Clew," legitimately present rationales justifying allegorical interpretations; but neither discusses the restraints that might be put on interpretation to achieve plausible historical interpretations. For the necessity to place limits on interpretation, see Joseph Margolis, *Art and Philosophy: Conceptual Issues in Aesthetics* (Atlantic Highlands, NJ: Humanities Press, 1980), 156–64; Frank Kermode, "Can We Say Absolutely Anything We Like?" and "Institutional Control of Interpretation," in *The Art of Telling: Essays on Fiction* (Cambridge, MA: Harvard University Press, 1983), 156–84; E. D. Hirsch, *Validity in Interpretation* (New Haven, CT: Yale University Press, 1967), 24–67; R. S. Crane, *The Languages of Criticism and the Structure of Poetry* (University of Toronto Press, 1955), 32–8; and Howard Weinbrot, "Historical Criticism, Hypotheses, and Eighteenth-Century Studies: The Case for Induction and Neutral Knowledge," in *Theory and Tradition in Eighteenth-Century Studies*, ed. Richard B. Schwartz (Carbondale: Southern Illinois University Press, 1990), 66–92.

4 John M. Wallace, "Dryden and History: A Problem in Allegorical Reading," *ELH* 36 (1969), 265–90, at 271. Or also as phrased by Wallace, "Whether the meaning we find in a text was put there by the author or is foisted on him by ourselves"; Wallace, "'Examples Are Best Precepts': Readers and Meanings in Seventeenth-Century Poetry," *Critical Inquiry* 1 (1974), 272–90, at 275.

5 Alan Roper, "Drawing Parallels and Making Applications in Restoration Literature," in Richard Ashcroft and Alan Roper, *Politics as Reflected in Literature. Papers Presented at a Clark Library Seminar, 24 January 1987* (Los Angeles, CA: William Andrews Clark Memorial Library, 1989), 29–65, at 52.

6 Hume, "The Politics of Opera," 42.

7 Robert D. Hume, *Henry Fielding and the London Theatre: 1728–1737* (Oxford: Clarendon Press, 1988), 77.

8 Or put another way, I am suggesting that for the political context of operas, we should not take just the concurrent world of political events, but the whole domain of politically engaged plays, poems, and satire of the era.

9 It is not that the modern interpretations of librettos need revision, have failed to find the correct allegorical key, or need recasting as personations or parallel histories, but that the underlying expectation is mistaken and leads to unhistorical readings of operas that show no signs of having been intended, written, or received as allegorical or political.

10 On the possibility (and desirability) of such historical scholarship, see Robert D. Hume, *Reconstructing Contexts: The Aims and Principles of Archaeo-Historicism* (Oxford University Press, 1999); Hume "The Aims and Limits of Historical Scholarship," *Review of English Studies*, n.s. 53(211) (2002), 399–422; Hume, "The Aims and Pitfalls of 'Historical Interpretation,'" *Philological Quarterly* 89 (2010), 353–82; Hume "Texts Within Contexts: Notes Toward a Historical Method," *Philological Quarterly* 71 (1992), 69–100; E. D. Hirsch Jr., *Validity in Interpretation*; and R. S. Crane, "The Multiplicity of Critical Languages," in *The Languages of Criticism and the Structure of Poetry* (University of Toronto Press, 1953), 3–38.

11 Neal Zaslaw, "The First Opera in Paris: A Study in the Politics of Art," in *Jean-Baptiste Lully and the Music of the French Baroque: Essays in Honor of James R. Anthony*, ed. John Hajdu Heyer (Cambridge University Press, 1989), 7–23, at 19.

For opera in Britain, the generic expectation that opera was topically concerned with the state and monarchs was instituted in John Buttrey, "The Evolution of English Opera between 1656 and 1695: A Re-investigation" (Ph.D. dissertation, Cambridge University, 1967); also Buttrey, "Dating Purcell's Dido and Aeneas," *Proceedings of the Royal Musical Association* 94 (1967/68), 57: "the new medium of English opera was not only topical, but … its topicality was concerned with King and State."

Other expressions reflecting the generic expectation are widespread; see Annette Landgraf: "das Musiktheater [war] ein wichtiges Medium, um politische Anspielungen in die öffentliche Diskussion einzubringen," in "Israel in Egypt: Ein Oratorium als Opfer der Politik," *Händel-Jahrbuch* 42/43 (1996/1997), 214; Ruth Smith: "Music was readily understood as a metaphor for politics … Eighteenth-century music drama was a prime vehicle for political innuendo … Granted, then, that it is reasonable to expect parallels in the librettos," in "Handel's Israelite Librettos and English Politics, 1732–52," *Göttinger Händel-Beiträge* 5 (1993), 195–215, at 203; and Udo Bermbach: "Wir wissen, dass italienische Opern in London stets als Vehikel politischer Anspielungen und kritischer Reflexionen fungierten und das legt die Vermutung nahe, dass ein solcher Zusammenhang auch für die Opern Händels gelten kann," in "'Dein

Wunsch zu regieren muß oberstes Gesetz sein' – Betrachtungen zu Händels Herrschergestalten," *Göttinger Händel-Beiträge* 12 (2008), 33–50, at 43.

12 Strohm, "Handel and his Italian Opera Texts," 35, 48.

13 See Reinhard Strohm: "Gewiss sind die Titelhelden aller drei Opern [*Riccardo I*, *Alessandro*, and *Admeto*] als Allegorien der hannoveranischen Herrscher zu lesen," in "Darstellung, Aktion and Interesse in der höfischen Opernkunst," *Händel-Jahrbuch* 49 (2003), 13–26, at 25; and Hans Dieter Clausen: "Da Opern von Anbeginn höfischer Repräsentation dienten, lag es nahe, in ihren Helden- und Herrschergestalten Abbilder des jeweiligen Souveräns zu sehen," in "Der Einfluß der Komponisten auf die Librettowahl der Royal Academy of Music (1720–1729)," in *Zur Dramaturgie der Barockoper: Bericht über die Symposien der Internationalen Händel-Akademie Karlsruhe 1992 und 1993*, ed. Hans Joachim Marx (Laabe: Laaber-Verlag, 1994), 55–72, at 60. In examining English operas, Hume, "The Politics of Opera," 42, finds the premise that rulers in the operas are to be identified with the reigning monarch "is not borne out by scrutiny of the texts. The results of such legislated application are mostly fatuous."

14 T. C. W. Blanning, *The Culture of Power and the Power of Culture: Old Regime Europe, 1660–1789* (Oxford University Press, 2002), 43–8 and 63–9.

15 Herbert Seifert, *Die Oper am Wiener Kaiserhof im 17. Jahrhundert*. Wiener Veröffentlichungen zur Musikgeschichte 25 (Tutzing: Hans Schneider, 1985); Seifert, *Der Sig-prangende Hochzeit-Gott: Hochzeitsfest am Wiener Hof der Habsburger und ihre Allegorik, 1622–1699*. Dramma per musica 2 (Vienna: Musikwissenschaftlicher Verlag, 1988); and Lorenzo Bianconi, *Music in the Seventeenth Century*, trans. David Bryant (Cambridge University Press, 1987), 228–31.

16 Carl B. Schmidt, "Antonio Cesti's *Il pomo d'oro*: A Reexamination of a Famous Hapsburg Court Spectacle," *Journal of the American Musicological Society* 29 (1976), 381–412.

17 Discussed in its role as *instrumentum regni* in Reinhard Strohm, "*Costanza e fortezza*: Investigation of the Baroque Ideology," in *I Bibinea: una famiglia in scena: da Bologna all'Europa*, ed. Daniela Gallingani (Florence: Alinea, 2002), 75–91; see p. 77, note 6 for further on the opera. Two works, *Cleofide* and *Teofane*, produced for the Dresden court of Frederick Augustus, Elector of Saxony and King of Poland, are similarly discussed in Blanning, *Culture of Power*, 63–9.

18 On political mythologizing of French opera, Robert M. Isherwood, *Music in the Service of the King: France in the Seventeenth Century* (Ithaca, NY: Cornell University Press, 1973), 208–38; Manuel Couvreur, *Jean-Baptiste Lully: Musique et dramaturgie au service du Prince* (Brussels: Marc Vokar, 1992), 325–97; Downing A. Thomas, *Aesthetics of Opera in the Ancien Régime, 1647–1785* (Cambridge University Press, 2002), 53–99; Zaslaw, "The First Opera in Paris," 7–23; Fritz Reckow, "Der inszenierte Fürst: Situationsbezug und Stilprägung der Oper im absolutistischen Frankreich," in *Die Inszenierung des Absolutismus: Politische Begründung und künstlerische Gestaltung höfischer Feste im Frankreich*

Ludwigs XIV, ed. Fritz Reckow (Erlangen: Erlanger Forschungen, 1992), 71–104; and Jean-Pierre Néraudau, *L'Olympe du Roi-Soleil: Mythologie et idéologie royale aux Grand Siècle* (Paris: Société d'édition "Les Belles Lettres," 1986).

19 Isherwood, *Music in the Service of the King*, 247.

20 For representative political allegory readings of many English operas, semi-operas, or masques, see Price, "Political Allegory in Late-Seventeenth-Century English Opera"; Price, "English Traditions in Handel's *Rinaldo*"; Andrew R. Walkling, "Performance and Political Allegory in Restoration England: What to Interpret and When," in *Performing the Music of Henry Purcell*, ed. Michael Burden (Oxford: Clarendon Press, 1996), 163–79; Walkling, "Politics and the Restoration Masque: The Case of *Dido and Aeneas*," in *Culture and Society in the Stuart Restoration, Literature, Drama, History*, ed. Gerald MacLean (Cambridge University Press, 1995), 52–69; and Walkling, "Political Allegory in Purcell's 'Dido and Aeneas,'" *Music and Letters* 76 (1995), 540–71. Many of these political interpretations of English opera are questioned effectively in Hume, "The Politics of Opera."

21 On its background, Christina Bashford, "Perrin and Cambert's 'Ariane, ou le mariage de Bacchus' Re-examined," *Music and Letters* 72 (1991), 1–16; and John Buttrey, "New Light on Robert Cambert in London, and his Ballet et Musique," *Early Music* 23 (1995), 198–220.

22 Price, "Political Allegory in Late-Seventeenth-Century English Opera," 6–7.

23 Price, "Political Allegory in Late-Seventeenth-Century English Opera," 8–9.

24 On *Albion and Albanius*, *The Works of John Dryden*, vol. XV: *Plays*, ed. Vinton A. Dearing (Berkeley: University of California Press, 1976), 323–55. See also Phillip Harth, *Pen for a Party: Dryden's Tory Propaganda in Its Contexts* (Princeton University Press, 1993), 254–8. A convenient summary of the allegorical plot is provided in Paul Hammond, "Dryden's *Albion and Albanius*: The Apotheosis of Charles II," in *The Court Masque*, ed. David Lindley (Manchester University Press, 1984), 169–83.

25 Harth, *Pen for a Party*, 254–8.

26 On allegory and politics of *King Arthur* and *Albion and Albanius*, James A. Winn, *John Dryden and His World* (New Haven, CT: Yale University Press, 1987), 393–4; Winn, *"When Beauty Fires the Blood": Love and the Arts in the Age of Dryden* (Ann Arbor, MI: University of Michigan Press, 1992), 254–304.

Curtis A. Price, *Henry Purcell and the London Stage* (Cambridge University Press, 1984), 289–319; Price, "Political Allegory in Late-Seventeenth-Century English Opera," 1–4, 10–17 (*King Arthur* as a backhanded compliment); Andrew Pinnock, "*King Arthur* Expos'd: A Lesson in Anatomy," in *Purcell Studies*, ed. Curtis Price (Cambridge University Press, 1995), 244–7; Howard Erskine-Hill, *Poetry of Opposition and Revolution: Dryden to Wordsworth* (Oxford: Clarendon Press, 1996), 21–4 (Oswald as William); and David Bywaters, *Dryden in Revolutionary England* (Berkeley: University of California Press, 1991), 75–93 (Jacobite reading of *King Arthur*). Christine Gerrard, *The Patriot Opposition to Walpole: Politics, Poetry, and National Myth, 1725–1742* (Oxford University Press, 1994), 119–20, 172–4, sees *King Arthur* as covertly Jacobitical.

Hume, "The Politics of Opera," 40–2, sees *King Arthur* as a work whose "*textual* reading, however, will not sustain anything like a clear and satisfying allegory on either side, patriotic or subversive" and that "finally shows us the difference between textual meaning and susceptibility to application."

27 Price, "Political Allegory in Late-Seventeenth-Century English Opera," 17–19.

28 Kathryn Lowerre, "A *ballet des nations* for English Audiences: *Europe's Revels for the Peace of Ryswick* (1697)," *Early Music* 35 (2007), 419–33.

29 On the transformations of *The British Enchanters*, Price, "Political Allegory in Late-Seventeenth-Century English Opera," 25–8.

30 For politics in Restoration literature in general, Jessica Munns, *Restoration Politics and Drama: The Plays of Thomas Otway, 1675–1683* (Newark: University of Delaware Press, 1995); Richard Braverman, *Plots and Counterplots: Sexual Politics and the Body Politic in English Literature, 1680–1730* (Cambridge University Press, 1993), 160–237; Susan J. Owen, *Restoration Theatre and Crisis* (Oxford: Clarendon Press, 1996); Steven N. Zwicker, *Lines of Authority: Politics and English Literary Culture, 1649–1689* (Ithaca, CT: Cornell University Press, 1993); Kevin Sharpe and Steven N. Zwicker, eds., *Politics of Discourse: The Literature and History of Seventeenth-Century England* (Berkeley: University of California Press, 1987); Sharpe and Zwicker, eds., introduction to *Refiguring Revolutions: Aesthetics and Politics from the English Revolution to the Romantic Revolution* (Berkeley: University of California Press, 1998); Robert D. Hume, *The Development of English Drama in the Late Seventeenth Century* (Oxford: Clarendon Press, 1976), 340–79; John Loftis, *The Politics of Drama in Augustan England* (Oxford: Clarendon Press, 1963), 7–35; Loftis, "Political and Social Thought in the Drama," in *The London Theatre World, 1660–1800*, ed. Robert D. Hume (Carbondale: Southern Illinois University Press, 1980), 253–85; Nancy K. Maguire, *Regicide and Restoration: English Tragicomedy, 1660–1671* (Cambridge University Press, 1992); Howard Erskine-Hill, *Poetry and the Realm of Politics: Shakespeare to Dryden* (Oxford: Clarendon Press, 1996); and Erskine-Hill, *Poetry of Opposition and Revolution*.

31 Phillip Harth, "Legends No Histories: The Case of *Absalom and Achitophel*," *Studies in Eighteenth-Century Culture* 4 (1975), 13–29, at 25.

32 *The Cambridge Companion to English Literature, 1650–1740*, ed. Steven N. Zwicker (Cambridge University Press, 1998), xi. And even more broadly, "There is an important sense in which no seventeenth-century literature is not also political"; Sharpe and Zwicker, eds., *The Politics of Discourse*, 3.

33 Loftis, *The Politics of Drama in Augustan England*, 1, 2.

34 Bianconi, *Music in the Seventeenth Century*, 221. Lorenzo Bianconi and Thomas Walker, "Production, Consumption and Political Function of Seventeenth-Century Italian Opera," *Early Music History* 4 (1985), 209–96, and Bianconi, *Music in the Seventeenth Century*, 161–263, analyze many contrasting

cases in detail. A briefer survey is given in Margaret R. Butler, "Italian Opera in the Eighteenth Century," in *The Cambridge History of Eighteenth-Century Music*, ed. Simon P. Keefe (Cambridge University Press, 2009), 203–71.

35 Bianconi, *Music in the Seventeenth Century*, 230.

36 For a survey, Robert D. Hume, "The Sponsorship of Opera in London, 1704–1720," *Modern Philology* 84 (1988), 420–32.

37 The work is untitled; Seifert, *Der Sig-prangende Hochzeit-Gott*, 48.

38 Seifert, *Der Sig-prangende Hochzeit-Gott*, 44–6.

39 Hume, "The Politics of Opera."

40 R. O. Bucholz, *The Augustan Court: Queen Anne and the Decline of Court Culture* (Stanford University Press, 1993), esp. 1–35, 202–51; Bucholz, "'Nothing but Ceremony': Queen Anne and the Limitations of Royal Ritual," *Journal of British Studies* 30 (1991), 288–323. Hannah Smith, "The Court in England, 1714–1760: A Declining Political Institution," *History* 90 (2005), 23–41, and Smith, *Georgian Monarchy: Politics and Culture, 1714–1760* (Cambridge University Press, 2006), reconsiders some of Bucholz's points, suggesting the court could still be a place of social and political significance.

41 Bucholz, *The Augustan Court*, 242, and Bucholz, "Nothing but Ceremony," 313.

42 On tradition of censorship of plays, Arthur F. White, "The Office of Revels and Dramatic Censorship during the Restoration Period," *Western Reserve University Bulletin* 34(13) (1931), 5–45.

43 Strohm discusses the London opera as if it were a court opera in "Darstellung, Aktion and Interesse."

44 Bianconi and Walker, "Production, Consumption and Political Function," 260, 264, 241.

45 Strohm, "Handel and his Italian Opera Texts," gives source librettos for Handel operas.

46 Adaptations included cutting recitative; inserting, deleting, and combining whole characters; modifying the plot; and adjusting the number of arias to reflect the status of the star singers.

47 See Swiney's correspondence with the Duke of Richmond in Elizabeth Gibson, *The Royal Academy of Music, 1719–1728: The Institution and Its Directors* (New York: Garland Publishing, 1989), 348–82.

48 In a letter of May 13, 1737, Sir John Buckworth, long active in the direction of opera companies and at the time involved with the Opera of the Nobility, wrote to the Earl of Essex in Turin in 1737 about an opera subject he had suggested; British Library, Add. MS 27,735, f. 177v.

49 Xavier Cervantes, "History and Sociology of the Italian Opera in London (1705–45): The Evidence of the Dedications of the Printed Librettos," *Studi Musicali* 27 (1998), 339–82.

50 Gibson, *The Royal Academy of Music*, 439–65.

51 Letter from Riva, Kensington, October 3, 1726, to Muratori; as trans. in R. A. Streatfeild, "Handel, Rolli, and Italian Opera in London in the Eighteenth Century," *Musical Quarterly* 3 (1917), 428–45, at 434.

52 Letter from Riva, Hanover, September 7, 1725, to Muratori; as trans. in Streatfeild, "Handel, Rolli, and Italian Opera," 433.

In the process of "deforming" the librettos for new settings in London, poets (Nicola Haym, Paolo Rolli, Samuel Humphreys, and others) shortened the librettos (by trimming recitative); adapted the librettos to changing casts by adding, enlarging, diminishing, or eliminating certain roles; substituted arias to flatter singers; or improved dramatic effectiveness.

53 Such a case has been made for Handel's *Ottone* in McLauchlan, "Lotti's 'Teofane' and Handel's 'Ottone.'" McLauchlan rightly points out: "For London audiences at performances of *Ottone*, there would have been no contemporary parallel with the marriage of Ottone and Teofane and obviously none of the allusion pertinent to the Saxons" (at 356); she reports some attempts by other scholars to relate the opera to political circumstances in Britain, but they are very tangential and unconvincing. The adaptations are described in Winton Dean, "The Genesis and Early History of *Ottone*," *Göttinger Händel-Beiträge* 2 (1986), 129–40.

54 The original circumstances are described in Blanning, *Culture of Power*, 62–4; McLauchlan, "Lotti's 'Teofane' and Handel's 'Ottone'"; and Michael Walter, "Italienische Musik al Repräsentationskunst der Dresdener Fürstenhochzeit von 1719," in *Elbflorenz; Italienische Präsenz in Dresden 16–19 Jahrhundert*, ed. Barbara Marx (Dresden: Verlag der Kunst, 2000), which reproduces the stage designs.

55 *The Generous Conqueror* (1702), A2v.

56 *Censor*, no. 93 (May 25, 1717; citing coll. edn.).

57 Jonathan Swift, *A Tale of a Tub*, 5th edn. (1710), 205 n.

58 Letter from John Gay (and Alexander Pope) to Jonathan Swift, November [7], 1726; in *The Correspondence of Jonathan Swift, D.D.*, ed. David Woolley, 4 vols. (Frankfurt am Main: Peter Lang, 1999–2007), no. 728, vol. III, 47.

59 See note 20 above.

60 J. P. Kenyon, *The Popish Plot* (London: Heinemann, 1972). On politics in the plays of the 1680s, Owen, *Restoration Theatre and Crisis*; Owen, "Interpreting the Politics of Restoration Drama," *Seventeenth Century* 8 (1993), and 67–97; and Hume, *The Development of English Drama*, 340–79.

61 J. R. Jones, *The First Whigs: The Politics of the Exclusion Crisis* (London: Oxford University Press, 1961). On the plot and its dramatization, Owen, *Restoration Theatre and Crisis*, 34–61; Matthew H. Wikander, "The Spitted Infant: Scenic Emblem and Exclusionist Politics in Restoration Adaptations of Shakespeare," *Shakespeare Quarterly* 37 (1986), 340–58.

62 Owen, "Interpreting the Politics of Restoration Drama"; developed in detail in her *Restoration Theatre and Crisis*, 200–74.

63 Michael Dobson, *The Making of the National Poet: Shakespeare, Adaptation and Authorship, 1660–1769* (Oxford: Clarendon Press, 1992), 62–90; Wikander, "The Spitted Infant"; and John M. Wallace, "Otway's *Caius Marius* and the Exclusion Crisis," *Modern Philology* 85 (1988), 363–72.

64 For other banned plays, Owen, *Restoration Theatre and Crisis*, 12; and *The Revels History of Drama in English*, vol. V: *1660–1750* (London: Methuen, 1976), 28.

65 Dobson, *The Making of the National Poet*, 63, 72, 73, 79, 81, 85. On how Shakespeare's *Richard II* was applied to Robert Walpole's ministry, see Thomas Davies, *Dramatic Miscellanies: Consisting of Critical Observations on Several Plays of Shakespeare*, new edn., 3 vols. (1785), vol. I, 150–4. In Davies' examples, it is specific lines of text that are seen as applying to Walpole.

66 On the politics of *Venice Preserv'd*, Thomas Otway, *Venice Preserved*, ed. Malcolm Kelsall (Lincoln: University of Nebraska Press, 1969), introduction; Munns, *Restoration Politics and Drama*, 166–75; Phillip Harth, "Political Interpretations of *Venice Preserv'd*," *Modern Philology* 85 (1988), 345–62; Owen, *Restoration Theatre and Crisis*, 29–38; John R. Moore, "Contemporary Satire in Otway's *Venice Preserved*," *PMLA* 43 (1928), 166–81; Harry M. Solomon, "The Rhetoric of 'Redressing Grievances': Court Propaganda as the Hermeneutical Key to *Venice Preserv'd*," *ELH* 3 (1986), 289–310; and A. M. Taylor, *Next to Shakespeare: Otway's "Venice Preserv'd" and "The Orphan," and Their History on the London Stage* (Durham, NC: Duke University Press, 1950), 39–72.

67 Otway, *Venice Preserved*, ed. Kelsall, 5.

68 For interpretations of *Venice Preserv'd*, *The Complete Works of Thomas Otway*, ed. Montague Summers, 3 vols. (London: Nonesuch Press, 1926), vol. I, lxxxviii; Moore, "Contemporary Satire in Otway's *Venice Preserved*"; Roswell G. Ham, *Otway and Lee: Biography from a Baroque Age* (New Haven, CT: Yale University Press, 1931), 185–200; Zera Fink, *The Classical Republicans: An Essay in the Recovery of a Pattern of Thought in Seventeenth Century England*, 2nd edn. (Evanston, IL: Northwestern University Press, 1962), 144–8; David Bywaters, "Venice, Its Senate, and Its Plot in Otway's *Venice Preserv'd*," *Modern Philology* 80 (1983), 256–63; and Solomon, "The Rhetoric of 'Redressing Grievances'." Bywaters' interpretation is endorsed by Judith Milhous and Robert D. Hume, *Producible Interpretations: Eight English Plays, 1675–1707* (Carbondale: Southern Illinois University Press, 1985), 173–6.

69 Harth, "Political Interpretations of *Venice Preserv'd*."

70 On the politics of *The Duke of Guise*, Harth, *Pen for a Party*, 188–205; *The Works of John Dryden*, vol. XIV: *Plays*, ed. Vinton A. Dearing and Alan Roper (Berkeley: University of California Press, 1992), 476–512; David Gunto, "Kicking the Emperor: Some Problems of Restoration Parallel History," *1650–1850: Ideas, Aesthetics, and Inquiries in the Early Modern Era* 3 (1997), 109–27; Roper, "Drawing Parallels and Making Applications in Restoration Literature," 48–51; and Owen, *Restoration Theatre and Crisis*, 124–7, 147–9, 169–71.

71 Thomas Hunt, *A Defence of the Charter, and Municipal Rights of the City of London* (1683); and Thomas Shadwell(?), *Some Reflections upon the Pretended Parallel in the Play Called The Duke of Guise* (1683).

72 In John H. Wilson, "Theatre Notes from the Newdigate Newsletters," *Theatre Notebook* 15 (1961), 81.

73 On *The Spanish Fryar*, Roper, "Drawing Parallels and Making Applications in Restoration Literature," 38–40; and Susan J. Owen, "The Politics of John Dryden's *The Spanish Fryar: or, the Double Discovery*," *English: The Journal of the English Association* 43(176) (1994), 97–113.

74 In John Dalrymple, *Memoirs of Great Britain and Ireland*, 4th edn., 4 vols. (1773–88), vol. III, 89.

75 Thomas Tickell, preface, *The Works of the Right Honourable Joseph Addison, Esq.*, 4 vols. (1721), vol. I, xiv.

76 Lady Mary Wortley Montagu; in Robert Halsband, "Addison's *Cato* and Lady Mary Wortley Montagu," *PMLA* 65 (1950), 1126.

77 "A *Prologue* to Cato. Written at the Time of the threaten'd Invasion from *Spain*, in 1717," in *Miscellaneous Poems*, collected by David Lewis, 2 vols. (1730), vol. I, 302–4.

78 John Loftis, "The Uses of Tragedy in Georgian England," in *The Stage in the 18th Century*, ed. J. D. Browning (New York: Garland Publishing, 1981), 10–22, at 17.

79 Colley Cibber, *An Apology for the Life of Cobby Cibber*, ed. Robert W. Lowe, 2 vols. (London: John C. Nimmo, 1889), vol. II, 130. But as one contemporary noted, the play can be called "*Whiggish* upon no other Account but upon the frequent Repetition of the Word *Liberty*"; in *Mr. Addison Turn'd Tory: or, the Scene Inverted: Wherein It Is Made Appear That the Whigs Have Misunderstood that Celebrated Author in His Applauded Tragedy, Call'd Cato* (1713), 21.

On contemporary reception and politics of *Cato*, M. M. Kelsall, "The Meaning of Addison's *Cato*," *Review of English Studies*, n.s. 17 (1966), 149–62; and David Walker, "Addison's Cato and the Transformation of Republican Discourse in the Early Eighteenth Century," *British Journal for Eighteenth-Century Studies* 26 (2003), 91–108.

80 Elizabeth, Countess of Bristol, to John, Earl of Bristol; Suffolk Record Office, Bury St. Edmunds, 941/46/10, 198. Other contemporary notices of the play's politics include a letter from George Berkeley to the Earl of Egmont, April 16, 1713, in *Berkeley and Percival: The Correspondence of George Berkeley and Sir John Percival*, ed. Benjamin Rand (Cambridge University Press, 1914), 113; letter from Thomas Burnet to George Duckett, May 9(?), 1713, in *The Letters of Thomas Burnet to George Duckett, 1712–1722*, ed. David Nichol Smith (Oxford: Roxburghe Club, 1914), 38 (Burnet will allow either Bolingbroke or Harley to be Cato "when they'll please to stab themselves, as he did"); and a manuscript newsletter, April 17/18, 1713 (Henry Snyder collection of newsletters, on loan at the William Andrews Clark Memorial Library, Los Angeles, BM 29/45 J-11, 55/237): "Elles est sur tout fort applaudie par le Party des Whigs á cause des Sentiments de Liberté et d'amour dela Patrie."

81 Prefixed to *The Unfortunate General: or, the History of the Life and Character of Cato* [?1713].

82 "The Key or Explanation to the History, and Play of Cato" (?1713), iv.

83 *Mr. Addison Turn'd Tory*, 3, pretends to defend Addison from the charge that he meant to give umbrage to the present ministry.

84 Cibber, *Apology*, 251.

85 John Dennis, *Remarks upon Cato*, 6.

86 Comment on Restoration plays was occasionally spread by manuscript newsletters, which contain the comments on the *Duke of Guise* quoted above.

87 The supposed case of *Floridante* will be discussed in Chapter 3.

88 Trowell, "Notes on Rinaldo."

Similar allegories relating the opera to the war against France are summarized in Price, "English Traditions in Handel's *Rinaldo*," 130–3. Price notes the Crusader interpretation "does not quite fit a template of contemporary events"; he offers additional interpretations (including one from a Jacobite perspective) and endorses such ambivalence in this "vigorous political work." Monod, "The Politics of Handel's Early London Operas," 455–6, sees the Crusaders paralleling Marlborough's victorious armies.

89 *Swift vs. Mainwaring: "The Examiner" and "The Medley*," ed. Frank H. Ellis (Oxford: Clarendon Press, 1985).

90 Monod, "The Politics of Handel's Early London Operas," 464–5.

91 Monod never points out how Teseo resembles William III or how the "flawed, misguided" and "despotic" Egeus resembles James II. Yet, Monod grants that Egeus' generosity in the *lieto fine* is "in stark contrast to James II." Egeus, in fact, is no worse than most absolute monarchs in operas. It is not clear (or shown relevant) how Theseus' suppression of a rebellion within Athens is a reference to how "the Whigs had crushed a Jacobite rebellion in 1708" in Scotland (both William III and James II were dead by then); the rebellion failed because the French fleet, with James left behind in France, never landed. Since Marlborough and Godolphin (both Tories) still headed the ministry, it is not clear how the repression of the rebellion can be laid to the Whigs, nor how a rebellion in a distant place correlates to an intra-city rebellion. Nor is it clear what parliamentary statute ("the will of the people") affirmed George's succession.

92 The date of the dedication (June 2, 1713) is no certain indication of the date of the premiere. Many librettos carry dedication dates at variance with that of the premiere.

93 J. Merrill Knapp, "The Libretto of Handel's 'Silla'," *Music and Letters* 50 (1969), 68–75.

94 D'Aumont's activities, including balls and masquerades, were widely reported in the newspapers and manuscript newsletters. None mention *Silla*. However, one newsletter reports that on the date of the supposed production of *Silla*, "This day ye duke de Aumont ye ffrench Ambr Nobly Entertained Sr Isaack Newton president of the Royall Society, ye two Secretaryes, ye Treasurer w.th sev.ll others of ye Society at Somerset House"; Newsletter LC 3622 (Henry Snyder collection of newsletters, on loan at the William Andrews Clark Memorial Library, Los Angeles).

95 Chisholm, "Handel's 'Lucio Cornelio Silla,'" 64–70. On the political functions of operas on Sulla, Robert C. Ketterer, "Senecanism and the 'Sulla' Operas of Handel and Mozart," *Syllecta Classica* 10 (1999), 214–33.

96 The Colman opera register is printed in Konrad Sasse, "Opera Register from 1712 to 1734 (Colman-Register)," *Händel-Jahrbuch* 5 (1959), 199–223.

97 Best known is Swift's *Examiner*, no. 27 (February 8, 1711), accusing him of avarice.

98 Harris, *Handel as Orpheus*, 185–6. Arguing that *Silla* allegorizes a future event essentially means no constraints may be put on the allegorical interpretations of a work.

99 C. S. Lewis, *Of Other Worlds: Essays and Stories*, ed. Walter Hooper (New York: Harcourt, Brace & World, 1967), 57–8. Wallace, "Dryden and History," 265, recognizes the temptation: "The more closely we read certain plays and non-dramatic poems, the more they seem to be offering covert advice on contemporary politics, and the greater is the temptation to translate their figures (in both senses) into topical allusions."

100 Rosamond Tuve, *Allegorical Imagery: Some Mediaeval Books and Their Posterity* (Princeton University Press, 1966), 330; or an example of what F. P. Lock, *The Politics of "Gulliver's Travels"* (Oxford: Clarendon Press, 1980), calls "a diversion of misplaced ingenuity"; or Thomas E. Maresca calls "*post-hoc* allegoresis" in "Personification vs. Allegory," in *Enlightening Allegory: Theory, Practice, and Contexts of Allegory in the Late Seventeenth and Eighteenth Centuries*, ed. Kevin L. Cope (New York: AMS Press, 1993), 21–39, at 22.

101 Richard Blackmore, preface to *Prince Arthur, an Heroick Poem* (1695); and John Hughes, "An Essay on Allegorical Poetry, &c.," prefixed to *The Works of Mr. Edmund Spenser*, ed. John Hughes, 6 vols. (1715), vol. I, xxiii–lvii.

102 On some of the relevant issues in allegorical interpretation, Tuve, *Allegorical Imagery*, esp. 3–55; Angus Fletcher, *Allegory: The Theory of a Symbolic Mode* (Ithaca, NY: Cornell University Press, 1964); Edward A. Bloom, "The Allegorical Principle," *ELH* 18 (1951), 163–90; Maresca, "Personification vs. Allegory"; Roper, "Drawing Parallels and Making Applications in Restoration Literature"; Wallace, "Examples Are Best Precepts"; Wallace, "Dryden and History"; Morton W. Bloomfield, "Allegory as Interpretation," *New Literary History* 3 (1971–72), 301–17 (on types of allegory); Richard Ashcroft, "The Language of Political Conflict in Restoration Literature," in Richard Ashcroft and Alan Roper, *Politics as Reflected in Literature*. Papers Presented at a Clark Library Seminar, 24 January 1987 (Los Angeles, CA: William Andrews Clark Memorial Library, 1989), 1–28; J. Douglas Canfield, "Royalism's Last Dramatic Stand: English Political Tragedy, 1679–89," *Studies in Philology* 82 (1985), 234–63; and Gunto, "Kicking the Emperor."

103 *The Works of Spenser*, ed. Hughes, vol. I, xxvii.

104 Blackmore, preface to *Prince Arthur*, b2r.

105 *The Works of Spenser*, ed. Hughes, vol. I, xxxiii.

106 On the prevailing assumption of epic as allegory, and use of allegory for moral lessons, see H. T. Swedenberg, Jr., *The Theory of the Epic in England, 1650–1800* (Berkeley: University of California Press, 1944), 16–17, 25–6, 155–60, 193–215, and 267–8. For Hughes, there is a "moral Sense couch'd under its [allegory's] Fictions" (*The Works of Spenser*, ed. Hughes, vol. I, xxxvi–xl). Cf. John Dennis: "A Dramatick Fable is a Discourse invented to form the Manners by Instructions disguised under the Allegory of an Action"; in *The Stage Defended, from Scripture, Reason, Experience, and the Common Sense of Mankind, for Two Thousand Years* (1726), 8.

107 Le Bossu, *Traité du poëme epique* (1693), 9–10: "L' Epopée est un discours inventé avec art, pour former les mœurs par des instructions déquisées sous les allégories d'une action importante."

108 *The Works of Spenser*, ed. Hughes, vol. I, xxxvi.

109 *The Works of Spenser*, ed. Hughes, vol. I, xlvii–li.

110 Hughes commended Addison and Steele for reviving allegorical writing and giving "an Idea ... of the Perfection to which this kind of writing is capable of being raised" (*The Works of Spenser*, ed. Hughes, vol. I, lvi). For allegories and dream-visions, see esp. the *Tatler* nos. 8, 48, 81, 97, 100, 102, 120, 123, 161, 194, and 237; and the *Spectator* nos. 3, 55, 63, 83, 159, 183, 225, 281, 301, 391, 392, 425, 455, 460, 463, 464, 499, 501, 511, 514, 524, 558, 587, 599, and 604. On allegory in the *Tatler*, Richmond P. Bond, *"The Tatler": The Making of a Literary Journal* (Cambridge, MA: Harvard University Press, 1971), 152–3.

111 In a similar survey of contemporary thought about allegory, Lock summarizes: "the taste and bent of the period [was] for short, self-contained, and internally consistent allegories whose purpose is not to conceal a meaning but to make a didactic point more pleasingly. This is the most typical use of allegory in early eighteenth-century literature"; Lock, *The Politics of "Gulliver's Travels,"* 96.

112 "Sed allegoria, quae est obscurior, aenigma dicitur; vitium meo quidem iudico, si quidem dicere dilucide virtus"; Quintilian, *Institutio Oratoria*, 8.6.5.2. *The Institutio Oratoria of Quintilian,* trans. H. E. Butler, 4 vols. Loeb Classical Library (Cambridge, MA: Harvard University Press, 1958), vol. III, 330–1.

113 *The Works of Spenser*, ed. Hughes, vol. I, liii and li.

114 Dryden, *Albion and Albanius*, preface, edition cited, 11. For other statements about the need for clarity in allegory, Richard Steele, *Tatler*, no. 194 (July 6, 1710); Joseph Addison, *Spectator*, no. 421 (July 3, 1712); Blackmore, preface to *Prince Arthur*. The author of the preface to the 1706 English translation of Traiano Boccalini's *De' ragguali di Parnaso* (1618) claimed that allegory was used to make morals and lessons clearer: "This way of conveying Truth by Allegory ... is observ'd to make more lively Impressions on the Reader than Reason in its Undress can do"; *Advices from Parnassus* (1706), iii.

115 *Cato Examin'd: or Animadversions on the Fable or Plot ... of Cato* (1713), 8, 16. Earlier he had stated, "Tragedy differs from History in this, the *Drama* consults not the Truth of what any one Person did say or do, but only the General Nature

of such *Qualities* of *Manners*, to produce such Words and Actions ... I therefore approve more of the Poet's rather inventing his own *Fable*; there being very few Historical Persons, that can be made *General*, and *Allegoric*" (at 8).

116 John Dennis, *Remarks on a Book Entitled, Prince Arthur, an Heroick Poem* (1696), 9. Henry Pemberton mentions, to dismiss, this universal view of allegorical names in *Observations on Poetry, Especially the Epic: Occasioned by the Late Poem upon Leonidas* (1738), 155.

117 Dennis, *The Stage Defended*, 7–8.

118 In Torquato Tasso, *Jerusalem Delivered*, trans. and ed. Ralph Nash (Detroit, MI: Wayne State University Press, 1987), 469–74.

119 "Sul Sentier della Gloria / Tu non devi arrestar' il Piè nel Corso"; I.i, pp. 4–5.

120 "Contaminata da' tuoi molli Amori"; III.iv, pp. 50–1.

121 John Arbuthnot, *The History of John Bull*, ed. Alan W. Bower and Robert A. Erickson (Oxford: Clarendon Press, 1976) (on how the allegorical narratives are a part of a program of political propaganda, xvii–xxii).

122 *True Briton*, nos. 15, 16, 20, and 55 (July 22 and 26, August 9, and December 9, 1723).

123 *Craftsman*, nos. 16, 61, and 299 (January 27, and September 2, 1727; March 25, 1732). On the *Craftsman*'s awareness of allegory as the safest form for political writing, see no. 75 (December 9, 1727). "The Allegory of the Tree of Corruption" was answered by the ministerial *British Journal*, no. 260 (September 16, 1727). Some other strict allegories in the *Craftsman* include a Persian letter containing an allegory on Great Britain (no. 150, May 17, 1729); and the Allegory of the Roches (no. 63, September 16, 1727), naming Knez (Prince) Menzikoff, but meaning Walpole, and explicated in no. 75 (December 9, 1727).

124 "The Vision of the Golden Rump" is an explication of a engraving; in *Common Sense*, nos. 7 and 8 (March 19 and 26, 1737). See Maynard Mack, *The Garden and the City: Retirement and Politics in the Later Poetry of Pope, 1731–1743* (University of Toronto Press, 1969), 143–9; Loftis, *Politics of Drama in Augustan England*, 139ff. Reproduced in Paul Langford, *Walpole and the Robinocracy*. The English Satirical Print, 1600–1832 (Cambridge: Chadwyck-Healey, 1986), no. 48; and Herbert M. Atherton, *Political Prints in the Age of Hogarth: A Study of the Ideographic Representation of Politics* (Oxford: Clarendon Press, 1974), plate 19.

125 On allegorical decorative painting in Britain, Edward Croft-Murray, *Decorative Painting in England, 1537–1837*, vol. I: *Early Tudor to Sir James Thornhill* (London: Country Life, 1962); and Jacob Simon, *English Baroque Sketches: The Painted Interior in the Age of Thornhill*, exhib. cat., Marble Hill House, Twickenham, May 1–July 7, 1974 (London: Greater London Council, 1974).

126 Known to those who had not traveled to France through Jean-Marc Nattier's engravings, *La Galerie du Palais du Luxembourg, peinte par Rubens, dessinée*

par les S. Nattier, et gravée par les plus illustres graveurs du temps (1710); and Moreau de Mautour, *Nouvelle Description de la Galerie du Palais du Luxembourg* (1704). On the allegorical program of the cycle, Susan Saward, *The Golden Age of Marie de' Medici* (Ann Arbor, MI: UMI Research Press, 1982) (on this panel in particular, 159–65); and Jacques Thuillier and Jacques Foucart, *Rubens' Life of Marie de' Medici*, trans. Robert E. Wolf (New York: Harry N. Abrams, 1970), no. 19, pp. 89–90.

127   *The Works of Spenser*, ed. Hughes, vol. I, xxxi.

128   On the ceiling and its iconographical program, Roy Strong, *Britannia Triumphans: Inigo Jones, Rubens, and Whitehall Palace*. Walter Neurath Memorial Lecture 1980 (London: Thames and Hudson, 1980); Per Palme, *Triumph of Peace: A Study of the Whitehall Banqueting House*. Figura no. 8 (1956) (Stockholm: Almquist & Wiksell, 1956), 225–62 and plates III–IX; David Howarth, *Images of Rule: Art and Politics in the English Renaissance, 1485–1649* (Berkeley: University of California Press, 1997), 35–8; and Croft-Murray, *Decorative Painting in England*, 34, 208–9, plates 58–62. The ceiling was known to contemporaries through an engraving by Simon Gribelin, "Ceiling of the Banqueting House at Whitehall," published in 1720.

129   The allegorical programs are explained in Allan Scott, *The Royal Naval College, Greenwich* (Watford: Woodmansterne Publications, 1987); and Croft-Murray, *Decorative Painting in England*, 71, 75–6, 268–9 (with plates).

130   Virgil L. Jones, "Methods of Satire in the Political Drama of the Restoration," *Journal of English and Germanic Philology* 21 (1922), 662–9, finds four types of content: (1) a parallel play casting ridicule, (2) typical character, (3) personation, and (4) satirical remarks. Hume, *The Development of English Drama*, 221, finds (1) personal references, (2) generalized warning, and (3) parallel play. Roper, "Drawing Parallels and Making Applications in Restoration Literature," distinguishes (1) parallels and (2) application. Owen, *Restoration Theatre and Crisis*, and "Interpreting the Politics of Restoration Drama," prefers to read politics in terms of themes and tropes. Hume, *Henry Fielding and the London Theatre*, distinguishes between topical allusion plays and application plays, and politicized plays and partisan plays. A variety of approaches to political meaning (moreso in terms of ideas and platforms than identification of persons and events) in Tudor drama are examined by David Bevington, *Tutor Drama and Politics: A Critical Approach to Topical Meaning* (Cambridge, MA: Harvard University Press, 1968), 1–27.

131   The following discussion draws on the important studies of Roper, "Drawing Parallels and Making Applications in Restoration Literature"; Wallace, "Dryden and History"; Wallace, "Examples Are Best Precepts"; Bloomfield, "Allegory as Interpretation" (on types of allegory); Maresca, "Personification vs. Allegory"; Lock, *The Politics of "Gulliver's Travels"*, Chapter 4: "Allegories and Allusions,"

89–122; Gunto, "Kicking the Emperor"; and William H. Youngren, "Generality, Science and Poetic Language in the Restoration," *ELH* 35 (1968), 158–87.

132 Wallace, "Dryden and History," 271–2, and Wallace, "Examples Are Best Precepts," 286.

133 Wallace, "Dryden and History," 265–7, 281. Recall how John Dennis said names in histories were meant to provide verisimilitude and that characters were to be taken as representing universal types.

134 Charles Rollin, *The Ancient History of the Egyptians, Carthaginians, Assyrians, Babylonians, Medes and Persians, Macedonians, and Greeks*, 13 vols. (1734–39), vol. IV, bk. 9, ch. 3, sec. 6; a translation of Rollin's *Histoire ancienne des Égyptiens, des Carthaginois, des Assyriens, des Babyloniens, des Mèdes, et des Perses, des Macédoniens, des Grecs*, 13 vols. (Paris, 1730).

135 Letter from Edward Barry, February 1, 1736/37, to the fifth Earl of Orrery; in *The Orrery Papers*, ed. the Countess of Cork and Orrery [E. C. Boyle], 2 vols. (London: Duckworth, 1903), vol. I, 194–5.

136 On Layer and the Atterbury Plot, G. V. Bennett, *The Tory Crisis in Church and State, 1688–1730: The Career of Francis Atterbury, Bishop of Rochester* (Oxford: Clarendon Press, 1975), esp. 223–75; Eveline Cruickshanks and Howard Erskine-Hill, *The Atterbury Plot* (Basingstoke: Palgrave Macmillan, 2004), 171–83; and Eveline Cruickshanks, "Lord North, Christopher Layer and the Atterbury Plot: 1720–23," in *The Jacobite Challenge*, ed. Eveline Cruickshanks and Jeremy Black (Edinburgh: John Donald, 1988), 92–106.

137 Probably *An Historical Narrative of the Tryals of Mr. George Kelly, and of Dr. Francis Atterbury; (late) Lord Bishop of Rochester* (1727).

138 Letter from Edward Barry, February 1, 1736/37, to the fifth Earl of Orrery; in *The Orrery Papers*, vol. I, 194–5.

139 Letter from Edward Barry, February 1, 1736/37, to the fifth Earl of Orrery; in *The Orrery Papers*, vol. I, 194–5.

140 The term is adapted from a use by Andrew Marvell; he remarked that "My Lord Shaftesbury and all his gang are sufficiently personated" in a play; quoted in Roper, "Drawing Parallels and Making Applications in Restoration Literature," 47. The more common term *personification* is inappropriate because rarely, if ever, are the operatic historical characters concretizations of abstractions, especially considering that the source librettos were written antecedent to, and without the current political figure in mind. On the need to avoid identifying allegory and personification, see Tuve, *Allegorical Imagery*, 3–55; Thomas E. Maresca, "Saying and Meaning: Allegory and the Indefinable," *Bulletin of Research in the Humanities* 83 (1980), 248–61; and Maresca, "Personification vs. Allegory."

141 "Instructions to Nicholas Nibble, Esq; for the Service of the good old Cause; or, the Art of writing Libels against the Government," *Weekly Register*, no. 67 (July 24, 1731). See also *The Art of Railing at Great Men: Being a Discourse upon Political Railers Ancient and Modern* (1723): "There is scarce a Character

of Antiquity that is remarkable for Pride, Avarice, Corruption, Ambition, or Domination (all Words of great Use to *Political Railers*) which has not been drawn forth in the blackest Colours, and by the Addition of Modern Incidents adapted to some of our Cotemporaries."

142 Nicholas Rowe, *Tamerlane, a Tragedy*, ed. Landon C. Burns, Jr. (Philadelphia: University of Pennsylvania Press, 1966), 6; and Loftis, *Politics of Drama in Augustan England*, 31–4.

143 J. Douglas Canfield, *Nicholas Rowe and Christian Tragedy* (Gainesville: University Presses of Florida, 1977), 46–9, 57. On the idealized and opposed characters of Tamerlane and Bajazet, Landon C. Burns, *Pity and Tears: The Tragedies of Nicholas Rowe* (Salzburg: Institut für Englishe Sprache und Literatur, 1974), 49–56.

144 Garth's "A Prologue Intended for Tamerlane" was widely reprinted; text from Pierre Danchin, ed., *The Prologues and Epilogues of the Eighteenth Century*. Part 1, vol. I (Nancy: Presses Universitaires de Nancy, 1990), 55.

145 *History of Timur-Bec, known by the Name of Tamerlaine the Great* (1723), dedication.

146 *Craftsman*, no. 455 (March 22, 1735).

147 Roper, "Drawing Parallels and Making Applications in Restoration Literature," 52. Hume distinguishes between textual or authorial meaning and the "susceptibility to application"; "The Politics of Opera," 42. Roper points out that presence of parallels implies authorial intent: "authors draw parallels, readers make application"; "Drawing Parallels and Making Applications in Restoration Literature," 52.

148 *True Briton*, no. 29 (September 9, 1723).

149 For other proposals for meaning and interpretation that invoke the interaction or convergence of multiple factors, see Irvin Ehrenpreis, *Literary Meaning and Augustan Values* (Charlottesville: University Press of Virginia, 1974), 39; Quentin Skinner, *Visions of Politics*, vol. I: *Regarding Method* (Cambridge University Press, 2002), 87; J. G. A. Pocock, "The Reconstruction of Discourse: Towards the Historiography of Political Thought," *Modern Language Notes* 96 (1961), 974; and Howard D. Weinbrot "Johnson's *London* and Juvenal's Third Satire: The Country as 'Ironic' Norm," *Modern Philology* 73(4) (May 1976, part 2), S56–S65. See also Lock's criteria for allegory, *The Politics of "Gulliver's Travels*," 89–122.

150 Fletcher, *Allegory*, 323. On "vision" allegories, see 348–50.

151 Despite the widely known (and misunderstood) intentional fallacy, intention is an essential component in understanding the meaning of verbal expressions; see John R. Searle, *Intentionality: An Essay in the Philosophy of Mind* (Cambridge University Press, 1983).

For some representative expositions of the intentionalist position, Hirsch, *Validity in Interpretation*; Hirsch, *The Aims of Interpretation* (University of Chicago Press, 1976); William Irwin, *Intentionalist Interpretation: A*

Philosophical Explanation and Defense (Westport, CT: Greenwood Press, 1999); and Stephen Knapp and Walter B. Michaels: "Against Theory," *Critical Inquiry* 8 (1982), 723–42 (and later replies to critics).

The principal argument against the intentionalist point of view is contained in the classic essay by W. K. Wimsatt and M. C. Beardsley, "The Intentionalist Fallacy," *Sewanee Review* 54 (1946), 468–88 (widely reprinted). The issues are explored in *On Literary Intention*, ed. and intro. David Newton-De Molina (Edinburgh University Press, 1976), and *Intention and Interpretation*, ed. Gary Iseminger (Philadelphia, PA: Temple University Press, 1992).

152 It is significant that when works with topical allegory, allusions, or parallels did appear in the seventeenth and eighteenth centuries, opportunistic publishers quickly produced keys to explicate them. Some of the best-known literary works provided with keys include Dryden's *Absalom and Achitophel* (issued with a key in 1708), Buckingham's play *The Rehearsal*, Samuel Garth's *The Dispensary* (1703), Jonathan Swift's *A Tale of a Tub* (1704), Joseph Addison's *Cato* (1713), John Arbuthnot's five *John Bull* pamphlets (1712), Alexander Pope's *The Rape of the Lock* (1712, 1714), Swift's *Gulliver's Travels* (1726), John Gay's *The Beggar's Opera* (1728), and Pope's *The Dunciad* (1728) and *Epistle to Burlington* (1733).

153 The supposed case of *Floridante* is discussed in Chapter 4.

154 For a clear statement, Ruth Smith, *Handel's Oratorios and Eighteenth-Century Thought* (Cambridge University Press, 1995), 187: "[Works] can have a single meaning or they can have two or more, aimed at different sectors of the audience, possibly one generally acceptable and overt, the other a minority view, 'coded' and disownable."

155 Harris, *Handel as Orpheus* (Sulla as Marlborough or Elector Georg Ludwig); Aspden, "Ariadne's Clew," 737, 757 (Theseus as William III or IV); and Duncan Chisholm, "New Sources for the Libretto of Handel's *Joseph*," in *Handel: Tercentenary Collection*, ed. Stanley Sadie and Anthony Hicks (Ann Arbor, MI: UMI Research Press, 1987), 182–208 (Joseph as George II, Frederick, Prince of Wales, or Robert Walpole). Harris' commitment to the strongly relativistic version of the doctrine is shown when she chides Ruth Smith for criticizing competing interpretations of a work; review of Smith, in *Journal of Modern History* 69 (1997), 340.

On the need to adjudicate interpretations, Frank Kermode, "Can We Say Absolutely Anything We Like?" and "Institutional Control of Interpretation," in *The Art of Telling: Essays on Fiction* (Cambridge, MA: Harvard University Press, 1983), 156–84; Christopher Butler, "On the Rivalry of Norms for Interpretation," *New Literary History* 20 (1988), 125–6; Hirsch, *Validity in Interpretation*, 24–67; and M. H. Abrams, *Doing Things with Texts: Essays in Criticism and Critical Theory* (New York: W. W. Norton, 1989), 126–7, 253–5.

156 See esp. Ehrenpreis, *Literary Meaning and Augustan Values*; Ehrenpreis, "Meaning: Implicit and Explicit," in *New Approaches to Eighteenth-Century Literature: Selected Papers from the English Institute*, ed. Phillip Harth (New

York: Columbia University Press, 1974), 117–55; and Ehrenpreis, *Acts of Implication: Suggestion and Covert Meaning in the Works of Dryden, Swift, Pope, and Austen* (Berkeley: University of California Press, 1980), 1–19.

157 On the plausibility of attempting such historical understanding, Hume, *Reconstructing Contexts*; Hume, "Texts Within Contexts"; Hume, "The Aims and Limits of Historical Scholarship"; John R. Searle, "Rationality and Realism, What Is At Stake?" *Daedalus* 122(4) (Fall 1993), 55–83; and Hirsch, *The Aims of Interpretation*, Chapters 5 and 9. Hume, *Reconstructing Contexts*, 9–10, defines the approach as Archaeo-Historicism, which is the attempt to "reconstruct specific contexts that permit the present-day interpreter to make sense of the cultural artefacts of the past and the conditions in which they were produced … [It] is devoted to the reconstruction of historical events and viewpoint from primary materials."

158 These examples are exceptions to the usual eighteenth-century practice that most critical comment on opera is about genre, not individual works.

159 John Dennis defended drama from Law's charges in *The Stage Defended*; see also *Law Outlaw'd: or, A Short Reply to Mr. Law's Long Declamation Against the Stage* (1726).

160 William Law, *The Absolute Unlawfulness of the Stage-Entertainment Fully Demonstrated* (1726), 23. Lewis Theobald's masque *Apollo and Daphne; or the Burgomaster Trick'd* played almost nightly from mid January through February 1726.

161 Quoted from the word book of the masque.

162 Law, *The Absolute Unlawfulness of the Stage-Entertainment*, 23.

163 "On Operas, and the Force of Music," *British Journal; or, The Traveller*, no. 17 (January 9, 1731).

164 "On Operas, and the Force of Music."

165 Unlike for Addison's later *Cato*, there are no commentaries or keys from 1707 suggesting contemporaries saw topical allegories or allusions in *Rosamond*. Brean Hammond, "Addison's Opera *Rosamond*: Britishness in the Early Eighteenth Century," *ELH* 73 (2006), 601–29, sees the opera "readable" as celebrating the recent union with Scotland. Luis R. Gamez, "Mocking the Meat It Feeds On: Representing Sarah Churchill's Hystericks in Addison's *Rosamond*," *Comparative Drama* 29 (1995), 270–85, sees the opera as allegorizing the Duchess of Marlborough's jealousy of her husband. Hammond (629, n. 64) rightly questions why "making the Duchess look ridiculous would serve any purpose." Hammond's reading is itself questioned in the *Scriblerian* 41 (2008), 5.

166 *Universal Spectator*, no. 352 (July 5, 1735).

167 *Universal Spectator*, no. 352 (July 5, 1735).

168 *Universal Spectator*, no. 352 (July 5, 1735).

169 Lowell Lindgren, "*Camilla* and *The Beggar's Opera*," *Philological Quarterly* 59 (1980), 44–61.

170 *Spectator*, no. 22 (March 26, 1711), Bond edn., vol. 1, 96.

171 *London Journal*, no. 382 (November 26, 1726). This issue prints the new prologue spoken at the revival, which makes no mention of politics.

172 Little is known of this Pearson, except that he sang treble at Cannons in 1717–21.

173 *Mist's Weekly Journal*, no. 87, December 17, 1726.

174 This phrase may be a joke. Mr. Pearson was a tenor; perhaps were he a castrato ("cut out"), he could sing more heroic roles (but of course could not then be married).

175 *Common Sense*, no. 46, December 17, 1737.

3 Politics in the Royal Academy of Music

1 On the relations of the Hanoverian electorate and the ministry of Harley and St. John, Edward Gregg, *The Protestant Succession in International Politics, 1710–1716* (New York: Garland Publishing, 1986).

2 Swift's note to "Verses on the Death of Dr Swift, D.S.P.D."; in *Jonathan Swift: The Complete Poems*, ed. Pat Rogers (New Haven, CT: Yale University Press, 1983), 855.

3 Henry St. John, Viscount Bolingbroke, September 1 or 2, 1714, to Bishop Atterbury; in James Macpherson, *Original Papers: Containing the Secret History of Great Britain*, 2 vols. (1775), vol. II, 651.

4 Linda Colley, *In Defiance of Oligarchy: The Tory Party, 1714–60* (Cambridge University Press, 1982), 21–3.

5 *Journals of the House of Commons* 18 (1714–1718), 14.

6 J. H. Plumb, *The Growth of Political Stability in England, 1675–1725* (London: Macmillan, 1967), 161.

7 Frank McLynn, *The Jacobites* (London: Routledge & Kegan Paul, 1985); and Bruce Lenman, *The Jacobite Risings in Britain, 1689–1746* (London: Eyre Methuen, 1980).

8 Donald Burrows and Robert D. Hume, "George I, the Haymarket Opera Company and Handel's *Water Music*," *Early Music* 19 (1991), 323–44.

9 On the abortive attempts to mount operas for the 1718–1719 season, Lowell Lindgren, "La carriera di Gaetano Berenstadt, contralto evirato (*c.*1690–1735)," *Rivista Italiana di Musicologia* 19 (1984), 36–112.

10 Elizabeth Gibson, *The Royal Academy of Music, 1719–1728: The Institution and Its Directors* (New York: Garland Publishing, 1989), 7–9; Gibson, "The Royal Academy of Music (1719–28) and its Directors," in *Handel Tercentenary Collection*, ed. Stanley Sadie and Anthony Hicks (Ann Arbor, MI: UMI Research Press, 1987), 139–40; Donald Burrows, *Handel* (New York: Schirmer, 1994), 106–7; and Burrows, *Handel and the English Chapel Royal* (Oxford University Press, 2005), 143–4, 167–9.

11 On the schism and royal feud, John M. Beattie, *The English Court in the Reign of George I* (Cambridge University Press, 1967), 225–40, 262–76; Basil Williams,

Stanhope: A Study in Eighteenth-Century War and Diplomacy (Oxford: Clarendon Press, 1932), 230–53, 266–7, 423–5; Ragnhild Hatton, *George I: Elector and King* (Cambridge, MA: Harvard University Press, 1978), 193–210, 244–6; W. A. Speck, "The Whig Schism Under George I," *Huntington Library Quarterly* 40 (1977), 171–9; and Jeremy Black, "Parliament and the Political and Diplomatic Crisis of 1717–18," *Parliamentary History* 3 (1984), 77–101. A principal primary source is *Diary of Mary Countess Cowper, Lady of the Bedchamber to the Princess of Wales*, ed. Spencer Cowper, 2nd edn. (London: John Murray, 1865).

12 Attacking Walpole and Townshend as dividers are Matthew Tindal, *The Defection Consider'd, and the Designs of Those, Who Divided the Friends of the Government* (1717); *An Answer to the Character & Conduct of R— W—, Esq; with an Exact Account of His Popularity* (1717); *The History of the Rise and Fall of Count Hotspur, with That of His Brother-in-Law, Colonel Headstrong* (1717); *An Epistle to R— W—, Esq; Occasion'd by a Pamphlet, Entitul'd, The Defection Consider'd* (1718); and *The Defection Farther Consider'd, Wherein the Resigners, As Some Would Have Them Sti'd, Are Really Deserters* (1718).

Defending Walpole and Townshend are *The Character & Conduct of R— W—, Esq; with an Exact Account of His Popularity* (1717); *An Impartial Enquiry into the Conduct of the Right Honourable Charles Lord Viscout T—* (1717); *Some Persons Vindicated against the Author of the Defection, &c.* (1718); *The Defection Detected; or, Faults Laid on the Right Side* (1718); and George Sewell, *The Resigners Vindicated; or, the Defection Re-Considered* [in two parts] (1718).

13 Burrows and Hume, "George I, the Haymarket Opera Company, and Handel's *Water Music*," 334.

14 Edward Raymond Taylor, "The Peerage Bill of 1719," *English Historical Review* 28 (1913), 243–59.

15 Judith Milhous and Robert D. Hume, "Heidegger and the Management of the Haymarket Opera, 1713–17," *Early Music* 27 (1999), 74; and David Hunter, "Bragging on *Rinaldo*: Ten Ways Writers have Trumpeted Handel's Coming to Britain," *Göttinger Händel-Beiträge* 10 (2004), 113–31.

16 Milhous and Hume, "Heidegger and the Management of the Haymarket Opera," 82.

17 Judith Milhous and Robert D. Hume, "The Charter for the Royal Academy of Music," *Music and Letters* 67 (1986), 50–8; Milhous and Hume, "New Light on Handel and The Royal Academy of Music in 1720," *Theatre Journal* 35 (1983), 149–67; and Gibson, *The Royal Academy of Music*.

18 Handel, letter of February 20, 1719, to his brother Michael Dietrich Michaëlsen: "des affaires indispensables et d'ou, j'ose dire, mà fortune depend"; in *The Letters and Writings of George Frideric Handel*, ed. Erich H. Müller (London: Cassell, 1935), 5.

19 O. E. Deutsch, *Handel: A Documentary Biography* (New York: W. W. Norton, 1955), 89–90.

20 The charter is printed and other aspects of the organization of the Academy are discussed in Milhous and Hume, "The Charter for the Royal Academy of Music." Most importantly, the charter reveals that the king proposed to settle £1,000 annually upon the Academy for the duration of its twenty-one-year charter, and details the Academy's clumsy and ill-conceived organization.

21 Abraham Rees, *The Cyclopædia; or, Universal Dictionary of Arts, Sciences, and Literature*, 39 vols. (1819), vol. IV, *s.v.* Bononcini. Burney cites seventy-three shareholders and the sum of £50,000, which is implausible. The amount was likely closer to £15,000.

22 A precise calendar of performances is not possible because newspapers are lacking for some days.

23 On the timing of *Radamisto*, see Donald Burrows' timeline in *Handel and the English Chapel Royal*, 167–70. With their Handel-centric focus, scholars have likely overstated the significance of the royal attendance at the premiere of *Radamisto*, which, after five performances of *Numitore*, was next in the queue for performance. No contemporary source makes any special mention of the significance of the choice of Handel's opera; the *Daily Post*, no. 180 (April 29, 1720), merely noted "On Monday [*recte:* Wednesday] Night his Majesty and the Prince were together at the Opera in the Hay-Market."

24 Reprinted in Milhous and Hume, "New Light on Handel," 165–7.

25 *The Cyclopædia*, vol. IV, *s.v.* Bononcini. Burney wanted to give a facsimile of each signature. The present location of the original deed and covenant Burney possessed is not known.

26 Thomas McGeary, "Farinelli's Progress to Albion: The Recruitment and Reception of Opera's 'Blazing Star,'" *British Journal for Eighteenth-Century Studies* 28 (2005), 339–61.

27 R. O. Bucholz, *The Augustan Court: Queen Anne and the Decline of Court Culture* (Stanford University Press, 1993), 1–35, 202–51; and Hannah Smith, *Georgian Monarchy: Politics and Culture, 1714–1760* (Cambridge University Press, 2006), 64–81.

28 See Smith, *Georgian Monarchy*, 81: "The political climate of early eighteenth-century Britain was, it would seem, not one where a concerted official programme for harnessing the arts to augment the Crown could flourish"; see also, 59–61, 123.

29 On types of Continental opera sponsorship, William C. Holmes, *Opera Observed: Views of a Florentine Impresario in the Early Eighteenth Century* (University of Chicago Press, 1993), 8–13; Lorenzo Bianconi, *Music in the Seventeenth Century*, trans. David Bryant (Cambridge University Press, 1987), esp. 161–263; and Lorenzo Bianconi and Thomas Walker, "Production, Consumption and Political Function of Seventeenth-Century Italian Opera," *Early Music History* 4 (1985), 209–96.

30 Horace, *Ars Poetica*, 208–11.

31 Charles B. Realey, *The Early Opposition to Sir Robert Walpole, 1720–1727* (Lawrence: University of Kansas, 1931), 1–67; and Plumb, *The Growth of Political Stability in England*.

32 John Carswell, *The South Sea Bubble*, rev. edn. (London: Alan Sutton, 1993); and P. G. M. Dickson, *The Financial Revolution in England: A Study in the Development of Public Credit, 1688–1756* (London: Macmillan, 1967), 90–198.

33 Carswell, *The South Sea Bubble*, 111–13, 118–19.

34 Diary of Arthur Onslow; in Historical Manuscripts Commission, *The Manuscripts of the Earl of Buckinghamshire* [etc.] (London: Her Majesty's Stationery Office, 1895), 504.

35 Eveline Cruickshanks and Howard Erskine-Hill, *The Atterbury Plot* (Basingstoke: Palgrave Macmillan, 2004); G. V. Bennett, *The Tory Crisis in Church and State, 1688–1730: The Career of Francis Atterbury, Bishop of Rochester* (Oxford: Clarendon Press, 1975), esp. 223–75; Paul S. Fritz, *The English Ministers and Jacobitism between the Rebellions of 1715 and 1745* (University of Toronto Press, 1975), 67–98; and Eveline Cruickshanks, "Lord North, Christopher Layer and the Atterbury Plot: 1720–23", in *The Jacobite Challenge*, ed. Eveline Cruickshanks and Jeremy Black (Edinburgh: John Donald, 1988), 92–106.

36 On Walpole's paranoia of Jacobites, G. V. Bennett, "Jacobitism and the Rise of Walpole", in *Historical Perspectives: Studies in English Thought and Society in Honour of J. H. Plumb*, ed. Neil McKendrick (London: Europa, 1974), 70–92.

37 On Walpole's exploitation of Jacobitism, Bennett, "Jacobitism and the Rise of Walpole."

38 The essays appeared from November 5, 1720, to July 27, 1723. They were collected and reprinted as *Cato's Letters*.

39 Clyve Jones, "The New Opposition in the House of Lords, 1720–3," *Historical Journal* 36 (1993), 309–29; and Jones, "William, First Earl Cowper, Country Whiggery, and the Leadership of the Opposition in the House of Lords, 1720–1723," in *Lords of Parliament: Studies, 1714–1914*, ed. R. W. Davis (Stanford University Press, 1995), 29–43.

40 The *True Briton* ran from June 3, 1723, to February 17, 1724. Wharton at first supported Cowper's new opposition in the Lords in 1720–21, but went over to the ministry between December 1721 and May 1723, and then opposed the ministry over the Atterbury affair. On government attempts to suppress the *True Briton* and other opposition papers, Hanson, *Government and the Press*, 36–83.

41 Plumb, *The Growth of Political Stability in England*, 158.

42 Charles Burney, "Sketch of the Life of Handel," in *An Account of the Musical Performances in Westminster-Abbey* (1785), 16.

43 Hans Dieter Clausen, "Der Einfluß der Komponisten auf die Librettowahl der Royal Academy of Music (1720–1729)," in *Zur Dramaturgie der Barockoper: Bericht über die Symposien der Internationalen Händel-Akademie Karlsruhe 1992 und 1993*, ed. Hans Joachim Marx (Laabe: Laaber-Verlag, 1994), 55–72, at 60:

"da die Oper nur in *einem* Theater vertreten war, spielte sich der Parteienstreit bei ihr innerhalb des Directoriums ab."

44 Clausen, "Der Einfluß der Komponisten," 60.

45 Deutsch, *Handel*, 148.

46 Jane Clark, "The Stuart Presence at the Opera in Rome," in *The Stuart Court in Rome: The Legacy of Exile*, ed. Edward Corp (Aldershot: Ashgate, 2003), 85–93, at 86. Clark uses this premise as the basis to find Jacobite political messages in opera plots.

47 Ellen T. Harris, "With Eyes on the East and Ears in the West: Handel's Orientalist Operas," *Journal of Interdisciplinary History* 36 (2006), 419–43, at 429; but see the Whig support for Bononcini indicated elsewhere.

48 Ellen T. Harris, ed., *The Librettos of Handel's Operas*, 13 vols. (New York: Garland, 1989), vol. III, xiv.

49 Riva, March 21, 1721, to Steffani; as transcribed and translated in Lowell Lindgren and Colin Timms, "The Correspondence of Agostino Steffani and Giuseppe Riva, 1720–1728, and Related Correspondence with J. P. F. von Schönborn and S. B. Pallavicini," *Royal Musical Association Research Chronicle* 36 (2003), letter no. 7, pp. 55–8: "Si è introdotto lo spirito maligno de' partiti, chè tanto naturale al genio inglese, nell'accademia di musica, in modocché al presente le cose vanno allo tranverso e vi è tutt'altro che armonia."

50 Riva, May 2, 1721, to Steffani; in Lindgren and Timms, "Correspondence of Steffani and Riva," letter no. 10, pp. 60–1: "L'Accademia di Musica è riuscita una specie di Comp[agni]a del Sud. Tutto andava a maraviglia nel principio, ma nel progresso vi è entrato il diavolo, che ha messo la discordia tra' cantori e tra i sottoscriventi e direttori. Si sono cominciate insolenza da una parte e dall'altra, secondo che ogni uno era portato dalla pazza passione." See also the mentions of dissention in the Academy in letters N, 11–13, 20, 28, and 47.

51 Von Fabrice, January 15, 1723, to Graf Flemming; in J. O. Opel, *Mitteilungen zur Geschichte der Familie des Tonkünstlers Händel*. Neue Mitteilungen aus dem Gebiet historisch-antiquarischer Forschungen 27 (Halle, 1889), printed in *Händel-Handbuch*, vol. IV, 113: *Dokumente zu Leben und Schaffen* (Kassel: Bärenreiter, 1985): "Il y a deux Factions, les uns pour Hendell et les autres pour Bononcini, les uns pour Cenesino, et les autres pour la Cossuna, qui sont aussy animés que les Whigs et Torys l'un contre l'autre, et qui partagent les Directeurs meme quelque fois."

52 Von Fabrice, March 10, 1724, to Graf Flemming; in Opel, *Mitteilungen*, printed in *Händel-Handbuch*, vol. IV, 122: "Les demelés entre les Directeurs et les party que tout le monde prend entre les Chanteurs et les Compositeurs donnent souvent des Scenes fort divertissantes au public."

53 *Weekly Journal: or Saturday's Post*, no. 273 (January 18, 1724). The mention of stock rising is a joke; the Academy shares are not known to have been traded.

54 Mary Delany, November 25, 1727, to Ann Granville; in Deutsch, *Handel*, 218.

55 *London Journal*, no. 306 (June 5, 1725).

56 Lists printed in Gibson, *The Royal Academy of Music*, 319–20, 346–7, and Gisbon, "The Royal Academy of Music (1719–28) and Its Directors."

57 *The History of Parliament. The House of Commons, 1715–1754*, ed. Romney Sedgwick, 2 vols. (New York: Oxford University Press, 1970), vol. I, 34.

58 Based on the party affiliations given in Clyve Jones, "The Impeachment of the Earl of Oxford and the Whig Schism of 1717: Four New Lists," *Bulletin of the Institute of Historical Research* 55 (1982), 66–87.

59 Colley, *In Defiance of Oligarchy*, 102–4.

60 Lowell Lindgren, "A Bibliographic Scrutiny of Dramatic Works Set by Giovanni and His Brother Antonio Maria Bononcini" (Ph.D. dissertation, Harvard University, 1972), 281–97; and Lindgren, "The Three Great Noises 'Fatal to the Interests of Bononcini,'" *Musical Quarterly* 61 (1975), 560–83. Lindgren is followed by, among others, Clausen, "Der Einfluß der Komponisten"; Winton Dean and J. Merrill Knapp, *Handel's Operas, 1704–1726*, rev. edn. (Oxford: Clarendon Press, 1995), 314; and Gibson, *The Royal Academy of Music*, 166–72, who extensively reproduces Lindgren's argument and documentation.

61 Lowell Lindgren, "Parisian Patronage of Performers from the Royal Academy of Music (1719–28)," *Music and Letters* 58 (1977), 4–28, at 14.

62 Clausen, "Der Einfluß der Komponisten," 60: "Letzlich scheint die Aufdeckung einer Rebellion zugunsten des katholischen Kronprätendenten der Stuart-Linie zu einer Schwächung der antigeorgischen Fraktion im Direktorium der Akademie und zur Entlassung Rollis und Bononcinis geführt zu haben."

63 Colley, *In Defiance of Oligarchy*, 204–38, has shown most Tories were not Jacobites and were by then Hanoverian Tories.

64 *Post Boy*, no. 5152 (July 28–31, 1722).

65 *Post Boy*, no. 5153 (July 31 to August 2, 1722).

66 Lindgren, "Bibliographic Scrutiny," 288; see also 287: "Had he [Atterbury] not planned and officiated at this funeral as Dean of Westminster, Giovanni Bononcini would in all probability not have been commissioned to write the anthem."

67 Atterbury, July 30 or August 3, 1722, to Alexander Pope; *The Correspondence of Alexander Pope*, ed. George Sherburn, 5 vols. (Oxford: Clarendon, 1956), vol. II, 129. See also Bennett, *The Tory Crisis in Church and State*, 255.

68 Frances Harris, *A Passion for Government: The Life of Sarah, Duchess of Marlborough* (Oxford: Clarendon Press, 1991), 244–5 (who notes the younger duchess' persistent attendance at the rehearsals).

   In 1896, John Wade had a search conducted of the chapter books at Westminster Abbey to ascertain who paid the charges of the funeral, but he reported "no evidence appears to prove by whom they were paid"; see William Coxe, *Memoirs of the Duke of Marlborough*, ed. John Wade, 3 vols. (London: George Bell, 1896), vol. III, 425 n. Wade cites other sources to the effect that the dowager duchess bore the charges. According to Thomas Lediard, *The Life of John, Duke of Marlborough*, 2nd edn. (1743), vol. II, 471, despite George I's offer to defray the funeral expenses, the duchess undertook all the preparations herself.

69 As transcribed in Lindgren, "Bibliographic Scrutiny," 282–3: "Giovan Bononcino … è stato scelto dal Re, e dalle due Duchesse, Madre [Sarah] e Figlia [Henrietta], a comporre la Musica in questa grande occasione."

70 Sidney, Earl of Godolphin, July 22, 1723, to the dowager Duchess of Marlborough; British Library. Blenheim Papers, v. 336, Add. MS 61,436, f. 58. A truncated and slightly different transcription is given in Lindgren, "Bibliographic Scrutiny," 286.

71 John Hawkins, *A General History of the Science and Practice of Music*, 5 vols. 1776 (1853 edn., reprint, New York: Dover, 1963), vol. II, 861. See also the Earl of Bristol's report of those invited to attend the rehearsal of the anthem; *Letter-Books of John Hervey, First Earl of Bristol*, ed. S. H. A. H., 3 vols. (Wells: Ernest Jackson, 1894), vol. II, 235.

72 Additional names to those in the printed subscription list are noted in Lindgren, "Bibliographical Scrutiny," 273.

73 W. A. Speck, "Politicians, Peers, and Publication by Subscription, 1700–1750," in *Books and Their Readers in Eighteenth-Century England*, ed. Isabel Rivers (Leicester University Press, 1982), 47–68, at 55.

74 *The Complete Letters of Lady Mary Wortley Montagu*, ed. Robert Halsband, 3 vols. (Oxford: Clarendon, 1965–67), vol. II, 13 and 52.

75 *The Diary of John Hervey, First Earl of Bristol. With Extracts from his Book of Expenses, 1688 to 1742*, ed. S. H. A. H. (Wells: Ernest Jackson, 1894), 158.

76 David Hunter, "Royal Patronage of Handel in Britain: The Rewards of Pensions and Office," in *Handel Studies: A Gedenkschrift for Howard Serwer*, ed. Richard G. King (Hillsdale, NY: Pendragon, 2009), 127–53, at 148, n. 68.

77 Pope, letter of January 27, 1722, to the Duchess of Buckingham; in Pope, *Correspondence*, vol. II, 99.

78 Lindgren, "Bibliographic Scrutiny," 286–96.

79 *British Journal*, no. 1 (September 22, 1722).

80 Pope, letter of September 22 [1722], to the Earl of Egmont; in Pope, *Correspondence*, vol. II, 135.

81 Earl of Egmont, letter of September 25 [1722], to Pope; in Pope, *Correspondence*, vol. II, 136. The bass singer Giuseppe Maria Boschi arrived in London in November 1720.

82 Performing forces from a word book for a performance of January 10, 1723; in Pope, *Correspondence*, vol. II, 135, n. 2.

83 *London Journal*, no. 181 (January 12, 1723).

84 Lindgren concedes the "reason is certainly plausible" but casts doubt on its accuracy because of factual errors elsewhere in the newspaper account of the rehearsals at Buckingham House; "Bibliographic Scrutiny," 292. It might also be noted that, back in September 1722, had the Royal Academy been suspicious of Bononcini's Jacobite connections with the Duchess of Buckingham, they would not have allowed use of their instrumental musicians in rehearsals continuing into January 1723.

85 Countess of Bristol, letter from Richmond, October 5, 1722, to the Earl of Bristol. Quoted here from the original letter copybook, Suffolk Record Office, Bury St. Edmunds, 941/46/11, 472–3. Lindgren quoted from the letter's reprint in *Letter-Books of John Hervey*, vol. II, 235.

86 Lindgren quotes a passage from Rolli's introduction to his translation of Richard Steele's *Conscious Lovers* indicating Bononcini and Rolli received a one-quarter reduction in their annual salary, and suggests Bononcini may have requested a benefit to compensate; Lindgren, "Bibliographic Scrutinty," 298.

87 Anastasia Robinson, letter of September or October 1722, to Giuseppe Riva; in Lindgren, "Parisian Patronage," 14, n. 26.

88 Lindgren, "Bibliographic Scrutiny," 297.

89 Anastasia Robinson, letter of September or October 1722, to Giuseppe Riva; in Lindgren, "Parisian Patronage," 14, n. 26.

90 Riva, letter of August 26, 1721, from London, to Steffani; as transcribed and translated in Lindgren and Timms, *Correspondence of Steffani and Riva*, letter no. 17, pp. 70–1: "Le cose dell'Accademia Musicale sono in sconcerto. Non hanno ancor finito di pagare i loro debiti della stagione. Oh che teste sono questi inglesi! Oh, e poi si lamentano che sono granellati da' forestiere! Se lo meritano, perché non hanno costanza ne loro impegni, e chi conosce la loro natura vede che bisogna prenderli al volo."

91 John, Lord Hervey, letter of June 14, 1731, to Stephen Fox; British Library. Holland House Papers, Add. MS 51,345, f. 33v.

92 The Earl of Egmont, characterizing Bononcini as "insolent" and "proud," recorded how the duchess demurred at paying for instrumentalists hired by Bononcini for her concerts (even though he was receiving £500 a year to direct her music); Bononcini took offense and left her employ. See Historical Manuscripts Commission, *Manuscripts of the Earl of Egmont. Diary of Viscount Percival afterwards First Earl of Egmont.* 3 vols. (London: His Majesty's Stationery Office, 1920–23), vol. I, 201–2 (cited as Egmont, *Diary*). Hawkins called Bononcini "a man of haughty and imperious temper"; Hawkins, *A General History of the Science and Practice of Music,* vol. II, 861.

93 Colin Haydon, *Anti-Catholicism in Eighteenth-Century England, c. 1714–80: A Political and Social Study* (Manchester University Press, 1993), 48, 87–90.

94 Reinhard Strohm, "Handel and his Italian Opera Texts," in *Essays on Handel and Italian Opera* (Cambridge University Press, 1985), 34–79, at 45.

95 On Walpole as divider of the Whig Party, see note 12 above.

96 "[cui suggetto] è il Nascimento della Romana Libertà: di quella Libertà che discacciata dalla sua sventurata gran Patria … trovato al fine, sicuro grande e glorioso Asilo ne' felici Regni della Maestà Vostra: Felicissimi Regni! poichè d'affatto diversa Condizione da tutti gli altri; godono veramente la Romana Libertà." I thank Carlo Vitali for assistance with this translation.

97 British Library. Portland Manuscripts, Add. MS 70415, f. 448r. The passage was first noticed by J. R. Clemens, who paraphrased Stratford's letter in "Handel and Carey," *The Sackbut* 11 (1930–31), 157–61, at 157.

98 Harris, "With Eyes on the East," 434.

99 Gibson, *The Royal Academy of Music*, 155.

100 Burrows, *Handel*, 110.

101 Quintilian, *Institutio Oratoria*, 5.10.95 and 5.14.14; in *The Institutio Oratoria of Quintilian*, trans. H. E. Butler, 4 vols. Loeb Classical Library (Cambridge, MA: Harvard University Press, 1958).

102 Gibson, *The Royal Academy of Music*, 155.

103 Harris, "With Eyes on the East," 434.

104 Konrad Sasse, "Die Texte der Londoner Opern Händels in ihren gesellschaftlichen Beziehungen." *Wissenschaftliche Zeitschrift der Martin-Luther-Universität Halle-Wittenberg*. Gesellschafts- und Sprachwissenschaftliche Reihe 4(5) (1955), 632: "spielten gewisse politische Strömungen hier noch eine Rolle."

105 Sasse, "Die Texte der Londoner Opern Händels": "Das neue Ministerium unter Walpole stand zwar wieder unter der Führung der Whigs, also der gleichen Partei, wie es vor der Regierung Bolingbrokes unter Leitung des Herzogs von Marlborough auch gestanden hatte, der seinerzeit unter ehrenrührigen Anschuldigungen von der Königin Anna entlassen worden war trotz seiner großen Verdienste als Feldherr im Spanischen Erbfolgekrieg" (at 632). "Dieses neue whigistische Ministerium unter Walpole verfolgte jedoch eine andere Politik als das alte unter Marlborough, denn dieser war ein Erzgegner Frankreichs gewesen und jener vertrat eine Verhandlungspolitik auch in diesem Falle" (at 632). "Bei der Parallelisierung des in Ungnade gefallenen Prinzen Floridante und des entlassenen Herzogs Marlborough findet neben der Übereinstimmung der erworbenen Kriegsverdienste auch das in der Oper angedeutete Gefahrenmoment für den König sein Gegenstück: Eine Verhandlungspolitik mit Frankreich, die der Entlassung des Herzogs gefolgt war, konnte dessen Regierung nicht auf die Dauer soweit im Schach halten, daß sie nicht – wie schon einmal 1708 – eine Erhebung der Stuarts noch einmal begünstigen würde. In der Tat sollte es 1744 wirklich dazu kommen" (at 632).

106 Frances Harris, "Parliament and Blenheim Palace: The House of Lords Appeal of 1721," *Parliamentary History* 8 (1989), 43–62.

107 Harris, *A Passion for Government*, 210–42.

108 To make the opera be opposing Walpole's pro-French policy seems to require assuming that, accepting the Floridant–Marlborough parallel, since a tyrant (Orontes) dismissed Floridant, who was later freed, the anti-French political position of Floridant's analog (Marlborough) is being endorsed. By this logic, Sasse avoids requiring Orontes to parallel George; as a result the opera would be taken as cautioning George that the pro-French posture of his ministry was dangerous and would lead to a Jacobite rising.

109 Strohm, "Handel and his Italian Opera Texts," 46; several names referring to the source libretto have been silently elided.

110 Pat Rogers, review in *British Journal of Eighteenth-Century Studies* 12 (1989), 246.

111 On the wisdom of a pro-French policy for George I, Jeremy Black, *British Foreign Policy in the Age of Walpole* (Edinburgh: John Donald, 1985), 2–4; Black, *The Collapse of the Anglo-French Alliance, 1727–1731* (Gloucester: Alan Sutton, 1987), 3–4; Black, *Natural and Necessary Enemies: Anglo-French Relations in the Eighteenth Century* (Athens: University of Georgia Press, 1986), 9–12; and Richard Lodge, "The Anglo-French Alliance 1716–31," in *Studies in Anglo-French History during the Eighteenth, Nineteenth, and Twentieth Centuries*, ed. Alfred Coville and Harold Temperley (Cambridge University Press, 1935), 3–18.

112 Strohm, "Handel and his Italian Opera Texts," 55. See also his expanded argument in "Darstellung, Aktion and Interesse in der höfischen Opernkunst," *Händel-Jahrbuch* 49 (2003), 13–26.

113 Strohm, "Handel and his Italian Opera Texts," 56.

114 On the coronation celebration and postponement, *Political State of Great Britain* 34 (June–December 1727), 171, 294, 329–51ff., and 446ff.; Smith, *Georgian Monarchy*, 100ff; César de Saussure, *A Foreign View of England in the Reigns of George I and George II: The Letters of Monsieur César de Saussure to His Family*, trans. Madame van Muyden (London: John Murray, 1902); and Andrew C. Thompson, *George II. King and Elector* (New Haven, CT: Yale University Press, 2011), 73–5.

115 *Daily Journal*, no. 2129 (November 9, 1727).

116 *The History of England Faithfully Extracted from Authentick Records*, 2nd edn., 2 vols. (1702), vol. I, 137; Laurence Echard, *The History of England. From the Entrance of Julius Cæsar and the Romans, To the End of the Reign of King James the First* (1707), 229 (this summary is repeated in Thomas Salmon, *A Review of the History of England*, 2 vols. [1724]).

117 Rapin de Thoyras, *The History of England*, trans. with notes by N. Tindal, 2nd edn., 2 vols. (1732), vol. I, 257. James Tyrrell, *The General History of England Both Ecclesiastical and Civil*, 2 vols. (1700), 571–3, concedes Richard's merits but notes his avarice and cruelty, and states "*England* suffer'd severely under his Government."

118 John, Baron Somers, *The True Secret History of the Lives and Reigns of all the Kings and Queens of England* (1702), 36–9.

119 *A Short History of Prime Ministers in Great Britain* (1733), 10.

120 John, Lord Hervey, *Ancient and Modern Liberty Stated and Compar'd* (1734), 9.

121 Winton Dean, *Handel's Operas, 1726–1741* (Woodbridge: Boydell & Brewer, 2006), 67. Dean, in general, agrees with Strohm in seeing the opera as linked to the British monarchy.

122 J. Merrill Knapp, "The Autograph of Handel's 'Riccardo Primo,'" in *Studies in Renaissance and Baroque Music in Honor of Arthur Mendel*, ed. Robert L. Marshall (Kassel: Bärenreiter, 1974), 331–58, at 334: "The link to George II was therefore a later fortuitous event and not one planned at the outset."

123 On the versions of the opera, Knapp, "The Autograph of Handel's 'Riccardo Primo'"; Dean, *Handel's Operas*, 65–79; *Riccardo Primo, Re d'Inghilterra*, ed. Terence Best (Kassel, Bärenreiter, 2005); and Suzana Ograjenšek, "From *Alessandro* (1726) to *Tolomeo* (1728): The Final Royal Academy Operas" (Ph.D. dissertation, University of Cambridge, 2005), 226–80. John Roberts has tentatively identified the librettist of the May version as Giovanni Sebastiano Brillani; "The Riddle of *Riccardo Primo*," *Händel-Jahrbuch* 58 (2012), 473–94.

124 For commendations of Richard's valor and clemency, II.vi, II.vii, II.ix, III.i, and III.vii; on the valor of Britons, II.vi, II.vii, and III.i. Ograjenšek, "From *Alessandro* (1726) to *Tolomeo* (1728)," 254 ff., argues the principal motive for revising the plot was not politics, but the absence of the singer Anna Dotti from the Royal Academy's roster, which required Richard to spend Act III fighting Isacus for Costanza.

125 Smith, *Georgian Monarchy*, 24–32.

126 I thank Carlo Vitali for assistance in this translation.

127 For sources of the trope, Aristotle, *Rhetoric*, 1.3 (1358a–1359a); and Pliny, *Epistulae*, 3.18.2–3. More recently, Francis Bacon's essay "Of Praise." On the Mirror for Princes topos, J. A. Burrow, *The Poetry of Praise* (Cambridge University Press, 2008), and a letter by Erasmus, quoted in J. H. Hexter, *The Vision of Politics on the Eve of the Reformation: More, Machiavelli and Seyssel* (New York: Basic Books, 1973), 13. For the Mirror for Princes, see note 31 in Chapter 8.

128 Harris, "With Eyes on the East," 419–21, 436. Harris' idea is endorsed by Katie Hawks, who uses it to provide an allegorical interpretation of *Riccardo primo* that sees it as related to the Gibraltar affair and a "reminder to the king of the strategic importance of small Mediterranean islands" and "to show support for oriental trade, for Gibraltar and for the British monarchy in the face of Franco–Spanish tyranny"; Hawks, "Looking for Richard: Why Handel Wrote *Riccardo Primo*," *Handel Institute Newsletter* 21(1) (Spring 2012), 5–7.

129 What needs to be shown is that for London the percentage of operas on oriental themes is significantly higher for the Royal Academy of Music than for other opera companies, periods, and court or theater repertories.

130 Harris mentions six directors who were notorious spendthrifts, gamblers, or avaricious as if, unpersuasively, this implied "the directors made their decisions largely on the basis of financial self-interest"; Harris, "With Eyes on the East," 421. Neither Sir John nor Sir Joseph Eyles were East India Company directors at the time when the Royal Academy operas began to feature Eastern locales. No documentation of any stock ownership or other financial investment in the oriental trade is given for any other directors.

131 Operas whose locations changed include *Floridante* (from Norway to Persia) and *Sosarme* (from Portugal to Asia minor).

132 Harris' essay, overall, does not effectively challenge Elizabeth Gibson's argument that aesthetic and ethical considerations, not financial ones,

were primary motivations that led patrons to become involved in the Royal Academy.

4   The opera house, allegory, and the political opposition

1 G. Malcolm to the Hon. John Molesworth, Summer 1724; in Manuscripts of M. L. S. Clements, in Historical Manuscripts Commission, *Reports of Manuscripts in Various Collections* (London: His Majesty's Stationery Office, 1913), vol. VIII, 379.

2 Charles B. Realey, *The Early Opposition to Sir Robert Walpole, 1720–1727* (Lawrence: University of Kansas, 1931), 105–85; Archibald S. Foord, *His Majesty's Opposition, 1714–1830* (Oxford: Clarendon Press, 1964). A retrospective history and justification of the opposition is given in John Perceval, Earl of Egmont, *Faction Detected, by the Evidence of Facts* (1743).

3 *The Parliamentary Diary of Sir Edward Knatchbull, 1722–1730*, ed. A. N. Newman, Camden Third Series 94 (1963), 43–5.

4 H. T. Dickinson, *Bolingbroke* (London: Constable, 1970), 173–80.

5 Nicholas Rogers, *Whigs and Cities: Popular Politics in the Age of Walpole and Pitt* (Oxford: Clarendon Press, 1989); and Alfred J. Henderson, *London and the National Government, 1721–1742: A Study of City Politics and the Walpole Administration* (Durham, NC: Duke University Press, 1945).

6 William Coxe, *Memoirs of Horatio, Lord Walpole* (1802), 152–4.

7 Isaac Kramnick, *Bolingbroke and His Circle: The Politics of Nostalgia in the Age of Walpole* (Cambridge, MA: Harvard University Press, 1968); Dickinson, *Bolingbroke*, 184–211; Foord, *His Majesty's Opposition*, 111–59; Quentin Skinner, "The Principles and Practice of Opposition: The Case of Bolingbroke versus Walpole," in *Historical Perspectives: Studies in English Thought and Society in Honour of J. H. Plumb*, ed. Neil McKendrick (London: Europa Publications, 1974), 93–128; and Simon Varey, *Henry St. John, Viscount Bolingbroke* (Boston, MA: Twayne, 1984).

8 *The Norfolk Gamester* (1734). The theater–ministry parallels are also employed in allegories of the players' revolt of 1733 (*St. James's Evening Post*, no. 2833 [November 24–27, 1733], and expanded in the *Grub-street Journal*, no. 211 [January 10, 1734]); and on Horatio Walpole's ambitions to join the ministry (*Craftsman*, no. 297 [March 11, 1732]).

9 Paul Langford, *Walpole and the Robinocracy. The English Satirical Print, 1600–1832* (Cambridge: Chadwyck-Healy, 1986); M. Dorothy George, *English Political Caricature to 1792: A Study of Opinion and Propaganda*, 2 vols. (Oxford: Clarendon Press, 1959), vol. I, 77–94; Herbert M. Atherton, *Political Prints in the Age of Hogarth: A Study of the Ideographic Representation of Politics* (Oxford: Clarendon Press, 1974), esp. 153–62, 167–72, 191–208, and plates 8–48; Mark Hallett, *The Spectacle of Difference: Graphic Satire in the Age of Hogarth* (New Haven, CT: Yale University Press, 1999), 131–67; Vincent Carretta, *The Snarling*

Muse: Verbal and Visual Political Satire from Pope to Churchill (Philadelphia: University of Pennsylvania Press, 1983), 20–61; and *Political Ballads Illustrating the Administration of Sir Robert Walpole*, ed. Milton Percival. Oxford Historical and Literary Studies 8 (1916).

10 *Lord Bolingbroke: Contributions to the "Craftsman,"* ed. and intro. Simon Varey (Oxford: Clarendon Press, 1982); and William Arnall, *The Case of Opposition Stated, Between the Craftsman and the People*, ed. and intro. Simon Varey (Lewisburg, PA: Bucknell University Press, 2003).

11 J. H. Plumb, *Sir Robert Walpole: The King's Minister* (London: Cresset Press, 1960), 141. Simon Varey cautions that although opposition political pamphlets certainly helped to stabilize public opinion, reassure the faithful, and lend authority to a political view, they never quite mobilized public opinion into action; see Arnall, *The Case of the Opposition Stated*, ed. Varey, xix.

12 See especially *Mist's Weekly Journal*, no. 34 (December 18, 1725), no. 80 (October 29, 1726), no. 87 (December 17, 1726), and no. 91 (January 14, 1727).

13 *Fog's Weekly Journal*, no. 311 (October 19, 1734), no. 335 (April 5, 1735), and no. 338 (April 26, 1735).

14 *A Further Report from the Committee … into the Conduct of Robert, Earl of Orford … the 30th of June, 1742* (1742), App. 13; also in *Journals of the House of Commons* 24 (1741–1745), 288–331. Laurence Hanson, *Government and the Press, 1695–1763* (London: Oxford University Press, 1936), 109, estimates that in 1731 the government spent £20,000 per annum on free mailing, printing, and publishing of newspapers.

15 Jonathan Swift, "To Mr. Gay on his being Steward to the Duke of Queensbury," line 4. On Walpole's patronage of writers, J. A. Downie, "Walpole, 'the Poet's Foe,'" in *Britain in the Age of Walpole*, ed. Jeremy Black (London: Macmillan, 1984), 171–88; and Tone S. Urstad, *Sir Robert Walpole's Poets: The Use of Literature as Pro-Government Propaganda, 1721–1742* (Newark: University of Delaware Press, 1999), 38–55. A retrospective defense of the Walpole ministry and its case against the opposition is given in *A Review of the Whole Political Conduct of a Late Eminent Patriot, and His Friends; for Twenty Years Last Past* (1743).

16 Hanson, *Government and the Press*, 67–70, 140.

17 Compiled by the ministerial writer William Arnall responding (presumably) to the *Freeholders Journal* and the *True Briton* to expose their dishonest rhetoric.

18 The "*Ironical* or *Mock Panegyrick*" exploits the truth that all men do have some vices and virtues; the writer then will "dwell entirely upon those which he [the victim] is known to *want*," and so will raise the "malignant Grin of your Readers"; in *The Art of Railing at Great Men*, 15.

19 *Craftsman*, no. 588 (October 15, 1737).

20 *The Art of Railing at Great Men*, 12.

21 Begun as a series in the *Craftsman*, no. 61 (September 2, 1727); see also *The History of the Norfolk Steward Continued* (1728).

22 *Craftsman*, no. 533 (September 18, 1736).

23 *Craftsman*, no. 571 (June 11, 1737).

24 *Craftsman*, no. 299 (March 25, 1732).

25 *Craftsman*, no. 16 (January 23–27, 1727). Other allegorical dream-visions are found throughout opposition journals: *Craftsman*, no. 55 (July 22, 1727), no. 273 (September 25, 1731), no. 295 (February 26, 1732), and no. 591 (November 5, 1737); *Mist's Weekly Journal*, no. 167 (June 29, 1728); and *Common Sense*, no. 15 (May 14, 1737).

26 *Common Sense*, nos. 7–8 (March 19 and 26, 1737). The engraving is reproduced and discussed in Langford, *Walpole and the Robinocracy*, no. 48; and Hallett, *The Spectacle of Difference*, 133–42, and elsewhere.

27 For example, *Craftsman*, no. 46 (May 20, 1727), no. 47 (May 27, 1727), no. 150 (May 17, 1729), no. 159 (July 19, 1729), no. 172 (October 18, 1729), and no. 311 (June 17, 1732); and *Mist's Weekly Journal*, no. 175 (August 24, 1728). The idea is expanded in George Lyttelton, *Letters from a Persian in England* (1735), including passing mention of castrato singers (Farinelli) and competing opera companies (3–5, 8–9).

28 *The Art of Railing at Great Men*, 16.

29 *Craftsman*, no. 7 (December 23–26, 1726), and no. 31 (March 20–24, 1727).

30 *Craftsman*, no. 7 (December 26–30, 1726).

31 Walpole as an evil minister and favorite, *The Sly Subscription: on the Norfolk Monarch* (1733); *The Norfolk Sting: or, the History and Fall of Evil Ministers* (1732); *Craftsman*, no. 51 (June 24, 1727), no. 97 (May 11, 1728), no. 105 (July 6, 1728), and no. 153 (June 7, 1729).

32 Eustace Budgell, *A Short History of Prime Ministers in Great Britain* (1733). The ministry replied in *A Review of the Short History of Prime Ministers* (1733).

33 The series "Memoirs of William Cecil Lord Burghley" in the *Daily Gazetteer* (from July 22 to October 14, 1737; October 21, 1737); the series was collected as *Memoirs of the Life and Administration of William Cecil Baron Burleigh* (1738).

34 *Craftsman*, no. 24 (February 24–27, 1727).

35 *Craftsman*, no. 24 (February 24–27, 1727).

36 Alexander Pope, *Epistle to Augustus* (1737), line 413.

37 William Shakespeare, *As You Like It*, II.vii.

38 *Craftsman*, no. 624 (June 24, 1738). The stage is compared to the world of politics in *Fog's Weekly Journal*, no. 106 (October 3, 1730); *Craftsman*, no. 194 (March 21, 1730), and no. 469 (June 28, 1735); *Common Sense*, no. 201 (December 13, 1740), and no. 242 (October 3, 1741) (ministry as puppet show); and *Politicks in Miniature: or, the Humours of Punch's Resignation* (1742).

39 Langford, *Walpole and the Robinocracy*, 31.

40 Diary of the Earl of Egmont; British Library, Add. MS 47,065, ff. 30v-31r. The entry should be "Thursday 23" (misdated by Egmont). The incident was widely reported in the newspapers; for example, the *Weekly Register*, no. 257 (January 25, 1735); *Grub-street Journal*, no. 265 (January 23, 1735); *Daily Advertiser*, no. 1240 (January 18, 1735); *Fog's Weekly Journal*, no. 325 (January 25, 1735);

London Evening Post, no. 1118 (January 16–18, 1735); and *Prompter*, no. 23 (January 28, 1735).

41 George II is compared to the adulterous King Solomon in a print "Solomon in his Glory"; in Langford, *Walpole and the Robinocracy*, no. 40; and Maynard Mack, *The Garden and the City: Retirement and Politics in the Later Poetry of Pope, 1731–1743* (University of Toronto Press, 1969), 133, plate 36.

42 The frontispiece is "The Downfall of Sejanus" and the title-page vignette illustrates the scene at the masquerade.

43 *The Doctrine of Innuendo's Discuss'd; or the Liberty of the Press Maintain'd* (1731); also in *Craftsman*, no. 2 (December 5–9, 1726), no. 7 (December 23–26, 1726), no. 31 (March 20–24, 1727), no. 68 (October, 21 1727), no. 75 (December 9, 1727), no. 80 (January 13, 1728), no. 135 (February 1, 1729), no. 140 (March 8, 1729), and no. 228 (November 14, 1730); *Free Briton*, no. 124 (April 13, 1732); *Daily Gazetteer*, no. 638 (July 7, 1737), no. 652 (July 26, 1737), and no. 774 (December 27, 1737); and *Common Sense*, no. 91 (October 28, 1738).

44 *The Crafts of the Craftsmen* (1736), 34.

45 *The Doctrine of Innuendo's*, 6 (also noting that "application makes the Ass").

46 *Craftsman*, no. 80 (January 13, 1728), and no. 220 (September 19, 1730).

47 John Loftis, *The Politics of Drama in Augustan England* (Oxford: Clarendon Press, 1963), 94–5.

48 The application of Macheath's character to Walpole is spelled out in *Memoirs Concerning the Life and Manners of Captain Macheath* (1728). The association of Walpole with Macheath has origins in 1725 when *Mist's Weekly Journal*, no. 7 (June 12, 1725), wrote about the highwayman Jonathan Wild as a "celebrated Statesman and Politician" and "a great Man."

49 *Craftsman*, no. 85 (February 17, 1728).

50 The following account draws on Jeremy Black, *The Collapse of the Anglo-French Alliance, 1727–1731* (Gloucester: Alan Sutton, 1987); Black, *British Foreign Policy in the Age of Walpole* (Edinburgh: John Donald, 1985); Stetson Conn, *Gibraltar in British Diplomacy in the Eighteenth Century* (New Haven, CT: Yale University Press, 1942); James F. Chance, *The Alliance of Hanover: A Study of British Foreign Policy in the Last Years of George I* (London: John Murray, 1923); Arthur M. Wilson, *French Foreign Policy during the Administration of Cardinal Fleury, 1726–1743* (Cambridge, MA: Harvard University Press, 1936); Basil Williams, "The Foreign Policy of England under Walpole," *English Historical Review* 15 (1900), 251–76, 479–94, 665–98; 16 (1901), 67–83, 308–27, 439–51; and Philip Woodfine, *Britannia's Glories: The Walpole Ministry and the 1739 War with Spain* (Woodbridge: Boydell & Brewer, 1998), 75–101.

51 Even as early as 1712, *Concordia Discors* argued it was not in Britain's interest to possess Gibraltar and Minorca.

52 Examples include Thomas Gordon, *Considerations Offered upon … the Importance of Gibraltar* (1720), and Gordon, *A Letter to the Independent Whig, Occasioned by His Considerations of the Importance of Gibraltar* (1720).

53 *Cato's Letters*, ed. Ronald Hamowy, 2 vols. (Indianapolis, IN: Liberty Fund, 1995), no. 1, vol. I, 38; also nos. 9 and 22.

54 The text of George's letter is given in William Cobbett, *Parliamentary History of England* (1722–32), vol. VIII, 695; and Conn, *Gibraltar in British Diplomacy*, 67–8.

55 Herbert Richmond, *The Navy As an Instrument of Policy, 1558–1727* (Cambridge University Press, 1953), 393–5.

56 *An Enquiry into the Reasons of the Conduct of Great Britain* (1727), 57, 55. An opposition rejoinder appeared as *Some Queries to the Author of the Enquiry into the Reasons of the Conduct of Great Britain* (1727).

57 *Occasional Writer. No. 1* (January 1727), 23 (from thirty-one-page edn.). For the importance of Gibraltar, *Mist's Weekly Journal*, no. 58 (June 4, 1726); and *Craftsman*, nos. 35–36 (April 3–7 and 7–10, 1727).

58 For example, *The Evident Approach of a War; and Something of the Necessity of It, in Order to Establish Peace, and Preserve Trade* (1727) argues the advantages of a war with Spain. *Reasons Against a War. In a Letter to a Member of Parliament* (1727) argues against going to war from a government position.

59 *Craftsman*, no. 21 (February 13–17, 1727).

60 *British Journal*, no. 232 (March 4, 1727). Almost two weeks later, the *British Journal*, no. 235 (March 25, 1727), also paid tribute to Italian opera by printing a poem by Henry Carey, "To Mr. *Handel*, on his *Admetus*"; also reprinted in Carey's *Poems on Several Occasions*, 3rd edn. (1729); and in O. E. Deutsch, *Handel: A Documentary Biography* (New York: W. W. Norton, 1955), 206. The letter of March 4, 1727, is reprinted in Elizabeth Gibson, *The Royal Academy of Music, 1719–1728: The Institution and Its Directors* (New York: Garland Publishing, 1989), 392–4.

61 *Craftsman*, no. 28 (March 10–13, 1727). The essay was reprinted as "On Luxury" in Bolingbroke's *A Collection of Political Tracts* (1747), 72–8, and later editions of his collected works.

62 For the conventional critique of luxury, John Sekora, *Luxury: The Concept in Western Thought, Eden to Smollett* (Baltimore, MD: The Johns Hopkins University Press, 1977).

63 *British Journal*, no. 241 (April 29, 1727).

64 Suzana Ograjenšek, "The Rival Queens," in the *Cambridge Handel Encyclopedia*, ed. Annette Landgraf and David Vickers (Cambridge University Press, 2009), 544–5; on how the rivalry has shaped modern opera scholarship, see Ograjenšek, "From *Alessandro* (1726) to *Tolomeo* (1728): The Final Royal Academy Operas" (Ph.D. dissertation, University of Cambridge, 2005), 11–15. On the roles Handel created for the two singers, C. Steven LaRue, *Handel and his Singers: The Creation of the Royal Academy Operas, 1720–1728* (Oxford: Clarendon Press, 1995).

65 *British Journal*, no. 15 (December 29, 1722).

66 *London Journal*, no. 192 (March 30, 1723).

67 *London Journal* (September 4, 1725); in Deutsch, *Handel*, 185.

68 *Mist's Weekly Journal*, no. 55 (May 14, 1726).

69 Prologue to revival of *Camilla* at Lincoln's Inn Fields (November 19, 1726); printed in the *London Journal*, no. 382 (November 26, 1726).

70 *Mist's Weekly Journal*, no. 86 (December 10, 1726).

71 Undated letter (?June 1727) from the Countess of Pembroke to Charlotte Clayton (Viscountess Sundon); Victoria and Albert Museum, National Art Library. Forster Collection, 48.E.14, 1–2. Lady Pembroke may be describing the final evening of the season, since her mention of Princess Amelia's being in the audience agrees with Zamboni's description of the final evening; see Lowell Lindgren, "Musicians and Librettists in the Correspondence of Gio. Giacomo Zamboni (Oxford, Bodleian Library, MSS Rawlinson Letters 116–138)," *Royal Musical Association Research Chronicle* 24 (1991), letter no. 209. The princess would be Caroline, daughter of the Princess of Wales.

72 The identification of the princess may be in error; in his letter of June 13 (OS) to Le Coq describing the event, Zamboni states it was Princess Amelia who was in the audience; see Lindgren, "Musicians and Librettists," letter no. 209. Or possibly both princesses attended.

73 *London Journal*, no. 410 (June 10, 1727); and the *British Journal*, no. 246 (June 10, 1727).

74 John, Lord Hervey, June 13, 1727, to Stephen Fox; Suffolk Record Office, Bury St. Edmunds, 914/47/4, 57.

75 The notoriety of the rivalry can be gauged by its coverage in the media (in addition to citations elsewhere in the text): *It Cannot Rain But It Pours: or London Strowed with Rarities* (1726) (often wrongly attributed to John Arbuthnot); *Services and Sufferings; or the Three Cuckoos* (1726); Bernard Mandeville, *The Fable of the Bees*, Part 2 (1729), 166; *An Epistle from S—r S—o to S—a F—a* (1727); Nicholas Amhurst, "(Polly Peachum:) A New Ballad" ("Of all the Belles") (reprinted in *The Twickenham Hotch-Potch* [1728], 38–9); Amhurst, *A Collection of Poems; Published in the Craftsman* (1731), 24–6; Henry Carey, "Polly Peachum" ("Of all the Toasts"), in *Poems on Several Occasions* (1729); Carey, *Mocking Is Catching, or, A Pastoral Lamentation for the Loss of a Man and no Man* ("As Musing I rang'd") [1726]; Carey, "The Beau Monde: or the Pleasures of St. *James's*," in *Poems on Several Occasions*, 3rd edn. [1729], 221–5 (frequently reprinted in other miscellanies, and as "To Caleb D'Anvers, Esq;" in the *Craftsman*, no. 49 [June 10, 1727]); *Mist's Weekly Journal*, no. 112 (June 10, 1727); Carey, *The Dragon of Wantley* (1737); Carey, *Faustina: or the Roman Songstress, A Satyr, on the Luxury and Effeminacy of the Age* (1726); "The Competition: Occasioned by the Success of the Beggar's Opera" ("Two nymphs the most renown'd Sir"), in *The Hive, a Collection of the Most Celebrated Songs*, 3rd edn., 3 vols. (1726–1729), vol. III, 168–9; "A Challenge from *C—oni* and *F—na*, to *Polly Peachum*," in *Letters in Prose and Verse, to the Celebrated Polly Peachum* (1728), 13; James-Moore Smythe, *The Rival Modes. A Comedy* (1727), 43; "Old *England*'s Garland; or, the

Italian Opera's Downfall," in *Miscellaneous Poems*, ed. David Lewis, 2 vols. (1730), vol. II, 78–81; "On the Famous Contests between Signora Cuzzoni, and Signora Faustina," MS poem in Bodleian Library MS. Rawl. Poetry 222, 13v (also printed in *A Collection of Poems*, ed. John Whaley [1732], 100); *La Staffetta Italiana: or, The Italian Post*, no. 7 (January 30, 1729); *Vivitur Ingenio: Being a Collection of Elegant, Moral, Satirical, and Comical Thoughts, on Various Subjects* (1726), 10; and *The Country Gentleman*, no. 18 (May 9, 1726).

The two are pictured in the prints *The Stage Medley* (1728) and *The Landing of Senesino* (1727), and in vignettes in George Bickham's *The Musical Entertainer* (1736–1739; coll. edn., 1738–1740), "On Loosing Their Toast and Butter" and "On Gallant Moor of Moor Hall."

76 *The Devil to Pay at St. James's* (1727), 3; reprinted in *The Miscellaneous Works of the Late Dr. Arbuthnot*, 2 vols. (1751 and 1770), vol. I, 213–23 (but not by Arbuthnot).

77 In *The Dramatic Works of Colley Cibber*, 5 vols. (1777), vol. IV, 371–81 (but probably not by Cibber). Not to be confused with *The Rival Queens*.

78 Owen Swiney, Venice, May 14, 1728 (NS), to the Duke of Richmond; in Gibson, *The Royal Academy of Music*, 379 (and see 254).

79 Mary, Countess of Pembroke (?June 1727), to Charlotte Clayton (Viscountess Sundon); Victoria and Albert Museum, National Art Library. Forster Collection, 48.E.14, 2. The king's message is also mentioned in a letter of June 6, 1727 (OS), to Jacques Le Coq in The Hague; in Lindgren, "Musicians and Librettists," letter no. 208.

80 John Hawkins, *A General History of the Science and Practice of Music*, 5 vols. 1776 (1853 edn. in 2 vols., reprint, New York: Dover, 1963), vol. II, 873.

81 *The History of Parliament. The House of Commons, 1715–1754*, ed. Romney Sedgwick, 2 vols. (New York: Oxford University Press, 1970), vol. II, 58 and 220, respectively. Simon Smith, Esq., is unidentified, although likely the opera subscriber in 1723; see Carole M. Taylor, "Italian Operagoing in London, 1700–1745" (Ph.D. dissertation, Syracuse University, 1991), 329.

82 Hawkins, *A General History of the Science and Practice of Music*, vol. II, 873, and the letter from the Countess of Pembroke to Charlotte Clayton (see note 79 above).

83 Reprinted in the *British Journal*, no. 235 (March 25, 1727) (probably not by Henry Carey).

84 The only alignment with politics comes from a remark by Johann Georg Keyssler several years later, who noted "the party which opposed the court espoused *Faustina*," which is contradicted by the reports above; see Keyssler, *Travels Through Germany, Bohemia, Hungary, Switzerland, Italy, and Lorrain*, 4 vols. (1756–57), letter from Venice, May 1730, vol. III, 263.

85 *A Foreign View of England in the Reigns of George I. & George II: The Letters of Monsieur César de Saussure to His Family*, trans. and ed. Madame Van Muyden (London: John Murray, 1902), 272.

86 *Craftsman*, nos. 33, 35, 36, and 45 (March 27–31, April 3–7, 7–10, and May 13, 1727).

87 Full or summary texts of the Preliminaries appeared in the *Daily Journal*, nos. 1994 and 1995 (June 5 and 6, 1727); *Craftsman*, no. 50 (June 17, 1727); *Daily Post*, no. 2402 (June 5, 1727); *Daily Courant*, no. 8005 (June 12, 1727); *British Journal*, no. 247 (June 17, 1727); and the *Political State of Great Britain* 33 (May 1727), 521–4.

88 Black, *British Foreign Policy in the Age of Walpole*, 163.

89 *Craftsman*, nos. 47–49 (May 27, June 3 and 10, 1727).

90 *Craftsman*, no. 49 (June 10, 1727); complete letter in Gibson, *The Royal Academy of Music*, 394–6.

91 See note 56 above.

92 Compare the text of Article 2 as printed in the *Daily Journal*, no. 1995 (June 6, 1727): "The Rights possessed by each of the contracting Parties, as well by Virtue of the Treaties of Utrecht, Baden, and the Quadruple Alliance as other Treaties and Conventions, before the Year 1725, and which do not concern the Emperor and States General, shall remain unaltered, unless it be found really necessary."

93 *Craftsman*, no. 54 (July 15, 1727); complete letter in Gibson, *The Royal Academy of Music*, 396–8.

94 *Craftsman*, no. 54 (July 15, 1727).

95 *Craftsman*, no. 54 (July 15, 1727).

96 *Craftsman*, no. 54 (July 15, 1727).

97 John, Lord Hervey, *Some Materials Towards Memoirs of the Reign of King George II*, ed. Romney Sedgwick, 3 vols. (London: Eyre and Spottiswoode, 1931), vol. I, 98.

98 Loftis, *The Politics of Drama in Augustan England*, 94.

99 *Craftsman*, no. 83 (February 3, 1728).

100 *London Journal*, no. 451 (March 23, 1728); complete letter in Gibson, *The Royal Academy of Music*, 398–401, and John Arbuthnot, *The Correspondence of Dr. John Arbuthnot*, ed. Angus Ross (Munich: Wilhelm Fink, 2006), no. 115, 276–9 (probably not by Arbuthnot).

101 *London Journal*, no. 452 (March 30, 1728). Philopropos refers to Addison's *Spectator*, no. 249.

102 *Weekly Journal; or British Gazetteer*, no. 149 (March 30, 1728).

103 *Craftsman*, no. 85 (February 17, 1728).

104 *Intelligencer*, no. 3 (May 25, 1728); in Jonathan Swift and Thomas Sheridan, *The Intelligencer*, ed. James Woolley (Oxford: Clarendon Press, 1992), 65. Swift's ideas are echoed in *Thievery-a-la-mode* (1728), 12–13, and *Memoirs of the Times; in a Letter to a Friend in the Country* (1737), 44.

105 *Craftsman*, no. 85 (February 17, 1728).

106 "A Key to the Beggar's Opera. In a Letter to Caleb Danvers, Esq."; in Christopher Bullock, *Woman's Revenge; or, a Match in Newgate*, 2nd edn. (1728), 69–76.

107 *Craftsman*, no. 87 (March 2, 1728).

108 *Craftsman*, no. 135 (February 1, 1729).

109 *Craftsman*, no. 153 (June 7, 1729).

110 William E. Schultz, *Gay's Beggar's Opera: Its Content, History & Influence* (New Haven, CT: Yale University Press, 1923), 139, 153, exaggerates when he writes, "Gay's opera, if it did not kill the rival species of stage entertainment, at least severely crippled it and … gradually weakened the influence of the Italian school and forced it from the stage."

111 *The Poems of Alexander Pope*, vol. III: *The Dunciad (1728) & The Dunciad Variorum (1729)*, ed. Valerie Rumbold (Harlow: Pearson, 2007), Pope's note to bk. 3, l. 326 (at p. 304). *La Staffetta Italiana: or, the Italian Post*, no. 7 (January 30, 1729) attributes the demise of Italian opera to both the Faustina–Cuzzoni rivalry and *The Beggar's Opera*.

112 Season productions as given in Gibson, *The Royal Academy of Music*, 262; since several dates are not covered by any surviving newspapers, figures are estimates.

113 On Gay's parody and burlesque of opera, Arthur V. Berger, "The Beggar's Opera, the Burlesque, and Italian Opera," *Music and Letters* 17 (1936), 93–105; Bertrand H. Bronson, "The Beggar's Opera," in *Facets of the Enlightenment* (Berkeley: University of California Press, 1968), 60–90; Edmond M. Gagey, *Ballad Opera* (New York: Columbia University Press, 1937), 16–19; Schultz, *Gay's Beggar's Opera*, 133–53; Pat Rogers, "Gay and the World of Opera," in *John Gay and the Scriblerians*, ed. Peter Lewis and Nigel Wood (New York: St. Martin's Press, 1988), 147–62; and Calhoun Winton, *John Gay and the London Theatre* (Lexington: University Press of Kentucky, 1993), 121–7.

114 Quotations from John Gay, *The Beggar's Opera*, ed. Edgar V. Roberts (Lincoln: University of Nebraska Press, 1969).

115 Rogers, "Gay and the World of Opera"; William A. McIntosh, "Handel, Walpole, and Gay: The Aims of *The Beggar's Opera*," *Eighteenth-Century Studies* 7 (1974), 415–33; Winton, *John Gay and the London Theatre*, 103–5; Bronson, "The Beggar's Opera," 77; and David Nokes, *John Gay: A Profession of Friendship* (Oxford University Press, 1995), 423–33. Peter Lewis, *John Gay: The Beggar's Opera* (London: Edward Arnold, 1976), 10–11, argues that Gay was generally an admirer of opera. Gay had friends (or former patrons) among the Royal Academy, including Lord Burlington; see Nokes, *John Gay: The Beggar's Opera*, 316–17. Todd Gilman argues the opera is more concerned to champion a viable form of native music drama; Gilman "*The Beggar's Opera* and British Opera," *University of Toronto Quarterly* 66 (1997), 539–61.

116 Gibson, *The Royal Academy of Music*, 255–6.

117 Gibson, *The Royal Academy of Music*, 267.

118 Gibson, *The Royal Academy of Music*, 269–71.

119 *Daily Courant*, nos. 8299 and 8312 (May 16 and 31, 1728); see also nos. 8292 and 8307 (May 8 and 25, 1728).

120 *Daily Courant*, no. 8312 (May 31, 1728).

121 *Daily Post*, nos. 2740 and 2747 (July 3 and 11, 1728); *Craftsman*, no. 104 (July 6, 1728); and *Mist's Weekly Journal*, no. 168 (July 6, 1728).

122 Undated list at the West Sussex Record Office, Goodwood MSS 143 and 144; in Gibson, *The Royal Academy of Music*, 278–79; and letter from Owen Swiney, Venice, May 14, 1728 (NS), to the Duke of Richmond; in Gibson, *The Royal Academy of Music*, 278, 378–80.

123 *London Evening Post*, no. 82 (June 15–18, 1728); and *Craftsman*, no. 103 (June 22, 1728).

124 Townshend to Stephen Poyntz, June 3/14, 1728; in William Coxe, *Memoirs of the Life and Administration of Sir Robert Walpole, Earl of Orford*, 3 vols. (1798), vol. II, 631. See also *British Diplomatic Instructions 1689–1789*, vol. VI: *France, 1727–1744*. Camden Third Series 43 (1930), 11, 19, 29, and 51.

125 For example, *Reasons for a War, in order to Establish the Tranquillity [sic] and Commerce of Europe* (February 10, 1729) and Nicholas Amhurst, *Some Farther Remarks on a Late Pamphlet, Intitled, Observations on the Conduct of Great-Britain* (March 5, 1729).

126 *Craftsman*, no. 105 (July 6, 1728).

127 *Craftsman*, no. 113 (August 31, 1728); complete letter in Gibson, *The Royal Academy of Music*, 401–4 (where it is signed "Phil-Harmonicus," following the collected edition).

128 *Craftsman*, no. 113 (August 31, 1728).

129 *Craftsman*, no. 113 (August 31, 1728).

130 The pamphlet was answered by *Fact against Falshood [sic]: or, Answer to the Norfolk Congress* (November 26, 1728). *Mist's Weekly Journal*, no. 166 (June 22, 1728), compared all the diplomats arriving at the Congress to those arriving "to the Ring of a Country Wrestling Match." The *Craftsman*, no. 104 (June 29, 1728), mocked the Congress as a source of ideas for John Rich's Harlequinades. See also *Quadrille to Perfection as Play'd at Soissons: or, The Norfolk Congress Pursu'd* (1728).

131 Opposition polemics include *The Craftsman Extraordinary. Being Remarks on a Late Pamphlet Intitled, Observations on the Conduct of Great Britain, &c.* (1729); *The Second Craftsman Extraordinary: Being Farther Remarks on a Pamphlet Lately Publish'd, Entitled, Observations on the Conduct of Great Britain* (1729); Bolingbroke, *The Crafts-man Extraordinary: Containing an Answer to the Defence of the Enquiry into the Reasons of the Conduct of Great Britain* (1729); and Nicholas Amhurst, *Some Farther Remarks on a late Pamphlet, Intitled, Observations on the Conduct of Great-Britain* (1729).

    Ministerial tracts include *Observations on the Conduct of Great-Britain, with Regard to the Negotiations and other Transactions Abroad* (1729); Benjamin Hoadly, *A Defence of the Enquiry into the Reasons of the Conduct of Great-Britain* (1729); *The Anti-Craftsman: Being an Answer to the Craftsman Extraordinary* (1729); and *An Enquiry into the Pretensions of Spain to Gibraltar* (1729). Most were published in time for the beginning of the parliamentary session.

132 For the ministry, Robert Walpole, *Observations upon the Treaty between the Crowns of Great-Britain, France, and Spain* (1730); *A Review of the Short*

View; and of the Remarks on the Treaty with Spain (1730); William Arnall, *The Free Briton Extraordinary: or, a Short Review of the British Affairs* (1730); *Some Remarks upon a Pamphlet intitled, A Short View of the State of Affairs* (1730); *A Review of a Pamphlet, entitled, Observations on the Treaty of Seville, Examined* (1730); and *The Treaty of Seville … impartially consider'd* (1730).

For the opposition, *Observations on the Treaty of Seville Examined* (1730); *A Letter to a Member of Parliament, Relating to the Secret Article … Concerning Gibraltar* (1730); *A Short View of the State of Affairs, with Relation to Great Britain* (1730); and Bolingbroke, *Observations on the Publick Affairs of Great-Britain. With some Toughts* [sic] *on the Treaty Concluded and signed (On What Terms God Knows) at Seville* (also titled *Observations on the Conduct of Great Britain in Publick Affairs* [1729]).

133 *Fog's Weekly Journal*, no. 64 (December 13, 1729).

134 *Craftsman*, no. 105 (July 6, 1728).

135 *Parrot*, no. 3 (October 9, 1728). The passage is reprinted in *Hell Upon Earth: or the Town in an Uproar* (1729), 26–7.

136 *London Evening Post*, no. 144 (November 7–9, 1728).

137 Anne, Countess of Albemarle, November 11, 1728, to the Duke of Richmond; in *A Duke and His Friends: The Life and Letters of the Second Duke of Richmond*, ed. Charles March, Earl of March, 2 vols. (London: Hutchinson, 1911), vol. I, 161.

138 Judith Milhous and Robert D. Hume, "New Light on Handel and The Royal Academy of Music in 1720," *Theatre Journal* 35 (1983), 153, 155, 164.

5   Handel's Second Academy

1 *London Evening Post*, no. 144 (November 7–9, 1728).

2 *London Gazette*, nos. 6743–44 (January 11–14 and 14–18, 1729).

3 Historical Manuscripts Commission, *Manuscripts of the Earl of Egmont. Diary of Viscount Percival afterwards First Earl of Egmont*, 3 vols. (London: His Majesty's Stationery Office (1920–23), vol. III, 329 (appendix) (January 18, 1729) (cited as Egmont, *Diary*). See also Paolo Rolli's letters of January 25 and February 4, 1729, to Senesino; in O. E. Deutsch, *Handel: A Documentary Biography* (New York: W. W. Norton, 1955), 234–8; Elizabeth Gibson, *The Royal Academy of Music, 1719–1728: The Institution and Its Directors* (New York: Garland Publishing, 1989), 280–4; and Donald Burrows, *Handel* (New York: Schirmer, 1994), 126–9.

4 Deutsch, *Handel*, 242–3; Johann Georg Keyssler, *Travels through Germany, Bohemia, Hungary, Switzerland, Italy, and Lorrain*, 4 vols. (1756–57), vol. III, 263–4.

5 *Craftsman*, no. 157 (July 5, 1729); Deutsch, *Handel*, 243–4.

6 *Fog's Weekly Journal*, no. 33 (May 10, 1729).

7 Judith Milhous and Robert D. Hume, "Box Office Reports for Five Operas Mounted by Handel in London, 1732–1734," *Harvard Library Bulletin* 26 (1978), 245–66; Milhous and Hume, "Handel's Opera Finances in 1732–3," *Musical Times* 125 (1984), 86–9; Robert D. Hume, "Handel and Opera Management in London in the 1730s," *Music and Letters* 67 (1986), 347–62; Judith Milhous, "Opera Finances in London," *Journal of the American Musicological Society* 37 (1984), 567–92; and Donald Burrows, "Handel and the London Opera Companies in the 1730s: Venues, Programmes, Patronage and Performers," *Göttinger Händel-Beiträge* 10 (2004), 149–65. Ilias Chrissochoidis, "'Hee-Haw … llelujah' Handel Among the Vauxhall Asses (1732)," *Eighteenth-Century Music* 7 (2010), 221–62, presents much new documentation about the Second Academy, but his interpretations must be accepted with caution.

8 Rolli to Senesino, January 25 and February 4, 1729; in Deutsch, *Handel*, 235 and 237. Chrissochoidis (note 7 above) suggests the Second Academy can be considered a court project.

9 John, Lord Hervey, December 2, 1729, to Stephen Fox; in *Lord Hervey and His Friends, 1726–38*, ed. Earl of Ilchester (London: John Murray, 1950), 41.

10 Earl of Shaftesbury, memoir; in Deutsch, *Handel*, 845.

11 Mary Delany, February 16, 1729, to her sister Ann Granville; in Deutsch, *Handel*, 238.

12 *Craftsman*, no. 168 (September 20, 1729).

13 Princess Amelia, October 23, 1729, to Lady Portland; in Richard G. King, "Two New Letters from Princess Amelia," *Händel-Jahrbuch* 40/41 (1994/1995), 169–71.

14 Paolo Rolli, November 6, 1729, to Giuseppe Riva, in Vienna; in Deutsch, *Handel*, 246.

15 Burrows, *Handel*, 131.

16 Phillip Lord, "The English-Italian Opera Companies, 1732–3," *Music and Letters* 45 (1964), 239–51; Roger Fiske, *English Theatre Music in the Eighteenth Century*, 2nd edn. (Oxford University Press, 1986), 130–45; and Judith Milhous and Robert D. Hume, "J. F. Lampe and English Opera at the Little Haymarket in 1732–3," *Music and Letters* 78 (1997), 502–31.

17 Aaron Hill, December 5, 1732, to Handel; in *The Works of the Late Aaron Hill, Esq.*, 2nd edn., 4 vols. (1754), vol. I, 174–5. On Hill's ideas about English dramatic music, Ruth Smith, *Handel's Oratorios and Eighteenth-Century Thought* (Cambridge University Press, 1995), 79–80.

18 The circumstances and date of the first performance are in doubt; see John Roberts, "The Composition of Handel's *Esther*, 1718–1720," *Händel-Jahrbuch* 55 (2009), 353–90.

19 Deutsch, *Handel*, 285.

20 Charles Burney, *An Account of the Musical Performances in Westminster-Abbey* (1785), 100.

21 *Daily Journal*, no. 3522 (April ?19, 1732). Burney, *Account of the Musical Performances in Westminster-Abbey*, 100–1, reports that the lack of staging ("even with books in the children's hands") was done to circumvent the Bishop of London's prohibition of a sacred subject in the opera house.

22 H. Diack Johnstone, "Handel and His Bellows-Blower (Maurice Greene)," *Göttinger Händel-Beiträge* 7 (1988), 208–17.

23 For Walpole's use of the Jacobite scare, G. V. Bennett, "Jacobitism and the Rise of Walpole," in *Historical Perspectives: Studies in English Thought and Society in Honour of J. H. Plumb*, ed. Neil McKendrick (London: Europa, 1974), 70–92. The *Craftsman* frequently exposed Walpole's fear of Jacobites; for example, no. 366 (July 7, 1733).

24 *Craftsman*, no. 319 (August 12, 1732); reprinted in *Lord Bolingbroke: Contributions to the "Craftsman,"* ed. Simon Varey (Oxford: Clarendon Press, 1982), 136–41, where the relation to the Belloni letter is not noted.

25 *Daily Post*, no. 3966 (June 9, 1732) (quoted); also in *Daily Advertiser*, nos. 423 and 424 (June 9 and 10, 1732). On the episode, Lowell Lindgren, "The Three Great Noises 'Fatal to the Interests of Bononcini,'" *Musical Quarterly* 61 (1975), 560–83, at 580–1, who suggests del Pò was "enriched" by a cabal intent on sabotaging Bononcini's concert series. Lindgren does not recognize the satiric nature of the Countryman's fictive letter, which lessens its use as a document for a cabal against Bononcini.

26 See notices in the *Daily Courant, Daily Post, London Evening Post*, and *Daily Journal* running from June 9 to June 24, 1732.

27 The *Daily Courant*, no. 5058 (June 26, 1732) reported: "On Saturday in the Evening her Majesty, his Royal Highness the Prince of Wales, and the Three Eldest Princesses, came to the Opera House in the Haymarket, and saw a new Pastoral Entertainment, composed by Signor Bononcini" (similar notice in the *Daily Advertiser*, no. 437 [June 26, 1732]). The notices suggest that Bononcini found a substitute soprano not, as Lindgren argues, that Strada's "refusal to sing forced cancellation of the serenata, and the substitute entertainment was a failure"; Lindgren, "The Three Great Noises," 579. The Colman opera register reports "Sig^r Senesino & 3 others Sung / the Queen. 3 Princesses & Pr. Wales pres^t"; see Konrad Sasse, "Opera Register from 1712 to 1734 (Colman-Register)," *Händel-Jahrbuch* 5 (1959), 199–223, at 220.

28 Contemporary accounts of the Corporation and scandal include *A Short History of the Charitable Corporation. From the Date of Their Charter, to … the frauds discovered in the management of their affairs* (1732); and *The Report of the Gentlemen Appointed by the General Court of the Charitable Corporation* (1732). See also George A. Aitken, *The Life and Works of John Arbuthnot* (Oxford: Clarendon Press, 1892), 138–41; and *The History of Parliament. The House of Commons, 1715–1754*, ed. Romney Sedgwick, 2 vols. (New York: Oxford University Press, 1970), vol. I, 470–1, vol. II, 21, 77–8, and 456–8.

29 William Cobbett, *Parliamentary History of England* (1722–1733), vol. VIII, 935–42, 1012–14, 1069–70, and 1077–166; complete documents reprinted in *The Several Reports, with the Appendix … from the Committee of the House of Commons, to Whom the Petition of the Proprietors of the Charitable Corporation … Was Referred* (1732).

30 *Journals of the House of Commons* 21 (1727–1732), 930. The relevant documents were reprinted in *Copy [of the] Letter, [from] Seignior John Angelo Belloni, to the Gentlemen of the Committee* (June [or later] 1732).

31 Supposedly, Belloni obtained Thomson's arrest, and made him give up to £30,000 in return for enjoying the remainder of his money; Lesley Lewis, *Connoisseurs and Secret Agents in Eighteenth Century Rome* (London: Chatto and Windus, 1961), 98.

32 As printed in the *Free Briton*, no. 131 (June 1, 1732).

33 *Journals of the House of Commons* 21 (1727–1732), 932.

34 *Free Briton*, no. 131 (June 1, 1732). The letter was reprinted in newspapers and disseminated throughout the nation in broadsheets; for example, *The Practices of the Pretender and his Agents at Paris and Rome* [Dublin, 1732]. The government's interpretation is also given in the *Daily Courant*, no. 5037 (June 1, 1732).

35 Earlier, Arnall had discussed the grammatical usage of *on* in French, and its ambiguous first- or third-person use.

36 *Free Briton*, no. 131 (June 1, 1732).

37 *Grub-street Journal*, nos. 127–129 (June 8, 15, and 22, 1732). The ministry's reading of the Belloni letter was also mocked in *Fog's Weekly Journal*, no. 188 (June 10, 1732). The purpose of the *Journal's* disputing the *Free Briton's* interpretation of the Belloni letter is admittedly obscure. Given the *Journal's* Tory and Jacobitical sympathies, there was merit in salvaging the Pretender's reputation from charges that he was sheltering the embezzler Thomson.

38 *Craftsman*, no. 319 (August 12, 1732).

39 Duke of Newcastle, April 12, 1731, to James, Lord Waldegrave; in Jeremy Black, *The Collapse of the Anglo-French Alliance, 1727–1731* (Gloucester: Alan Sutton, 1987), 202.

40 Jeremy Black, "Jacobitism and British Foreign Policy, 1731–5," in *The Jacobite Challenge*, ed. Eveline Cruickshanks and Jeremy Black (Edinburgh: John Donald, 1988), 142–60, at 144, 147; Black, *The Collapse of the Anglo-French Alliance*, 202–4; and Jeremy Black and Armin Reese, "Die Panik von 1731," in *Expansion und Gleichgewicht: Studien zur europäischen Mächtepolitik des ancien régime*, ed. Johannes Kunisch (Berlin: Dunker & Humbolt, 1986), 69–95. Neither the invitations to the Pretender or Jacobites nor invasion took place, and the crisis was defused by August.

41 Historical Manuscripts Commission, *The Manuscripts of the Earl of Buckinghamshire* [etc.] (London: Her Majesty's Stationery Office, 1895), 465.

42 The example of over-reading also satirizes Walpole's method of deciphering the correspondence of the Atterbury plotters, which was also satirized in Swift's account in *Gulliver's Travels* (1726) of the academicians of Lagado finding secret meanings in texts (Book 3, Chapter 6). On mocking the over-reading of innocuous texts, *Grub-street Journal*, no. 258 (December 5, 1734); the *Craftsman*, no. 10 (January 2–6, 1727), carried a mock advertisement for "the true *Political Perspective*" (telescope), which concludes, "Beware of *Pretenders*, for such are abroad."

43 On the Excise, Paul Langford, *The Excise Crisis: Society and Politics in the Age of Walpole* (Oxford: Clarendon Press, 1975); and *The Historical Register* 18 (1733), 130–68, 241–5, and 258–336. On the polemical literature about the Excise, E. Raymond Turner, "The Excise Scheme of 1733," *English Historical Review* 42 (1927), 34–57.

44 *Political Ballads Illustrating the Administration of Sir Robert Walpole*, ed. Milton Percival. Oxford Historical and Literary Studies 8 (1916), 61–81; Paul Langford, *Walpole and the Robinocracy*. The English Satirical Print, 1600–1832 (Cambridge: Chadwyck-Healey, 1986), plates nos. 22–32; M. Dorothy George, *English Political Caricature to 1792: A Study of Opinion and Propaganda*, 2 vols. (Oxford: Clarendon Press, 1959), vol. I, 81–3; and Herbert M. Atherton, *Political Prints in the Age of Hogarth: A Study of the Ideographic Representation of Politics* (Oxford: Clarendon, 1974), 153–62, plates 11–16.

45 Illustrated in Langford, *Walpole and the Robinocracy*, no. 23; the ballad is *Political Ballads*, ed. Percival, no. 24. The print is explicated by a dream vision in the *Craftsman*, no. 345 (February 10, 1733).

46 Charles Delafaye to the Earl of Essex at Turin, January 18, 1733: British Library, Add. MS 27732, ff. 93v–94r.

47 Nicholas Rogers, *Whigs and Cities: Politics in the Age of Walpole and Pitt* (Oxford: Clarendon, 1989), 51–5; Kathleen Wilson, *The Sense of the People: Politics, Culture and Imperialism in England, 1715–1785* (Cambridge University Press, 1995); and Langford, *The Excise Crisis*, 151–71.

48 William Coxe, *Memoirs of of the Life and Administration of Sir Robert Walpole*, 3 vols. (1798), vol. III, 401.

49 The Excise was not actually defeated; Walpole allowed it to die because the order of the day was never called for.

50 *Historical Register* 18 (1733), 140. Reports of celebration over the defeat of the Excise are collected in the *Bee*, no. 11 (1733), 475–76, 507–10, 517–18.

51 For example, *The Honest Electors, Court Legacy, Rome Excis'd, The Sturdy Beggars, The Commodity Excis'd, The Stage Juggler*, and *Lord Blunder's Confession* (all 1733), and Henry Fielding's farce *Eurydice Hiss'd* (1737).

52 Earl of Shaftesbury, memoir; in Deutsch, *Handel*, 845. The editorial addition corrects what seems a muddled account, for only if Handel had not reckoned *Deborah* into the fifty operas the subscribers had already paid for, would he be justified in charging an admission price, to which they objected.

53 Lady Irwin, March 31, 1733, to Lord Carlisle; Castle Howard Archives, Yorkshire, J8/1/252. Lady Irwin apparently enclosed a copy of the epigram. Transcribed and printed here by kind permission of the Howard family.

54 As translated in Jeremy Black, "Lord Bolingbroke's Operatic Allegory," *The Scriblerian* 16 (1984), 97–9.

55 *Daily Journal*, no. 3821 (April 2, 1733).

56 *Daily Advertiser*, nos. 661–664 (March 14–17, 1733). Similar advertisements in the *Daily Journal* and the *Daily Post*.

57 *Daily Advertiser*, no. 666 (March 20, 1733).

58 Advertisements in the *Daily Journal* beginning March 22, 1733.

59 First printed in the *Bee*, no. 7 (March 24, 1733); also in Deutsch, *Handel*, 309.

60 Identifications from a copy at the Cambridge University Library; see *Lord Bolingbroke: Contributions to the "Craftsman"*, 215, n. 3.

61 Complete letter in Deutsch, *Handel*, 310–13; *Lord Bolingbroke: Contributions to the "Craftsman,"* 149–52; and George E. Dorris, *Paolo Rolli and the Italian Circle in London, 1715–1744* (The Hague: Mouton, 1967), 103–6.

62 *Bee*, no. 10 (April 14, 1733), 405.

63 A contemporary key is provided in Count Degenfeld's dispatch; see Black, "Lord Bolingbroke's Operatic Allegory."

64 See note 61.

65 At the time, Italian operas were only produced by Handel and Heidegger at the Haymarket Theatre.

66 The bass Antonio Montagnana.

67 George II was known for his temper and flying into rages of fury; he often kicked courtiers; see especially "The Festival of the Golden Rump," reproduced in Langford, *Walpole and the Robinocracy*, no. 48.

68 The soprano Anna Maria Strada del Pò.

69 One common customs fraud was entering more tobacco than actually was recorded or weighed; see *The Rise and Fall of the Late Projected Excise, Impartially Considered* (1733).

70 Sometime previously, Handel seems to have instituted a new system of admission for season ticket holders. Instead of admission on the basis of the season ticket, subscribers had to appear at a special office on the day of the performance to receive their ticket. This would ensure more accurate accounting and prevent doorkeepers of the boxes admitting non-subscribers in return for a tip; see Milhous and Hume, "Box Office Reports for Five Operas," 250–1.

71 The opposition and merchants complained about the long time required to adjudicate and appeal Excise disputes.

72 The opposition objected that a merchant charged with violating the law had to prove his own innocence and had no right of trial by jury; in short, the Excise office was like the inquisition. See Turner, "The Excise Scheme of 1733," 52.

73 [William Pulteney], *The Late Excise Scheme Dissected* (1734), 62.

74 [Pulteney], *The Late Excise Scheme Dissected*, 35 and 62; *A Review of the Excise-Scheme* (1733), 32; and Turner, "The Excise Scheme of 1733," 52. For a ministerial defense, [?Robert Walpole], *Vindication of the Conduct of the Ministry*, 32–5.

75 William Pulteney, in *The Second Part of an Argument Against Excises* (1733), 33–4, cites the hardships and sufferings of merchants under the existing excise laws, which caused some to abandon their trade and would cause others to do the same if excise laws were extended.

76 Most of those who voted for the Excise were placemen beholden to Walpole for offices.

77 There are occasional accounts of Handel leaving Britain (some have him following Anne to Holland). See letter of Richard Pococke, Venice, June 13, 1734 (writing on June 7): "Hendel is laid on his back by Heddeger, & goes over with yᵉ Princess of orange"; British Library, Add. MS 19,939, ff. 15–16. The *Daily Advertiser*, no. 719 (May 21, 1733), reported "As there are to be no Italian Opera's here next Season, several of the most eminent Performers both Vocal and Instrumental, will attend her Royal Highness to Holland," possibly including Handel.

78 *Lord Bolingbroke: Contributions to the "Craftsman,"* 215, n. 2; Chrissochoidis, "Hee-Haw … llelujah," 255. Burrows, *Handel*, 176–7, reprints an extract as painting "an extravagant picture of public reaction to the price rises for *Deborah.*"

79 John, Lord Hervey, *Some Materials Towards Memoirs of the Reign of King George II*, ed. Romney Sedgwick, 3 vols. (London: Eyre and Spottiswoode, 1931), vol. I, 160–1 (cited as Hervey, *Memoirs*).

80 In Turner, "The Excise Scheme of 1733," 45.

81 Sir Thomas Robinson, April 14, 1733, to Lord Carlisle; in Historical Manuscripts Commission, *The Manuscripts of the Earl of Carlisle, Preserved at Castle Howard* (London: Her Majesty's Stationery Office, 1897), 110 (cited as *Carlisle Manuscripts*); also described in a letter from Col. Charles Howard, April 12, to Lord Carlisle, 108.

82 *A Review of the Excise-Scheme*, 51. The ministerial pamphlet *A Letter from a Member of Parliament for a Borough in the West* (1733), 31, asserted Walpole was "utterly free from all Signs of Perturbation and Fear."

83 See the print "Julius II" in Langford, *Walpole and the Robinocracy*, no. 10.

84 *Remarks on Fog's Journal, of February 10. 1732/3. Exciting the People to an Assassination* (1733), 6–7. Other ministerial replies on assassination include the *London Journal*, no. 712 (February 17, 1733), and the *Free Briton*, no. 180 (May 13, 1733). The ministry continued to accuse the opposition of planning Walpole's assassination; see *Daily Courant*, no. 5369 (June 22, 1733); *Free Briton*, no. 268 (December 19, 1734); and *Daily Gazetteer*, no. 120 (November 15, 1735).

85 *Fog's Weekly Journal*, no. 227 (March 10, 1733). *Fog's* returned to the Vasconcellos parallel and hints of assassination in issues nos. 227, 230, 231, and 240 (March

10 and 31, April 7 and June 9, 1733). After the Excise's postponement, the *Craftsman*, no. 355 (April 21, 1733), revisited assassination once again to humiliate Walpole: "As to the *Projector* Himself, I can only hope [he will] use a little more Caution, for the future, how He provokes the Patience of the People. This will be the only effectual Way for Him to sleep in quiet, without being haunted with continual Dreams of *Murder* and *Assassination*."

86 *Fog's Weekly Journal*, no. 223 (February 10, 1733).

87 *Giulio Cesare* (libretto of 1732 revival), II.vi.

88 The significant difference in the last line, "The Excise was obtain'd, but poor Deborah lost," suggests the poem was written before the withdrawal of the scheme. A manuscript copy of the epigram is in the Brotherton Library, University of Leeds, MS Lt q 20, f. 11v.

89 Because Paolo Rolli owned an Italian translation of the letter, Dorris, *Paolo Rolli and the Italian Circle in London*, 107–12, suggests Rolli did write the original, which Bolingbroke then translated for publication. However, the allegory fits so well with allegories in the *Craftsman*, displays such an accurate knowledge of contemporary politics, and serves Bolingbroke's polemical purpose so well, that Rolli is unlikely to be the author. More likely, someone translated the satire for the benefit of Senesino, who at the time no doubt delighted in Handel's difficulties.

90 John Henley, *Hyp-Doctor*, no. 123 (April 10, 1733). On the *Hyp-Doctor*'s ministerial writings, Graham Midgley, *The Life of Orator Henley* (Oxford: Clarendon Press, 1973), 217–18. Henley's public lecture on the *Hyp-Doctor* paper is described in the *Daily Journal*, no. 3828 (April 10, 1733), as "The present Condition of Musick in all Parts: A Defense of Deborah."

91 Letter from Col. Charles Howard, April 10, 1733, to the Earl of Carlisle; in *Carlisle Manuscripts*, 107; *Fog's Weekly Journal*, no. 241 (June 16, 1733); and Egmont, *Diary*, vol. I, 387 (June 16, 1733). The Earl of Burlington's voluntarily resignation of his posts on May 3 was due not to opposition to the ministry over the Excise, but out of pique that the king broke a promise to offer him the first available cabinet post. See letter of Col. Charles Howard to the Earl of Carlisle, May 8, 1733; in *Carlisle Manuscripts*, 114–15; and Hervey, *Memoirs*, vol. II, 188–9. Lady Burlington kept her place as lady-in-waiting.

92 *Craftsman*, no. 355 (April 21, 1733). On Chesterfield's role in the Excise and its aftermath, *The Letters of Philip Dormer Stanhope 4th Earl of Chesterfield*, ed. Bonamy Dobrée, 6 vols. (London: King's Printer's Edition, 1932), vol. I, 66–72. Chesterfield's letter to the king is printed in vol. II, 265–6 (reprinted from Hervey's *Memoirs*).

93 *Free Briton*, nos. 183 (quoted), 184, and 186 (May 24 and 31, June 14, 1733). The *Craftsman* replied in nos. 362 and 364 (June 9 and 23, 1733).

94 For example, when the *Grub-street Journal*, no. 181 (June 14, 1733), printed the report of Senesino's farewell speech, it added this editorial comment: "*My brother* [i.e., journalist] *calls* Senesino Senoseni, *because he is grown old*."

95 *Daily Advertiser*, no. 737 (June 11, 1733).

96 Winton Dean, "Handel's *Sosarme*, a Puzzle Opera," in *Essays on Opera* (Oxford: Clarendon Press, 1990), 45–73, at 49, 51, 59.

97 "Es bestanden dort am Hofe starke Spannungen zwischen dem König und dem Prinzen von Wales. So beruht auch die Opera auf solchen Spannungen zwischen dem König Haliate und seinem Sohn Argone"; Konrad Sasse, "Die Texte der Londoner Opern Händels in ihren gesellschaftlichen Beziehungen," *Wissenschaftliche Zeitschrift der Martin-Luther-Universität Halle-Wittenberg. Gesellschafts- und Sprachwissenschaftliche Reihe* 4(5) (1955), 627–46, at 642.

98 Reinhard Strohm, "Handel and his Italian Opera Texts," in *Essays on Handel and Italian Opera* (Cambridge University Press, 1985), 34–79, at 64.

99 Bolingbroke, letter of November 29, 1735, to William Wyndham; in Coxe, *Memoirs of the Life and Administration of Sir Robert Walpole*, vol. I, 427.

6 Rival opera companies and Farinelli in Madrid

1 *Daily Post*, no. 4288 (June 13, 1733); repeated in the *Daily Advertiser*, no. 740 (June 14, 1733).

2 *Daily Advertiser*, no. 743 (June 18, 1733); repeated the following day.

3 *Daily Advertiser*, no. 747 (June 22, 1733).

4 Dowager Duchess of Leeds, July 4, 1733, to the Duke of Leeds; British Library, Add. MS 28,050, ff. 217–18.

5 *Daily Advertiser*, no. 760 (July 7, 1733). The *Daily Advertiser* reported again, no. 913 (January 2, 1734): "Signora Cuzzona is expected over here from Turin in about a Month's time."

6 Probably John-Nicola Matteis; see Simon Jones, "The Legacy of the 'Stupendous' Nicola Matteis," *Early Music* 29 (2001), 563.

7 *Daily Advertiser*, no. 840 (October 9, 1733).

8 See notices in the *Daily Advertiser*, nos. 857 and 859 (October 29 and 31, 1733). The *Daily Courant*, no. 5481 (October 31, 1733), explicitly states the Prince of Wales was among the royal family.

9 See advertisements in the *Daily Advertiser* (for example, no. 904 [December 22, 1733]).

10 Charles Jennens, December 13, 1733, to John Ludford; in Anthony Hicks, "A New Letter of Charles Jennens," *Göttinger Händel-Beiträge* 4 (1991), 254–7. Prior to Jennens' writing, Handel had skipped three of his usual Tuesday or Saturday performances (November 27 and December 1 and 11). He gave only two more performances of *Caio Fabbricio* (December 15 and 22) before pausing for the holidays.

11 Thomas McGeary, "Farinelli's Progress to Albion: The Recruitment and Reception of Opera's 'Blazing Star,'" *British Journal for Eighteenth-Century Studies* 28 (2005), 339–61.

12 Hints of the received account are still found in Donald Burrows, *Handel* (New York: Schirmer, 1994) 171, 176.

13 Averyl Edwards, *Frederick Louis, Prince of Wales, 1707–1751* (London: Staples Press, 1947), still reliable, is now complemented by Frances Vivian, *A Life of Frederick, Prince of Wales: A Connoisseur of the Arts*, ed. Roger White (Lewiston, NY: Edwin Mellen Press, 2006).

14 Lady Mary Wortley Montagu, November 25, 1716 (OS), from Hanover, to the Countess of Bristol; in *The Complete Letters of Lady Mary Wortley Montagu*, ed. Robert Halsband, 3 vols. (Oxford: Clarendon Press, 1965–67), vol. I, 286.

15 Anne, Viscountess Irwin, January 18, 1729, to the Earl of Carlisle; in Historical Manuscripts Commission, *The Manuscripts of the Earl of Carlisle, Preserved at Castle Howard* (London: Her Majesty's Stationery Office, 1897), 55 (cited as *Carlisle Manuscripts*).

16 Historical Manuscripts Commission, *Manuscripts of the Earl of Egmont. Diary of Viscount Percival afterwards First Earl of Egmont*, 3 vols. (London: His Majesty's Stationery Office, 1920–23), vol. II, 267 (May 1, 1736) (cited as Egmont, *Diary*).

17 Christine Gerrard, "Queens-in-waiting: Caroline of Anspach and Augusta of Saxe-Gotha as Princesses of Wales," and John L. Bullion, "'To Play What Game She Pleased without Observation': Princess Augusta and the Political Drama of Succession, 1736–56," in *Queenship in Britain 1660–1837*, ed. Clarissa Campbell Orr (Manchester University Press, 2002), 153–5 and 207–15.

18 Kimerly Rorschach, "Frederick, Prince of Wales (1707–1751) as a Patron of the Visual Arts: Princely Patriotism and Political Propaganda," 2 vols. (Ph.D. dissertation, Yale University, 1985); Rorschach, "Frederick, Prince of Wales: Taste, Politics and Power," *Apollo* 134 (1991), 239–45; Rorschach, "Frederick, Prince of Wales (1707–51) as Collector and Patron," *Walpole Society* 55 (1989/1990), 1–76; Stephen Jones, *Frederick, Prince of Wales and His Circle*, exhibition catalog, Gainsborough's House, June 6–July 26, 1981 (Sudbury: Gainsborough's House, 1981); and Vivian, *A Life of Frederick, Prince of Wales*.

19 Christopher White, *The Dutch Pictures in the Collection of Her Majesty the Queen* (Cambridge University Press, 1982), l–li.

20 Ray Desmond, *Kew: The History of the Royal Botanic Gardens* (Kew: The Harvill Press with the Royal Botanic Gardens, 1995), 27–8.

21 Brian Allen, *Francis Hayman* (New Haven, CT: Yale University Press, 1987), 4–7, 65–6, 122, fig. 6.

22 Vivian, *A Life of Frederick, Prince of Wales*, 452–62.

23 Pat Rogers, "Book Dedications in Britain, 1700–1799: A Preliminary Survey," *British Journal for Eighteenth-Century Studies* 16 (1993), 222.

24 Peggy Daub, "Music at the Court of George II (*c.*1727–1760)," (Ph.D. dissertation, Cornell University, 1985); and Derek McCulloch, "Royal Composers: The Composing Monarchs That Britain Nearly Had," *Musical Times* 122 (1981), 525–9, with response by Daub, "Handel and Frederick," *Musical Times* 122 (1981), 733.

25 *London Daily Post, and General Advertiser*, no. 24 (November 30, 1734). The opera was likely the Nobility opera's next new production, Handel's *Ottone*, produced on December 10, 1734.

26 Anecdotes of Handel and Frederick are collected in Thomas McGeary, "Handel and the Feuding Royals," *Handel Institute Newsletter* 17 (Autumn 2006), 5–8.

27 Farinelli, May 23, 1735, from London, to Conte Pepoli, in Bologna; in Carlo Broschi Farinelli, *La solitudine amica: lettere al conte Sicinio Pepoli*, ed. Carlo Vitali and Francesca Boris (Palermo: Sellerio Editore, 2000), letter no. 46, p. 138.

28 Anne, Viscountess Irwin, February 1, 1729, to the Earl of Carlisle; in *Carlisle Manuscripts*, 56.

29 Egmont, *Diary*, vol. I, 387 (June 24, 1733). Lady Betty Germain reported in January or February 1734 that "the Prince talks as violently and publicly against Sir Robert as ever"; Historical Manuscripts Commission, *Report on the Manuscripts of Mrs. Stopford-Sackville*, 2 vols. (London: His Majesty's Stationery Office, 1904), vol. I, 157 (cited as *Stopford-Sackville Manuscripts*).

30 John, Lord Hervey, *Some Materials Towards Memoirs of the Reign of King George II*, ed. Romney Sedgwick, 3 vols. (London: Eyre and Spottiswoode, 1931), vol. I, 273 (cited as Hervey, *Memoirs*).

31 John, Lord Hervey, *Memoirs of the Reign of George the Second*, ed. John W. Croker, 3 vols. (London: Bickers and Son, 1884), vol. I, 319, n. 11; also reported in William Coxe, *Memoirs of the Life and Administration of Sir Robert Walpole*, 3 vols. (1798), vol. I, 522.

32 William Cobbett, *Parliamentary History of England* (1733–37), vol. IX, 1220–5; Coxe, *Memoirs of the Life and Administration of Sir Robert Walpole*, vol. I, 524.

33 Egmont, *Diary*, vol. II, 267 (May 1, 1736).

34 First edition in 1909; citing R. A. Streatfeild, *Handel*, 2nd edn. (London: Methuen, 1910), 124–6. Streatfeild was somewhat anticipated by Fritz Volbach's account: "Der Prinz von Wales jedoch, der in heftiger Opposition gegen seinen Vater stand, schlug sich zur Gegenpartei"; in *Georg Friedrich Händel*, 2nd edn. (Berlin: Harmonie Verlagsgesellschaft für Literatur und Kunst, 1907), 61. The Volbach–Streatfeild account was taken up in Friedrich Chrysander, *G. F. Händel*, 2nd edn., 3 vols. (Leipzig: Breitkopf & Härtel, 1919), vol. II, 325.

35 Henry Curties, *A Forgotten Prince of Wales* (London: Everett, [1912]), 116.

36 Newman Flower, *George Frideric Handel: His Personality and His Times* (London: Cassell & Co., 1923), 203.

37 *Daily Advertiser*, nos. 673 and 679 (March 28 and April 4, 1733); *Daily Courant*, no. 5286 (March 19, 1733); and *Daily Journal*, no. 3821 (April 2, 1733).

38 Vivian, *A Life of Frederick, Prince of Wales*, 99.

39 Flower, *George Frideric Handel*, 206–7. O. E. Deutsch, *Handel: A Documentary Biography* (New York: W. W. Norton, 1955), 304, states on no authority that the June 15 meeting "was called by Frederick, Prince of Wales, in opposition to the King, Handel's permanent protector." The entry in *The New Grove Dictionary of Music and Musicians*, 20 vols. (1980), vol. VIII, 93, similarly reports that the

June 15 meeting was held "at the instigation of the Prince of Wales, in traditional opposition to his father (and Handel's protector) the king."

40 Suffolk Record Office, Bury St. Edmunds, 941/47/13, vol. I, 250; full entry in Hervey, *Memoirs*, vol. I, 273.

41 Suffolk Record Office, Bury St. Edmunds, 941/47/13, vol. I, 251; full entry in Hervey, *Memoirs*, vol. I, 273.

42 Alan Yorke-Long, "The Opera of the Nobility" (Oxford University, dissertation presented for the Osgood Memorial Prize, 1951), provided a systematic reconsideration of the traditional account. His account is amplified and extended below. See also Thomas McGeary, "Handel, Prince Frederick, and the Opera of the Nobility Reconsidered," *Göttinger Händel-Beiträge* 7 (1998), 156–78.

43 Hervey's accounts of persons and personalities should not be accepted without corroboration; see Hans Gerig, *Die Memoiren des Lord Hervey als historische Quelle* (Inaugural dissertation, Albert-Ludwigs-Universität zu Freiburg i. Br., 1936), 72–7; Vivian, *A Life of Frederick, Prince of Wales*, 182–5.

44 Robert Halsband, *Lord Hervey: Eighteenth-Century Courtier* (New York: Oxford University Press, 1974), 98–9, 122–3, 127–9, 135–6; Vivian, *A Life of Frederick, Prince of Wales*, 174–85, 195–7.

45 The conventional account revolving around Frederick poaching Hervey's mistress Anne Vane is no longer considered convincing. The most careful account by Stephen Taylor and Hannah Smith, "Hephaestion and Alexander: Lord Hervey, Frederick, Prince of Wales, and the Royal Favourite in England in the 1730s," *English Historical Review* 124(507) (2009), 283–312, argues a combination of Hervey's sense of betrayal at being displaced in Frederick's favor by George Dubb Doddington, Frederick's discomfort with Hervey's role as a Walpole supporter, and Frederick's awareness that association with Hervey could be a political and social liability due to public attacks on Hervey's sexuality caused their falling out.

46 Hervey, *Memoirs*, vol. I, xiii–xiv.

47 In addition to the comments in passing, see the comparison of Frederick to Nero in Hervey, *Memoirs*, vol. I, 308–11, vol. III, 858–75. A manuscript poem, "Norfolk House" (Oxford, Bodleian Library, MS. Firth c. 16, 307), is attributed "By L.ᵈ Harvey. 1738" (or at least represents sentiments a contemporary thought could be Hervey's), and roundly defames Frederick:

> To Norfolk House Lords Knights & Beaux repair
> To view that matchless Thing Great Britain's Heir;
> It fawns, it grins & prattles to the Crew,
> And whispers mighty Threats against Sʳ Blue [Robert Walpole];
> Then struts & nods and gives itself Applause
> As if it meant to act by Faith & Laws;
> But Men of Sense the Idol Calf despise
> And know that every Word it speak it lies.

> Avert, ye Gods! our Country's future Smart
> Bad is it's Head, but ten Times worse it's Heart!

Norfolk House was Frederick's residence from 1737 to 1741.

48 On the roles of Delawarr and Cowper in the Nobility opera, Carole M. Taylor, "Italian Operagoing in London, 1700–1745" (Ph.D. dissertation, Syracuse University), 190–244.

49 Delawarr, June 16, 1733, to the Duke of Richmond; West Sussex Record Office. Goodwood MS 103, ff. 173–5. Deutsch, *Handel*, 303–4, misdates the letter as from January 1733.

50 Duke of Newcastle, September 1733, to the Earl of Essex in Turin; British Library, Add. MS 27,732, f. 246r.

51 Count Heinrich von Bünau, December 22, 1733, in Dresden to Zamboni in London; as trans. in Lowell Lindgren, "Musicians and Librettists in the Correspondence of Gio. Giacomo Zamboni, Oxford, Bodleian Library, MSS Rawlinson Letters 116–138." *Royal Musical Association Research Chronicle* 24 (1991), letter no. 344, 154.

52 Paolo Rolli, December ?26, 1733, to Antonio Cocchi in Florence; as trans. in Lindgren, "Musicians and Librettists," 155.

53 Duke of Chandos, March 25, 1734, to Lord Delawarr; Huntington Library, San Marino, CA, ST 57, v. 44, 47–8. Chandos, like others at the time, uses "Academy of Musick" to refer to the opera company at the King's Theatre.

54 Dispatch from Caspar Wilhelm von Borcke, January 1, 1734 (OS), to King Friedrich Wilhelm I; in Ernst Friedlaender, "Einige archivalische Nachrichten über Georg Fried. Händel und seine Familie," *Mittheilungen für die Mozart-Gemeinde in Berlin*, 2(13) (February 1902), 102–7, at 103–4: "Letztern Sonnabend wurde der Anfang der neuen *Opera* gemachet, welche die *Noblesse entreprenniret* hat, nachdem Sie mit der *conduite* des *Directeurs* von der alten *Opera, Händel*, nicht zufrieden gewesen, und denselben zu *abbaissiren* eine neue angeleget, welche über zweyhundert Persohnen *subscribiret*, und jegliche 20 *Guineés* dazu *praenumeriret* haben. Auf dem *Piquet* der *subscribenten* ist der erste Sänger, Nahmens *Senesino*, gepräget, mit der Ueberschrift: *Nec pluribus impar*" (translation provided). The motto is that of Louis XIV: "Not unequal to many [suns]."

55 In a letter to Sarah Cowper, January 2, 1734, Joseph Atwell described the Nobility opera's silver ticket: "a Scene is represented with Senesino, drest like a Heroe, in a Singing Posture"; Hertfordshire Archives and Local Studies, D/EP F234, 279. He noted how mortified Louis XIV would be, to see his motto applied to an opera singer.

56 Alluding to the disputed election of the King of Poland, which embroiled Continental Europe, but in which Walpole managed to keep Britain uninvolved.

57 *Do You Know What You Are About? or, A Protestant Alarm to Great Britain* (1733), 14, 16–17.

58 *Daily Advertiser*, no. 840 (October 9, 1733).

59 Konrad Sasse, "Opera Register from 1712 to 1734 (Colman-Register)," *Händel-Jahrbuch* 5 (1959), 222–3.

60 Abbé Prévost, *Le Pour et contre*, 3(16) (1733), 23: "On sçait déja que Senesino broüillé irréconciliablement avec M. Handel, a formé un schisme dans la Troupe, & qu'il a loüé un Théâtre séparé pour lui & pour ses partisans."

61 Prévost, *Le Pour et contre*, 3(41) (1734), 257–8: "M. Handel, toujours soutenu par le Roi & la Famille Royale … & tous les Seigneurs de la Cour idolâtres du Signor *Senesino*, prodiguent les guinées pour l'élever au-dessus de son Rival."

62 Thomas Bowen, January 24, 1734, to the Earl of Essex; British Library, Add. MS 27,738, f. 103.

63 *Grub-street Journal*, no. 211 (January 10, 1734) (articles dated November 28, 1733). An abbreviated version of the articles appears in the *St. James's Evening Post*, no. 2823 (November 24–27, 1733). Suzanne Aspden, "Ariadne's Clew: Politics, Allegory, and Opera in London (1734)," *Musical Quarterly* 85 (2001), 735–70, errs in claiming that the allegories demonstrate the political partisanship of the rival opera companies.

64 Thomas Bowen, July 8, 1733, to the Earl of Essex in Turin; British Library, Add. MS 27,738, f. 114v.

65 Not by John Arbuthnot; reprinted in Deutsch, *Handel*, 344–58. From the pro-Handel camp also came the satirical print "The Windy Bum"; see Thomas McGeary and Xavier Cervantes, "Handel, Porpora, and the Windy Bum," *Early Music* 29 (2002), 607–16.

66 One foreign observer erroneously put the rivalry as between Handel and Heidegger; see letter by Jacob Friedrich, Freiherr von Bielfeld, February 7, 1741, in London; in *Letters of Baron Bielfeld*, 4 vols. (1770), vol. IV, 43–4.

67 Earl of Shaftesbury, memoir; in Deutsch, *Handel*, 846.

68 John Mainwaring, *Memoirs of the Life of the Late George Frederic Handel* (1760), 114.

69 John Hawkins, *A General History of the Science and Practice of Music*, 5 vols. 1776 (1853 edn. in 2 vols., reprint, New York: Dover, 1963), vol. II, 875–6. Hawkins does mention that Porpora did dedicate his *Twelve Italian Cantatas* (1735) to Frederick, adding "who had taken part with him in the dispute with Handel" (vol. II, 877). But the statement overlooks Frederick's simultaneous patronage of Handel.

70 Charles Burney, *A General History of Music*, 4 vols. 1776–89; ed. Frank Mercer, 2 vols. (1935, reprint, New York: Dover, 1957), vol. II, 781. In the later "Sketch of the Life of Handel," Burney uses the anonymous *Harmony in an Uproar* (1734) to amplify the rivalry and identify its partisans, but adds nothing further on the motivation or Frederick's role; prefixed to *An Account of the Musical Performances in Westminster-Abbey* (1785), *22–*23.

71 William Coxe, *Anecdotes of George Frederick Handel and John Christopher Smith* (1799), 19.

72 The Nobility opera did move over to the King's Theatre for the 1734–35 season, whereas Handel entered a partnership with John Rich at Covent Garden. On Handel's relations with the Opera of the Nobility, Donald Burrows, "Handel and the London Opera Companies in the 1730s: Venues, Programmes, Patronage and Performers," *Göttinger Händel-Beiträge* 10 (2004), 149–65. On the opera companies, Judith Milhous, "Händel und die Londoner Theaterverhältnisse im Jahr 1734," in *Gattungskonventionen der Händel-Oper: Bericht über die Symposien der internationalen Händel-Akademie Karlsruhe 1990 und 1991* (Karlsruhe: Laaber-Verlag, 1992), 117–37.

73 Jacques Carré, "Lord Burlington's Book Subscriptions," in *Lord Burlington – The Man and His Politics: Questions of Loyalty*, ed. Edward Corp (Lewiston, NY: Edwin Mellen Press, 1998), 129–30; and Eveline Cruickshanks, "The Political Career of the Third Earl of Burlington," in *Lord Burlington: Architecture, Art and Life*, ed. Toby Barnard and Jane Clark (London: Hambledon Press, 1995), 201–15.

74 Deutsch, *Handel*, 304, on no authority states that Richmond became a director.

75 John Byrom, *The Private Journal and Literary Remains of John Byrom*, ed. Richard Parkinson; *Chetham Society* 34 (1855), 608 (gone to Hanover with the king, May 17, 1735); and *Daily Gazetteer*, no. 69 (September 17, 1735).

76 *Daily Advertiser*, no. 817 (September 12, 1733).

77 Hawkins, *A General History of the Science and Practice of Music*, vol. II, 911.

78 McGeary, "Farinelli's Progress to Albion." See also notice in the *London Evening Post*, no. 1037 (July 11–13, 1734).

79 Suffolk Record Office, Bury St. Edmunds, 941/47/13, vol. I, 251; full entry in Hervey, *Memoirs*, vol. I, 274.

80 Hervey, *Memoirs*, vol. I, 273.

81 Dispatch from von Borcke, January 1, 1734 (OS), to King Friedrich Wilhelm I; in Friedlaender, "Einige archivalische Nachrichten," 104: "Es wurde diese neue *Opera* erstlich die *Opera* der Rebellen genennet. Weilen aber bey der ersten *Ouverture* der gantze Hof zugegen war, alss ist Sie dadurch *legitim*iret und *loyal* geworden."

82 John, Lord Hervey, St. James's, November 25, 1735, to Mrs. Charlotte Digby; in *Lord Hervey and His Friends, 1726–38*, ed. the Earl of Ilchester (London: John Murray, 1950), 238.

83 *Daily Advertiser*, no. 1523 (December 15, 1735). The composer was Francesco Maria Veracini, who wrote three operas for the Nobility opera. No newspaper reports the anticipated attendance, suggesting again the newspapers under-report royal attendance (see following note).

84 Based on the pattern of newspaper accounts and command performances matched against payments in royal account books; see Donald Burrows and Robert D. Hume, "George I, the Haymarket Opera Company and Handel's *Water Music*," *Early Music* 19 (1991), 323–44, at 326–9.

85 In Richard G. King, "Handel's Travels in the Netherlands in 1750," *Music and Letters* 72 (1991), 372–86, at 384. In early 1734, one of the seasons in which he gave equal bounties to both companies, Lady Betty Germain reported: "the Prince was as eager and pressed me as earnestly to go to Lincoln's Inn Fields opera as if it had been a thing of great moment to the nation"; in *Stopford-Sackville Manuscripts*, vol. I, 157.

86 For the Granville family, Deutsch, *Handel*, 418; for Egmont, see his *Diary*; for the Wentworth family (including Handel's future librettist Newburgh Hamilton), the Wentworth Papers, British Library, Add. MS 22,229, f. 75; Add. MS 31,145, ff. 133, 135, 357.

87 Thomas Coke, December 20, 1736, to the Earl of Burlington; in H. Avray Tipping, "Four Unpublished Letters of William Kent in the Possession of Lord Spencer," *Architectural Review* 63 (1928), 180–3, 209–11, at 210.

88 *David e Bersabea*, *Festa d'Imeneo*, *Issipile*, *Adriano in Siria*, *Orfeo*, *Ottone*, *Mitridate*, *Ifigenia in Aulide*, *Polifemo*, and *Onorio*; see Peggy Daub, "Queen Caroline of England's Music Library," in *Music Publishing and Collecting: Essays in Honor of Donald W. Krummel*, ed. David Hunter (Urbana-Champaign: Graduate School of Library and Information Science, 1994), 131–65, at 148–50.

89 *Orfeo* (1736) and *Onorio* (1736) at the Henry E. Huntington Library, San Marino; *Polifemo* (1735) at the William Andrews Clark Memorial Library, Los Angeles; and *David e Bersabea* (private collection).

90 Princess Anne's account books; in King, "Handel's Travels in the Netherlands," 378–9.

91 Vivian, *A Life of Frederick, Prince of Wales*, 263, 446. In May 1736, the Earl of Egmont reported Frederick was resolved not to run into debt and was economizing for his wedding; Egmont, *Diary*, vol. II, 267 (May 1, 1736).

92 See note 85 above.

93 Handel received a payment for its composition from the Treasurer of the Chamber; David Hunter, "Royal Patronage of Handel in Britain: The Rewards of Pensions and Office," in *Handel Studies: A Gedenkschrift for Howard Serwer*, ed. Richard G. King (Hillsdale, NY: Pendragon), 127–53, at 148, n. 68.

94 *Old Whig: or, the Consistent Protestant*, no. 58 (April 15, 1736).

95 *London Daily Post, and General Advertiser*, no. 478 (May 13, 1736). Sir John Buckworth reported: "the Prince could not be persuaded to go to it, but order'd a play at Drury Lane, which carry'd away most of the Company, though the rest of the Royal Family were at Covent Garden, by this you will perceive, that our Theatrical Warr is as furious as ever, we have much the advantage for next year, having near a hundred Subscribers already, and the Subscription in the Prince's Hands, who labours hard for our Interest; Handel has not begun his yet, and I question, whether his vanity will permit him, to sollicit one"; letter to the Earl of Essex, May 13, 1736; British Library, Add. MS 27,735, f. 177r.

96 The report in the *Daily Journal*, no. 5686 (May 15, 1737), that Frederick and Augusta would attend the second performance of *Atalanta* may be

inaccurate since their presence is not corroborated in other newspapers. Deutsch, *Handel*, 408, states (probably on the basis of this item) that the couple probably attended the second performance on May 15. The report in the *Daily Journal*, no. 5703 (June 3, 1736), that the couple attended the June 2 performance of *Atalanta* is also not corroborated.

97 *London Daily Post, and General Advertiser*, no. 625 (November 1, 1736).

98 *London Daily Post, and General Advertiser*, no. 631 (November 8, 1736).

99 Aspden, "Ariadne's Clew," 738–9.

100 Aspden, "Ariadne's Clew," 739, n. 12. The two literary reports adduced are misinterpreted. The items in the *St. James's Evening Post*, no. 2823 (November 24–27, 1733), and the *Grub-street Journal*, no. 211 (January 10, 1734), deal with the players' rebellion of 1733, not the rival opera company. In *Harmony in an Uproar* (1734), what Aspden calls "partisan" is just the rivalry between the two companies; a single, passing, ironic mention of "our most noted Spirits of Sense and Patriotism" is too general to denote the political opposition.

101 Charles Burney, *The Present State of Music in France and Italy*, 2nd edn. (1773), 224.

102 Sir John Buckworth, May 13, 1736, to the Earl of Essex; British Library, Add. MS 27,735, 177r.

103 *Daily Post*, no. 4455 (December 25, 1733). The opera would formally open on December 29 at Lincoln's Inn Fields.

104 *London Daily Post, and General Advertiser*, no. 24 (November 30, 1734). *Ottone* was a revival of Handel's *Ottone*, which had its first Nobility opera performance on December 10.

105 *Daily Advertiser*, no. 1286 (March 13, 1735).

106 *Grub-street Journal*, no. 276 (April 10, 1735) (news for April 7).

107 On the gifts, McGeary, "Farinelli's Progress to Albion," 349–50.

108 Royal Music Library, British Library: RM 22 m 29–31, RM 23 a 1–3, RM 23 a 7–9, and RM a 4–6, respectively. On bills for their binding, Thomas McGeary, "Pope and Frederick, Prince of Wales: Gifts and Memorials of Friendship," *Scriblerian* 33 (2000), 40–7.

109 For the opposition, *A Letter from a Member of Parliament … upon the Motion to Address His Majesty to Settle 100,000 l. per Annum on His Royal Highness the Prince of Wales* [1737] and *Lords Protest on the Motion to Address His Majesty to Settle 100,000 l. per Annum on the Prince of Wales* [1737]; for the government, see *An Examination of the Facts and Reasonings Contain'd in a Pamphlet intitled, A Letter from a Member of Parliament* (1739).

110 Cobbett, *Parliamentary History of England* (1733–1737), vol. IX, 1352–454.

111 According to a letter from Wasner to Count Zinzendorf, March 15, 1737 (NS): "The Prince of Wales continuing to wait on the King and Queen as usual, there is reason to hope the consequences, that were apprehended from what lately

happened in Parliament, will be prevented, and that the ill intentioned will find no opportunity of making use of this misunderstanding for their private views." The National Archives, SP 107/21.

112 On the feud and expulsion, Hervey, *Memoirs*, vol. III, 756–93, 807–27, 838–9; Philip C. Yorke, *The Life and Correspondence of Philip Yorke, Earl of Hardwicke, Lord High Chancellor of Great Britain*, 3 vols. (Cambridge University Press, 1913), vol. I, 169–82; Coxe, *Memoirs of the Life and Administration of Sir Robert Walpole*, vol. I, 533–46; and Egmont, *Diary*, vol. II, 425ff. How the feud affected Handel and Prince Frederick is examined in McGeary, "Handel and the Feuding Royals," 5–8.

113 So strong was the king's displeasure and desire to humiliate his son that he commanded that his edict and all the letters exchanged between him and Frederick be printed in newspapers and magazines and distributed to members of parliament, foreign ministers, and courts throughout Europe. The letters were published as *Letters … That Passed between the King, Queen, Prince and Princess of Wales; on Occasion of the Birth of the Young Princess* (1737), and in *The Political State of Great Britain* 54 (November 1737), 477–88.

114 Robert O. Bucholz, *The Augustan Court: Queen Anne and the Decline of Court Culture* (Stanford University Press, 1993), 247–8.

115 On the theatrical productions relating to the wedding, see Emmett L. Avery, "A Royal Wedding Royally Confounded," *Western Humanities Review* 10 (1956), 153–64; and Michael Burden, "The Wedding Masques for Anne, the Princess Royal," *Miscellanea Musicologica. Adelaide Studies in Musicology* 17 (1990, 87–113.

116 The case for the rivalry is put by Aspden, "Ariadne's Clew." The emphases of the plots of the two operas are so different, it is not clear on what points the productions rival. A true rivalry might consist in two settings of the same libretto (as in the case of *The Judgment of Paris* [1701]), whose libretto by Congreve was set in a competition by Eccles, Finger, Daniel Purcell, and Weldon). There is no contemporary comment comparing the two operas.

117 Aspden, "Ariadne's Clew," 756–57. She points to various allegorizations and potential satire present in other texts and iconography of William and Anne as a warrant for her allegorical reading; but none cited use the myth of Theseus and Ariadne, and it does not follow that the operas are also allegorical.

118 Hervey, *Memoirs*, vol. I, 194.

119 *Daily Advertiser*, no. 971 (March 11, 1734); and *Daily Journal*, no. 4102 (March 11, 1734).

120 British Library, Add. MS 24,399, f. 16r.

121 The consensus was that greed sent him on to Madrid. For example, Charles Philippe d'Albert, *Mémoires du Duc de Luynes sur la Cour de Louis XV (1735–1758)*, 17 vols. (Paris: Firmin Didot Frères, Fil et Cie., 1860–65), vol. I, 364: "mais ne trouvant pas apparemment ces présents assez considérables, il jugea à propos d'aller en Espagne chercher un établissement plus avantageux"; and Jean

Frederic Phelypeaux de Maurepas, *Mémoires du Comte de Maurepas*, 4 vols. (1792), vol. IV, 236: "ne se trouvant pas assez récompensé, il alla en Espagne chercher un meilleur traitement." It is likely that the Conde de Montijo, the former Spanish Ambassador to Britain, had extended the invitation to Farinelli on behalf of the Spanish Queen Elisabeth Farnese.

122 Farinelli's progress to Madrid and its use in partisan propaganda is explored in greater detail in Thomas McGeary, "Farinelli in Madrid: Opera, Politics, and the War of Jenkins' Ear," *Musical Quarterly* 82 (1998), 383–421.

123 His arrival at Madrid in summer 1737 was noted and reported on by the diplomatic community (for British reports, see McGeary, "Farinelli in Madrid"). The French minister the Comte de Vaulgrenant described Farinelli's reception on August 12, in his weekly correspondence to the minister of foreign affairs, Denis Amelot de Chaillou: "Leurs Maj.ˢ Cath.ᵉˢ se donnent en Particulier tous les soirs une heure de récreation a entendre chanter le fameux farinelli"; Paris, Archives du Ministère des Affaires Etrangères, Correspondance Politique, Espagne, vol. 442, f. 163v. The substance of this report was repeated on August 19 (f. 182v).

124 The principal sources are Burney, *A General History of Music*, vol. II, 815–16; and Burney, "Carlo Broschi," in Abraham Rees, *The Cyclopædia; or, Universal Dictionary of Arts, Sciences, and Literature*, 39 vols. (1819). The cure probably was not complete; see McGeary, "Farinelli in Madrid."

125 Vaulgrenent wrote to Amelot on August 26, 1737: "Leurs Majestes Cath.ᵉˢ sont si Contentes du Musicien farinelly et prennent tant de plaisir a L'entendre, quelles se sont determinées a le garder, et luy ont delcaré Elles mêmes quelles ne Luy permettroient pas de retourner en Angleterre, Il ne s'est pas fait presser pour se soumettre a Leurs Volontez"; Paris, Archives du Ministère des Affaires Etrangères, Correspondance Politique, Espagne, vol. 442, ff. 207v–208r.

126 On the background of the Depredations Crisis, Philip Woodfine, *Britannia's Glories: The Walpole Ministry and the 1739 War with Spain* (Woodbridge: Boydell & Brewer, 1998), 75–101; Jean O. McLachlan, *Trade and Peace with Old Spain, 1667–1750* (Cambridge University Press, 1940), 78–121; Richard Pares, *War and Trade in the West Indies, 1739–1763* (Oxford University Press, 1936), 14–43; and Ernest G. Hildner, Jr., "The Rôle of the South Sea Company in the Diplomacy Leading to the War of Jenkins' Ear, 1729–1739," *Hispanic American Historical Review* 18 (1938), 321–41.

127 For example, *London Evening Post*, nos. 1517, 1544–45, 1548–49, 1552, 1560, 1566 (August 4–6, October 6–8, 8–11, 15–18, 18–20, 25–27, November 12–15, 26–29, 1737); *Daily Post*, nos. 5640, 5649 (October 8 and 19, 1737); *Common Sense*, nos. 38, 42, 44 (October 22, November 19, December 3, 1737); *Old Whig: or, the Consistent Protestant*, no. 137 (October 20, 1737); and *Craftsman*, nos. 589, 591–93 (October 22, November 5, 12, 19, 1737).

128 *Craftsman*, nos. 603, 605, 607–08, 610–11 (January 28, February 11 and 25, 4, 18, and March 25, 1738).

129 *Daily Gazetteer*, no. 722 (October 27, 1737).

130 *Common Sense*, no. 32 (September 10, 1737). The writer continues the theater–politics parallel in an afterthought: "I just now heard, that Expresses are sent to diverse Parts of the Kingdom, to summon the Directors of the Academy together, in order to concert proper Measures, at this critical Juncture; though some are of Opinion, this grand Affair ought to be solemnly debated at the approaching Congress at *Nimirow*, and his Excellency Mynheer *Handel*, be forthwith appointed First Plenipotentiary on this important Occasion."

131 A similar charge is made in Weddell, *A Voyage up the Thames* (1738): "The Polite Part of the Nation [is] in Tears; who are, in all Appearance, more enraged at *Iberia* for preventing his [Farinelli's] Return, than on any *other* Account" (dedication).

132 Letter from Robert Marsham, second Baron Romney, London, September 6, 1737, to the Duke of Leeds; British Library, Add. MS 28,051 f. 316r.

133 *Craftsman*, no. 591 (November 5, 1737).

134 Beginning with *Harlequin-Horace* (1731), Miller's writings show an increasing sympathy to the opposition cause; his oppositional satires include *Seasonable Reproof* (1735), *Are These Things So?* (1740), and *The Year Forty-One. Carmen Seculare* (1741). His *Miscellaneous Works in Verse and Prose* (1741) was dedicated to Prince Frederick. On January 29, 1740, the ministerial John "Orator" Henley's *Hyp-Doctor* (no. 482) included Miller among the minor prophets of the opposition who preached politics to ministers of state. His widow described his refusing a government offer in Theophilis Cibber, *The Lives of the Poets of Great Britain and Ireland*, 5 vols. (1753), vol. V, 332–4.

   On the pamphlet war set off by Miller, see Ian Gordon, introduction to James Miller, *Are These Things So?* Augustan Reprint Series 153 (1972); Bertrand Goldgar, *Walpole and the Wits: The Relation of Politics to Literature, 1722–1742* (Lincoln: University of Nebraska Press, 1976), 210–11; Maynard Mack, *The Garden and the City: Retirement and Politics in the Later Poetry of Pope, 1731–1743* (University of Toronto Press, 1969), 194–200; and Paula J. O'Brien, "The Life and Works of James Miller, 1704–1744" (Ph.D. dissertation, Westfield College, University of London, 1979).

135 The farce was performed twice on January 26 and 28, 1738; the application to the Lord Chamberlain is dated January 12, 1738; see *Catalogue of the Larpent Plays in the Huntington Library*, comp. Dougald MacMillan (San Marino, CA: Huntington Library Press, 1939), no. 3, p. 1.

136 James Miller, *The Coffee-House*, 8–9. The song was reprinted (text only) as "The Loss of Faronello" in Miller, *Miscellaneous Works*, 109–10. It was frequently printed separately with its music (as "England's Lamentation for the Loss of Farinello") and in *Calliope, or English Harmony*, 2 vols. [?1737–?1745], no. 178, as well as on several single-sheet songs. Similar sentiments are expressed in Henry Carey's "The Beau's Lamentation for the Loss of Farrinelli," in his

Musical Century, 2 vols. (1737–1740), vol. II, 5, and in passing in the song "As musing I rang'd in the Meads all alone," in *The Syren*, 3rd edn. (1739), 363–4.

137 Henry E. Huntington Library, San Marino, CA, LA 3. The objectionable lines were restored in the printed play (p. 9).

138 *Common Sense*, no. 45 (December 10, 1737).

139 Dulness had figured in Pope's *Dunciad* (1728); the Goddess of Nonsense appeared in Fielding's *The Author's Farce* (1730).

140 *Common Sense*, no. 45 (December 10, 1737).

141 *Nonsense of Common-Sense*, no. 3 (January 3, 1738); also reprinted in Mary Wortley Montagu, *Essays and Poems*, ed. Robert Halsband (Oxford: Clarendon Press, 1977), 114–20. On Lady Mary as pro-ministry writer, Halsband, *The Life of Lady Mary Wortley Montagu* (Oxford: Clarendon, 1956), 165–71. Halsband did not recognize the name Balducci, who was mentioned several months earlier in the *Craftsman*, no. 588 (October 15, 1737), as a maker of mathematical statues. The writer proposes Balducci could make statues to sit in Parliament, an implication that Walpole's placemen are nothing but automatons who do his bidding on command. His Italian figures are also mentioned in the *London Daily Post, and General Advertiser*, no. 1131 (June 14, 1738).

142 Cobbett, *Parliamentary History of England* (1737–1739), vol. X, 561–643 (Commons), and 729–87 (Lords). The *Gentleman's Magazine* 8 (March 1738), 163–4, fanned the issue by printing a list of fifty-one ships seized or plundered since 1728.

143 *Daily Post*, nos. 5775, 5788, 5790, 5800 (March 15 and 30, 1738, April 1 and 13 [quoted], 1738); and *London Evening Post*, nos. 1618–19, 1621 (March 28–30 [quoted], March 30 to April 1, April 4–6, 1738); by April, the number had swelled to seventy-one. See also McLachlan, *Trade and Peace with Old Spain*, 107; and Woodfine, *Britannia's Glories*, 130–4.

144 The truth of the incident is hard to establish. However, J. K. Laughton, "Jenkins' Ear," *English Historical Review* 4 (1889), 741–9, has found several contemporary letters citing Jenkins losing his ear. The *Craftsman*, no. 259 (June 19, 1731), and *Fog's Weekly Journal*, no. 137 (June 19, 1731), carried near-contemporary accounts of the torture of Captain Jenkins that mention the severing of his ear.

145 Jenkins never appeared before the Commons; see Philip Woodfine, "The Anglo-Spanish War of 1739," in *The Origin of War in Early Modern Europe*, ed. Jeremy Black (Edinburgh: John Donald, 1987), 185–209, at 196; Cobbett, *Parliamentary History of England* (1737–1739), vol. X, 638–40.

146 Cobbett, *Parliamentary History of England* (1737–1739), vol. X, 586.

147 *Common Sense*, no. 70 (June 3, 1738). See also *Common Sense*, no. 62 (April 8, 1738), and the *Daily Post*, no. 5852 (June 13, 1738); item repeated in *Common Sense*, no. 72 (June 17, 1738). *Common Sense*, no. 73 (June 24, 1738), reiterates

the foolishness of British adulation for Farinelli and Italian opera during his first season.

148 *Common Sense*, no. 70 (June 3, 1738).

149 On the plan, the negotiations leading to the Convention of the Pardo, and its ultimate collapse, McLachlan, *Trade and Peace with Old Spain*, 110–21; Woodfine, *Britannia's Glories*, 154–209; and Woodfine, "The Anglo-Spanish War of 1739," 200–5.

150 Representative opposition tracts include *The British Sailor's Discovery: or the Spanish Pretensions Confuted* (1739); Hugh Hume-Campbell, Earl of Marchmont, *A State of the Rise and Progress of Our Disputes with Spain* (1739); Richard Copithorne, *The English Cotejo: or, the Cruelties, Depredations, and Illicit Trade Charg'd upon the English* (1739); *England's Triumph: or, Spanish Cowardice Expos'd* (1739); George Lyttelton, *Considerations upon the Present State of Our Affairs, at Home and Abroad* (1739); *Ministerial Prejudices in Favour of the Convention, Examin'd and Answer'd* (1739); *Peace and No Peace* (1739); William Pulteney, *A Review of All that hath Pass'd between the Courts of Great Britain and Spain* (1739); Benjamin Robins, *Observations on the Present Convention with Spain* (1739); and *Some Remarks on a Pamphlet Intitled Popular Prejudices against the Convention and Treaty with Spain* (1739).

151 Representative ministerial tracts include *An Address to the Merchants of Great-Britain: or, a Review of the Conduct of the Administration* (1739); *An Apology for the Minister* (1739); *Common Sense: Its Nature and Use* (1738); Thomas Gordon, *An Appeal to the Unprejudiced, Concerning the Present Discontents Occasioned by the Late Convention with Spain* (1739); *Popular Prejudices against the Convention and Treaty with Spain, Examin'd and Answer'd* (1739); *The Spanish Merchant's Address to all Candid and Impartial Englishmen* (1739); Horatio Walpole, *The Convention Vindicated from the Misrepresentations of the Enemies of Our Peace* (1739); and Walpole, *The Grand Question, Whether War, or No War, with Spain, Impartially Consider'd* (1739).

152 Woodfine, *Britannia's Glories*, 217–18.

153 For the years of the two companies, the library of the family of Earl Cowper had librettos of only operas produced by the Opera of the Nobility; see the eleven-volume set of librettos with the Panshanger family bookplate, University of California, Los Angeles, Music Library, Special Collections.

154 For later oratorio and opera attendance, Carole Taylor, "Handel and Frederick, Prince of Wales," *Musical Times* 125 (1984), 89–92.

155 In later years, *c.*1746–50, Frederick was assembling a collection of manuscript scores of Handel's anthems and oratorios; see Donald Burrows, "The 'Granville' and 'Smith' Collections of Handel Manuscripts," in *Sundrey Sorts of Music Books: Essays on The British Library Collections*, ed. Chris Banks, Arthur Searle, and Malcolm Turner (London: The British Library, 1993), 231–47, at 238–44.

7   Politics, theater, and opera in the 1730s

1 Cobham's extended political family included Thomas Pitt, Richard Grenville, William Pitt (Pitt the elder, later Earl of Chatham), George Lyttelton, and George and James Grenville. Lyttelton had been introduced to the Prince of Wales in 1732 and became an equerry, close adviser, and finally his secretary in 1737. On the formation of Cobham's opposition, and the early careers of its members, Lewis M. Wiggin, *The Faction of Cousins: A Political Account of the Grenvilles, 1733–1763* (New Haven, CT: Yale University Press, 1958), esp. 1–15 and 84–97; Basil Williams, *The Life of William Pitt, Earl of Chatham*, 2 vols. (London: Longmans, Green, and Co., 1914), vol. I, 45–71; and Peter Douglas Brown, *William Pitt, Earl of Chatham: The Great Commoner* (London: George Allen & Unwin, 1978), 30–45.

2 Christine Gerrard, *The Patriot Opposition to Walpole: Politics, Poetry, and National Myth, 1725–1742* (Oxford University Press, 1994), 127–9.

3 Mabel H. Cable, "The Idea of a Patriot King in the Propaganda of the Opposition to Walpole, 1735–1739," *Philological Quarterly* 18 (1939), 119–30; H. T. Dickinson, "Bolingbroke: 'The Idea of a Patriot King'," *History Today* 20 (1970), 13–19; Isaac Kramnick, *Bolingbroke and His Circle: The Politics of Nostalgia in the Age of Walpole* (Cambridge, MA: Harvard University Press, 1968), 33–5, 163–9; and Gerrard, *The Patriot Opposition to Walpole*, 185–229. For text, *Bolingbroke: Political Writings*, ed. David Armitage (Cambridge University Press, 1997), 217–94.

4 For the poet David Mallet, Lyttelton procured the place of undersecretary to the prince at £200; James Thomson received a pension of £100 from the prince in 1737; see Rose Mary Davis, *The Good Lord Lyttelton: A Study in Eighteenth Century Politics and Culture* (Bethlehem, PA: Times Publishing Co., 1939), 48–74.

5 Tone S. Urstad, *Sir Robert Walpole's Poets: The Use of Literature as Pro-Government Propaganda, 1721–1742* (Newark: University of Delaware Press, 1999), esp. 172–230; and David H. Stevens, *Party Politics and English Journalism, 1702–1742* (Menasha, WI: Collegiate Press, 1961).

6 Looking back on the seasons, the vigorously ministerial *Hyp-Doctor* (no. 502, June 10, 1740), charged that the Patriots made politics theatrical (by their "clapping and hissing as in the theatre" in the Commons debates), and "endeavoured to make the Theatre Political, by *Edward and Eleonora*, *Pasquin*, *Gustavus Vassa*, *Arminius*, the *Golden Rump*, *Tom Thumb* the *Great*, and about a hundred Farces that might be mentioned."

7 James J. Lynch, *Box, Pit, and Gallery: Stage and Society in Johnson's London* (Berkeley: University of California Press, 1953), 247–50.

8 Thomas Davies, *Dramatic Miscellanies: Consisting of Critical Observations on Several Plays of Shakespeare*, new edn., 3 vols. (1785), vol. I, 152–3.

9 *The Doctrine of Innuendo's Discuss'd, or The Liberty of the Press Maintain'd* (1731), 15.

10 John, Lord Hervey, *Some Materials Toward Memoirs of the Reign of King George II*, ed. Romney Sedgwick, 3 vols. (London: Eyre and Spottiswoode, 1931), vol. I, 98 (cited as Hervey, *Memoirs*).

11 The play's application is that evil ministers will finally receive just punishment by a wise king. *Remarks on an Historical Play, called The Fall of Mortimer. Shewing Wherein the Said Play May Be Term'd a Libel Against the Present Administration* (1731) points out the parallels and charges that the play shows a prime minister taking bribes and selling the interest of his king and country. The play is defended in *The History of Mortimer ... Occasion'd by It's Having Been Presented as a Treasonable Libel* (1731).

12 *Fog's Weekly Journal*, nos. 137 and 142 (June 19 and July 24, 1731).

13 Robert D. Hume, *Henry Fielding and the London Theatre, 1728–1737* (Oxford: Clarendon Press, 1988), 77–104; and Hume, "Henry Fielding and Politics at the Little Haymarket, 1728–1737," in *The Golden and Brazen World: Papers in Literature and History, 1650–1800*, ed. John M. Wallace (Berkeley: University of California Press, 1985), 79–124 (esp. 95–104).

14 Hume, *Henry Fielding and the London Theatre*, 213.

15 When revised as *The Grub-Street Opera* (pub. 1731), the play was suppressed.

16 See Fielding's "To the Right Honourable Sir Robert Walpole" (1730). On Fielding's politics and of his plays, Thomas R. Cleary, *Henry Fielding: Political Writer* (Waterloo: Laurier University Press, 1984); Hume, *Henry Fielding and the London Theatre*; Hume, "Henry Fielding and Politics at the Little Haymarket"; Bertrand A. Goldgar, *Walpole and the Wits: The Relation of Politics to Literature, 1722–1742* (Lincoln: University of Nebraska Press, 1976), 150–6; and Thomas Lockwood, "Fielding and the Licensing Act," *Huntington Library Quarterly* 50 (1987), 379–393.

17 Cleary, *Henry Fielding: Political Writer*, 1–12, 69–73, 75–116; and Martin C. Battestin, with Ruthe R. Battestin, *Henry Fielding: A Life* (London: Routledge, 1989), 165–7, 173–7, 183–5.

18 Vincent J. Liesenfeld, *The Licensing Act of 1737* (Madison: University of Wisconsin Press, 1984), 23–59; Hume, *Henry Fielding and the London Theatre*, 192–9.

19 *Weekly Miscellany*, no. 117 (March 8, 1735).

20 William Cobbett, *Parliamentary History of England* (1733–1737), vol. IX, 948.

21 *Craftsman*, no. 469 (June 28, 1735).

22 Historical Manuscripts Commission, *Manuscripts of the Earl of Egmont. Diary of Viscount Percival afterwards First Earl of Egmont*, 3 vols. (London: His Majesty's Stationery Office 1920–23), vol. II, 375 (March 22, 1737) (cited as Egmont, *Diary*). None of the newspapers saw the play as partisan or oppositional at the time; see Goldgar, *Walpole and the Wits*, 152–3.

23 Brean S. Hammond, "Politics and Cultural Politics: The Case of Henry Fielding," *Eighteenth-Century Life* 16 (February 1992), 76–93.

24 *Daily Gazetteer*, no. 584 (May 7, 1737).

25 On the politics in the *Historical Register*, Cleary, *Henry Fielding: Political Writer*, 96–102; Hume, *Henry Fielding and the London Theatre*, 234–38; and Goldgar, *Walpole and the Wits*, 153–5.

26 Henry Fielding, *The Historical Register For the Year 1736 and Eurydice Hissed*, ed. William W. Appleton (Lincoln: University of Nebraska Press, 1967), quoting Act I (pp. 16, 36, 37).

27 On the politics of *Eurydice Hiss'd*: Cleary, *Henry Fielding: Political Writer*, 102–6; Hume, *Henry Fielding and the London Theatre*, 237–9; Goldgar, *Walpole and the Wits*, 153–5.

28 Egmont, *Diary*, vol. II, 390 (April 18, 1737).

29 Liesenfeld, *The Licensing Act of 1737*, 91–122.

30 *Daily Gazetteer*, no. 584 (May 7, 1737).

31 *Common Sense*, no. 16 (May 21, 1737); and *Daily Gazetteer*, no. 608 (June 4, 1737).

32 Liesenfeld, *The Licensing Act of 1737*, 123–55; John Loftis, *The Politics of Drama in Augustan England* (Oxford: Clarendon Press, 1963), 128–53; Hume, *Henry Fielding and the London Theatre*, 242–60; Liesenfeld, ed., *The Stage and the Licensing Act, 1729–1739* (New York: Garland, 1981), introduction; and L. W. Conolly, *The Censorship of English Drama, 1737–1824* (San Marino, CA: Huntington Library Press, 1976).

33 The farce was probably based on the obscene and treasonous "The Vision of the Golden Rump," the allegory that had recently appeared in *Common Sense*, nos. 7–8 (March 19 and 26, 1737) and was illustrated in the print "The Festival of the Golden Rump," which is reproduced in Paul Langford, *Walpole and the Robinocracy*. The English Satirical Print, 1600–1832 (Cambridge: Chadwyck-Healey, 1986), no. 48; Herbert M. Atherton, *Political Prints in the Age of Hogarth: A Study of the Ideographic Representation of Politics* (Oxford: Clarendon Press, 1974), no. 19; and Liesenfeld, ed., *The Stage and the Licensing Act* (including the *Common Sense* essays).

34 Most of the surviving word books are in the Larpent Collection at the Henry E. Huntington Library; see Douglas McMillan, *Catalogue of the Larpent Plays in the Huntington Library* (San Marino, CA: Huntington Library Press, 1939); and Conolly, *The Censorship of English Drama*.

35 Letter by Col. John Cope, May 28, 1737, to Edward Weston; Historical Manuscripts Commission, *Reports on the Manuscripts of the Earl of Eglinton* [etc.] (London: Eyre and Spottiswoode, 1885), 267.

36 The renown of Chesterfield's speech (admired even by the government partisans John, Lord Hervey and Colley Cibber) has led to the mistaken idea that there was strong opposition to the bill. On the speech and the debate, Liesenfeld, *The Licensing Act of 1737*, 147–55; 232, n. 93. Also writing against the Act are the *Craftsman*, nos. 569–70, 572–73, 577 (May 28, June 4, 18, and 25, July 30, 1737); and *Fog's Weekly Journal*, no. 3, n.s. (June 18, 1737).

37 A letter by A. Z. in *Common Sense*, no. 18 (June 4, 1737), repeats the substance of Chesterfield's argument.

38 *Daily Gazetteer*, nos. 608–9, 611–15, 617, 625, 635–36, 638, 644–45, and 654 (June 4, 6, 8–11, 13, 15, and 24, and July 6–7, 9, 16, 18, and 30, 1737). The ministry and opposition continued their sparring over the bill through the following year; see *Common Sense*, nos. 49, 61, and 90–91 (January 7, April 1, and October 21 and 28, 1738); *Craftsman*, no. 602 (January 21, 1738), and no. 613 (April 8, 1738); and *Daily Gazetteer*, no. 774 (December 27, 1737).

39 Letter dated May 30; in *Fog's Weekly Journal*, no. 3, n.s. (June 18, 1737).

40 *Craftsman*, no. 570 (June 4, 1737).

41 *Craftsman*, no. 573 (June 25, 1737).

42 *Common Sense*, no. 67 (May 13, 1738).

43 On the widespread and varied use of the story, see Elizabeth Rawson, *The Spartan Tradition in European Thought* (Oxford: Clarendon Press, 1969).

44 *Common Sense*, no. 10 (April 9, 1737). Lyttelton also wrote a poem "To Mr. Glover; On his Poem of Leonidas," in *The Works of George Lord Lyttelton*, 3 vols. (1776), vol. 3, 193–6, and other editions of his works.

45 For prominent places of Patriot rhetoric, see bk. 1, ll. 34–5, 75–76, 126–59, bk. 4, ll. 17–55, 320–47, bk. 7, ll. 293–5, 404–45, and bk. 8, ll. 105–8.

46 *Weekly Miscellany*, nos. 227, 228, and 230 (April 29, May 6 and 20, 1737).

47 Maynard Mack, *Alexander Pope: A Life* (New York: W. W. Norton, 1985), 758–60; and James Sambrook, *James Thomson, 1700–1748: A Life* (Oxford: Clarendon Press, 1991), 188–200.

48 Thomas Davies, *Memoirs of the Life of David Garrick*, new edn., 2 vols. (1780), vol. II, 31–40.

49 Davies, *Memoirs of Garrick*, vol. II, 32.

50 Samuel Johnson, *Lives of the English Poets*, ed. George B. Hill, 3 vols. (Oxford: Clarendon Press, 1905), vol. III, 286; and Alan D. McKillop, "Thomson and the Licensers of the Stage," *Philological Quarterly* 37 (1958), 448–53, at 448.

51 James Thomson, *Liberty, the Castle of Indolence, and Other Poems*, ed. James Sambrook (Oxford: Clarendon Press, 1986), 19 (edition quoted); James Thomson, *The Castle of Indolence and Other Poems*, ed. Alan D. McKillop (Lawrence: University of Kansas Press, 1961), 159–60.

52 *Daily Journal*, no. 2514 (January 28, 1729); *Fog's Weekly Journal*, no. 19 (February 1, 1729); and *Free Briton*, no. 37 (August 13, 1730).

53 Thomson, *Liberty, the Castle of Indolence, and Other Poems*, 31–147; and McKillop, "Ethics and Political History in Thomson's *Liberty*," in *Pope and his Contemporaries: Essays Presented to George Sherburn*, ed. James C. Clifford and Louis A. Landa (Oxford: Clarendon Press, 1949), 215–29.

54 Alan D. McKillop, *The Background of Thomson's "Liberty."* Rice Institute Pamphlet 38(2) (July 1951). The agreement of *Liberty* with opposition polemic is made explicit in the *Craftsman*, no. 476 (August 16, 1735).

55　Strong anti-Walpole lines at pt. 5, ll. 99–114; on the effects of dependency on wealth, luxury, and corruption at pt. 5, ll. 157–99.

56　James Thomson, October 10, 1732, from Paris, to Lady Hertford: in James Thomson, *Letters and Documents*, ed. Alan Dugald McKillop (Lawrence: University of Kansas Press, 1958), 83.

57　See line numbers in James Thomson, *The Seasons*, ed. James Sambrook (Oxford: Clarendon Press, 1981): *Autumn* 1037–81 (Cobham, Stowe Gardens, and the Temple of Virtue), *Spring* 904–62 (George Lyttelton), *Autumn* 1048 (William Pitt), *Winter* (Chesterfield), 656–90.

58　*Liberty, the Castle of Indolence, and Other Poems*, 301–2, 427–8. The ode was published simultaneously in several newspapers.

59　*Daily Gazetteer*, no. 704 (October 6, 1737). The *Political State of Great Britain* 54 (October 1737), 361–2, 400–4, noted the ode had "occasioned some extraordinary political Reflections" and reprinted the ode and the *Daily Gazetteer* essay.

60　On the politics of *Agamemnon*, *The Plays of James Thomson, 1700–1748: A Critical Edition*, ed. John C. Greene, 2 vols. (New York: Garland, 1987), vol. I, cxxi–cxxxi (edition quoted); and Sambrook, *James Thomson*, 175, 184–5.

61　Davies, *Memoirs of Garrick*, vol. II, 32.

62　The copy submitted to the licenser (Henry E. Huntington Library, LA 4), has numerous revisions. None show any sign of being made by the licenser or to avoid incendiary politics; all seem made to cut characters and shorten or improve the drama.

63　Loftis, *The Politics of Drama in Augustan England*, 151.

64　The six objectionable lines are included in the printed text. The prologue was not included in the text submitted to the licenser.

65　*The Plays of David Mallet*, ed. Felicity A. Nussbaum (New York: Garland, 1980), xix–xxiv.

66　Davies, *Memoirs of Garrick*, vol. II, 34. *Mustapha* is not present in the Larpent Collection.

67　*Observations on the Present Taste for Poetry* (1739), 22.

68　Frances Thynne Seymour, Countess of Hertford, from London, February 22. 1739 (OS), to Henrietta Louisa Jeffreys, Countess of Pomfret; Archives of the Duke of Northumberland at Alnwick Castle, DNP MS 111, 36. The full correspondence (with inexact and altered transcriptions) can be found in *Correspondence between Frances, Countess of Hartford [sic] (afterwards Duchess of Somerset) and Henrietta Louisa, Countess of Pomfret between the Years 1738 and 1741*, ed. W. M. Bingley, 2nd edn., 3 vols. (London: Richard Phillips, 1806), vol. I, 97 (cited as *Hartford-Pomfret Correspondence*).

69　Countess of Pomfret, April 15, 1739 (NS), from Montserrat, to Countess of Hertford; Alnwick Castle, DNP MS 111, 49.

70　On the politics of *Mustapha*, Sambrook, *James Thomson*, 190–1; and *The Plays of David Mallet*, ed. Nussbaum, xxiii.

71 *Gustavus Vasa* is not present in the Larpent Collection.

72 W. A. Speck, "Politicians, Peers, and Publication by Subscription, 1700–1750," in *Books and Their Readers in Eighteenth-Century England*, ed. Isabel Rivers (New York: St. Martin's Press, 1982), 47–68, at 58–9; and Goldgar, *Walpole and the Wits*, 181.

73 Countess of Hertford, March 16/27, 1739, London, to Countess of Pomfret; Alnwick Castle, DNP MS 111, 46.

74 Benjamin Victor, undated, to Sir William Wolseley; in Benjamin Victor, *Original Letters, Dramatic Pieces, and Poems*, 3 vols. (1776), letter no. 11, vol. I, 33. On the politics of *Gustavus Vasa*, Liesenfeld, ed., *The Stage and the Licensing Act*, xxv–xxviii; and Alexander Pettit, "Anxiety, Political Rhetoric, and Historical Drama under Walpole," *1650–1850: Ideas, Aesthetics, and Inquiries in the Early Modern Era* 1 (1994), 109–36, at 127–30.

75 The prologue was reprinted in *Common Sense*, no. 114 (April 7, 1739), to demonstrate the only merit of the play was not in its being banned.

76 *Daily Gazetteer*, no. 1216 [=1214] (May 15, 1739).

77 J. C. D. Clark, *Samuel Johnson: Literature, Religion and English Cultural Politics from the Restoration to Romanticism* (Cambridge University Press, 1994), 166. A Jacobitical reading is also given by Howard Erskine-Hill, *Poetry of Opposition and Revolution: Dryden to Wordsworth* (Oxford: Clarendon Press, 1996), 129–32.

78 Howard Weinbrot, "Johnson, Jacobitism, and the History of Nostalgia," *Age of Johnson* 7 (1996), 163–211, at 185–6.

79 The pamphlet is based on *The Lives of Roger Mortimer, Earl of March, and of Robert, Earl of Oxford, &c.* (1711). A similar strategy is employed in *The Fate of Favourites; Examplified in the Fall of Villiers, Duke of Buckingham* (1734).

80 See advertisements in *Common Sense*, no. 115 (April 14, 1739); *Daily Advertiser*, no. 1569 (April 18, 1739); and *Daily Post*, no. 6117 (April 18, 1739).

81 *Country Correspondent* [No. 3]: *Humbly Address'd to Gustavus Vasa, Esq* (May 1739), 8, 30.

82 Davies, *Memoirs of David Garrick*, vol. II, 33–4. The copy submitted to the licenser is at the Henry E. Huntington Library, LA 12.

83 Sambrook, *James Thomson*, 194.

84 Subscription advertisements in *Common Sense*, no. 115 (April 14, 1739); and *London Daily Post, and General Advertiser*, nos. 1395, 1398, and 1399 (April 18, 21, and 23, 1739).

85 On the politics of *Edward and Eleonora*, Sambrook, *James Thomson*, 195–6; and *The Plays of James Thomson*, ed. Greene, vol. I, cxxxix–cxliv.

86 These lines, additions to the fair copy submitted to the licenser, may have been intended to increase the topicality of the play.

87 Countess of Pomfret, February 25, 1739 (NS), from Montserrat, to Countess of Hertford; Alnwick Castle, DNP MS 111, 33.

88 *The History of the Life and Death of Sultan Solyman the Magnificent, Emperor of the Turks, and of his Son Mustapha. Inscrib'd to the Spectators of* "*Mustapha*" (1739); *The History of the Life and Actions of Gustavus Vasa, Deliverer of His Country. Recommended to the Spectators of a Tragedy on that Subject, Now in Rehearsal* (1739); and *The History of the Life and Reign of the Valiant Prince Edward … and his Princess Eleonora. On which history, is founded a play, written by Mr. Thomson, call'd, Edward and Eleonora* (1739).

89 *Daily Gazetteer*, nos. 1188 [= 1186] and 1200 [=1198] (April 12 and 26, 1739). On these essays, McKillop, "Thomson and the Licensers of the Stage," 448–53.

90 *Daily Gazetteer*, nos. 1216 [=1214], 1221 [=1219], 1224 [=1223], and 1232 [=1230] (May 15, 21, and 24, and June 2, 1739).

91 Henry E. Huntington Library, LA 8. In Act IV, before the entrance of Sigismund, someone crossed out (too heavily to be read now) the four lines following "The power of Varus ever to retrieve," which are not in the printed play.

92 Kimerly Rorschach, "Frederick, Prince of Wales (1707–1751), as a Patron of the Visual Arts: Princely Patriotism and Political Propaganda," 2 vols. (Ph.D. dissertation, Yale University, 1985), vol. I, 168–71.

93 Clark, *Samuel Johnson: Literature and Cultural Politics*, 156.

94 On the mythology of the play and for a refutation of Clark's Jacobite interpretation, see Weinbrot, "Johnson, Jacobitism, and the History of Nostalgia," 183–5.

95 On operas on the Arminius subject, Robert Ketterer, *Ancient Rome in Early Opera* (Urbana: University of Illinois Press, 2009), 132–49. On Arminius as representative of German liberty, Samuel Kliger, *The Goths in England: A Study in Seventeenth Century Thought* (Cambridge, MA: Harvard University Press, 1952), 56–7, 98–101; and W. Bradford Smith, "German Pagan Antiquity in Lutheran Historical Thought," *Journal of the Historical Society* 4 (2004), 351–74.

96 Tacitus, *Annals*, 1. 54–65.

97 Reinhard Strohm, "Handel and his Italian Opera Texts," in *Essays on Handel and Italian Opera* (Cambridge University Press, 1985), 34–79, at 73.

98 Konrad Sasse, "Die Texte der Londoner Opern Händels in ihren gesellschaftlichen Beziehungen," *Wissenschaftliche Zeitschrift der Martin-Luther-Universität Halle-Wittenberg*. Gesellschafts- und Sprachwissenschaftliche Reihe 4(5) (1955), 627–46, at 643: "Dieses Werk handelt zunächst von dem gesellschaftlichen Aufstieg eines Mannes vom einfachen Landmann zum ruhmbekränzten Helden. Das ist insofern typisch, als damit von der Möglichkeit eines solchen Aufstieges für jedermann aus dem Volke die Rede ist."

99 Strohm, "Handel and his Italian opera Texts," 74.

100 This reading of *Giustino* accords with the historians' view of Britain as a stable, oligarchic society; see Chapter 1, note 35.

101 On the elite status of opera, David Hunter, "Patronizing Handel, Inventing Audiences: The Intersection of Class, Money, Music and History," *Early Music* 30 (2000), 33–49.

102 *The Plays of James Thomson*, ed. Greene, vol. I, clii–clxiii, and vol. II, 301–15 (edition quoted); *The Plays of James Thomson*, ed. Percy G. Adams (New York: Garland, 1979), xxiii–xxvii; Sambrook, *James Thomson*, 200–5; *The Plays of David Mallet*, ed. Nussbaum, xxv–xxxiii; and Thomson, *The Castle of Indolence and Other Poems*, ed. McKillop, 176–82.

103 On Aaron Hill and James Miller, Ruth Smith, *Handel's Oratorios and Eighteenth-Century Thought* (Cambridge University Press, 1995), 70–80, 134–5, 192–4.

104 On the political debate, Isaac Kramnick, "Augustan Politics and English Historiography: The Debate on the English Past, 1730–35," *History and Theory* 6 (1967), 33–56. On the origins of what he calls "the mythology of a golden Saxon past," see Christopher Hill, "The Norman Yoke," in *Puritanism and Revolution: Studies in Interpretation of the English Revolution of the 17th Century* (New York: Schocken, 1964), 50–122.

105 *Craftsman*, no. 479 (September 6, 1735).

106 On the politics of *Alfred*, *The Plays of James Thomson*, ed. Greene, vol. I, cliii–clxiii; Sambrook, *James Thomson*, 202–4; Michael Burden, *Garrick, Arne and the Masque of Alfred: A Case Study in National, Theatrical and Musical Politics* (Lewiston, NY: Edwin Mellen, 1994), 16–24; and Alan D. McKillop, "The Early History of *Alfred*," *Philological Quarterly* 41 (1962), 311–24.

107 *London Magazine* 9 (August 1740), 393–4.

108 Countess of Hertford, September 10, 1740 (OS), from Richkings, to Countess of Pomfret; Alnwick Castle, DNP MS 111, 322. The countess is referring to the words italicized in the Hermit's speech (p. 31) in the 1740 printed play text.

109 Elizabeth [Robinson] Montagu, August 11, 1740, to Sarah Robinson; in *Elizabeth Montagu, the Queen of the Blue-Stockings: Her Correspondence from 1720 to 1761*, ed. Emily J. Climenson, 2 vols. (London: John Murray, 1906), vol. I, 54. The Mr. Grenville is likely one of Lord Cobham's relations.

110 The 1741 manuscript version submitted for licensing is at the Henry E. Huntington Library, LA 27; the text is given in *The Plays of James Thomson*, ed. Greene, vol. II, 351–81. The topical patriotic and political sentiments are especially expanded in the second act.

8 The opera stage as political history

1 John Dennis, *Essay on the Opera's after the Italian Manner, which are about to be Establish'd on the English Stage* (1706), 7.

2 *Fog's Weekly Journal*, no. 338 (April 26, 1735).

3 *The Touch-Stone: or ... Essays on the Reigning Diversions of the Town* (1728), 2–3. The author is likely Robert Samber; see Lowell Lindgren, "Another Critic Named Samber Whose 'particular historical significance has gone almost entirely unnoticed,'" in *Festa Musicologica: Essays in Honor of George J. Buelow*, ed. Thomas J. Matheisen and Besnito V. Rivera (Stuyvesant, NY: Pendragon Press, 1995), 407–34.

4 [Henry Stonecastle], *Universal Spectator, and Weekly Journal*, no. 352 (July 5, 1735).

5 *An Oration, in Which an Enquiry is Made Whether the Stage Is, or Can Be Made a School for Forming the Mind to Virtue; and Praising the Superiority of Theatric Instruction Over Those of History & Moral Philosophy. With Reflections on Opera* (1734), 50–2; a translation by John Lockman of Charles Porée, *Theatrum Sit Ne, Vel Esse Possit Schola Informandis Moribus Idonea?* [1733] (1734).

6 Cicero, *De Oratore* 2.9.36.

7 On the *ars historica* tradition, Anthony Grafton, *What Was History? The Art of History in Early Modern Europe* (Cambridge University Press, 2007); Rüdiger Landfester, *Historia Magistra Vitae* (Geneva: Librairie Droz, 1972); George H. Nadel, "Philosophy of History before Historicism," *History and Theory* 3 (1964), 291–315 (reprinted in *Studies in the Philosophy of History*, ed. Nadel (New York: Harper Torch, 1965), 49–73); Reinhart Koselleck, "Historia Magistra Vitae: Über die Auflösung des Topos im Horizont neuzeitlich bewegter Geschichte," in *Vegangene Zukunft: Zur Semantik geschichtlicher Zeiten* (Frankfurt: Suhrkamp, 1979), 38–66 (trans. in *Futures Past: On the Semantics of Historical Time*, trans. Keith Tribe (Cambridge, MA: MIT Press, 1985), 21–38); Beatrice Reynolds, "Shifting Currents in Historical Criticism," *Journal of the History of Ideas* 14 (1953), 471–92; Giorgio Spini, "Historiography: The Art of History in the Italian Counter Reformation," in *The Late Italian Renaissance*, ed. Eric Cochrane (New York: Harper Torch, 1970), 91–133; Eckhard Kessler, "Das rhetorische Modell der Historiographie," in *Formen der Geschichtsschreibung*, ed. Reinhart Koselleck *et al.* (Munich: Deutscher Taschenbuch, 1982), 37–85; Blair Worden, "Historians and Poets," *Huntington Library Quarterly* 68 (2005), 71–93; John L. Brown, *The Methodus ad Facilem Historiarum Cognitionem of Jean Bodin: A Critical Study* (Washington DC: Catholic University Press, 1939), 46–85, 162–94; and Donald R. Kelley, "The Theory of History," in *The Cambridge History of Renaissance Philosophy*, gen. ed. Charles B. Schmitt (Cambridge University Press, 1988), 746–61.

   On the *ars historica* in England, Joseph M. Levine, *The Battle of the Books: History and Literature in the Augustan Age* (Ithaca, NY: Cornell University Press, 1991), 267–82; Philip Hicks, *Neoclassical History and English Culture: From Clarendon to Hume* (New York: St. Martin's Press, 1996), esp. 7–11; J. H. M. Salmon, "Precept, Example, and Truth: Degory Wheare and the *ars historica*," in *The Historical Imagination in Early Modern Britain*, ed. Donald R. Kelley and David H. Sacks

(Washington DC: Woodrow Wilson Center Press, 1997), 11–36; and Isaac Kramnick, intro., *Lord Bolingbroke: Historical Writings* (University of Chicago Press, 1972).

Some English examples are Degory Wheare, *The Method and Order of Reading Both Civil and Ecclesiastical Histories* (trans. from Latin) (1685 and later edns.); Langlet du Fresnoy, *A New Method of Studying History* (trans. from French) 2 vols. (1728); and Charles Rollin, *The Method of Teaching and Studying the Belles Lettres* (trans. from French), 2nd edn., 4 vols. (1737), vol. III, 184–208 ("Rules and Principles for the Study of Profane History").

8 On the superiority of example over precept, William H. Youngren, "Generality, Science and Poetic Language in the Restoration," *ELH* 35 (1968), 158–87. For representative contemporary discussions, William Davenant, "The Author's Preface," *Gondibert* [1651]; John Dryden, "The Gounds of Criticism in Tragedy," preface to *Troilus and Cressida* (1679); John Dennis, *Remarks on a Book Entitled, Prince Arthur* (1696), 4–7; *A Defense of Dramatick-Poetry* (1698), 71; Richard Blackmore, *Essays Upon Several Subjects*, 2 vols. (1716–1717), vol. I, 33–4; Henry Pemberton, *Observations on Poetry, Especially the Epic: Occasioned by the Late Poem upon Leonidas* (1738), 139–40, 146–7, 154; and Samuel Johnson, *Rambler*, no. 4 (March 31, 1750).

9 Dionysius of Halicarnassus, *De Arte Rhetorica* 11.2.19.

10 Seneca, *Epistulae Morales*, 6.5: "Longum iter est per praecepta, breve et efficax per exempla." Sallust, *Bellum Jugurthinum*, 4.5–6, told how Romans contemplated images of their ancestors and were inflamed with desire for virtue and to strive for glory. For Quintilian, the Greeks bear the palm for precepts, but the Romans produce more striking examples of moral performance, which is far greater (*Institutio Oratoria*, 12.2.29).

11 Cornelius Nepos, *The Lives of Illustrious Men,* 2nd edn. (1685), b5v.

12 John Dryden, *Dedication of the Æneis* (1697); in *The Works of John Dryden*, vol. V: *Poems: The Works of Virgil in English 1697* (Berkeley: University of California Press, 1987), 267.

13 Richard Steele, *Tatler*, no. 98 (November 24, 1709). See also *Tatler*, nos. 3, 8, 99 (April 16 and 28, November 26, 1709).

14 *Fog's Weekly Journal*, no. 98 (August 8, 1730).

15 *British Journal, or The Traveller*, no. 17 (January 9, 1731). See also: "If some great and laudable Story were express'd in pompous Verse, set to apt, harmonious Sounds, finely executed Vocally and Instrumentally, and enliven'd with proper Dances; on such an occasion, the music Theatre would prove a School proper for exiting in us a love for Virtue"; in *Historia Litteraria: or, an Exact and Early Account of Valuable Books* 4 (1733), 426 (review of Charles Porée, *Theatrum sit ne, vel esse possit Schola informandis moribus idonca?* [1733]).

16 Giovanni Botero, *Ragion di stato* (1589), 49.

17 Livy, *Ab Urbe Condita*, 1.1; Livy, *The Early History of Rome*, trans. Aubrey de Sélincourt (London: Penguin Books 1960), 34: "omnis te exempli documenta in

inlustri posita monumento intueri; inde tibi tuaeque rei publicae quod imitere capias, inde foedum inceptu, foedum exitu, quod vites" (Loeb edition, vol. I, 6). For Sir William Temple, the "great Ends of History" and the "chief Care of all Historians" are to "argue the Virtues or Vices of Princes, [and] serve for Example or Instruction to Posterity"; in *An Introduction to the History of England* (1695), 301.

18 Tacitus, *Annals,* 3.65; Tacitus, *The Annals of Imperial Rome*, trans. Michael Grant, rev. edn. (London: Penguin Books, 1989), 150; "quod praecipuum munus annalium reor ne virtutes sileantur utque pravis dictis factisque ex posteritate et infamia metus sit" (Loeb edition, vol. II, 624).

19 Livy, *Ab Urbe Condita*; Plutarch, *Lives*; Valerius Maximus, *Factorum et Dictorum Memorabilium*; Petrarch, *De Viris Illustribus* (1337) (epitomes of the lives of great men); Boccaccio, *De Casibus Virorum Illustrium* (On the Fates of Famous Men) and *De Mulierbius Claris* (On Famous Women) (both 1374). On the Roman tradition of canonic exemplars, H. W. Litchfield, "National *Exempla Virtutis* in Roman Literature," *Harvard Studies in Classical Philology* 25 (1914), 1–71 (lists persons and their virtues); and J. Rufus Fears, "The Cult of Virtues and Roman Imperial Ideology," *Aufstieg und Niedergang der römischen Welt.* II.17.2 (1981), 827–948. On exemplary figures as models for Renaissance readers, Timothy Hampton, *Writing from History: The Rhetoric of Exemplarity in Renaissance Literature* (Ithaca, NY: Cornell University Press, 1990).

20 *The Mirror for Magistrates*, ed. Lily N. Campbell (Cambridge University Press, 1938).

21 For example, Carlo Paschal, *Virtutes et Vitia hoc est Virtutum et Vitiorum Definitiones Descriptiones Characterers* (1615).

22 Jean Bodin, *Methodus ad Facilem Historiarum Cognitionem* (1566): "certissimáque rerum expetendarum ac fugiendarum præcepta conflantur" (b1r); in *Method for the Easy Comprehension of History*, trans. Beatrice Reynolds (Columbia University Press, 1945), 9. On use of precepts in training in virtue, Joan Marie Lechner, *Renaissance Concepts of the Commonplaces* (New York: Pageant Press, 1962), 201–25; and Salmon, "Precept, Example, and Truth."

23 On the role of *sententiae*, "Of Sentences," in Pierre Le Moyne, *Of the Art Both of Writing & Judging of History* (trans. of *De l'Histoire*) (1695), 134–51; on their use in oratory, Quintilian, *Institutio Oratoria*, 8.5.

24 On reception of Tacitus, Kenneth C. Schellhase, *Tacitus in Renaissance Political Thought* (University of Chicago Press, 1976); Else-Lilly Etter, *Tacitus in der Geistesgeschichte des 16. und 17. Jahrhunderts* (Basel: Helbing & Lichtenhahn, 1966); *The Cambridge History of Political Thought, 1450–1700*, ed. J. H. Burns (Cambridge University Press, 1991), 484–90. Examples of volumes of maxims extracted from Tacitus include Filippo Cavriana, *Discorsi ... sopra i primi cinque libri di Cornelio Tacito* (1597); Arnoldus Clapmarius, *De Arcanis Rerumpublicarum* (1624); Girolamo Frachetta, *Il seminario de governi di stato et di guerra* (1624); and Fabio Frezza, *Massime regole, et precetti di stato, & di guerra* (1616).

25 Justus Lipsius, *Politicorum sive Civilis Doctina Libri Sex* (1589); trans. as *Politica: Six Books of Politics or Political Instruction*, ed. and trans. Jan Waszink (Assen, The Netherlands: Koninklijke van Gorcum, 2004).

26 The French translation, *Discours politiques et militaires sur Corneille Tacite*, trans. Laurens Melliet (1619), appends a list of the Tacitean *sententiae*.

27 For English examples, *The Quintesence of Wit, Being a Corrant Comfort of Conceites, Maximies, and Poleticke Devices* (English trans., selected by Francisco Sansovino) (1590); and Robert Dallington, *Aphorismes Civill and Militaire* (1613 and later edns.); and William Hatchett, trans., *The Morals of Princes: or, an Abstract of the Most Remarkable Passages Contain'd in the History of all the Emperors Who Reign'd in Rome* (1727). On use of fables for history, Annabel Patterson, *Fables of Power: Aesopian Writing and Political History* (Durham, NC: Duke University Press, 1991).

28 On active reading, Anthony Grafton, *Commerce with the Classics: Ancient Books and Renaissance Readers* (Ann Arbor: University of Michigan Press, 1997), 203–8 (Johannes Kepler as reader of Tacitus); Lisa Jardine and Anthony Grafton, "'Studied for Action': How Gabriel Harvey Read His Livy," *Past and Present* 129 (1990), 30–78 (Gabriel Harvey); Kevin Sharpe, *Reading Revolutions: The Politics of Reading in Early Modern England* (New Haven, CT: Yale University Press, 2000), esp. 101–5, 177–8, 183–4, 186, 190, 192–9, 217, 261–5, 277–8, 320–3 (Sir William Drake's reading practice); Sharpe, *Sir Robert Cotton, 1586–1631: History and Politics in Early Modern England* (Oxford University Press, 1979), 235–40 (Sir Robert Cotton's collection of maxims).

29 On the commonplace book tradition, Ann Moss, *Printed Commonplace-Books and the Structure of Renaissance Thought* (Oxford: Clarendon Press, 1996); Lipsius, *Politicorum* (edn. cited), 152–55; and Lechner, *Renaissance Concepts of the Commonplaces*, 154–70. On their assembly, Erasmus, *De Duplici Copia Verborum ac Rerum* (1512). Degory Wheare described how to extract aphorisms from history, "Of the Manner of Collecting the Fruits of History," in *The Method and Order of Reading Both Civil and Ecclesiastical Histories* (1685 and later edns.). Jean Bodin's *Methodus* discussed how to "gather flowers from History" ("flores historiarum legere," *ii).

   Representative collections include Erasmus, *Adagiorum Collectanea* (edns. between 1500 and 1533); Polydore Vergil, *Adagiorum* (1541); Jan Gruter, *Loci Communes: Sive Florilegium* (1624); and Lipsius, *Politicorum*.

30 Lipsius, *Politicorum* (citing book and chapter).

31 On the influence of Seneca and the Roman monarchial tradition for the education of Renaissance princes (the *bonus princeps*) and the Mirror for Princes genre, Peter Stacey, *Roman Monarchy and the Renaissance Prince* (Cambridge University Press, 2007), esp. 37–41, 173–204. See also Hampton, *Writing from History*, 31–80; Quentin Skinner, "Political Philosophy," in *The Cambridge History of Renaissance Philosophy*, ed. Charles Schmitt (Cambridge University Press, 1988), 389–452, at 431–4, 443–5; and Skinner, *The Foundations of Modern Political Thought*, vol. I: *The Renaissance* (Cambridge University Press, 1978),

116–28, 214–21; Hans-Otto Mühleisen and Theo Stammen, eds., *Politische Tugendlehre und Regierungskunst. Studien zum Fürstenspiegel der Frühen Neuzeit* (Tübingen: M. Niemeyer, 1990); Mühleisen and Stammen, eds., *Fürstenspiegel der Frühen Neuzeit.* Bibliothek des deutschen Staatsdenkens 5 (Frankfurt a/M: 1996); Rainer A. Müller, "Die deutschen Fürstenspiegel des 17. Jahrhunderts. Regierungslehren und politische Pädagogik," *Historische Zeitschrift* 240 (1985), 571–597; Bruno Singer, *Die Fürstenspiegel in Deutschland im Zeitalter des Humanismus und der Reformation* (Munich: Wilhelm Fink, 1980) (Germany only); Girolamo Cotroneo, *I trattatisti dell' "Ars historica"* (Naples: Giannini, 1971).

    The Mirror for Princes genre and opera is touched on briefly in Udo Bermbach, "Die Verwirrung der Mächtigen: Herrschertungenden und Politik in Georg Friedrich Händels Londoner Opern," in *Wo Macht ganz auf Verbrechen ruht: Politik und Gesellschaft in der Oper* (Hamburg: Europäische Verlangsanstalt, 1997), 38–63.

32 Erasmus, *The Education of a Christian Prince*, trans. Neil M. Cheshire and Michael J. Heath (Cambridge University Press, 1997); Niccolò Machiavelli, *The Prince*, trans. and ed. Quentin Skinner and Russell Price (Cambridge University Press, 1988). Other convenient examples are Giovanni Botero, *Ragion di stato* (1589) (*The Reason of State*, trans. P. J. and D. P. Waley (London: Routledge & Kegan Paul), with *sententiae* drawn from Livy, Tacitus, and others); and Claude de Seyssel, *La Monarchie de France* (*The Monarchy of France*, trans. H. H. Hexter, ed. Donald R. Kelley (New Haven, CT: Yale University Press, 1981)).

33 Francis Bacon, *The Advancement of Learning* (1623), 2.4.2.

34 Aristotle, *Poetics*, 1451b. Paradigmatic examples of the notion of poetic justice are Thomas Rymer's applications of Aristotle to the tragedies of Shakespeare in *A Short History of Tragedy* (1692/93), esp. Chapter 7.

35 Philip Sidney, *Sir Philip Sidney's Defense of Poetry*, ed. Lewis Soens (Lincoln: University of Nebraska Press, 1970), 16–18.

36 John Dryden, *Dedication of the Æneis* (1697); in *The Works of Dryden*, vol. V: *Poems*, 298.

37 John Dennis, *Remarks upon Cato* (1713), 6.

38 On the general avoidance of tragic endings in Italian *opera seria*, Michael F. Robinson, "How to Demonstrate Virtue: The Case of Porpora's Two Settings of *Mitridate*," *Studies in Music from the University of Western Ontario*, 7(1) (1982), 47–64 at 50–1.

39 Niccolò Machiavelli, *The Prince*, trans. and intro. George Bull (London: Penguin Books, 1961), chapter 14, p. 47: "Il principe leggere le istorie, e in quelle considerare le azioni degli uomini eccellenti; vedere come si sono governati nelle guerre; esaminare le cagioni delle vittorie e perdite loro, per potere queste fuggire e quelle imitare."

40 John Dryden, "The Life of Plutarch," in *The Works of John Dryden*, vol. XVII: *Prose, 1668–1691* (Berkeley: University of California Press, 1971), 270–1. This is the principle of uniformitarianism in history.

41 *The History of Timur-Bec, known by the name of Tamerlaine the Great*, trans. Petis de la Croix, 2 vols. (1723), dedication. See also the dedication and preface to William Wotton, *The History of Rome, from the Death of Antonious Pius, to the Death of Severus Alexander* (1701), written for William, Duke of Glocester; and the dedication to Frederick, Prince of Wales, in Thomas Gordon, trans., *The Works of Tacitus*, 2nd edn., 4 vols. (1737), vol. III, iii–xxiv.

42 John Clarke, preface, Suetonius, *XII Cæsaris ... or, the Lives of the Twelve First Roman Emperors* (1732), v.

43 Cicero, *On Duties*, ed. M. T. Griffin and E. M. Atkins (Cambridge University Press, 1991). On the persistence of the Ciceronian virtues, Rosemond Tuve, "Notes on the Virtues and Vices," *Journal of the Warburg and Courtauld Institutes* 26 (1963), 264–303 (in the Medieval and Christian traditions); Quentin Skinner, *Visions of Politics*, vol. II: *Republican Virtues* (Cambridge University Press, 2002), 10–159; Skinner, *The Foundations of Modern Political Thought*, vol. I: *The Renaissance*, 87–101.

44 Cicero, *De Officiis*, esp. 1.5–29. A briefer discussion in *De Inventione*, 2.53–54, and *Tusculanarum Disputationum*, 3.16–18 and 36–37.

45 For *clementia* (mercy), the most extended discussion is Seneca, *De Clementia*; "Of Mercy," in Seneca, *Moral and Political Essays*, ed. and trans. John M. Cooper and J. F. Procopé (Cambridge University Press, 1995), 119–64.

46 Sallust, *Bellum Catilinae*, 10.1: "ubi labore atque iustitia"; in *Sallust*, trans. J. C. Rolfe. Loeb Classical Library (Cambridge, MA: Harvard University Press, 1947), 17.

47 Cicero, *De Republica*, 6.13: "omnibus, qui patriam conservaverint, adiuverint, auxerint, certum esse in caelo definitum locum, ubi beati aevo sempiterno fruantur"; in Cicero, *The Republic and The Laws*, trans. Niall Rudd (Oxford University Press, 1998), 88.

48 Cicero, *De Officiis*, 1.57: "omnes omnium caritates patria una complexa est, pro qua quis bonus dubitet mortem oppetere, si ei sit profuturus?"; in *De Officiis*, trans. Walter Miller. Loeb Classical Library (Cambridge, MA: Harvard University Press, 1968), 61. Cicero ranks one's duties from country, parents, children, family, to kinsmen.

49 Quoting Thomas Gordon, "Discourses," prefixed to Tacitus, *Works*, 2 vols. (1728), vol. I, 27.

50 William Paterson, *Arminius* (1737), I.iv.

51 The danger of effeminacy – a concern for fashion, cosmetics, and luxury – was that it rendered the male ill suited for the rigors of military service.

52 On prevailing concepts of female honor and virtue, Diane Willen, "Gender, Society and Culture, 1500–1800," *Journal of British Studies* 37 (1998), 451–60.

53 See also the example of Polissena in *Radamisto* (1720), II.ix–x.

54 On moral choices testing the hero's devotion to duty or to private passion and love, Robert C. Ketterer, *Ancient Rome in Early Opera* (Urbana: University of Illinois Press, 2009).

55 On the same theme, Horatio to Irene in *Muzio Scevola* (1721), III.vi.

56 Likewise, Stilicon, in *Onorio* (1736), must execute his own son for treason (II.v).

57 *Muzio Scevola* (1721), dedication: "Cui suggetto … è il Nascimento della Romana Libertà: di quella Libertà che discacciata dalla sua sventurata gran Patria, tontò ricovrarsi in tutte quasi le rimanenti Parti del Mondo: ma o ristetta ed oppressa da Pochi, o vinta e profugata da un Solo; saria sempre andata raminga tra selve e capanne; se non avesse trovato al fine, sicuro grande e glorioso Asilo ne' felici Regni della Maestà Vostra: Felicissimi Regni! poichè d'affatto diversa Condizione da tutti gli altri; godono veramente la Romana Libertà: mentre i Popoli la possiedono, i Tribuni c' invigilano, i Patrizij la disendono, il Sovrano la protégé"; trans. provided.

58 John Trenchard and Thomas Gordon, *Cato's Letters*, 2 vols., ed. Ronald Hamowy (Indianapolis, IN: Liberty Fund, 1995), nos. 84–85, vol. II, 607–18.

59 While most of the ideas are also discussed in the many political treatises of the period, for convenience, reference will be made to Natural Law theory. On Natural Law: *The Cambridge History of Political Thought*, ed. Burns, 561–652; Kund Haakonssen, *Natural Law and Moral Philosophy: From Grotius to the Scottish Enlightenment* (Cambridge University Press, 1996); T. J. Hochstrasser, *Natural Law Theories in the Early Enlightenment* (Cambridge University Press, 2000); Heinrich A. Rommen, *The Natural Law: A Study in Legal and Social History and Philosophy*, trans. Thomas R. Hanley (Indianapolis, IN: Liberty Fund, 1998); Otto Gierke, *Natural Law and the Theory of Society, 1500–1800*, trans. Ernst Barker (Cambridge University Press, 1950); Norberto Bobbio, *Thomas Hobbes and the Natural Law Tradition*, trans. Daniela Gobetti (University of Chicago Press, 1993); Michael P. Zuckert, *Natural Rights and the New Republicanism* (Princeton University Press, 1994); and Richard Tuck, *Natural Rights Theories: Their Origin and Development* (Cambridge University Press, 1979), 63.

60 John Selden, *De Jure Naturali et Gentium* (1640); Samuel Pufendorf, *De Jure Naturæ et Gentium* (1672) and its abridgement/compendium *De Officio Hominis et Civis Legem Naturalem* (1673); Richard Cumberland, *De Legibus Naturæ Disquisitio Philosophica* (1672); Thomas Hobbes, *De Cive* (1642); Hobbes, *Leviathan* (1651); and John Locke, *Two Treatises on Government* (1690). Representative British treatises (some of which reconcile Natural Law with Divine authority and are anti-Hobbesian) include Samuel Parker, *A Demonstration of the Divine Authority of the Law of Nature* 1681); Robert Ferguson, *A Brief Justification of the Prince of Orange's Descent* (1688); James Tyrrell, *A Brief Disquisition on the Law of Nature, according to Dr. Cumberland's Latin Treatise* (1701); Richard Blackmore, "An Essay upon the Laws of Nature,"

in *Essays upon Several Subjects* (1716), 355–419; and *A Dissertation on the Law of Nature, the Law of Nations, and the Civil Law in General* (1723).

61 Grotius, *De Jure Belli ac Pacis*, 1.1; Pufendorf, *De Jure Naturæ et Gentium*, 2.3.11, 7.2; Pufendorf, *De Officio*, 2.6–7; Hobbes, *Leviathan*, 1.13–15,18; Hobbes, *De Cive*, chapters 1 and 5; and Locke, *Two Treatises on Government*, 2.2, 2.7.89, 2.8.95–99, 2.9.

62 Pufendorf, *De Officio*, 2.6.9, 2.11.3, 2.16–17, 2.18.2–5; Pufendorf, *De Jure Naturæ et Gentium*, 7.2.8.

63 In *Leviathan*, 1.14–15, Hobbes identified nineteen laws of nature.

64 Cicero, *De Legibus*, 3.3. Cf. Plato, *Republic*, I.342e; and Pufendorf, *De Officio*, 2.11.3.

65 On absolutist thought, *The Cambridge History of Political Thought*, ed. Burns, 347–73; and James Daly, "The Idea of Absolute Monarchy in Seventeenth-Century England," *Historical Journal* 21 (1978), 227–50, who defines absolute monarchy as where the monarch has no superior, is not elected, is not to be resisted, has a right to occupy the throne, has a right to govern without consent, takes full extent of the powers of the throne, stretches rights to questionable lengths, and tries to enforce legal rights against popular opposition.

66 Jean Bodin, *Six Livres*, 1.8–10; Hobbes, *Leviathan*, 2.29. Pufendorf, similarly, thought there should be a single, unmixed sovereignty; see *De Jure Naturæ et Gentium*, 7.5.12–15. See Julian H. Franklin, *Jean Bodin and the Rise of Absolutist Theory* (Cambridge University Press, 1973); *The Cambridge History of Political Thought*, ed. Burns, 298–309; and Bobbio, *Thomas Hobbes and the Natural Law Tradition*, 49–62.

67 *The Cambridge History of Political Thought*, ed. Burns, 351–5; Pufendorf, *De Officio*, 2.8.4; Pufendorf, *De Jure Naturæ et Gentium*, 7.5.9.

68 On the contrasts, Gordon J. Schochet, "Patriarchalism, Politics and Mass Attitudes in Stuart England," *Historical Journal* 12 (1969), 413–41; and S. E. Finer, *The History of Government from the Earliest Times*, 3 vols. (Oxford University Press, 1997), vol. III, 1307–74. John Miller, "The Potential for 'Absolutism' in Later Stuart England," *History*, 69(226) (1984), 187–207, shows the English made a caricature of the nature of the French monarchy, which did have some practical restraints.

69 Peter Laslett, introduction to *Patriarcha and Other Political Works of Sir Robert Filmer* (Oxford: Basil Blackwell, 1949); James Daley, *Sir Robert Filmer and English Political Thought* (University of Toronto Press, 1979); Johann P. Sommerville, introduction to Robert Filmer, *Patriarcha and Other Writings* (Cambridge University Press, 1991); John N. Figgis, *The Divine Right of Kings*, new edn. with intro. by G. R. Elton (New York: Harper & Row, 1965); and Gordon J. Schochet, *Patriarchalism in Political Thought* (New York: Basic Books, 1975). On the persistence of divine right ideas in England, W. A. Speck, *Reluctant Revolutionaries: Englishmen and the Revolution of 1688* (Oxford University Press, 1988).

70 James Tyrrell, *Patriarcha non Monarcha. The Patriarch Unmonarch'd* (1681); Algernon Sidney, *Discourses Concerning Government* (1698); and Locke, *Two Treatises on Government* (Treatise 1).

71 Pufendorf, *De Officio*, 2.9.6–7; Pufendorf, *De Jure Naturæ et Gentium*, 7.6.7, 7.6.9, 7.6.11; Franklin, *Jean Bodin*, 70–92; Glenn Burgess, *Absolute Monarchy and the Stuart Constitution* (New Haven, CT: Yale University Press, 1996); and Preston King, *The Ideology of Order: A Comparative Analysis of Jean and Thomas Hobbes* (New York: Harper Row, 1974), 73–157 and 161–252.

72 Thomas Gordon, trans., *The Works of Tacitus*, 2nd. edn., 4 vols. (1737), vol. III, xxi.

73 Rightful heirs are restored, for example, in *Antioco* (1711), *Astarto* (1720), *Dario* (1725), *Demetrio* (1737), *Floridante* (1721), *Giustino* (1737), *Lotario* (1729), *Ormisda* (1730), *Parthenius* (1738), *Radamisto* (1720), *Rodelinda* (1725), *Siroe* (1728, 1736), *Teuzzone* (1727), and *Tolomeo* (1728).

74 On the possibility of females as good rulers, Lipsius, *Politicorum*, II.3 and 17.2.

75 On resistance: *The Cambridge History of Political Thought*, ed. Burns 159–253; Skinner, *The Foundations of Modern Political Thought*, vol. II: *The Age of Reformation*, 189–238, 302–48; Frank Grunert, "Sovereignty and Resistance: The Development of the Right of Resistance in German Natural Law," in *Natural Law and Civil Sovereignty: Moral Right and State Authority in Early Modern Political Thought*, ed. Ian Hunter and David Saunders (Basingstoke: Palgrave Macmillan, 2002), 123–38; *A Defence of Liberty Against Tyrants: A Translation of the Vindiciae Contra Tyrannos by Junius Brutus*, intro. by Harold J. Laski (Gloucester, MA: Peter Smith, 1963); *Vindiciae, Contra Tyrannos: or, Concerning the Legitimate Power of a Prince Over the People, and of the People Over a Prince*, ed. and trans. George Garnett (Cambridge University Press, 1994); and Franklin, *Jean Bodin*, 43–4.

76 Lois G. Schwoerer, "The Right to Resist: Whig Resistance Theory, 1688 to 1694," in *Political Discourse in Early Modern Britain*, ed. Nicholas Phillipson and Quentin Skinner (Cambridge University Press, 1993), 232–52; Speck, *Reluctant Revolutionaries*, 139–65; H. T. Dickinson, *Liberty and Property: Political Ideology in Eighteenth-Century Britain* (New York: Holmes and Meier, 1977), 62–5, 77–9, 125–32; Julian H. Franklin, *John Locke and the Theory of Sovereignty: Mixed Monarchy and the Right of Resistance in the Political Thought of the English Revolution* (Cambridge University Press, 1978), esp. 89–98; and J. P. Kenyon, "The Revolution of 1688: Resistance and Contract," in *Historical Perspectives: Studies in English Thought and Society*, ed. Neil McKendrick (London: Europa Publications, 1974), 43–69.

77 Hervey, *Ancient and Modern Liberty Stated and Compar'd* (1734), 46. Hervey, writing as a member of the Whig ministry, carefully puts limits on the right of resistance; he condemns a "general Doctrine of *Resistance*" that would "keep the People for ever on the Brink of Insurrection and Rebellion."

78 Grotius, *De Jure Belli ac Pacis*, 1.4.7.15; Pufendorf, *De Jure Naturæ et Gentium* 7.8.1; Pufendorf, *De Officio*, 2.9.4; and Locke, *Two Treatises on Government*, 2.18.204.

79 Bodin, *Six Livres*, 2.5, p. 307 (English trans., 225); Franklin, *Jean Bodin*, 51 and 93–5 (Bodin did allow resistance to usurpers who had no title to exercise authority (Franklin, *Jean Bodin*, 95)); Filmer, *Patriarcha*, ed. Laslett, 19 and chapter 9 (refuting Grotius); Hobbes, *Leviathan*, 2.24; Hobbes, *De Cive*, 12.3, 18.3; Pufendorf, *De Jure Naturæ et Gentium*, 7.5.12–15; and Pufendorf, *De Officio*, 2.9–10. Locke did reserve this right to the people.

80 Pufendorf, *De Jure Naturæ et Gentium*, 7.8.5–6; Pufendorf, *De Officio*, 2.9.4; and Grunert, "Sovereignty and Resistance," 127–8. John Locke's doctrine of popular sovereignty (*Two Treatises on Government*, 2.19) was considered too radical in its day and generally rejected by British writers of the time.

81 Grotius, *De Jure Belli ac Pacis*, 1.4.2: "Et naturaliter quidem omnes ad arcendam à se injuriam jus habent resistendi, ut supra diximus. Sed civili societate ad tuendam tranquillitatem instituta … Potest igitur civitas jus illud resistendi promiscuum publicæ pacis & ordinis causa prohibere: Et quin voluerti, dubitandum non est, cum aliter non posset finem suum consequi. Nam si maneat promiscuum illud resistendi jus, non jam civitas erit, sed dissociata multitude"; trans. in Hugo Grotius, *De Jure Belli ac Pacis* (1646 edn.). The Classics of International Law no. 3, 2 vols. (Oxford: Clarendon Press, 1913–1925), vol. II, 139.

82 Bodin, *Six Livres*, 2.5, 299 (English trans., 219); Grotius, *De Jure Belli ac Pacis*, 1.4.11; Pufendorf, *De Jure Naturæ et Gentium*, 7.8.6–7; Hobbes, *De Cive*, 12.3; Locke, *Two Treatises on Government*, 2.18.209–10.

83 Pufendorf, *De Jure Naturæ et Gentium* (1688 edn.), 7.8.6: "populus contra extremam vim eamque injustam principis sese defendere possit; quæ defensio ubi bene successerit, libertatem quoque comitem ducit. Quippe cum dominus, dum in hostem abit, subjectum ab obligatione adversus se videatur ipse absolvere"; trans. in Samuel Pufendorf, *De Jure Naturæ et Gentium*. The Classics of International Law no. 17, 2 vols. (Oxford: Clarendon Press, 1934), vol. II, 1110. Pufendorf limits resistance to cases of self-defense; see Grunert, "Sovereignty and Resistance," 127–8.

84 *The Cambridge History of Political Thought*, ed. Burns, 193–218; Skinner, *The Foundations of Modern Political Thought*, vol. II: *Republican Virtues*, 191–238.

85 Bodin, *Six Livres*, 2.5.

86 Bodin, *Six Livres*, 2.4: "Or la plus noble différence du Roy & du Tyran est, que le Roy se conforme aux loix de nature: & le tyran les foule aux pieds: l'un entretient la pieté, la justice, & la foy: l'autre n'a ny Dieu, ny soy, ny loy: l'un fait tout ce qu'il pense servir au bien public, & tuition des subjects: l'autre ne fait rien que pour son proffit particulier, vengeance, ou plaisir"; English trans. [1606], 212. On recognizing the difference between a (legitimate) prince and a tyrant, Erasmus, *The Education of a Christian Prince* (edn. cited), 25–31. A tyrant rules only for his self-interest, not the people's (Lipsius, *Politicorum*, 309; and Aristotle, *Politics*, 3.5.1 and 4.8.3); for Seneca the difference lies in extending mercy (*De Clementia*, 1.12.3, and 1.13).

87 Bodin, *Six Livres*, 2.5: "aussi est chose tresbelle & magnifique à un Prince, de prendre les armes pour venger tout un peuple injustement opprimé par la

cruauté d'un tiran"; English trans. [1606], 220. See also the the fourth question in *Vindiciae, Contra Tyrannos* (1580).

88 Grotius, *De Jure Belli ac Pacis*, 2.20.40: "Sciendum quoque est reges, & qui par regibus jus obtinent, jus habere pœnas poscendi non tantum ob injurias in se aut subditos suos commissas, sed & ob eas quæ ipsos peculiariter non tangunt, sed in quibusvis personis jus naturæ aut gentium immaniter violantibus"; trans. in edn. cited, vol. II, 504.

89 Mirror for Princes (see note 31).

90 Quoted from 4th, enlarged edn. (1730). See also Thomas Hearne, *Ductor Historicus: or a Short System of Universal History*, 4th edn., 2 vols. (1724), vol. I, 97–102.

91 Erasmus, *Institutio Principis Christiani* (1516); Francesco Patrizi, *De Regno et Regis Institutione* (1531).

92 Lipsius, *Politicorum*; Botero, *Ragion di stato*; Francesco Guicciardini *Ricordi politici e civili* (*Maxims and Reflections of a Renaissance Statesman*, trans. Mario Domani [New York: Harper Torchbooks, 1965]). On development of the concept of reason of state, Maurizio Viroli, *From Politics to Reason of State: The Acquisition and Transformation of the Language of Politics, 1250–1600* (Cambridge University Press, 1992), 126–200, 238–80.

93 Cicero, *Pro M. Marcello Oratio*, 3: "animum vincere, iracundiam cohibere, victoriam temperare … non ego eum cum summis viris comparo, sed simillimum do iudico"; in *The Speeches of Cicero*, ed. and trans. N. H. Watts. The Loeb Classical Library (London: William Heinemann, 1931), 428–9.

94 Similar examples are presented in Richard King, "Classical History and Handel's *Alessandro*," *Music and Letters* 77 (1996), 34–63.

95 Cicero, *De Officiis*, 2.12. On the "Clement Prince" in opera, see Ketterer, *Ancient Rome in Early Opera*.

96 Seneca, *De Clementia*, 1.3.2: "Nullam ex omnibus virtutibus homini magis convenire, cum sit nulla humanior"; trans. in Seneca, *Moral and Political Essays*, ed. Cooper and Procopé, 131.

97 Niccolò Machiavelli, *Il Principe*, chapter 17: "che ciascumo principe debbe desiderare di essere tenuto pietoso"; *The Prince*, trans. Bull, 51.

98 Augustine, *De Civitate Dei*, 9.5: "alienae miseriae quaedam in nostro corde compassio qua utique si possumus subvenire compellimur"; in *The City of God Against the Pagans*, trans. David S. Wiesen, 7 vols. Loeb Classical Library (Cambridge, MA: Harvard University Press, 1968), vol. V, 168–9.

99 Seneca, *De Clementia*, 2.3.1: "Clementia est temperantia animi in potestate ulciscendi vel lenitas superioris adversus inferiorem in constituendis poenis"; in *Moral Essays*, trans. John W. Basore, 3 vols. Loeb Classical Library (London: Heinemann, 1928), 434–5.

100 On pity in the Stoics, Traute Adam, *Clementia Principis: Der Einfluß hellenistischer Fürstenspiegel auf den Versuch einer rechtlichen Fundierung des Principates durch Seneca* (Stuttgart: Ernst Klett Verlag, 1970), 20–39 and

82–118; and Ford L. Battles and André M. Hugo, *Calvin's Commentary on Seneca's "De Clementia,"* Renaissance Society of America (Leiden: E. J. Brill, 1969), 367. Also especially, Cicero, *Tusculanarum Disputationum*, 4.8 and 3.10; Seneca, *De Clementia*, 2.4.4; and Quintilian, *Institutio Oratoria*, Book I, Prooemium, and 6.2.

101 A classic example is the speech of Marcus Cato in Aulis Gellius, *Noctium Atticarum*, 6.3.47. More recently, Grotius, *De Jure Belli ac Pacis*, 3.11.7. In operas, see *Ormisda* (1730), I.xv, and *Serse* (1738), I.xii.

102 On pardons in the British legal system, J. H. Baker, "Criminal Courts and Procedure at Common Law 1550–1800," and J. M. Beattie, "Crime and the Courts in Surrey 1736–1753," in *Crime in England, 1550–1800*, ed. J. S. Cockburn (Princeton University Press, 1977), 15–48 and 155–87; *Albion's Fatal Tree: Crime and Society in Eighteenth-Century England*, ed. Douglas Hay *et al.* (London: Allen Lane, 1975), 17–63, 43–9; and J. M. Beattie, *Crime and the Courts in England, 1660–1800* (Princeton University Press, 1986), 430–9.

103 Quoted from *The Grand Exemplar … Of His Sacred Majesty King George … with the Declaration and Coronation Oath* (1715), 25.

104 William Blackstone, *Commentaries on the Laws of England* (1765), 4.31.391.

105 Blackstone, *Commentaries*, 4.31.390.

106 The Transportation Act, which sent convicts to the North American and West Indian plantations, was passed in 1719.

107 In Surrey, for example, between 1736 and 1753, for those 179 people guilty of capital property offenses, 51.4% were pardoned and transported. And in London, between 1749 and 1771, of 1,121 condemned, 443 (40%) were pardoned; by the end of the century, only one-quarter of death sentences were carried out. See Baker, "Criminal Courts and Procedure at Common Law," 44–5; Beattie, "Crime and the Courts in Surrey 1736–1753," 179–81; and Thomas R. Forbes, "A Study of Old Bailey Sentences between 1729 and 1800," *Guildhall Studies in London History* 5(1) (October 1981), 26–35.

108 Philip Ayres, *Classical Culture and the Idea of Rome in Eighteenth-Century England* (Cambridge University Press, 1997).

109 The issue was a reply to Joseph Addison's *Freeholder*, no. 10 (January 23, 1716), on the subject of the arbitrary monarch Mulai Ismail (1646–1726), Emperor of Morocco.

110 On the "Fifteen" and punishments and executions, John Baynes, *The Jacobite Rising of 1715* (London: Cassel, 1970); Margaret Sankey, *Jacobite Prisoners of the 1715 Rebellion: Preventing and Punishing Insurrection in Early Hanoverian Britain* (Aldershot: Ashgate, 2005); and Daniel Szechi, *1715: The Great Jacobite Rebellion* (New Haven, CT: Yale University Press, 2006).

111 Sankey, *Jacobite Prisoners of the 1715 Rebellion*, 151–2, 99–116, shows how clemency actually did effect loyalty among those receiving it.

112 Ayres, *Classical Culture and the Idea of Rome*, 1–47.

Epilogue

1 David Hunter, "Miraculous Recovery? Handel's Illnesses, the Narrative Tradition of Heroic Strength and the Oratorio Turn," *Eighteenth-Century Music* 3 (2006), 253–67. The principal consequence of Handel's ill health would have been his inability to direct long performance seasons. Hunter also examines other explanations for Handel's turn from opera to oratorio. See also Ilias Chrissochoidis, "Handel Recovering: Fresh Light on His Affairs in 1737," *Eighteenth-Century Music* 5 (2008), 237–44.

2 Fourth Earl of Shaftesbury, letter of June 11, 1737, to James Harris; in Donald Burrows and Rosemary Dunhill, *Music and Theatre in Handel's World: The Family Papers of James Harris, 1732–1780* (Oxford University Press, 2002), 31–2.

    On these seasons, the rival opera companies, and Handel's turn to oratorios: Carole Taylor, "Handel's Disengagement from the Italian Opera," in *Handel Tercentenary Collection*, ed. Stanley Sadie and Anthony Hicks (Ann Arbor, MI: UMI Research Press, 1987), 165–81; Taylor, "Italian Operagoing in London, 1700–1745" (Ph.D. dissertation, Syracuse University, 1991), 245–308; Donald Burrows, "Handel and the London Opera Companies in the 1730s: Venues, Programmes, Patronage and Performers," *Göttinger Händel-Beiträge* 10 (2004), 149–65; and Ilias Chrissochoidis, "Handel at a Crossroads: His 1737–1738 and 1738–1739 Seasons Re-examined," *Music and Letters* 90 (2009), 599–635.

3 *London Daily Post and General Advertiser*, no. 1113 (May 24, 1738), and no. 1167 (July 26, 1738).

4 On Middlesex's operatic productions, Carole Taylor, "From Losses to Lawsuit; Patronage of the Italian Opera in London by Lord Middlesex," *Music and Letters* 68 (1987), 1–25.

5 Horace Walpole, letter of November 2, 1741, to Horace Mann; in *Yale Edition of Horace Walpole's Correspondence*, ed. W. S. Lewis, 48 vols. (New Haven, CT: Yale University Press, 1937–1983), vol. XVII, 186.

6 See especially the letter from John Christopher Smith, July 28, 1743, to the Earl of Shaftesbury; in Betty Matthews, "Unpublished Letters Concerning Handel," *Music and Letters* 40 (1959), 261–8; and Donald Burrows, *Handel* (New York: Schirmer, 1994), 273–4. For the opposition to Handel, David Hunter, "Margaret Cecil, Lady Brown: 'Persevering Enemy to Handel' but 'Otherwise Unknown to History,'" *Women and Music* 3 (1999), 43–58; and Chrissochoidis, "Handel at a Crossroads."

7 On the waning months of the Walpole ministry and the aftermath of his resignation, John B. Owen, *The Rise of the Pelhams* (London: Methuen, 1957), 1–40; R. Harris, "A Leicester House Political Diary, 1742–43," *Camden Miscellany* 31, 4th ser., 44 (1992), 373–411; Lewis M. Wiggin, *The Faction of Cousins: A Political Account of the Grenvilles, 1733–1763* (New Haven, CT: Yale University Press, 1958), 51–102; Historical Manuscripts Commission, *Manuscripts of the Earl of Egmont. Diary of Viscount Percival afterwards First Earl of Egmont*, 3 vols. (London:

His Majesty's Stationery Office, 1920–23), vol. III, 232–50 (cited as Egmont, *Diary*); and William Cobbett, *Parliamentary History of England* (1741–43), vol. XII, 188–404.

8 Richard Glover, *Memoirs by a Celebrated Literary and Political Character*, new edn. (London: John Murray, 1814), 1.

9 George L. Lam, "Walpole and the Duke of Newcastle," in *Horace Walpole: Writer, Politician, and Connoisseur*, ed. Warren H. Smith (New Haven, CT: Yale University Press, 1967), 57–84; and *The Life and Correspondence of Philip Yorke, Earl of Hardwicke, Lord High Chancellor of Great Britain*, ed. Philip C. Yorke, 3 vols. (Cambridge University Press, 1913), vol. I, 190–4, 229–77.

10 William Coxe, *Memoirs of the Life and Administration of Sir Robert Walpole, Earl of Orford,* 3 vols. (1798), 250–1; Helen S. Hughes, *The Gentle Hertford: Her Life and Letters* (New York: Macmillan Co., 1940), 185; and Egmont, *Diary*, vol. III, 238–40.

11 *Craftsman*, no. 816 (February 20, 1741).

12 John, Lord Hervey, *Miscellaneous Thoughts on the Present Posture both of our Foreign and Domestic Affairs* (1742), 26–7 (citing eighty-page edition). He attributed the make-up of the new Parliament to "the Weight and Industry of the P. of W."

13 J. H. Plumb, *The Growth of Political Stability in England, 1675–1725* (London: Macmillan, 1967), 158 (quoted); Geoffrey Holmes, "Sir Robert Walpole," in *Politics, Religion and Society in England, 1679–1742* (London: Hambledon, 1986), 163–80; H. T. Dickinson, *Walpole and the Whig Supremacy* (London: English Universities Press, 1973), 191–2; Owen, *The Rise of the Pelhams*, 38–40; and P. G. M. Dickson, *The Financial Revolution in England: A Study in the Development of Public Credit, 1688–1756* (London: Macmillan, 1967), 199–204.

14 Vincent Carretta, *The Snarling Muse: Verbal and Visual Political Satire from Pope to Churchill* (Philadelphia: University of Pennsylvania Press, 1983), 173–251.

Select bibliography

Primary Sources

Manuscript Sources

Archives of the Duke of Northumberland at Alnwick Castle

Archives du Ministère des Affaires Etrangères, Paris, Correspondance Politique, Espagne

Bodleian Library
    MS. Firth
    MS. Rawlinson

British Library
    Additional Manuscripts
    Blenheim Papers
    Essex Papers
    Holland House Papers
    Portland Manuscripts
    Wentworth Papers

Castle Howard Archive, Yorkshire

Duchy of Cornwall Office (London)
    Household Accounts

Hertfordshire Archives and Local Studies
    Panshanger Papers

Henry E. Huntington Library
    Stowe Papers

Suffolk Record Office, Bury St. Edmunds
    Hervey Manuscripts

University of Leeds, Brotherton Library

Victoria and Albert Museum, National Art Library
    Forster Collection

West Sussex Record Office
    Goodwood Manuscripts

Periodicals

Bee: or Universal Weekly Pamphlet

British Journal
Censor
Common Sense
Country Gentleman
Craftsman (Country Journal: or, the Craftsman)
Daily Advertiser
Daily Courant
Daily Gazetteer
Daily Journal
Daily Post
Examiner
Fog's Weekly Journal
Free Briton
Freeholders Journal
Gentleman's Magazine
Grub-street Journal
Historical Register
Hyp-Doctor
Intelligencer
Journals of the House of Commons
La Staffetta Italiana: or, the Italian Post
London Daily Post, and General Advertiser
London Evening Post
London Gazette
London Journal
London Magazine
Mist's Weekly Journal
Nonsense of Common-Sense
Old Whig: or, the Consistent Protestant
Parliamentary History of England
Parrot
Political State of Great Britain
Post Boy
Prompter
Spectator
St. James's Evening Post
Tatler
True Briton
Universal Spectator, and Weekly Journal
Weekly Journal: or British Gazetteer
Weekly Journal: or Saturday's Post
Weekly Miscellany
Weekly Register: or, Universal Journal

Italian Opera Librettos

Given by Italian title, year of London (unless noted) premiere, composer, and librettist.

Arsinoe (1705; Clayton, Motteux/Stanzani)

Camilla (1706; Bononcini, Swiney/Stampiglia)

Rosamond (1707; Clayton, Addison)

Thomyris (1707; pasticcio, Motteux)

Isacio tiranno (1710, Venice; Lotti, Briani)

Antioco (1711; Gasparini, Pariati/Zeno)

Rinaldo (1711; Handel, Hill/Rossi)

Teseo (1713; Handel, Haym)

Lucio Cornelio Silla (1713; Handel, ?)

La caccia in Etolia (1715; Chelleri, Valeriani)

Tito Manlio (1717; pasticcio, ?)

Teofane (1720, Dresden; Lotti, Pallavicino)

Numitore (1720; Porta, Rolli)

Radamisto (1720; Handel, Haym/Lalli)

Narciso (1720; D. Scarlatti, Rolli/Capece)

Astarto (1720; Bononcini, Rolli/Zeno and Pariati)

Arsace (1721; Orlandini, Rolli/Salvi)

Muzio Scevola (1721; Amadei, Bononcini, Handel; Rolli/Minato and Stampiglia)

L'Odio e l'amore (1721; Bononcini, Rolli/Noris)

Floridante (1721; Handel, Rolli/Silvani)

Crispo (1722; Bononcini, Rolli/Lemer)

Griselda (1722; Bononcini, Rolli/Zeno)

Ottone, re di Germania (1723; Handel, Haym/Pallavicino)

Cajo Marzio Coriolano (1723; Ariosti, Haym/Pariati)

Erminia favola boschereccia (1723; Bononcini, Rolli/?Petrosellini)

Flavio, re di Longobardi (1723; Handel, Haym/?Noris or ?Stampiglia)

Farnace (1723; Bononcini, ?Lalli/Morari)

Vespasiano (1724; Ariosti, Haym/Corradi)

Giulio Cesare in Egitto (1724; Handel, Haym/Bussani)

Calfurnia (1724; Bononcini, Haym/Braccioli)

Aquilio Consolo (1724; Ariosti, ?Haym/Silvani)

Tamerlano (1724; Handel, Haym/Piovene)

Artaserse (1724; Ariosti, Haym/Zeno and Pariati)

Rodelinda, regina de' Longobardi (1725; Handel, Haym/Salvi)

Dario (1725; Ariosti, ?Haym)

Elpidia, overo li rivali generosi (1725; Handel, arr., ?Haym/Zeno)

Elisa (1726; Popora, ?Haym)

Scipione (1726; Handel, Rolli/?Salvi)

Alessandro (1726; Handel, Rolli/Mauro)

Lucio Vero, imperator di Roma (1727; Ariosti, ?Haym/Zeno)

Admeto, re di Tessaglia (1727; Handel, Rolli or Haym/Mauro)

Astianatte (1727; Bononcini, Haym/Salvi)

Teuzzone (1727; Ariosti, ?Haym/Zeno)

Riccardo primo, re d'Inghilterra (1727; Handel, Rolli/Briani)

Siroe, re di Persia (1728; Handel, Haym/Metastasio)

Tolomeo, re di Egitto (1728; Handel, Haym/Capece)

Lotario (1729; Handel, Salvi)

Partenope (1730; Handel, Stampiglia)

Ormisda (1730; pasticcio, Zeno)

Venceslao (1731; pasticcio, Zeno)

Poro, re dell'Indie (1731; Handel, Metastasio)

Ezio (1732; Handel, Metastasio)

Sosarme, re di Media (1732; Handel, Salvi)

Lucio Papirio, dittatore (1732; Handel, arr., Zeno)

Catone in Utica (1732; Handel, arr., Metastasio)

Arianna in Nasso (1733; Porpora, Rolli)

Orlando (1733; Handel, Capece)

Semiramide riconosciuta (1733; Handel, arr., Metastasio)

Cajo Fabbricio (1733; Hasse, Zeno)

Arianna in Creta (1734; Handel, Pariati)

Arbace (1734; Handel, arr., Metastasio)

Oreste (1734; Handel, arr., Barlocci)

Fernando (1734; Arrigoni, Rolli/Gigli)

Il Parnasso in festa (1734; Handel, ?)

Enea nel Lazio (1734; Porpora, Rolli)

Artaserse (1734; Hasse and Broschi, Metastasio)

Ariodante (1735; Handel, Salvi)

Polifemo (1735; Porpora, Rolli)

Issipile (1735; Sandoni, Cori/Metastasio)

Alcina (1735; Handel, Ariosti)

Ifigenia in Aulide (1735; Porpora, Rolli)

Adriano in Siria (1735; Veracini, Cori/Metastasio)

Mitridate (1736; Porpora, Cibber/Lee)

Orfeo (1736; Porpora, Rolli)

Onorio (1736; Campi, Lalli)

Festa d'Imeneo (1736; Porpora, Rolli)

Atalanta (1736; Handel, Valeriano)

Siroe, re di Persia (1736; Hasse, Metastasio)

Merope (1737; ?, Cori/Zeno)

Arminio (1737; Handel, Salvi)

Demetrio (1737; Pescetti, Cori/Metastasio)

Giustino (1737; Handel, Beregan/Pariati)

Didone (1737; Handel, arr., Metastasio)
La clemenza di Tito (1737; Veracini, Cori/Metastasio)
Sabrina (1737; pasticcio, Rolli)
Berenice (1737; Handel, Salvi)
Demofoonte (1737; Duni, Cori/Metastasio)
Arsace (1737; pasticcio, Rolli/Salvi)
Faramondo (1738; Handel, Zeno)
La conquista del vello d'oro (1738; Pescetti, Rolli)
Alessandro Severo (1738; Handel, Zeno)
Parthenius (1738; Veracini, Rolli)
Serse (1738; Handel, Zeno)
Angelica e Medoro (1739; Pescetti, Metastasio)
Giove in Argo (1739; Handel, Lucchini)
Diana and Endimion (1739; Pescetti, ?)
Mericle e Selinante (1740; pasticcio, Rolli)
Olimpia in Ebuda (1740; Hasse, Rolli)
Imeneo (1740; Handel, Stampiglia)
Busiri, overo il trionfo d'amore (1740; Pescetti, Rolli)
Deidamia (1741; Handel, Rolli)
Alessandro in Persia (1741; Galuppi, Vanneschi)
Penelope (1741; Galuppi, Rolli)
Scipione in Cartagina (1742; Galuppi, Vanneschi)
Meraspe, o l'Olimpiade (1742; Pergolesi, Rolli/Metastasio)
Ceffalo e Procri (1742; pasticcio, Rolli)

Printed Sources

Following are principal printed sources cited in text or notes; topical political pamphlets cited in notes are excluded. Location is London, unless given.

Addison, Joseph. *Cato* (1713).
    The Works of the Right Honourable Joseph Addison, Esq. Ed. Thomas Tickell. 4 vols. (1721).
Amhurst, Nicholas. *A Collection of Poems; Published in the Craftsman* (1731).
Arbuthnot, John. *The Miscellaneous Works of the Late Dr. Arbuthnot*. 2 vols. (1751 and 1770).
The Art of Railing at Great Men: Being a Discourse upon Political Railers Ancient and Modern (1723).
Aston, Walter. *The Restauration of King Charles II* (1732).
Bickham, George. *The Musical Entertainer* (1736–1739; coll. edn. 1738–40).
Blackmore, Richard. *Prince Arthur, an Heroick Poem* (1695).
Boccalini, Traiano. *Advices from Parnassus* (1706).
Bononcini, Giovanni. *Cantate e duetti* (1721).
Brooke, Henry. *Gustavus Vasa, the Deliverer of His Country* (1739).

Budgell, Eustace. *A Short History of Prime Ministers in Great Britain* (1733).

Bullock, Christoper. *Woman's Revenge; or, a Match in Newgate*. 2nd edn. (1728).

Burney, Charles. *An Account of the Musical Performances in Westminster-Abbey* (1785).

    The Present State of Music in France and Italy. 2nd edn. (1773).

Calliope, or English Harmony. 2 vols. [?1737–?1745].

Carey, Henry. *The Dragon of Wantley* (1737).

    Faustina: or the Roman Songstress, A Satyr, on the Luxury and Effeminacy of the Age (1726).

    Mocking is Catching, or, A Pastoral Lamentation for the Loss of a Man and no Man [1726].

    The Musical Century. 2 vols. (1737–1740).

    Poems on Several Occasions (1729; 3rd edn. 1729).

Cato Examin'd: or Animadversions on the Fable or Plot … of Cato (1713).

Cibber, Colley. *The Dramatic Works of Colley Cibber*. 5 vols. (1777).

A Collection of Poems. Ed. John Whaley [1732].

Copy [of the] Letter, [from] Seignior John Angelo Belloni, to the Gentlemen of the Committee … Appointed to Inspect the Affairs of the Charitable Corporation (1732).

Country Correspondent [No. 3]: *Humbly Address'd to Gustavus Vasa, Esq.* (1739).

Coxe, William. *Anecdotes of George Frederick Handel and John Christopher Smith* (1799).

    Memoirs of the Life and Administration of Sir Robert Walpole, Earl of Orford. 3 vols. (1798).

Dalrymple, John. *Memoirs of Great Britain and Ireland*. 4th edn., 4 vols. (1773–88).

Davies, Thomas. *Dramatic Miscellanies: Consisting of Critical Observations on Several Plays of Shakespeare*. New edn., 3 vols. (1785).

    Memoirs of the Life of David Garrick. New edn., 2 vols. (1780).

de Mautour, Moreau. *Nouvelle Description de la Galerie du Palais du Luxembourg* (1704).

de Thoyras, Rapin. *The History of England*. Trans. with notes by N. Tindal. 2nd edn., 2 vols. (1732).

Dennis, John. *Essay on the Opera's after the Italian Manner, which are about to be Establish'd on the English Stage* (1706).

    Remarks on a Book Entitled, Prince Arthur, an Heroick Poem (1696).

    Remarks upon Cato (1713).

    The Stage Defended, from Scripture, Reason, Experience, and the Common Sense of Mankind, for Two Thousand Years (1726).

The Devil to Pay at St. James's (1727).

The Doctrine of Innuendo's Discuss'd; or the Liberty of the Press Maintain'd (1731).

Dryden, John. *Albion and Albanius* (1685).

    King Arthur (1691).

    The Spanish Fryar (1680).

Dryden, John, and Nathaniel Lee. *The Duke of Guise* (1682).

Echard, Laurence. *The History of England. From the Entrance of Julius Cæsar and the Romans, To the End of the Reign of King James the First* (1707).

An Epistle from S—r S—o to S—a F—a (1727).

The Fate of Favourites; Examplified in the Fall of Villiers, Duke of Buckingham (1734).

The Fate of Favourites: or, a Looking-Glass for S*****. Addressed to the Subscribers of Gustavus Vasa, the Deliverer of His Country (1739).

Fielding, Henry. *The Author's Farce* (1730).

    Eurydice Hiss'd: or a Word to the Wise (1737).

    The Grub-Street Opera (1731).

    The Historical Register for the Year 1736 (1737).

    Pasquin: A Dramatic Satire on the Times (1736).

    The Welsh Opera (1731).

Friedrich, Jacob, Freiherr von Bielfeld. *Letters of Baron Bielfeld*. Trans. "Mr. Hooper." 4 vols. (1770).

Gay, John. *The Beggar's Opera* (1728).

    Polly (1729).

Glover, Richard. *Leonidas* (1737).

Gribelin, Simon. *Ceiling of the Banqueting House at Whitehall* (1720).

Harmony in an Uproar (1734).

Hatchett, William. *The Fall of Mortimer* (1731).

Hell Upon Earth: or the Town in an Uproar (1729).

Hervey, John, Lord. *Ancient and Modern Liberty Stated and Compar'd* (1734).

Hill, Aaron. *The Works of the Late Aaron Hill, Esq.* 2nd edn., 4 vols. (1754).

An Historical Narrative of the Tryals of Mr. George Kelly, and of Dr. Francis Atterbury; (late) Lord Bishop of Rochester (1727).

The History of England Faithfully Extracted from Authentick Records. 2nd edn., 2 vols. (1702).

The History of Mortimer … Occasion'd by It's Having Been Presented as a Treasonable Libel (1731).

The History of Tamerlaine the Great (1723).

The History of the Life and Actions of Gustavus Vasa, Deliverer of His Country. Recommended to the Spectators of a Tragedy on that Subject, Now in Rehearsal (1739).

The History of the Life and Death of Sultan Solyman the Magnificent, Emperor of the Turks, and of his Son Mustapha. Inscrib'd to the Spectators of "Mustapha" (1739).

The History of the Life and Reign of the Valiant Prince Edward … and his Princess Eleonora. On which history, is founded a play, written by Mr. Thomson, call'd, Edward and Eleonora (1739).

The History of the Norfolk Steward Continued (1728).

History of Timur-Bec, known by the Name of Tamerlaine the Great (1723).

The Hive, a Collection of the Most Celebrated Songs. 3rd edn., 3 vols. (1726–1729).

It Cannot Rain But It Pours: or London Strowed with Rarities (1726).

Keyssler, Johann Georg. *Travels through Germany, Bohemia, Hungary, Switzerland, Italy, and Lorrain*. 4 vols. (1756–57).

Law Outlaw'd: or, A Short Reply to Mr. Law's Long Declamation Against the Stage (1726).

Law, William. *The Absolute Unlawfulness or the Stage-Entertainment Fully Demonstrated* (1726).

Le Bossu. *Traité du poëme epique* (1693).

Lediard, Thomas. *The Life of John, Duke of Marlborough*. 2nd edn. (1743).

Letters in Prose and Verse, to the Celebrated Polly Peachum (1728).

Letters … That Passed between the King, Queen, Prince and Princess of Wales; on Occasion of the Birth of the Young Princess (1737).

The Lives of Roger Mortimer, Earl of March, and of Robert, Earl of Oxford, &c. (1711).

Lyttelton, George. *Letters from a Persian in England* (1735).

  The Works of George Lord Lyttelton. 3 vols. (1776).

Macpherson, James. *Original Papers: Containing the Secret History of Great Britain* (1775).

Mainwaring, John. *Memoirs of the Life of the Late George Frederic Handel* (1760).

Mallet, David. *Alfred* (1740).

  Mustapha (1739).

Mandeville, Bernard. *The Fable of the Bees* (1714).

Memoirs Concerning the Life and Manners of Captain Macheath (1728).

Miller, James. *Miscellaneous Works in Verse and Prose* (1741).

Miscellaneous Poems. Collected by David Lewis. 2 vols. (1730).

Mr. Addison Turn'd Tory: or, the Scene Inverted: Wherein It Is Made Appear That the Whigs Have Misunderstood that Celebrated Author in His Applauded Tragedy, Call'd Cato (1713).

Nattier, Jean-Marc. *La Galerie du Palais du Luxembourg, peinte par Rubens, dessinée par les S. Nattier, et gravée par les plus illustres graveurs du temps* (1710).

The Norfolk Gamester (1734).

The Norfolk Sting: or, the History and Fall of Evil Ministers (1732).

An Oration, in Which an Enquiry is Made Whether the Stage Is, or Can Be Made a School for Forming the Mind to Virtue; and Praising the Superiority of Theatric Instruction Over Those of History & Moral Philosophy. With Reflections on Opera. Trans. John Lockman (Trans. of Charles Porée, *Theatrum Sit Ne, Vel Esse Possit Schola Informandis Moribus Idonea?* [1733])(1734).

Otway, Thomas. *Venice Preserv'd, or a Plot Discovered* (1682).

Paterson, William. *Arminius* (1740).

Pemberton, Henry. *Observations on Poetry, Especially the Epic: Occasioned by the Late Poem upon Leonidas* (1738).

Perceval, John, Earl of Egmont. *Faction Detected by the Evidence of Facts* (1743).

Pope, Alexander. *The Dunciad* (1728).
  The Dunciad Variorum (1729).
  Epistle to Augustus (1737).
The Practices of the Pretender and his Agents at Paris and Rome [1732].
Prevost, Abbé. *Le Pour et contre* (1733–34).
Quadrille to Perfection as Play'd at Soissons: or, The Norfolk Congress Pursu'd (1728).
Remarks on an Historical Play, called The Fall of Mortimer. Shewing Wherein the Said Play May Be Term'd a Libel Against the Present Administration (1731).
Remarks on Fog's Journal, of February 10. 1732/3. Exciting the People to an Assassination (1733).
The Report of the Gentlemen Appointed by the General Court of the Charitable Corporation (1732).
A Review of the Short History of Prime Ministers (1733).
Rollin, Charles. *The Ancient History of the Egyptians, Carthaginians, Assyrians, Babylonians, Medes and Persians, Macedonians, and Greeks.* 13 vols. (1734–39).
  Histoire ancienne des Égyptiens, des Carthaginois, des Assyriens, des Babyloniens, des Mèdes, et des Perses, des Macédoniens, des Grecs. 13 vols. (1730).
Rowe, Nicholas. *Tamerlane* (1701).
Salmon, Thomas. *A Review of the History of England.* 2 vols. [1724].
Services and Sufferings; or the Three Cuckoos (1726).
Shadwell, Thomas(?). *Some Reflections upon the Pretended Parallel in the Play Called The Duke of Guise* (1683).
A Short History of Prime Ministers in Great Britain (1733).
A Short History of the Charitable Corporation. From the Date of Their Charter, to … the frauds discovered in the management of their affairs (1732).
The Sly Subscription: on the Norfolk Monarch (1733).
Smythe, James-Moore. *The Rival Modes. A Comedy* (1727).
Somers, John, Baron. *The True Secret History of the Lives and Reigns of all the Kings and Queens of England* (1702).
The Spanish Merchant's Address to all Candid and Impartial Englishmen (1739).
Spenser, Edmund, *The Works of Mr. Edmund Spenser*. Ed. John Hughes. 6 vols. (1715).
Swift, Jonathan. *Gulliver's Travels* (1726).
  A Tale of a Tub (1704); 5th edn. (1710).
The Syren. 3rd edn. (1739).
Temple, William. *An Introduction to the History of England* (1695).
Theobald, Lewis. *Apollo and Daphne; or the Burgomaster Trick'd* (1726).
Thievery-a-la-mode (1728).
Thomson, James. *Agamemnon* (1738).
  Britannia (1729).
  Edward and Eleonora (1739).
  Liberty (1735–36).

The Seasons (1730).

Sophonisba (1730).

The Touch-Stone: or ... Essays on the Reigning Diversions of the Town (1728).

The Twickenham Hotch-Potch (1728).

Tyrrell, James. *The General History of England Both Ecclesiastical and Civil.* 2 vols. (1700).

The Unfortunate. General: or, the History of the Life and Character of Cato [?1713].

Victor, Benjamin. *Original Letters, Dramatic Pieces, and Poems.* 3 vols. (1776).

Vivitur Ingenio: Being a Collection of Elegant, Moral, Satirical, and Comical Thoughts, on Various Subjects (1726).

Weddell. *A Voyage up the Thames* (1738).

Secondary Sources

This list gives the principal secondary sources dealing with opera, theater history, British politics, and the major political, musical, and literary persons in this study.

Aitken, George A. *The Life and Works of John Arbuthnot.* Oxford: Clarendon Press, 1892.

Arbuthnot, John. *The Correspondence of Dr. John Arbuthnot.* Ed. Angus Ross. Munich: Wilhelm Fink, 2006.

The History of John Bull. Ed. Alan W. Bower and Robert A. Erickson. Oxford: Clarendon Press, 1976.

Arnall, William. *The Case of Opposition Stated, Between the Craftsman and the People.* Ed. and intro. Simon Varey. Lewisburg, PA: Bucknell University Press, 2003.

Ashcroft, Richard. "The Language of Political Conflict in Restoration Literature." In Richard Ashcroft and Alan Roper. *Politics as Reflected in Literature.* Papers Presented at a Clark Library Seminar, 24 January 1987. Los Angeles, CA: William Andrews Clark Memorial Library, 1989, pp. 1–28.

Aspden, Suzanne. "Ariadne's Clew: Politics, Allegory, and Opera in London (1734)." *Musical Quarterly* 85 (2001), 735–70.

Atherton, Herbert M. *Political Prints in the Age of Hogarth: A Study of the Ideographic Representation of Politics.* Oxford: Clarendon Press, 1974.

Avery, Emmett L. "A Royal Wedding Royally Confounded." *Western Humanities Review* 10 (1956), 153–64.

Ayers, Philip. *Classical Culture and the Idea of Rome in Eighteenth-Century England.* Cambridge University Press, 1997.

Bashford, Christina. "Perrin and Cambert's 'Ariane, ou le mariage de Bacchus' Re-examined." *Music and Letters* 72 (1991), 1–16.

Battestin, Martin C., with Ruthe R. Battestin. *Henry Fielding: A Life.* London: Routledge, 1989.

Beattie, John M. *The English Court in the Reign of George I.* Cambridge University Press, 1967.

Bennett, G. V. "Jacobitism and the Rise of Walpole." In *Historical Perspectives: Studies in English Thought and Society in Honour of J. H. Plumb.* Ed. Neil McKendrick. London: Europa, 1974, pp. 70–92.

  The Tory Crisis in Church and State, 1688–1730: The Career of Francis Atterbury, Bishop of Rochester. Oxford: Clarendon Press, 1975.

Berger, Arthur V. "The Beggar's Opera, the Burlesque, and Italian Opera." *Music and Letters* 17 (1936), 93–105.

Bermbach, Udo. "'Dein Wunsch zu regieren muß oberstes Gesetz sein'—Betrachtungen zu Händels Herrschergestalten." *Göttinger Händel-Beiträge* 12 (2008), 33–50.

  "Die Verwirrung der Mächtigen: Herrschertungenden und Politik in Georg Friedrich Händels Londoner Opern." In *Wo Macht ganz auf Verbrechen ruht: Politik und Gesellschaft in der Oper.* Hamburg: Europäische Verlagsanstalt, 1997, pp. 38–63.

Betz, Sigmund A. E. "The Operatic Criticism of the *Tatler* and *Spectator.*" *Musical Quarterly* 31 (1945), 318–30.

Bianconi, Lorenzo. *Music in the Seventeenth Century.* Trans. David Bryant. Cambridge University Press, 1987.

Bianconi, Lorenzo, and Thomas Walker. "Production, Consumption and Political Function of Seventeenth-Century Italian Opera." *Early Music History* 4 (1985), 209–96.

Black, Jeremy. *British Foreign Policy in the Age of Walpole.* Edinburgh: John Donald, 1985.

  The Collapse of the Anglo-French Alliance, 1727–1731. Gloucester: Alan Sutton, 1987.

  George II: Puppet of the Politicians? University of Exeter Press, 2007.

  "Jacobitism and British Foreign Policy, 1731–5." In *The Jacobite Challenge.* Ed. Eveline Cruickshanks and Jeremy Black. Edinburgh: John Donald, 1988, pp. 142–60.

  "Lord Bolingbroke's Operatic Allegory." *Scriblerian* 16 (1984), 97–9.

  Natural and Necessary Enemies: Anglo-French Relations in the Eighteenth Century. Athens: University of Georgia Press, 1986.

Blanning, T. C. W. *The Culture of Power and the Power of Culture: Old Regime Europe, 1660–1789.* Oxford University Press, 2002.

Bloom, Edward A. "The Allegorical Principle." *ELH* 18 (1951), 163–90.

Bloomfield, Morton W. "Allegory as Interpretation." *New Literary History* 3 (1971–72), 301–17.

Bond, Richmond P. *"The Tatler": The Making of a Literary Journal.* Cambridge, MA: Harvard University Press, 1971.

Brewer, John. *The Sinews of Power: War, Money, and the English State.* London: Century Hutchinson, 1988.

Britain in the First Age of Party, 1680–1750: Essays Presented to Geoffrey Holmes. Ed. Clyve Jones. London: Hambledon Press, 1987.

Bronson, Bertrand H. "The Beggar's Opera." In *Facets of the Enlightenment.* Berkeley: University of California Press, 1968, pp. 60–90.

Brown, Peter Douglas. *William Pitt, Earl of Chatham: The Great Commoner.* London: George Allen & Unwin, 1978.

Bucholz, R. O. *The Augustan Court: Queen Anne and the Decline of Court Culture.* Stanford University Press, 1993.

   "'Nothing but Ceremony': Queen Anne and the Limitations of Royal Ritual." *Journal of British Studies* 30 (1991), 288–323.

Burden, Michael. *Garrick, Arne and the Masque of Alfred: A Case Study in National, Theatrical and Musical Politics.* Lewiston, NY: Edwin Mellen, 1994.

   "The Wedding Masques for Anne, the Princess Royal." *Miscellanea Musicologica. Adelaide Studies in Musicology* 17 (1990), 87–113.

Burney, Charles. *A General History of Music.* 4 vols. 1776–1789. Ed. Frank Mercer. 2 vols. New York: Dover, 1957.

Burrows, Donald. "The 'Granville' and 'Smith' Collections of Handel Manuscripts." In *Sundrey Sorts of Music Books: Essays on The British Library Collections.* Ed. Chris Banks, Arthur Searle, and Malcolm Turner. London: The British Library, 1993, pp. 231–47.

   Handel. New York: Schirmer, 1994.

   Handel and the English Chapel Royal. Oxford University Press, 2005.

   "Handel and the London Opera Companies in the 1730s: Venues, Programmes, Patronage and Performers." *Göttinger Händel-Beiträge* 10 (2004), 149–65.

Burrows, Donald, and Robert D. Hume. "George I, the Haymarket Opera Company and Handel's *Water Music.*" *Early Music* 19 (1991), 323–44.

Butler, Margaret R. "Italian Opera in the Eighteenth Century." In *The Cambridge History of Eighteenth-Century Music.* Ed. Simon P. Keefe. Cambridge University Press, 2009, pp. 203–71.

Buttrey, John. "The Evolution of English Opera between 1656 and 1695: A Re-investigation." Ph.D. dissertation, Cambridge University, 1967.

Bywaters, David. *Dryden in Revolutionary England.* Berkeley: University of California Press, 1991.

Cable, Mabel H. "The Idea of a Patriot King in the Propaganda of the Opposition to Walpole, 1735–1739." *Philological Quarterly* 18 (1939), 119–30.

The Cambridge Companion to Handel. Ed. Donald Burrows. Cambridge University Press, 1997.

The Cambridge Handel Encyclopedia. Ed. Annette Landgraf and David Vickers. Cambridge University Press, 2009.

Canfield, J. Douglas. *Nicholas Rowe and Christian Tragedy.* Gainesville: University Presses of Florida, 1977.

   "Royalism's Last Dramatic Stand: English Political Tragedy, 1679–89." *Studies in Philology* 82 (1985), 234–63.

Cannon, John. *Aristocratic Century: The Peerage of Eighteenth-Century England.* Cambridge University Press, 1985.

Carswell, John. *The South Sea Bubble.* Rev. edn. London: Alan Sutton, 1993.

Catalogue of the Larpent Plays in the Huntington Library. Comp. Dougald MacMillan. San Marino, CA: Huntington Library Press, 1939.

Cervantes, Xavier. "History and Sociology of the Italian Opera in London (1705–45): The Evidence of the Dedications of the Printed Librettos." *Studi Musicali* 27 (1998), 339–82.

'"Tuneful Monsters': The Castrati and the London Operatic Public, 1667–1737." *Restoration and 18th Century Theatre Research*, 2nd ser., 13 (1998), 1–24.

Chance, James F. *The Alliance of Hanover: A Study of British Foreign Policy in the Last Years of George I.* London: John Murray, 1923.

Chisholm, Duncan. "Handel's 'Lucio Cornelio Silla.'" *Early Music* 14 (1986), 64–70.

Chrissochoidis, Ilias. "Handel at a Crossroads: His 1737–1738 and 1738–1739 Seasons Re-examined." *Music and Letters* 90 (2009), 599–635.

"Handel Recovering: Fresh Light on His Affairs in 1737." *Eighteenth-Century Music* 5 (2008), 237–44.

'"Hee-Haw … llelujah' Handel Among the Vauxhall Asses (1732)." *Eighteenth-Century Music* 7 (2010), 221–62.

Chrysander, Friedrich. *G. F. Händel.* 2nd edn., 3 vols. Leipzig: Breitkopf & Härtel, 1919.

Cibber, Colley. *An Apology for the Life of Cobby Cibber.* Ed. Robert W. Lowe. 2 vols. London: John C. Nimmo, 1889.

Clark, J. C. D. *English Society, 1688–1832: Ideology, Social Structure and Political Practice during the Ancien Regime.* Cambridge University Press, 1985. Second edition in 2000 with the title *English Society, 1660–1832: Religion, Ideology, and Politics during the Ancien Regime.*

Clark, Jane. "For Kings and Senates Fit." *Georgian Group Journal* (1989), 55–63.

'"His Zeal Is Too Furious': Lord Burlington's Agents." In *Lord Burlington – The Man and His Politics: Questions of Loyalty.* Ed. Edward Corp. Lewiston, NY: Edwin Mellen Press, 1998, pp. 181–97.

"Lord Burlington Is Here." In *Lord Burlington: Architecture, Art and Life.* Ed. Toby Barnard and Jane Clark. London: Hambledon Press, 1995, pp. 251–310.

"The Mysterious Mr Buck: Patronage and Politics, 1688–1745." *Apollo* 129 (May 1989), 317–22, 371.

"Palladianism and the Divine Right of Kings: Jacobite Iconography." *Apollo* 135 (April 1992), 224–9.

"The Stuart Presence at the Opera in Rome." In *The Stuart Court in Rome: The Legacy of Exile.* Ed. Edward Corp. Aldershot: Ashgate, 2003, pp. 85–93.

Clausen, Hans Dieter. "Der Einfluß der Komponisten auf die Librettowahl der Royal Academy of Music (1720–1729)." In *Zur Dramaturgie der Barockoper: Bericht über die Symposien der Internationalen Händel-Akademie Karlsruhe 1992 und 1993*. Ed. Hans Joachim Marx. Laabe: Laaber-Verlag, 1994, pp. 55–72.

Cleary, Thomas R. *Henry Fielding: Political Writer*. Waterloo, Ontario: Wilfrid Laurier University Press, 1984.

Clemens, J. R. "Handel and Carey." *The Sackbut* 11 (1930–31), 157–61.

Colley, Linda. *In Defiance of Oligarchy: The Tory Party, 1714–60*. Cambridge University Press, 1982.

Conn, Stetson. *Gibraltar in British Diplomacy in the Eighteenth Century*. New Haven, CT: Yale University Press, 1942.

Conolly, L. W. *The Censorship of English Drama, 1737–1824*. San Marino, CA: Huntington Library, 1976.

Correspondence between Frances, Countess of Hartford [sic] (afterwards Duchess of Somerset) and Henrietta Louisa, Countess of Pomfret between the Years 1738 and 1741. Ed. W. M. Bingley. 2nd edn., 3 vols. London: Richard Phillips, 1806.

Couvreur, Manuel. *Jean-Baptiste Lully: Musique et dramaturgie au service du Prince*. Brussels. Marc Vokar, 1992.

Coxe, William. *Memoirs of Horatio, Lord Walpole* (1802).
  Memoirs of the Duke of Marlborough. Ed. John Wade. 3 vols. London: George Bell, 1896.

Cruickshanks, Eveline. "Lord North, Christopher Layer and the Atterbury Plot: 1720–23." In *The Jacobite Challenge*. Ed. Eveline Cruickshanks and Jeremy Black. Edinburgh: John Donald, 1988, pp. 92–106.
  "The Political Career of the Third Earl of Burlington." In *Lord Burlington: Architecture, Art and Life*. Ed. Toby Barnard and Jane Clark. London: Hambledon Press, 1995, pp. 201–15.

Cruickshanks, Eveline, and Howard Erskine-Hill. *The Atterbury Plot*. Basingstoke: Palgrave Macmillan, 2004.

Curties, Henry. *A Forgotten Prince of Wales*. London: Everett [1912].

Danchin, Pierre. Ed. *The Prologues and Epilogues of the Eighteenth Century*. Part 1, vol. I. Nancy: Presses Universitaires de Nancy, 1990.

Daub, Peggy. "Handel and Frederick." *Musical Times* 122 (1981), 733.
  "Music at the Court of George II (c.1727–1760)." Ph.D. dissertation, Cornell University, 1985.
  "Queen Caroline of England's Music Library." In *Music Publishing and Collecting: Essays in Honor of Donald W. Krummel*. Ed. David Hunter. Urbana–Champaign, IL: Graduate School of Library and Information Science, 1994, pp. 131–65.

Daunton, M. J. *Progress and Poverty: An Economic and Social History of Britain, 1700–1850*. Oxford University Press, 1995.

Davis, Rose Mary. *The Good Lord Lyttelton: A Study in Eighteenth Century Politics and Culture*. Bethlehem, PA: Times Publishing Co., 1939.

de Saussure, César. *A Foreign View of England in the Reigns of George I & George II: The Letters of Monsieur César de Saussure to His Family.* Trans. and ed. Madame Van Muyden. London: John Murray, 1902.

Dean, Winton. *Handel's Operas, 1726-1741.* Woodbridge: Boydell & Brewer, 2006.

"Handel's *Sosarme*, a Puzzle Opera." In *Essays on Opera.* Oxford: Clarendon Press, 1990, 45–73.

Dean, Winton, and Merrill Knapp. *Handel's Operas, 1704-1726.* Rev. edn. Oxford: Clarendon Press, 1995.

Deutsch, O. E. *Handel: A Documentary Biography.* New York: W. W. Norton, 1955.

Dickinson, H. T. *Bolingbroke.* London: Constable, 1970.

"Bolingbroke: 'The Idea of a Patriot King.'" *History Today* 20 (1970), 13–19.

Liberty and Property: Political Ideology in Eighteenth-Century Britain. New York: Holmes and Meier, 1977.

The Politics of the People in Eighteenth-Century Britain. New York: St. Martin's Press, 1995.

"Popular Politics in the Age of Walpole." In *Britain in the Age of Walpole.* Ed. Jeremy Black. London: Macmillan, 1984, pp. 45–68.

Dickson, P. G. M. *The Financial Revolution in England: A Study in the Development of Public Credit, 1688-1756.* London: Macmillan, 1967.

Dobson, Michael. *The Making of the National Poet: Shakespeare, Adaptation and Authorship, 1660-1769.* Oxford: Clarendon Press, 1992.

Dorris, George E. *Paolo Rolli and the Italian Circle in London, 1715-1744.* The Hague: Mouton, 1967.

Downie, J. A. "Swift's Politics." In *Proceedings of the First Münster Symposium on Jonathan Swift.* Ed. Hermann J. Real and Heinz J. Vienken. Munich: Wilhelm Fink, 1985, pp. 47–58.

"Walpole, 'the Poet's Foe.'" In *Britain in the Age of Walpole.* Ed. Jeremy Black. London: Macmillan, 1984, pp. 171–188.

Dryden, John. *The Works of John Dryden*, vol. XIV: *Plays.* Ed. Vinton A. Dearing and Alan Roper. Berkeley: University of California Press, 1992.

The Works of John Dryden, vol. XV: *Plays.* Ed. Vinton A. Dearing. Berkeley: University of California Press, 1976.

Edwards, Averyl. *Frederick Louis, Prince of Wales, 1707-1751.* London: Staples Press, 1947.

Erskine-Hill, Howard. *The Augustan Idea in English Literature.* London: E. Arnold, 1983.

Poetry of Opposition and Revolution: Dryden to Wordsworth. Oxford: Clarendon Press, 1996.

The Social Milieu of Alexander Pope: Lives, Example, and the Poetic Response. New Haven, CT: Yale University Press, 1975.

Farinelli, Carlo Broschi. *La solitudine amica: lettere al conte Sicinio Pepoli.* Ed. Carlo Vitali and Francesca Boris. Palermo: Sellerio Editore, 2000.

Feiling, Keith G. *The Second Tory Party, 1714–1832*. London: Macmillan and Co., 1938.

Fielding, Henry. *The Historical Register for the Year 1736 and Eurydice Hissed*. Ed. William W. Appleton. Lincoln: University of Nebraska Press, 1967.

Fiske, Roger. *English Theatre Music in the Eighteenth Century*. 2nd edn. Oxford University Press, 1986.

Fletcher, Angus. *Allegory: The Theory of a Symbolic Mode*. Ithaca, NY: Cornell University Press, 1964.

Flower, Newman. *George Frideric Handel: His Personality and His Times*. London: Cassell & Co., 1923.

Foord, Archibald S. *His Majesty's Opposition, 1714–1830*. Oxford: Clarendon Press, 1964.

Friedlaender, Ernst. "Einige archivalische Nachrichten über Georg Fried. Händel und seine Familie." *Mittheilungen für die Mozart-Gemeinde in Berlin* 2(13) (February 1902), 102–7.

Fritz, Paul S. *The English Ministers and Jacobitism between the Rebellions of 1715 and 1745*. University of Toronto Press, 1975.

Gagey, Edmond M. *Ballad Opera*. New York: Columbia University Press, 1937.

Gay, John. *The Beggar's Opera*. Ed. Edgar V. Roberts. Lincoln: University of Nebraska Press, 1969.

George Frideric Handel: Collected Documents. Ed. Donald Burrows, Helen Green, John Greenacombe, and Anthony Hicks. Cambridge University Press, forthcoming.

George, M. Dorothy. *English Political Caricature to 1792: A Study of Opinion and Propaganda*. 2 vols. Oxford: Clarendon Press, 1959.

Gerig, Hans. *Die Memoiren des Lord Hervey als historische Quelle*. Inaugural dissertation, Albert-Ludwigs-Universität zu Freiburg i. Br., 1936.

Gerrard, Christine. *The Patriot Opposition to Walpole: Politics, Poetry, and National Myth, 1725–1742*. Oxford University Press, 1994.

"Queens-in-waiting: Caroline of Anspach and Augusta of Saxe-Gotha as Princesses of Wales." In *Queenship in Britain 1660–1837*. Ed. Clarissa Campbell Orr. Manchester University Press, 2002, pp. 143–61.

Gibson, Elizabeth. *The Royal Academy of Music, 1719–1728: The Institution and Its Directors*. New York: Garland Publishing, 1989.

"The Royal Academy of Music (1719–28) and its Directors." In *Handel Tercentenary Collection*. Ed. Stanley Sadie and Anthony Hicks. Ann Arbor, MI: UMI Research Press, 1987, pp. 136–64.

Gilman, Todd. "*The Beggar's Opera* and British Opera." *University of Toronto Quarterly* 66 (1997), 539–61.

"The Italian (Castrato) in London." In *The Work of Opera: Genre, Nationhood, and Sexual Difference*. Ed. Richard Dellamora and Daniel Fischlin. New York: Columbia University Press, 1997, pp. 49–70.

Glixon, Beth, and Jonathan Glixon. *Inventing the Business of Opera: The Impresario and His World in Seventeenth-Century Venice*. New York: Oxford University Press, 2006.

Goldgar, Bertrand A. *Walpole and the Wits: The Relation of Politics to Literature, 1722–1742*. Lincoln: University of Nebraska Press, 1976.

Gregg, Edward. *The Protestant Succession in International Politics, 1710–1716*. New York: Garland Publishing, 1986.

Gregory, Jeremy, and John Stevenson. *Britain in the Eighteenth Century, 1688–1820*. London: Longman, 2000.

Gunn, J. A. W. *Beyond Liberty and Property: The Process of Self-Recognition in Eighteenth-Century Political Thought*. Kingston, Ontario: McGill-Queen's University Press, 1983.

Gunto, David. "Kicking the Emperor: Some Problems of Restoration Parallel History." *1650–1850: Ideas, Aesthetics and Inquiries in the Early Modern Era* 3 (1997), 109–27.

Hallett, Mark. *The Spectacle of Difference: Graphic Satire in the Age of Hogarth*. New Haven, CT: Yale University Press, 1999.

Halsband, Robert. *The Life of Lady Mary Wortley Montagu*. Oxford: Clarendon Press, 1956.

   Lord Hervey: Eighteenth-Century Courtier. New York: Oxford University Press, 1974.

Hammond, Brean S. "Politics and Cultural Politics: The Case of Henry Fielding." *Eighteenth-Century Life* 16 (February 1992), 76–93.

Handel, George Frideric. *The Letters and Writings of George Frideric Handel*. Ed. Erich H. Müller. London: Cassell, 1935.

Händel-Handbuch, vol. IV: *Dokumente zu Leben und Schaffen*. 4 vols. Kassel: Bärenreiter, 1985.

Hanham, Andrew. "'So Few Facts': Jacobites, Tories and the Pretender." *Parliamentary History* 19 (2000), 233–57.

Hanson, Laurence. *Government and the Press, 1695–1763*. London: Oxford University Press, 1936.

Harris, Ellen T. *Handel as Orpheus: Voice and Desire in the Chamber Cantatas*. Cambridge, MA: Harvard University Press, 2001.

   "With Eyes on the East and Ears in the West: Handel's Orientalist Operas." *Journal of Interdisciplinary History* 36 (2006), 419–43.

   Ed. *The Librettos of Handel's Operas*. 13 vols. New York: Garland, 1989.

Harris, Frances. "Parliament and Blenheim Palace: The House of Lords Appeal of 1721." *Parliamentary History* 8 (1989), 43–62.

   A Passion for Government: The Life of Sarah, Duchess of Marlborough. Oxford: Clarendon Press, 1991.

Harris, Tim. *Politics Under the Later Stuarts: Party Conflict in a Divided Society, 1660–1715*. Harlow: Pearson Education, 1993.

Harth, Phillip. "Legends No Histories: The Case of *Absalom and Achitophel*." *Studies in Eighteenth-Century Culture* 4 (1975), 13–29.

  Pen for a Party: Dryden's Tory Propaganda in Its Contexts. Princeton University Press, 1993.

  "Political Interpretations of *Venice Preserv'd*." *Modern Philology* 85 (1988), 345–62.

Hatton, Ragnhild. *George I: Elector and King*. Cambridge, MA: Harvard University Press, 1978.

Hawkins, John. *A General History of the Science and Practice of Music*. 5 vols. 1776. Reprint of 1853 edn. 2 vols. New York: Dover, 1963.

Hawks, Katie. "Looking for Richard: Why Handel Wrote *Riccardo Primo*." *The Handel Institute Newsletter* 23(1) (Spring 2012), 5–7.

Haydon, Colin. *Anti-Catholicism in Eighteenth-Century England, c.1714–80: A Political and Social Study*. Manchester University Press, 1993.

Henderson, Alfred J. *London and the National Government, 1721–1742: A Study of City Politics and the Walpole Administration*. Durham, NC: Duke University Press, 1945.

Hervey, John, Earl of Bristol. *The Diary of John Hervey, First Earl of Bristol. With Extracts from his Book of Expenses, 1688 to 1742*. Ed. S. H. A. H. Wells: Ernest Jackson, 1894.

  Letter-Books of John Hervey, First Earl of Bristol. Ed. S. H. A. H. 3 vols. Wells: Ernest Jackson, 1894.

Hervey, John, Lord. *Lord Hervey and His Friends, 1726–38*. Ed. Earl of Ilchester. London: John Murray, 1950.

  Memoirs of the Reign of George the Second. Ed. John W. Croker. 3 vols. London: Bickers and Son, 1884.

  Some Materials Towards Memoirs of the Reign of King George II. Ed. Romney Sedgwick. 3 vols. London: Eyre and Spottiswoode, 1931.

Hill, Brian W. *The Growth of Parliamentary Parties, 1688–1742*. Hamden: Archon Books, 1976.

Historical Manuscripts Commission. *The Manuscripts of the Earl of Buckinghamshire* [etc.]. London: Her Majesty's Stationery Office, 1895.

  The Manuscripts of the Earl of Carlisle, Preserved at Castle Howard. London: Her Majesty's Stationery Office, 1897.

  Manuscripts of the Earl of Egmont. Diary of Viscount Percival afterwards First Earl of Egmont. 3 vols. London: His Majesty's Stationery Office, 1920–23.

  Reports of Manuscripts in Various Collections. London: His Majesty's Stationery Office, 1913.

  Reports on the Manuscripts of the Earl of Eglinton [etc.]. London: Eyre and Spottiswoode, 1885.

The History of Parliament. The House of Commons, 1715–1754. Ed. Romney Sedgwick. 2 vols. New York: Oxford University Press, 1970.

Holmes, Geoffrey. "The Achievement of Stability: The Social Context of Politics from the 1680s to the Age of Walpole." In *The Whig Ascendancy: Colloquies on Hanoverian England.* Ed. John Cannon. London: Edward Arnold, 1981, pp. 1–22.

British Politics in the Age of Anne. Rev. edn. London: Hambledon Press, 1987.

The Making of a Great Power, Late Stuart and Early Georgian Britain, 1660–1722. London: Longman, 1993.

Holmes, Geoffrey, and Daniel Szechi. *The Age of Oligarchy: Pre-Industrial Britain, 1722–1783.* London: Longman, 1993.

Holmes, William C. *Opera Observed: Views of a Florentine Impresario in the Early Eighteenth Century.* University of Chicago Press, 1993.

Horwitz, Henry. "Parties, Connections, and Parliamentary Politics, 1689–1714: Review and Revision." *Journal of British Studies* 6 (1966–67), 45–69.

Hughes, Helen. *The Gentle Hertford: Her Life and Letters.* New York: Macmillan, 1940.

Hume, Robert D. "The Aims and Limits of Historical Scholarhip." *Review of English Studies,* n.s. 53(211) (2002), 399–422.

The Development of English Drama in the Late Seventeenth Century. Oxford: Clarendon Press, 1976.

"Handel and Opera Management in London in the 1730s." *Music and Letters* 67 (1986), 347–62.

"Henry Fielding and Politics at the Little Haymarket, 1728–1737." In *The Golden and Brazen World: Papers in Literature and History, 1650–1800.* Ed. John M. Wallace. Berkeley: University of California Press, 1985, pp. 79–124.

Henry Fielding and the London Theatre, 1728–1737. Oxford: Clarendon Press, 1988.

"The Politics of Opera in Late Seventeenth-Century London." *Cambridge Opera Journal* 10 (1998), 15–43.

Reconstructing Contexts: The Aims and Principles of Archaeo-Historicism. Oxford University Press, 1999.

"The Sponsorship of Opera in London, 1704–1720." *Modern Philology* 84 (1988), 420–32.

Hunter, David. "Bragging on *Rinaldo*: Ten Ways Writers have Trumpeted Handel's Coming to Britain." *Göttinger Händel-Beiträge* 10 (2004), 113–31.

"Margaret Cecil, Lady Brown: 'Persevering Enemy to Handel' but 'Otherwise Unknown to History.'" *Women and Music* 3 (1999), 43–58.

"Patronizing Handel, Inventing Audiences: The Intersection of Class, Money, Music and History." *Early Music* 30 (2000), 33–49.

"Royal Patronage of Handel in Britain: The Rewards of Pensions and Office." In *Handel Studies: A Gedenkschrift for Howard Serwer.* Ed. Richard G. King. Hillsdale, NY: Pendragon, 2009, pp. 127–53.

Innes, Joanna. "Jonathan Clark, Social History, and England's Ancien Regime." *Past and Present* 115 (May 1987), 165–200.

Isherwood, Robert M. *Music in the Service of the King: France in the Seventeenth Century.* Ithaca, NY: Cornell University Press, 1973.

The Jacobite Challenge. Ed. Eveline Cruickshanks and Jeremy Black. Edinburgh: John Donald, 1998.

Jones, Clyve. "The New Opposition in the House of Lords, 1720–3." *Historical Journal* 36 (1993), 309–29.

"William, First Earl Cowper, Country Whiggery, and the Leadership of the Opposition in the House of Lords, 1720–1723." In *Lords of Parliament: Studies, 1714–1914*. Ed. R. W. Davis. Stanford University Press, 1995, pp. 29–43.

Jones, Stephen. *Frederick, Prince of Wales and His Circle*. Exhibition catalog, Gainsborough's House, June 6 – July 26, 1981. Sudbury, Suffolk: Gainsborough's House, 1981.

Ketterer, Robert C. *Ancient Rome in Early Opera*. Urbana: University of Illinois Press, 2009.

"Senecanism and the 'Sulla' Operas of Handel and Mozart." *Syllecta Classica* 10 (1999), 214–33.

King, Richard G. "Classical History and Handel's *Alessandro*." *Music and Letters* 77 (1996), 34–63.

"Handel's Travels in the Netherlands in 1750." *Music and Letters* 72 (1991), 372–86.

"Two New Letters from Princess Amelia." *Händel-Jahrbuch* 40/41 (1994/1995), 169–71.

Knapp, J. Merrill. "The Autograph of Handel's 'Riccardo Primo.'" In *Studies in Renaissance and Baroque Music in Honor of Arthur Mendel*. Ed. Robert L. Marshall. Kassel: Bärenreiter, 1974, pp. 331–58.

"The Libretto of Handel's 'Silla.'" *Music and Letters* 50 (1969), 68–75.

Knif, Henrik. *Gentlemen and Spectators: Studies in Journals, Opera and the Social Scene in late Stuart London*. Helsinki: Finnish Historical Society, 1995.

Kramnick, Isaac. *Bolingbroke and His Circle: The Politics of Nostalgia in the Age of Walpole*. Cambridge, MA: Harvard University Press, 1968.

Landgraf, Annette. "Israel in Egypt: Ein Oratorium als Opfer der Politik." *Händel-Jahrbuch* 42/43 (1996/1997), 213–21.

Langford, Paul. *The Excise Crisis: Society and Politics in the Age of Walpole*. Oxford: Clarendon Press, 1975.

A Polite and Commercial People: England, 1727–1783. Oxford: Clarendon Press, 1989.

Public Life and the Propertied Englishman, 1689–1798. Oxford: Clarendon Press, 1991.

Walpole and the Robinocracy. The English Satirical Print, 1600–1832. Cambridge: Chadwyck-Healey, 1986.

LaRue, C. Steven. *Handel and his Singers: The Creation of the Royal Academy Operas, 1720–1728*. Oxford: Clarendon Press, 1995.

Lenman, Bruce. *The Jacobite Risings in Britain, 1689–1746*. London: Eyre Methuen, 1980.

Lewis, Peter. *John Gay: The Beggar's Opera*. London: Edward Arnold, 1976.

Liesenfeld, Vincent J. *The Licensing Act of 1737*. Madison: University of Wisconsin Press, 1984.

Ed. and intro. *The Stage and the Licensing Act, 1729–1739*. New York: Garland, 1981.

Lindgren, Lowell. "A Bibliographic Scrutiny of Dramatic Works Set by Giovanni and His Brother Antonio Maria Bononcini." Ph.D. dissertation, Harvard University, 1972.

"Critiques of Opera in London, 1705–1719." *Il melodramma italiano in Italia e in Germania nell' età barocca*. Contributi musicologici del Centro Ricerche dell' A.M.I.S.-Como 9. Como (1995), 145–65.

"Musicians and Librettists in the Correspondence of Gio. Giacomo Zamboni, Oxford, Bodleian Library, MSS Rawlinson Letters 116–138." *Royal Musical Association Research Chronicle* 24 (1991).

"Parisian Patronage of Performers from the Royal Academy of Music (1719–1728)." *Music and Letters* 58 (1977), 4–28.

"The Three Great Noises 'Fatal to the Interests of Bononcini.'" *Musical Quarterly* 61 (1975), 560–83.

Lindgren, Lowell, and Colin Timms. "The Correspondence of Agostino Steffani and Giuseppe Riva, 1720–1728, and Related Correspondence with J. P. F. von Schönborn and S. B. Pallavicini." *Royal Musical Association Research Chronicle* 36 (2003).

Lock, F. P. *The Politics of "Gulliver's Travels."* Oxford: Clarendon Press, 1980.

Swift's Tory Politics. London: Duckworth, 1983.

Lockwood, Thomas. "Fielding and the Licensing Act." *Huntington Library Quarterly* 50 (1987), 379–93.

Lodge, Richard. "The Anglo-French Alliance 1716–31." In *Studies in Anglo-French History during the Eighteenth, Nineteenth, and Twentieth Centuries*. Ed. Alfred Coville and Harold Temperley. Cambridge University Press, 1935, pp. 3–18.

Loftis, John. "Political and Social Thought in the Drama." In *The London Theatre World, 1660–1800*. Ed. Robert D. Hume. Carbondale: Southern Illinois University Press, 1980, pp. 253–85.

The Politics of Drama in Augustan England. Oxford: Clarendon Press, 1963.

The London Stage, 1660–1800: A Calendar of Plays, Entertainments & Afterpieces. Ed. Arthur Scouton. 11 vols. Carbondale: Southern Illinois University Press, 1960–68.

Lord Bolingbroke: Contributions to the "Craftsman." Ed. Simon Varey. Oxford: Clarendon Press, 1982.

Lord, Phillip. "The English-Italian Opera Companies, 1732–3." *Music and Letters* 45 (1964), 239–51.

Lynch, James J. *Box, Pit, and Gallery: Stage and Society in Johnson's London*. Berkeley: University of California Press, 1953.

Mack, Maynard. *Alexander Pope: A Life*. New York: W. W. Norton, 1985.

The Garden and the City: Retirement and Politics in the Later Poetry of Pope, 1731–1743. University of Toronto Press, 1969.

Maresca, Thomas E. "Personification vs. Allegory." In *Enlightening Allegory: Theory, Practice, and Contexts of Allegory in the Late Seventeenth and Eighteenth Centuries*. Ed. Kevin L. Cope. New York: AMS Press, 1993, pp. 21–39.

McGeary, Thomas. "Farinelli in Madrid: Opera, Politics, and the War of Jenkins' Ear." *Musical Quarterly* 82 (1998), 383–421.

"Farinelli's Progress to Albion: The Recruitment and Reception of Opera's 'Blazing Star.'" *British Journal for Eighteenth-Century Studies* 28 (2005), 339–61.

"Gendering Opera: Italian Opera as the Feminine Other in England, 1700–42." *Journal of Musicological Research* 14 (1994), 17–34.

"Handel and the Feuding Royals." *The Handel Institute Newsletter* 17 (Autumn 2006), 5–8.

"Handel, Prince Frederick, and the Opera of the Nobility Reconsidered." *Göttinger Händel-Beiträge* 7 (1998), 156–78.

"Verse Epistles on Italian Opera Singers, 1724–1736." *Royal Musical Association Research Chronicle* 33 (2000), 29–88.

"'Warbling Eunuchs': Opera, Gender, and Sexuality on the London Stage." *Restoration and 18th Century Theatre Research*, 2nd ser., 7 (1992), 1–22.

McIntosh, William A. "Handel, Walpole, and Gay: The Aims of *The Beggar's Opera*." *Eighteenth-Century Studies* 7 (1974), 415–33.

McKillop, Alan D. "The Early History of *Alfred*." *Philological Quarterly* 41 (1962), 311–24.

"Thomson and the Licensers of the Stage." *Philological Quarterly* 37 (1958), 448–53.

McLachlan, Jean O. *Trade and Peace with Old Spain, 1667–1750*. Cambridge University Press, 1940.

McLauchlan, Fiona. "Lotti's 'Teofane' (1719) and Handel's 'Ottone' (1723): A Textual and Musical Study." *Music and Letters* 78 (1997), 349–90.

McLynn, Frank. *The Jacobites*. London: Routledge & Kegan Paul, 1985.

Midgley, Graham. *The Life of Orator Henley*. Oxford: Clarendon Press, 1973.

Milhous, Judith. "Händel und die Londoner Theaterverhältnisse im Jahr 1734." In *Gattungskonventionen der Händel-Oper: Bericht über die Symposien der internationalen Händel-Akademie Karlsruhe 1990 und 1991*. Karlsruhe: Laaber-Verlag, 1992, pp. 117–37.

"Opera Finances in London." *Journal of the American Musicological Society* 37 (1984), 567–92.

Milhous, Judith, and Robert D. Hume. "Box Office Reports for Five Operas Mounted by Handel in London, 1732–1734." *Harvard Library Bulletin* 26 (1978), 245–66.

"The Charter for the Royal Academy of Music." *Music and Letters* 67 (1986), 50–8.

"Construing and Misconstruing Farinelli in London." *British Journal for Eighteenth-Century Studies* 28 (2005), 361–85.

"Handel's Opera Finances in 1732-3." *Musical Times* 125 (1984), 86–9.

"Heidegger and the Management of the Haymarket Opera, 1713–17." *Early Music* 27 (1999), 65–84.

"New Light on Handel and The Royal Academy of Music in 1720." *Theatre Journal* 35 (1983), 149–67.

A Register of English Theatrical Documents, 1660-1737. 2 vols. Carbondale: Southern Illinois University Press, 1991.

Monod, Paul K. *Jacobitism and the English People, 1688-1788.* Cambridge University Press, 1989.

"The Politics of Handel's Early London Operas, 1711–1718." *Journal of Inter-disciplinary History* 36 (2006), 445–72.

Montagu, Mary Wortley. *The Complete Letters of Lady Mary Wortley Montagu.* Ed. Robert Halsband. 3 vols. Oxford: Clarendon Press, 1965–67.

Namier, Lewis. *The Structure of Politics at the Accession of George III.* 2nd edn. London: Macmillan, 1957.

The New Grove Dictionary of Music and Musicians. 2nd edn. Ed. Stanley Sadie and John Tyrrel. 20 vols. London: Macmillan, 2001.

The New Grove Dictionary of Opera. Ed. Stanley Sadie and Christina Bashford. 4 vols. London: Macmillan, 1992.

The New Grove Handel. Ed. Winton Dean with Anthony Hicks. New York: W. W. Norton, 1983.

Nokes, David. *John Gay: A Profession of Friendship.* Oxford University Press, 1995.

O'Gorman, Frank. "The Recent Historiography of the Hanoverian Regime." *Historical Journal* 29 (1986), 1005–20.

Ograjenšek, Suzana. "From *Alessandro* (1726) to *Tolomeo* (1728): The Final Royal Academy Operas." Ph.D. dissertation, University of Cambridge, 2005.

The Orrery Papers. Ed. the Countess of Cork and Orrery [E. C. Boyle]. 2 vols. London: Duckworth, 1903.

Owen, Susan J. "Interpreting the Politics of Restoration Drama." *Seventeenth Century* 8 (1993), 67–97.

"The Politics of John Dryden's *The Spanish Fryar: or, the Double Discovery.*" *English: The Journal of the English Association* 43(176) (1994), 97–113.

Restoration Theatre and Crisis. Oxford: Clarendon Press, 1996.

Pares, Richard. *War and Trade in the West Indies, 1739-1763.* Oxford University Press, 1936.

Percival, Milton. *Political Ballads Illustrating the Administration of Sir Robert Walpole.* Oxford Historical and Literary Studies 8 (1916).

Pettit, Alexander. "Anxiety, Political Rhetoric, and Historical Drama under Walpole." *1650-1850: Ideas, Aesthetics, and Inquiries in the Early Modern Era* 1 (1994), 109–36.

Pittock, Murray G. H. *Jacobitism*. New York: St. Martin's Press, 1998.

> *Poetry and Jacobite Politics in Eighteenth-Century Britain and Ireland*. Cambridge University Press, 1994.

Plumb, J. H. *The Growth of Political Stability in England, 1675–1725*. London: Macmillan, 1967.

> *Sir Robert Walpole: The Making of a Statesman*. Boston: Houghton Mifflin: 1956.

> *Sir Robert Walpole: The King's Minister*. London: Cresset Press, 1960.

Pocock, J. G. A. "1660 and All That: Whig-Hunting, Ideology and Historiography in the Work of Jonathan Clark." *Cambridge Review* 108(2298) (October 1987), 125–8.

Pope, Alexander. *The Correspondence of Alexander Pope*. Ed. George Sherburn. 5 vols. Oxford: Clarendon Press, 1956.

> *The Poems of Alexander Pope*, vol. III: *The Dunciad (1728) & The Dunciad Variorum (1729)*. Ed. Valerie Rumbold. Harlow: Pearson, 2007.

Porter, Roy. "English Society in the Eighteenth Century Revisited." In *British Politics and Society from Walpole to Pitt, 1742–1789*. Ed. Jeremy Black. New York: St. Martin's Press, 1990, pp. 29–52.

Prest, Wilfred. *Albion Ascendant: English History, 1660–1815*. Oxford University Press, 1998.

Price, Curtis A. "English Traditions in Handel's *Rinaldo*." In *Handel Tercentenary Collection*. Ed. Stanley Sadie and Anthony Hicks. Ann Arbor, MI: UMI Research Press, 1987, pp. 120–37.

> *Henry Purcell and the London Stage*. Cambridge University Press, 1984.

> "Political Allegory in Late-Seventeenth-Century English Opera." In *Music and Theatre: Essays in Honour of Winton Dean*. Ed. Nigel Fortune. Cambridge University Press, 1987, pp. 1–29.

Realey, Charles B. *The Early Opposition to Sir Robert Walpole, 1720–1727*. Lawrence: University of Kansas Press, 1931.

Reckow, Fritz. "Der inszenierte Fürst: Situationsbezug und Stilprägung der Oper im absolutistischen Frankreich." In *Die Inszenierung des Absolutismus: Politische Begründung und künstlerische Gestaltung höfischer Feste im Frankreich Ludwigs XIV*. Ed. Fritz Reckow. Erlangen: Erlanger Forschungen, 1992, pp. 71–104.

Rees, Abraham. *The Cyclopædia; or, Universal Dictionary of Arts, Sciences, and Literature*. 39 vols. (1819).

Richmond, Herbert. *The Navy as an Instrument of Policy, 1558–1727*. Cambridge University Press, 1953.

Roberts, John. "The Story of Handel's *Imeneo*." *Händel-Jahrbuch* 47 (2001), 337–84.

Rogers, Nicholas. "Riot and Popular Jacobitism in Early Hanoverian England." In *Ideology and Conspiracy: Aspects of Jacobitism, 1689–1759*. Ed. Eveline Cruickshanks. Edinburgh: John Donald, 1982, pp. 70–88.

Whigs and Cities: Popular Politics in the Age of Walpole and Pitt. Oxford: Clarendon Press, 1989.

Rogers, Pat. "Gay and the World of Opera." In *John Gay and the Scriblerians.* Ed. Peter Lewis and Nigel Wood. New York: St. Martin's Press, 1988, pp. 147–62.

Romano, Dennis. "Why Opera? The Politics of an Emerging Genre." *Journal of Interdisciplinary History* 36 (2006), 401–9.

Roper, Alan. "Drawing Parallels and Making Applications in Restoration Literature." In Richard Ashcroft and Alan Roper. *Politics as Reflected in Literature.* Papers Presented at a Clark Library Seminar, 24 January 1987. Los Angeles, CA: William Andrews Clark Memorial Library, 1989, pp. 29–65.

Rorschach, Kimerly. "Frederick, Prince of Wales (1707–1751) as a Patron of the Visual Arts: Princely Patriotism and Political Propaganda." 2 vols. Ph.D. dissertation, Yale University, 1985.

"Frederick, Prince of Wales (1707–51) as Collector and Patron." *Walpole Society* 55 (1989/1990), 1–76.

"Frederick, Prince of Wales: Taste, Politics and Power." *Apollo* 134 (1991), 239–45.

Rosand, Ellen. *Opera in Seventeenth-Century Venice: The Creation of a Genre.* Berkeley: University of California Press, 1991.

"Seneca and the Interpretation of *L'Incoronazione di Poppea.*" *Journal of the American Musicological Society* 38 (1985), 34–71.

Rousseau, G. S. "Revisionist Polemics: J. C. D. Clark and the Collapse of Modernity in the Age of Johnson." *Age of Johnson* 2 (1988), 421–50.

Ruttkay, Kállmán G. "The Critical Reception of Italian Opera in England in the Early Eighteenth Century." *Studies in English and American Philology* 1 (1971), 93–169.

Sambrook, James. *James Thomson, 1700–1748: A Life.* Oxford: Clarendon Press, 1991.

Sasse, Konrad. "Die Texte der Londoner Opern Händels in ihren gesellschaftlichen Beziehungen." *Wissenschaftliche Zeitschrift der Martin-Luther-Universität Halle-Wittenberg.* Gesellschafts- und Sprachwissenschaftliche Reihe 4(5) (1955), 627–46.

"Opera Register from 1712 to 1734 (Colman-Register)." *Händel-Jahrbuch* 5 (1959), 199–223.

Schmidt, Carl B. "Antonio Cesti's *Il pomo d'oro*: A Reexamination of a Famous Hapsburg Court Spectacle." *Journal of the American Musicological Society* 29 (1976), 381–412.

Schultz, William E. *Gay's Beggar's Opera: Its Content, History & Influence.* New Haven, CT: Yale University Press, 1923.

Seifert, Herbert. *Die Oper am Wiener Kaiserhof im 17. Jahrhundert.* Wiener Veröffentlichungen zur Musikgeschichte 25. Tutzing: Hans Schneider, 1985.

Der Sig-prangende Hochzeit-Gott: Hochzeitsfest am Wiener Hof der Habsburger und ihre Allegorik, 1622–1699. Dramma per musica 2. Vienna: Musikwissenschaftlicher Verlag, 1988.

Sharpe, Kevin, and Steven N. Zwicker. Eds. *Politics of Discourse: The Literature and History of Seventeenth-Century England*. Berkeley: University of California Press, 1987.

"Sir John Plumb's 'Growth of Political Stability': Does it Stand?" In *Albion* 25 (1993), pp. 237–77.

Skinner, Quentin. "The Principles and Practice of Opposition: The Case of Bolingbroke versus Walpole." In *Historical Perspectives: Studies in English Thought and Society in Honour of J. H. Plumb*. Ed. Neil McKendrick. London: Europa Publications, 1974, pp. 93–128.

Visions of Politics, vol. I: *Regarding Method*. Cambridge University Press, 2002.

Smith, Hannah. "The Court in England, 1714–1760: A Declining Political Institution." *History* 90 (2005), 23–41.

Georgian Monarchy: Politics and Culture, 1714–1760. Cambridge University Press, 2006.

Smith, Ruth. "Handel's Israelite Librettos and English Politics, 1732–52." *Göttinger Händel-Beiträge* 5 (1993), 195–215.

Handel's Oratorios and Eighteenth-Century Thought. Cambridge University Press, 1995.

Speck, W. A. *Stability and Strife: England, 1714–1760*. Cambridge, MA: Harvard University Press, 1977.

Tory & Whig: The Struggle in the Constituencies, 1701–15. London: Macmillan, 1970.

"The Whig Schism Under George I." *Huntington Library Quarterly* 40 (1977), 171–9.

"Whigs and Tories Dim Their Glories: English Political Parties under the First Two Georges." In *The Whig Ascendancy: Colloquies on Hanoverian England*. Ed. John Cannon. London: Edward Arnold, 1981, pp. 51–70.

Stevens, David H. *Party Politics and English Journalism, 1702–1742*. Menasha, WI: Collegiate Press, 1961.

Streatfeild, R. A. *Handel*. 2nd edn. London: Methuen, 1910.

"Handel, Rolli, and Italian Opera in London in the Eighteenth Century." *Musical Quarterly* 3 (1917), 428–45.

Strohm, Reinhard. *"Costanza e fortezza*: Investigation of the Baroque Ideology." In *I Bibiena: una famiglia in scena: da Bologna all'Europa*. Ed. Daniela Gallingani. Florence: Alinea, 2002, pp. 75–91.

"Darstellung, Aktion and Interesse in der höfischen Opernkunst." *Händel-Jahrbuch* 49 (2003), 13–26.

"Handel and his Italian Opera Texts." In *Essays on Handel and Italian Opera*. Cambridge University Press, 1985, pp. 34–79.

"Rulers and States in Hasse's *Drammi per Musica*." In *Dramma per Musica: Italian Opera Seria of the Eighteenth Century*. New Haven, CT: Yale University Press, 1997, pp. 270–93.

Swedenberg, H. T., Jr. *The Theory of the Epic in England, 1650–1800*. Berkeley: University of California Press, 1944.

Swift, Jonathan. *Jonathan Swift: The Complete Poems*. Ed. Pat Rogers. New Haven, CT: Yale University Press, 1983.

Swift, Jonathan, and Thomas Sheridan. *The Intelligencer*. Ed. James Woolley. Oxford: Clarendon Press, 1992.

Szechi, David. *Jacobitism and Tory Politics, 1710–14*. Edinburgh: John Donald, 1984.

Taylor, Carole M. "Handel and Frederick, Prince of Wales." *Musical Times* 125 (1984), 89–92.

"Handel's Disengagement from the Italian Opera." In *Handel: Tercentenary Collection*. Ed. Stanley Sadie and Anthony Hicks. Ann Arbor, MI: UMI Research Press, 1987, pp. 165–81.

"Italian Operagoing in London, 1700–1745." Ph.D. dissertation, Syracuse University, 1991.

Taylor, Stephen. "British Politics in the Age of Holmes." *Parliamentary History* 8 (1989), 132–41.

Taylor, Stephen, and Hannah Smith. "Hephaestion and Alexander: Lord Hervey, Frederick, Prince of Wales, and the Royal Favourite in England in the 1730s." *English Historical Review* 124(507) (2009), 283–312.

Thomas, Downing A. *Aesthetics of Opera in the Ancien Régime, 1647–1785*. Cambridge University Press, 2002.

Thomas, Peter D. G. "Party Politics in Eighteenth-Century Britain: Some Myths and a Touch of Reality." *British Journal for Eighteenth-Century Studies* 10 (1987), 201–10.

Thompson, Andrew C. *George II. King and Elector*. New Haven, CT: Yale University Press, 2011.

Thompson, E. P. "Patrician Society, Plebeian Culture." *Journal of Social History* 7 (1974), 382–405.

Thomson, James. *The Castle of Indolence and Other Poems*. Ed. Alan D. McKillop. Lawrence: University of Kansas Press, 1961.

Letters and Documents. Ed. Alan Dugald McKillop. Lawrence: University of Kansas Press, 1958.

Liberty, the Castle of Indolence, and Other Poems. Ed. James Sambrook. Oxford: Clarendon Press, 1986.

The Plays of James Thomson. Ed. Percy G. Adams. New York: Garland, 1979.

The Plays of James Thomson, 1700–1748: A Critical Edition. Ed. John C. Greene. 2 vols. New York: Garland, 1987.

The Seasons. Ed. James Sambrook. Oxford: Clarendon Press, 1981.

Timms, Colin. "Handelian and Other Librettos in Birmingham Central Library." *Music and Letters* 65 (1984), 141–67.

Tipping, H. Avray. "Four Unpublished Letters of William Kent in the Possession of Lord Spencer." *Architectural Review* 63 (1928), 180–3, 209–11.

Trowell, Brian. "Notes on Rinaldo." In program book for Metropolian Opera, New York, production. *Stagebill* 11(5) (January 1984).

Turner, E. Raymond. "The Excise Scheme of 1733." *English Historical Review* 42 (1927), 34–57.

Tuve, Rosamond. *Allegorical Imagery: Some Mediaeval Books and Their Posterity*. Princeton University Press, 1966.

Urstad, Tone S. *Sir Robert Walpole's Poets: The Use of Literature as Pro-Government Propaganda, 1721–1742*. Newark: University of Delaware Press, 1999.

Varey, Simon. *Henry St. John, Viscount Bolingbroke*. Boston, MA: Twayne, 1984.

Vickers, David. "Handel's Performing Versions: A Study of Four Music Theatre Works from the 'Second Academy' Period." Ph.D. dissertation, The Open University, 2007.

Vivian, Frances. *A Life of Frederick, Prince of Wales: A Connoisseur of the Arts*. Ed. Roger White. Lewiston, NY: Edwin Mellen Press, 2006.

Volbach, Fritz. *Georg Friedrich Händel*. 2nd edn. Berlin: Harmonie Verlagsgesellschaft für Literatur und Kunst, 1907.

Walcott, Robert. *English Politics in the Early Eighteenth Century*. Oxford: Clarendon Press, 1956.

Wallace, John M. "Dryden and History: A Problem in Allegorical Reading." *ELH* 36 (1969), 265–90.

"'Examples Are Best Precepts': Readers and Meanings in Seventeenth-Century Poetry." *Critical Inquiry* 1 (1974), 272–90.

Weinbrot, Howard. "Johnson, Jacobitism, and the History of Nostalgia." *Age of Johnson* 7 (1996), 163–211.

"Johnson's *London* and Juvenal's Third Satire: The Country as 'Ironic' Norm." *Modern Philology* 73(4), part 2 (1976), S56–S65.

Wiggin, Lewis M. *The Faction of Cousins: A Political Account of the Grenvilles, 1733–1763*. New Haven, CT: Yale University Press, 1958.

Williams, Basil. "The Foreign Policy of England under Walpole." *English Historical Review* 15 (1900), 251–76, 479–94, 665–98; 16 (1901), 67–83, 308–27, 439–51.

The Life of William Pitt, Earl of Chatham. 2 vols. London: Longmans, Green, and Co., 1914.

Stanhope: A Study in Eighteenth-Century War and Diplomacy. Oxford: Clarendon Press, 1932.

Wilson, Arthur M. *French Foreign Policy during the Administration of Cardinal Fleury, 1726–1743*. Cambridge, MA: Harvard University Press, 1936.

Wilson, Kathleen. *The Sense of the People: Politics, Culture and Imperialism in England, 1715–1785*. Cambridge University Press, 1995.

Winn, James A. *John Dryden and His World*. New Haven, CT: Yale University Press, 1987.

"When Beauty Fires the Blood": Love and the Arts in the Age of Dryden. Ann Arbor: University of Michigan Press, 1992.

Winton, Calhoun. *John Gay and the London Theatre*. Lexington: University Press of Kentucky, 1993.

Woodfine, Philip. "The Anglo-Spanish War of 1739." In *The Origin of War in Early Modern Europe.* Ed. Jeremy Black. Edinburgh: John Donald, 1987, pp. 185–209.

    Britannia's Glories: The Walpole Ministry and the 1739 War with Spain. Woodbridge: Boydell & Brewer, 1998.

Yorke, Philip C. *The Life and Correspondence of Philip Yorke, Earl of Hardwicke, Lord High Chancellor of Great Britain.* 3 vols. Cambridge University Press, 1913.

Yorke-Long, Alan. "The Opera of the Nobility." Dissertation presented for the Osgood Memorial Prize, Oxford University, 1951.

Youngren, William H. "Generality, Science and Poetic Language in the Restoration." *ELH* 35 (1968), 158–87.

Zaslaw, Neal. "The First Opera in Paris: A Study in the Politics of Art." In *Jean-Baptiste Lully and the Music of the French Baroque: Essays in Honor of James R. Anthony.* Ed. John Hajdu Heyer. Cambridge University Press, 1989, pp. 7–23.

Zwicker, Steven N. *Lines of Authority: Politics and English Literary Culture, 1649–1689.* Ithaca, NY: Cornell University Press, 1993.

Index

Lightning Source UK Ltd.
Milton Keynes UK
UKHW030636290520
364072UK00009B/128